ISLAMIC SOCIETY AND THE WEST

ISLAMIC SOCIETY AND THE WEST

A Study of the Impact of Western Civilization on Moslem Culture in the Near East

BY

SIR HAMILTON GIBB AND HAROLD BOWEN

Volume One

ISLAMIC SOCIETY IN THE EIGHTEENTH CENTURY

PART I

Issued under the auspices of the Royal Institute of International Affairs

OXFORD UNIVERSITY PRESS
LONDON NEW YORK TORONTO

Oxford University Press, Amen House, London E.C.4
GLASGOW NEW YORK TORONTO MELBOURNE WELLINGTON
BOMBAY CALCUTTA MADRAS KARACHI LAHORE DACCA
CAPE TOWN SALISBURY NAIROBI IBADAN ACCRA
KUALA LUMPUR HONG KONG

FIRST EDITION 1950
REPRINTED 1951, 1957, 1960 AND 1963

PRINTED IN GREAT BRITAIN

AUTHORS' NOTE

THE present volume, containing the first half of the prolegomena to our projected study of the Islamic Society and the West, went to press shortly before the outbreak of war. During the war years, the remainder of our material was sent to the United States for safe keeping. Since its return in 1946, revision of the second part has proceeded as steadily as the pressure of post-war duties would permit, and it is hoped that it will appear in print with no great delay. In order to facilitate the use of this part by itself, an index has been added to this volume.

ADDITIONAL NOTE

On issuing this offset reprint, the authors wish to draw attention to the corrections supplied by Professor Bernard Lewis in *Bulletin of The School of Oriental and African Studies*, Vol. XVI, Part 3 (1954), pp. 599-600.

CONTENTS

PART I

CONTENTS OF PART II

Vowels and Diphthongs

a, e, i, o, u	As in English.
i̊	A hard *i* (Turkish only).
ö, ü	As in German (Turkish only).
â, î, û	Long vowels (Arabic and Persian words only).
aw	In Arabic pronounced as *ow* in 'how'; in Turkish pronounced *ev*.
ay, ey	As English *y* in 'why'; in colloquial Arabic sometimes as *ey* in 'whey'

The Arabic article is rendered by *el* or *al* (the assimilation of the *l* to a following *d*, *n*, *r*, *s*, *t*, or *z* being neglected), but in the middle of compound phrases by *ul* (Turkish *ül*).

Proper names are spelled according to Arabic and Turkish pronunciation respectively; thus Arabic Muḥammed, Turkish Meḥmed. Standardized English spellings are retained for well-known place-names, e.g. Cairo, Mecca, Ḥijâz, and in such terms as Janissary.

In a certain number of common terms it has been found necessary to retain the distinctive Arabic and Turkish vocalizations, thus *multazim* and *mutawallî* (Arabic), *mültezim* and *mütevelli* (Turkish).

NOTE ON TRANSLITERATION

THE character and scope of this book have raised a peculiar problem of transliteration of Arabic and Turkish words. The natural impulse of the Orientalist is to use a standard system of transcription, such as that of the Royal Asiatic Society and the British Academy. But this simple course meets with an insuperable obstacle in the Latin alphabet officially adopted by the Turkish Republic, which we are bound to use in dealing with modern Turkey. It is obvious that we cannot spell one and the same word *khwāja* in the first volume and *hoca* in the third. For the same reason we cannot adopt the former spelling for Arabic words and the latter for Turkish, especially since a large proportion of technical Turkish terms are in fact Arabic. The most educated of Western readers cannot be expected to know the technical terms of Oriental languages and to recognize them in a variety of orthographic disguises.

We have therefore taken the matter boldly into our own hands and have worked out a system of transliteration which preserves, in all but minor points, the official Turkish spelling and yet offers an exact transcription of the Arabic sounds. If some slight inconsistencies remain, it is hoped that they are such as to offer no difficulty to the reader.

Consonants

b	ب	As in English;[1] in Turkish pronounced as *p* (and so written in the official system) at the end of a word.
c	ج	As English *j* in 'jam'.
ç	چ	As English *ch* in 'church' (Turkish only).
d	د	As in English; in Turkish pronounced as *t* at the end of a word and after unvoiced consonants.[2]
ḏ, ẕ	ذ	In Classical Arabic as *th* in 'that'; in colloquial Arabic and Turkish as *z*.
ḍ	ض	In Arabic like a thickened *d*; in Turkish pronounced as *z*.
f	ف	As in English.
g	گ	As in English, but before *â* and *û* as *gy* (Turkish only).

[1] The English equivalents are, of course, only approximate.

[2] In a few Turkish words the initial *d* was represented by ط.

ğ	غ	Like the rolled *r* in French, but deeper.[1]
h	ه	As in English, but never silent.
ḥ	ح	Like a strongly whispered *h*; in Turkish pronounced as *h*.
ḫ	خ	A scraped guttural *h*: in Turkish pronounced as *h*.
j	ژ	As English *s* in 'treasure' (Turkish only).
k	ك	As in English: but in Turkish pronounced as *ky* before *â* and *û*.
ḳ	ق	A guttural *k*; in Turkish pronounced as *k* (never as *ky*).
l	ل	As in English.
m	م	As in English.
n	ن	As in English.
ñ	ڭ	A nasal *n* (Turkish only).
p	پ	As in English (Turkish only).
r	ر	As in northern English.
s	س	As in English.
ṣ	ص	In Arabic like a thickened *s*; in Turkish pronounced as *s*.
ş	ش	As English *sh*.
ṯ, s̱	ث	In Classical Arabic as *th* in 'thin'; in colloquial Arabic and Turkish as *s*.
t	ت	As in English.
ṭ	ط	In Arabic like a thickened *t*; in Turkish pronounced as *t*.
v	و	As in English (in Turkish words only).
w	و	In Arabic pronounced as in English; in Turkish pronounced as *v*.
y	ی	As in English.
z	ز	As in English.
ẓ	ظ	In Arabic like a thickened *z* (in 'Irâḳ like *ḍ*); in Turkish pronounced as *z*.
ẕ	ذ	See *ḏ*.
'	ء	The glottal stop, neglected in Turkish at the beginning and end of a word.
'	ع	In Arabic a harsh guttural intonation; in Turkish neglected, or pronounced as the glottal stop.

[1] After *e*, *i*, *ö*, *ü* in Turkish words, this letter is sounded as an English *y*, and forms a diphthong: thus *seğmen* is pronounced as 'seymen'.

INTRODUCTION

WHEN we were entrusted with the task of surveying the effects of the Western impact upon Turkey and its former Arab provinces since the beginning of the nineteenth century, we had no idea of the formidable nature of the commission, or of the obstacles which were to confront us. The first hint of these was conveyed in the initial work of preparing a bibliography. A complete bibliography of this field has not yet been, and probably never will be, compiled, but the few partial bibliographies which exist demonstrate that the mass of publications dealing with these countries since 1800 is staggering. Even in the limited ground covered by René Maunier's classified *Bibliothèque Économique, Juridique et Sociale de l'Égypte Moderne* (1798–1916)[1] the number of books and articles listed (in French, English, Italian, and German, but excluding Arabic and Greek) amounts to 6,695. When there are added to these the published works relating to Turkey, Syria, and 'Irâḳ, it is evident that twenty thousand titles would be a low estimate for the period to 1919, and those written since 1919 probably amount to as many again.[2] When, however, one begins to examine such of them as are within reach, one does not take long to discover that an enormous proportion are quite negligible owing to their obvious deficiencies: lack of intimate experience, ignorance of the language of the country, reliance upon hearsay, unfamiliarity with the historical background, and so forth. The three-decker narratives of travel so popular in the early nineteenth century, no less than the hundreds of more recent travel-sketches, abound in these faults. Even the works of residents for a longer or shorter period do not always escape them, and are apt to suffer in addition from the acceptance of 'official' views, or, on the contrary, from an unreasoning depreciation of all the local institutions. A further criticism which must be made against the vast majority of these books and articles is their concentration either upon political events or upon external description of the society concerned (and that chiefly in the cities), while neglecting all investigation into its inner mechanism and laying bare of the forces at work to maintain or to transform it. Even such a book as Lane's *Modern Egyptians*, with all its excellences, falls short of the ideal in many respects, as, for example, in relation to economic life and industry; much more so, then, such a work as Cromer's *Modern Egypt*.

[1] *Publications spéciales de la Société Sultanieh d'Économie Politique*, &c., i, Cairo, 1918.

[2] The series of bibliographies of the literature dealing with the Mandated Territories since 1919, and published under the auspices of the American University of Bairut (Social Science Series), comprises eight fasciculi.

A more serious deficiency is the comparative absence of detailed and original monographs on many of the social problems with which our study is concerned. Later writers have too often accepted the pronouncements of their predecessors without question, while the Turkish, and still more the Arabic, materials have too often been neglected. At the same time research has been hampered by the inaccessibility of archives and documentary materials. It is true that within very recent years a little has been done towards remedying this defect. Under the enlightened auspices of the late King Fu'âd, a start has been made with the classification and publication of the state archives in Cairo;[1] and in Syria the collection of documents relating to the years 1830–40 made by Dr. Asad Rustum at the American University of Bairut[2] is an excellent example of what can be accomplished by private initiative. But these touch only the fringes of the problem, and there is every reason to fear that unless steps are taken within a very short time to form local archives, not only of political and judicial but also of educational and commercial documents, much valuable material will be permanently lost.

Another deficiency, the importance of which will not be lost on those who realize the influence of the individual personality in the introduction of new ideas and the working of new measures, is the absence of intimate biographies in Arabic and Turkish literature. In Arabic the only considerable work of this kind, Şeyḫ Raşîd Riḍâ's biography of Şeyḫ Muḥammad ʿAbduh, cumbrous and ill digested though it is, serves to show the immensity of this gap which can now never be filled. Biographical sketches, it is true, there are in plenty, but they are all confined to externals. In Turkish it is not until the end of the nineteenth century that memoirs of value are to be met with.

These criticisms do not all apply equally to every period, region, or field of study. In some fields, such as those of administration and law, the published materials are probably sufficient to enable a satisfactory study to be made. On the other hand, despite the crucial importance of education and the large numbers of Western educational institutions in the East, it is a scarcely credible fact that no thorough study yet exists of education in either Egypt or Syria.[3] It is true that a good deal of ground has been covered by official reports and by a number of private observers. But while much

[1] J. Deny, *Sommaire des Archives Turques du Caire*, Cairo, 1930; *Recueil des Firmans Imperiaux Ottomans addressés aux Valis et aux Khédives d'Égypte*, Cairo, 1934.

[2] *Materials for a Corpus of Arabic Documents relating to the History of Syria under Mehemet Ali Pasha*, 5 volumes, Beirut, 1930, etc.

[3] Since these lines were written, the first volume has appeared of Dr. J. Heyworth-Dunne's *Introduction to the History of Education in Modern Egypt* (London, 1939).

valuable material may be derived from these sources, it is open to question how far they correspond to the purposes of this study. It must be insisted again that the object in view is an organic study of the life of the Moslem societies, and the forces, ideals, and tendencies at work within them. The function of official reports is a different one, and their analyses of existing conditions are generally written with an eye to administrative action in a desired direction, whereas the investigation now projected is in its essence purely objective. The prime condition for any satisfactory work is the full and unprejudiced examination of all the relevant facts without attempting to place upon them any construction which will fit them into agreement with preconceived ideas.

The descriptions of contemporary observers, on the other hand, lack the fundamental basis of the present programme, the tracing of social evolution and the bearing of this process upon present conditions. But there are two sources which, rightly used, may serve as very valuable indications and mirrors of social development. One of these is the series of annual statistical reports published by the Turkish government since tne establishment of the Republic, and by the Egyptian government regularly since 1909, although statistical records of varying kinds go back as far as 1870. It is obviously, of course, not the statistics in themselves which are of value for us so much as the comparison of them over a period of years. The other source is that formed by the literary productions of successive periods, especially in the periodical press and the field of imaginative literature. Of all sources this has been the most neglected, yet, with due allowance for its limitations, it will often supply the most candid and revealing commentary on the real moral and intellectual forces at work within each community. But to utilize it requires, in still greater degree than most of the subjects included in our research programme, and in addition to a sound knowledge of the nuances of Turkish and Arabic, the rare ability to pick out the telling facts and sound clues from an intolerable deal of second-hand rubbish.

It began, therefore, to dawn upon us that, so far from being overcultivated, much of our field of study was practically virgin soil. From this preliminary survey also it became clear that the subject could not be at once handled concisely in vertical sections, but required an historical treatment at some length. Three divisions were obviously indicated: (*a*) a survey of the social institutions in Turkey and its Arab provinces, prior to the introduction of Western influences; (*b*) an examination of the circumstances and immediate effects of the Western impact since the beginning of the nineteenth century; (*c*) an investigation into the actual conditions and forces in play. At the same time by establishing a uniform system of vertical divisions for all periods, the historical treatment could be resolved into a series of cross-sections, by means of which the original plan would be maintained as far as possible. The next step was to draw up the list of vertical divisions, or, in other words, to break the field up into a number of manageable, and more or less self-contained, compartments. To draw rigid boundaries is, of course, impossible, as the interrelations of the various social functions make a certain overlapping inevitable. The most natural system which suggested itself was one based on a dual principle of demarcation: firstly, an occupational division leading up to government and administration, followed by a cultural division cutting across all classes and groups. On this basis a complete scheme was prepared, indicating under each head the particular problems which call for investigation. Although, for reasons which will appear later, this scheme does not represent the actual programme of our study, it seems worth while to reproduce it here, inasmuch as it may serve to indicate the general lines of our research.

I. *The Family.*

The obvious basis of any complete social investigation must be the study of the social unit constituted by the family. The problems involved are many: the structure and ramifications of the family, including (where it is found) the joint family system in which several generations live under the same roof; the mutual rights and duties of its members; its internal jurisdiction; the relationships contracted by marriage and adoption; the effects of the system of inheritance; the forms of ownership of movable and immovable property, whether private or communal; and demographic statistics, where they are available. In addition to these descriptive features, however, it is one of the most important tasks of the investigator to analyse what may be called the spirit of the family, to discover the nature and strength of the ties which unite the members of the family, not only in the direct line of descent but also with collateral branches, and the social effects of these ties, as, for example, in the formation of closed and rival groups, the duty of blood-revenge, the transmission of functions by inheritance and marriage, and the tendency towards nepotism. This naturally hangs together with the manner in which the family is linked up with the next larger group, the clan, the village, the guild, &c., and it may be found necessary to subdivide the study of the family in consequence, treating the village family, the industrial family, the professional family, and so on, as separable units of different types. The further investigation of the subject, in accordance with the scheme outlined above, will be concerned with the changes introduced during the nineteenth and early twentieth centuries into the structure, functions, and spirit of these families, either through administrative action, or by personal initiative as the result of education and social changes (more especially amongst women), and the place of the family and strength of family ties in the social structure of to-day. A valuable supplement to this study (which would throw light also on many other problems considered below) could be made by the compilation of histories of notable or extensive family groups, tracing changes in structure, occupation, &c., and their relations with other groups.

II. *The Village.*

Next to the family the most important social unit in all Moslem countries outside Arabia is the village or agricultural community; yet it has hitherto been one of the most neglected. No Moslem writer, in either medieval or modern times, has condescended to describe the organization of village life in his country, and for the purpose of this investigation the great bulk of the materials must be sought in the works of Western observers. A further difficulty is that the village communities in the different countries are not uniform in type, the organization of the village in Egypt, for example, being quite distinct from that in Palestine, Syria, 'Irâḳ, or Turkey, while within Egypt itself, again, the village of the upper valley diverges considerably from the typical *'ezba* of the Delta.

Whether these differences may prove in the end to be important or negligible will depend on the character of the social institutions linked up with them. The main points for investigation include the distribution of population and land between landowners, tenant farmers, free cultivators, and labourers; the mutual relations, social and economic, and the rights and duties of each of these sections; internal jurisdiction (e.g. punishments inflicted without recourse to law courts or police officials) and its sanctions, the administrative machinery within the village, including methods of assessment and of payment of taxation, and its relations with provincial or district authorities; usages and institutions which maintain the solidarity of the village, or the existence of group rivalries within the village or between neighbouring villages; and the changes which may have affected the village community in some or all of these aspects.

A second field of study is afforded by the economic aspects of the agricultural community; the original methods, implements, and organization of agriculture (including irrigation); the nature and yield of crops and methods of disposal of the surplus; the organization of village markets and periodical fairs; the introduction of new cultures and implements; changes in means of transport and methods of marketing; the provision of credit by money-lenders and landbanks; the introduction of co-operative schemes; changes in village education; and the effects of these upon the village and the rural economy.

II*a*. *The Beduins.*

This includes the relations between the nomadic tribes and the settled areas; the functions of the tribesmen as breeders of live stock, in supplying transport for caravans, and as auxiliary troops; the control and settlement of the tribes; and especially the legacy of nomadism in the social and legal institutions of the people.

III. *Industry.*

Neglected though the rural community has been, it has fared well in comparison with the organization of native industry in Western Asia and Egypt. This criticism applies even more to the organized industries than to the coarse village industries, which have generally been included by Western writers in their descriptions of the village economy. In the following scheme it is rather the organized industries in the cities and provincial towns that are in view, though in many cases the remarks apply to both.

The first subject of study must be the unit of industry, the workshop: its organization, staffing, equipment, &c., and the various forms of industrial enterprise (individual workshops, home industries, grouped or large-scale industrial plants under capitalist control, and industrial *waḳfs*). Then come the distribution of industries, sources of raw materials, and methods of disposal of their products, and all the social aspects of industrial life: the organization of guilds or industrial corporations, their means of recruitment, functions, and internal jurisdiction; their status and relations with other groups and with the administrative authorities (especially the *muḥtasib*); government monopolies; methods and distribution of taxation.[1]

The study of the later developments of native industry will include, on the economic side, the factors which have contributed to the decline of certain industries and the maintenance of others, such as the introduction of Western industrial products; transference of markets; improvements in means of transport; changes in the volume and direction of purchasing power; provision of capital and credit facilities; the introduction of machinery and Western industrial methods; the results of administrative action (imposition of tariffs, development of industrial education, &c.);

[1] A study of the corporations will necessarily embrace a wider field than industry, and take in all professional corporations from *'Ulemâ*, merchants, and revenue clerks to beggars, dancers, and monkey-trainers. These professional lines of demarcation may serve also as the basis of a very interesting and important linguistic investigation.

the advance of industrial technique; the preparation of industrial statistics; and on the social side, the suppression or disappearance of the industrial corporations; the rise of new types of industrial associations; changes in the status of industry and in the personnel of industrial undertakings; and the effects of mechanization on the character of the industrial population.

IV. *Commerce.*

The commercial organization of the Western Asiatic lands even before the ninteenth century was, to all appearances, peculiarly complicated owing to the international character it had already assumed. The trading relations of the European countries with the Levant have been fully investigated by MM. Charles-Roux and others, but the commercial intercourse between Turkey and Greece, Syria, Egypt, the Sudan, the Mağrib, Arabia, and 'Irâḳ still remains an unworked field. It is too often believed that the discovery of the Cape route to India resulted in the commercial stagnation of the Levant, but while it certainly reduced the volume of transit trade, a very lively interchange of local products was still maintained, and strong and wealthy mercantile communities were to be found in all the principal cities. It is on the history of these communities, rather than on the actual commodities concerned, that investigation is mainly required. That, in spite of their composite character, they formed organized bodies is clear from the records available; but the structure of these organizations, and their relations with the industrial guilds on the one hand and with the administration on the other, require to be cleared up, together with the arrangements in force for credit and exchange, the forms of commercial contracts, the working of commercial law, and the systems of import and export duties, customs, *wekâlas*, &c.

In connexion with later developments, further investigation is needed on such points as the competition of European commerce and commercial houses, the effects of administrative regulation and introduction of commercial tribunals, and the modernization of commercial methods and organization, formation of Chambers of Commerce, changes in the social status of merchants, and so on. Within this field should be included also the development of modern banking and exchange systems, and their relations with commercial enterprise

V. *The City.*

By this heading is meant the study of the communal structure and institutions of the city as a whole, apart from that of the individual groups of which it is composed, and which are dealt with under separate headings. Spengler, it will be remembered, declared that the Eastern city 'has no soul', meaning that it was a conglomeration of units, not a complex and living organism. Whatever truth may be attached to this observation, some form of organization was clearly demanded and in existence. Starting with the division of the city into numerous, and generally self-contained, wards, *ḥâras*, markets, &c., each with its own responsible *Şeyḫ* or chief, this organization doubtless included provisions for the maintenance of law and order, some sort of policing and sanitary services, and at least the rudiments of a civic life and spirit. Since the beginning of the nineteenth century the study of the city takes on an increasing importance. The expansion of the cities and their external transformation, the breaking down of old divisions, the establishment of municipalities and municipal services, form one aspect of this; the other, and even more important, is connected with the rise of the middle class, the development of intellectual life in the cities, the extension of their influence, their relations with the rural districts and the effects of their predominating position in social and political movements.

VI. *The Army.*

The old military organizations in the Ottoman Empire and in Egypt have often been described in detail, and ample materials are available in consequence for a study of the composition, equipment, and internal structure of the military forces. There is still room, however, for an investigation into the place of the military classes in the social life of their communities, the privileges which they enjoyed, their relations with other groups (particularly the artisans and the '*Ulemâ*), the attitude adopted towards them by the other sections of the population, and their religious affiliations (such as, notably, the connexion between the Janissaries and the Bektâşî order).

Similarly, in connexion with the progressive introduction of Western organization, discipline, training, and equipment into the army, it is necessary not only to consider the effects of this process upon the character and efficiency of the military and naval forces themselves, but also to deal with their wider social consequences. On the one hand, the army served as an important channel of Western penetration, through the appointment of foreign missions and instructors and the organization of medical and sanitary services, the promotion of technical training, and the necessity of providing modern equipment. On the other hand, attention needs to be given to the social status and influence of the armed forces, and in particular to the part played by members of the military forces in the social and political movements in their countries.

VII. *Government and Administration.*

It may appear, at first sight, that the whole subject of government has been so fully handled already as to leave little room for fresh investigation. But this is far indeed from being the case, however minutely the external organization of government may have been described. We know, in fact, exceedingly little of the inner relations between the government and the people, and it is only on the basis supplied by the results of the preceding investigations into the circumstances of the different sections of the population (including the *'Ulemâ*—see the following section) that a really satisfactory study of this delicate and difficult problem can be undertaken. It can scarcely be doubted that government, in its administrative aspect, was not merely a set of forms imposed upon the people by the will of the conqueror, but an organism intimately associated with the structure of society and the character and ideas of the governed, and that there was a constant interplay between governors and governed. It is necessary to clear the ground of the misconceptions engendered by the abuse of European terms such as despotism and autocracy, and to submit all the traditional organs and usages of government to re-examination, in order to bring out the underlying ideas and relations, and the principles which guided their working. Such a study involves the most intricate analysis of psychological forces, and is perhaps the most difficult of all the investigations propounded in this scheme. It would also be desirable to lead on from this to a consideration of the reasons for the evident decay of administration visible during the latter half of the eighteenth century, and to examine whether this was symptomatic of a break-down of the whole system or whether sufficient elements of vitality remained to reform and reconstruct it without the intervention of European institutions and ideas.

Until such a preliminary study of the traditional functions, ideals, and psychology of government in the Moslem world has been undertaken, the further investigation of the social reactions to the administrative and political changes of more recent times will be hopelessly handicapped, and the investigator will be largely working in the dark. For while certain obvious changes have been brought about by the spread of Western ideas (both the liberal ideas of the nineteenth century and the newer totalitarian ideas of the twentieth), by constitutional and bureaucratic developments, and the delimitation of functions between government departments, the provision of social services, economic changes, and the like, it remains true to a large extent that inherited and ingrained characteristics cannot be easily eradicated. The same considerations apply also to the study of the social effects of the more strictly political movements, including the rise of nationalist parties, the reactions to Western political control, and the mutual relations of the Islamic countries.

VIII. *Religion.*

In discussing the place of religion in social life two distinct, though of course closely related, aspects have to be investigated. One is the influence of the religious ideals and religious ethic in the lives of individuals of all classes and in the social groups, singly and collectively, and the extent to which customary usages and elements foreign to Islâm were bound up with them. The other is concerned with the organization, usages, and functions of institutional religion. In this field the *'Ulemâ* naturally come first, and in spite of all that has been written on the subject there is still need for much research into the organization, recruitment, education, and status of the *'Ulemâ*, especially during the period from the sixteenth to the eighteenth centuries (for example, in regard to the prevalence of hereditary transmission of religious functions and the purchase of religious offices), and their relations with the central and local governments, the administration of law, the religious orders, and the population of the cities and the rural districts. Scarcely less important are the numerous *ṭarîḳas* or orders of *derwîşes*, their structure, rituals, distribution, and special associations with and influence over particular groups, military and occupational, both in the cities and in the villages. But it would be a serious mistake to limit the study of institutional religion to these two classes of professional 'men of religion'. One must rather visualize it as a vast corporation which included within itself all the other corporations, and formed the uniting link between them by calling out and focusing the sentiment of loyalty. Each lesser group had therefore its own place in, and its own contribution to make to, the religious structure, from the Sultan to the peasant. It is this communal aspect of religion which has been chiefly neglected and which calls for investigation, together with its external manifestations in public rituals, festivals, the constitution of *waḳfs*, and other means of serving and maintaining the common religious life and its institutions, and the limitations and disturbances arising from the presence of dissident Moslem sects.

It is from this point of view also that the history of religious developments from the end of the eighteenth century requires to be followed up. The disturbance of the old system by administrative interference and social and economic changes, the effect of such movements as Wahhâbism, the Sanûsîya, Mahdism, Pan-Islamism, and the reformist agitations, of Christian missionary activity, of changes in religious education and the machinery of religious organization, of the infiltration of Western ideas both within and without the ranks of the professional *'Ulemâ*, and the activities of the religious orders, are all worthy of study in themselves, but their full influence can only be estimated when they are correlated with the religious life of the community as a whole.

IX. *Education.*

The traditional structure of education and of law (see section X) can hardly be divorced entirely from religion, but in view of the subsequent separation between the three fields, it is necessary to include them under individual headings. The old educational organization, not only on account of the preponderance of religious students and subjects, but even more strongly because of the prevailing conceptions as to the basis and purpose of education, was very closely bound up with the organization of the *'Ulemâ*. A detailed study is required, nevertheless, in order to clear up many points on which our ideas are at present confused and inadequate, such as the existence and staffing of *madrasas* in the smaller towns, the teaching of other than religious subjects, the education of the military and official classes, and especially the literature and literary pursuits of the seventeenth and eighteenth centuries.

From this point onwards, the strictly religious aspect of education tends to fall into the background, owing to the increasing introduction of Western educational methods, as the result of educational missions to Europe, the multiplication of European and technical schools, and the creation of government educational services. These in turn give rise to a vast number of social problems arising out of the organization of education itself and of its social effects. They are too many to be even summarized here,[1] and amongst them may be mentioned only—as the most important—the rise of new ideals and aims of education, the relative influence of religious, government, private, and foreign schools, the persistence or weakening of group distinctions, the place of European languages in education, its effects upon the spoken and literary language, and the consequences of the education of girls. Closely connected also with the subject of education is the whole field of intellectual development, including not only literature, but also science, medicine, art and music, and technical equipment.

[1] See, for a fuller discussion, the article on 'Social Reactions in the Moslem World', in *Journal of the Royal Central Asian Society*, Oct. 1934.

X. *Law.*

It has already been noted that the traditional conceptions of law and the public legal administration were closely related to the field of religion, but the association of law with institutional religion was much less close than is commonly believed. It is true that the only tribunals whose competence and theoretical authority were unrestricted and universally accepted were the *Şer'î* courts administered by the *Kâḍîs* and their substitutes, and equally true that the only written law was the *Şerî'a*. An objective study of the working of these courts and the functions and status of *Kâḍîs* and *Muftîs* in the old Ottoman organization is consequently much to be desired. But the most casual student cannot fail to be struck by the fact that the *Şer'î* courts were not called upon to adjudicate in large areas of what we should regard as the field of law. The organization of society in innumerable small self-contained groups created an equal number of local jurisdictions for the handling of disputes between members of the same group. This involves us in the apparently endless field of customary law as it was applied in the villages, among the industrial corporations, &c., which has never yet been investigated in Western Asia.[1] Arising out of this is the conflict between customary law and the *Şerî'a* and the extent to which they were influenced by one another. Another very important limitation upon the application of the *Şerî'a*, particularly in criminal cases, was the authority vested in the officers of the army and the public administration to adjudicate and to condemn offenders, even to death, without the intervention of any *Kâḍî* or legal officer, and not infrequently without trial of any kind. Finally, an investigation is necessary into the whole question of the public conception of the nature of law, the psychology of the popular attitude towards it, and its practical application and enforcement.

The development of legal practice and administration during the nineteenth century and after raises, in consequence, many complex social problems. The establishment of military codes, in the first place, and later on the attempts to codify civil and criminal law, and introduction of Western codes and principles of law, involve consideration of the relations of these codes and principles to the accepted rules of both *Şer'î* and customary law, of the effects of the changes in judicial administration, organization, and procedure upon the popular attitude to law, and the rise of new conceptions of criminality. Another important aspect of the same process is furnished by the rapid evolution of a new

[1] There is, however, an extensive literature in Dutch upon the customary law applied in Indonesia—see the article ''Ādat law' in the *Supplement* to the *Encyclopaedia of Islâm*.

class of trained and practising lawyers, exercising a wide social and political influence, and saturated with Western legal ideas, the diversity of which adds still more to the complexity of the situation.

These ten headings comprise the more important problems affecting the social life and development of the Moslem peoples of Western Asia during the last two centuries. But in order to complete the cross-section of Moslem society in Western Asia, two special features remain to be listed, in so far as they affect the social structure.

XI. *Slavery.*

Three aspects are of importance: the place and function of slaves in the old economy (as domestic servants, labourers, and soldiers), the social effects of the abolition of slavery, and the evolution of public opinion and religious doctrine in their attitude towards slavery.

XII. *Non-Moslem minorities.*

The question of the traditional status of the non-Moslems in the Asiatic countries is probably less important for our purpose than an investigation into the actual functions, occupations, conditions of life, and organization of the various Christian and Jewish communities, prior to the nineteenth century, and their social and economic relations with the Moslems of all classes, with the local governments, and with the European merchant houses. During the nineteenth century their closer contact with Europeans and greater readiness to take advantage of European education and the new economic methods widened on the one hand their fields of activity, giving them greater importance in the social economy, and on the other hand invested them with a new function as carriers of European ideas at second hand. This series of social and cultural interactions has already been partially investigated, but requires more detailed analysis of its extension and effects. In the third place, in more recent years, the social aspects and reactions of the political relationships between Moslem and non-Moslem groups offer a wide, though somewhat delicate, field of study.

The mere setting out of such a scheme as this is enough to show how vast is the field and how backward the state of socio-historical research in this area, how premature therefore any composite study of the social evolution in Turkey and Western Asia. To carry it out fully would occupy a whole staff of research workers for many years and would involve a lengthy series of stages.

The first requirement is a series of monographs on the individual problems, which, while dealing in the first place with each area separately, would eventually embrace the relations and contacts between the separate regions and bring out the likenesses and differences in their reactions to similar intrusive forces. An essential element, however, is that there should not only be collected the relevant facts, but that there should be a study of the significance of these facts in the life of the individual and for the evolution of the society as a whole. Only on the basis of such a monographic treatment can sure progress be made towards a final synthetic study of the problems as a whole, under such general heads as rationalization and the release of individuality. Farther than these, into the significance of the process on the plane of world history, we need not go. But the fundamental condition is speed, for the materials, in the form of oral tradition and casual documents, are growing less year by year. Ten years hence there will be large gaps difficult to fill, twenty years hence they will be impossible to fill at all.

It remains to indicate the relation of our own study to this complete and ideal scheme. That the former can represent only a part of the latter needs neither explanation nor apology; what part, however, has naturally been determined by the circumstances of our work. There are large areas in each section of the field which can be investigated only in the East, by patient collection of oral tradition and search for manuscript materials, and by prolonged immersion in oriental life. These methods are of necessity ruled out for those who, like us, are limited to occasional visits to the field of our research. Our main sources must consequently be such published work, including that written in Turkish and Arabic, as is accessible to us, supplemented by the data derived from personal contacts. As the value and proportions of these sources vary from period to period, so the breadth and depth of our study must vary also, and there are some few sections of the field (notably that of the family) from which we are excluded almost entirely. But such imperfections, great as they are, are inevitable in what is in effect a pioneer study, and we shall feel that we have attained our end if our work does anything to stimulate or to contribute to that more thorough research which has been outlined above.

These considerations apply with special force to the materials contained in this first volume. In attempting to present a composite survey of the original institutions and social organization of the Ottoman Empire at the end of the eighteenth century, we were hampered from the first by the fact that no thorough study of the old social structure of the Islamic lands has yet been made. It was consequently impossible to superimpose the data derived from eighteenth-century sources upon an existing picture. The need for a clearly defined starting-point of our investigation was, however, the more clamant, because examination revealed that the narratives of the eighteenth-century travellers and the biased pronouncements of nineteenth-century writers and apologists for Meḥmed ʿAlî were profoundly unsatisfactory. On the other hand, the materials available for a more thorough, objective, and analytic treatment of the eighteenth century are scanty and ill distributed. Only for one country is there anything approaching an adequate description, an island of firm ground amidst a treacherous and uncharted morass. This is the brilliant collection of monographs written by the savants who accompanied Bonaparte's expedition to Egypt, and collected in the four stately volumes of the *Description de l'Égypte, État Moderne.* Their peculiar merits are due to the rare combination of personal talents with intimate experience of the administration during the French occupation, a combination which could not be expected to recur elsewhere. The only comparable work, Mouragea d'Ohsson's *Tableau Général de l'Empire Ottoman*, presents a much more external and theoretical picture, which the books of de Tott, Thornton, and others supplement only to a slight extent. For Syria, Palestine, and ʿIrâḳ there is nothing which corresponds to these works until a much later date.

Yet all these writers, not excluding the savants of the *Description*, were in one respect little better than the eighteenth-century travellers. Moslem society was too close-knit and exclusive to permit of real and intimate social contact with Europeans. To fill this gap it is necessary to have recourse to Turkish and Arabic sources. Since, however, the archive materials are unclassified or inaccessible, we have been compelled to fall back on published works, but these too are by no means extensive.

None of the Turkish works that we have used deals exclusively with the eighteenth century. The works of some of the official annalists do so indeed; but they are concerned almost entirely with political events, and are swollen with rhetorical embellishments to such enormous length that we have neglected them in favour of two nineteenth-century accounts of the period, in which most, if not all, of the material contained in them and relevant to our purpose is embodied. These are the 'History' of Aḥmed Cevdet Paşa and 'The Consequences of Events' (*Netâ'icü'l-Vuḳû-ʿât*) of Seyyid Muṣṭafâ Nûrî Paşa, both composed after the reforms of Maḥmûd II had largely transformed the face of their country. The first and introductory volume of Cevdet Paşa's work, and the appendices to the various sections into which Seyyid Muṣṭafâ's is divided, furnish us with a general account of the central government, the administration of the provinces, the army, the navy, and the 'learned profession'. Cevdet Paşa's purpose in composing his introduction was indeed similar to our own: to provide a background against which he might depict the events of the period to which his remaining volumes are devoted—the period immediately subsequent to that which we have chosen for our survey. He provides this background by describing the corruption into which the various institutions in question had fallen since their heyday in the sixteenth century; a procedure that we too have been obliged to adopt, in order to make their condition in the eighteenth century intelligible. Seyyid Muṣṭafâ's work is a general history of the Ottoman Empire from its rise, the appendices to the various sections of which describe these same institutions at various epochs of rise and decline. The period at which both authors wrote was just sufficiently remote from that of our survey, on the one hand to necessitate their explaining points that earlier authors might have taken for granted, and on the other to allow of their understanding, as later authors might have been less well able to understand, the conditions they describe. If they exhibit any prejudice, it is in favour of the reforms of the early nineteenth century, with the result that they perhaps tend to depict the anterior age in too sombre colours.

For information concerning the Imperial Household our chief source has been the 'History' of 'Aṭâ (Ṭayyâr-zâde Aḥmed), another work of the mid-nineteenth century. For many details of the organization of city life, particularly that of the trade-guilds, we have drawn on a modern work, the 'Code of Municipal Affairs' (*Mecellei Umûru Beledîye*) by 'Os̱mân Nûrî, the first volume of which is based largely on documents of the sixteenth, seventeenth, and eighteenth centuries. Other modern studies used are: 'The Economics of the Turkish Village' (*Türkiye Köy Iḳtiṣâdiyâtî*) by Isma'îl Ḫüsrev, part of which deals with agricultural conditions in Anatolia in the feudal age; 'Bulgaria under Turkish Rule' (*Türk Idâresinde Bulgaristan*), 'The Tribes of the Turks in Anatolia' (*Anadoluda Türk Aşîretleri*), 'The Life of Istanbul in the Twelfth Century of the Hegira' (*Hicrî on ikinci 'aṣîrda Istanbul Ḥayâtî*), 'The Life of Istanbul in the Thirteenth Century of the Hegira' (*Hicrî on üçüncü 'aṣîrda Istanbul Ḥayâtî*)—all these consisting of contemporary state papers edited with introductions by Aḥmed Refîḳ; and 'Mohammedanism in Anatolia' (*Anadoluda Islâmiyet*), by Professor Köprülüzâde Meḥmed Fu'âd, which, though in the main a study of pre-Ottoman conditions, deals with the Bektaşî and other orders of mystics by which Ottoman history was so profoundly influenced. Finally, though this list is not exhaustive, we may mention the various collections of *Ḳânûns*, published in the

Revue Historique of the Institut d'Histoire Ottomane (*Ta'rîḫi Osmânî Encümeni Mecmû'asî*) and the 'Review of National Studies' (*Millî Tetebbü'ler Mecmû'asî*).

The published Arabic materials relating to the eighteenth century are still fewer. The first place amongst them belongs to the minute and faithful record of the Egyptian Şeyḫ 'Abdul-Raḥmân el-Cabartî, a sober chronicle which presents the view of an educated, relatively enlightened, and on the whole impartial observer of the last decades of Mamlûk rule, the French expedition, and the first fifteen years of Meḥmed 'Alî's government. In its wide range of detail it contains a great many observations of importance for the social history of his times, and while some of them are only half intelligible without the aid of the *Description*,[1] they constitute a most valuable supplement and corrective to the monographs of the French savants. A contemporary record of events in Syria was compiled by the Amîr Ḥaidar Aḥmad Şihâb,[2] but it falls somewhat below the level of Cabartî's chronicle in breadth of view, and is (unfortunately for our purposes) more interested in the Lebanon than in Syria proper. Nevertheless, it preserves, apart from the writer's own observations, a number of documents of importance for our purpose. In the absence of an inner-Syrian chronicle, we have had recourse to a work of a different kind, the biographical dictionary of notable personages and scholars of the twelfth century of the Moslem era (A.D. 1689–1786) compiled by the *Muftî* of Damascus, Muḥammad Ḫalîl el-Murâdî, who died in 1791.[3] In this work, following a traditional pattern of Islamic compilation, there are to be found about a thousand biographical notices, varying in length from three or four lines to ten or twelve pages, of men of various countries and walks of life, but especially of Syrian scholars. Within its own limits, such a book as this gives a far more vivid picture of the social and intellectual life of its period than any descriptive narrative, and it will be seen that it has supplied an unexpectedly large variety of facts relating to these. Nevertheless, all these compositions, with their predominantly political and scholastic interests, leave large sections of Islamic society almost out of view, and cannot compensate for the absence of archives and family records. The relations between the individual and the social group on the one hand, and on the other the inter-relations of the groups

[1] For this reason, and also because of many omissions, the French translation made by four Egyptians (*Merveilles biographiques et historiques*, Cairo, 1888–96) is a most unsatisfactory substitute for the original text in any thorough study.

[2] *Le Liban à l'époque des Amirs Chihab*, published by Dr. A. Rustum and F. E. Boustany, 3 volumes, Beyrouth, 1933.

[3] *Silk el-Durar fi a'yân el-ḳarn el-ṯânî 'aşar*, 4 volumes, published at Cairo, 1874–83.

within the social system as a whole, are not clearly reflected, and remain somewhat intangible in consequence.

Thanks, however, to the combination of the European and Oriental sources, it is possible to make a direct investigation into the social structure and problems of Turkey and of Egypt in the eighteenth century. For the other countries, it is necessary to adopt for the time being a more indirect method, either expanding the scattered data by analogy from the situation in Turkey and Egypt, or working backwards by inference from the later changes and innovations. Since little or no research has been directed so far along these lines, the survey contained in our first volume can be regarded only as a tentative and partial exposition, based on a very inadequate documentation, and with many lacunae which we hope may be filled up in part in the later portions of our study. In particular, two very important aspects of social life, namely the position and functions of women and of slaves, have been held over for fuller treatment in connexion with the movements toward emancipation.

Finally, we have deliberately confined ourselves as closely as possible to making a plain factual survey, and have resisted the temptation to elevate the discussion to a philosophic level. Current views on Turkey and Egypt in the eighteenth century so abound with misconceptions, which we ourselves shared at the outset of our study, that it is our first duty to marshal for others the data which have led us to very different conclusions. Moreover, the tentative nature of our enterprise warns us that any generalizations would be premature, and might even result in misrepresentations as serious as those which we hope to have done something to remove.

CHAPTER I

THE OTTOMAN EMPIRE AND THE SACRED LAW

IT is our business to investigate the gradual transformation of Moslem society in the Ottoman Empire under Western influences.[1] Our first care, therefore, must be to fix on a date at which we may view that society before the process in question began. This is not altogether easy; partly because the Ottoman Empire[2] was at no period, like the societies of the Far East, wholly cut off from contact with Europe; partly because certain parts of the Empire were sooner influenced than others; and partly because the process was at first comparatively slow. Throughout the long period of its strength the Ottoman government attracted a stream of Europeans to its service, who brought with them ideas foreign to its Moslem culture. Sometimes the result was noticeable, as, for instance, in the reforms undertaken in certain divisions of the armed forces in the early eighteenth century. But it was not until the latter part of that century that any systematic imitation of European techniques was undertaken. Until then even the leaders of the governing class were conscious of no inferiority in comparison with Europe. It was only the experience of two disastrous wars, lasting one from 1767 to 1774 and the other from 1788 to 1792, that induced a change of attitude. Even during the earlier of these two campaigns, however, the Sultan of the time turned to certain Europeans resident in his capital for advice and aid. And though the innovations then introduced were of no wide range and were later more or less abandoned, they were indicative enough of what was to come to merit inclusion in the later part of our study rather than in our introductory survey of Ottoman society in what was still, so to speak, its pure state. For this reason we have chosen the period of peace that preceded the declaration of war on Russia in 1767—actually a peace of unprecedented length, enduring, as it did, at least in Europe, no less than thirty years—as that regarding which our introductory survey may be best undertaken.

During this period the Empire comprised the following territories: in Europe, the whole Balkan peninsula up to the Danube

[1] Ottoman. Derived from the name 'Osmân (Arabic, 'Uṯmân), the Turkish adjective being *'Osmanlî*, the Arabic *'Uṯmânî*.

[2] The Ottoman Turks took to referring to the realm of the Sultans as an 'Empire' (*Imparaṭorluḳ*) only under the influence of European writers. In older times it was generally called *Devleti 'Alîye* (Arabic, *el-Dawla el-'Alîya*), 'the high state' or *Salṭanati Senîye* (Arabic, *el-Salṭana el-Sanîya*), 'The Sublime Sultanate'.

(except for certain strongholds in Albania), Bosnia, the principalities of Moldavia and Wallachia, Bessarabia, and the whole north coast of the Black Sea, including the Crimean peninsula; in Asia, all Asia Minor and Armenia, Western Kurdistan, the 'Irâḳ, Mesopotamia, Syria, the Ḥijâz, Laḥsâ, and the Yemen; in Africa, Egypt, Tripoli, Tunis, and Algiers; and, finally, Cyprus, Crete, and the islands of the Aegean. It had earlier included other territories still, namely most of Hungary and Transylvania, Podolia, Georgia, Dağistân, Sûrwân, and part of Azerbâycân. On the other hand, after losing the Morea to Venice in 1699, it had regained it in 1718, and after losing some territory round Belgrade south of the Danube and part of Wallachia to Austria in 1718, it had regained them in 1739. Russia, again, had already for a time held the fortress of Azov and so reached the Black Sea, but had been obliged to retrocede it in 1711, by the Treaty of the Pruth; and for fifteen years in the early seventeenth century Bağdâd had been recovered by the Ṣafevids of Persia.

In comparison with the territories that still owed the Sultans allegiance, therefore, those that they had lost were of small extent. But these losses, particularly in Europe, and even where they had been but temporary, were ominous. Moreover, certain parts of the Empire were more loosely attached than others; and the adherence of others again was now no more than nominal. These irregularities were due partly to the circumstances in which the incorporation of the various provinces had been effected and to subsequent political developments, and partly to the fact that the Empire had been built up in accordance with certain Moslem principles, which allowed a considerable elasticity in the relationship of its component parts. It owed its structure, indeed, to the guidance provided by these principles for those who controlled its destinies, in the particular circumstances in which it had grown and maintained itself in being. We may here digress, accordingly, to consider what these principles were, and in what authoritative exposition they were embodied.

According to the first of them, the world is conceived as being divided into two parts, the Domain of Islâm, and the Domain of War.[1] It is the duty of true-believers, where they can, to extend the first at the expense of the second. The Domain of War has two kinds of inhabitants: People of Scripture[2] (Christians, Jews, and Zoroastrians) and idolaters. Idolaters must accept Islâm or die. People of Scripture, however, may retain their own religion and become subjects of the Moslem ruler, if they will agree to pay a special tax for the privilege. The Moslem ruler may also, if he so wishes, accept this tax as a tribute from whole 'Scriptural'

[1] *Dâr el-Islâm* and *Dâr el-Ḥarb* (Arabic). [2] *Ahl el-Kitâb* (Arabic).

populations, who thus attach themselves in a vassal capacity to the Domain of Islâm.

According to a second principle, mankind is divided into free and bond; and slaves may be either born or made. But this principle depends on the first. For though inhabitants of the Domain of Islâm may be born slaves, none, either Moslems or people of Scripture, may be enslaved. Masters may, and as men of virtue should, free their slaves in time, and may buy slaves from one another. But all newly enslaved persons must be non-Moslem inhabitants of the Domain of War.

These principles were embodied in the Sacred Law of Islâm, the *Şerî'a*, which had been constructed during the first centuries of its history by theologians and jurists from the precepts of the *Ḳur'ân*, traditions concerning the practice of the Prophet and his Companions, and custom sanctioned by general consent. From the earliest times, however, differences of opinion, theological, legal, liturgical, and political, had appeared among the Moslems; and owing to the adherence of some to one opinion, some to another, they had split into many sects, and schools within sects. It is necessary, therefore, for us to consider some of them briefly, in order to make clear which varieties of opinion regarding the *Şerî'a* were dominant in the Ottoman Empire.

A large majority of Moslems were from early times so far agreed as to consider themselves orthodox. These called themselves *Sunnî*, followers of (the Prophet's) practice.[1] The most important bodies of their opponents, in contrast, were called by them *Şî'î*, 'sectarian'.[2] The Umayyad and 'Abbâsid Caliphs, or successors of the Prophet as rulers of Islâm, were orthodox. And until early in the tenth century A.D. the Sectarians, with unimportant exceptions, failed to achieve their political aims—for the differences that divided them from the orthodox were as much political as religious. Hence 'Sectarianism' in its various forms was given a revolutionary colour and came, then and in later ages, to appeal to the dissatisfied.

During the tenth and eleventh centuries Sectarian revolutionary movements made great headway. The unity of Islâm was completely disrupted; various Şî'î dynasties were founded; and Şî'î missionaries carried on a vigorous propaganda. At the same time a new colour was given to the religion by the spread of mysticism (*Taṣawwuf*, Sufism),[3] among orthodox and sectaries alike. Now it was at this time that Turkish tribes began their migrations into Persia and other lands of the Caliphate. The

[1] *Sunna*.

[2] From *el-Şî'a*, the Sect (*par excellence*), i.e. the adherents of 'Alî ibn Abî Ṭâlib, the Prophet's son-in-law, and his descendants. The word 'Shia' is often used erroneously as an adjective.

[3] See below, ch. xiii.

bulk of them were more or less recent converts; but with their tribal life they conserved many heathen practices; and the brand of Islâm to which they were most easily attracted was one sometimes orthodox in name, but at the same time strongly tinged with both Şî'î and mystical elements. The dynasty under whose leadership their migrations were effected, however, took up for its own ends the championship of the 'Abbâsid Caliphs against the heterodox princes who for a century had kept them in ignominious subjection, and again united a large part of the Moslem world under one orthodox government. Now this dynasty, the Selcuḳid, was, through its offshoot of Asia Minor, the parent, so to speak, of the House of 'Os̱mân. And this tradition of adherence to orthodoxy formed part of the legacy inherited from it by the Ottoman Sultans. As we shall see, the Moslem Turkish-speaking section of Ottoman society was penetrated, in varying degrees according to class, with the mystical-heterodox conception of Islâm that had appealed to the earliest Turkish invaders and had since continued to appeal to their successors. The government, on the other hand, set its face sternly against the toleration of open heterodoxy within the Empire, particularly from the beginning of the sixteenth century, when a 'Sectarian' state was set up in Persia.

For the first six centuries of Islâm the *Şerî'a*, the Sacred Law of the orthodox, retained a gradually diminishing fluidity. Its nature depended upon two chief points: the determination of the sources upon which it should be founded, and their interpretation. By the turn of the ninth-tenth century the traditions of primitive practice on which it was largely based were beginning to be finally determined with the recognition of six collections as canonical. And by this time also the interpreters both of Tradition and of the *Ḳur'ân*, in their legal rather than theological aspects, had grouped themselves into four schools. The differences between these schools gave rise to passionate disputes; but they were all, nevertheless, regarded as orthodox. The Selcuḳid Sultans were personally attached from the first to the most liberal of the four, the Ḥanefî;[1] and this attachment again was inherited from them by the Ottoman state. The other schools were still tolerated; but the Ḥanefî interpretation of the Sacred Law was that officially adopted. It was adopted, moreover, as a system no longer to be modified. Fresh interpretations were no longer admitted. In a famous phrase it was said, 'the Gate of Interpretation has been shut'.[2] The final touches to the immutable edifice of the Law were given, as far as the Ḥanefî section of Ottoman society was concerned, in the fifteenth and sixteenth centuries,

[1] So called after its founder, Abû Ḥanîfa (A.D. 696–767).
[2] *Ictihâd ḳapisi ḳapandi.*

with the composition of two books, 'The Pearls' and 'The Confluence of the Seas',[1] in which were collected and reduced to order of a sort the opinions of all the most celebrated Ḥanefî doctors of times gone by.

The *Şerî'a* was, in theory, all-embracing. It was not merely a religious law, like the canon law of Christendom, outside the scope of which a civil law might regulate some mundane affairs. Yet it was based on traditions of life in a society very different from that which came into being even with the first great expansion of Islâm. There were many activities concerning which it gave no detailed guidance. In pre-Ottoman times practice in these matters was built up into no code of regulations; it was merely customary, and varied according to time and place. The Ottoman Sultans, however, erected a more elaborate governmental system than their predecessors. All Ottoman society was divided into clearly defined groups; and it was by virtue of their membership of such groups that the relationship of individuals to the government was conditioned. In order, therefore, to define the obligations entailed by this relationship, as also the status, the duties, the emoluments, the dress, &c., of persons actually in the government service, regulations were issued by the Sultans under the name *Ḳânûn*. It was not held, however, that the Sultans' *Ḳânûns* constituted a secular law, rival to the *Şerî'a*, nor, especially, that they applied to a sphere outside the *Şerî'a's* scope. They were merely regulations applying to matters undefined by the *Şerî'a*, with the rulings of which they were, of course, supposed not to conflict.[2] The *Şerî'a* itself was held by Ottoman jurists to cover the 'enactments' embodied in *Ḳânûns* by its concession of a power of initiative to the head of the state, to be exercised, in harmony with its provisions, for the good of the community. This initiative, known as *'Urf*, was naturally exemplified by the monarch's day-to-day commands, so that *Ḳânûns* were merely particular registered instances of its exercise. Again, *Ḳânûns* sometimes embodied customs (*'Âdât*) established before their conquest in various parts of the Empire, so that as well as by the *Şerî'a*, the duties of the Sultans' subjects were defined by *Ḳânûns* embodying *'Urfî* and *'Âdî* laws; moreover, other *'Âdât*, not so embodied, played an important part in determining the administration of justice, even though, strictly speaking, they were not held to be

[1] *al-Durar* (or, in full, *Durar al-ḥukkâm fî şarḥ ğurar al-aḥkâm*) by Meḥmed ibn Firâmurz, known as Molla Ḫusrev, d. 1480, and *Multaḳâ'l-Abḥur* by Ibrahîm ibn Muḥammad el-Ḥalabî, d. 1549.

[2] Thus in the heading of the *Ḳânûnnâme* of Süleymân the Magnificent (*M.T.M.* i. 49 sq.) the following words occur: 'The Imperial *Ḳânûnnâme*, whose agreement with the holy *Şerî'a* has been established' (*Ḳânûnnâmei sulṭânî (dir) ki şer'i şerife muvâfaḳati muḳarrer olup . . .*).

legally binding. Finally, though the Gate of Interpretation was declared to be shut, the pressure of events could not but force it continually ajar. For there existed a special class of legal experts whose function it was to consider public and private problems submitted to them, and to issue rulings upon the line of conduct to be taken. These rulings were to be based upon the provisions of the *Şerî'a*; but in all but formal cases the very fact that they were demanded implied that these provisions were not explicit. In issuing their rulings, therefore, the experts were forced, though they might not admit it, to exercise a prerogative held to have vanished with the great doctors of the past. And that their interpretations were a real addition to the Law, which should guide their successors, is shown by their collection and use.

The Sacred Law made no provision for the conquest of territory by one Moslem ruler from another. Its sources all dated from a time when Islâm had been a political unity; and even during the later days of its 'interpretation', though this unity was disrupted, the 'Abbâsid Caliphate still covered, at least nominally, all but some regions at its extremities. Hence conquests by one Moslem ruler from another were practically disregarded by the Sunnî theorists of the *Şerî'a*, who only demanded that the *de facto* rulers should be Sunnî too. And by its gradual incorporation of all the Western countries formerly included in the Caliphate, the Ottoman Empire came in fact to correspond more and more closely to the ideal Moslem state. For the conquests in Europe, on the other hand, the Law had ready the precedent set up by the original expansion of Islâm outside the limits of Arabia.

This new accession to the Domain of Islâm was divided, as was permissible, into two parts: territories under the direct control of the central administration, and territories paying tribute. All the European possessions of the eighteenth century were of the first type except three, the republic of Dubrovnik or Ragusa, and the two Rumanian principalities of Moldavia and Wallachia. Dubrovnik was purely tributary; the Ottoman government exercised no control whatever over its internal affairs. The principalities, on the other hand, though tributary also, were governed by *Voyvodas* or *Hospodars*, appointed by the Ottoman government. Up to the year 1716 the *Boyars*, or landowners, of each principality had elected a native *Voyvoda*, their choice then being submitted for ratification to Istanbul. But since, during the war with Russia that ended in 1711 both the then incumbents were found to be intriguing with the enemy, this arrangement was put an end to; and thenceforward *Voyvodas* were chosen from among the Greek families of the Phanar quarter of Istanbul. There were no Moslem officials appointed to posts in the principalities, except in a number of frontier fortresses. These were occupied by permanent garrisons; and their presence necessitated that also of various civil functionaries.

The Ḫanate of the Crimea was on a different footing, since it had been Moslem territory before its inclusion in the Empire. The southern part of the peninsula had been conquered by the Ottomans in the fifteenth century, and brought under the central government. In the remainder, which included a large region on the 'mainland', the Tatar *Ḫans* maintained their rule, but acknowledged the Sultans as their suzerains. The ruling family, the Girey Ḫans, as they were called, occupied a special position in Ottoman esteem, since it was an offshoot of the Golden Horde, and so descended from the redoubtable Mongol, Çingiz Ḫan. If the House of 'Os̱mân should die out—and owing to the extraordinary laws that regulated the succession, such an event was by no means improbable—it was agreed that the throne should pass to the Gireys.

Provinces exceptionally governed were not confined to Europe. In the first place the three regencies of North Africa, on the one hand, and, on the other, the 'Şerîfate' of Mecca, were upon much the same footing as the Ḫanate of the Crimea. For both the locally elected *Dayîs* of Algiers, Tunis, and Tripoli, and the *Şerîfs* of the Holy City, acknowledged the suzerainty of the Sultans, who confirmed them in office. But none of them were tributary; on the contrary, they were all recipient of gifts from the Porte. In the case of the *Dayîs* these gifts were occasional and took the shape of munitions of war. In that of the *Şerîfs*, who were honoured not only for their long pre-Ottoman possession of Mecca but for their descent from the Prophet, they were annual and delivered on the occasion of the arrival of the Pilgrimage caravans. The government of Medina, the other holy city, was again peculiar. It was always conferred on one of the leading black eunuchs of the Sultan's palace. Finally, there were certain regions in Kurdistan and Albania, inhabited by semi-nomad tribes, that were governed through their chieftains.

The administration of the rest of the Empire, though Egypt exhibited certain peculiarities, was more or less uniform, provincial governors being appointed to each province and district from Istanbul for a term of office. Actually, at the period of our survey, the control of the central government was scarcely more than nominal in some Asiatic regions even of this category. But we may defer mention of them until we come to deal with the provincial administration in detail. Before doing so we propose to describe the structure of the central government, beginning with its centre and pivot, the monarch himself.

CHAPTER II

CALIPHATE AND SULTANATE

THE importance which was attached, both by the Ottoman governing class and by the mass of the Moslem population, to the *Şerî'a* and the Islamic tradition, and the extent to which at least outward conformity with them was sought after, render it necessary to explain, in regard to nearly every aspect of social life, the traditions and ideals which were inculcated by these authoritative guides. More especially is this required in regard to the functions of the ruler, since it is on his person that both the political thought and the political practice of Islâm have been concentrated from the beginning. The Ottoman Sultanate was the heir of nine hundred years of history, during which the Islamic conception of monarchy had evolved from the practice of the Prophet Muḥammad with the aid of the traditions of ancient Arabia and Persia, the theories of Plato and Aristotle, the theoretical deductions of the Sunnî jurists, and the necessities of practical government. Each of these left its mark on the complex of ideas which clustered round the monarchy, though without changing its essential character.

The form of government set up by Muḥammad at Medîna represents a transitional stage between Arab tribalism and monarchy in the strict sense. The essential function of government in Arabia, as represented by the tribal shaikhs, was the settlement of disputes by arbitration, and the application of tribal customary law. Executive authority they had not, either in war or peace, nor had they any legislative power. For Muḥammad also the basis of government was the judicial function, strengthened in his case by his divinely inspired authority and doubled by the legislative function, peculiar to himself in his capacity as Prophet (or, in the Islamic view, promulgator of the divine legislation). But with Muḥammad the executive function was for the first time combined with the judicial function, and, what is still more important, this combination of functions was inherited by his successors, in virtue of their position as head of the Islamic community. On the other hand, the legislative function came to an end, Islamic Law henceforth taking the place of Arab customary law, and even the right of interpreting Islamic Law was gradually withdrawn from them and vested before the 'closing of the gate of interpretation' in the body of *'Ulemâ* or students of the spiritual legacy of Muḥammad (i.e. the *Ḳur'ân* and the Traditions of the Prophet).[1]

[1] The Şî'î theory diverged from this by attributing continued legislative authority to the divinely inspired Imâms, descended from Muḥammad through the marriage of his daughter Fâṭima to his cousin 'Alî.

By the time when, in the middle of the eighth century, the 'Abbâsid Caliphate[1] established itself in 'Irâḳ, this division of functions had become traditional, and though an attempt was made by certain Caliphs to challenge it and claim the right of interpretation, the '*Ulemâ* were successful in maintaining their prerogative. The 'Abbâsid Caliphs, however, emphasized their exclusive possession of the executive and judicial functions to a still greater degree than their predecessors, the former by the centralization of government, the latter by their personal appointment or confirmation of the *ḳâḍîs* in all districts and by the revival of the old Persian custom of holding regular courts of appeal for the hearing of 'grievances' (*maẓâlim*). It was during this period that there was formulated the classical doctrine of the Caliphate, which was to determine, once and for all, the orthodox Islamic view of the relations between the sovereign and the subjects. Into this, in view of the nineteenth-century developments, we must go in some detail.

It is important to observe that the Sunnî canonists who codified (if the term may be used) the accepted legal prescriptions in regard to the Caliphate were not at liberty to develop their system by simple theoretical deduction from the sources. On the contrary, they were tied hand and foot. On the one hand, the dogma of the divine guidance of the Community, and the necessity of avoiding any conclusion which would prove the Community to have fallen away from the Sacred Law (and its judicial and religious activities, consequently, to be void), compelled them to condone the historical process. On the other hand, the same reasons counselled a prudent vagueness in making provision for cases which had not yet arisen in practice. Consequently the Sunnî theory had from the first (and this is of the greatest importance for an understanding of its later development) the character of an apologia for the *status quo nunc*, no matter what the actual state of affairs might be. In essentials, the view which they put forward was that the Caliph or Imâm is the representative or upholder of the Sacred Law; that his office is indispensable and of divine institution, although the holder is elected thereto by human agency;[2] that as the Sacred Law is one and indivisible so also is the Caliphate;[3] and that as the Law is binding on all Moslems

[1] 'Caliph' and 'Caliphate' are accepted English forms of the Arabic words *ḫalîfa* (abbreviated from *ḫalîfat rasūli'llâh*, 'successor of the Apostle of God') and *ḫilâfa*, pronounced in Turkish *hilâfet*, 'succession'. Such forms as Khalif, Khalifat, and the like are spurious.

[2] Not by the body of the people, but by a small group of specially qualified and authoritative electors, or even by the nomination of his predecessor. This election was subsequently confirmed by the *bey'a* or oath of allegiance taken by all office-holders and men of rank.

[3] A number of reputable canonists, however, from the fourth century

without question or qualification, so also is allegiance to the Caliph and obedience to his commands (except when these are contrary to the Law). It was held that the Caliph must be a male, free, and of age and normal physical capacities, possessed of a certain degree of piety and of legal knowledge and perception,[1] capable of directing the public administration and of leadership in war. Moreover, though he might delegate the performance of certain of his functions to qualified persons, he could not divest himself of his ultimate responsibility for all the actions of government. The further provision that none but members of the Meccan tribe of Ḳorayş were eligible for the office was a restriction arising from the monopoly hitherto held by them and consequent 'Consensus' on the point, but one about which several canonists were already uneasy. Finally it was admitted that a Caliph guilty of immorality or grave heresy thereby violated the 'contract' which he was held to have made with the electors and became deserving of deposition; but the jurists carefully abstained from specifying any tribunal or body which was competent to declare him deposed, and were forced (though with evident dislike) to admit the legality of forcible deposition, being too honest to allow that the customary formal *fetwâ* of deposition had any validity apart from the military force behind it.[2] Moreover, the strict doctrine of the liability of the Imâm to deposition was modified considerably by the fact that his subjects were enjoined to obey even an unjust and tyrannical ruler, and were forbidden to revolt and withdraw their allegiance. The standard expression of this view is found in a saying of as early as the first century, attributed to the saintly el-Ḥasan of Baṣra.

'The Prophet said "Do not abuse those who bear rule. If they act uprightly, they shall have their reward, and your duty is to show gratitude. If they do evil, they shall bear the burden, and your duty is to endure patiently. They are a chastisement which God inflicts upon those whom He will; therefore accept the chastisement of God, not with indignation and wrath, but with humility and meekness".'[3]

onwards, allowed the coexistence of more than one Caliph in lands so far apart that there was no practical possibility of any enforcing his sole authority: cf. Bağdâdî, *Uṣûl el-Dîn*, I, p. 274, and Ibn Ḫaldûn I, 3, §26.

[1] This was the nearest approach made by the Sunnî jurists to the recognition of an interpretative function in the Caliphate, but it was closely limited by further definition. As for a 'spiritual function' attaching to the Caliphs, no Sunnî jurist admitted, nor even apparently conceived of, such an idea. It is noteworthy that when, in the last century of the 'Abbâsid Caliphate, this conception was put forward by the temporal Sultans, it was indignantly rejected by the Caliphs and the '*Ulemâ*; cf. Barthold, *Turkestan down to the Mongol Invasion*, p. 347.

[2] Cf. Mâwardî, p. 32 (tr. Fagnan, p. 40).

[3] Abû Yûsuf, *Kitâb el-Ḫarâc*, p. 11 (tr. Fagnan, p. 14). It is authoritatively laid down in the standard exposition of the Sunnî creed by el-Aş'arî (*c.* 300):

The Caliphate is thus, in the theory of the canonists, a limited absolutism, inasmuch as the Caliph-Imâm, while subject to no other control so long as he carries out his duties faithfully, stands *vis-à-vis* the *Şerî'a*, which it is beyond his power to modify or even to interpret, to which he is subject, and which prescribes the principles in accordance with which he must govern. But the doctrine of political quietism, and the absence of any effective check upon his arbitrary action, except by the dangerous expedient of rebellion, turned the canonists' theory of a bilateral contact into an academic archaism, and substituted for it in practice an absolutism limited only by the fear of armed revolt.

This affirmation of the monarchical principle was supported, perhaps even more powerfully, by the survival of other and older practices. Of these the most influential were the traditions of the old Persian Empire, which fixed an impassable gulf between the sovereign and subjects and taught the 'divine right of kings' in its most absolute form, subject only to open apostasy.[1] The revival of these Persian traditions by the 'Abbâsid Caliphs coincided with the beginnings of the codification of the juristic theory, and appeared in many details of usage, such as the practice of seclusion. Their influence is seen, even more clearly than in the writings of the canonists, in the numerous 'Mirrors of Princes', or manuals of government and court etiquette, which were written in Arabic during the Middle Ages.[2] Since these books present what may be called the practical ethics of the official classes, and consequently reflect their views and ideals, they are peculiarly valuable for our present purpose. It is true that the personal predilections of the writers individually tend to blur the outlines of any composite picture, but there are certain features which stand out clearly from the variety of expositions and which we are justified in regarding as the corner-stones of their theoretical structure. Temporal sovereignty is a social necessity; there is no other means whereby the social order may be maintained in the face of human greed and violence. Hence the office of kingship is of divine institution, and obedience to the ruler is a part

'We uphold the prayer for peace for the Imâms of the Muslims and submission to their office, and we maintain the error of those who hold it right to rise against them whensoever there may be apparent in them a falling-away from right. We are opposed to armed rebellion against them and civil war' (D. B. Macdonald, *Development of Muslim Theology*, p. 298).

[1] Cf. T. W. Arnold, *The Caliphate*, pp. 48 sqq.; Christensen, *L'Empire des Sassanides* (Copenhagen, 1907), pp. 79–80.

[2] Of these works, the most popular were the Indian and Persian works translated by Ibn el-Muķaffa' (eighth century A.D.), the *'Uyûn el-Aḫbâr* of Ibn Ķuteyba (ninth century), the *Sirâc el-Mulûk* of el-Ţarţûşî (d. 1126), and the *Kîmiyâ' el-Sa'âda* of el-Ğazâlî (d. 1111). See the study by G. Richter, *Studien zur arabischen Fürstenspiegel*, Leipzig, 1932.

of religion. As supreme judge and sole executive, the fundamental qualities of a good king are justice and munificence: 'The excellence of kings is in giving, their nobility in forgiving, and their pride in equity.' Justice is commended ideally on religious and ethical grounds, but practically on the ground that sooner or later an unjust and tyrannical ruler stands to forfeit his throne. Munificence is 'one of the pillars of kingship, its foundation, its crown, and its adornment'. It is much more than generosity, which is mere 'willingness to spend'; it means that the ruler must shrink from amassing wealth and must give away all that he has. But the prime object of his munificence must be his army: 'The king's enemy is his treasury and his friend is the army; when one is strong the other is weak.' Throughout their works, however, there runs an apologetic note. Thus and thus should kingship be; alas, kingship in being is but a poor compromise between the ideal and human imperfection, and tolerable only because the sole alternative is anarchy. The responsibilities of sovereigns are so terrible that the good life is all but unattainable to them: 'Paradise and Sovereignty are never united.' Men must thus learn to endure the evils arising from sovereignty; it is like rain, which may bring loss and destruction to caravans, towns, and ships, but is withal the life of the earth and its inhabitants. 'Sixty years of tyranny are better than an hour of civil strife.'

The grim realism, of pagan rather than Islamic inspiration, which underlies these expositions received a further reinforcement from the most famous of Moslem *wezîrs*, whose 'Book of Government' was the fountain-head of political wisdom for twenty-five generations of Persian and Turkish rulers.[1] In outward form, Niẓâm ul-Mulk sought to summarize the lessons of history for the guidance of his master, the Selcuḳid Sultan Melik-Şâh (reigned A.D. 1072–92), and to weave them into a series of practical maxims which should ensure the well-being of the state. It is a system completely centralized on the *pâdişâh*. The fief-holders form a second estate, a military aristocracy 'over the heads of the people' and bound to the person of the *pâdişâh*; the civil and religious officials, the third estate, are merely his tools in the matter of administration; the fourth and last estate consists of the passive body of taxpayers. That they have rights against the state, or even an interest in it, is an idea never expressed, possibly never entertained, by the writer. It would be hard to find a more complete contrast in spirit to the constitutional theory of the canonists than this amalgam of Persian tradition and Turkish military institutions, for all the outward religious conformity of the Niẓâm. Here is no divinely ordained system, directed to

[1] Niẓâm ul-Mulk, *Siyâset-Nâme*, ed. and tr. Ch. Schefer, Paris, 1891–1893.

the well-being of all men in this world and the next, and based on a contract between ruler and ruled. It is a theory of rights acquired by force and maintained by force, a state whose institutions are inspired by suspicion and mistrust. The *pâdişâh* fears the troops on whom his power is based, and distrusts the officials by whom he administers his territories; loyalty is discounted, and honesty can be secured only by threat of punishment.

It will be observed that already, in these works, it is no longer the Caliph who is represented as sovereign, but the temporal authority, the 'Sulṭân', or in the old Persian terminology, the 'Pâdişâh'. The Caliphate had indeed, since the middle of the tenth century, lost all executive authority, and there were not wanting those who suggested that the whole structure elaborated by the jurists had fallen to the ground, and that the Caliphate was no longer in existence. But the jurists, though forced by the march of events to modify their theory, refused to give it up altogether. To do so was tantamount to an admission that the community was living in sin. A means of escape from the dilemma with which they were confronted was offered by the Caliphs' practice of granting a diploma to the temporal rulers; by this means, the government of those who seized power by military force was regarded as legitimated and the fiction of the Caliph as the fountain of authority maintained. By the end of the eleventh century, however, the great theologian el-Ğazâlî, with his usual frankness and robust common sense, breaks through the sham and defines the position as facts had made it.

'An evildoing and barbarous sulṭân, so long as he is supported by military force, so that he can only with difficulty be deposed and that the attempt to depose him would cause unendurable civil strife, must of necessity be left in possession and obedience must be rendered to him, exactly as obedience must be rendered to emîrs. . . . We consider that the Caliphate is contractually assumed by that person of the 'Abbâsid house who is charged with it, and that the function of government in the various lands is carried out by means of Sulṭâns, who owe allegiance to the Caliph. . . . Government in these days is a consequence solely of military power, and whosoever he may be to whom the holder of military power gives his allegiance, that person is the Caliph. And whosoever exercises independent authority, so long as he shows allegiance to the Caliph in the matter of his prerogatives of the *Ḫuṭba* and the *Sikka*,[1] the same is a sulṭân, whose commands and judgments are valid in the several parts of the earth.'[2]

These concessions, he explains elsewhere, 'are involuntary, but necessity makes lawful what is prohibited'.[3]

[1] i.e. by having his name mentioned in the bidding-prayer in the mosques and on the coinage—the two traditional external attributes of sovereignty in Islâm.

[2] *Iḥyâ' 'ulûm el-dîn*, ii. 124.

[3] *Kitâb el-Iḳtiṣâd fi'l-I'tiḳâd*, p. 107.

This accommodation prepared the way for the final step. The Sultanate had forced itself into the canonical theory of government, subject only to the theoretical suzerainty of the Caliphate, and had already taken over the greater part of the prerogatives of the latter, at the same time throwing over its own former obligations. The Caliphate, as el-Ğazâlî clearly shows, had become a mere symbol for the legitimation of rights acquired by force. When, in 1258, the Caliphate of Bağdâd was extinguished by the Mongols, its disappearance scarcely affected the political theory of the canonists. Now that election and confirmation were out of the question, it remained only to declare that rights acquired by force were legitimate in themselves and that military power could constitute a valid Imâmate. The setting-up of a nominal 'shadow-Caliphate' at Cairo made no difference, since few if any of the jurists of the period recognized it.[1] It was, in fact, a chief *ḳâḍî* of Egypt itself who consecrated secular absolutism in the final exposition of the canonical theory. After summarizing the classical methods of election and nomination of the Imâm he proceeds:

'As for the third method [of acquisition of the Imâmate], that whereby the contract is made by oath of allegiance exacted by force, this is when a person possessed of military power exercises compulsion. If the office of Imâm is vacant at the time, and one who is not fitted for it aspires to it and compels people by his might and his armies [to accept him] without [receiving] an oath of allegiance or without nomination by his predecessor, his office [literally 'bey'a'] is contractually assumed and obedience is to be rendered to him, in order that the unity of the Muslims may be preserved. That he should be barbarous or evildoing[2] no way invalidates this, in the most authoritative view. When the Imâmate is thus contractually assumed by one person by means of force and military superiority, and thereafter there arises another who overcomes the first by his might and his armies, then the first is deposed and the second becomes Imâm, for the reasons of the wellbeing and unity of the Muslims which are stated above.'[3]

Such a doctrine, however, which practically amounted to divorcing the Imâmate or sovereign power from the Sacred Law which it was supposed to represent and uphold, could not be accepted

[1] See Arnold, *The Caliphate*, pp. 99–102. This point is of great importance in view of the later fiction that the last of the shadow-Caliphs had devolved his office upon the Ottoman Sultans. Even the Egyptian Mamlûks themselves, in the middle of the fifteenth century, had assumed the title of 'Grand Imâm', in spite of the continued existence of their 'Abbâsid protégés; cf. Wiet, *Précis*, ii. 250, and A. N. Poliak in *Revue des Études Islamiques*, ix (1935), p. 236, n. 3.

[2] In Santillana, *Istituzioni di Diritto* . . . (Rome, 1926), i. 24, there are inserted after this the words 'or even a slave or a woman' (*che sia perfino uno schiavo od una donna*), for which, however, there seems to be no authority in the text.

[3] Badr el-Dîn Ibn Cemâ'a, *Taḥrîr el-aḥkâm fî tadbîr ahl el-Islâm*, ap. *Islamica*, Bd. vi, p. 357. Ibn Cemâ'a was chief Ḥanefî *ḳâḍî* of Egypt from 1291 to 1294 and 1309 to 1327.

as an adequate solution by Moslem opinion. More especially in the Perso-Turkish lands of Eastern Islâm, which had been severed from the Arabic lands by the irruption of the heathen Mongols and the destruction of the older traditions, and where a long struggle had to be waged for the restoration of the supremacy of the *Şerî'a*, some other doctrine more applicable to their own conditions and aspirations was felt to be necessary. The old canonical theory was obviously out of court, and another view (afterwards accepted as the official doctrine by the Ḥanefî jurists of the Ottoman Empire)[1] that the genuine Caliphate had come to an end with the fourth of Muḥammad's successors failed to satisfy the need felt by the Sunnî community for a present and visible Imâm. There was in existence, however, another body of doctrine which had found supporters even during the period of the 'Abbâsid Caliphate, though never countenanced by the official jurists. This doctrine, which had arisen in philosophical circles under Platonic influence, sought to equate the theory of the philosopher-king with the Islamic Caliph-Imâm, administering the *Şerî'a* under the guidance of divine wisdom.

In its original form[2] it obviously ran counter to the Sunnî theory to some extent, and found favour chiefly in philosophical and Şî'î circles. But when stripped of its theosophic elements and brought into line with orthodox views, it supplied the later Sunnî jurists with a practical and satisfactory basis for the political and religious structure of the community.

'The governor is a person distinguished by divine support, that he may lead individual men to perfection and provide a corrective order for them. The philosophers designate him "the absolute sovereign", and the moderns [i.e. the Islamic philosophers] call him the Imâm and his function the Imâmate. Plato calls him "The controller of the world" and Aristotle calls him "the civic man".'[3]

Sovereignty (so the argument runs) is a gift divinely bestowed upon a selected person. Government may be either righteous or unrighteous. The righteous government, which 'regards its subjects as children and friends' and labours for their temporal and spiritual welfare, is the Imâmate; the unrighteous government is the rule of force, which treats its subjects as beasts of burden

[1] See Arnold, *The Caliphate*, p. 163.

[2] e.g. in el-Fârâbî's version of the *Republic*, entitled *Ârâ' ahl el-Medîna el-fâḍila*.

[3] Celâl ul-Dîn el-Dawwânî, *Aḫlâḳ-i Celâlî*, tr. W. F. Thompson, *Practical Philosophy of the Muhammadan People* (London, 1839), pp. 322 sqq. El-Dawwânî belonged to a learned family of Şâfi'î jurists and was himself a *ḳâḍî* in the province of Fârs, where he died in 1502/3 (see Browne, *Lit. Hist. Persia*, iii. 444). This ethical treatise of his was one of the most popular and widely read books in the eastern Islamic world.

and slaves.[1] Consequently, every righteous ruler who governs with justice and enforces the *Şerî'a* is entitled to the style and prerogatives of the Caliphate. It is this theory, and not the 'classical' theory, which underlies the use of the terms Caliph and Caliphate in the later Perso-Turkish world; Dawwânî, it should be observed, did not invent it, but merely gave it final and acceptable expression because of his personal reputation.[2] For some two centuries before his time the term 'Caliphate' in one form or another had been applied in relation to a number of Moslem rulers (including the Ottoman Sultans), probably with some such connotation, as contrasted with the heathen Mongols and those rulers who maintained the Mongol code.[3] That it was, so to speak, in the air at this period seems to be proved by the fact that at the other end of the Islamic world, in North-west Africa, the Mâlikite *ķâḍî* and historian Ibn Ḫaldûn (d. 1406) came to the identical conclusion.[4]

Henceforward Caliphate and Sultanate were to all intents and purposes synonymous terms. But it should be remarked that, on the other hand, the Sultan was practically never addressed or referred to as *Imâm* or *Ḫalîfa* in ordinary or in official usage. Contemporary writers in the seventeenth and eighteenth centuries speak of Constantinople indiscriminately as *dâr ul-ḫilâfa* or *dâr us-salṭana*;[5] the Sultan is referred to either by that title or by the Persian title 'Pâdişâh of Islâm'. As late as 1813, after Meḥmed 'Alî's reconquest of Mecca and Medîna on behalf of his Ottoman suzerain, the official formula to be employed in the *ḫuṭba* is given as 'The Sulṭân, son of the Sulṭân, son of the Sulṭân, Maḥmud Ḫan, son of the Sulṭân 'Abd ul-Ḥamîd Ḫan, son of the Sulṭân Aḥmed Ḫan, the Warrior for the Faith, Servitor of the Two Noble Sanctuaries'.[6] That the Ottoman Sultan was the universal Caliph of Islam, after the manner of the Caliphs of Medîna, Damascus, and Bağdâd, was an idea entertained by no responsible jurist.[7]

1 Ibid., pp. 377 sqq.

2 It is especially noteworthy that the Ottoman Sultan Bâyezîd II sent a complimentary letter and gift to Dawwânî, and that the famous Ottoman jurist 'Abdul-Raḥmân Çelebî actually studied under him for seven years.—Browne, op. cit. iii. 423.

3 Cf. T. W. Arnold, *The Caliphate*, ch. ix: 'Assumption of the Title Khalīfah by Independent Muslim Princes', and ch. xi: 'The Ottomans and the Caliphate'.

4 Prolegomena of Ibn Ḫaldûn, bk. iii, ch. 25 (de Slane's translation, i. 385 ff., misinterprets a crucial distinction).

5 Murâdî, i. 25, 32, 50, *et pass.*, sometimes also *dâr el-mulk*, i. 41.

6 Cabartî, iv. 178/ix. 23. It is curious to find in Murâdî the application of archaic Sultanian (*not* Caliphial) titles to the Ottomans, e.g. Muṣṭafâ III is called 'The Sulṭân, favoured by Divine Support and Victory (Abu'l-ta'yîd wa'l-ẓafar), Niẓâm ul-Dîn Muṣṭafâ Ḫan' (i. 258); and 'Abd ul-Ḥamîd I is 'The Very Great Sulṭân, favoured by Divine aid (Abu'l-naṣr), Ğiyâṯ ul-Dawla wa'l-Dîn 'Abd ul-Ḥamîd Ḫan' (i. 228).

7 This view is apparently contradicted by the expressions occasionally found

Unexpected confirmation of this view is supplied by a striking passage in the work of el-Murâdî. It may have been remarked that while the later jurists freely use the term 'Caliphate' they are careful to avoid the historic title borne by the early Caliphs, *Amîr ul-Mu'minîn*, 'Commander of the Faithful'. Only once does this title reappear in the literature of the Ottoman dominions in the eighteenth century, and it is then applied not to an Ottoman Sultan but to a Grand Mughal of India. In his brief notice of Awrangzêb (reigned 1659–1707), el-Murâdî qualifies him as 'Sultan of India in our time, the *Amîr ul-Mu'minîn* and their Imâm, the Stay of the Muslimîn and their Support, the Warrior on the Path of God, . . . who has no equal among the kings of Islâm in this age in uprightness of conduct, fear of God, and zeal in religion'.[1] Here, it is evident, the true and original conception of the Caliphate breaks through, and in a flash reveals the other as but a legal fiction. There might be many *Ḫalîfas*, but only he is *Amîr ul-Mu'minîn* who 'brings victory to the Faith, who has destroyed the unbelievers in his land and asserted his authority over them, who has overthrown their temples, reduced their polytheism to weakness, given his aid to Islâm and made the word of God uppermost'.[2]

Except in so far, then, as the obligation to maintain the *Şerî'a* was concerned (an obligation, for the rest, more loyally accepted by the Ottoman Sultans than by any previous universal Islamic dynasty), it may be concluded that the general conception of the powers and functions of the monarchy in the Ottoman Empire was but little affected by Islamic ideas. The Selcuḳids had been thoroughly impregnated with Persian doctrines which fitted in but too well with Turkish views based upon the military organization of the Turkish tribe, and these they had passed on to their Ottoman successors. The main function of the 'World-Creator'—

in Turkish works; e.g. the exordium to the *Ḳânûn-nâme* of Süleymân: 'The *Ḫaḳan* of the face of the earth and *Ḫalîfa* of the Apostle of the Lord of the Universe, the King of the kingdoms of the World and overshadowing shade over all mankind, . . . the possessor of the Supreme Imâmate and the glorious Sulṭân [i.e. temporal sovereignty], Inheritor of the Great Caliphate'; but this language is typical of the bombastic phraseology used in such passages, and is not to be taken as expressing either fact or juristic theory. Even more remarkable, for example, is the exordium to the work of the eighteenth-century Tripolitan chronicler Ibn Ǧalbûn, who applies the terms 'Shadow of God' and '*Ḫalîfa*' to the local Ḳaramanlî prince, and in the same breath affirms the suzerainty of the Ottomans.—E. Rossi, *La Cronaca . . . di Ibn Ǧalbûn*, Bologna, 1936, p. 26.

[1] Murâdî, iv. 113–14. It should be remembered that el-Murâdî was chief Ḥanefî muftî of Damascus, and in personal relations with Sultan 'Abd ül-Ḥamîd and the Turkish *'Ulemâ*.

[2] A similar significance is to be attached to the occasional application of the title Amîr ul-Mu'minîn to the earlier Ottoman sultans; see H. A. R. Gibb in *Archives d'Histoire du Droit Oriental*, vol. iii, (Wetteren, 1948), 406 ff.

ḫünkâr, one of the favourite titles of the Ottoman Sultans—was to keep the world on its axis by seeing that his army was paid and that no class of his subjects trespassed upon the rights and duties of any other class. The weaker the personal authority and influence of a Sultan, the more rigidly was he held to the strict observance of traditional customs and usages.

By the time of our survey the Ottoman Sultanate had been in existence over four hundred years, in the course of which it had passed, politically, through a number of phases. These fall naturally into two divisions, the first comprising the reigns of the first ten Sultans and ending with that of Süleymân the Magnificent.[1] For with his reign the era of conquest virtually came to an end, though certain comparatively minor additions, offset by far greater losses, were made to the Empire in later reigns. And simultaneously decay set in, gathering force, particularly in the reign of Süleymân's grandson, Murâd III (1574–95). The Millennium of the Hegira was completed during the reign of Murâd; and later Turkish historians are fond of taking this picturesque date as a turning-point. But both Murâd and his father, Selîm II, called the Sot, belong to the second category of Sultans, among whom there were no more than one or two exceptions, in that they ceased to control affairs as their energetic forefathers had done. Most of the Sultans of the second period applied themselves more or less exclusively to pleasure or devotion, according to their tastes, and left matters of supreme moment to ministers who had not always received office for their merits.

If the Sultans of the second period were remarkable chiefly for ineffectiveness, this was due largely to the singularity of their upbringing. The early Ottomans, like other Turkish rulers before them, had been wont to give princes of the blood royal provincial governments. But this, instead of satisfying the princes' ambition, often encouraged them to make a bid for the throne by revolt. The Sultans were safe not even from the schemes of sons, let alone brothers and cousins. To do away with sons would be to imperil the dynasty; but short of this the throne was the thing; and Meḥmed the Conqueror issued a *Ḳânûn* enjoining his descendants to mark their accession with a slaughter of their brothers.[2] The *Ḳânûn* was obeyed up to the end of the sixteenth century; but

[1] This epithet is not of Turkish usage, which gives him instead that of *Ḳânûnî*—the *Ḳânûn*-maker. The period comprised in these ten reigns began about 1300 and ended with the death of Süleymân in 1566.

[2] See *O.T.E.M.* 1912, No. 14, Appendix, 27 (*Ḳânûn-nâmei Âli* '*Oṣmân*) *Ve her kimseneye evlâdimdan salṭanet muyesser ola, ḳarndaşlarini niẓâmi 'alem için ḳatl etmek munâsibdir. Ekṣeri 'ulemâ daḫi tecvîz etmişdir. Onunla 'âmil olalar.* 'And to whomsoever of my sons the Sultanate shall pass, it is fitting that for the order of the world he shall kill his brothers. Most of the '*Ulemâ* allow it. So let them act on this.'

then a substitute was invented.[1] From that time on all princes but the sons of the reigning Sultan were confined in special pavilions in the palace and were denied all communication with the outside world. Their lives were spent in the company of a few eunuchs, slave-girls, and pages, from whom they gained what knowledge of the world they could. They were, it is true, sometimes supplied with instructors, but only for such studies as the *Ḳur'ân*, astrology, and official composition;[2] and generally acquired from them as well an outlook of extreme conservatism and a horrified contempt of all things non-Moslem. Moreover, any children, male or female, born to them by slave-concubines —who for this reason were as a rule above the child-bearing age—were not allowed to live. All the princes living, therefore, were the sons of the reigning Sultan or his predecessors.

From the beginning of the fourteenth to the beginning of the seventeenth century, the Sultanate had passed from father to son in thirteen generations. But at the death of Aḥmed I in 1617 none of his sons were yet of age—and no minor had ever succeeded. Aḥmed's brother, Muṣṭafâ I, was accordingly preferred before his children—despite the fact that, though a major, he was mad. And at the same time a *Ḳânûn* was promulgated regulating the succession for the future, which practically ensured that every Sultan should have spent part of his life in the crippling seclusion we have described. For it was then laid down that when the throne fell vacant, it should pass to the eldest surviving male member of the imperial house. And this in fact during the next century and a half brought about the succession of brothers, uncles, and cousins (who by the other *Ḳânûn* had been mewed up in their 'cages')[3] to the immediate exclusion of sons (who were not) on all but one occasion.

The one exception was Meḥmed IV, who in 1648 succeeded his father Ibrahîm at the age of seven years, because he was the sole Ottoman prince alive. And the case is interesting, because it follows that all the subsequent Sultans were the descendants of Ibrahîm, who, if not actually mad, was at least eccentric to the verge of madness.[4] Since the fall of the Ottoman dynasty has

[1] According to Juchereau (i. 17–18) the seclusion of princes was decreed by Süleymân I, but only begun in the reign of Murâd III. D'Ohsson places it in the reign of Aḥmed I. Muṣṭafâ I owed his life to the relaxation of the *Ḳânûn* (see *Encyclopaedia of Islam*, art. 'Muṣṭafā I'). But it is to be remarked that his successor Murâd IV killed three of his brothers (ibid., art. 'Murād IV').

[2] See Juchereau de Saint-Denys, *Les Révolutions de Constantinople*, i. 17 sq.

[3] The princes' pavilions were each surrounded by a garden enclosed in a high wall. They were hence called *Ḳafes* (Arabic), a cage.

[4] The private life of Ibrahîm might make an amusing study. He once levied a special tax to pay for the import of sables from Russia so that he might cover the walls of his apartments with them, and was pleased to encase his beard in a network of diamonds.

permitted, and even encouraged, the laying of blame on the Sultans for many of the woes of the Empire, some play has been made with the fact that for over two hundred and fifty years it was ruled by the descendants of Ibrahîm. As a matter of fact actual madness appeared only in one of them.[1] When the seclusion system was brought to an end, indeed, several estimable princes mounted the throne in turn. And if some of these were inclined on occasion to display symptoms of waywardness, there were many other circumstances to explain it.

The Sultans of the second period, though they were often little more than ciphers, yet remained potential autocrats. For no rival power grew up so strong that an energetic occupant of the throne might not realize this potentiality. But their autocracy, limited in theory by the Sacred Law, was also limited in practice by their liability to deposition. And in this respect the weakening of their power during the second period may be illustrated by a comparison. Whereas during the first period only one Sultan was obliged to abdicate (and that by his son and successor), during the second —up to the date of our survey—no less than six Sultans either abdicated or were deposed, two of them also being murdered. Nor was it their successors that were responsible for these depositions, which were oftenest brought about by the soldiery of the capital.

It is true that several of these Sultans were made scapegoats for the defeat of their armies in the field, and were innocent of anything more unusual than negligence. But two, who raised opposition by their conduct, are interesting from our point of view, since their fate portended things to come. Thus 'Os̱mân II was deposed and killed in 1622 largely because he had meditated the destruction of the Janissaries (already required, though not achieved for another two centuries); and Aḥmed III was forced to abdicate in 1730 as the result of what was in part a social revolution,[2] provoked by the ostentatious luxury of his court, which was rendered the more distasteful to his subjects by its faintly European flavour.[3]

The Sultans, then, though some of them played but a small part in affairs, remained so far the pivot of the Empire that its destinies lay in their hands. But the two checks on their will remained in being. In the future they must perform the difficult feat of harmonizing innovations, if they should deem them necessary, with the set prescriptions of the Law, and steer clear of conflicts with those who might deprive them of their throne.

[1] In Murâd V, whose deposition on this ground (whether or not it was justified) led to the accession of his brother, the famous 'Abd ül-Ḥamîd II.

[2] Cf. *Encyclopaedia of Islam*, 'Maḥmūd I'.

[3] He encouraged his courtiers, for instance, to build pavilions on the hills round the *Kâğidḫâne* (the Sweet Waters of Europe) in imitation of Marly. These, after his fall, were destroyed with gusto by the people—see De Tott, *Memoirs*, i. 5.

CHAPTER III

THE RULING INSTITUTION

I. INTRODUCTION

HAVING sketched the position of the Sultans in the Ottoman polity, we may next turn to the organization by which they ruled. In its nature this organization was to a great extent traditional: its main features were inherited from the Persian system, already somewhat 'Turkified', adopted by the Selcuḳids, which had itself been inherited, with modifications, from the 'Abbâsids through the Ġaznawids. But the Ottoman system of government had features peculiar to itself; and these seem to have been due to the geographical situation of the Ottoman state in its early days. From the earliest times of Islâm the greatest monarch of the Domain of War had been the Byzantine Emperor. An attempt at the conquest of Constantinople had been made in the first century of the Hegira; and it had remained ever since an intermittent ambition of Moslem rulers so placed as to be able to dream of undertaking it. The prestige of Byzantium in Moslem eyes was immense. When, therefore, first all its former dependencies, and finally the city itself, fell to the Ottoman conquerors, it was inevitable that their conception of statecraft should be affected by that of the state they had overthrown. The adaptation was made the easier, moreover, by the fact that for centuries the Moslem and Byzantine forms of civilization had reacted strongly on one another, so that, largely through the growth of Armenian influence in the management of Byzantine affairs, the Empire had been progressively Easternized. There was, indeed, hardly one Ottoman institution but was modelled on those existing in one or another former and contemporary Moslem state. But they were welded in the new realm into a more consistent, and especially a more thoroughly organized, whole; and in this circumstance it is difficult not to detect Byzantine influence. The excessively bureaucratic character of Ottoman administration reflects, indeed, what we are accustomed to regard as Byzantinism *par excellence*. The notion of *Ḳânûn* framing was an Ottoman innovation—and the very word is 'canon' in disguise. The recognition of the Sultan's *'urf* initiative was another—and, though this would certainly have consorted well with the despotic power expected of the traditional Persian monarch, it was, in all likelihood, actually accorded in imitation of the Emperors.

It was only after the conquest of Constantinople in the mid-fifteenth century that the Ottoman institutions that already existed were regularized in the manner characteristic of the hey-day of the Empire. But this is not to say that it was only then that they were Byzantinized, even though the process of 'Byzantinization' was then intensified. For it was not until the Sultans had conquered the whole Balkan peninsula, which, if it was no longer politically subject to the Emperors, yet looked exclusively to Constantinople for its culture, that they, the Sultans, effected any notable additions in Asia to the territory under their sway.

The Byzantine aspect of the Ottoman government must not, however, be exaggerated.[1] It was essentially what had come in the course of time to be regarded as typically Moslem. But in so far as it was affected by Byzantine precedents, the fact that the Sultans made their first notable conquests in Europe, and not in Asia, is significant. The direction in which they launched their earliest campaigns, moreover, influenced the character of their rule and institutions in other ways.

The course that these conquests took was almost fortuitous. War between Moslem rulers had for long been much more common than war against the infidel. Indeed, in Moslem history there had been only three considerable enlargements of the Domain of Islâm: the original Arab conquests, the campaigns of the Ǧaznawids in India, and the penetration of the Selcuḳid Turks into Asia Minor; whereas, from the eclipse of the ʿAbbâsid Caliphate at the beginning of the tenth century, the world of Islâm had been continually ravaged by what to a Moslem theorist could scarcely appear as other than civil wars. But the state formed by ʿO̱smân in the last years of the thirteenth century—one of a number of small Turkish principalities (and by no means the largest of them) that sprang up in Asia Minor as the hold on that territory of the Mongols, or Tatars, declined—was situated on what was then a frontier of Islâm. The lands surrounding it, both within the pale and without it, were in a state of upheaval. It was evident to the Ottomans that their position could be maintained only by arms, and could best be defended by expansion; and the Moslem doctrine of the obligation to increase the Domain of Islâm determined what direction this expansion should take. The earliest Sultans, indeed, loved the rival Turkish chieftains that were their neighbours within the pale little more than the infidels that confronted them outside it. But many of their supporters were imbued with missionary zeal; and others were bound by strong religious ties to the subjects of the other Turkish chieftains.[2] It was, therefore, into the Domain of

[1] See Köprülüzade, 'Biẓans'in O̱smanli Mu'esseselerine Te'ṣiri', in *Türk Ḥuḳuḳ ve Iḳtiṣat Mecmuasi*, i.

[2] Gibbons, in *The Foundations of the Ottoman Empire*, emphasizes the fact

War that they pressed, and won the spoils for which all were eager, virtuously, from the infidels.

Owing to the direction that this expansion took not only was a certain Byzantinism impressed from its beginnings on the growing Ottoman state, but, even more important, its military character was preserved for good. For though the frontier of Islâm was thereby advanced, the centre of the new state was advanced simultaneously;[1] and it thus remained, as it were, a frontier organization, with all the obligation of military preparedness that this necessitated. Moreover, the expansion was so rapid as to forbid an assimilation of the infidel populations included within the new frontiers. A military government was necessary on this account as well, therefore: to keep the peace between them and hold them down.[2]

The history of the Empire's foundation is still the subject of some controversy. But it is certain that in its origins it was as much a popular-religious as a dynastic enterprise. As time went on, however, and the Sultans came to rule over wider and wider territories, the dynastic aspect gained on the popular. The fervour for conquest waned in the people; and the supply of voluntary fighters diminished, both from this cause, and as a result of casualties. To some extent, also, the interests of the Sultans diverged from those of even their Moslem subjects. Like other dynasts before them, they felt the need of forces attached exclusively to the throne. These seem to have been the chief reasons for the acquisition, during the fifteenth and sixteenth centuries, by the Ottoman government of an extraordinary character.

As we have mentioned, the Sacred Law regarded mankind as being divided into free and bond, and laid it down as a principle that the only persons eligible for enslavement were non-Moslem inhabitants of the Domain of War. Born slaves existed within the Domain of Islâm, and might be bought and sold; but the supply always tended to decline owing to manumission and the free status of children borne by slave women to free masters. The acquisition of slaves by the inhabitants of the Domain of Islâm as a whole,

that the other Turkish emirs of Asia Minor made no effort to aid the Ottomans, towards whom they were clearly rather hostile than friendly. But he overlooks the importance of the *Aḫi* organization in determining the mutual relations of all these Turkish rulers. This social-religious 'society of virtue' had centres in all the cities of Anatolia, and was hostile to all governments alike. It appears to have been quite strong enough to prevent any serious warfare among the chieftains, and at the same time to have played a preponderant role in launching the Ottoman enterprise, by way of a Holy War. It was only after the formation of the Janissaries (see below, p. 43) that the Ottoman Sultans could afford to disregard the ties that bound many of their own subjects and those of their Turkish rivals, and attack the latter. For the *Aḫis*, see below, p. 64.

[1] The capital was moved from Eski-şehir to Bursa, and then from Bursa to Adrianople,

[2] See *Encyclopaedia of Islam*, art. 'Turks'.

therefore, was dependent upon their capture or purchase outside its bounds. Another provision of the Law allotted one-fifth of the booty, including prisoners, taken in campaigns against the infidel, to the Imâm. And from the earliest times the Ottoman Sultans were so far regarded as Imâms as to be able to exercise this privilege.[1] They thus found themselves to have a large and ever-growing number of slave prisoners at their disposal. It was usual at first for them to sell these slaves. As the supply of volunteer fighters diminished, however, they bethought them of converting those that were suitable into soldiers. But towards the end of the fourteenth century, again, large-scale conquests in Europe came to an end for the time being. A great part of the Sultans' energies was taken up with the extension of their dominions in Moslem Asia, where no prisoners of war might legitimately be enslaved. If they were to keep their army up to strength, then, they must draw slave recruits from some other source.

In the meantime the Ottoman forces had come to fall into two groups: those paid in cash from the Sultans' treasury, and those given land with the right to collect taxes and dues from its inhabitants.[2] And though both of them seem originally to have been composed of free-born Moslems, these gradually ceased to take service in the first, as the employment of slaves in it became more and more common. Thus the paid army, as distinct from the feudal cavalry (which formed the majority of the land-holding soldiery), came to be almost exclusively a slave corps, the personal property of the Sultans.

At this point the Sultans might, perhaps, have contented themselves with the possession of a large feudal army and a slave bodyguard. This, indeed, was more or less the policy followed at its prime by the dynasty from which they derived their traditions of government—the Selcuḳid. For the purchase and employment of slaves as soldiers was far from being an Ottoman eccentricity, having been common even under the ʿAbbâsid Caliphs. The Sultans might now, then, have recruited the latter from the diminished, but not quite exhausted supply of prisoners of war, supplemented by purchase at home or abroad. But by this time, conquest had become a fatal tradition; and if such forces might have sufficed for the maintenance of order within the Empire (which then included only the Balkan Peninsula and Asia Minor), even though, by now, the interests of the Sultans had so far diverged from those of the people as to have given birth to a certain antagonism be-

[1] According to Aḥmed Râsim, iii. 1236, notes, from the time of Murâd I. The price of a prisoner (called *Bedeli Esâret*) was then established at 125 *aḳçes* or pieces of silver. (For the currency, see below, chap vii.)

[2] The first were known as *ʿÖlûfeli*, 'stipendiary' or 'pay-drawing' (from the Arabic *ʿAlûfa*, 'fodder')—see, e.g., A. Djevad, *État Militaire Ottoman*, 15–16.

tween them, it was not enough as well for the achievement of further expansion.

The Sultans therefore pitched on a new expedient, which had the great merit of costing nothing in cash, but the serious defect of being contrary to the Sacred Law. They decided to make periodical levies of the unmarried male children of their Orthodox Christian[1] subjects, taking them from their parents at between the ages of ten and twenty, reducing them to the status of slaves, and training them for the service of the state.

In the Sultans' eyes this system had one immense advantage. The children so enrolled were wholly dependent on them. They were drawn from the least dangerous class of their subjects, and were, in any case, almost entirely cut off from their former associations. Hence the enrolment system—*devşirme*, as it was called—led to a further development. Whereas in its earlier days the administration of the growing Empire had been conducted by free Moslems, now these were almost without exception replaced by the Sultans' slaves on an ever larger scale, until nearly every post, in what has been described as the 'Ruling Institution' of the Empire, was filled either by a Christian conscript or by a slave otherwise acquired.[2]

It is unfortunate that we should be obliged to use the word 'slave' for persons of this status. For it is appropriate only in some ways. Slaves in Islâm are, or were, the property of the masters, who had absolute rights over them. But their servitude carried with it scarcely any social inferiority. No distinction was made between the sons of slave women born to a free master and those whose mothers were also free. Indeed, most of the 'Abbâsid Caliphs of Bağdâd, to say nothing of minor dynasts, were born of slave mothers; and, from the mid-fifteenth century onwards, so were all the Ottoman Sultans.[3] Moreover, the history of Islâm shows several examples of slave dynasties—that is to say, dynasties of monarchs either enslaved or born in slavery, from a slave father as well as a slave mother—the most celebrated being those of the Egyptian *Mamlûk* Sultans, contemporary with the Ottomans of the 'first' period. In such a world little obloquy could attach to the status. And so to the Ottomans there seemed nothing outrageous

[1] According to Cevdet, i. 90, the Christians subjected to the *Devşirme* were Albanians, Bosnians, Bulgarians, and Armenians. The Armenians, however, were legally exempt from it, since they were not orthodox—see Lybyer, 34, and below, chap. xiv.

[2] See *Encyclopaedia of Islam*, arts. 'Dewshirme', 'Turks'; Hasluck, *Christianity and Islam under the Sultans*, ii. 493. The term 'Ruling Institution' is an invention of A. H. Lybyer. See his *Government of the Ottoman Empire*, p. 36.

[3] According to Gibbons, op. cit. 183, Bâyezîd I was the last Sultan to contract a formal marriage. D'Ohsson, vii. 63, however, states that both Murâd II and Meḥmed II married princesses. Ibrahîm married also, but a slave of his *Ḥarem*.

in the system they erected wherein half the highest positions in the state were held by slaves. Nevertheless, its effect was to exclude from them all the Sultans' free Moslem subjects. The Sultans' slaves—the *Ḳapî Ḳullarî*, 'Slaves of the Porte', as they were called[1] —nearly all adopted Islâm, indeed, not because they were forced to do so, but because they could not otherwise obtain any influential position. Nevertheless, for the ambitious it was a positive advantage to be born an unbeliever. And in the long run this was more than free-born Moslems were prepared to put up with.

The employment of slaves in the administration as well as in the army was nothing new in Islamic history either. But never before had free Moslems been all but entirely excluded from it. No doubt the fact that they were so excluded in this case may be connected with another: namely, that the proportion of non-Moslems in the Ottoman population (particularly before the Asiatic conquests of the sixteenth century) was unprecedentedly high. For the loyalty of these infidels could be expected to be at best but grudging; so that, unloved as they were, at the same time, by so many of the Moslems under their rule, the Sultans were perhaps possessed of relatively fewer dependable subjects than any of the dynasts their predecessors. The institution of the *Ḳapî Ḳullarî*, therefore, may be held to have corresponded to a special need. It at once served to protect the Sultans from overthrow by a subject population exceptionally liable to disaffection, and to secure to the non-Moslem section of this population—though by a method well calculated to obscure the advantages of this privilege to its beneficiaries—a place in the state machine commensurate with its preponderant numbers.

The Moslems, to be sure, had another institution as their equally exclusive field—that of the *'Ulemâ*, the students of the *Şerî'a*.[2] But the Ottoman Empire was a Moslem state in which it was paradoxical that any institution should be reserved for the infidel born. How the Moslems contrived to rebel we shall describe later. Suffice it here to say that by the eighteenth century the whole system of a slave-manned Ruling Institution had been swept away. Free Moslems had captured nearly all the posts it formerly included—

[1] *Ḳapî* means 'gate' or 'door' in Turkish, *Ḳul* 'slave'. The use of a word meaning 'door' to denote a royal court is Persian in origin, and is due to the custom whereby the monarch would sit in the great archway before his palace to receive petitions and do justice. As well as the Turkish *Ḳapî*, the Arabic *Bâb* and the Persian *Där* are found in various Ottoman phrases with this significance. See *Encyclopaedia of Islam*, art. 'Der'. It was only in later times that the Porte—Sublime Porte (*Bâbî 'Alî*)—came to denote the head-quarters of the government as opposed to the Sultan's court. Though it properly embraced every person of slave status in the Sultan's service, the term *Ḳapî Ḳullarî* was applied particularly to the paid as opposed to the feudal troops—see Hammer, *Staatsverwaltung*, p. 189.

[2] See below, ch. ix.

and with disastrous results. At the same time this change had never been acknowledged. In this, as in many other matters, there was a general tacit agreement to shut the eye to realities which compared disquietingly with dreams of the past. So the whole apparatus of this Ruling Institution still existed, hardly changed at all, on paper. And, odder still, every one that belonged to it was held still to be a slave of the Sultan, though only a small minority were really eligible to be any such thing. The conventional slavery of the rest had a painfully real quality, however. It was actual enough to cost them what may be termed their civil rights. By entering the Sultan's service they still became his property: he could take their lives without legal process, and confiscate what he would of their wealth when they died—or before.[1]

II. THE ARMY

What we have referred to as the 'Ruling Institution' corresponds more or less to a category defined by some Moslem authors when considering the structure of their society. They contrast the military and civil employees of the ruler with the *'Ulemâ*, calling the first 'Men of the Sword'[2] and the second 'Men of the Pen'.[3] And in some ways the term 'Men of the Sword' is a good name for the members of the Ruling Institution, since it brings out the essentially military character of the Ottoman government. But the term must be taken in the sense of 'Men supporting the Sword of Government', so that it may include the whole personnel of the Sultan's court and the central and provincial administration. Thus it must embrace all the secretaries and accountants of this personnel, wielders of pens though they were, because of the character of their offices. In this view the real 'Men of the Pen' were the professors of mosque colleges, those who administered and expounded the Sacred Law, ministers of religion, physicians, &c., whom we are to deal with in a later section.[4] Our present task is to describe the structure of the Ruling Institution in further detail. But since, as we have remarked, by the eighteenth century it had largely changed its nature whilst preserving its form, we must start by sketching its original constitution, and then note how, why, and in what respects this had changed.

The Ruling Institution, apart from the Sultan himself, included the officers of his household, the executive officers of his government, the whole body of the army, 'standing' and feudal, and the navy. In the hey-day of Ottoman rule all posts in it, except most of those in the feudal army and the navy, were as a rule filled by the *Ḳapï Ḳullarï*, either conscripted by *Devşirme* or acquired in some other manner.

[1] See D'Ohsson, vii. 148.
[2] *Ehl ul-Seyf*.
[3] *Ehl ul-Ḳalem*
[4] Below, chs. viii–x.

We propose first to deal with the army, the court, and the central government, leaving the provincial administration and the navy to subsequent sections. For the first three cannot conveniently be dealt with separately, owing to the facts that the personnel of the court and the central government and that of the 'standing', as opposed to the feudal, forces was recruited from the same source (the *Ḳapî Ḳullarî*), and that some members of it were often employed now in one now in the others. But in order to deal with these two main divisions of the army consecutively, we must begin our review with the feudal troops. And this will require a short description of the fief-system on which they depended—though we shall return to this again in connexion with agriculture and the life of the peasantry.

(*a*) *The Feudal Forces*

A feudal system was adopted very early in the career of the Ottoman dynasty, possibly, indeed, at its very beginning. Its main purpose was to provide a livelihood for various categories of soldiery alternative to that of maintaining them as a standing force. It involved, as in Europe, the grant of land to these warriors. In return they were bound to do military service when called upon, and for this purpose to equip and mount not only themselves, but also, usually, a number of retainers varying with the size of each holding. The fiefs thus created were worked partly by the holders, partly by the peasants that lived on them as tenants. Their holders derived a livelihood from them in the shape of the crops, &c., that they grew themselves, and of the tithes and dues imposed on the peasantry.

The system was not, in Islâm, an Ottoman invention. The granting of fiefs on these terms to fighting men had first become common during the period of the break-up of the Caliphate, but had assumed a character more nearly similar to that which they bore under the Ottoman régime during the Selcuḳid era.[1] The system had been adopted in these earlier times chiefly as a method of relieving the Treasury from the burden of tax-collection and the payment of troops in cash, and was maintained by the Ottoman Sultans largely for the same purposes. While the Empire was being swiftly enlarged by fresh conquests, moreover, it had another virtue. It imposed control by a class of Moslem knights, attached to the conquerors, on the rural populations of the provinces so incorporated, and, in most regions where it was introduced, prevented the conquests from assuming the character of a simple military occupation, by attaching these knights to the land. Hence, except where

[1] See Hammer, *Staatsverfassung*, 337; Tischendorf, *Das Lehnswesen*, chap. i; *Encyclopaedia of Islam*, art. '*Iḳṭâ*''; Becker. *Steuerpacht und Lehnswesen*.

religious distinctions precluded this—perpetuated as these distinctions were by the privileges granted to People of Scripture under the rules of the Sacred Law—knights and peasants came at length to regard themselves, whatever their racial origins may have been, as of one people.

In most parts of those provinces, both European and Asiatic, that were included in the Sultan's dominions before the sixteenth century, a feudal system very similar was already in being. So like was it, indeed, that many historians have believed the Ottoman to be derived from the Byzantine. And in so far as that employed by the Selcuḳids of Asia Minor (from which the Ottoman was immediately imitated) differed from the system of the parent dynasty of Persia and the 'Irâḳ, it did so probably by the contagion of Byzantine usage. For not only had Asia Minor actually remained part of the East Roman Empire until its conquest by the Selcuḳids (thereby differing from all the other provinces in their control), but, after the conquest, which was no more than partial, it continued to march with territory that was Byzantine still. Moreover, in so far as the Ottoman system differed again from that of the Selcuḳids of Asia Minor, it can scarcely have been otherwise than by a further 'Byzantinization'. The subject, indeed, as part of the whole problem of the influence of Byzantine on Ottoman institutions, is still controversial.[1] But in any case the existence in the provinces conquered by the Ottomans in Europe of a system so much resembling that which they had 'inherited' cannot but have made the application of the latter considerably easier than it would otherwise have been.

Fiefs in the Ottoman system went by various names. In general they were known as *Dirliks*, that is to say, 'livings'.[2] The great majority of them were created to support these knights, cavalrymen, for whom the term used in Turkish was of Persian origin, *Sipâhî*;[3] and in this case they went by the names *Timar*[4] and *Zi'âmet*,[5] according as the revenues they yielded were small or large. Fiefs of higher yield than *Zi'âmets* were known as *Ḫâṣṣ* (meaning 'special').[6] Some of the latter, the largest of all, formed the Sultan's private property, the so-called *Ḫavâssi Hümâyûn*;[7]

[1] See Köprülüzade, op. cit., section 'Timar'; *Encyclopaedia of Islam*, arts. 'Timar' and 'Ze'āmet'.

[2] Strictly speaking, *Dirlik* has a wider meaning. It was applied to any means of livelihood afforded by the Sultan to those that served him, whether in the shape of cash or land. See Seyyid Muṣṭafâ, i. 100.

[3] The word corrupted in French to *Spahi*, in English to *Sepoy*.

[4] It appears to be doubtful whether this word is of Turkish or of Greek origin. See *Encyclopaedia of Islam*, s.v.

[5] From Arabic *Zi'âma*, used for such a fief because its holder was termed *Za'îm*, meaning originally 'the spokesman of a group', and later applied, particularly in Egypt, to certain officials.

[6] Also Arabic.

[7] *Hümâyûn*, Persian, meaning originally 'blessed, sacred, fortunate', and so 'royal'.

and others were granted to members of the imperial family: princesses, ladies of the *Ḥarem*, &c. The remaining *Ḫâṣṣes* and a certain number of smaller fiefs of both classes appertained to offices, changing hands as their incumbents succeeded one another. In this they contrasted with those held by *Sipâhîs*, which were, so to speak, personal holdings and even, within limits, heritable. *Ḫâṣṣes*, *Ziʿâmets*, and *Timars* constituted the fiefs proper. But there were other holdings that partook of the nature of fiefs. Thus certain lands had their revenues set aside for special purposes, such as the support of the wardens of fortresses and of local garrisons, or that of the Admiralty at Istanbul. These were known as *Yurtluḳs* and *Ocaḳlîḳs*.[1] Moreover, there were various other types of so-called *ʿAskerîs*,[2] that is soldiery, though some of them performed only auxiliary services, to whom small parcels of land were granted on which they were excused the payment of dues and tithes. We shall deal with them later.

Many of the fiefs appertaining to offices yielded revenues to persons unconnected directly with the armed forces. The system, indeed, was primarily financial rather than military. Our present concern, however, is with the army. We will confine ourselves at present, therefore, to a consideration of those fiefs that provided a livelihood for the *Sipâhîs* and their superior officers.[3] *Timars* and *Ziʿâmets* existed only in those provinces of the Empire directly governed from Istanbul, and not even in all of these.[4] Nor were the rules regarding them precisely similar in all regions. So that the following details may not be considered as applying universally.

The distinction between a *Ziʿâmet* and a *Timar* was financial. A fief yielding revenue amounting to from 2,000 or 3,000 to 19,999 *aḳçes*[5] a year was called a *Timar*, one yielding more, up to 99,999 *aḳçes*, a *Ziʿâmet*. Both might be made up of two parts:

[1] *Yurt* (Turkish) means 'home' or 'tent' or 'estate'. *Ocaḳ* (also Turkish) means primarily 'hearth', but was used for each of the various corps of the *Ḳapî Ḳullarî*, of which much of the nomenclature was derived from the processes of cooking (see Appendix A (A)). Hence 'hearth' came to denote a corps centre or rallying-point, and so its whole establishment. The attributive *luḳ*, *liḳ* here signifies 'belonging to' and so 'the domains of' the *Yurt* or *Ocaḳ*.

[2] *ʿAskerî* (Arabic) 'military', from *ʿAsker*, a corruption of the Persian *Läşkär*, 'an army'. All government servants, except clerks, 'Learned' and other, were, the Ruling Institution having a military basis, called *ʿAskerî*, being thereby distinguished from *Reʿâyâ* or subjects proper (see below, p. 158).

[3] The revenues accruing to the holders of such fiefs were called *'Mâlî Muḳâtele*, 'fighting money', from *Mâl*, 'property, money', and *Muḳâtala*, verbal noun from Ḳâtala, 'he fought, contested', both Arabic. See ʿAyni ʿAli in Tischendorf, 88.

[4] See below, p. 147.

[5] Or 'aspres'—a piece of silver (for the currency see below, ch. vii). In the European provinces 3,000 *aḳçes* was the lower limit, in the Asiatic 2,000—according to ʿAyni ʿAli in Tischendorf, 89–90. In the *Ḳânûn-nâme* published in *O.T.E.M.*, No. 15, Appendix, 11, however, fiefs yielding no more than 1,000 *aḳçes* are mentioned.

namely the 'original' holding, called *Ḳılıç*,[1] and additions, called *Teraḳḳî*,[2] granted one at a time so as to yield one-tenth of the revenues derived from the *Ḳılıç*. The parts of the fief composed of these additions were called *Ḥiṣṣa*,[3] and, unlike the *Ḳılıç*, might, on its falling vacant, be again detached from it and added to other holdings. This rule was framed with the object of encouraging *Sipâhîs* to perform their duties satisfactorily. For apart from the fact that if they failed to do so they might be temporarily or permanently deprived, good conduct was rewarded by the grant of such *Teraḳḳîs*. It was the ambition, indeed, in early times at least, of ordinary 'Timariot' *Sipâhîs* to rise to the rank of *Za'îm*, the holder of a *Zi'âmet*.

As we shall see, the superior officers of the *Sipâhîs* were the provincial governors; and originally the grant of fiefs lay with those of highest rank, the *Beylerbeyis*.[4] When granting a fief the *Beylerbeyis* would provide its holder with a diploma of title, called *Berât*.[5] In 1530, however, during the reign of Süleymân the Magnificent, the central government partially withdrew this right. Thenceforward, except in the case of the smallest *Timars*, it reserved the issue of *Berâts* to itself. The *Beylerbeyis* now merely provided the candidate for a fief with a memorandum or note of recommendation called *Teẕkere*.[6] This was presented at a special office at the capital,[7] and, if the candidate was found to be deserving of the grant, he received his diploma thence. From this time forth, accordingly, there were two types of *Timar*: those to obtain which such *Teẕkeres* were necessary—which for this reason were known as *Teẕkereli* or 'Note' *Timars*, and those to obtain which they were not—which were in contrast known as *Teẕkeresiz* or 'Noteless'.[8] In a few provinces only those yielding less than 3,000 *aḳçes* a year were noteless. In others, however, notes were required only when the *Timar* yielded 5,000 or 6,000.[9] At the same time, these

[1] *Ḳılıç* (Turkish), 'sword'. This nucleus of a fief was so called because its revenues were considered enough to support the *Sipâhî* himself, and hence provided one 'sword' for the Sultan in war.

[2] *Teraḳḳî* (Arabic), verbal noun from *Teraḳḳâ*, 'he rose, progressed, advanced'.

[3] *Ḥiṣṣa* (Arabic), 'lot, portion'—falling to some one in a partition of property.

[4] For *Beylerbeyis* see below, p. 139. The *Ḳânûn-nâme* of the Conqueror (*O.T.E.M.*, No. 14, Appendix, 22) refers to the granting of fiefs by them as follows: *Ve eṭrâfta beylerbeyiler timar ve zi'âmeti tevcîh edip 'arḍ etsinler. 'Arḍlari maḳbûl olsun.* 'And in the provinces, when the *Beylerbeyis* have granted *Timars* and *Zi'âmets*, let them report (or show the fact). Let their reports be accepted.'

[5] See below, p. 122.

[6] *Teẕkira* (Arabic), from *Ẕakara*, 'he mentioned, he reminded'.

[7] The *Defter-ḫâne*—see below, p. 127.

[8] '*Li*' here implying 'with' or 'requiring', and '*Siz*' meaning 'without'.

[9] The figures were: 6,000 in the *Eyâlets* (see below, p. 141) of Rumelia, Buda, Bosnia, Temeşvar, Diyâr Bekr, Erḍerûm, Damascus, Aleppo, Bağdâd, and Şehrizor; 5,000 in those of Anatolia and the Archipelago; and 3,000 in those of Ḳaramân, Mer'aş, and Sivas.—'Ayni 'Ali in Tischendorf, 89–90.

provisions regarded only such grants as were made either to persons that had already held fiefs, or who became eligible to hold them as heirs of former holders.[1] If a man was granted a fief for the first time, not being eligible in this manner, a *Berât* from the central government had to be obtained even when the revenues yielded by the *Timar* in question would otherwise have ranked it as 'noteless'.[2] Such a novice would, in fact, generally be granted a 'noteless' fief; for the establishment of these regulations under Süleymân resulted in the division of *Timar* holders into two categories corresponding to the 'note' and 'noteless' categories of their holdings. Thenceforward only the holders of 'Note' *Timars* were regarded as worthy of the name *Sipâhî*. The rest were called merely *Timarcı*, 'Timariot'.[3] This distinction was no more than official, however. In common parlance, which for the sake of convenience we propose to follow, it was ignored: all fief holders, including even *Za'îms*, being referred to indifferently as *Sipâhîs*.

In return for the revenues they thus enjoyed, *Sipâhîs* were obliged to go on campaign when summoned, though in later times, at least, they were permitted to compound with a payment. But their conditions of service were not uniform. Some were always obliged to obey the call to arms,[4] others served in rotation.[5] The lowest category of *Sipâhîs* went on service unaccompanied, mounted, wearing a breastplate and bringing a tent. But those that derived as much as twice the minimum yield of a *Timar* were obliged to bring with them a fully equipped and mounted man-at-arms (*Cebeli*);[6] and for every further 3,000 *akçes* of income they had to furnish one more *Cebeli*, so that their train might consist of as many as five. The regulations were similar for *Za'îms*, except that the sum for each *Cebeli* in their case was 5,000 *akçes*,[7] with an initial allowance of the same amount for themselves. Their train might, therefore, consist of eighteen men. They were subjected to no kind of regular training; but the authorities were fairly well assured, as long as the regulations were observed, that the feudatories called to service would be capable of performing it, since fiefs might be granted only to the sons or descendants of *Sipâhîs* or *Cebelis*, who from their childhood were brought up in the tradition of arms.

[1] For the inheritance of fiefs see below, ch. v.

[2] A Berât of this kind was called *Ibtidâ Berâtî*—*Ibtidâ* (Arabic) meaning 'beginning'.—'Ayni 'Ali in Tischendorf.

[3] Lybyer, 103.

[4] These were called *Eşkincis*—from *Eşmek*, 'To ride to war'.

[5] These were called *Bi-nevbet*—'in turn' (Arabic).

[6] From the Persian *Coba*, 'a coat of mail', itself derived from the Arabic *Cubba*, 'a man's garment'.

[7] It seems odd that *Za'îms* should have been obliged to furnish relatively fewer *Cebelis* than Timariots, who enjoyed smaller revenues. Perhaps it was because the equipment of *Za'îms* and their followers was much more elaborate.

The officers of the *Sipâhîs* below the provincial governors, who commanded them on campaign and with whom we shall deal in our section on the provincial administration, were of three ranks. The highest were the *Alay-beyis*.[1] These were elected by the feudatories of each province (*Sancaḳ*), whom it was their duty to muster for a campaign. They were granted *Ziʿâmets*, on a life tenure; were provided each with a standard and drum; and had the immediate command of the regiments in which the said *Sipâhîs* were organized.[2] It was on their recommendation that appointments to vacant holdings were made. Below them came the *Çeri-baṣis* or *Su-baṣîs*,[3] who were chosen from among the *Zaʿîms* of each of the smaller administrative districts called *Ḳaḍâ*,[4] where, in peace time, they performed the duties of police. The third rank of officers was that of the *Çeri-Sürücüs*,[5] who enrolled and policed the *Sipâhîs* when on campaign.

In normal circumstances, when a *Sipâhî* died his *Ḳîlîç* passed to his son, even though the latter were a minor. In this case, however, he must be represented on campaign by a *Cebeli*. If the *Sipâhî* were childless, or left only sons incapable of discharging feudal obligations, the fief fell vacant; and its revenues were collected for the Treasury, pending a re-grant by an official called *Mevḳûfâtçî*.[6] The *Ḳîlîç* was then granted to the most deserving of the late *Sipâhî's Cebelis*, the *Ḥiṣṣa* parts of the fief being added, by way of *Taraḳḳî*, to the holdings of *Sipâhîs* of lower rank than that of the deceased.[7] Presumably these grants were usually earned by valour in the field. Two of the younger sons of most *Sipâhîs* also had a prescriptive right to the *Ḥiṣṣa* parts of vacant *Timars*, as had also the sons of certain *Ḳapi Ḳulus*, the size of the holdings they were granted (which might even be of the *Ziʿâmet* category) depending on the rank attained by their fathers.[8]

---

[1] *Alay Beyis*. *Alay* (Turkish) means 'an array or formation of troops'.
[2] See below, p. 146.
[3] *Çeri* and *Su* both mean 'troops'. Hence *Yeni Çeri* (Janissary), 'new troops'.
[4] A *Ḳaḍâ* is the districts under the jurisdiction of a *Ḳâḍî* or judge—see below, p. 153.
[5] i.e. 'troop-drivers'.
[6] A fief between the death of an heirless holder and a re-grant was said to be *Mevḳûf*, 'retained'. For the *Mevḳûfâtçi* see below, p. 130, n. 7
[7] According to Seyyid Muṣṭafâ, i. 121, however, it was only *Timars* whose revenues exceeded 15,000 *aḳçes* and *Ziʿâmets* yielding between 30,000 and 40,000 *aḳçes* that were so split up.
[8] The size of the holdings conferred on the sons of both *Ṣubaṣis* and *Sipâhîs* depended partly on that of their father's holding, partly on the manner of his death: if he was killed on service, they received larger holdings than if he died in his bed. See Hammer, *Staatsverfassung*, 352 sq. The *Ḳânûn-nâme* of the Conqueror (*O.T.E.M.*, No. 14, Appendix, 20–1) makes the following provisions for the sons of *Ḳapi Ḳulus*: (1) The sons of *Vezîrs* (other than the Grand *Vezîr*) and *Sancaḳ Beyis* (see below, p. 138) are to receive *Ziʿâmets* of 30,000 *aḳçes'* revenue. (2) The sons of *Çavuṣes* (see below, p. 87) are to receive *Timars* of

The *Sipâhîs'* chief source of livelihood was the tithes and dues that they were authorized to collect from the peasantry settled on their holdings; and with this right of collection they enjoyed seigneurial jurisdiction over the peasants, who, as we shall see, were virtually serfs. Hence a general exodus of *Sipâhîs* at a call to arms would have jeopardized the order of the country-side. In order to avoid this inconvenience, therefore, one in every ten was permitted to remain at home. Moreover, if the *Sipâhîs* that went on campaign were obliged to remain in winter quarters, some of them were allowed to return and collect the revenues that had meanwhile accrued to themselves and their fellows, since they were otherwise unprovided for.

The total force furnished by the *Sipâhîs* with their *Cebelis* (including the *Cebelis* supplied both by the military *Ḫâṣṣ* fiefs enjoyed by the higher commanders with whom we have not yet dealt and by zealots who sometimes equipped contingents of as many as fifty apiece beyond what was obligatory) is said to have numbered at one time some two hundred thousand. According to this computation it would appear that the majority were Asiatic; though the province (*Eyâlet*) of Rumelia provided some eighty thousand as against the thirty thousand odd forthcoming from that of Anatolia. These figures seem, however, to be based on little more than guess-work. Other authorities put the total force of the territorial troops during the hey-day of the Empire at no more than one hundred and forty or fifty thousand. It seems likely that the Ottoman authorities themselves could never be certain of the exact numbers at their disposal.

The Ottoman feudal system seems to have differed from that of western Europe chiefly in that the principal feudatories held their lands temporarily, in virtue of their offices. Less than half the lands concerned appear to have appertained to the *Sipâhîs*, who alone enjoyed any hereditary rights.[1] Hence the monarchy was exposed to little danger from the rivalry of this class of its tenants-in-chief. In later days, as we shall see, provincial dynasts did rise to such power as threatened that of the central government. But they were in no case upstart *Sipâhîs*. On the contrary they were rebellious office-holders who defied ejection at a time when the central government had grown too feeble to oppose

10,000 *akçes*. Detailed provisions for the sons of *Sancak Beyis* and *Beylerbeyis*, issued to a *Beylerbeyi* of Rumelia under Süleymân I, are given in Hammer, op. cit., 364 sq.

[1] See Seyyid Muṣṭafâ, i. 120, who states that in a typical *Sancak* (see below, p. 138) the revenue lands might be distributed as follows: one-fifth *Ḫâṣṣ* fiefs, one-tenth *Zi'âmets*, two-fifths *Timars*, one-tenth *Ocakliks* and *Yurtluks*, one-fifth *Awkâf* (see below, p. 237). It will be remembered that some *Zi'âmets* and *Timars* appertained, like *Ḫâṣṣes*, to offices. See above, p. 48.

them with success. As long as the Sultans engaged in war with powers unprovided with trained troops, the feudal levies formed perhaps the most important and formidable part of their forces.[1] But their attachment to the land was always disadvantageous—as was that of their European counterparts—since they were inevitably reluctant to leave their holdings and eager to return to them. Hence a *sine qua non* of their effectiveness was the maintenance of its authority over them by the central government. When this was relaxed they soon declined into uselessness.[2]

So much, at present, for the *Sipâhîs*. But before turning to the 'standing' army, we may deal briefly with those other so-called *'Askerîs* whom we have referred to[3] as holding land—the more appropriately in that all of them likewise were free, and most of them were Moslem—and with certain nomad and other warriors, who, being again free Moslems, may best be treated of here.

The first category of settled *'Askerîs* was that of the *Müsellems*. They appear originally to have been nomad also and of Turkish race. But, in return for undertaking to do the Sultans regular service, they were each granted a small parcel of land, on which they were excused the payment of tithes and dues—hence their name *Müsellem* which means 'exempt'.[4] They supported themselves by working their land, receiving no pay. Their position thus resembled that of the *Sipâhîs*, like whom they were cavalrymen; but, unlike the *Sipâhîs*, they worked their holdings entirely themselves, and derived no part of their livelihood from the collection of taxes. When they were called up for service, therefore, they had for the time being to be otherwise provided for. Hence they were organized in teams, called *ocaḳ*,[5] each of which consisted of three or four men.[6] One man served at a time; and the others, as his auxiliaries—*Yamaḳs*—furnished him with a sum of money according to their means[7] and a tithe of their crops. The *Müsellems*, again like the *Sipâhîs*, were commanded by *Çeri-başîs*[8] and subject to the authority of the provincial governors.

[1] See Cevdet, i. 90—*Devleti 'aliyenin en cesîm ḳuvveti 'askerîyesi erbâbi timar ve zi'âmet idi*, 'The strongest military force of the Sublime State were the holders of *Timars* and *Zi'âmets*'.

[2] This account of the feudal *Sipâhîs* is taken from Ḳoçu Bey (Behrnauer, *Z.D.M.G.* xv. 279 sq.); Seyyid Muṣṭafâ, i. 120–3; Cevdet, i. 90–1; Hammer, *Staatsverfassung*, 337 sq.; Belin, 'Régime des Fiefs Militaires', *J.A.*, 6th Series, xv. 230 sq.; D'Ohsson, vii. 372 sq.; Tischendorf, 39 sq., 89 sq. ('Ayni 'Ali); Lybyer, 101–2; *Encyclopaedia of Islam*, art. 'Timar'. See further pp. 189–190.

[3] See above, p. 48.

[4] *Musellem* (Arabic) means 'granted'—of a contested point or of a right—and hence (in Persian usage) 'dispensed from public burdens'.

[5] *Ocaḳ* (Turkish) meaning 'hearth'—see above, p. 48, n. 1.

[6] So Aḥmed Refîḳ. The *Ḳânûn* cited below shows numbers varying in different places.

[7] These contributions were called *Ḫarcliḳ*; 'expense money'. Rich *Yamaḳs* gave 50–60 *aḳçes*; middling 30–40; poor 10–20.

[8] See above, p. 51.

The holdings of the *Müsellems* were distributed about both the 'original' provinces, Rumelia and Anatolia. Those of the other 'settled' *'Askerîs* that we are here concerned with, on the other hand, seem to have been confined either to one or the other. Thus the troops known as *Yaya* or *Piyâde*,[1] infantry, whose status as regards land-holding was similar to that of the *Müsellems*, were to be found only in Anatolia;[2] whereas two other categories, called *Voynuk* and *Doğancî*, were exclusively Rumelian.

The *Voynuks*[3] were Bulgarians, both Moslem and Christian. Their duty consisted in rearing and tending the horses of the imperial stables and those of various high officials and grandees. Their organization resembled that of the *Müsellems* in that they paid no taxes and were commanded by *Çeri-başis* (headed in their case by a *Voynuk Beyi*), but differed from it in having no framework of *ocaks*. They had instead a reserve,[4] by promotion from which their numbers were kept up to strength.[5] As for the *Doğancîs*,[6] or Hawkers, they seem to have been mostly Bulgarians also. Their privileges were similar to those of the *Voynuks*. Their service consisted in raising falcons for the use of the Sultan and his court.[7]

The earliest *Müsellems* and *Yayas* were, as we have indicated, probably Türkmen nomads that the Sultans desired at once to settle, reward, and maintain for future service by granting them land. For such Türkmens, many of whom were then recent immigrants into Western Asia Minor from farther east, and whose chief desire was the acquisition of booty, formed perhaps the chief ingredient in the composition of the armies that achieved the

---

[1] Meaning, in Turkish and Persian respectively, 'on foot'.

[2] *O.T.E.M.*, No. 17, 43 sq. (*Kânûns* regarding *Müsellems* and *Yayas*). That of the *Yayas* shows that their *ocaks* were of from six to seven men. See, too, Hammer, *Staatsverfassung*, 209, and Aḥmed Refîḳ, *Türk Aşîretleri*, Introduction, vii–viii. According to the latter authority, the *Yayas* and *Müsellems* of Anatolia numbered 26,500, 8,900 being available for service at a time. Cevdet, i. 91, following Ḳoçu Bey (?—see Behrnauer, op. cit., 282), puts the *Yürüks* (see below) and *Müsellems* of Rumelia together at 5,000 or 6,000 and 40,000 with their *Yamaks*, and the *Yayas* of Anatolia at 3,000 or 4,000 and 30,000 with their *Yamaks*. Seyyid Muṣṭafâ, i. 146–7, states, erroneously, that the *Müsellems* were confined to Anatolia, that they numbered some 50,000, and were commanded in war by a *Mîri Müsellemân*. Ḳoçu Bey (Behrnauer, loc. cit.) states that the *Yayas* were commanded by fourteen *Yaya Başis* drawn from the Janissaries. *Yaya Başis* are also mentioned in the *Kânûn* cited above.

[3] *Voynuk* = *'Askerî*, being derived from the Slav root signifying war, &c., that occurs also in the word *Voyvoda*, likewise used in Turkish (see below, p. 198).

[4] The men of this reserve were called *Voynuk Zevâ'idi*—'supernumeraries of the *Voynuks*'.

[5] *M.T.M.* i. 108, 308–9; Aḥmed Refîḳ, *Türk Idâresinde Bulgaristan*, 3, 6; D'Ohsson, vii. 378–9. The latter states that in his time the *Voynuks* numbered 6,000, 800 serving yearly at the capital as grooms.

[6] *Doğan* means a lanner hawk.

[7] Aḥmed Refîḳ, op. cit. 3.

earliest Ottoman conquests.[1] Their subsequent settlement was, however, no more than partial. Many of them, maintaining their tribal relationships, continued to lead a pastoral life that necessitated seasonal migrations. And these *Yürüks*, or nomads,[2] were still employed by the Sultans in war no less than the settled *Müsellems* and *Yayas*.

Their organization, again, was similar. They, too, were commanded in war-time by *Çeri-Başis*, headed by *Yürük-Beyis*, were subject to the authority of the provincial governors, and were divided into *ocaks* of thirty.[3] The men of each *ocak* served in rotation, five at a time, and were supported whilst on service by the contributions of the remainder, who constituted their *Yamaks*. The *Yürüks*, unlike the other *'Askerîs* we have been considering, were not exempt from taxation. On the contrary, not only were they obliged to pay various pastoral dues, but in peace time a fixed contribution was exacted from each *ocak* in lieu of service.[4] They were to be found in both Rumelia and Anatolia, the majority in the latter province.[5]

The organization of all these "*'Askerî*" corps belonged to the early centuries of the Empire. They all declined in importance, even the feudal *Sipâhîs*, with the institution and growth of the slave army. By the sixteenth century neither the *Müsellems*, the *Yayas*, nor the *Yürüks* were any longer employed for actual fighting, though they were still obliged to accompany the armies on campaign. Instead they discharged less glorious duties, such as dragging guns, levelling roads, digging trenches, carrying provisions, and casting cannon balls. Indeed, the *Yayas* seem already to have all but disappeared, their holdings being eventually converted into a special type of *Timar*.[6] And various other types of soldiery who played a part in the earlier Ottoman campaigns were likewise either absorbed into or superseded by the *Ḳapî Ḳullarî* as their numbers and influence grew. Such were the

[1] The *Yayas* are said to have been instituted by the second Sultan, Orḫan (1321–60) as the first infantry of the dynasty, and to have been given lands only when displaced by the Janissaries—see D'Ohsson, vii. 308. Cf. Belin, *Régime des Fiefs*, 224–5, who, however, supposes them to have held land on a *Müsellem* basis from the first.

[2] *Yürük* is from *Yürümek* (Turkish), 'to walk, to wander'.

[3] So, apparently, in the time of Süleymân I. In an earlier *Ḳânûn*, of Meḥmed II (1488), the *Yürüks* are referred to as being organized in *ocaks* of twenty-four —see Aḥmed Refîḳ, *Türk Aşîretleri*, Introduction, v.

[4] The dues payable by the *Yürüks* were those called *Otlaḳ Resmi* (Pasture Due), *'Âdeti Ağnâm* (Sheep Custom), and *Ağil Resmi* (Pen Due). In peace time each *ocaḳ* had to pay 600 *aḳçes* a year.—*M.T.M.* i. 306. 307, 308; Aḥmed Refîḳ, op. cit. vi.

[5] Aḥmed Refîḳ, op. cit. v. Both Cevdet, i. 91, and Seyyid Muṣṭafâ, i. 147, mention the *Yürüks* and the *Müsellems* together, Seyyid Muṣṭafâ stating that the *Yürüks* were confined to Rumelia and were commanded by a *Mîri Yürükân*.

[6] Cevdet and Seyyid Muṣṭafâ, loc. cit.; D'Ohsson, vii. 308–9.

Aḳincîs, Rumelian volunteer scouts or pioneers, who in early times raided into enemy country in front of the main army and rewarded themselves by pillage.[1] Their function was in later times discharged by Tatars subject to the Crimean *Ḫans*.[2] Or the *'Azebs* ('Bachelors'), first used as infantry, later as munition-carriers, and finally incorporated in the 'standing' *ocaḳ* of the *Cebecis*;[3] the *Cânbâzân* ('Soul-stakers'), *Dîvânegân* ('Madmen'), and other volunteer troops, who, after robbing the infidels of the Domain of War were only too apt to do the same by true-believers at home.[4] On the other hand, as the standing army itself declined during the seventeenth and eighteenth centuries, still other types of soldiery were enrolled to supplement their waning strength. We shall refer to these later.

(b) The Janissaries

We may now return to the *Ḳapî Ḳullarî*. Most of these, as we have indicated, were in the Golden Age of the Empire, the late fifteenth and the sixteenth centuries, conscripted from among the Sultan's Orthodox Christian subjects, and reduced, illegally (from the standpoint of the *Şerî'a*), to slavery. Caught young, these slaves were all put through a rigorous course of training, both mental and physical. They were chosen in the first place for the likelihood of their physique; in the course of their training their aptitudes were studied; and each was given a post for which he seemed suited. The most promising in body and mind, but particularly in mind, were selected as *Iç Oğlans*[5] or pages, and placed for special training either in one of the old imperial palaces at Brusa and Adrianople, or in special palace schools at Ġalaṭa and in Istanbul itself.[6] They were finally admitted to the Sultan's

---

[1] *Aḳinci* from *Aḳin* (Turkish), 'a raid, an onslaught'. Cevdet and Seyyid Muṣṭafâ, loc. cit., state that there were 20,000 registered *Aḳincis* under an *Aḳinci Beyi*. Their authority seems to be Ḳoçu Bey (see Berhnauer, op. cit. 282). On campaign the *Aḳincis'* numbers would be swollen to 40,000 or 50,000 by volunteers.

[2] Seyyid Muṣṭafâ, ii. 96.   [3] Zinkeisen, iii. 202; D'Ohsson, vii. 309.

[4] See Aḥmed Râsim, i. 501–2, note.

[5] Turkish, literally, 'Inside Boys'. Cf. below, p. 78.

[6] Seyyid Muṣṭafâ, i. 88, states that 'they were educated in the palaces of Adrianople, Brusa, Gallipoli and Ġalaṭa'. But as regards Ġalata, he seems to have confused these *Iç Oğlans* with the *'Acemî Oğlans* (see below, p. 57). This confusion may be due to the fact that new arrivals in the page-schools were also called *'Acemîs* (see 'Aṭâ, i. 138 sq.). There were certainly *'Acemî Oğlans* proper at Gallipoli, since one of their officers was called *Gelibolu Ağasi* (see below, App. A (A)). Cf. also Aḥmed Cevâd, who states (243, note) that a quarter of the town of Gallipoli was still called 'Acemî Oğlanlar in his time. For the College of Ibrahîm Paşa in Istanbul, opened only under Süleymân I, see below, ch. xi. At Adrianople, at least also from the reign of Süleymân, there were both *Iç* and *'Acemî Oğlans* (see *Encyclopaedia of Islam*, art. 'Edirne', where reference is made to the conversion by this Sultan of the 'Old Palace' into an *'Acemî-Oğlan* barracks). According to foreign accounts of the early sixteenth century there were

own palace, where, according to merit, they were promoted through various grades of more or less menial service, the most successful becoming the personal attendants of the monarch, his 'Gentlemen of the Privy Chamber'.[1] But they were trained meanwhile in the arts, not only of the courtier, but of the administrator and the commander, since it was from among the chosen of the chosen that the higher posts of government were filled.[2]

It is not, however, the *Iç Oğlans* with whom we are here immediately concerned, since they were not of the army, but of the Household. Our business is with the remainder of the conscripts, who went by the name of *'Acemî Oğlans* (literally 'Foreign Boys').[3] The latter were subjected to a different kind of schooling, designed principally to harden them. Those unable to speak Turkish were first placed in the service of feudal *Sipâhîs* in Anatolia;[4] but all were sooner or later brought to Istanbul. There they were scrutinized again, and appointed to various duties according to their capacities. Many of them were now drafted into the *ocaḳ* of the Gardeners,[5] whose members, as we shall see, performed a large variety of duties other than that indicated by this name. And in this service they too formed for the time being part of the personnel of the Imperial Household, as did also those that were placed in the *ocaḳ* of the Wood-cutters[6] and other departments of the palace service. But from this a certain number passed out into the *ocaḳ* of the Armourers[7] and its branches, and so returned to soldiering. Others of the *'Acemî Oğlans*, again, were given employment in the *ocaḳ* of the Admiralty, serving both at the capital and at Gallipoli,[8] or in the public offices of Istanbul; and

three or four hundred *Iç Oğlans* in training both at Adrianople and Ğalaṭa.—Lybyer, 72, notes. We have discovered no other information regarding the school at Brusa. Lybyer, loc. cit., also states that they were placed in the households of important government officials and provincial governors. But we have not found any Turkish references to this practice. Possibly Spandugino, the authority for this statement, is likewise really referring here not to *Iç Oğlans* but to *'Acemî Oğlans*, some of whom were in fact placed in the service of the governors of *Eyâlets*, and on the *Ḫâṣṣes* of the *Ḳul Kâḫyasi* (see below, p. 60), the *Istanbul Ağasi* (below, p. 60), and other Janissary officers.—Aḥmed Cevâd, 242.

[1] *Ḫaṣṣ Odalis*—see below, p. 80.

[2] See *'Aṭâ*, i. 138 sq. Among other things they were instructed in the *Ḳur'ân* and the *Şerî'a*, in Arabic and Persian, in archery, musketry, and military science, in horsemanship and javelin-throwing (*cerîd-bâzî*) and in music.

[3] So called because they were of non-Moslem birth. Cf. the Black eunuch *'Acemî Ağas*, Appendix B (A).

[4] Lybyer, 79. Cf. Aḥmed Cevâd, 244, citing Ḳoçu Bey. According to Aḥmed Cevâd, 242, this method of dealing with *Devşirme* recruits was resorted to only in earlier times, before barracks enough to house them had been built.

[5] *Bostancis* (see below, p. 84).—Aḥmed Cevâd, 243; Seyyid Muṣṭafâ, i. 149; Lybyer, 81.

[6] *Balṭacis* (see below, p. 86).—Aḥmed Cevâd, loc. cit.

[7] *Cebecis* (see below, p. 67).

[8] Aḥmed Cevâd, 244; Lybyer, 803. Cf. Seyyid Muṣṭatâ, i. 146.

yet others, it seems, were hired out to private persons as labourers.[1] But the destiny of most was enrolment in the standing infantry, the celebrated corps of the Janissaries.

It is still uncertain precisely when and how the Janissaries were founded. For the long-credited account furnished by historians of the Ottoman Golden Age seems to be false in important particulars.[2] The earliest conquests were carried out largely by the aid of Moslem enthusiasts and freebooters. The first infantry placed by the Sultans on a regular footing was that called *Yaya* or *Piyâde*, which as we have seen was maintained by fiefs confined to Anatolia.[3] It seems likely that *Yayas* were the Sultans' personal troops, the nucleus, together with the feudal cavalry, of the conquering forces, though it is possible that from the beginning the Ottoman, like most previous Moslem rulers, had also a slave bodyguard. But they can hardly have had the resources necessary for the maintenance of a large body of paid troops. Hence the feudal character both of the *Sipâhîs* and the *Yayas*. The *Yayas*, however, were lacking in docility, and being at once foot-soldiers and feudal, could not be used conveniently in operations far from the situation of their fiefs. It was natural, therefore, that the Sultans should replace them, as soon as they could, by infantry so recruited and organized as to avoid these disabilities. The opportunity to do so occurred in the third quarter of the fourteenth century. The first Ottoman raids into Europe brought the Sultans much booty and many prisoners. The latter became slaves by the mere fact of capture. So those of them that by age and physique were suitable might be turned into soldiers, who might in turn be paid from these newly acquired revenues.[4]

Such would appear to be the manner in which these 'New Troops', *Yeni-çeris*, Janissaries, came into being. And there are indications that their organization was modelled on, or at least influenced by, that of a religious movement to which the Ottoman enterprise owed much of its first vigour. We shall refer in greater detail to this movement, whose devotees were called singly *Ahi*[5]

[1] Lybyer, loc. cit.

[2] This credits Orhan (d. 1360) with their creation, makes the institution of the *Devşirme* conscription contemporary, and tells of the blessing of the first recruits by the *Derviş* Ḥâccî Bektaş (see below, p. 64). The latter incident has been proved apocryphal (see, e.g., Köprülüzade, *Anadolada Islâmiyet*, 87; *Les Origines du Bektachisme*, 21–4; Giese, *Zeitschrift für Semitistik*, 1924, 266).

[3] Above, p. 54.

[4] Giese, op. cit. 264, 266 (citing one of the earliest—later fifteenth-century—Ottoman historians, 'Aşık Paşa-Zâde); *Encyclopaedia of Islam*, arts. 'Murād I', 'Turks'.

[5] Properly, according to Giese, op. cit. 256, *Aki*, a Turkish word meaning 'generous' or 'chivalrous', and so corresponding to the Arabic *Fatâ*, plural *Fityân*. It is generally taken for its Arabic homonym, meaning 'My brother', the members of a famous earlier society having called themselves *Ihwân*,

and collectively *Ahl al-Futuwwa* (People of Chivalry or Virtue), in a later chapter.[1] Here it is enough to say that, in so far as the first Ottoman conquests were undertaken from religious motives, many of the townsmen that harboured them, including possibly persons closely connected with ʿOs̱mân I himself, were members of this society.[2] Hence it would seem that the Janissaries were first established before the occurrence of that cleavage between the beliefs of the Sultans and those of their Moslem subjects to which we have referred above, though the Sultans were later to rely on them for protection against the insurrections to which this cleavage was in time to give rise. The Janissary corps, or *ocaḳ*, as it existed in later times, however, was an amalgamation of three distinct bodies. One of these, the corps of the *Seğmens*,[3] was created independently at the end of this same century, and was placed under the authority of the Janissary commander only after the conquest of Constantinople.[4] The remaining two seem, if the duties allotted to them respectively in later times may be taken to throw some light on their origin,[5] to have been more closely allied; they were called *Cemâʿat*[6] (Company or Assemblage) and *Bölük*[7] (Division).

However that may be, the Janissaries of whatever division were all *Ḳapî Ḳullarî*, that is to say the Sultan's slaves, from the first. But it was almost certainly not until more than half a century after the creation of the *ocaḳ* that the *Devşirme* conscription was introduced.[8] After its introduction most of the conscripts were destined to become Janissaries, though not all, as we have indicated. Nor were the Janissaries exclusively recruited from the conscripts; they were still recruited partially from boys taken in war or simply

brethren. The proper singular, however, would be *Aḫ*. ʿOs̱mân Nûrî, i. 65, suggests that *Aḫi* may be a corruption of *Ağa*.

[1] Below, ch. xiii. The Janissary costume, particularly the peculiar cap, but also the trousers, was derived from that of the *Aḫis*. Other resemblances to the *Aḫis* have been noted in the short knives worn by Janissaries, in their use of the word *Yoldaş* ('fellow wayfarer', *yol* being equivalent to *Ṭarîḳat*) in reference to one another, and in the fact that celibacy was enjoined on them (till retirement)—Giese, op. cit. 259. The curious hierarchy of the *orta* officers, which was not 'pyramidal' as in most military organizations (that is to say, the lower the rank, the more numerous its holders)—a feature that D'Ohsson, vii. 320, notes as an inconvenience—may also point to a derivation from the *Aḫi* lodges, as may the fact that the Janissaries had the privilege of being punished by their own officers.

[2] Giese, op. cit. 257; *Encyclopaedia of Islam*, art. 'Turks'.

[3] *Sägbân*, of which this word is a Turkish corruption, means in Persian 'Dog-Keeper'.

[4] *Encyclopaedia of Islam*, art. 'Muḥammad II'. Cf. D'Ohsson, vii. 39–40. According to Hammer, *Staatsverwaltung*, 191, 208, *Seğmen* was the name given to the Ottoman infantry before the creation of the Janissaries.

[5] See Appendix A (A). [6] Arabic. [7] Turkish.

[8] Probably by Murâd II (succeeded 1421) before 1438—Giese, op. cit. 267; *Encyclopaedia of Islam*, arts. 'Dewshirme', 'Turks'.

bought. The *Devşirme* then was no such essential feature of the Janissary organization as has been generally stated. And if, when it was eventually abandoned, the Janissaries soon decayed, it was rather because this abandonment resulted in the admission of free men into a body designed for slaves.

As finally constituted the *ocaḳ* consisted of one hundred and ninety-six companies of variable size, called *Orta.*[1] One hundred and one of these made up the *Cemâ'at*,[2] sixty-one the *Bölük*, and thirty-four the *Seğmen* division. The whole was now commanded by an *Ağa*, the *Ağa* of the Janissaries (*Yeniçeri Ağasi*), to whom the commander of the *Seğmens*, the *Seğmen Başi*, and the commander of the *Bölük*, the *Ḳul Kâhyasi*,[3] acted as adjutants. These three officers, together with the commanders of three special *ortas*, made up a general council, or *Dîvân*, for the corps. They were known as the *Ocaḳ Ağasis*.[4]

Next below them stood a number of *orta*-commanders who acted in various capacities as general officers either of the whole corps or of parts of it; a secretary, the *Yeniçeri Kâtibi*; and finally an officer called the *Ağa* of Istanbul, who commanded the thirty-four *ortas*, supplementary to the establishment of the

[1] *Orta* means, literally, 'centre'. At an intermediate stage between the foundation of the corps and its final constitution there were 165 *ortas* (Aḥmed Cevâd, 27). When precisely the number was increased to 196 seems not to be known. It still stood at the lower figure in the reign of Süleymân the Magnificent, at least at its beginning, and the establishment was then of about 12,000 men—see Lybyer, 95, note. Seyyid Muṣṭafâ, i. 141, states that at the accession of Murâd III in 1574 the corps consisted of 20,000 men; Ḳoçu Bey (cited by Aḥmed Cevâd, 90) that it then consisted of 13,599 men. But Seyyid Muṣṭafâ's figure (which is confirmed by Hammer; see Lybyer, loc. cit.) includes the *'Acemî Oğlan ortas*; so perhaps these two estimates do not conflict. In this case, the addition would seem to have been made later. Unhappily we do not know to which of the three divisions it was made. If it was made to the *Cemâ'at* it must have been before 1591, since in that year the Bektaşîs were affiliated to the 99th *orta* of this division (see below, p. 65). We know that a great addition was made to the establishment of the Janissaries during the reign of Murâd III (see, e.g., Seyyid Muṣṭafâ, loc. cit.) in 1583. Moreover, Cevdet, cited by Aḥmed Cevâd, loc. cit., puts the establishment (presumably minus the *'Acemî Oğlans*) at 27,000 in the middle of this reign. Murâd died in 1594. 1583 may well, therefore, have been the date of the increase in the number of *ortas*.

[2] Up to the reign of Murâd IV, when the 65th *orta* was suppressed for its participation in the murder of that Sultan's predecessor, 'Oṣmân II.—D'Ohsson, vii. 213. According to Hammer, op. cit., 195–6, 219, the *Bölük* comprised 62 and the *Seğmens* 33 *ortas*.

[3] Literally, Intendant of the Slaves, no doubt short for *Ḳapî Ḳulu Kâhyasi*. He was known more familiarly as the *Kâhya Beyi*. *Kâhya* is the Turkish version of the Persian *Kat-ḫudâ*, literally 'lord of the house' or 'major-domo'. In Turkish as written in the Arabic character the Persian spelling was preserved, though the pronunciation had already been corrupted. We shall come across the word *Kâhya* in many different uses.

[4] D'Ohsson, vii. 315. According to Seyyid Muṣṭafâ, i. 143, they were known also as *Ḳaṭâr Ağalari*, *Ağas* of the train or file, because each of the five lower offices led by promotion to that above it.

ocaḳ proper, of the *'Acemî Oğlans*, from which all three divisions were recruited indifferently.[1]

The *Ağa* of the Janissaries was a personage of the first importance, partly because his corps was the most powerful military instrument at the Sultan's disposal, partly because he acted also as Chief of Police in Istanbul itself. He was *ex officio* a member of the Council of State, and took precedence of all ministers below the rank of *vezîr*, which he might enjoy himself, and of all other generals whatever.[2] In war he had the privilege of commanding the *ocaḳ* only when the Sultan went on campaign in person. Otherwise he sent a deputy to act on the orders of the general directing the operations.[3] Up to the beginning of the sixteenth century the *Ağas* were chosen from among the officers of the corps itself. Selîm I, however, who suffered from the insubordination of the Janissaries on campaign, sought to curb it by reversing this rule; and thenceforward for almost a hundred years the *Ağas* were appointed from the Imperial Household.[4] When the earlier practice was reverted to, either the *Seğmen Başî* or the *Ḳul Kâhyasî* was regularly promoted to the *Ağalîḳ*. And eventually the *Ḳul Kâhyasî* came to be regarded as the *Ağa's* chief lieutenant, though in earlier times the *Seğmen Başî* had held this position. The *Seğmen Başî* preserved only one notable right: that of acting in the *Ağa's* absence as his deputy, or *Ḳâ'im-maḳâm*.

The *ortas* of all three divisions and also, probably, of the *'Acemî Oğlans* came, even if they had not been so originally, to be organized alike. At first, apparently, they were small, and even in later times their establishment was commonly of no more than a hundred men.[5] These were divided into three grades, the highest consisting of pensioners who no longer went to war. Each *orta* was commanded by an officer called *Çorbacî*,[6] with six subordinates

[1] See below, App. A (A).

[2] Except on feast days, when the generals of the *Sipâhî* and *Siliḥdâr Bölüks*, which were of more ancient institution than the Janissary, had precedence of him.—D'Ohsson, vii. 351; *M.T.M.* i. 524–5 (*Ḳânûn-nâme* of 'Abdu'r-Raḥmân Tevḳî'î).

[3] D'Ohsson, loc. cit.

[4] D'Ohsson, vii. 314.

[5] Lybyer, 96, cites Chalcocondyles as stating that in his time—the reign of Meḥmed II—the *ortas* had each an establishment of 50 men. In the late eighteenth century, of those stationed at the capital it was supposed to be 100, and of those stationed in the provinces 300 men, in peace-time; whereas in war the establishment of such *ortas* as were sent on campaign was increased to 500.—D'Ohsson, vii. 320, 331. These increases, as we shall see, were effected by hasty enrolments; and few men but the officers were then permanently maintained in fact. The regulations referred to by D'Ohsson were not enforced for some time before he wrote, and may date from considerably earlier. According to Hammer, op. cit., 195, the average strength of *ortas* was 400 men, of whom 200 were capable of fighting. He does not state, however, at what period this was so.

[6] From *Çorba*, 'soup', 'stew', from Persian *Şorba*, the latter perhaps in turn derived from the Arabic root *Şaraba*, 'to drink'. See Appendix A for the probable origin of this title.

and a number of sub-officers.[1] Each, moreover, had a clerk to keep its rolls, and an *Imâm*, or prayer-leader. The men, besides pay, scaled according to their grades, though increased for distinguished service,[2] and rations, were supplied by the state with clothes. In peace-time, however, owing to their aptitude for insurrection they were not provided with arms. Even in war-time, though the state maintained an arsenal, they were permitted, by a curious custom, to choose the weapons that took their fancy. Nevertheless, while the Empire was at its height, they were well trained in archery and the use of small fire-arms, and were extremely well disciplined. In the Turkish phrase, 'forty were to be led by a hair'.[3] Their decorous and submissive bearing is remarked by European observers of the age.[4] Though the corps as a whole, feeling its power, was ready even as early as the fifteenth century to exact largess from Sultans whenever opportunity offered, the discipline in which its men were held by their officers was maintained with ease as long as they continued to be recruited all but exclusively from the *Devşirme* conscripts and other slaves. For then their life was wholly bound up with the *ocaḳ*. They entered it at a tender age; they were entirely cut off from communication with their relatives; they were obliged to live entirely in barracks. They were forbidden to marry until attaining the rank of pensioner. Though the sons of married pensioners were already, on occasion, admitted into the corps, they were too few, and chosen with too much care, to compromise the spirit induced in the rest of its personnel by the observance of these regulations.[5]

The Janissaries seem to have been founded as a bodyguard for the Sultan and consequently to have followed him about wherever he went. But as the corps increased in size, though a considerable number of *ortas* continued to be stationed at the Sultan's place of residence, most of them were posted to provincial garrisons, where they were subjected to the command of the local governors. In either case every *orta* came eventually to be lodged in a so-called Room (*Oda*),[6] most of the *ortas* stationed in Istanbul being housed in two large barracks, called the Old and the New Rooms (*Eski Odalar* and *Yeni Odalar*). These rooms, however, comprised not only sleeping-quarters for the officers and men, but also kitchens and storehouses. On campaign a large tent served each *orta* as its *oda*. Both the barrack-rooms and these

[1] Cf. below, App. A (A).

[2] Seyyid Muṣṭafâ, i. 142. Cf. Hammer, op. cit. 217–18.

[3] '*Ḳirḳ bir ḳil ile yedilir*', see Cevdet, i. 97.

[4] e.g. Busbecq.

[5] D'Ohsson, vii. 328, 332–3, 341–2, 346, 353; Aḥmed Cevâd, 54 sq.; *Encyclopaedia of Islam*, art. 'Janissaries'.

[6] Cf. below, p. 78, for the 'Chambers', also called *Oda*, of the 'Inside Service'. Owing to the accommodation of each *orta* in an *oda* the latter word was sometimes used for the former.

tents were decorated conspicuously with the sign, a key, an anchor, a fish, a flag, a mace, of the *orta* to which it belonged. In later times at least the men used also to have these signs tattooed on their arms and legs.[1]

One of the main concerns of the Sultans in early times was to confine the attention of the Janissaries to their proper duties: fighting and the preservation of order. The regulation admitting only persons of slave status into the *ocaḳ*, after a training begun when such recruits were still of a tender age, ensured in them an ignorance of money-making crafts, and was reinforced by another that forbade them later to engage in such crafts and in any form of trade.[2] The government, moreover, as we shall see, procured all the commodities required for the rationing of the Janissaries direct from the producers, without resorting to 'civilian' middlemen, and engaged, possibly even for the *orta*-men stationed in the capital, certainly for those that were sent on campaign, a number of men from those guilds whose members produced such manufactured articles as the Janissaries might have need of.[3] If, therefore, the latter disregarded the prohibition in question, they did so under no valid pretext. The artisans so engaged ceased, apparently, to belong to their original guilds, but formed others, one for each industry, under the aegis of the *ocaḳ*. They were not, probably, regarded as forming part of the Janissary establishment proper, but seem to have enjoyed some of the privileges attaching to Janissary status, such as immunity from arrest and punishment by the 'civil' authorities.[4]

More remarkable persons also attached to, but not actually forming part of, the *ocaḳ* were some *Dervişes* of the Bektaşî order. What this order was, indeed what *Dervişes* in general were, we shall describe later.[5] But we may here consider how they were connected with the Janissaries, since, particularly in later times, this connexion was both close and important. Indeed, the Janissaries were commonly known as the 'Bektaşî soldiery';[6] and the

[1] Seyyid Muṣṭafâ, i. 142; D'Ohsson, vii. 347; Aḥmed Cevâd, 47.

[2] See Seyyid Muṣṭafâ, i. 140, for two stories exhibiting the wrath of Selîm I at the idea of the son of a merchant's being admitted into the corps and at that of Janissaries' engaging in trade. Cf. Aḥmed Cevâd, 64 sq., 73–4, and 'Oṣmân Nûrî, i. 620.

[3] See Appendix A (A).

[4] See 'Oṣmân Nûrî, i. 621 and again 637. It may be, however, that the persons here mentioned as enjoying such immunity were not the guildsmen in question, but either ordinary Janissaries that, in defiance of the regulations, engaged in trade, or ordinary artisans affiliated to the *ocaḳ* in the manner of later times.

[5] Ch. xiii below.

[6] '*Asḳeri Bektaşîye*; or 'the *ocaḳ* of the Bektasîs' (*Bektaşîye Ocaği*), as by Ṣari Meḥmed, see Wright, *Ottoman Statecraft*; or 'the Children of Ḥâccî Bektaş' (*Ḥâccî Bektaş Oğullari*)—see *Encyclopaedia of Islam*, art. 'Bektash'.

traditional account of their foundation gives Ḥâccî Bektaş,[1] the saint from whom the order takes its name, a prominent part in it, stating that he blessed the first recruits, placing his sleeve on their heads, and so inspired them to adopt their peculiar head-dress with its pendant tube.[2] This account, as we have already stated, has been proved fictitious. Ḥâccî Bektaş can have had nothing to do with the foundation of the Janissaries personally for the good reason that he died quite a century before they were ever thought of.[3] And though the Bektaşî order, for its part, was not organized until much later—some time in the fifteenth century[4]—it was partly in response to the preaching and under the leadership of earlier *Dervişes* of the same type that the first Ottomans set out on their career of conquest. But another part of the responsibility for this enterprise belonged to the *Aḫis* of the Society of Virtue already referred to, whose doctrine had a mystical basis similar to that of the *Dervişes*, though otherwise developed; and, as will be remembered, it was on the organization of the *Aḫis*—from whose head-dress, incidentally, the cap of the Janissaries was really derived[5]—that the Janissary organization was in some degree modelled. The beliefs entertained by the Janissaries, as far as they were inherited from the *Aḫis*, had, therefore, something in common with those of the *Dervişes* from the first. Indeed, it is even considered probable that the story of the blessing by Ḥâccî Bektaş of the first Janissary recruits reflects a truth: that the *Dervişes* (of the type referred to) regarded the New Troops with benevolence, and invoked the blessing of their dead patron upon them.[6] As time went on, moreover, the way was left clearer for the *Dervişes* by the gradual dissolution of the *Aḫi* society—a dissolution that may, actually, have been hastened by its connexion with the Janissaries. For it had always been even more closely connected with the guilds that had for centuries controlled the commerce and industry of Moslem cities.[7] But, as we have seen, the Janissaries were expressly forbidden to engage in commerce and industry. And the very peculiarity of this prohibition—for soldiers, after all, are not apt in general to turn artisan—may indicate that the Sultans, on account of their gradual conversion to a comparatively strict Sunnism, came to view the connexion between the Janissaries and the *Aḫis* with suspicion, since the doctrine of the *Aḫis*, if nominally Sunnî also, was fundamentally

[1] The term *Ḥâccî*, properly *Ḥâcc*, denotes one that has performed the *Ḥacc*, or Pilgrimage to Mecca.

[2] See, e.g., Aḥmed Cevâd, 24 sq. and *Encyclopaedia of Islam*, art. 'Janissaries'.

[3] Köprülüzade, *Les Origines du Bektachisme*, 21.

[4] Ibid.

[5] Giese, op. cit. 261.

[6] Köprülüzade, *Origines*, 24; *Anadoluda Islâmiyet*, 88.

[7] For guilds see below, ch. vi.

heterodox.[1] The *Aḫis*, in any case, ceased to exert any political influence after the fourteenth century.[2] Thenceforward it was again only in the trade guilds that their system was still practised.[3] But if such was the intention of the Sultans, they failed, eventually, to guide the *ocaḳ* into the straight path of orthodoxy, or at least to keep it there. For the Bektaşîs were even more heterodox than the *Aḫis*; and by some means,[4] whether or not they profited by the latters' decline, they succeeded, as heirs of the *Dervişes* that had originally blessed the foundation of the *ocaḳ*, in establishing a patronage of it, at first ignored officially, but finally recognized. The Bektaşî order seems to have been formed during the fifteenth century; but it was not until the end of the sixteenth that this official recognition was accorded. In 1591, however, the order was declared to be affiliated to the ninety-ninth *orta* of the *Cemâʿat*, the rank of *Çorbacî* in which was conferred on its Grand Master; and eight Bektaşî *Dervişes* were thenceforward lodged and fed in the *oda* of this company, which was situated in the 'New' Barracks at Istanbul. These used to pray for the Empire and its arms, and to march before the *Ağa* on parades of ceremony, dressed in green, their leader crying 'God is Bountiful!'[5] and the rest answering '*Hû!*',[6] meaning 'He is'. For this reason these *Dervişes* were known as *Hû-keşân*, 'Criers of "He is" '.[7]

The official connexion of the Bektaşîs with the Janissaries hence belongs to the period of decline, which we propose to deal with later. And there is reason to believe that the disruption of discipline in the *ocaḳ*, which contributed in no small measure to this decline, was at least encouraged by some of the antinomian tenets of the Bektaşîs.[8] Perhaps we may on this ground conclude,

[1] According to Köprülüzade, see *Origines*, 16, *Anadoluda Islâmiyet*, 67 (citing observations of Massignon and Huart in support of this opinion). It is, however, combated by Giese, op. cit. 255.

[2] Giese, op. cit. 267–8. Köprülüzade, *Anadoluda Islâmiyet*, 85, attributes the decline of the *Aḫis* as a political force to the foundation in ever-growing numbers of Orthodox colleges (*Madrasa*).

[3] For the *Futuwwa* inheritance of the Ottoman guilds see particularly ʿOşmân Nûrî, i. 518 sq.

[4] Possibly it was over the *Cemâʿat ortas* stationed in the provinces that the Bektaşîs first established their influence. For the Bektaşîs were of the 'rural' type of *Derviş* (see below, ch. xiii); and it was to a *Cemâʿat orta* that they were eventually affiliated.

[5] *Kerîm Allah*.

[6] For Arabic *Huwa*.

[7] D'Ohsson, iv. 673, vii. 325.

[8] Aḥmed Cevâd, 61, 64, in a section dealing with Rule 4 of 'the fundamental *Ḳânûn* of the Janissaries', which required them 'never to deviate from the prescriptions of Saint Ḥâccî Bektaş', states that 'l'odjak qui disait vouloir suivre les préceptes de la Secte du Saint-Bektach, adopta certaines habitudes, telle que l'usage du vin, contraires aux prescriptions des vrais principes de la foi et de la loi sacrée'. Cf. below, ch. xiii, on the addiction to wine-drinking of *Dervişes*.

therefore,—thus bearing out a conclusion come to on others[1]—that it was not until a short time before the said recognition that the Bektaşîs gained a hold over the Janissaries firm enough to affect their conduct.

The *Ağa* of the Janissaries, as well as being a general, was a police officer. In this capacity he was responsible for the maintenance of order and the protection of property in most of Istanbul proper.[2] Only the Sultan's palace and a quarter adjacent were, indeed, outside his jurisdiction. This latter quarter, and all the area surrounding the capital, were under the similar control of other military officers. For there existed no independent police force either here or in the provinces. Hence, the duties that would have devolved on such a force were performed in peace-time by Janissary *ortas* and detachments and by other standing troops. In the area under the control of the *Ağa* they were performed by the *ortas* stationed at the capital. When these went on campaign, the place of these *ortas* was taken by those of the *'Acemî Oğlans*. This area, for police purposes, was divided into a number of districts, in each of which an *orta* was stationed for one year at a post, and from this patrols were sent out in perpetual rotation into all the markets, streets, and alleys within the district in question.[3] Not only the *Ağa* himself and the commanders of the *ortas* so posted, but also six other general officers of the *ocaḳ* and another officer of slightly lower rank were concerned with police duties. The corps also supplied two bodies of detectives for the preservation of good order and decorum and the prevention and punishment of crime.[4]

(*c*) *The Artillery and Armourers*

The organization of the Janissaries was not much affected by the introduction of fire-arms, which occurred, probably, near the beginning of the fifteenth century. Their manufacture, however, and the use of cannon brought about the creation of three special corps, recruited, like the Janissaries, from the *'Acemî Oğlans*. The men of these *ocaḳs* were called, in the order of their creation, *Ṭopçus*, or Gunners—*Ṭop* meaning a cannon—*Ṭop 'Arabacis*,[5] or Gun-carriage drivers, and *Cebecis*,[6] or Armourers.

The first two of these three *ocaḳs* were created by Murâd II

[1] By Hasluck, *Christianity and Islam under the Sultans*, 490. Hasluck's conclusion is that the legend connecting Ḥâccî Bektaş with the Janissaries was of late invention, appearing first in the works of the historians Taşköprüzade and 'Âli, who both died in the latter half of the sixteenth century.

[2] i.e. excluding Eyyub, Ğalaṭa, and Üsküdar.

[3] D'Ohsson, vii. 348–9.

[4] See Appendix A (B).

[5] From *'araba*, 'a wheeled carriage', Arabic (post-classical).

[6] From *Cebe* 'armour' or 'arms'. Cf. *Cebeli*, above, p. 50, n. 6.

(1421–51), during whose reign ordnance was first employed in a siege.[1] It had already been used in Western Europe for the best part of a hundred years; but how it was introduced into the Ottoman Empire, and whether the first Ottoman cannons were of home manufacture, appears to be uncertain. In any case native foundries were established by this Sultan, and produced bronze guns of large size, projecting stone balls, which played a decisive part in the reduction of Constantinople by his successor. The earliest European ordnance was immobile; it was not until the Hussite wars that field artillery was used to any great extent. The creation of the *Ṭop ʿArabacî* corps shows, however, that the Ottomans adopted patterns capable of being moved from the first. Both *Ṭopçus* and *Ṭop ʿArabacîs*, it may be noted, were infantry. Hence, indeed, the necessity for the *ʿArabacîs*. It was not until the end of the eighteenth century that a corps of mounted artillery was created, on a French model.

The functions of the Armourers were various. Primarily they were concerned with the manufacture and repair of arms and munitions for the infantry. But they had also to guard the army transport and stores on campaign. Their *ocaḳ* was created by Meḥmed the Conqueror.[2] It consisted originally of seven hundred men, as did also the *ocaḳ* of the *Ṭopçus*; whereas the *Ṭop ʿArabacîs* numbered three thousand.[3] Each *ocaḳ* had an organization similar to that of the Janissaries, that of the *Cebecis*, if not the others, being divided likewise into two sections, called *Bölük* and *Cemâʿat*, both comprising a number of *ortas*.[4] Each *ocaḳ*, again, was commanded by an *Ağa* called, in the case of the Gunners *Ṭopçu Başî*, in that of the Drivers *Ṭop ʿArabacî Başî*, in that of the Armourers *Cebeci Başî*; and was provided with a *Kâḫya* and a secretary.[5] The *ortas* of all three were stationed, some in the capital, some in the provinces.[6] For those stationed in the capital each *ocaḳ* had its barracks.

[1] So D'Ohsson, vii. 364. He states that ordnance was first used by the Ottomans at the siege of Semendria. It is sometimes stated (e.g. by ʿAbdu'r-Raḥmân Şeref, in his *Ta'riḫi Devleti ʿOsmâniye*, i. 105) that it was used by Murâd I at the battle of Kossovo.

[2] D'Ohsson, vii. 362; Juchereau, i. 83; Aḥmed Râsim, i. 98, note; ʿOsmân Nûrî, i. 916. Hammer, *Staatsverwaltung*, 224, states that the *Cebeci ocaḳ* was as old as, if not older than, the *Ṭopçu*, and also that its original establishment was 600.

[3] According to D'Ohsson, vii. 362–4.

[4] Ibid.; Cevdet, i. 89; Seyyid Muṣṭafâ, i. 144 (stating that all three *ocaḳs* had *ortas*, *bölüks*, and officers like the *ocaḳ* of the Janissaries); Aḥmed Râsim, i. 99, note.

[5] See Lybyer (Ramberti), 252. The *Ṭopçu Başî* and *ʿArabacî Başî* were chosen from the officers of their respective corps. The *Cebeci Başî* was appointed from among the *Ḳapîcî Başîs*, a category of officers belonging to the Imperial Household (see below, p. 83). D'Ohsson, 368–9.

[6] The *Cebecis* stationed in frontier fortresses, but particularly those in Egypt, were commonly called *ʿAzebs* (literally, 'bachelors'—see above, p. 56).

The *Ṭopçu Başî*, as well as commanding the Gunners, controlled the arsenal just referred to and also the powder-magazines (*Barud-ḫâne*)[1] at Salonika, Gallipoli, and the capital.[2] Both the arsenal and the powder-magazines, however, had independent government inspectors;[3] and the arsenal had a technical director, called *Döküċü Başî*[4] (Head Founder or Caster). Owing to the ease with which copper was obtainable in the Empire, ordnance continued up to beyond the date of our survey to be wrought in bronze instead of iron (as was usual in Europe).[5] In the earlier part of the sixteenth century, however, when the use of cast-iron balls was introduced, the huge cannon hitherto wrought for the projection of stone balls gave way to others of smaller size.

Under Süleymân the Magnificent the establishment of both the *Ṭopçu* and *Cebeci ocaḳs* was increased, to two thousand and fifteen hundred men respectively. That of the *Ṭop ʿArabacîs* remained at the original figure, even, apparently, in later times, when the other *ocaḳs* were greatly expanded.[6] By the reign of Süleymân two other small *ocaḳs* had also come into being, namely those of the *Ḫumbaracîs* (Mortar-bombardiers) and the *Lağîmcîs* (Sappers).[7] The *ocaḳ* of the *Ḫumbaracîs* is said to have originally formed part of the *Ṭopçu* corps;[8] but both *Ḫumbaracîs* and *Lağîmcîs*, instead of receiving pay from the Treasury, were provided with military fiefs.[9] As we shall see, the *Ḫumbaracîs* were reorganized early in the eighteenth century under the direction of a celebrated French convert to Islam.[10]

The *Ṭopçu Başî* and the *Cebeci Başî*, again, were, like the *Ağa* of the Janissaries, responsible for the policing of certain areas. That under the jurisdiction of the *Ṭopçu Başî* consisted of Bey Oğlu or Péra, and the quarter round the arsenal itself.[11] That under the jurisdiction of the *Cebeci Başî* consisted of the quarters of

[1] *Barud* (Turkish), 'gunpowder'.

[2] See Cevdet, vi. 126, for the amalgamation of the three in 1792, and Juchereau, i. 63, for the removal of the powder-magazine and the foundry from the authority of the *Ṭopçu Başî* under Selim III.

[3] Called *Ṭop-ḫâne Nâẓiri* and *Barud-ḫâne Emînis*. (See D'Ohsson, vii. 196.)

[4] From *Dökmek*, Turkish, 'to cast, to form in a mould'.—Aḥmed Râsim, i. 99. ʿOsmân Nûrî, i. 921, identifies the *Döküċü Başî* with the *Ḫumbaracî Başî* (see below).

[5] Juchereau, i. 70.

[6] See Lybyer (Ramberti), 252; and D'Ohsson, vii. 362–4.

[7] *Ḫumbara*, Persian (? from *Ḫom*, 'a jar'), 'a mortar, a trough'. *Lağîm*, Turkish, 'an underground tunnel, a mine, a sewer'.

[8] They are not mentioned by Ramberti (see Lybyer, loc. cit.).

[9] So Juchereau, i. 71. D'Ohsson, vii. 369, states that up to 1732 the corps consisted of 300 men provided with military fiefs. He places both *Ḫumbaracîs* and *Lağîmcîs* in a special category of troops outside the framework of the (original?) six corps of the standing army, viz. the Janissaries, the *Ṭopçus*, the *Ṭop ʿArabacîs*, the *Cebecis*, and two cavalry *ocaḳs* with which we have not yet dealt.

[10] The Comte de Bonneval, Aḥmed Paşa. See below, p. 187.

[11] ʿOsmân Nûrî, i. 920.

Aya Ṣofya, the 'Stable Gate' referred to above, and another, called Ḥoca Paşa.[1] Presumably these police duties were discharged by the men of the *ortas* stationed in the capital, as in the case of the Janissaries.

(*d*) *The Cavalry*

The rest of the standing army was made up of six cavalry divisions. These are said to have been of older creation even than the Janissaries.[2] Two of them, indeed, seem to show this antiquity in their name: *'Ölûfeci*, 'Men drawing pay',[3] since this evidently distinguishes them from the rest of the troops, who, as we have seen, were originally all feudal. Moreover, two of the other divisions were called *Ğurebâ*, 'strangers',[4] because they were recruited from 'foreign' Moslems, that is to say Moslems that came from beyond the bounds of Ottoman rule, to seek their fortune, material or spiritual, in the Sultans' wars against the infidels. It is true that they continued to be so recruited at least until late in the sixteenth century.[5] Nevertheless, this participation of 'foreign' Moslem enthusiasts was especially characteristic of the early campaigns of expansion. These divisions were known as the Four *Bölüks*,[6] one of the *'Ölûfecis* and one of the *Ğurebâ* being known as 'of the Right',[7] and the other two as 'of the Left',[8] because of the positions they took up with respect to the Sultan on the field of battle. The remaining two divisions seem to have been created slightly later.[9] They enjoyed greater honour and were larger than the Four *Bölüks*.[10] The men of the first, which again was larger and more honoured than the second and took up a position on the Sultan's right in war, were called simply *Sipâhîs*—as if

[1] Ibid. 916. [2] D'Ohsson, vii. 364, 366; Lybyer, 98.

[3] Cf. "*Ölûfeli*', p. 42. n. 2 above. [4] Arabic, plural, from *Ğarîb*, 'strange'.

[5] See Lybyer, 98–9, and note.

[6] *Bölükâti Erba'a*—a fine linguistic mixture. The Turkish *Bölük* is given an Arabic plural *ât* and put in the Persian *iḍâfet* construction with the Arabic *Erba'a* 'four.' There seems to be some confusion in the use of this term. According to Seyyid Muṣṭafâ (e.g. i. 63) it was applied to the *'Ölûfecis* and the *Ğurebâ*. Lybyer, 98, writes as if 'the four' were the *Sipâhîs*, the *Silihdârs*, the *'Ölûfecis*, and the *Ğurebâ*.

[7] *'Ölûfeciyâni Yemîn* and *Ğurebâi Yemîn*.

[8] *'Ölûfeciyâni Yesâr* and *Ğurebâi Yesâr*.

[9] According to D'Ohsson, vii. 365. Seyyid Muṣṭafâ, loc. cit., implies that they were of earlier creation saying that the 'Four *Bölüks*' were added to them. According to Zinkeisen, iii. 175, a standing cavalry was first created under Orḫân and was reorganized under his successor, Murâd I, by Timur-Ṭaş Paşa. 'Abdu'r-Raḥmân Şeref, i. 104, puts the organization of the *Sipâhîs* down to this latter officer. Perhaps, therefore, we may take it that the Four *Bölüks* were created under Orḫân, and the *Sipâhîs* and *Silihdârs* under Murâd. But just as the early history of the Janissaries is obscure, so is that of the cavalry.

[10] Together they formed the first grade of the cavalry, the *'Ölûfecis* forming the second, and the *Ğurebâ* the third.—Seyyid Muṣṭafâ, i. 144. For their numbers and pay in the time of Süleymân see Lybyer in passages cited below.

they were cavalry-men *par excellence*, for in fact all the standing as well as the feudal cavalry was generally referred to by this term.[1] Those of the second were called *Silihdârs*, 'Sword- or Weapon-bearers',[2] and operated on the Sultan's left.[3]

The *Sipâhîs*, *Silihdârs*, and *'Ölûfecis* were recruited from among the Janissaries and part of the Imperial Household.[4] Their organization seems to have been imitated in some degree from that of the feudal cavalry. Thus each man had to train and take on campaign two or more armed and mounted slaves, maintained at his own expense like the *Cebelis* of the fief-holders.[5] Moreover, the *Silihdârs*, by way of privilege, were actually provided with fiefs.[6] Each division was commanded by an *Ağa*,[7] appointed from the Imperial Household, who was assisted by four other general officers and one or more secretaries. The men of the *Sipâhîs* and *Silihdârs*, if not of the other divisions, were organized in squadrons of twenty, each with its commander and sub-officers.[8] Unlike the Janissaries and other infantry corps, the cavalry were not provided with barracks. Most of them lived in villages near the capital, in order to use the local pasture for their horses.[9] Only the *Ağas* and other general officers of the divisions appear to have had quarters in Istanbul, since the attendance of some was required several times a week at the palace.[10]

The original establishment of the cavalry divisions is put at different figures by various authors.[11] But it appears that during

[1] Lybyer (Ramberti), 250. Ramberti and other foreigners refer to them as *Sipâhî Oğlans* (Cavalry Boys). Cf. 'Abdu'r-Raḥmân Şeref, loc. cit., this author calling them *Ebnâi Sipâhîyân* (*Sipâhîs*' sons). The equivalent Turkish of this phrase would, however, be *Sipâhî Oğullari*.

[2] Cf. below, p. 124, n. 4.

[3] Lybyer (Ramberti), 251. Cf. D'Ohsson, vii. 367, for the later subordination of the *'Ölûfecis* and *Ġurebâ* of the left to the *Silihdârs*.

[4] From the *Iç Oğlans* (see below, p. 78) other than *Ḫâṣṣ Odalis* (see below, p. 80), and from the officers of the infantry *ocaḳs*. The *'Ölûfecis* received recruits also from the irregular troops.—D'Ohsson, vii. 366; Lybyer, 78, 98; Seyyid Muṣṭafâ, i. 144; Juchereau, i. 86; Zinkeisen, iii. 177.

[5] Lybyer, 98, citing foreign sixteenth-century accounts. Neither Seyyid Muṣṭafâ nor D'Ohsson refers to these armed slaves.

[6] Lybyer (Ramberti), 251. Cf. Juchereau, i. 86.

[7] Called *Sipâhîler Ağasi*, *Silihdârlar Ağasi*, &c., and, collectively, *Bölük Ağalari*.

[8] So Seyyid Muṣṭafâ, i. 144. D'Ohsson, vii. 368, states that they had quarters in the capital and at Adrianople and Brusa.

[9] See Appendix A (A).

[10] See *M.T.M.* i (The *Ḳânûn-nâme* of 'Abdu'r-Raḥmân Tevḳî'î), 506, 511, 512 for attendance of the *Bölük Ağasis* at Thursday, Imperial, Audience, and Pay-distribution *Dîvâns*.

[11] The Four *Bölüks* are said to have originally numbered 2,400 men (D'Ohsson, vii. 365; cf. Zinkeisen, iii. 175, who puts the original standing *Sipâhîs*, in the more general sense of the word, at '*kaum 2500 Mann*'). Seyyid Muṣṭafâ, i. 144, asserts that the establishment of the *Bölüks* (all six) was 7,000 up to the time of Süleymân I, which if the 'Four' were maintained at 2,400 would leave 4,600 for the *Sipâhîs* proper and *Silihdârs*. Zinkeisen, iii. 176, however, states that after his conquest of Egypt and Syria, Selîm I raised the total to 8,000,

the reign of Süleymân the Magnificent it stood at between ten and twelve thousand, excluding the attendant slaves, who brought it up to between forty and fifty thousand.[1] At that time, therefore, it was actually larger than that of the Janissaries. Moreover, the men of the superior divisions, being drawn from the *Iç Oğlans*, the pages of the Household, were held in far greater honour than those of the infantry. The possession of slaves no doubt enhanced their prestige; and they were noted for the magnificence of their dress and accoutrements, which put those not only of the Janissaries but also of the feudal cavalry in the shade.[2] They were far, however, from being merely decorative. For not only were they expert in the care of horses—and that in a society in which horses were highly prized[3]—but were incomparable bowmen.[4] As we shall see, the palace pages were trained from childhood in archery, and no doubt proficiency in markmanship was exacted from those pages that were promoted to service in the *Bölüks*. It was partly, indeed, the very excellence of their bowmanship that led to their decline. For when, already late, it was sought in 1548 to provide two hundred of them with pistols and carbines in the campaign undertaken in that year against the Şâh Ṭahmäsp of Persia, the men were so much mocked by their companions and pained at the dirt of the powder, that the new weapons had to be withdrawn, and were not generally adopted by the cavalry till the end of the century.[5]

III. THE IMPERIAL HOUSEHOLD

A description of the Imperial Household may not seem to deserve much space in that of Ottoman society as a whole. For it was a comparatively small body confined to the Sultan's palace in the capital. In fact, however, it was a model for the households of all the grandees of the Empire who copied it as far as their means and etiquette permitted, and even to some extent for those of humbler Moslems. Also it formed a training college for administrators and officers,[6] by whose appointment to positions of influence in both the capital and the provinces its spirit was spread far and wide. On this account alone, therefore, it deserves attention.

comprising 3,500 *Sipâhîs*, 2,500 *Silihdârs*, 1,000 *'Ölûfecis*, and 1,000 *Ğurebâ*. D'Ohsson's figures (vii. 364, 365): 10,000 for the *Sipâhîs* and 8,000 for the *Silihdârs* under the earlier Meḥmed II, must, as is suggested by Lybyer, if they are to be trusted, include the men-at-arms furnished by the men of those corps.

[1] Lybyer, 99. [2] Zinkeisen, iii. 169.

[3] Ibid. 170–2. [4] Ibid. 173. [5] Ibid. 174.

[6] See, for instance, 'Aṭâ, 41: '*Serâyi Hümâyûn bir mektebi 'umûmî ittiḫâẕ olunaraḳ*', 'The Imperial Palace being turned into a general school'. Cf. Lybyer, 75.

The constitution of the Imperial Household was conditioned by two main features of the Sultans' way of life, namely their maintenance of a *Harem* and their adherence to the old Persian tradition of kingly conduct. The seclusion of women, though of ancient origin in the countries of the Middle East, had been adopted early in Islam and had of course become a very striking characteristic of Moslem society. It may, however, be worth while here to point out that it was not essentially connected with the practice of polygamy as sanctioned by the *Şerî'a.* For any Moslem of even the humblest pretensions to culture, though he might have only one wife, or might be unmarried, as long as he had women dependent on him, would keep them secluded from male society. The *Ḥarem* was merely the instrument of this seclusion. For the word, which means 'forbidden', hence 'sacred', and so, virtually 'taboo', was primarily applied, in this connexion, to the apartments in any Moslem house in which the women lived. It was used only secondarily of their inmates; and this solely because the very mention of woman was itself so far taboo among the polite that in order to avoid it they would resort equally to such a word as 'house'.

Part of the royal palace—the *Serây*[1]—was therefore set aside as a *Ḥarem.* But the rest was further divided into two sections. Persian influence in the Islamic tradition of sovereignty tended to remove the monarch from the sight of his subjects except on occasions of ceremony. Hence such hours of his life as were not spent in the *Ḥarem* itself were usually spent in his private apartments. Provision had therefore to be made for the latter in the layout of the *Serây,* which thus came to consist of an outer court, an inner court, and the *Ḥarem.* Moreover, so jealously separated were they, that special rooms were in each case set aside for a transition from one to the other. Hence the Sultan's audience chamber was located between the outer and inner courts, so that he might maintain his seclusion as far as this was compatible with being seen by dignitaries, native and foreign, at all, while the latter were excluded from the private apartments proper. And between the inner courts and the *Ḥarem*, into which no one but himself, eunuchs, and women were allowed to penetrate, there were rooms known collectively as the *Mâ-beyn*,[2] where he was waited on by his male entourage for such intimate purposes as being robed and having his head shaved.

The *Serây* being so divided, its personnel was divided similarly—into the *Ḥarem*, the Inner, and the Outer Services.

[1] Persian. The application of the Italian version of this word 'seraglio' to the *Ḥarem* alone is quite unwarranted by Moslem usage.

[2] Arabic 'what is between'.

(*a*) *The Ḥarem*

The *Ḥarem* was the sphere of the women and the eunuchs that guarded them. Its centre was, of course, the Sultan's family—his wives and concubines, and their children. In early times the Sultans had been in the habit of marrying princesses, Moslem and Christian, often more than one at a time, but never more than the canonical four. The last Sultan so to marry, however, was Meḥmed the Conqueror; and though two later Sultans, of the first half of the seventeenth century, had married Moslem 'commoners'—one a freed slave—their successors abandoned marriage altogether. The law prescribes no limits to the number of concubines a man may entertain. The Sultans, however, confined themselves as a rule also to four,[1] who, after they finally abandoned the contraction of marriages, were treated with all the consideration and ceremony of legal wives; these ladies were known as *Ḳadîns*,[2] and formed the highest class of the female personnel of the *Ḥarem*. Each had separate apartments and a staff to serve her, and saw her companion *Ḳadîns* only on ceremonial occasions. The *Ḳadîns* were ranked by seniority, first, second, third, and fourth,[3] each rank carrying with it the enjoyment of a higher income than that below it.

It naturally made a great difference to the estimation in which *Ḳadîns* were held, if they bore children to the monarch. To bear a son, again, was more praiseworthy than to bear a daughter: ladies successful in so doing were called *Ḫâṣṣekî Sulṭâns*,[4] thereby being approximated to real *Sulṭâns*[5]—the title given to imperial daughters —whereas those that bore only female children were called merely *Ḫâṣṣekî Ḳadîns*. But the position of greatest consideration to which a *Ḳadîn* might rise was that of mother to a Sultan (*Vâlide Sulṭân*),[6]

[1] In later times, at least. Some earlier monarchs are said to have had more than three hundred concubines during their reigns; and Murâd III (1574–95) had no less than 130 children as a result of this extravagance. If the Sultan took one of the *Gediklis* (see below, p. 74) as a concubine without raising her to the status of *Ḳadîn* (see below), she was known as *Ḫâṣṣ Odaliḳ* or *Iḳbâle*. The word Odalisk is a corruption of *Odaliḳ*, which means 'appertaining to the room'. *Iḳbâle* is from the Arabic *Iḳbâl*, 'good fortune' (D'Ohsson).

[2] *Ḳadîn*, in Turkish, means simply 'woman'.

[3] Called, according to 'Oṣmân Bey, *Les Femmes en Turquie*, a somewhat sensational work, *Büyük, Ikinci, Ortanca*, and *Küçük*, i.e. Big, Second, Middle, and Little.

[4] Derived from the Arabic *Ḫâṣṣ* (see above, p. 47) through the Persian, *Ḫâṣṣagî* in that language meaning primarily 'speciality', 'peculiarity', hence 'excellence' and hence again 'a favourite'. The Turkish word appears to be merely a mispronunciation due to the ambiguity of the Arabic script. It was also applied to some categories of Ottoman soldiery (see below, p. 84).

[5] The Sultans being referred to usually as *Pâdişâh* (see above, p. 34). When used of them the word preceded their names, as Sulṭân Aḥmed, Sulṭân Selîm, whereas in the case of princesses it was placed after their names, as Ḫadîce Sulṭân, Esmâ Sulṭân. The Arabic word had originally an impersonal meaning, 'power', 'authority'.

[6] i.e. 'Princess Mother', from Arabic *Wâlida*.

since the Sultans invariably treated their mothers with the utmost reverence; and it was customary for these ladies to issue their commands direct to the Grand *Vezîr*. In later times they invariably rose to this height from comparative obscurity, however, owing to the rarity with which son then succeeded father on the throne. For *Ḳadîns* that had once borne the Sultan a child, if he should tire of them, or if they should survive him, were removed from the so-called 'New' *Serây* to the Old;[1] and only those returned that had the good fortune to see their sons ascend the throne.

Below the *Ḳadîns* came four other categories of women slaves, the highest being that of the *Gediklis* (privileged).[2] It was from among the *Gediklis* that the *Ḳadîns* were chosen, as were also the two principal female office-holders of the *Ḥarem*, the Lady Intendant[3] and her assistant and deputy, the Treasurer.[4] The Lady Intendant was responsible for the discipline, and the Treasurer, under her, for the economy, of the establishment. The *Gediklis* waited on the Sultan personally, a number of them holding offices corresponding to those of the pages of the Privy Chamber that we shall describe below, whereas the next rank of slave-women[5] waited on the Sultan's mother, the *Ḳadîns* and their children. The third category, again, was that of the Pupils,[6] slave-girls recently arrived, who were trained in such arts as reading, writing, sewing, embroidery, music, and dancing, so that they might fill vacancies in the higher ranks when the need arose. The last category was composed of servants,[7] who seldom rose above it; whereas the women of the higher categories gradually worked their way up.

Owing to the rules of the *Şerî'a* regarding slaves, all the women of the *Ḥarem* were invariably foreigners. Up to the seventeenth century many of them were European prisoners of war: thus Ḫurrem Sulṭân, known to Europe as Roxelana, the famous *Ḳadîn* of Süleymân the Magnificent, was Russian; and the powerful

[1] The old *Serây* was a Byzantine building repaired by Meḥmed the Conqueror and used by him immediately after the conquest. The new *Serây* was built by him in 1468.—'Aṭâ, i. 39, 56. It, too, incorporated some already existing buildings—ibid. 41 sq. It is that now known as *Ṭop Ḳapî Serâyi*, the 'Seraglio' *par excellence*. The old *Serây* occupied the site of the present University of Istanbul. Up to the time of Süleymân the Magnificent the Sultans divided their time when in the capital between the two palaces. It was only then that the New *Serây* was adopted as their sole residence.—'Aṭâ, i. 57.

[2] *Gedik* (Turkish) signifies 'gap', and hence 'exception (to a rule)'. 'privilege'. We shall meet the word in various other connexions.

[3] *Kâḫya Ḳadînî*.

[4] Called *Ḫazîne-dâr Ustâ*, from Arabic *Ḫazîna*, 'treasure', with Persian ending *dâr*, 'possessing', 'managing'. *Ustâ* is also a Persian word, properly *Ustâḏ*, meaning 'master', master-workman. Hence, through Arabic, the Spanish Vd.—*Usted*.

[5] Called *Ustâ*—see note above.

[6] *Şâgird* (Persian)—a word applied to both sexes.

[7] Called *Câriye* (Arabic)—from the root 'to run': a young and active girl; especially applied to slaves.

Vâlides of Meḥmed III and the brothers Murâd IV and Ibrahîm were respectively Venetian and Greek.[1] From the end of the sixteenth century, however, the majority were recruited from the Caucasus, partly because the women of that region were especially admired for their beauty, partly because their people entered willingly into this profitable slave-trade. The majority, again, were then bought for the palace service through the Customs Commissioner of the capital, in which case they would enter the *Ḥarem* usually at the age of ten or eleven. But some were presented to the Sultans by rich officers and others, after they had already been trained in various accomplishments.[2]

Most of the women thus introduced into the *Ḥarem* eventually left it. For, as we have mentioned, Moslem law and custom enjoined the virtuous to manumit their slaves;[3] and in accordance with this precept the Sultan would regularly grant their freedom to inmates of the *Ḥarem*, in which case they became eligible for marriage. On a Sultan's death, his childless *Ḳadîns* were frequent beneficiaries of this favour, and since, though they then left it, they and other such freedwomen continued to have the *entrée* to the *Ḥarem*, they were eagerly sought in marriage by ambitious intriguers for the influence with which this contact endowed them. For as in later times the Sultans led a retired life, so they came to be swayed in their decisions by the members of their entourage, male and female. A word from a *Ḳadîn* often worked wonders; and *Ḳadîns* might be prompted by their ex-colleagues. Female influence on public affairs reached its zenith in the reign of the eccentric Ibrahîm.[4] Then certain ladies of the *Ḥarem* succeeded in obtaining even the government of provinces, which they administered through deputies, whom, of course, they never saw. For none of them, from *Ḳadîns* to servants, were allowed outside the palace walls except when some of them accompanied the Sultans on a visit to one of the smaller summer palaces. Indeed, they seldom went beyond the limits of the *Ḥarem* itself: they had to obtain the Sultan's special permission even to walk in the Palace gardens; and on all such excursions elaborate precautions were taken to prevent any unauthorized person from catching sight of them.

The *Ḥarem* walls themselves, however, enclosed a number of open courts and small gardens. The Sultan had his own pavilion in the midst of the enclosure, containing his bedroom and a large reception room, where he performed many of his religious duties and entertained his married female relatives. Moreover, he, his

[1] *Encyclopaedia of Islam*, arts. 'Khurrem', 'Murād III', 'Muḥammad III', 'Kösem'.

[2] D'Ohsson, vii. 63–4; Lybyer, 57.

[3] See above, p. 21.

[4] See above, p. 37.

Ḳadîns, the Lady Intendant, and the Treasurer each had a separate bath-house, the remainder of the women using one in common. The *Ḥarem* was in fact a little village; and in it the Sultan was treated with almost superhuman reverence. It was etiquette for none of the women to meet his eye unsummoned: at his approach all had to hide. In order to give warning of his movements, the monarch always wore slippers soled with silver, to make a clatter on the marble pavements.[1]

The *Ḥarem* was guarded and its affairs to some extent directed by eunuchs. From the early fifteenth century[2] to the end of the sixteenth the eunuchs employed in the chief posts of this service were White, being for the most part Caucasians like the *Ḥarem* women themselves. During the reign of Murâd III, however—a reign that we have already had occasion to mention as a turning-point in the fortunes of the Empire—the three highest of these posts were for the first time conferred on Negroes; and though the Whites recovered their influence for a time, from the following reign onwards they remained subordinate to the Blacks, and were even, at the beginning of the eighteenth century, obliged to yield in influence to the Chief of the Pages. At this time, indeed, during the reign of Aḥmed III (1703–30), an attempt was made by a Grand *Vezîr*[3] to suppress the use of eunuchs in the palace altogether. He sent orders to Egypt that the castration and presentation of Negro slaves to the Sultan must cease. But, as if by a reaction, after this minister's death, the Black eunuchs came to exercise an unprecedented ascendancy over the Sultans. And so up to the time of our survey their head, the *Dârü'l-Seʿâdet Ağasî* (*Ağa* of the House of Felicity), more usually referred to as the *Ḳizlar Ağasî* (*Ağa* of the Women), continued to be esteemed the principal officer of the whole palace, and actually ranked third in the Empire —after the Grand *Vezîr*, whose communications with the Sultan passed through his hands, and the *Şeyḫü'l-Islâm*[4]—as a *Vezîr*, or *Paşa* of three *Ṭuğs*.[5] The White eunuchs were now employed only in connexion with the Inside Service, which they had always supervised; and the guardianship of the *Ḥarem* devolved entirely on the Blacks. Moreover, the *Ḳizlar Ağasî* now took control of the pious

[1] Most details of this account of the *Ḥarem* are taken from D'Ohsson, vii. 62 sq. He obtained his information from the husbands of former inmates that had been freed and married (see above, p. 75). His inquiries on this subject cost him more trouble and presents than those required for all the rest of the work (see op. cit. vii. 85, note). Hammer's account, in *Staatsverwaltung*, 63 sq., bears him out, as far as it goes, in most particulars.

[2] According to the *History* of ʿAṭâ, i. 34, 36, it was Murâd II (1421–51) that first employed White eunuchs for the guardianship of the *Ḥarem*. This passage cited by Aḥmed Râsim, ii. 273, note.

[3] Damad Çorlulu ʿAlî Paşa. Actually in 1716.

[4] See below, ch. viii.

[5] See below, p. 139.

foundations (*Awḳâf*) of the Two Holy Cities,[1] an office, hitherto held by the Chief of the Whites, that vastly enhanced the prestige of its occupant. In their administration he was aided both by certain functionaries of the Outside Service whose corps he commanded and by certain 'learned men'.[2]

In the eighteenth century there were in all about two hundred Black eunuchs employed in the Sultan's *Ḥarem*. But others, also under the control of the *Ḳizlar Ağasi* and forming part of the corps, were employed at the 'Old' palace, in the apartments of the royal princes, and in the Households of married princesses. They were for the most part presented to the Sultans by the governors of Egypt,[3] who were emulated by other provincial governors. Otherwise they were bought; but in either case those newly acquired, while they were being educated by their superiors, were used as guards for the door of the *Ḥarem*, next which they lived in dormitories. Having completed their education, they might then rise through four grades, while holding which they acted as under-officers, to the command of this guard, the highest post to be obtained by mere seniority. And in the course of this promotion they might be employed by one or other of the *Ḳadîns* in the *Ḥarem* itself, since each was entitled to the services of several eunuchs. The remaining offices were filled by favour, accorded for personal merit, as indeed was that of the *Ağa* himself. The next most important of these posts was that of Treasurer, which carried with it, like the *Ağa's*, the rank of *Vezîr*.[4]

(*b*) *The Inside Service*

So much for the *Ḥarem*. We may now emerge into the third court of the palace, the Domain of the Pages and White eunuchs. The word 'Page' may give the impression that the persons to whom we apply it were all adolescent; and in early times even the senior pages were, in fact, seldom more than twenty-five years of age.[5] Later, however, after the abandonment of the *Devşirme* in the seventeenth century, the system formerly in force, by which they were early promoted to posts in the Outside Service, the army or

[1] i.e. Mecca and Medina, called 'the two *Ḥarems*' (*Ḥarameyn*), a use of the word illustrative of its meaning as explained above, p. 72.

[2] See below, ch. viii.

[3] They were selected from the slaves brought to Egypt by the annual caravans from Darfur and Sennar (see below, p. 305). The younger boys were castrated during the journey at Abu Tig, near Aswan, the operators being Copts, since castration is forbidden by Islamic law (see Girard, 632).

[4] 'Aṭâ, i. 37, 159, 160, 257 sq., and D'Ohsson, iv. 54–6, 58–61. These authors' accounts of the transference of power over the *Ḥarem* from the White eunuchs to the Black differ in several particulars. We have followed that of 'Aṭâ. For further particulars of the eunuchs' organization see Appendix B.

[5] See Lybyer, 78, citing Postel. They used to remain in whatever post they finally attained only seven years.—D'Ohsson, vii. 53.

the administration, was abandoned; and the senior pages were then usually men of sixty years or more.[1] In Turkish the pages were referred to as *Iç Ağas*, 'Inside *Ağas*', that is, officers of the Imperial Interior Service, the *Enderûnî Hümâyûn*,[2] only novices being designated by the term *Iç Oğlan* that we have used above.

As we have remarked, the White eunuchs originally guarded the *Ḥarem* as well. But from their first employment they seem also to have been responsible for the pages; and at any rate in the sixteenth century the four lower of their five chief offices corresponded with the four departments into which the Interior or Inside Service was divided. The lowest of these departments was composed of two chambers called 'Great' and 'Little'.[3] The others, in order of increasing importance, were called the 'Privy Larder',[4] the 'Imperial Treasury',[5] and the 'Privy Chamber'.[6] Each was controlled by one of these four White eunuchs, assisted by a number of others.[7]

The chief White eunuch was called either *Bâbü's-Se'âdet Ağasî* (Officer of the Gate of Felicity) or more simply *Ḳapî Ağasî* (Officer of the Gate).[8] Until displaced by his Black rival, he was no doubt occupied largely with *Ḥarem* matters. But even after the fall of the Whites from favour, the *Ḳapî Ağasî* had under his immediate command a company of from thirty to forty *Ḳapî Oğlanîs* (literally 'Gate Boys'); while the eunuch that controlled the lowest department also commanded the guard proper of forty other eunuchs.[9] The four departments were also known as Dormitories (*Ḳoğuş*), since it was in dormitories that all the pages except the principal officers of the Privy Chamber (each of whom had a separate pavilion)[10] were accommodated, as were also the White eunuchs. The pages were further grouped in messes of ten, a White eunuch presiding over each.[11]

The Inside Service seems to have been first generally organized in this manner by Meḥmed the Conqueror.[12] It appears, however, that Selîm I reformed much of it in detail after his conquest of Syria and Egypt; and he endowed the Privy Chamber with greater

[1] 'Aṭâ, i. 162, 208.

[2] From Persian *Ändärûn*, 'within'. Hammer, op. cit. 11, refers somewhat confusingly to the Inside Service as *Der Äussere Hofstaat*.

[3] *Büyük ve Küçük Odalar*—also called in early times *Eski ve Yeni Odalar* (Old and New Rooms). They were of equal standing: see Lybyer, 78, citing Ramberti.

[4] *Kilârî Ḫâṣṣ*. [5] *Ḫazînei Hümâyûn*. [6] *Ḫâṣṣ Oda*.

[7] See Appendix B (B).

[8] *Bâb* being the Arabic, *Ḳapî* the Turkish for 'gate'.

[9] Aḥmed Râsim, i. 184–5, note.

[10] So D'Ohsson, vii. 49. Hammer, op. cit. 12, states that only the *Kapî Ağasî* had a separate dwelling.

[11] 'Aṭâ, i. 34, 160.

[12] Reference is made to it in his *Ḳânûn-nâme*; see Appendix B.

importance than it had hitherto possessed by forming its pages into a guard of honour for the Prophet's Cloak and other relics, which the Sultan brought to Istanbul from Mecca on the submission of the Ḥijâz.[1]

After undergoing a preliminary training in one of several colleges, of which the most important was Galaṭa Serâyi,[2] founded by Selîm's father Bâyezîd II, the *Iç Oğlans* were admitted as probationers into the Great and Little Chambers, where their education was continued.[3] Their instruction was in the hands of visiting professors (*Ḫocas*),[4] of the White eunuchs,[5] and of pages that had attained the age of thirty and a certain standard of proficiency.[6] When it was completed, they were given actual employment in this lowest department, and rose thence, sometimes by mere seniority, sometimes by favour shown to talent, either through the Larder or the Treasury, or else direct, to the Privy Chamber.

The Larder and the Treasury were chiefly concerned, as their names indicate, the first with the service of the Sultan's meals, the second with his private, as opposed to the state, treasure. As for the Great and Little Chambers, in the seventeenth century they were converted into a fourth department, known as the 'Campaign Chamber',[7] owing to the fact that some of its members then acted as laundrymen to the Sultan when on campaign. Its staff, however, included barbers, turban-folders, and musicians as well. Indeed, apparently anomalous duties came to be allotted to many of the pages in all the departments. Some account of these, and of their organization as a whole—which was excessively complicated—is given below.[8]

Among the pages of each of the lower departments there were several office-holders with special titles; the remainder were further divided into two or more grades; and each department was controlled, under the supervision of its White eunuchs, by a *Kâḫya*, appointed from the Privy Chamber. Some of these subordinate pages also waited on their superiors as coffee-makers, pipe-lighters, messengers, &c.; and others—for instance, forty valets,[9] serving under a page of the Privy Chamber—came into direct contact with

[1] 'Aṭâ, i. 30, 73 sq., 94, 98.

[2] Ibid. 72 sq. Other training centres were the old palace at Adrianople and the palace of Ibrahîm Paşa, founded under Süleymân, on the site of the Sulṭân Aḥmed Mosque.—*Encyclopaedia of Islam*, art. 'Edirne'; D'Ohsson, vii. 47; 'Aṭâ, i. 112.

[3] 'Aṭâ, i. 137.

[4] From the Persian *Ḫwâcâ*—ibid. 75.

[5] Ibid. 160.

[6] Ibid. 138, 139. Such pages were known as *Lalas*, like the Black eunuchs mentioned in App. B (A). The novices were taught manners, reading, writing, and various military accomplishments; but the talents of individuals were carefully studied and appropriately used. See Lybyer, 76 sq.—account based on Menavino and Ricaut.

[7] *Seferli Odasi*.

[8] Appendix B (B) (2), 'The Lower Chambers'.

[9] *Çoḳadârs*; see App. A (B).

the Sultan, despite their relatively humble position. The Inside Service also included a number of mutes and dwarfs, attached to all four departments. Both were used as messengers, the mutes attending the Sultan during confidential interviews.[1]

The Privy Chamber itself was staffed by some forty pages called *Ḫâṣṣ Odalis*. According to one account, as guardians of the Prophet's Cloak, their number was brought up to the auspicious figure of forty by the inclusion of the Sultan himself.[2] The principal *Ḫâṣṣ Odalis* waited on him in the apartments known as the *Mâ-beyn*;[3] and were for this reason styled *Mâ-beyncis*. These were his personal attendants *par excellence*, by whom he was shaved, dressed, served at table, and so on. Up to the end of the seventeenth century the *Mâ-beyncis* were headed, as indeed was the *Ḫâṣṣ Oda* as a whole, by the chief page, to whom we have already referred: the *Siliḥdâr Ağa*, or Sword-bearer.[4] But during the reign of Aḥmed III, when, as we have mentioned, an attempt was made by a Grand *Vezîr* to suppress the employment of eunuchs in the palace,[5] the Inside Service was partially reorganized, and the office of Sword-bearer (which this minister had earlier held) was exalted to a height unknown before. The death of this Grand *Vezîr* was followed by a reaction in favour of the Black eunuchs. Nevertheless, thenceforward the Sword-bearer replaced the chief White eunuch as head of the Inside Service altogether; and the pages of the Privy Chamber immediately inferior to him were excused *Mâ-beynci* duty and converted into his lieutenants.[6] The White eunuchs that formerly controlled each of the four chambers were similarly displaced; the *Kâḫyas* of the lower chambers were made responsible to the Sword-bearer for their management; and a *Ḫâṣṣ Odali* called *Ağa* of the Key[7] was charged with a like responsibility for the Privy Chamber.

Mâ-beyn service was now performed by no more than a dozen of the *Ḫâṣṣ Odalis*, though with the help of numerous assistants from the lower chambers; and these *Mâ-beyncis* were regarded as inferior to the principal pages of the Privy Chamber. Yet two of them in particular, the Head Valet[8] and the Confidential Secretary,[9] exercised an influence scarcely inferior to that of the Sword-bearer —owing to the close contact with the Sultan into which they were brought by the nature of their duties.

[1] The mutes were called *Dil-siz* ('tongueless'), the dwarfs *Cüce*—'Aṭâ, i. 171–2; D'Ohsson, vii. 46–7.

[2] D'Ohsson states that the *Ḫâṣṣ Oda* was composed of thirty-nine pages, the Sultan being reckoned as a fortieth; 'Aṭâ that the pages numbered forty without the *Siliḥdâr*, to say nothing of the Sultan himself—see Appendix B (B) 3. Meḥmed II is said to have had thirty-two *Ḫâṣṣ Odalis*—Lybyer, 127, note.

[3] See above, p. 72. [4] See above, p. 70. [5] See above, p. 76.

[6] See Appendix B (B) 3. [7] *Anaḫtar Ağasi*.

[8] *Baş Çoḳadâr*. [9] *Sirr Kâtibi*.

This reorganization diminished the power of the White eunuchs to vanishing point. After their ejection from the *Ḥarem*, they had retained their inspectorship of various pious foundations and their superintendence of the pages; but now they were deprived of these functions also. Their offices were, to be sure, retained: there was still a *Ḳapi̊ Ağasi̊* with *Ağas* corresponding to each of the chambers. But all they did was to supervise the pages' food and to some extent the education of novices.[1] Thus Ğalaṭa Serâyi̊ was left in charge of a eunuch; and, as formerly, it was the holder of this office that succeeded to that of *Ḳapi̊ Ağasi̊*.[2]

Ğalaṭa Serâyi̊ had in the two centuries of its existence been repeatedly closed and reopened,[3] the *Iç Oğlans* during the periods of its closure being received direct into the Campaign Chamber.[4] After the reorganization it remained open up to the period of our survey, before which, indeed, it was enlarged and repaired, under Maḥmûd I; and the education given to the pages both at Ğalaṭa and in the palace itself was much improved. The pages were by then, of course, no longer *Devşirme* conscripts but Moslems, often members of families prominent in the capital,[5] who remained slaves only technically. No doubt it was the employment of such born Moslems, instead of slave converts, that led to the growth in power of the Sword-bearers during the seventeenth century and the eventual relegation of the White eunuchs to a position of inferiority.

In considering the ups and downs of the influence exercised on the Sultans by the White eunuchs, the Black eunuchs, and the pages, we may observe that up to the time when the Sultans adopted a life of seclusion, the White eunuchs were supreme, dominating both the *Ḥarem* and the Inside Service; but that when the Sultans did so retire, they came to favour both the Blacks and the pages at the White eunuchs' expense. We may also perhaps suppose that the influence of the *Ḥarem* proved more potent than that of the pages, since the chief Black eunuch, its guardian, emerged from the struggle as the Sword-bearer's superior. For,

[1] See Appendix B (B) I.

[2] ʿAtâ, i. 81, 160–2, 164–5.

[3] For the vicissitudes of Ğalaṭa Serâyi̊ see ʿAṭâ, i. 78-80:

Founded by Bâyezîd II, it was
Closed by Selîm II, 1566–1574,
Reopened by Murâd III, 1574–1595,
Closed by Aḥmed I, 1603–1617,
Reopened by ʿOṣmân II, 1618–1622,
Closed under Meḥmed IV, 1648–1687,
by Köprülü Meḥmed Paşa,
Reopened by Aḥmed III 1703–1730,
Restored and enlarged by Maḥmûd I, 1730–1754.

[4] On at least one occasion when it was closed some of the pupils were drafted into the cavalry *Bölüks* (see above, p. 69).—ibid.

[5] Juchereau, i. 166.

whereas in his struggle with the *Ḳapî Aǧasî* of the day the Sword-bearer to whom the reorganization was due obtained the transference to himself of the right to convey communications between the Sultan and his ministers—a right that very greatly enhanced the importance of his post—in the reaction against his later attempted suppression of the eunuchs, his successors were obliged to yield it in turn to the chief Black, their subordination to whom they were required to mark by kissing the hem of his robe.[1]

(c) The Outside Service

The Outside Service of the Household differed from the Inside in not being exclusively concerned with palace affairs. For, unlike those of the Inside Service, its members came into direct contact with officers of the army and officials of the administration. Indeed, no very clear line was drawn between such officers and officials on the one hand and these servants of the Household on the other. Thus, in tables of precedence all three appear in an order that altogether disregards the types of duty each performed. Some of the duties performed by Outside Servants were, indeed, no less military or administrative than those performed by officers or officials unconnected with the Household. This confusion was due to the fact that, except for the feudal troops, the whole military and administrative organization of the Empire had developed from a state in which it was manned by members of the Sultan's immediate entourage.

This being so, it is not surprising to find that the Outside Service included a vast number of persons of very diverse employments. Not all of them even resided within the limits of the palace enclosure; some were regarded as being attached to the Janissaries; others were not *Ḳapî Ḳullarî* at all, but members of the learned profession, while certain groups were under the orders of the Inside *Aǧas* and the Black and White eunuchs. The 'Learned Men' we shall deal with when considering their kind. The rest we propose to consider more or less in order of declining importance, though this was not in all cases constant between the fifteenth and eighteenth centuries.

Most of the principal officers of the Outside Service were numbered among the so-called '*Aǧas* of the Stirrup'.[2] There seem

---

[1] 'Aṭâ, i. 161, 265; D'Ohsson, vii. 54.

[2] *Üzengi Aǧalari* or *Aǧayâni Rikâbi Hümâyûn*. The word stirrup was used metaphorically, not only under the Ottomans but also under the Selcuḳids, for the Sultan or his presence—apparently because in earlier times the ruler had received petitions and litigants on horseback (see Hammer, op. cit. 60)—and under the Ottomans, by extension, for cavalcades and audiences at which he appeared. The title *Üzengi Aǧalari* might therefore be translated '*Aǧas* of the Imperial Presence'. It was, however, also applicable more literally, since some of these

to have been seventeen of these *Ağas* in the time of the Conqueror of whom nine were the chief generals of the standing army.[1] Of the remainder, however, all but four had lost this rank by the eighteenth century, whereas another officer had by then been promoted to it; so that the *Ağas* of the Stirrup, apart from the generals, then numbered five.[2] The four that had held the rank of *Ağa* from the beginning were the Standard Bearer (*Mîr 'Alem*), the Great and Little Masters of the Horse (*Büyük ve Küçük Mîr Aḫorlar*), and the Intendant of the Door Keepers (*Ḳapîcîlar Kâhyasî*). The additional officer was the Chief Gardener (*Bostancî Başî*).

The Standard Bearer, who always retained his position as principal officer of the Outside Service, besides taking charge of the Imperial Standard and the Sultan's particular emblem of six *Ṭuğs* or horse-tails,[3] presented similar emblems to provincial governors on their appointment. He was also responsible for the palace military band,[4] and in later times commanded an important corps of special messengers called for historical reasons Chief Doorkeepers (*Ḳapîcî Başîs*).[5]

The Great Master of the Horse commanded all the personnel of the imperial stables, and controlled all the imperial pasturages on either side of the Bosphorus: it was under his orders that the *Voynuḳ 'Askerîs* performed their duties. The Little Master, as well as assisting in the command of the stables, had as his particular charge the supply of pack animals to the Inside pages and the care of the imperial carriages.[6] The Intendant of the Doorkeepers was responsible for the guardianship of the gates in the wall bounding the middle or second Court of the *Serây*. He also acted as master of ceremonies at the assemblies of State called Imperial *Dîvân*, together with an official who in early times was, like himself, an *Ağa* of the Stirrup, but by the eighteenth century had ceased to be so ranked owing to the fact that his duties came to be connected more closely with the Grand *Vezîr* than with the Sultan: namely the Chief Pursuivant (*Çavuş Başî*).[7]

Ağas had the privilege of aiding the Sultan to mount his horse, two of them holding the stirrups. See *Encyclopaedia of Islam*, art. 'Rikāb', and App. B (c) 1.

[1] viz. the *Ağa* of the Janissaries, the commanders of the six 'standing' cavalry divisions (*Bölük Ağalarî*), the *Ṭopçu Başî* and the *Cebeci Başî*.

[2] D'Ohsson, vii. 14–18 and 'Aṭâ, i. 74 agree on this number. 'Aṭâ, however, replaces the *Bostancî Başî* by the *Baş Ḳapîcî Başî* (see below). We follow D'Ohsson; but for an explanation of this uncertainty see Appendix B (c) 3 (i).

[3] See below p. 139. [4] The *'Alem Mehteris*; see Appendix B (c) 6.

[5] D'Ohsson, vii. 14; *O.T.E.M.*, No. 13, Appendix, 11, notes. For the *Ḳapîcî Başîs* see Appendix, B (c) 2 (i).

[6] *O.T.E.M.*, No. 13, Appendix, 12, note; D'Ohsson, vii. 33; 'Aṭâ, i. 302.

[7] D'Ohsson, vii. 17; *O.T.E.M.*, No. 13, Appendix 15. The *Kânûn-nâme* of 'Abdu' r-Raḥmân Tevḳî'î (1676) defining the order of ceremonies for an Imperial *Dîvân*, states that the *Çavuş Başî* and the *Ḳapîcîlar Kâhyasî* receive the

The Chief Gardener, though raised late to Stirrup rank, and always remaining inferior to the Standard Bearer, enjoyed in fact greater influence in the palace than any of his fellows, partly because it was under his direction that delinquent officials were put to the question or executed, partly because over two thousand men, employed in many different ways, came under his control. These men were known as Gardeners (*Bostancîs*) because their corps was first formed to undertake the conversion of the rough ground about the palace into gardens and vegetable plots. In fact, however, only a few of them did gardener's work. Most of them were watchmen or guards of the pavilions scattered about the palace grounds, of some of the gates in the surrounding wall, or of numerous small ports round the Golden Horn, the Bosphorus, and part of the Sea of Marmara. Those posted at the ports both controlled the shipping that put in at them and acted as local police, the *Bostancî Başî*, by their agency, being responsible for the policing of all this area, of which he was the Inspector, as also the Inspector of the forests and watercourses that it comprised. The most notable divisions of the *Bostancî* corps were those of the *Ḫâṣṣekîs*, who acted principally as one of the Sultan's bodyguards, and the *Ṣandalcîs*, or boatmen, who rowed his barge. Other divisions consisted of porters and grooms; while the Chief Gardener also supervised the supply of fowls, sheep, &c., to the imperial kitchens, the removal of refuse from the palace and its precincts, and the conduct of the story-tellers, jugglers, and musicians maintained for the amusement of the Sultan and his entourage. It is doubtful, however, whether the men employed in these latter ways were accounted as *Bostancîs* proper. The *Bostancîs* proper were recruited, like the Janissaries, of whose corps, indeed, they were held to form part, from the *ʿAcemî Oğlans*. They used, on occasion, to accompany the Sultan on campaign, but were never employed as fighting troops.[1]

Next in importance after the *Ağas* of the Stirrup in the Outside Service were five commissioners (*Emîns*),[2] the first being the Commissioner of the City (*Şehir Emîni*).[3] This functionary had two principal duties: the registration of expenditure in the imperial palaces[4] and the supervision of buildings in the capital and of its

dignitaries entering the second court at the *Orta Ḳapî*, and gives further particulars of their duties at this gathering.—*M.T.M.* i. 506 sq. It was the especial duty of the *Ḳapîcîlar Kâḫyasî* to carry the messages called *telḫîṣ* (cf. below, p. 122) from the Grand *Vezîr* to the Sultan on these occasions: ibid. 526.

[1] D'Ohsson, vii. 27–30; Lybyer, 130–1. For further particulars see Appendix B (c) 3.

[2] Arabic, *Amîn*, 'faithful, a confidential agent'; plural, *Umanâ*. The word is often translated by 'Intendant', which we have used for *Kâḫya*.

[3] *Şehir*, from the Persian *Şähr*, 'city'.

[4] Oşmân Nûrî, i. 1363–4. This author prints a document dated 1527, in

water-supply; among the minor officials by whom he was assisted the most notable were, accordingly, the Chief Architect (*Mi'mâr Başî*) and the Water Inspector (*Ṣu Nâẓiri*). The *Şehir Emîni* was, therefore, like most of the other commissioners, not merely a palace servant, but what we should regard as an official of the local administration, if such a body had existed. It did not, however. It was not until late in the nineteenth century that the Istanbul area was endowed with a government of its own, distinct from that of the court on the one hand and the central administration on the other.

The second of the commissioners was the Commissioner of the Mint (*Ḍarb-ḫâne*[1] *Emîni*), which was situated in the grounds of the *Serây*, not far from the Imperial Gate. His staff consisted in the eighteenth century of twelve *ustâs* (masters) and some five hundred workmen; but it seems likely that in earlier times the establishment was smaller, since at that time various provincial mints, later abolished, were in existence.[2] The commissioner's activities were checked by an official of the public treasury, but he was essentially an officer of the Household. The Sultan derived a considerable private revenue from the mint by the simple device of forcing the exploiters of gold, silver, and copper mines to hand over their entire yield to the mint at a price far below its current value. The *Ḍarb-ḫâne Emîni* received one-tenth of this profit.[3]

The other three commissioners were concerned with food-supplies. The first of them, the Commissioner of the Kitchen (*Maṭbaḫ Emîni*), and the third, his assistant, termed Secretary of the Royal Expenditure (*Maṣrefi Şâhriyârî Kâtibi*),[4] dealt with the provisioning of the palace, while the second, the so-called Barley Commissioner (*Arpa Emîni*), had wider responsibilities. He appears in the first place to have been charged with the supply of fodder to the stables,[5] but had also the appointment and to some extent the control of the officials who purchased grain at fixed prices in the provinces for consumption at the capital.[6]

which the *Şehir Emîni* is charged with the supervision of supply purchases for the palaces of Ibrahîm Paşa and Ğalaṭa, and quotes a description by the historian Na'îmâ of the plight to which the inmates of Ğalaṭa Serâyî were reduced during the reign of Ibrahîm (1640–8), owing to the insufficiency of the funds at the disposal of the *Şehir Emîni*. Cf. D'Ohsson, vii. 255. For further details see Appendix B (c) 4.

[1] Pronounced *Zarb-hane* in Turkish.

[2] e.g. Adrianople. It possessed a mint from the beginning of the fifteenth to the middle of the seventeenth century and again for a short time under Muṣṭafâ II (1695–1703). See *Encyclopaedia of Islam*, art. 'Edirne'.

[3] D'Ohsson, vii. 252–4.

[4] Ibid. 20 and 195 calls him simply '*Massraf-Schehriyari*', 'Aṭâ i. 290, *Maṣref Kâtibi*.

[5] D'Ohsson, vii. 20.

[6] See 'Oṣmân Nûrî, i. 769–90 and 773. These officials were more closely controlled, however, by the *Ḳâḍî* of Istanbul, to whom complaints about their conduct were addressed.

The officers of the Outside Service below the rank of *Emîn* were, at least by the eighteenth century, of little importance. They were then grouped in three categories, of which the first consisted of four chief falconers,[1] the next again of four functionaries dependent on the chief Black eunuch,[2] and the last of six others, four of whom were dependent on the Commissioner of the Kitchens and the other two on the Inside 'Chamber of the Larder'.[3] But apart from all these individuals and their numerous subordinates, there were also about a dozen bodies of men more or less independent, though usually commanded likewise by some officer or other of the Inside Service or the *Ḥarem*, some of which deserve rather more attention.

One of the most notable of these independent bodies was the *ocaḳ* of the Wood-cutters (*Balṭacis*),[4] which had been instituted even before the conquest of Constantinople. Its members were then employed in the levelling of roads, the draining of swamps, and the felling of trees. But after the conquest, though they continued to discharge these duties when the Sultans went to war in person, they were converted into guards of the *Ḥarem*; and the corps was divided into two parts, one of which was stationed at the Old and the other at the New *Serây*. The first division was commanded by the chief eunuch,[5] who was assisted by some of its senior members in the administrations of the pious foundations in his care. The second was commanded by the Sword-bearer,[6] the chief of the Pages, its members going by a curious name: *Zülüflü Balṭacîlar*, or 'Lock-wearing wood-cutters', because they wore a long thin lock of hair on each side of their faces.[7] The men of both divisions were originally recruited from the *'Acemî Oğlans*.[8]

Of the rest of these 'independent' bodies several were quite small and unimportant, their members being concerned with such matters as the water-supply of the palace and the furnishing of sheep for sacrifice at the yearly Feast of *Ḳurban*.[9] Others, again, consisted of artisans such as tailors, mat-makers, furriers, and cobblers.[10] The remaining *ocaḳs* of higher standing were four corps of

[1] Called *Şahinci Başi*, *Çaḳirci Başi*, *Doğanci Başi*, and *Atmacaci Başi*; see Appendix B (c) 2 (ii).

[2] Called *Çadir Mehteri Başi*, *Ḥazînedâr Başi*, *Bâzergân Başi*, and *Pişkeşci Başi*; see Appendix B (c) 5.

[3] Called *Çaşni-gîr Başi*, *'Alem Mehteri Başi*, *Ekmekci Başi*, *Kilâr Ağasi*, *Aşci Başi*, and *Ḥalvâci Başi*; see Appendix B (c) 4 (ii) and 6.

[4] From *Balṭa* (Turkish), an axe.

[5] The *Ḳizlar Ağasi* (Black) in late times, no doubt the *Ḳapi Ağasi* (White) earlier. Cf. above, p. 78.

[6] The *Siliḥdâr Ağa*; see above, p. 80.

[7] *Zülüflü* from the Persian *Zolf*, meaning a down-hanging lock of hair.

[8] For further particulars and references see Appendix B (c) 7 (i).

[9] *Ḳurban Bayrami*, the Feast of Sacrifice—called in Arabic *'Îdu'l-Aḍḥâ*, falling on the 10th of *Ẓu'l-Ḥicca*, the lunar month of pilgrimage. For these small *ocaḳs* see Appendix B (c) 7 (ii).

[10] See Appendix B (c) 7 (iii).

guards. These were called respectively *Ṣolaḳs*, *Peyks*, *Çavuşes*, an *Muteferriḳas*.

The *Ṣolaḳ* guard we have already referred to. It consisted of four companies, originally archers,[1] each one hundred strong, recruited from the Janissary *ortas* of the same name, and was commanded by a *Ṣolaḳ Başî* assisted by two lieutenants. The *ocaḳ* of the *Peyks*,[2] likewise commanded by a *Peyk Başî*, was smaller, consisting of one hundred and fifty men. These two corps constituted the Sultan's bodyguard *par excellence*, and were accordingly provided with uniforms of peculiar magnificence. Their duties, however, came to be purely ceremonial: sixty of the *Ṣolaḳs* and thirty of the *Peyks* surrounded the monarch when he rode in procession, while four *Ṣolaḳs* were always in attendance at the palace.[3] The *Çavuşes*[4] also took part in these processions, which, indeed, they led. Their *ocaḳ*, however, was considerably larger, consisting of fifteen companies each of forty-two men, which did guard duty at the palace in rotation.

The *Çavuşes* had been employed in the first centuries of Ottoman rule as messengers, for the conveyance of the Sultan's orders to provincial governors and commanders. But this duty came in later times to be performed by various other functionaries, ordinary messages being then usually carried by Tatars from the Crimea, and extraordinary by *Ḳapicî Başis*.[5] Hence the *Çavuşes* were now employed as guards and attendants, on the one hand, and, on the other, as ushers in the law courts of the Grand *Vezîr*. That the duties they performed were of these two types was due to the similar double employment of their commander, the Chief Pursuivant (*Çavuş Başî*), to whom we have already alluded.[6] For as well as being, together with the Intendant of the Doorkeepers, a master of court ceremonies, the *Çavuş Başî* was vice-president of this law court. We shall therefore have more to say of him when considering the central administration.[7]

Muteferriḳa means 'separated',[8] and is thought to have been

[1] *Ṣolaḳ* means left-handed—from *Ṣol* (Turkish) left—with reference, presumably, to the holding of the bow in the left hand.

[2] Persian for messenger.

[3] D'Ohsson, vii. 25–7, 33; 'Aṭâ, i. 309; *O.T.E.M.*, No. 14, Appendix, 27, notes; Aḥmed Râsim, i. 358, note.

[4] For the significance of the word *Çavuş* see Appendix B (c) 2 (iv).

[5] 'Aṭâ, i. 170, enumerates the officials employed in later times as couriers thus: *Tatars*, *Ḳiz-bekcis*, *Ḫâṣṣekîs*, *Muteferriḳas*, *Za'îms*, *Silîḥşûrs*, *Ḳapici Başis*, *Baş Ḳapici Başis*, *Mîr 'Alems*, *Ḳapicilar Kâḫyasis*, *Mîr Aḫors*, and *Bostanci Başis*. Presumably officers as important as the latter four were sent only on missions of the greatest gravity. For *Muteferriḳas* see below. *Silîḥşûr* was another name for a 'standing' *Sipâhî*.

[6] Above, p. 83.

[7] For further particulars of the *Çavuşes* and for references see Appendix B (c) 2 (iv).

[8] Arabic, the form of the verb of which this is a participle meaning 'to separate oneself, or to be separated'.

applied to men of this guard because they were employed on 'special' or 'various' duties.[1] In the first half of the sixteenth century they numbered between one and two hundred, but in the second their establishment was more than doubled.[2] They were highly paid and were mounted and magnificently accoutred, each owning a number of armed slave retainers, after the manner of the 'standing' *Sipâhîs*. Indeed, they are referred to by foreign writers as the Sultan's 'Noble Guard': they never left his side when he went on campaign, and performed no military service but on these occasions. Only *Ḫâṣṣ Odalîs*, the sons of eminent *Ḳapî Ḳullarî* and, exceptionally, the relatives of tributary rulers, such as the Hospodars, were admitted to the corps.[3]

Both the *Çavuşes* and the *Muteferriḳas* were divided into two classes, those that received pay from the Treasury and those that subsisted on fiefs. In early times the latter ranked lower than the former; but with the rise in importance of the Grand *Vezîrs* to whose service they were attached, they came to eclipse their paid colleagues. The feudal *Muteferriḳas* had an independent commander, the *Muteferriḳa Başî*.[4]

IV. THE OTTOMAN NAVY

The Ottoman state inherited no naval traditions from its forerunners. Both the 'Great' Selcuḳid dynasty and its offshoot of Ḳonya established their rule exclusively by warfare on land; and though their territory included some seaboards, they conquered these by advances from the interior. Some of the small Turkish dynasties that rose to power at the same time as the Ottoman, whose territory lay on the coasts of Asia Minor, indulged in piracy and raids on the islands and coasts of the Aegean. Not so the Ottomans—for the reason that their original dominions were situated inland. And though, as soon as they had won their way to the sea from the original centre of their rule, they chose to extend their dominions by continuing to fight the Christians in Europe rather than their co-religionists in Asia, and so were obliged to cross the Straits, they did so in ships hired from the Greeks. It was not for another century that they began building ships for themselves, or considered using them for the consolidation of the enormous conquests they had effected in the meantime.

The Serbian Empire at whose expense the greater part of these conquests had been made relied likewise exclusively on its armies.

[1] *Encyclopaedia of Islam*, art. 'Mutafarriḳa'.

[2] Lybyer, 129. According to Zinkeisen, iii. 181–2, they numbered 100 during the earlier part of Süleymân's reign; between 250 and 300 during the later; and between 400 and 500 during the reign of Selîm II.

[3] Zinkeisen III, 181–3; Lybyer, loc. cit.

[4] For further particulars and references see Appendix B (c) 7 (iv).

The Ottomans were able, therefore, to overthrow it without resort to naval armaments, as they were later to defeat the Wallachian, Moldavian, Hungarian, and other exclusively terrestrial powers. The Byzantines, however, were another matter: they had always maintained a navy; indeed, their possession of large seaboards and many islands necessitated it; and they still did so on a small scale, even after the restoration of the Palaeologi, though the territory under their control had by then been immensely reduced. Without ships the Ottomans could scarcely have destroyed their power. Still less could they have expelled the Venetians and Genoese from the many regions in the Levant of which they had possessed themselves since the Crusades first gave them the opportunity of developing their commerce. For their whole might was based on their navies: it was only late in Venetian history, for instance, that a policy of expansion on the Italian mainland was adopted by the Republic. In fine, warships were necessary to the Sultans for the conquest of a large part of what was to become their Empire and for the retention of the conquests that they had already achieved on land.

Both Venice and Genoa played important parts in the later history of the Byzantine Empire. Thus, to go no farther back than the time of the Fourth Crusade, the Genoese were then the allies of the Comneni, who had granted them settlements and privileges for services rendered, whereas the Venetians, their rivals, sided with the Crusaders. It was the warships of Venice, indeed, that made possible the establishment of the short-lived Latin Empire (1204); and, for providing them, the Venetians repaid themselves by taking no less than three-eighths of the Comneni's dominions, so that by this stroke alone they acquired large dependencies in the Levant. Thereafter they embarked on a series of wars with the Genoese, in the course of which the latter aided the Palaeologi to re-establish a Greek dynasty at Constantinople (1261), but which ended in triumph for the Venetians (1380). By the time, therefore, that the Ottomans were in a position to embark on naval warfare, neither the Genoese nor the Byzantines could offer them any formidable opposition. They found that the chief obstacle to the rounding off of their conquests on the European mainland and in the islands that surrounded it was Venice.

It is true that some of these islands and places on the continent were still held by relicts of the Latin and Greek Empires. But these had virtually no means of defending their possessions from Ottoman onslaughts by sea. Yet without naval armaments the Ottomans could not conquer them; and it was in most cases necessary for the security of the Ottoman dominions that they should be conquered. Only Venice was capable of withstanding such a movement. It may therefore be said that the Ottoman navy was brought into being to defeat the Venetian. In the event, over a long stretch of time, the Venetians were defeated, for of all their whilom Balkan and Aegean possessions there was not one but fell to the Sultan's forces. Once in being, the Ottoman navy was employed in other adventures, farther afield: in the western Mediterranean, in the Black and Red Seas, even in the Indian Ocean and the Persian Gulf. But these were not foreseen by Murâd II, in whose reign the first warships were constructed for the ejection of the Venetians from various coastal regions of the Balkan peninsula.

That no naval activity was engaged in by Murâd's predecessors was due to the fact that their Empire, despite its rapid expansion, possessed few seaboards conquered from inland. It was only when, after overrunning most of the Balkan peninsula, the Ottomans began to conquer or absorb the Turkish principalities of Asia Minor which had arisen about the same time as their own, that such regions fell, by land warfare or negotiation, into their hands. This process was interrupted by the incursion of Timur. Hence it was only in the reign of Murâd II, when Ottoman control over most of the acquisitions of Bâyezîd I had been re-established, that the Sultan's ownership of these maritime territories could be put to use. In them there already existed a tradition of sea adventure. But none of these principalities had been strong enough to engage in actual warfare. In most cases, indeed, it seems improbable that the rulers themselves had any policy of naval activity. It was rather some of their subjects that sought profit from the capture of rich merchantmen, preferably infidel. What the Sultans now acquired, in fact, was a number of new subjects well versed in seamanship, who lived by piracy.

They had no interest in suppressing this piracy, except in so far as it affected their own commerce. On the contrary, it was probably because of its existence that they first bethought themselves of making war by sea as well as by land. Murâd built ships at his own expense. But these were no more than supplementary to those already owned by the private sea-captains of his newly won ports. This was the doubtful inspiration of the Ottoman navy. It is no wonder, then, that for the next century of its career, privateers were conspicuous in the expeditions embarked on at the Sultan's orders, and that, even later, experience as a corsair continued to be the best, indeed almost the only effective, preparation for high command at sea. But in allotting a large share of its activities to privately owned ships the Ottoman navy was by no means peculiar. All medieval navies consisted partly of the ruler's own ships, partly of merchantmen embargoed for service in time of war. Privateers of all nations, moreover, were apt to indulge in piracy. If piracy was more prevalent in the Mediterranean than elsewhere, it was because that sea formed a no-man's-area between Christendom and Islâm, which were held by both to be at perpetual warfare; so that attacks on enemy traders at least might be justified as legitimate operations.

If the Sultans were unable to embark on naval warfare until they had acquired certain seaboards; and if these seaboards had already long been held by Turkish-speaking Moslem rulers; it might be expected that the Ottoman navy, when it came into being, would have a peculiarly Turkish, or at least Moslem, character. This was not so, however. It was, on the contrary, a faithful copy of the navies of Italy, so faithful that nearly all the words used to describe its personnel and material were corruptions of the corresponding Italian terms.[1] This was probably due principally to the recent dominance of the Italians in the Levant, so that even if the corsair subjects that the Sultans now acquired were Moslem or Greek, they had been to school with the Venetians and Genoese. But it was certainly reinforced by the policy of Meḥmed II. For by way of reward for their help in effecting his restoration in 1261, the Emperor Michael VII Palaeologus had permitted the Genoese established in Ğalaṭa to govern that suburb of the capital as an autonomous colony;[2] and, on the conquest, Meḥmed II engaged them to aid him in the development of his navy.[3] It is not clear how generally this Genoese influence was exerted, or how long it lasted. Shipbuilding and navigation must have been the arts in which it was most felt. But, as we shall see, the crews of the galleys then used were made up chiefly of men-at-arms and rowers, the mariners employed being few; and it was only as mariners that the Genoese would have figured. This may account for the fact that, as the terminology of the Ottoman navy shows, its Italian models were finally given as it were a Turkish veneer.

In the course of Ottoman history up to the time of our survey there were three periods at which the navy was especially active. The first followed on the conquest of Istanbul and lasted up to the end of the fifteenth century. Its most important feature was the conversion of the Black Sea into an Ottoman lake. This was accomplished, first, by the destruction of the Byzantine principality which, originally established by the Comneni at Trebizond after their expulsion from Constantinople by the Crusaders, had

[1] Cf. D'Ohsson, vii. 420.

[2] *Encyclopaedia of Islam*, art. 'Constantinople'.

[3] Juchereau, i. 100.

been maintained there ever since in independence of the Palaeologi, and, secondly, by the subjugation of the Crimean *Ḫanate* and its dependencies. The achievement affected the Sultans' naval policy profoundly. For well over a century they were able, because of it, to neglect the defence of the Black Sea entirely, and whenever they wished to do so, to concentrate all their ships in the Aegean.

During the remainder of this first period of activity the energies of the navy were chiefly expended in reducing some coastal districts and islands in and round the Balkan peninsula.[1] Then there was a lull. Selîm I, while engaging in his campaigns against Persia and the Egyptian Mamlûks, was anxious to avoid embroiling himself elsewhere, and forbade his sea captains to harass the shipping and raid the coasts of the Christian powers. At the same time it was he that transferred naval head-quarters from their original seat at Gallipoli to the capital, and there he opened a ship-yard, in which the building of vessels larger than any hitherto employed was begun.[2]

The second and most brilliant period of naval activity was indeed prepared by him. It opened suitably enough with the ejection from Rhodes of the Knights of St. John (1522), whose livelihood both spiritual and material was derived from piratical raids on Moslem shipping and coastal settlements; and, lasting throughout the great reign of Süleymân the Magnificent, continued into that of his son, Selîm II. Ḫayru'd-Dîn, known to Europe as Barbarossa, was its most notable figure. He is indeed the hero of Ottoman sea history. Barbarossa began his career as a freebooter; and one of his earliest piratical voyages ended in his possessing himself of Algiers.[3] On his subsequently asking aid of the Sultan, the latter, when sending it, created him *Beylerbeyi* of the province, which was held to have been thereby added to the Empire. Such was the haphazard foundation of the North-African Regencies, so called. For Barbarossa himself afterwards took Tunis;[4] and Tripoli was brought under Ottoman suzerainty

[1] The captain Kemâl Re'îs was the chief figure of this period—see *Encyclopaedia of Islam*, s.v. Two of the Ionian islands were occupied by a fleet commanded by the ex-Grand *Vezîr*, Gedik Aḥmed Paşa, in 1480.—Ibid., art. 'Aḥmed Pasha'.

[2] Cevdet, i. 131.

[3] Together with his brother Aruc, in 1516. Algiers and its neighbourhood had since the beginning of the century fallen into the hands of the Spaniards, who, having driven the Moors from Spain, were now pursuing their crusade in North Africa. The Spaniards soon recovered Algiers; but Barbarossa took possession of it definitely in 1529; and his successors gradually deprived the Spaniards of all their conquests except Oran, which they held until the eighteenth century.—*Encyclopaedia of Islam*, art. 'Algeria'.

[4] In 1534. He lost it next year. It was retaken in 1569, lost again in 1573, retaken in 1574, and finally made dependent on the Porte in 1587.—*Encyclopaedia of Islam*, art. 'Tunis'.

by one of his successors in the office of Lord High Admiral, or *Ḳaptan Paşa.*[1] Süleymân conferred this on Barbarossa in 1533, later summoning him to Istanbul, where he devoted much care to the construction of ships and the organization of the fleet. It was during his term as *Ḳaptan* that the last islands of the Aegean were conquered for the Sultan,[2] and that Süleymân made the first European alliance contracted by the House of 'O͟smân, with France against the Empire. Barbarossa commanded the fleet sent to co-operate with that of François I in the siege of Nice (1543), and devoted much of his energies during the last years of his life (he died in 1546) to ravaging such of the Emperor's possessions in Spain and Italy as were accessible from the sea. It was indeed largely owing to his influence at the Porte that this French alliance was concluded. And since the alliance led to the drawing-up of the first Capitulations, he may be said to have been in a manner responsible for the creation of these celebrated instruments, whereby the relations of the Ottoman Empire with the states of Europe were to be regulated for so long a period.[3]

While Barbarossa was alarming the powers of Europe in the Mediterranean, and also after his death, Ottoman warships were used for expeditions in quite another direction. After their discovery of the Cape route in 1488, the Portuguese lost little time in making it serve the two principal aims of their policy. These were to secure for themselves as much as they could of that trade with the Middle and Far East from which they had hitherto been excluded, and to prosecute the attacks on Islâm (now from another direction) by which their kingdom had been built up. Within a few years of their first appearance in the Indian Ocean, they had established posts on both the east coast of Africa and the west coast of India at the expense of the Arab traders who had long maintained prosperous settlements in each area, and by their conquest of Socotra (1506) and Hormuz (1515) were able to cut the two sea routes, passing through the Red Sea and the Persian Gulf, by which the products of India and the Farther East had hitherto been exchanged for those of Europe and the Levant.[4] The Moslem potentates that suffered most grievously from this diversion of trade were the Mamlûks of Egypt and Syria, through whose dominions both trade routes were continued, and the Ṣafevids of Persia, who were then in possession of 'Irâḳ. Though the Portuguese entered into relations with the

[1] Viz. Ḳoca Sinan Paşa, with the help of the famous corsair Ṭorğud in 1551.—*Encyclopaedia of Islam*, art. 'Tripoli'.

[2] Except Chios (Saḳîz) which was taken only by Piyale Paşa in 1565–6.—Cevdet, i. 146.

[3] For accounts of Barbarossa see Cevdet, i and *Encyclopaedia of Islam*, art. 'K͟hair al-Dīn'.

[4] Depping, ii. 266 sq.

Ṣafevids (whom they knew to be hostile to the Ottoman arch-enemy), expeditions were sent out to oppose them not only from Suez (Suways) but also from al-Baṣra. And after the Ottoman conquest of Egypt, several further attempts were made, at the instance of Süleymân the Magnificent. All failed. Their only favourable result was to extend his empire over most of the Yemen, including 'Aden, and over part of the west coast of the Red Sea, where for a time in the sixteenth century, and somewhat precariously, an *Eyâlet* of Abyssinia was brought into being, which included, however, only two maritime *Sancaḳs*, of Maṣṣawa' and Suwâkin. Presumably these expeditions were undertaken with Egyptian ships, though they were led by Ottoman (as opposed to Egyptian) commanders. But neither the commanders nor their ships were able to compete with the Portuguese.[1] It is evident, however, from their being undertaken at all, that the Porte, which had relied until so late in its career entirely on its armies, was by now well aware of the importance of naval armaments. And that it owed the possessions it now acquired on both shores of the Red Sea to the use of such armaments was subsequently proved when, later in the sixteenth century, being weak at sea, it lost them.[2]

The last important event of this second period of Ottoman naval activity was the conquest of Cyprus from the Venetians under Selîm II. But this was followed immediately by the famous battle of Lepanto (Ine Baḫtî in Turkish), in which almost half the fleet was destroyed.[3] This damage was repaired almost within a year.[4] Nevertheless, the Ottoman fleet ceased from the time of this defeat to be a menace to Europe. The principal reason for this decline, as indeed for the defeat itself, was the appointment of a succession of courtiers inexperienced in sea warfare to the post of *Ḳaptan*. And, oddly enough, the adoption of this policy is traceable to the outstanding fame of Barbarossa. For when he first appeared in the capital as the hero of

[1] The chief expeditions were those of: (1) Ḫâdim Süleymân Paşa, 1535–8: conquest of Zebîd, 'Aden, and Lâhic, and siege of Diu; (2) Piri Re'îs, 1547: reconquest of 'Aden (meanwhile revolted), sack of Masḳaṭ, and siege of Hormuz; and (3) Sīdī 'Alī, 1553: sent to bring back ships left by Piri at al-Baṣra, he defeated the Portuguese at Hormuz and Masḳaṭ, but was driven by storms on to the Indian coast. See Cevdet, i. 132, 143–4; 'Aṭâ, ii. 20; *Encyclopaedia of Islam*, arts. "Aden', "Alī', 'Lāhedj', 'Piri Re'īs', 'Sulaimān I', 'Sulaimān Pasha Khādim', 'Zabīd'.

[2] Cf. Cevdet, i. 155.

[3] A large part of the fleet had already returned to Istanbul for the winter.—Cevdet, i. 148. Lepanto is known in Ottoman history as *Şingin Donanma Seferi*, 'The Sunk Fleet Campaign'.

[4] Uluc 'Alī (see below, p. 95), appointed *Ḳaptan* immediately after Lepanto at which he was present, constructed eight docks near the Admiralty and laid down 158 galleys during the following winter; so that, next year, he was able to emerge into the Mediterranean with a fleet of no less than 8 (new) *Mavnas* and 234 *Kadirğas*. The next two years saw further increases.—Cevdet, i. 150–1.

many triumphant encounters with the infidel, he was at once admitted to the chief councils of state. Thenceforth he and his successors in the *Ḳaptanlıḳ* which, as we shall explain, had hitherto been a comparatively humble office, were recognized *ex officio* as members of the Imperial *Dîvân*. Its other members, however, were all persons trained either for statesmanship or for the service of the Sacred Law. Barbarossa's qualifications for high politics, on the other hand, were entirely personal, and unlikely to be possessed by other sea captains. After his death, accordingly, it became customary to appoint as *Ḳaptan* a *Ḳapı Ḳulu*, whereas hitherto the post had been occupied by corsairs or other persons of maritime experience;[1] and few, if any, of the persons so appointed were in the least versed in naval affairs. Moreover, whereas hitherto the *Ḳaptans* had always been subordinate to a general (*serdâr*) appointed to command expeditions at sea, just as *serdârs* were appointed to command armies when the Sultan did not take the field in person, now this practice was discontinued.[2] Indeed, the new *Ḳaptans* virtually took the place of the old *serdârs*. For, at least to start with, they were usually accompanied by an adjutant experienced in sea warfare.[3] But the final responsibility now lay entirely with the *Ḳaptan*, as it had not with the *serdârs*; and it was the insistence of the *Ḳaptan* at the battle of Lepanto, against the advice of his adjutant, that the Ottoman ships should leave harbour and break through the Allied fleet blockading it, that brought about the disaster.[4]

Even so the system was not permanently reformed, though immediately after the battle, in which the *Ḳaptan* was drowned, an experienced corsair was appointed to succeed him. This man, known as Uluc ʿAlī, remained in office until his death fifteen years later, and engaged in a number of expeditions in the Mediterranean, one of which resulted in the reconquest of Tunis for the Sultan.[5]

[1] Except for one *Ḳapı Ḳulu* of the time of Meḥmed II, viz. Şehîd Maḥmûd Paşa (later Grand *Vezîr*)—d. 1467–8. He was the third person to hold the office of *Ḳaptan*. On Barbarossa's death Ṣoḳollu Meḥmed Paşa was appointed, as fourteenth holder of the office. See ʿAṭâ, ii. 189; cf. Cevdet, i. 141. All the *Ḳaptans* from the death of Barbarossa to the date of Lepanto were *Ḳapı Ḳulları*, viz. Ṣoḳollu, Sinan Paşa (1548), Piyale Paşa (1554), Mu'ezzinzâde ʿAli Paşa (1568): Cevdet, i. 141–3, 147; *Encyclopaedia of Islam*, art. 'Piāle Pasha'.

[2] Seyyid Muṣṭafâ, ii. 114; *Encyclopaedia of Islam*, art. 'Ḳapudān'. It may be noted, however, that when the attack of 1564 on Malta was being planned, a *Serdâr* was appointed besides the *Ḳaptan*, and that both were cautioned not to disregard the advice of the adjutant, Ṭorğud. They did so, with the result that the attack failed.—Cevdet, i. 146.

[3] For instance, this same Ṭorğud, who virtually directed operations for the successors of Barbarossa in the *Ḳaptanlık*. He also led expeditions independently. Süleymân even desired to appoint him *Ḳaptan*, but was dissuaded by Rüstem Paşa, the Grand *Vezîr*.—Cevdet, i. 141–3, 145.

[4] Cevdet, i. 149.

[5] Uluc ʿAlī was Italian by birth, having been captured in a raid and made to

But though the ships lost at Lepanto were replaced quickly, the old aggressive spirit, which had for long so greatly alarmed the powers of Europe, seems to have departed in its fullness from the Ottoman navy.[1] After Uluc 'Alī's death the *Ḳaptanlïḳ* again became a perquisite of the court. And it was not until half-way through the next century that the Sultans' ships engaged in warfare of serious consequence.[2]

The occasion of the renewed activity was the campaign undertaken to conquer Crete from the Venetians, an enterprise that naturally depended for its success on the superiority of the Ottoman fleet. This superiority was achieved only with difficulty after many reverses, one of which, in 1656, was held to be scarcely less disastrous than Lepanto.[3] It was because the Sultans' ships were in none too good trim, indeed, that the conquest took the unconscionably long time of twenty-five years (1644–69).[4] The chief difficulties to be surmounted were the construction, and particularly the use, of adequate sailing-ships. For in the wars of the sixteenth century the type of vessel used for actual fighting by all the contending navies in the Mediterranean was the galley: a ship provided indeed with sails to be used when no enemy was in sight, but rowed, when operations were on hand, by banks of oarsmen.[5] Ships propelled by sail alone had been in use for a century, but they were used almost if not quite exclusively for transport. In the meantime, however, the Venetians had taken to imitating the naval powers whose ships operated in the Atlantic and other oceans, where rowed galleys were useless, and, though they still

serve in the galleys. Being converted to Islâm, he rose to be *Beylerbeyi* of Tripoli and Algiers in turn and took part in the battle of Lepanto. His name appears in Italian works as Ochialy.—*Encyclopaedia of Islam*, art. 'Ochialy'.

[1] The navy was weakened by the loss at Lepanto of skilled mariners rather than of ships. This was such that next year the *Ḳaptan* was careful to avoid any collision with the enemy.—Cevdet, i. 150.

[2] Under Aḥmed I the *Ḳaptan* Ḫalîl Paşa Ḳayṣariyeli won a minor victory against the Maltese near Cyprus in 1609, and in 1614 reasserted the Porte's authority in Tripoli.—*Encyclopaedia of Islam*, art. 'Khalīl Pasha'.

[3] The *Ḳaptan* responsible was Ṣari Ken'ân Paşa, who was promptly dismissed and thrown into jail.—*Encyclopaedia of Islam*, art. 'Ken'ān Pasha'.

[4] Cf. Cevdet, i. 152.

[5] There were more than ten different kinds of galleys (Turkish, *Çekdiri*, *çekdirir*) in use in the Ottoman navy. They were classed according to the number of places for oarsmen that each contained. Starting from the smallest, the following names are given: (i) *Ḳirlanğiç* (Turkish for 'swallow'), (ii) *Firḳata* (from Italian '*fregatta*'), (iii) *Pergende* (meaning in Persian 'dispersed'), whether this reading is correct seems uncertain, however, (iv) *Ḳâlite*, (v) *Ḳadirğa*. All the preceding are classed as light: *Ince Donanma*. (vi) *Mavna*, (vii) *Baştarda* (Italian *Bastarda*, French *Bâtardelle*), (viii) *Küke* or *Küve*. This type seems to have had the hull of a *Mavna* and the superstructure of a *Ḳalyon* or sailing-ship proper. *Kükes* were first built in the last quarter of the fifteenth century. They were double-decked, carried two large guns (in the prow), and were manned by 2,000 men-at-arms and rowers.—Aḥmed Râsim, i. 247 sq., notes; cf. Cevdet, i. 129–30; Hammer, *Staatsverwaltung*, 282.

used galleys as well,[1] possessed by now a formidable array of this new type of sailing-craft. With these, at the beginning of the Crete campaign, they were able to blockade the Dardanelles and so cut off the forces operating in Crete from direct communication by sea with Istanbul. To oppose these sailing-ships the Porte thereupon set about building similar ones of its own;[2] and with such success that the blockade was kept at least intermittent enough to allow of the campaign's being brought to a successful conclusion. The new ships, however, proved less useful than had been hoped owing to the shortage of experienced mariners to navigate and manœuvre them, since the tactics used with sail were quite different from those used with galleys; and even during the latter stages of the war, the Porte decided to concentrate its main efforts in shipbuilding on galleys of the traditional type. Moreover, the use of sailing-ships had necessitated the organization of a separate staff at the Admiralty; and this was unwelcome to those who held offices of older creation. Hence, when peace was re-established, the construction of sailing-ships fell gradually into disuse at Istanbul, though it was maintained in the Regencies and Egypt;[3] and it was not resumed until war with Venice threatened again, in 1681—and then too late.[4]

For though, in the great war that finally broke the Ottoman power as a menace to Europe, the navy contrived on several occasions to inflict defeat on the Venetians, it was unable to prevent them from recovering that hold on the Morea which it had originally been brought into being to destroy. Meanwhile also the Porte had felt itself obliged, owing to the threat of a Russian advance towards Azov, to devote part of its naval strength to the Black Sea,[5] and even to maintain a flotilla on the Danube.[6] And so, by 1700, since the total number of its ships was now considerably

[1] Cevdet, i. 151.

[2] To the sailing-ships (*Ḳalyon*, i.e. 'galleon') of the Ottoman navy the following names were given: *Ḳaraḳa, Barca, Ḳaravela, Poliḳa, Burtun*. *Ḳaraḳas* of from 1,500 to 2,000 tons were built during the reign of Süleymân I, but their use was thereafter abandoned. Those built in 1644 for the Cretan war were of the type *Burtun*, carrying from 40 to 50 guns. Other types were built from 1651.—Aḥmed Râsim, i. 251–2, notes; cf. Cevdet, i. 129, 151; Hammer, loc. cit.

[3] Cevdet, i. 152–4.

[4] Seyyid Muṣṭafâ, ii. 97, iii. 91. The ships now built were of the type *Ḳapaḳ* (literally, Turkish, 'a lid, a cover'—here 'two-decker'?), carrying 80 guns, and three-deckers (*üç enbârli*) carrying 110 guns.—Aḥmed Râsim, i. 252, notes. Seyyid Muṣṭafâ, ii. 97, says that there were ten ships in all now built of from 45 to 50 *zirâ'̄s*, or cubits, in length. If the cubit intended is the architect's (there were three others), these lengths would be about 110 and 123 feet. On the other hand, Seyyid Muṣṭafâ states, in iii. 91, that only six ships were now built, adding, however, that the number was later increased.

[5] D'Ohsson, vii. 425.

[6] Cevdet, i. 156. Ships called *Şayḳa* and *Üstü Açiḳ* are mentioned as belonging to it. Redhouse defines *Şayḳa* as 'a particular kind of sea-going boat used in the Black Sea'. Cf. Hammer, loc. cit.

smaller than it had been a century before, that available for operations in the Aegean and Mediterranean was barely a quarter of what it had then been. The reign of Aḥmed III, however, which followed on the disastrous Peace of Carlovitz, began with a strenuous effort at reform in various departments of Ottoman public life; and several new sailing-ships were constructed, with which, as if to revive memories of ancient glory, a raid was actually made on the coast of Spain and an attack on Malta.[1] In the Porte's last war with Venice, moreover, the navy contributed to the victory by which the Morea was restored to the Empire.[2] And it entered on the long peace that lasted up to the period of our survey by being further augmented. The navy, however, was actually at peace twenty-one years longer than the army,[3] since it played no part in the war with Austria that was concluded by the treaty of Belgrade in 1738; and this tranquillity was no less demoralizing to its personnel than to that of the land forces. For during this period the commanders of the fleet devoted much of their energies to the oppression of the islanders that were subject to their jurisdiction.[4] They also proved themselves so far incapable of defending Ottoman shipping from the depredations of pirates, that the Porte was obliged to engage foreign assistance for this purpose. Finally, both they and the officials charged with the building of ships misused the funds that were allotted to naval expenditure; and the latter prepared unpleasant surprises for the government and its employees by permitting the use of unseasoned timber.[5] It is not to be wondered at, therefore, that, as we shall see, the navy failed to distinguish itself in the war with Russia by which the peace was disrupted, indeed, that it suffered a total and wholly unnecessary destruction.

When, on the fall of Constantinople to the Crusaders in 1204, Venice, in return for her services in bringing about that event, acquired many ports and islands in the Levant, her rulers instituted a feudal system, imitated from their allies, by which to govern them. These feudatories enjoyed the rights conferred on them in return for maintaining order in these dependencies and on the surrounding seas, for the benefit of Venetian trade. For the discharge of the latter duty ships were required, to man which the feudatories drew on the local populations. The name by which these sailors

[1] Cevdet, loc. cit. The ships built under Aḥmed III were three-deckers and 'caravellas' (Turkish, *Ḳaravela*). The fashion was now adopted of giving men-of-war fanciful names, such as *Tuḥfetu'l-Mulûk* (Arabic, 'The Gift of Kings'); *Fâtiḥi Baḥrî* (Perso-Arabic, 'Sea-Conqueror'); *Berîdu'l-Ẓafer* (Arabic, 'The Courier of Victory').

[2] Seyyid Muṣṭafâ, iii. 91.

[3] No naval engagement took place between 1717 and 1768.

[4] Eton, 276–7.

[5] Cevdet, i. 157–8.

went in Venice was *Levantino*. Throughout this area the term Levantine, or *Levantino*, thus came to mean specifically a sailor. It was corrupted in Turkish to *Levend*. Hence the crews of the Ottoman navy and the privateers with which it was so closely associated were known as *Levends*, most of them being, like the Venetian *Levantini*, of Greek, Dalmatian, and Albanian origin.[1]

Presumably these *Levends* were supported from the proceeds of piracy and raids in which the privateers and even the government ships engaged; and it was found that, for the latter at least, they were intolerably ill-disciplined as well as very doubtfully loyal. The Porte accordingly sought to replace them by crews of a more dependable type. But this problem was never in fact satisfactorily solved throughout the course of Ottoman naval history. For the *Levends* proper seem mostly to have been seafaring men by upbringing, in contrast to the soldiers of various types that were chosen in turn to serve in their stead; nor were the latter given any such training as would supply the defect of this inexperience. The earliest soldiers posted to replace the *Levends* were of the type called *'Azeb*, irregular infantry neither feudal nor paid, like the Janissaries, by the Porte. The first regular enrolment for service with the fleet was of four hundred in the reign of Bâyezîd II.[2] But they seem to have possessed most of the defects of the *Levends*—in that their similar dependence on booty made for indiscipline—without the advantages of the *Levends'* familiarity with life at sea. Consequently, towards the end of the sixteenth century, the Porte began to employ feudal *Müsellems* and *Yürüks* for naval service instead of them. These troops, it will be remembered, had come to be used as auxiliary labour gangs with the army, the members of each of their small *ocaḳs* serving in turn. The same rotatory system was preserved for those that were now employed with the fleet. But they again proved to be unsatisfactory sailors—though for a reason opposite to that which had caused the Porte to discard their predecessors, viz. that since their livelihood depended on their tax-free farms, their interest lay rather in these than in the duties they were now made to perform. Hence yet another expedient was resorted to. These *Müsellems* and *Yürüks* were no longer asked to serve in person; but each *ocaḳ* was required to make a yearly contribution to the funds of the Admiralty.[3] This measure deprived them of their characteristic status, which allowed them to serve the Sultans instead of paying them taxes: they became in fact, if not in name, *Re'âyâ* from having been *'Askerîs*. But for the first time the Admiralty was endowed with the means of enrolling paid crews, on whom it might have imposed a proper discipline.

[1] *Encyclopaedia of Islam*, art. 'Lewend'.
[2] Ibid.
[3] Seyyid Muṣṭafâ, iii. 92.

Unfortunately, its officers proved incapable of turning the means thus acquired to advantage. By this time Ottoman institutions as a whole had fallen far into decay, and the former good order in which the standing army in particular was maintained had been disrupted. Instead of employing the funds at its disposal for the maintenance and training of a regular corps of seamen, the Admiralty adopted a procedure that was calculated to afford it the least possible benefit. Just as even in Europe it was customary up to the end of the eighteenth century for armies to winter without fighting, so among the Mediterranean navies, and indeed those of the Oceanic powers, it had always been considered advisable for large ships to return to their bases in the early autumn and re-emerge only in the late spring. Every year, accordingly, before the date[1] on which the fleet embarked on its summer cruise, the Admiralty would send out, into the islands and coastal districts that composed the *Eyâlet* of the *Ḳaptan Paşa*, a number of recruiting officers, who would offer six months' pay to any men that chose to enrol themselves. The result was that the force assembled for embarkation in the Sultan's ships during that period consisted of men without regular occupation, who might never before have had any experience either of fighting or of the sea, and might never seek it again.[2] These 'Standard Troops',[3] as they were called—because each recruiting officer enrolled them under the standard that marked his office—were in fact nothing better than a rabble, whose presence at a naval engagement was all but a guarantee of defeat. This method of recruitment continued in force up to, and just past, the period of our survey.[4]

From antiquity up to the eighteenth century, as long as galleys were anywhere used, their crews consisted, apart from officers, of men-at-arms, seamen, and rowers. Galleys were provided with but a few sails, which were used only when no engagement was on hand. For in a fight they were manœuvred for ramming or boarding enemy vessels—operations that could be effected only by the use of oars. Consequently, the seamen required were few, the rowers and the fighting men many.[5] It seems that the original

[1] i.e. *Rüzi Ḫiḍr*, St. George's Day, April 23rd (O.S.). The day of return was *Rüzi Ḳâsim*, St. Demetrius's Day, October 26th (O.S.). These days were held to divide summer from winter. For the identification of Moslem and Christian saints see chapter on *Dervişes*, below.

[2] According to Seyyid Muṣṭafâ, iii. 192, the money furnished by the *Yürüks* and *Müsellems* provided pay for from 8,000 to 10,000 men.

[3] In Turkish '*Bayraḳ* '*Askerî*'.

[4] Seyyid Muṣṭafâ, iv. 11.

[5] The crew of a medium-sized galley of the type called *Ḳadirğa* is said to have been made up as follows: oarsmen, 196; men-at-arms, 100; seamen, 30; officers, 3. The seamen included helmsmen (*Dümenci*), boatswains (*Yelkenci*), carpenters, caulkers, and 20 makers or tenders of tools (*Alatcilar*), headed by an *Oda Başî* (cf. above, p. 62). From the incomplete data supplied by Cevdet, the corresponding figures for a large galley of the *Mavna* type work out at

Levends were employed as all three, but that by the sixteenth century their successors had been almost entirely relieved of both rowing on the one hand and fighting on the other. The rowing of galleys, being an exceedingly hard and unpleasant labour, came to be confided to men who could be forced to perform it. These were, chiefly, adult prisoners of war[1] (who, in accordance with the provisions of the Sacred Law, were by their capture reduced to slavery) and criminals, condemned, as in some Christian states, to serve in the galleys by way of penal servitude.[2] Similarly, the fighting that ensued on the boarding of enemy ships, or on disembarkation on enemy coasts, was now usually confided to regular troops: companies of Janissaries or feudal *Sipâhîs* from the *sancaḳs* that made up the *Eyâlet* of the *Ḳaptan*.[3] It was perhaps the use of such feudal contingents at sea that prompted the Porte to employ the *Yürüks* and *Müsellems* in its men-of-war. But these, in the division of labour that we have described, were engaged mainly in such tasks as hauling anchors, serving guns, and acting at the orders of the master-mariners. The employment of Janissaries and feudal *Sipâhîs* for naval expeditions was at length abandoned, partly, no doubt, because both types of soldiery became more and more disorganized, but partly also because, with the development of naval gunnery and the abandonment of galleys in favour of sailing-ships, it became otiose.[4] In so far, therefore, as by the eighteenth century the rowed galley had become obsolete, the only persons employed in warships, apart from the officers and more or less trained overseers (whom we are about to describe), were these same 'Standard Troops'. Hence they came also to be generally referred to merely as *Ḳalyoncus*, 'galleon-men' or sailors, *par excellence*.[5]

approximately: oarsmen, 357; men-at-arms, 175; seamen, 55; officers, 6; while those for the *Ḳaptan's Baştarda* work out at: oarsmen, 497; men-at-arms, 250; seamen, 76; officers, 8.—Cevdet, i. 130.

An Ottoman fleet usually consisted (in the sixteenth century?) of: (*a*) 1 *Baştarda*, crew 800; 6 *Mavnas*, crews, 3,600 (600 each); 40 *Ḳadirğas*, crews 12,000 (300 each); total 16,400. Of this total, 10,500 were oarsmen; 5,300 were men-at-arms; and 600 were seamen. (*b*) 20 light ships, in each of which there were 100 men-at-arms. In such a fleet of 67 ships, therefore, there were in all over 7,000 men-at-arms.—Aḥmed Râsim, i. 249–50, notes.

The first fleet prepared for the conquest of Cyprus consisted of 10 *Mavnas*, 180 *Ḳadirğas*, and 170 *Barcas* (sailing-ships—presumably for transport only); the second of 250 galleys (*Mavnas* and *Ḳadirğas*). Cevdet, i. 148. The allied fleet at Lepanto, according to Cevdet, consisted of 200 small and 7 large galleys, 20 small and 2 large sailing-ships.

[1] Children taken in war being sent to the Imperial palaces for education as pages, &c. Cossacks and Christian corsairs in particular were drafted for service in the galleys.—Seyyid Muṣṭafâ, i. 146.

[2] D'Ohsson, vii. 437.

[3] Seyyid Muṣṭafâ, i. 146. These *Za'îms* and *Timariots* were registered separately in the *Deryâ Ḳalemi*, or Sea Department.

[4] Cf. Seyyid Muṣṭafâ, iii. 92.

[5] Nevertheless they were distinguished by various names, according to the duties they performed: viz. *Ḳalyoncus* proper, i.e. seamen; *Levends*, i.e. marines;

The first officer to be appointed *Ḳaptan Paşa* was a certain Balṭa Oğlu Süleymân, whom the Conqueror rewarded by this elevation for his services at the siege of Constantinople.[1] The office carried with it, up to the time of Barbarossa, the rank of *Beylerbeyi* (with two *Ṭuğs*). For as well as being an admiral, the *Ḳaptan* was a provincial governor—of the *Sancaḳ* of Gallipoli, to which were attached the *Ḳaḍâs* of Ğalaṭa and Izmid (Nicomedia).[2] Ğalaṭa came under his jurisdiction presumably on account of its Genoese population, which, as we have mentioned, was called upon by the Conqueror for assistance with the navy; and Izmid because it embraced the best sources of timber for shipbuilding. From the time of the admission of Barbarossa as a member of the Imperial *Dîvân*, however, the *Ḳaptans* enjoyed the rank of *Vezîr* (with three *Ṭuğs*);[3] and as the navy gradually won for the Sultan all the former dependencies of Venice, &c., in the Levant, nearly all these islands and coastal districts alike were brought under the *Ḳaptan's* jurisdiction to form, eventually, an *Eyâlet*, called *Eyâleti Baḥri Sefîd* (the *Eyâlet* of the White—that is, the Aegean or the Mediterranean—Sea). This *eyâlet* was divided up, like its fellows, into *sancaḳs*, the *Sancaḳ Beyis* of which were called Sea *Beys* (*Deryâ Beyleri*). It was under them that the feudal *Sipâhîs* served with the fleet. Later, when this service was discontinued, each of them was charged with the supply and upkeep of a man-of-war.[4]

The *Ḳaptan Paşa* was *Beylerbeyi* of Gallipoli because Gallipoli was the seat of the original dockyard. And even after naval headquarters were removed in 1516 to Istanbul, he continued to direct the new dockyard at the Admiralty (*Tersâne*), situated in the suburb of Ğalaṭa eventually called *Ḳâsim Paşa*, on the Golden Horn—which indeed, from this circumstance, is known in Turkish as 'Admiralty Strait' (*Tersâne Boğazî*).[5] Hence the *Ḳaptan* had immediately under him, on the one hand, a number of officers commanding vessels, and, on the other, a number of officials in charge of Admiralty affairs. But of the organization of either before the displacement of galleys by sailing-ships little appears to be known. All persons on the Admiralty pay-list—who are said to have numbered no more than 2,364 during the reign of

Ṭopçus, i.e. gunners; and '*Aylaḳcis*'. D'Ohsson, vii. 426. D'Ohsson states that the *Aylaḳcis* were more experienced seamen entrusted with manœuvres; but Redhouse gives the word's meaning as 'unemployed, casual worker'.

[1] *Encyclopaedia of Islam*, art. 'Ḳapudān Pas̲h̲a'.

[2] Ibid. Ğalaṭa up to the beginning of the sixteenth century was not distinguished from Péra, the whole area going by the former name.—*Encyclopaedia of Islam*, art. 'Constantinople'.

[3] Hammer, op. cit. 286–5. The *Ḳaptans* had precedence over all the other *vezîrs*, ranking immediately after the Grand *Vezîr* and the *Şeyḫü'l-Islâm*.—*Encyclopaedia of Islam*, art. 'Ḳapudān Pas̲h̲a'.

[4] See D'Ohsson, vii. 424.

[5] *Encyclopaedia of Islam*, art. 'Constantinople'.

Murâd III, for example—were then regarded as forming an *ocaḳ* (*Tersâne Ocaġî*).[1] They included captains, mates, marine officers, gunners, and guards. With the gradual abandonment of galleys, however, an order of precedence for the officers commanding the chief sailing-ships was at first unofficially, and at length officially, established. The abandonment of galleys affected the organization of Admiralty head-quarters also.[2] So it is impossible to say whether its officers, as we find them at the end of the eighteenth century, had existed prior to this change or not.

Just as *Levend* was a corruption of the Venetian *Levantino*, and *Ḳaptan* or *Ḳapîdan* (as it was in early times pronounced and always written) of the Venetian *capitano*, so were the names given to the chief sailing-ships of the Ottoman navy; viz. in order, *Ḳapîdana*, *Patrona*, and *Riyala*, derived from the Italian. Their commanders were called *Ḳapîdana Beyi*, *Patrona Beyi*, &c., all three being subordinate to the commander of the *Ḳaptan Paşa's* galley of the type known as *Baştarda* (also of Italian origin), since, even when galleys were no longer in general use, this was maintained (until 1764) as a ceremonial vessel.[3] These three men-of-war, of which alone the commanders enjoyed the title *Bey*, were known as Flag-ships (*Sancaḳ Gemileri*), the rest being called Ships of the Line (*Alay Gemileri*).[4] The *Paşa* had as his chief lieutenant for the management of the Admiralty a commissioner, appointed from among the *Ḫocas* of the *Dîvân*, called *Tersâne Emîni*. It was he that directed the construction,

[1] Seyyid Muṣṭafâ, i. 145–6. Employees of the Admiralty also went commonly by the name of *'Azeb*, owing to the employment of *'Azebs* with the fleet at one time. *Levend* was loosely used in a similar way. According to Hammer, op. cit., 280, 288, the term *'Azeb* was properly applied only to the paid (*'Olûfeli*) Admiralty guard, the men of which, however, served also on the ships of the *Ḳaptan*, the *Kâḫya* (see below, p. 104, n. 1), and the '*Agas der Holz- und Steinschiffen*'. The *'Azebs*, again according to him (op. cit., 287), were organized in companies (*Bölüks*), each commanded by a *Re'îs*, consisting of 280 men, except those of the *Ḳaptan*, the *Kâḫya*, and the *Beys*, which consisted of 350.

[2] It was reorganized in 1682.—Cevdet, i. 155.

[3] For some time after sailing-ships began to replace galleys as the chief type of warship, the *Ḳaptan* continued to command from his *Baştarda*, the '*Ḳaptan* of the sailing-ships' (*Ḳalyonlar Ḳaptanî*), whom Cevdet describes as having taken the place of the earlier *Serdâr*, sailing in the *Ḳapîdana*. Later, with the complete abandonment of galleys, the Admiral's flagship was known simply as *Paşa Gemisi* (the Paşa's ship), ranking, of course, above the *Ḳapîdana*. The *Ḳapîdana Beyi* now became merely the chief subordinate commander.—Cevdet, i. 157.

[4] D'Ohsson, vii. 424 sq. *Ḳapîdana*, *Patrona*, and *Riyala* were derived respectively from the Venetian *galea capitana* (flagship), *galea padrona* (second-in-command), and *galea reale*.—*Encyclopaedia of Islam*, art. 'Riyala'. Ordinary warships were commanded by *Ḳaptans*, chosen from the *Re'îses*, commanders of *Bölüks* (see above, note 1),—Hammer, op. cit., 287. They were promoted to be *Vardiyan Başis* and 'Imperial' *Re'îses*. *Vardiyan* is from the Italian *guardiano*, and appears to be connected with the use of galley-slaves. Perhaps the *Vardiyan Başîs* and Imperial *Re'îses* were the commanders of the principal galleys, before the adoption of sailing-ships.

repair, and armament of ships, and, through another commissioner (*Enbârlar Emîni*) and an inspector (*Enbârlar Nâẓiri*), apparently subordinate to him, was responsible for all naval stores. The Admiralty had also an Intendant (*Tersâne Kâhyasi*) who commanded its guards, a Clerk of the Ships (*Ḳalyonlar Kâtibi*), a record-keeper (*Tersâne Re'îsi*), and a paymaster (*Sergi Emîni*). The Harbour Master (*Liman Re'îsi*), who also enjoyed the title of *Bey*, completes the list of its officials.[1]

Like other provincial governors, the *Ḳaptan Paşa* had a *Dîvân*, which sat in his mansion at the Admiralty.[2] He was also responsible for public order in Ġalaṭa and Ḳâsim Paşa, just as the *Ağa* of the Janissaries, the *Bostanci Başi*, the *Cebeci Başi*, and the *Ṭopçu Başi* were responsible for other districts in the capital and its vicinity. To enforce it he used a system similar to theirs: of guard-houses from which patrols would make rounds of neighbouring streets and markets. Only in the district under the jurisdiction of the *Ḳaptan Paşa* these police were called 'sailors', and seem actually to have been officered by sea-captains. We read at least of nightly patrols, in the seventeenth century, conducted by no less than thirty-five such captains. The prison in which convicts condemned to the galleys were confined when on shore was situated near the *Ḳaptan's Dîvân*-house. It was controlled immediately by the Intendant of the Admiralty.[3]

On the Admiralty pay-roll in the eighteenth century, besides these officers and officials, were all the subordinate commanders, the master mariners and master gunners, the *Paşa's çavuş*, the head *Ağa*, and a number of *Çavuşes* under him—about one thousand persons in all, so it is said.[4] Up to the reign of Maḥmûd I (1730–54) the lack of skilled seamen was partially supplied by an arrangement come to with the captains of certain merchant ships plying in the Ottoman ports of the Levant. They and their crews were engaged to serve with the fleet in war time, in return for a remission of the payment of customs duties in time of peace. By this compact the Admiralty procured the services of some

[1] D'Ohsson, vii. 435. Hammer, op. cit., 286–7, mentions a *Kâhya* apart from, and superior to, the *Tersâne Kâhyasi*; also a *Tersâne Kâtibi*, a *Tersâne Rüznameci*, a *Mahzen Kâtibi* (perhaps equivalent respectively to the *Ḳalyonlar Kâtibi*, the *Tersâne Re'îsi*, and the *Sergi Emîni*, none of whom figure in his list), a *Liman Kâtibi* (equivalent to the *Liman Re'îsi*?), and a *Zindân Kâtibi*, '*Sekretär des Bagno*', presumably in charge of the registers of galley-slaves.

[2] *Encyclopaedia of Islam*, art. 'Ḳapudān Pasha'.

[3] 'Os̱mân Nûrî, *Belediye*, i. 915–16.

[4] Seyyid Muṣṭafâ, iii. 91. The members of this paid personnel were called *Gedikli Ḳalyoncular*, 'exceptional sailors'—exceptional because of being so paid. According to Hammer, op. cit., 288, in the seventeenth century (?) the '*Azebs* numbered 1,364, the caulkers (*Ḳalfatcis*), who were recruited from the '*Acemî Oğlans*, 500 or 600, and the gunners 40 or 50 (having earlier numbered 500 or 600 also).

two thousand experienced mariners—though the accounts left by European observers of the manner in which merchant shipping was navigated rather later in the century suggest that even these professional sailors were possessed of no remarkable skill. During Maḥmûd's reign, however, the Admiralty was deprived even of this. In order to increase the Sultan's revenues from the customs dues, a commissioner (*Gümrük Emîni*) of the reign insisted that they should be paid on the cargoes borne in these ships.[1] Henceforward, accordingly, the Admiralty had to rely on the officers and seamen on its own pay-roll. This deprivation no doubt contributed to the inefficiency of the navy in the ensuing war with Russia.

By attaching many islands and coastal regions to the *Ḳaptan's eyâlet*, Süleymân had sought to provide the navy with sufficient resources.[2] In the eighteenth century these *sancaḳs* still supplied the Admiralty with contributions in kind;[3] but they were not enough to meet all its wants; and the remainder had to be provided for from the *Mîrî*.[4] Nor were their revenues such as to satisfy the *Ḳaptans* of the age. So, like other great officers of state, they were in the habit of augmenting them by the sale of places—in this case captaincies—usually to hangers-on at court. The captains then sold subordinate posts, and so on;[5] with the result that the officers of every grade went indeed so far as to sail on the yearly summer cruise—which the islanders and inhabitants of the ports that they called at dreaded as a plague of locusts—but could count as scarcely more than passengers. Navigation they left to provincial Greek pilots, who worked, however, in the most disadvantageous circumstances. For not only were they obliged to engage totally inexperienced assistants, picked up at the eleventh hour in the streets of the capital, so that they accounted themselves lucky to dispose of the service of Christian slaves and Maltese corsair prisoners; but they were threatened with death for the least misadventure.[6] Misadventures were common. For these pilots were quite unequal to the management of men-of-war, few of them knowing even the use of the compass or how to take meridian observations.[7] Nor were their difficulties lessened by the build of the ships they were engaged to navigate, though, as was generally agreed among European students of the time, the Ottomans showed greater ability in building ships than in manning

[1] Seyyid Muṣṭafâ, iii. 92–3.

[2] Juchereau, i. 101. Under Bâyezîd II a special tax had been imposed on Istanbul and other cities to pay for shipbuilding.—Seyyid Muṣṭafâ, i. 65.

[3] Though the Admiralty finances had been reformed in 1682 by Ḳara Muṣṭafâ Paşa, the Grand *Vezîr*.—Cevdet, i. 155.

[4] Thornton, i. 42, 44.

[5] Juchereau, i. 102.

[6] Juchereau, i. 102–3; Eton, 77–8.

[7] Eton, 208–9.

them.[1] Two types of ship were in use: caravellas and frigates.[2] They are said to have been too high decked, too short, and ill-rigged. And though they were fast sailers,[3] their lower-tier guns were so placed as to be easily submerged in the slightest gale.[4] Their ordnance in particular was defective. For not only were they frequently mounted with guns of varying calibre, but the ammunition supplied was no less frequently found to fit none even of these variegated guns.[5]

This is a dark picture. But though it is chiefly derived from the descriptions of Europeans, most of whom were imbued with prejudices against the Grand Signor and his co-religionists, it is supported by Ottoman writers themselves. From all accounts one point at least emerges clearly: that what contemporary Europeans called 'Turks'—that is, Turkish-speaking Moslems—did not shine as sailors:[6] the navy being very strikingly dependent, in its seafaring as opposed to its military aspect, on Greeks from the islands and coasts of the Aegean and Arabic-speaking Moslems from the North African Regencies. And in this judgement the fact is evidently reflected that the Ottoman navy was not, if such an expression may be used, an indigenous Ottoman product. No doubt few great powers have been maritime in origin, as were Venice and Genoa. Even the Portuguese, of whom in their era of empire-building a Chinese is reported to have said that they were, like fish, bound to expire if removed from the water, built up their sea power after having won their kingdom from the Moors by warfare on land. But not only was the Ottoman case similar in this to the Portuguese; the Ottoman state was also conditioned in an extraordinary manner by the traditions of its forerunners, who had no naval organization at all. Hence the Sultans' navy had always something about it of the anomalous. That its admiral should be at the same time a provincial *paşa* was not, in the circumstances, inconvenient, odd though it may seem. His introduction into the *Dîvân*, on the other hand, was attended, as we have remarked, with disastrous consequences. Yet the fact that the navy stood in this manner outside the framework of the Ruling Institution as determined by inherited tradition proved eventually of advantage not only to itself but to governmental institutions as a whole. The point is noticed by an eighteenth-century European; and it was true: the navy having

[1] Thornton, i. 292–3; cf. Eton, 77–8.

[2] Juchereau, i. 101; Eton, 75. In Turkish these ships were called *Ḳaravela* and *Firḳata* (the latter term having earlier been applied also to a galley—see above, p. 96, n. 5).

[3] Eton, 77–8.

[4] Tott, iii. 20; cf. ibid. ii. 250 and Eton, 83.

[5] Tott, iii. 21; Juchereau, i. 102–3.

[6] Thornton, i. 77–8, it is true, considered the 'Turks' the equals of the Greeks in navigation.

been adopted from the infidels, fewer prejudices stood in the way of its reform than in that of any other state service.[1] It was accordingly in the navy, and by a *Ḳaptan*, that some of the earliest and most striking reforms were introduced.

V. THE CENTRAL ADMINISTRATION

The central administration of the Empire was modelled on those of former Moslem states. Its pattern was the administration of the 'Abbâsid Caliphate—which was itself much influenced by Sasanian traditions—as modified in turn by the Ġaznevids and the Selcuḳids. In all these organizations there were three principal departments, though subdivision sometimes disguised the scheme of their arrangement. This was, so to speak, triangular. At the apex of the triangle stood the ruler's general deputy, most often, though not invariably, called *wazîr*, or, as pronounced in Turkish, *vezîr*. At its other points stood two principal officials, who managed, one everything to do with correspondence, the registration of documents, and the issue of commands and regulations, and the other everything to do with the reception of revenues and their expenditure.[2] In all cases the officials of the latter two departments were subordinate to the holder of the first office. We shall therefore start with a description of this.

The office of *wazîr* dated from the early days of Islâm, and is thought to have been an inheritance from the Sasanian Empire.[3] Ever since the term had come into use in early 'Abbâsid days, every Moslem ruler of any actual, if not theoretical, independence had had his *wazîr*;[4] and as a rule the grander the monarch the more important had been the minister, not merely because the whole state concerned was more powerful, but because of the rela-

[1] Eton, 79.

[2] Ibn Ḫaldûn in the famous Introduction to his *History* explains that 'affairs of state and their administration do not exceed four', i.e. are of only four kinds, namely, (i) defence (both of the state from external attacks and of the people from internal disorders, including crime), (ii) correspondence and the issuing of orders, (iii) finance, and (iv) the preservation of the monarch from importunate petitioners; (i) being the province of the *Wazîr*, (ii) that of the Secretary (*Kâtib*), (iii) that of the Treasurer (*Ṣâḥib el-mâl wa'l-cibâya*, literally 'The master of the money and tax-collection'), and (iv) that of the Chamberlain (*Ḥâcib*). Ibn Ḫaldûn goes on to explain, however, that under the 'Abbâsids the first three departments were all subordinated to the *Wazîr*, only the fourth remaining outside his competence.—*Kitâb el-'ibar*, i. 197–9. The fourth department was represented in the Ottoman scheme by the Imperial Household.

[3] The word is now usually derived from the Pehlevi *vçir*, meaning 'judge', not, as is commonly stated, from the Arabic root *wazara*, 'to bear a burden'. The Arabic adaptation of the word is, however, pre-Islamic, since in the Ḳur'ân (Sûra 20. v. 30, &c.) the term is applied to Aaron.

[4] Their predecessors, the Umayyad Caliphs, had employed merely *kâtibs*, 'secretaries'. Ibn Ḫaldûn, loc. cit., refers to the employment by the Umayyads of *wazirs*; but this appears to be incorrect.

tions between minister and monarch. For as, under the influence of Persian example, growing grandeur had repeatedly encouraged Moslem dynasts to become more and more unapproachable, so the real control of their realms devolved more and more on their *wazîrs.* The authority of *wazîrs* varied in fact between what certain Moslem theorists of government have called 'the Wazîrate of Execution' and 'the Wazîrate of Delegation'.[1] The minister whose authority was executive merely carried out the monarch's commands. He whose authority was delegated acted on his own initiative, though he continued of course to be responsible to the monarch for his actions. This distinction does not seem, however, to have been formal. The initiative of ministers, under Ottoman rule, at least, seems in practice merely to have varied inversely with the vigour of their masters, except when the latter were so much preoccupied by the waging of war as to have little time left for the consideration of other affairs.

Under the earliest Sultans their chief ministers were called, not *vezîr*, but *pervâne*, or *pervâneci*,[2] a usage inherited from the Selcuḳids of Ḳonya.[3] The title *vezîr* indeed was first conferred on a military commander;[4] and, perhaps on account of the precedent thereby set up, continued, or at least soon after came, to denote the highest rank—as opposed to an office—in the hierarchy of the Ruling Institution, a rank which several persons, including the chief minister, might hold simultaneously. Nevertheless, the title *pervâneci* implied no especial subordination of its holders to the Sultan's orders. For the ministers of the earliest reigns enjoyed the greater independence in the management of affairs, as the Sultans they served were occupied in almost ceaseless warfare. Consequently, when under Meḥmed the Conqueror *ḳânûns* were drawn up, or collected,[5] defining the position and functions of the various officers of state, the chief minister was referred to as the

[1] *Wizâret el-tenfîẓ* and *wizâret el-tafwîḍ*; see e.g. el-Mâwardî, *el-Aḥkâm el-Sulṭânîya* (trans. Fagnan, 24), and Ibn Ḫaldûn (loc. cit.).

[2] *Pervâne* (Persian) has among many others the meanings of both 'a commander or inspector' and 'a royal patent or diploma'. Hence its use without the Turkish ending *ci* (here signifying 'one that issues') in the first sense, and with it in the second, to denote a minister.

[3] *Encyclopaedia of Islam*, art. 'Wazīr'; Köprülüzade, *Selcuḳliler Zamanînda Anadoluda Türk Medeniyeti* (*M.T.M.* ii. 204).

[4] *Encyclopaedia of Islam*, art. 'Wazīr'. Timurtaş, the commander in question, may, as is here suggested, have been regarded as the first Ottoman Grand (*Ulu*) *Vezîr*, but hardly in the sense in which that term was later understood. For he seems never to have been the Sultan's *Pervâneci*, but merely the first *paşa* of three *ṭuğs* (see below, p. 139), and principal *Beylerbeyi* (cf. art. 'Tīmūrtāsh').

[5] Though no *ḳânûn-nâmes*, or collections of *ḳânûns*, earlier than the reign of Meḥmed II have come to light, individual *ḳânûns* are known to have been promulgated by that Sultan's predecessors; see *O.T.E.M.*, No. 13, Appendix 3 (introduction to the *Ḳânûn-nâmei Âlî 'Osmân*).

Sultan's 'absolute representative'.[1] Moreover, owing to the peculiar distinction now attached to the vezîrate as a rank, he was called no longer *pervâneci*, but Great or Greatest (whence our 'Grand') *Vezîr* (*Ulu Vezîr* or *Vezîri A'ẓem*).[2] The Ottomans thus reverted to earlier Moslem practice in entitling their chief minister *vezîr*, but were obliged to modify it by qualifying the title with the epithet 'Great' because they had already modified it by conferring the title on several persons at once as a mere mark of rank.

Up to the time of the conquest of Constantinople the office of chief minister had been filled by free Moslems, beginning, under Orḫân, with that Sultan's reputed brother, 'Alâ'u'l-Dîn.[3] One family in particular, Çandârlî by name, had at intervals served Orḫân's successors for four generations in this capacity, its fourth representative, indeed, being actually in office when the conquest took place.[4] Meanwhile, however, the Sultans, as we have indicated, had adopted, with the growth of their dominions, an ever more autocratic mode of rule, to support which they had brought into being the Household and the standing army, manned almost exclusively by their slaves, and now largely recruited by the *devşirme* levy, that we have described. That the chief office of the Ruling Institution should be held by a free Moslem was by this time, therefore, something of an anomaly. Meḥmed is said to have regarded the prestige acquired by the Çandârlîs with some jealousy,[5] to have borne a personal grudge against his minister, Ḫalîl Paşa, and to have suspected him of being in treacherously close relations with the Byzantine court.[6] However that may be, he dismissed and executed him in the very year of the conquest, and chose in his place a *Ḳapî Ḳulu*, Maḥmûd Paşa 'Adenî.[7]

Thereafter, though another Çandârlî served Meḥmed's successor for a short period,[8] the Grand *Vezîrs*, as long as the Ruling Institution was maintained on a servile basis, were regularly chosen from among the slave officials. And from the date of the conquest to the later days of Süleymân the Magnificent—some hundred

[1] *Vekîli Muṭlaḳ* (Arabic, *el-wakîl el-muṭlaḳ*).

[2] *Ulu*, Turkish. *A'ẓem*, superlative of Arabic *'Aẓîm*.

[3] *Encyclopaedia of Islam*, art. "Alā al-Dīn Pāshā'.

[4] *Encyclopaedia of Islam*, art. 'Čendereli'. The four ministers in question were: (i) Ḳara Ḫalîl—served Murâd I; (ii) his son 'Alî—served Bâyezîd I; (iii) his son Ibrahîm—served Meḥmed I and Murâd II; (iv) his son Ḫalîl—served Murâd II and Meḥmed II. Various spellings of the name are given, viz. Çendereli, Cendereli, Çenderli, Çandârlî. The latter, which we have used, seems to be favoured by modern Turkish historians.

[5] Seyyid Muṣṭafâ, i. 56–7.

[6] *Encyclopaedia of Islam*, art. 'Čendereli'.

[7] 'Aṭâ, ii. 4. According to D'Ohsson, vii. 152, Meḥmed, after ridding himself of Ḫalîl Çandârlî, sought to dispense with the services of a *vezîr* altogether. He appointed Maḥmûd Paşa only after eight months.

[8] Ibrahîm the son of Ḫalîl served Bâyezîd II from 1497 to 1499 (see *Encyclopaedia of Islam*, art. 'Čendereli').

years—they approximated more closely than at any other period to the ideal '*vezîrs* of execution'. For Meḥmed II, Selîm I, and Süleymân were rulers of peculiar vigour. But owing to the retirement of Süleymân towards the end of his reign into a comparative seclusion, and still more to the preoccupation of his successors with private extravagance, the *Vezîrs*—henceforth generally known as *Ṣadrî A'ẓem* (Greatest Dignitary)[1]—though still *Ḳapi Ḳulus*, then came into their own. Nevertheless, with the exception, perhaps, of Damad Ṣokollu Meḥmed Paşa, who ruled the Empire for thirteen years after the death of Süleymân,[2] and the four members of the Köprülü family, who saved it from collapse at the end of the seventeenth century,[3] the Grand *Vezîrs* were unable effectively to replace the Sultans of the great days. In the first place, the *Vezîrs*' tenure of office, which had always been dependent upon the Sultans' continued favour, was made many times more precarious than before, when the factors attendant on the Sultans' retirement came into play. For their retirement placed the Sultans at the mercy of the *Ḥarem* and the eunuchs, from whose intrigues their knowledge of the world, especially after the institution of the 'cage' system,[4] was too slight to protect them: hence the attempt by Çorlulu 'Alî Paşa, recorded above, to reduce the eunuchs' influence.[5] And in the second, no substitute for governmental genius such as was displayed by two at least of the Köprülüs, even the first of whom was only conventionally a *Ḳapi Ḳulu*,[6] was any

[1] *Encyclopaedia of Islam*, art. 'Ṣadr A'ẓam'. The title was habitually contracted to *Ṣadr-A'ẓem* by omission of the '*iḍâfet*', just as *Ḳâḍî-'asker* was contracted from *Ḳâḍîi 'Asker*.

[2] Grand *Vezîr* from 1565 (a year before the accession of Selîm II) to his murder in 1579 (five years after the accession of Murâd III). He was a Bosnian by birth, Soḳollu being the Turkicized form of his real name Sokolevich. He was *damad*, 'son-in-law', by his marriage with Esmiḥan Sulṭân, daughter of Selîm II. —*Encyclopaedia of Islam*, art. 'Soḳollu'. The year of his elevation to the Grand Vezîrate appears to be wrongly given in this article as 1568, which was two years later than the death of Süleymân, whom he served in this capacity for fifteen months.

[3] (i) Meḥmed Paşa, Grand *Vezîr* from 1656 to his death in 1661; (ii) his son Fâḍil Aḥmed Paşa, Grand *Vezîr*, in immediate succession to his father, from 1661 to his death in 1676; (iii) Fâḍil Muṣṭafâ Paşa, son of (i), Grand *Vezîr* from 1689 till killed on campaign in 1691; (iv) Ḥüseyn Paşa, nephew of (i), Grand *Vezîr* from 1697 to his retirement in 1702. The family was of Albanian origin. Meḥmed Paşa distinguished himself particularly by the energy with which he restored the Empire to order; Fâḍil Aḥmed by his generalship; Fâḍil Muṣṭafâ and Ḥüseyn by their economic reforms. It was under Ḥüseyn that the Peace of Carlovitz was signed with Russia, Austria, Poland, and Venice.

A fifth member of the family, Nu'mân Paşa, son of Muṣṭafâ, served as Grand *Vezîr* from 1702 to 1710, but was less successful and was dismissed in the latter year. He became a *damad* by marrying 'Â'işe Sulṭân, the sister of Muṣṭafâ II. —*Encyclopaedia of Islam*, art. 'Köprülü'.

[4] See above, p. 37.

[5] See above, p. 76.

[6] He was apparently a Moslem by birth and owed his first employment—in the *Ḥalvâ-ḫâne* of the Outside Service of the Household (see App. B (c) 2 (iii))

longer available after the system of education for office and advancement by merit was corrupted.

The Grand *Vezîr*, though he was the Sultan's 'absolute representative', had no direct authority over two important institutions of state, namely, the Imperial Household and the 'Learned Profession'.[1] But otherwise he was all-powerful, controlling all appointments both in the army and the administration central and provincial alike.[2] He was further required not only to manage the affairs of the army but also, if necessary, to command it in war, and, like the generals of the various infantry corps, to supervise the preservation of law and order in the capital. Moreover, he represented the Sultan as chief dispenser of justice, in virtue of the latter's office as *Imâm*. In the early days of the Empire the Sultans, emulating some previous Moslem dynasts, had dispensed justice in person.[3] But they had usually done so with the assistance of *Şer'î* magistrates, since even if they gave decisions according to their conception of what was just, or in deference to some established custom, such decisions were supposed to conform with the rulings, or the implicit intentions, of the *Şerî'a*. So when the Grand *Vezîrs* came to take their place, and presided over the highest court of law, they did so likewise in company with *Şer'î* magistrates, to whom they handed over cases actually provided for in the *Şerî'a*—and so admitting of no arbitrary solution—and whose advice they might seek regarding others.[4] But the authority of the minister on the one hand, and of the magistrates on the other, was not mutually exclusive. On the contrary, the authority of both extended over all the cases brought before the court: that of the *Vezîr* in virtue of his general mandate from the Sultan-*Imâm*, that of the magistrates because the *Şerî'a* was supposed to be amplified, rather than supplemented, by *'urfî* and *'âdî* rulings.[5] Nevertheless, the position of the *Vezîr* being superior to that of the magistrates, he was likely to settle all cases in any way doubtful. As we shall see, this undefined division, or overlapping, of powers prevailed also in the provinces, where the Sultan was

—to a meeting with a fellow townsman employed in the Imperial Kitchens—see 'Aṭâ, ii. 68.

[1] The Learned Profession was under the control ot the *Şeyḫü'l-Islâm* and the two *Ḳâḍî-'askers* (see below, ch. ix).

[2] D'Ohsson, vii. 156; Hammer, *Staatsverwaltung*, 82–3.

[3] Up to the reign of Meḥmed the Conqueror (see Seyyid Muṣṭafâ, i. 59), like the Selcuḳid Sultans of Ḳonya (see Köprülüzade, '*Selcuḳliler Zamaninda Anadoluda Türk Medeniyeti*, *M.T.M.* ii. 199 sq.). See above, p. 27.

[4] The judges concerned were: (*a*) the *Ḳâḍî-'askers* of Rumelia and Anatolia at Friday and Imperial *Dîvâns* (held, up to the mid-seventeenth century on Saturdays, Sundays, Mondays, and Tuesdays, thereafter only on Sundays and Tuesdays); (*b*) the *Ḳâḍîs* of Istanbul, Eyyub, Ğalaṭa, and Üsküdar at Wednesday *Dîvâns*. (See *M.T.M.* i. 501, 503, 506—*Ḳânûn-nâme* of 'Abdu'r-Raḥmân Tevḳî'î.)

[5] See above, p. 23.

represented by the local governors. It was equally responsible for the fact that, when, as chief guardian of law and order in the capital, the Grand *Vezîr* went his weekly rounds of the markets, to ensure the proper observance of craft and trade regulations, and to apprehend and punish criminals and wrongdoers, he was, as we have remarked, accompanied by the *ḳâḍî* of the capital.[1]

The Sultan signalized the delegation of his powers to the Grand *Vezîr* by confiding to him his signet ring,[2] with which various important depositories were sealed. And a demand for its return was the sign of his dismissal from office. The ministers of early times would wear this ring on their fingers. Those of later times kept it in a cloth of gold purse in their pockets.[3] The Sultan further honoured the Grand *Vezîr* by allowing members of his Household to wait on him. Thus the *Ağas* of the Stirrup would do so once a week; and the Grand *Vezîr* would be escorted between his own residence and the palace by the *Çavuş Başî* and a number of his men.[4] Moreover, the Grand *Vezîrs* had several peculiar rights. Thus they alone might correspond with the sovereign;[5] they alone might, like the Sultans, when placed in command of the army, carry the Prophet's Standard to war.[6] In later times, indeed, as they became more powerful in fact, so their position became more august. Thus all functionaries, 'learned' and 'lay' alike, except the *Şeyḫü'l-Islâm*, were obliged on entering the minister's presence to kiss the hem of his robe;[7] and whereas they

[1] The Grand *Vezîr* made his ordinary rounds after the Wednesday *Dîvân* (see *M.T.M.* i. 503 sq.). By D'Ohsson's time, however, the *Ḳâḍî* of Istanbul no longer accompanied him—vii. 157. Cf. Hammer, op. cit., 85.

[2] So historians will refer to the elevation of Grand *Vezîrs* by saying: 'He attained the signet of the Sovereign of the World' (*Nâ'ili muhru şahriyâri cehân olmuştu*).—'Aṭâ, ii. 137.

[3] Seyyid Muṣṭafâ, i. 59; D'Ohsson, vii. 153–4; Hammer, op. cit., 94–5; Lybyer, 166. The depositories sealed with the imperial signet were the financial record store (*Mâliye Defter-ḫânesi*), the Outside Treasury of the *Serây* (*Diş Ḫazîne*), and the general archive store (*Defter-ḫâne*). The so-called Journal Bag (*Rüznâme Kîsesi*) was likewise sealed with it. Apparently this contained records of the rulings pronounced in the *Vezîr's* court (see *M.T.M.* i. 507, 509, 512—*Ḳânûn-nâme* of 'Abdu'r-Raḥmân Tevḳî'î). In early times the signet was delivered to the Grand *Vezîr* in his own mansion by a court official, but from the reign of Aḥmed I it was presented to him by the Sultan in person. When the Sultan desired to dismiss a *Vezîr* he likewise sent a court official, usually the *Ḳapîcîlar Kâḫyasî*, to retrieve it.—Grand *Vezîrs*, on dismissal, were obliged to leave the capital immediately.

[4] Lybyer, 166, citing 'Âlî, with reference to the practice of the reign of Meḥmed II. The *Ḳânûn-nâme* of 'Abdu'r-Raḥmân Tevḳî'î shows that by the seventeenth century the *Ağas* of the Stirrup attended at all *Dîvâns*. But they (and the *Bölük* commanders) then waited on the Grand *Vezîr* on Thursday mornings also, when there was no *Dîvân*, perhaps by way of preserving this privilege (see *M.T.M.* i. 506—The Thursday *Ḳânûn*).

[5] *M.T.M.* i. 499 ('Abdu'r-Raḥmân); Hammer, op. cit., 93.

[6] Ibid. 500.

[7] D'Ohsson, vii. 154. The *Vezîr* usually prevented them from doing so, out of courtesy, presenting his hand instead.

were all accessible at any time to any member of the public in their offices, the Grand *Vezîr* might only be approached by the eminent after they had applied for an interview, except when he sat in his law court or held public audience once a month.[1] But perhaps the most striking evidence of the transference of leadership, if not of ultimate power, from the Sultans to the Grand *Vezîrs* in later times was the creation of the Sublime Porte. For till then all the chief affairs of state were attended to in the Sultan's palace. The Grand *Vezîr* then had only a private house, where he dealt with minor matters. But in 1654 Meḥmed IV presented Derviş Meḥmed Paşa with an official residence, which was thenceforth, under the names *Paşa Ḳapîsî* (the *Paşa's* Gate) and *Bâbî 'Âlî* (High Gate, or, more pompously, Sublime Porte),[2] inhabited by that minister and his successors. This vast building was not however, only a residence, for the Grand *Vezîr*, his family, his household, and his guards. It was also a public office, at which their duties were discharged by all the chief functionaries of the administration except those which dealt that matters of finance.[3]

As we have explained, the title *vezîr* was applied, by the fifteenth century, to a number of persons simultaneously. These were usually provincial governors of the highest grade; for with the title the Sultan delegated full authority to them; so that they might issue imperial orders called *Fermân*,[4] and in some cases might strike coins in his name. Under Meḥmed the Conqueror, however, the rank was conferred also on officers other than the Grand *Vezîr* resident in the capital. This innovation was made partly because the Sultan and the Grand *Vezîr* were frequently absent, either together or singly, on campaign, and partly in order to provide them with councillors of fit dignity. For when the Grand *Vezîr* was placed in command of the army, some one had to take his place. When the Sultan commanded the army himself, the Grand *Vezîr* accompanied him; and so some one had to be left in charge at the capital. Finally, when the war was in Europe, it was thought desirable to charge some important officer with the maintenance of security in Asia, and, when it was in Asia, with the maintenance of security in Europe. Hence at first two, and later, in the sixteenth century, as many as nine, *Vezîrs* were created, who, when the need arose, were employed in these various

[1] Ibid. 176–7.

[2] For Arabic *el-Bâb el-'Âlî*. Hammer, op. cit., 95, considers it probable that the name *Bâbi 'Âlî* was applied earlier to the Sultan's palace, and was transferred to that of the Grand *Vezîr* together with effective power.

[3] D'Ohsson, vii. 158, 174 sq.; *Encyclopaedia of Islam*, art. 'Constantinople'.

[4] Seyyid Muṣṭafâ, i. 91. They also had the right to draw the Sultan's monogram called *Ṭuğra* on documents (see below, p. 117).

ways. Owing to the fact that the councils at which they assisted were habitually held in a domed chamber in the palace, they came to be known as *Ḳubbe* (Dome) *Vezîrs*. They were numbered: Second *Vezîr*, Third *Vezîr*, and so on. Sometimes they were given command of forces on minor expeditions, in which case they were entitled *Serdâr* for the occasion. Each would maintain a considerable body of household troops, which they would station, part at their mansions in the capital, part on their estates in the neighbourhood, where they kept their tents, pack animals, and war equipment. They would use these as their bodyguards on campaign, and would set out in the company of a number of Janissary *ortas* and some divisions of the standing cavalry, being joined at their destination by the local governors with their household and feudal troops.[1] *Vezîrs* appointed to replace the Grand *Vezîr* when he was commanding in the field were called *Ḳâ'im-maḳâm*.[2] It was generally the Second *Vezîr* that was given this duty. He enjoyed for the time being almost all the authority of a Grand *Vezîr* except in the area where the army was operating, though less than his pomp. For since most of the principal officers and officials of the administration would accompany the Grand *Vezîr* on campaign, the *Ḳâ'im-maḳâm* had to support him at home only the officers and officials that were also appointed to replace them. This curious system dated from the days when the Sultans led their armies to war in person. Their chief ministers followed them, leaving substitutes at the capital. And in later times it was continued even when the Sultans remained at home and the Grand *Vezîrs* commanded. As wars were extremely frequent and the Grand *Vezîrs* did generally command, the appointment of *Ḳâ'im-maḳâms* was common; so that in biographies of Grand *Vezîrs* we often find that immediately before their elevation to the highest rank they had held that of *Ḳâ'im-maḳâm*. *Ḳâ'im-maḳâms* were also appointed during the 'interregnums' that occurred when a new Grand *Vezîr* was promoted from some provincial governorship.[3]

As well as on the *Ḳubbe Vezîrs* the rank of *vezîr* was also from the later fifteenth century conferred on certain other high dignitaries of state.[4] And the number of persons holding it was gradually multiplied, especially after the decline of Ottoman institutions had set in, to such an extent that the rank no longer bore its former prestige. Hence in the middle of the seventeenth century the *Ḳubbe Vezîrs* were reduced in number, and early in the eighteenth were abolished altogether. Thenceforward there

[1] *M.T.M.* i. 499–500 (*Ḳânûn-nâme* of 'Abdu'r-Raḥmân Tevkî'î); Seyyid Muṣṭafâ, i. 59; D'Ohsson, vii. 212; *Encyclopaedia of Islam*, art. 'Wazīr'.

[2] Literally, 'standing in the station (of)'. Cf. above, p. 61.

[3] D'Ohsson, vii. 158; *M.T.M.* i, loc. cit.; Hammer, op. cit., 96, 136–7.

[4] For instance, the *Nîşâncı* and the *Defterdâr* (see below, pp. 124–128).

were seldom more than four or five persons, including the prime minister, of vezirial rank in the capital; and at least two of these were members of the Household—one of them being the *Ḳîzlar Ağasî*—who had to do with public affairs only unofficially. The remaining *vezîrs* were now as heretofore all governors of provinces.[1]

We may now pass on to the structure of the central administration proper. As we have mentioned, governmental business in former Moslem states had generally been divided between two main sections of state officials, one of whom dealt with correspondence, the issue of orders, &c., and the other with financial matters. Thus the 'Abbâsids and the 'Great' Selcuḳids had each had a Correspondence Office and an Office for the Issue of Orders on the one hand, and a Finance Office on the other;[2] and the Ottomans imitated them fairly exactly. Under the early 'Abbâsids again each of these offices was called *dîwân*.[3] But early in the tenth century when the Caliphs first fell under the domination of rebel rulers and controlled only a comparatively small area, and that no more than nominally, they no longer required an elaborate administrative machine. All these *dîwâns* therefore were amalgamated in one;[4] and henceforward the word *dîwân*, as applied to a government office, acquired a new significance: it now meant the administration in general as opposed to the ruler's court or household. Hence another name for the *wazîr* came to be, as under the Great Selcuḳids, *Ṣâḥib* (Head of the) *Dîvân*. Under the offshoot dynasty of Ḳonya, however, the word seems to have undergone a further change in application. At any rate as well as the *Ṣâḥib Dîvân* (who was an official other than the *Pervâneci*) there were, under these Selcuḳid rulers, both a Registrar of Properties (*Emvâl Deftercisi*) and a Privy Secretary (*Münşi'i Ḫâṣṣ*):[5] so that *dîvân*, under this dynasty, would seem to have been applied to what later, under the Ottomans, was a department of the office of the Grand *Vezîr* himself: his chancery or secretariat.[6] But

[1] Aḥmed Râsim, ii. 309; Seyyid Muṣṭafâ, ii. 91; D'Ohsson, vii. 212; Hammer, op. cit., 81.

[2] (i) Correspondence Office called *Dîwân el-Resâ'il* ('Abbâsids) and *Dîvân-e Inşâ* (Selcuḳids). (ii) Office for Issue of Orders called *Dîwân el-Tawḳî'* ('Abbâsids) and *Dîvân-e Ṭuğrâ* (Selcuḳids). (iii) Finance Office called *Dîwân el-Ḫarâc* (Revenue) ('Abbâsids), *Dîwân el-Nafaḳât* (Expenditure) ('Abbâsids), *Dîvân-e Istîfâ* (Selcuḳids).

[3] The word (of Persian derivation) having had originally the significance of 'register'. See *Encyclopaedia of Islam*, s.v.

[4] See Bowen, *Life and Times of 'Ali ibn 'Îsà*, 393.

[5] See Köprülüzade, *Selcuḳliler Zamanînda Anadoluda Türk Medeniyeti*, 204. Under the 'Great' Selcuḳids the Head of the Correspondence Office was also called *Munşi'*. For these references to their government see, e.g., Niẓâm el-Mulk, *Siyâset Nâme*, and el-Bundârî, *Zubdat el-Nuṣra*.

[6] This chancery was indeed called *Dîvânî Hümayûn Ḳalemi* (Secretarial

under the Ottomans the word no longer denoted either this or any other particular department, or the administration as a whole. It denoted instead an official assembly, particularly that held at the palace and presided over by the Grand *Vezîr*. And we may conveniently digress at this point to consider this usage in greater detail, since the status of many officials of the administration depended largely on their inclusion in or exclusion from these palace *dîvâns*.

In this new sense *dîvân* seems primarily to have been applied to public audiences of the Sultans. In early times they held these principally to dispense justice, but also to receive the homage of their ministers, to give audiences to ambassadors, and to preside over the distribution of pay to their standing troops. Up to the reign of Meḥmed the Conqueror they continued to appear for the first and last of these purposes, as well as for the others, in public. But owing, it is said, to the lack of due deference shown to that Sultan by a petitioner on one occasion, Meḥmed resolved to abandon this practice. He delegated his duties of judge to his Grand *Vezîr*; but in order to maintain full control over the latter's conduct in court caused a window to be pierced in the wall of the chamber where the court was held, from which, concealed by a grille, he might watch its proceedings unobserved.[1] This chamber, which from its dome gave their name to the *Ḳubbe Vezîrs*, stood in the Middle or Second Court of the palace, the province of the Outside Service. And from the date of Meḥmed's withdrawal from the presidency of the court, he and his successors ceased to appear in it. For whether or not he had done so before, henceforth they sat for audiences in another room,[2] just within the Gate of Felicity, which led into the Inner Court. Such audiences, however, were always preceded by the holding of assemblies in the Dome Chamber, presided over by the Grand *Vezîr*; and it was to these that the term *dîvân* was chiefly applied, though it covered also the receptions, when these followed them, in the Audience Chamber. But since the proceedings invariably began with the consideration of petitions by the prime minister and the Learned

Department of the Imperial *Dîvân*—the Arabic word *Ḳalem* being used metaphorically for such a department. Cf. below, p. 127, n. 9); but the *dîvân* here referred to is the Grand *Vezîr's* assembly and court.

[1] See Seyyid Muṣṭafâ, i. 59.

[2] Called *'Arḍ* (pronounced *arz*) *Odasî*, *'arḍ* (Arabic) meaning 'presentation' (of petitions) and hence 'audience'. The withdrawal by Meḥmed from public presidency of the court occurred very soon after he had taken up residence in the palace, so the arrangement here described existed virtually from the beginnings of the *Serây's* history. Whether the court was already held actually in the afterwards famous Dome Chamber, however, we have not been able to ascertain. Certainly the contrivance of a grille would seem to have dated from this change in the Sultan's habits. 'Aṭâ, i. 59, mentions the Dome Chamber under his section on Meḥmed II but does not give the date of its construction.

Men that assisted him, in a more restricted sense it came to denote merely his court of justice.[1] More generally, on the other hand, it was applied to the meetings of any body of officials. Thus the councils of the general staff of the Janissaries were likewise termed *dîvân*.

The Correspondence Office of the 'Abbâsids was represented in the Ottoman administration by the Grand *Vezîr's* Chancery, referred to above. And both excluded, but worked in concert with, a department for the Issue of Orders. The function of the latter office under the 'Abbâsids seems to have been to examine, and if necessary to correct, documents emanating from the former, and to affix to them some sign indicating that they were issued with the ruler's authority. A similar office existed in the Great Selcuḳid administration, its chief official being called *Ṭuğrâ'î*, because the ruler's sign in this case was called *ṭuğra*. The Ottoman ruler's sign was likewise called *ṭuğra*: it was an intricate monogram of each Sultan's name and was used not only on documents but on coins. One of the two principal officials that ranked next (excluding the *Ḳubbe Vezîrs*) after the Grand *Vezîr*, accordingly, was the *Nîşâncî*, or Affixer of the Sign.[2] For though under the 'Abbâsids and Selcuḳids the Affixer of the Sign was of less account than the official in charge of the Correspondence Office,[3] under the Ottomans he was not. The Chancery itself was of greater account than the office of the *Nîşâncî*, but because of its direct supervision by the Grand *Vezîr* its principal functionary, called *Re'îsü'l-Kuttâb* (Chief of the Secretaries),[4] was in early Ottoman days of comparatively humble standing, and only attained to a prominent position, approximating to that of his 'Abbâsid and Selcuḳid prototypes, in the period of decline. Moreover, owing to the conservatism with which old forms were clung to under the Sultans, even then the *Re'îs* was never officially recognized as the equal of the *Nîşâncî*, though in fact he had become far more important.

The *Re'îsü'l-Küttâb* was thus the Grand *Vezîr's* lieutenant for the direction of his Chancery. But the Grand *Vezîr* had another general lieutenant, who, though of slighter public eminence, actually ranked above the *Re'îs*: he was called *Kâḫya Bey*.[5] Moreover, owing to the assumption of the Sultan's judicial functions by the

[1] For the ceremonial observed at *Dîvâns* of Audience, the payment of troops, and the reception of ambassadors see the *kânûn-nâme* of 'Abdu'r-Raḥmân Tevḳî'î, *M.T.M.* i.

[2] Further details regarding the *Nîşâncî* and *ṭuğra* and the sources consulted regarding them are given below.

[3] The Selcuḳid *Ṭuğrâ'î* was certainly inferior to the *Munşî'*. See el-Bundârî, loc. cit., for the pre-eminence of the *Munşî'* and *Mustawfî*.

[4] Arabic: *kuttâb* is the plural of *kâtib*. See the article in the *Encyclopaedia of Islam*.

[5] i.e. Intendant. For the word *Kâḫya* see above, p. 60, n. 3.

Grand *Vezîr*, the *Çavuş Başî*, whose primary duty it was to conduct proceedings at the sittings of the court in which these functions were performed, came to attend more generally on the minister than on the monarch and so to be regarded as yet another of his lieutenants: it is for this reason that the *Çavuş Başî* appears not only as an officer of the Household but as a functionary of the administration.[1] In D'Ohsson's description the *Kâhya Bey*, the *Re'îsü'l-Küttâb*, and the *Çavuş Başî* figure as three ministers, below the Grand *Vezîr*, whereas the *Nîşâncî* and the Head of the Finance Department figure only as Councillors of State.[2] But this designation was not applied to them in Ottoman parlance. D'Ohsson seems only to have applied it in order to give his readers an idea of their actual importance in the government by comparing them to the ministers of European states. They had gained this importance only as the importance of the Grand *Vezîr* itself had increased, in virtue of being his lieutenants. It was never recognized officially; and so neither the *Kâhya* nor the *Re'îs* ever gained a seat in the *Dîvân*, whereas the *Nîşâncî* and the Head of the Finance Department had each had one from early times. Nevertheless, we may most conveniently begin our description of the administration in detail with an account of these three lieutenants, in virtue of the prestige they derived from their immediate attachment to the Grand *Vezîr*. D'Ohsson places the *Kâhya* first, the *Re'îs* second, and the *Çavuş Başî* third. Officially, however, the *Çavuş Başî* was superior to the *Re'îs*,[3] while the *Kâhya Bey*, for reasons that will appear, had no standing at all. This being so, we propose to deal first with the *Çavuş Başî*, but to leave the *Re'îs* till last, owing to his closer connexion with other officials.

In late times the *Çavuş Başî* performed a variety of duties. They all had their origin, however, in his command of the *Çavuşes*. These had originally attended the sittings of the Sultan's court of justice for the purpose of seeing to the execution of the rulings there pronounced; and they continued so to attend after the presidency of this court had devolved on the Grand *Vezîr*. The *Çavuş*

[1] Cf. above, p. 83.

[2] D'Ohsson, vii. 159 sq. Hammer, op. cit., 101, 126, follows D'Ohsson in describing the *Kâhya*, the *Re'îs*, and the *Çavuş Başî* as ministers, and even states that they were formally raised to this rank by the Grand *Vezîr* Ibrahîm under Aḥmed III (reigned 1703–30). He does not inform us, however, what Turkish word was used as the equivalent of 'minister'; and apart from the fact that the *Dîvân* was not reorganized to give these 'ministers' a place corresponding to their alleged elevation, the Turkish sources that we have consulted do not seem to bear him out.

[3] See *O.T.E.M.*, No. 13, Appendix, p. 12, and No. 14, Appendix, p. 18 (*kânûn-nâmei 'Âli 'Oṣmân*), the *Çavuş Başî* ranked directly after the *Bölük Ağalari* (see above, p. 83, n. 1), whereas the *Re'îs*, though above all the other secretaries, ranked below the *Şehir Emîni* (see above, p. 84).

Başî gave them the necessary orders, and so played an important part in the proceedings of the court. By the eighteenth century he had come indeed to be regarded as its vice-president, and as such would hold preliminary sittings in order to save the minister's time both by making abstracts of the cases to be considered by him and by deciding which cases should be so considered and which should be brought before inferior tribunals. D'Ohsson describes him also as Minister of Police. But this is a misleading description. As we have seen, the duty of preventing crime and assuring the maintenance of order in the capital and the area surrounding it was performed by various general officers.[1] The police duty performed by the *Çavuş Başî* was still only that of executing sentences pronounced by the Grand *Vezîr* and the 'learned' magistrates that were otherwise charged with the dispensation of justice. It is true that for this purpose he had at his orders the Janissary officers called *Muḥḍir Ağa*, *'Assâs Başî*, and *Ṣubaşî*,[2] who, as we have remarked, were among those that were charged with more general police functions; but the *Çavuş Başî* was concerned in no way with the prevention, but only with the punishment, of delinquencies. It was the duty of the *Çavuşes* under him to marshal petitioners, litigants, and accused persons in the Grand *Vezîr's* court, to carry messages, and to execute certain sentences. Each of the fifteen companies of forty-two men into which their corps was divided was commanded by an officer, attached to the Grand *Vezîr's* staff;[3] and the whole corps was controlled by a Commissioner and a Secretary,[4] whose duties included the detention of highly placed, and particularly of 'learned', persons at their office. It was through the Commissioner that the *Çavuş Başî* transmitted his commands. The Secretary, for his part, registered the cases sent by the Grand *Vezîr* to inferior courts, together with the names of the *Çavuşes* charged with so transmitting them.[5]

Owing to his supervision of procedure at the Grand *Vezîr's* court the *Çavuş Başî* came also more or less to control the action of two officials called *Teẕkereci*,[6] whose duty it was alternately to read the petitions submitted for the minister's judgement, and note his decisions. The *Teẕkerecis* were officials of considerable importance. D'Ohsson places them first among his six 'Secretaries of State'.[7] Their official standing, however, was quite low. In the

1 Above, pp. 66, 104.

2 See Appendix A (B).

3 Below, Appendix C.

4 *Çavuşlar Emîni* and *Çavuşlar Kâtibi*.

5 D'Ohsson, vii. 166–7, 174; Seyyid Muṣṭafâ, i. 60; Hammer, op. cit., 119.

6 Cf. *Teẕkereli* above, p. 49. The *Teẕkeres* here concerned were the petitioners presented for consideration. The *Teẕkerecis* were entitled *Büyük* (Great) and *Küçük* (Little) respectively. D'Ohsson calls them 'Maîtres des Requêtes'.

7 The others being the *Mektûpçu* the *Teşrîfâtçi* the *Beylikçi*, and the *Kâẖya Kâtibi*, cf. Hammer, op. cit., 127.

Ḳânûn-nâme of Meḥmed the Conqueror they appear as taking precedence only of the *Re'îs's* clerks, and some way below that functionary himself.[1] As well as their duties in the *Vezîr's* court, they had that of drawing up the orders he sent out to the various government departments.[2]

The Grand *Vezîr's Kâh̲ya* was originally one of his personal servants, having nothing direct to do with the administration. But as the grandeur and responsibilities of the prime ministry increased, so the *Kâh̲ya*ship gained both in prestige and authority, till in the end it came to be filled regularly by high officers of state.[3] The *Kâh̲ya Bey*, as he was by this time called,[4] was then usually referred to as *Ağa Efendimiz* 'our *Ağa-Efendi*'.[5] He was the Grand *Vezîr's* general deputy, but particularly in home and military affairs.[6] Thus on feast days, when the functionaries of the Porte in general had a holiday, the *Kâh̲ya Bey* was obliged to remain on duty while the Grand *Vezîr* paid a round of ceremonial calls, to represent him in case of sudden crisis.[7] Moreover, besides having himself two secretaries, one for general correspondence and the collection of dues accruing to himself and the Grand *Vezîr* called *Kâh̲ya Kâtibi*,[8] and the other, called *Ḳara Ḳulaḳ*,[9] for messages passing between himself and the minister, he controlled also the Grand *Vezîr's* general secretary, called *Mektûpçu*,[10] and the *Teşrîfâtçi*,[11] or Master of Ceremonies. The latter, who had several assistants, kept registers of court ceremonial and of the prerogatives enjoyed by the various functionaries of state.[12]

[1] *O.T.E.M.*, No. 14, Appendix, p. 18.

[2] *M.T.M.* i. 502 (Friday *Dîvân*), 508 (Imperial *Dîvân*); D'Ohsson, vii. 169; Seyyid Muṣṭafâ, i. 60; Hammer, op. cit., 128.

[3] Aḥmed Râsim, ii. 313, note.

[4] To distinguish him from the Janissary officer of the same title (see above, p. 60, n. 3) he was called in full *Vezîr Kâh̲ya Beyi*.

[5] Aḥmed Râsim, loc. cit. *Ağa Efendi* is a curious combination, since *Efendi* was applied generally to 'Men of the Pen', both *'Ulemâ* and government secretaries, and *Ağa* to 'Men of the Sword'. Hammer, op. cit., 135, states that the *Kâh̲ya Bey* and the *Çavuş Başi* ranked as *Ağas*, whereas the *Re'îs* ranked as an *Efendi*.

[6] D'Ohsson, vii. 159. Cf. Hammer, op. cit., 103 *seq.*

[7] D'Ohsson, vii, 175–6. Cf. Hammer op. cit., 136.

[8] i.e. Secretary of the *Kâh̲ya*.—D'Ohsson, vii. 170; Hammer, op. cit., 132–3.

[9] D'Ohsson, vii. 175, note. Hammer, op. cit., 107. For the meaning of *Ḳara Ḳulaḳ* see Appendix C.

[10] D'Ohsson, viii, 169. *Mektûpçu* from Arabic *mektûb*, 'what is written, a letter'; and so, with Turkish consonantal change and ending, 'letter-writer'. Compare *Kâtib*, from the same Arabic root, 'he that writes'. Hammer, op. cit., 131, differs from D'Ohsson in placing the *Mektûpçu* under the supervision, not of the *Kâh̲ya*, but of the *Re'îs*.

[11] *Teşrîf*, Arabic verbal noun from *şarrafa*, 'he showed honour to', hence 'ceremony'—in plural with Turkish ending.

[12] D'Ohsson, vii. 170; Hammer, op. cit., 131–2. Hammer states that up to the reign of Aḥmed III the *Teşrîfâtçi's* office formed part of the Finance Department, and was only then transferred to the Sublime Porte.

The particular subordination of the *Kâhya*, the *Mektûpçu*, and the *Teşrîfâtçi* to the Grand *Vezîr* was marked by the fact that whereas the *Re'îs* and the *Çavuş Başi* usually dined at the *Vezîr's* table, they dined daily apart and together, even in the late eighteenth century.[1] Yet by this time they were all, in fact, of eminence. For D'Ohsson is able not only to describe the *Kâhya* as first minister, but to describe the *Mektûpçu*, the *Teşrîfâtçi*, and even the *Kâhya Kâtibi* as three of the six Secretaries of State. The *Kâhya*, these lesser officials, and many of the clerks of their respective departments subsisted largely from the shares they received of the presents offered to the Grand *Vezîr* by persons freshly appointed to government employments. They were also allowed rations from the *Vezîr's* kitchens.[2] The *Kâhya*ship, indeed, was exceedingly remunerative in later times. Many of its holders contrived to make their fortunes while in office.[3]

The *Re'îsü'l-Küttâb*, as his name implies, was primarily the principal secretary of the Chancery. Yet his authority seems even in early times to have extended beyond the Chancery proper and to have included a control of the principal secretaries of the Treasury and others,[4] though at the same time his official position, as we have indicated, was comparatively humble. The business of the Chancery consisted in the conservation of all *ḳânûns* other than those concerned with finance and fief-holding, the preparation of all imperial orders other than those concerned with financial matters, and the issue of brevets of authority, which went by various names according to their nature, to all provincial governors, military fief-holders, 'learned' office holders of various classes,[5] *Ḳapici Başis*,[6] secretaries of the administration, and beneficiaries of pensions derived from religious endowments. The department that had to do with the conservation of the *ḳânûns* and the preparation of imperial orders was called *Beylik*, a word thought to be a corruption of *Bitik*, meaning 'Document';[7] and it is perhaps an indication that the *Beylik* was originally synonymous with the Chancery as a whole that the latter was managed under the supervision of the *Re'îs* by another official called *Beylikçi*. The issue of brevets, however, was at least in later times confided to two departments other than the *Beylik*, one of which was called *Taḥvîl*[8]

[1] D'Ohsson, 176.

[2] Aḥmed Râsim, ii. 357, note.

[3] Ibid. ii. 312, note.

[4] *O.T.E.M.*, No. 14, Appendix, 18 (*Ḳânûn-nâmei Âli 'Osmân*). D'Ohsson, vii. 166, states that this was still so in his time.

[5] i.e. of *Mollâs*, *Ḳâḍîs*, *Müderrises*, *Imâms*, and *Mütevellis* (see below, ch. ix.)

[6] Above, p. 83.

[7] Obsolete in Ottoman Turkish—see Redhouse, s.vv.

[8] Arabic *taḥwîl*. Verbal noun from *ḥawwala*, 'he transferred', and so 'transference, translation'.

and the other *Rü'ûs*,[1] because the brevets issued to the first two classes of 'learned' functionaries went by the first name, and those issued to minor 'learned' men, *Ḳapîcî Başîs*, and secretaries of the administration, went by the second. Brevets issued to provincial governors were called *berât*,[2] those to military fief-holders *ḍabṭ fermânî*.[3] They were the concern also of the *Taḥvîl* office. Authorizations to draw pensions on religious foundations were likewise called *berât*, but they were issued by the office of *Rü'ûs*. In the eighteenth century the Chancery employed about one hundred and fifty clerks, of three grades.[4] Controlling them were six officials, subordinate to the *Beylikçi*.[5]

Besides his control of the Chancery, however, the *Re'îs* had two other duties, the first of which was the drawing up of the communications called *telḫîṣ* from the Grand *Vezîr* to the Sultan.[6] And for the discharge of this duty the *Re'îs* had another assistant, who, because he also signed receipts for the dues payable by newly installed military fief-holders with the word '*âmed*',[7] was known as the *Âmedci*. The *Re'îs's* second duty apart from the management of the chancery was to deal with foreign affairs, for which purpose he had to employ an interpreter.[8] In the middle period of Ottoman history, however—that is to say, from the conquest to the onset of decay—the relations of the Porte with foreign powers were comparatively simple: the Sultan merely dictated his wishes and declared war if they were not respected; so in these times the *Re'îs* was little preoccupied with such matters. Even when a treaty was first concluded with infidel France, and when the first European ambassadors took up residence at the Gate of Felicity, the Grand *Vezîrs* themselves carried out the negotiations involved, the *Re'îses*

[1] Literally 'heads'—Arabic, plural of *ra's*. In Turkish 'a commission, diploma'.

[2] From Arabic *berâ'a*, 'immunity, privilege', and hence a diploma conferring the same.

[3] Pronounced in Turkish *Zapt*. *Ḍabṭ* (Arabic), 'holding, maintenance'. *Fermân* (Persian), 'order'.

[4] *Kâtibs* (secretaries), *Şâgirds* (pupils, cf. p. 74 for *Ḥarem* women called also by this name), and '*Scharhlus*' (so D'Ohsson—Hammer has '*Scharhli*' *Şâriḫlîs*? *Şarḥlîs*?—we have not been able to ascertain the meaning of this word).

[5] These were:
(i) The *Ḳânûncu*. He looked up *Ḳânûns* relevant to any problem that arose. (ii) The *I'lâmcî* ('notifier'—from Arabic *i'lâm*, verbal noun from *a'lama*, 'he informed'). He drew up reports on such problems. (iii) The *Mümeyyiz* 'Investigator'—from Arabic *Meyyeza*, 'he separated (something from something)'. He examined and corrected documents prepared by the clerks: (iv), (v), and (vi) three *Kîsedârs* ('purse-bearers'—from Arabic *kîs*, 'a purse'), one for each department. The *Re'îs* also had an independent *Kîsedâr* of his own.

[6] Above, p. 84. See also Appendix C.

[7] Meaning, in Persian, 'It has come' (or, more strictly, 'came').

[8] *Tercümân*. Properly *tarcumân*, Arabic, a word of Aramaic origin. Corrupted to the familiar 'Dragoman' through the Greek pronunciation. The *Re'îs's* interpreter was called 'Interpreter of the *Dîvân*'—*Dîvân Tercümânî*.

merely keeping record of them, as they did of every other vezirial transaction. But gradually, as with the Sultan's retirement from the personal direction of affairs the Grand *Vezîrs* had the more to manage, and as relations with European states grew more complicated and demanded continuous attention and ingenuity, the responsibility for their conduct fell more and more on the *Re'îses*. And since *Re'îses* were seldom well informed regarding European politics, or the status, or even sometimes the whereabouts, of European states, they came to rely for advice and in negotiation more and more on their Interpreters. Up to the middle of the seventeenth century these Interpreters were usually Europeans that had turned Moslem. But by that time leading Greek Orthodox families of the Phanar quarter of the capital had begun to europeanize themselves in some degree, and were able to provide the requisite knowledge. Thenceforward, accordingly, the post of Interpreter was regularly held by a member of one of these families; and when early in the eighteenth century the Porte took, as we have related, to appointing Phanariots likewise to the Hospodarships of the Rumanian Principalities, the holder of the Interpretership was regularly chosen for whichever of these two offices fell vacant. The Interpreter's duty was to translate notes addressed by foreign envoys to the Porte and vice versa, and to interpret both for the *Re'îs* when he engaged in negotiations with such envoys, and for the Grand *Vezîr* and the Sultan when they received them in audience.[1] In later times at least, also, they used often to carry on negotiations independently, and so acquired a position of great consequence in the esteem of foreigners.

When the various offices subordinate to the *Re'îs* were created is not clear: presumably from time to time as the need for them arose with the increase of business.[2] It is improbable that they all existed in the time of Meḥmed II; and their creation doubtless contributed to the *Re'îs's* advancement. This in the main, however, was due in the first place to his attachment to the Grand *Vezîr*—to the circumstance indeed that he was still officially a 'servant'—so that with the *Vezîr's* other servants he came to be recognized, so to speak, unofficially as a public figure of mark. In the second place, and even more, it was due to the ever-increasing importance of foreign affairs in the councils of the Empire. Foreign observers of later times were apt perhaps to attribute an eminence to the

[1] *M.T.M.* i. 517–18 (*Ḳânûn-nâme* of 'Abdu'r-Raḥmân Tevḳî'î—*Ḳânûn* of the *Re'îsü'l-Küttâb*); D'Ohsson, vii. 159–66; Hammer, op. cit., 110, sq., 131; Lybyer, 184–5; *Encyclopaedia of Islam*, art. 'Terdjumān'.

[2] Seyyid Muṣṭafâ, i. 91, states that the number of *ḳalems* was increased as time went on; and Aḥmed Râsim, ii. 358–9, note, contrasts posts such as those of the *Âmedci* and *Mektûpçu*, for which fiefs were not provided, with others of earlier foundation, for which they were.

Re'îs Efendi that he scarcely enjoyed in the eyes of his compatriots, because next to the Grand *Vezîr* he was brought most constantly to their attention, whereas most contemporary Ottomans knew little and cared less about the Domain of War. But he was undoubtedly of far greater influence on the conduct of affairs than either of his two fellow 'ministers'.

We have now accounted for all the officials that stood, under the Grand *Vezîr*, at the apex of the governmental triangle. And we have noticed that most of the business that in Moslem administrations in general was dealt with by officials standing at one of the points of the base—namely, those that controlled correspondence, the registration of documents, and the issue of commands and regulations—came in the Ottoman scheme under the more immediate purview of the prime minister. We may now, accordingly, pass on to describe the departments that did in fact stand at this point in the Ottoman administration, the most distinguished official of which was, as we have already indicated, the *Nîşâncı*, the Affixer of the Sign.

The use of a royal cipher (*tawḳî'*, *tevḳî'*) was inherited by the Ottomans from the 'Abbâsids, that of a *ṭuğra*—a specifically Turkish badge—from the Selcuḳids; and the latter came into use in the Ottoman Empire as early as the reign of Orḫân in the fourteenth century.[1] But it was not till the reign of Meḥmed II, after the conquest, that the office of *Nîşâncı*—or *Tevḳî'î*,[2] as he was also called—was created.[3] At first the new official would seem to have been given some authority both over the Chancery and its head, the *Re'îs*, and over another department, that of the *Defter-ḫâne*, in which all documents relating to fiefs were preserved, and *its* head, the *Defter Emîni*, or Commissioner of the Register.[4] The latter office was in any case always independent of the Grand *Vezîr* in a way that the Chancery was not.[5] The above-mentioned authority arose from the nature of the *Nîşâncı's* duties, as then

[1] *Encyclopaedia of Islam*, art. 'Ṭug̲h̲rā'. See now also P. Wittek, "Notes sur la Tughra ottomane" in *Byzantion XVIII* (1948), pp. 311–334, where a list is given of published reproductions of *ṭoğras* of the Sultans from Orḫân to Maḥmûd II.

[2] *Nîşâncı* is from the Persian *nîşân*, 'sign', with Turkish ending. *Tevḳî'î* is from *tevḳî'* as above. 'Abdu'r-Raḥmân Tevḳî'î, whose *Ḳânûn-nâme* we have frequently quoted, was thus a *Nîşâncı*.

[3] See *O.T.E.M.*, No. 13, Appendix, 5 (Introduction to the *Ḳânûn-nâme* of Meḥmed II—*Ḳânûn-nâmei Âli 'Os̲mân*).

[4] See Seyyid Muṣṭafâ, i. 58. The word *defter* is a corruption of the Greek *diphthera*, a parchment, register, or book—*Encyclopaedia of Islam*, s.v. So *Defter-dâr*, 'register-keeper' (cf. *Silîḥ-dâr*, *Ḫazîne-dâr*, above, pp. 70 and 74, n. 4); *Defter-ḫâne*, 'register-house'.

[5] See Aḥmed Râsim, ii. 358, where the *Defter-ḫâne* is represented as forming one of the three fundamental departments of state, together with the *Dîvân* (meaning here the *Vezîr's* chancery) and the Finance Office (*Ḫazîne*, literally, 'Treasury').

defined. For though his primary function was the tracing of the *ṭuğra* on official documents of various kinds, he was at first empowered as well to examine and correct them, comparing them on the one hand with such *ḳânûns* as existed on the topics to which they referred, and, on the other, in special cases, modifying *ḳânûns* to harmonize with decrees newly issued. But in order to fulfil this duty the *Nîşânci* was obliged to consult the archives, which were kept in part by the *Beylikçi*, as we have seen, and in part by the *Defter Emîni*.

Owing to his power of altering documents to harmonize with already existent *ḳânûns*, the *Nîşânci* in these early times came to be compared with the 'learned' functionary, the *Muftî*,[1] whose function it was to state whether any projected action harmonized with the Sacred Law: the *Nîşânci* was therefore regarded as 'the *Muftî* of *Ḳânûns*'.[2] But he differed from his 'learned' counterpart in being authorized, on occasions, to alter the texts to which such references were made. He might do so, however, only upon receiving a special order called *taṣḥîḥ fermâni* (Correction Order),[3] on which the Grand *Vezîr* drew the *ṭuğra* with his own hands (so that such orders might not be confected by the *Nîşânci* himself). After making the required alteration and returning the *ḳânûn* to the archives, the *Nîşânci* would preserve the *taṣḥîḥ fermâni* to justify his action.[4]

The discharge of these duties required considerable erudition on the part of *Nîşâncis*. They were therefore chosen, in these early days, either from among a certain class of 'Learned Men',[5] or were promoted from the office of *Re'îs* or from that of Head of the Finance Department. Nevertheless, the latter, the *Defterdâr*, as he was called, was held to be of equal dignity with the *Nîşânci* unless the *Nîşânci* had been elevated either to the Vezîrate

[1] See below, ch. x, iii.

[2] See *M.T.M.* i. 516 (*Ḳânûn-nâme* of 'Abdu'r-Raḥmân Tevḳî'î).

[3] *Taṣḥîḥ*, Arabic, verbal noun from *ṣaḥḥaḥa*, 'he corrected'. In the *Encyclopaedia of Islam*, art. 'Ṭug̲h̲rā', this operation—*taṣḥîḥ*—on the part of the *Nîşânci* is represented as a verification rather than a correction of *ḳânûns*: that is to say that these orders authorized the *Nîşânci* merely to compare current orders with *ḳânûns* to ensure their harmonization. But it hardly seems likely that orders of such dignity as these *taṣḥîḥ fermânlari* evidently were should have authorized the *Nîşânci* to do no more than inspect the *ḳânûns*. For such an inspection must surely have been one of his routine duties, involved in his right of correcting the documents submitted to him. Moreover, we know that from time to time alterations *were* made in *ḳânûns* (cf. *O.T.E.M.*, No. 13, Appendix), and that the *Nîşânci* was commonly charged with the redaction of the collections of *ḳânûns* known as *ḳânûn-nâmes* (see *Encyclopaedia of Islam*, loc. cit.). It may be presumed, therefore, that such alterations were likewise the business of the *Nîşânci*, that authorization to make them would be conveyed with some solemnity, and that precautions would be taken to prevent unauthorized alterations.

[4] *M.T.M.*, loc. cit.

[5] *Müderrises* (professors) of *Dâḫil* and *Ṣaḥn* rank (see below, ch. xi).

or to a rank next below it.[1] In this case his superiority to the *Defterdâr* was officially acknowledged;[2] but in any case he is usually placed, in accounts of the ceremonial to be observed at *dîvâns*, at which both were entitled to seats, before the *Defterdâr*.[3] And by the middle of the seventeenth century his official superiority to that official seems to have increased. For in a *ḳânûn-nâme* of that period we find him seated (at such *dîvâns*) on the Grand *Vezîr's* right, whereas the *Defterdâr* is seated on his left.[4]

By this time, nevertheless, the *Nîşâncî's* real importance had suffered a decline. His office, as we have seen, constituted some kind of check on the proceedings of the Grand *Vezîr*, since even 'Correction orders' could only be issued with the Sultan's knowledge; and by the middle of the seventeenth century the Sultans had retired from the conduct of affairs, leaving the Grand *Vezîrs* in charge. Most posts in the administration were by then conferred by favour, often on unsuitable persons; and whether or not because the Grand *Vezîrs* preferred to weaken the *Nîşâncî's* authority, the office was now usually given to *Ḫâṣṣ Odalîs* or *Ağas* of the Stirrup and formed a stepping-stone to no less incongruous a post than the Admiralty.[5] So far the *Nîşâncîs* still possessed the right, whether they often exercised it or not, to control and correct the documents submitted to them for adornment with the *ṭuğra*. But under Aḥmed III this right was officially abolished.[6] On the other hand, the *Nîşâncî* now had the drawing of the *ṭuğra* as his exclusive privilege, whereas up to the reign of Ibrahîm he had shared it with the *Ḳubbe Vezîrs*, who in early times, when the *Nîşâncîs* were occupied with less mechanical duties, had often relieved them in this one.[7] Otherwise the office became a sinecure, like a number of others that we shall refer to in their places, retaining, like them, only conventional eminence. Meanwhile, the office of *Defter Emîni*, for other causes, had likewise declined in importance to an almost equal degree. In the eighteenth century, therefore, the two were conferred for life, unlike those of the rest of the administration, being held alternately by two functionaries, year by year.[8]

[1] The rank of *Beylerbeyi* of Rumelia (see below, p. 141).
[2] *O.T.E.M.*, No. 13, Appendix, 13–14 (*Ḳânûn-nâme* of Meḥmed II).
[3] Seyyid Muṣṭafâ, i. 58; Aḥmed Râsim, i. 156, note.
[4] *M.T.M.* i. 508 (*Ḳânûn-nâme* of 'Abdu'r-Raḥmân Tevḳî'î).
[5] Seyyid Muṣṭafâ, ii. 90; Aḥmed Râsim, ii. 312, note.
[6] D'Ohsson, vii. 192.
[7] *M.T.M.* i. 499 (*Ḳânûn-nâme* of 'Abdu'r-Raḥmân Tevḳî'î); Seyyid Muṣṭafâ, i. 91; *Encyclopaedia of Islam*, art. 'Ṭughrā'. A *Ḳubbe Vezîr*, in his capacity of sign-affixer, was called *Ṭuğra-keş*, '*Ṭuğra*-Drawer' (from Persian *kaşîdan*, 'to draw'). According to Hammer, *Staatsverwaltung*, 133, in his day it was by an assistant to the *Nîsâncî*, also called *Ṭuğra-keş*, that documents were actually adorned with the monogram.
[8] Aḥmed Râsim, ii. 314–15, note.

The *Defter-ḫâne*, managed by the *Defter Emîni*, was divided into three departments. The first of these, called *Icmâl* (Summary),[1] dealt with the documents in which the limits of all provinces and their subdivisions, and of all fiefs, were defined. The second, called *Mufaṣṣal*,[2] dealt with similar documents regarding private property; and the third, called *Rüznâme*,[3] with changes in fief-holding. In the late eighteenth century it was staffed by about a hundred clerks.[4] By that time, however, its importance had very greatly declined, owing to the decay into which the Ottoman feudal system had fallen. For the existence of the *Defter-ḫâne* side by side with and independently of the Finance Department corresponded, of course, with the maintenance of some state employees, including troops, on a feudal basis, while the rest were paid for their services in money. But this feudal scheme, which, as we have explained, allowed its beneficiaries to collect tithes and dues on the lands assigned to them, required little attention in comparison with that which it was necessary to devote to the finances proper, even though in early times the number of persons supported by fiefs was far greater than that of the recipients of pay and allowances. And so from the first the *Defter Emîni* was an official much inferior to the *Defterdâr*; indeed his office was then a regular stepping-stone to the Finance Department.[5] In precedence he seems at first to have ranked after the *Cebeci* and *Ṭopçu Başîs*,[6] and immediately above the *Şehir Emîni*.[7] Except the *Nîşâncî* and the *Defterdâr*, he was then the most highly placed of all the secretaries (as opposed to the *Ağas*—of the army and the Household), being superior by two places to the *Re'îsü'l-Küttâb*.[8] Nevertheless, he seems to have been generally regarded as of less eminence than the *Re'îs*, partly, perhaps, because not only did he (like the *Re'îs*) have no seat at the *Dîvân*, he did not even appear at it. Thus in Turkish accounts of the structure of the administration six officials (called *Ḳalem Ricâlî*, or Heads of Departments)[9] are mentioned as holding the chief

[1] Arabic.

[2] Literally, 'detailed' (Arabic), i.e. a detailed register. Redhouse, s.v., referring to this register, explains it as 'a detailed doomsday-book of Turkey, containing a list of every separate estate; also, name of the office where this register is kept'.

[3] *Rüznâme* (Persian, from *roz*, 'day', and *nâme*, 'a book, a document, a letter'), 'a day-book, a journal' (cf. below, p 130). Generally one recording receipts and disbursements. Here one recording day-to-day transferences of fiefs.

[4] D'Ohsson, vii. 193; Lybyer, 172.

[5] *O.T.E.M.*, No. 14, Appendix, 17 (*Ḳânûn-nâmei 'Âlî 'Osmân*).

[6] Above, pp. 67–68.

[7] Above, p. 84.

[8] Ibid., pp. 18, 22.

[9] *Ḳalem* (Arabic), 'a reed, a reed-pen'. The term *Ahl el-Ḳalem*, 'People of the Pen', being used to mean employees of government departments, *ḳalem*, by a semantic transition, comes to denote such departments collectively (as here), or singly, in which case its plural *aḳlâm* is used also. *Ricâl* (also Arabic) is the plural of *Racul*, 'man'. In Turkish it is used particularly of important persons, as '*Ricâli Devlet*', 'statesmen'.

places—*Menâṣibi Sitte* (the Six Posts)[1]—in it; and of these six posts the *Re'îs* is shown as holding the third (after the *Nîşâncî* and the Head *Defterdâr*) and the *Defter Emîni* the fourth; while the fifth and sixth are held by two minor *Defterdârs*.[2] These six officials all appear in D'Ohsson's account, but arranged in another order. The *Re'îs*, as we have seen, is elevated by him to the dignity of minister, whereas the other five are called Councillors of State. And of these five D'Ohsson gives the first three places to the *Defterdârs* (though the second two were mere sinecures by his time), the fourth to the *Nîşâncî*, and the fifth to the *Defter Emîni*.[3] The *Defter Emîni*, it may be noted, like the *Re'îs*, the *Çavuş Başî*, and the *Nîşâncî*, had as his secretary and messenger a *Kîsedâr*.[4]

If we have placed the *Defter Emîni* at the *Nîşâncî's* end of our imaginary administrative triangle it is because he was regarded as in some degree coming under the authority of that functionary, whereas he had little, apparently, to do with the *Defterdâr*. But in fact he stood as it were between the two, since the matters with which his registers dealt were exclusively economic. In considering his department, therefore, we may imagine ourselves to have moved towards the third point of the triangle, at which we now arrive.

The *Defter Emîni* and the *Defterdâr*, as their styles indicate, were both concerned with the keeping of *Defters* or registers; but those under the control of the *Defterdâr* referred to all the revenues accruing in money and kind to the central treasury, to such expenditure of these funds as was necessary, to the storage and use of surpluses, and to the procuring of other resources on the occurrence of a deficit. This being so the business of his department required the attention of many more officials and clerks than those employed in all the other departments of the administration put together, the more so in that the Finance Department had, apart from a large number of accountancy bureaux, both a chancery of its own, called *Mâliye Ḳalemi*,[5] and a court in which disputes that arose between the government and private persons regarding monetary matters were tried. The Finance

[1] *Menâṣib* (Arabic), plural of *menṣab*, 'a station', from *naṣaba*, 'he set, he planted'.

[2] Seyyid Muṣṭafâ, ii. 90; Aḥmed Râsim, i. 381, note.

[3] D'Ohsson, vii. 192–3.

[4] See *M.T.M.* i. 515 (*Ḳânûn-nâme* of 'Abdu'r-Raḥmân Tevḳî'î—*Ḳânûn* of the *Nîşâncî*).

[5] Cf. p. 127, n. 9, above. *Mâliye* is from the Arabic *Mâl*, 'riches, money'. The adjectival forms *mâlî*, *mâlîya*, however, are not classical. The latter is used substantivally in Turkish with the meanings 'finance, financial affairs': so *Mâliye Ḳalemi*, 'Department, or Bureau, of Finance'. The Finance Office, inclusive of all the departments controlled by the *Defterdâr*, was usually referred to as the *Ḥazînei 'Âmire*, 'the State Treasury'.

Office was housed, not in the Sublime Porte, but in a building of its own. And just as an alternative name for the Sublime Porte was *Paşa Ḳapîsî*, so this building was called *Defterdâr Ḳapîsî*: 'the Gate of the *Defterdâr*'.[1]

The *Defterdâr* was from the time of the conquest an official of the first consequence. As we have seen, he ranked as equal with the *Nîşâncî* immediately (excluding the *Ḳubbe Vezîrs* and the chief 'learned men') after the Grand *Vezîr*. And if the *Nîşâncî* was regarded as the 'first between equals' because of his authority to draw the imperial cipher, the *Defterdâr* was otherwise distinguished as the sole official of the administration who had the right of presenting petitions to the Sultan in person.[2] At that time the Empire consisted only of 'Rumelia' and 'Anatolia'. But already the *Defterdâr* was provided with an assistant to deal with the finances of Anatolia, so that those of Rumelia were regarded as the *Defterdâr's* especial province.[3] Under Bâyezîd II the assistant was entitled *Defterdâr* also—'of the second class';[4] and when in the sixteenth century vast additions were made to the Empire, still other *Defterdârs* were appointed to manage the finances of the newly conquered territories.[5] These seem all, however, to have been subordinate to the *Defterdâr* of Rumelia; and when on the loss of Hungary at the end of the seventeenth century, the *Defterdârlîḳ* that had been created under Süleymân the Magnificent to

[1] Up to 1708 the Finance Office was housed in a mansion then appointed as a residence for a *Sulṭân*; from 1708 to 1755 in the *Yere-batan Serây* (built over the vaulted Byzantine cistern that still goes by that name: 'the Palace sinking into the ground'); and thereafter in a building in the outer court of the Imperial *Serây*, its archives then being stored next the Mosque of Sulṭân Aḥmed and the office of the *Nîşâncî*. Hammer, *Constantinopolis und der Bosporus*, 329–30

[2] *O.T.E.M.*, No. 13, Appendix, 14 (*Ḳânûn-nâmei Âli 'Oşmân*). The other persons thus privileged were the *Ḳâḍî-'askers* and the White eunuchs.

[3] Aḥmed Râsim, i. 154, note; *Encyclopaedia of Islam*, art. 'Defterdār'.

[4] D'Ohsson, vii. 261. 'Of the second class'—*Şaḳḳi Sânî* (Arabic), *şaḳḳ* meaning 'fissure', and so 'section'. According to Hammer, op. cit., 143, a *Defterdârî Şaḳḳi Sânî* was appointed only in 1576 under Murâd III, and was known also as *Muḳâṭa'a Defterdârî*, '*Defterdâr* of Leases' (for *muḳâṭa'as* or 'leases' see below). But Hammer's account is not very clear, since, having mentioned the creation of an earlier *Defterdârlîḳ* of Aleppo, he then ignores the latter, and also places the *Defterdârî Şaḳḳi Sânî* after the *Anadolu Defterdârî* and so third, despite his style.

[5] It is usually stated that in the sixteenth century there were four *Defterdârs*, one for Rumelia, one for Anatolia, one for Syria, Egypt, and Diyâr Bekir (created by Selîm I), and one for Hungary and the Danubian area (created by Süleymân I)—see D'Ohsson, 261; Lybyer, 168; *Encyclopaedia of Islam*, art. 'Defter'. 'Aṭâ, i. 96, however, states that Selîm I created *Defterdârliks* not only for Damascus (i.e. Syria), but also for Aleppo, Bosnia, and Erḍerum; and Hammer, op. cit., 144, that (as well as those of Rumelia, Anatolia, Aleppo, the Danube, Damascus, Diyâr, and Erḍerum) there were in later times others for Tripoli of Syria, Sivas, and Ḳaraman. D'Ohsson, loc. cit., adds that under Selîm II and Murâd III every province (*eyâlet*) had its *defterdâr*. But possibly these (and some of those mentioned by Hammer) were provincial *Mâl Defterdârîs*, not resident at the capital—see below, p. 150.

control the various provinces lying along the Danube was suppressed, the *Defterdâr* of Rumelia, or *Baş Defterdâr* (as he had always been called) assumed responsibility for the finances of the entire Empire. Two other *Defterdârlıḳs* remained in being. But thenceforth they were sinecures, conferred, like the posts of *Nîşâncı* and *Defter Emîni*, for life.[1]

In the time of Meḥmed the Conqueror the *Baş Defterdârlıḳ* was open to persons holding the offices of *Defter Emîni*, *Şehir Emîni*, *Ḳâḍî* (of a certain rank), and *Re'îsü'l-Küttâb*. Like the *Nîşâncı*, the *Defterdâr* might already be elevated to the rank of *vezîr*. At the beginning of the Conqueror's *Ḳânûn-nâme* he is mentioned, like and directly after the Grand *Vezîr*, as the Sultan's deputy (*vekîl*) for finance, the Grand *Vezîr* being, however, his inspector (*nâẓir*). In money matters, it is further stated, there is no appeal against the *Defterdâr's* decision; and he, like the Grand *Vezîr* and the *Ḳâḍî-'askers* only, has the right to issue orders adorned with the *ṭuğra* (always, of course, regarding financial affairs).[2]

D'Ohsson, in his 'Tableau', gives a complete description of the Finance Office as it existed in his day. But it is clear from the names of the various bureaux into which part of it was divided that these had been created from time to time as new types of business arose to be dealt with. Whether some of these bureaux had during the period of their activity come under the control of one or other of the lesser *Defterdârs*, and whether there had earlier been yet other bureaux, suppressed when their services were no longer required, we have not been able to discover. It is clear, at any rate, that they had never been thoroughly reorganized. And so we find business distributed very unsystematically between them.

It seems probable that there were originally four types of bureau, if we exclude both the chancery mentioned above and a special bureau—that of the *Ta'rîḫçi* (or Dater)[3] where all documents emanating from the others were dated. These four types were called respectively *Rüznâme* (Day-Book),[4] *Muḥâsebe* (Accountancy),[5] *Muḳâbele* (Check),[6] and *Mevḳûfât* (Contributions in Kind).[7] The Accountancy departments kept records of receipts

[1] D'Ohsson, vii. 261–2; Aḥmed Râsim, ii. 315.
[2] *O.T.E.M.*, Nos. 13 and 14, Appendix, 10, 16, 17 (*Ḳânûn-nâmei Âli 'Oṣmân*).
[3] *Ta'rîḫ* (Arabic), 'date'. [4] Cf. above, p. 127.
[5] Arabic.
[6] From Arabic *ḳâbala*, one meaning of which is 'he collated, or compared'—for instance, one manuscript with another.
[7] From Arabic *mawḳûf*, 'stopped, immobilized'—applied to these contributions because they were 'immobilized' as far as those that furnished them were concerned: they could neither use them themselves nor trade in them, just as property was otherwise *mawḳûf* by the act—*waḳf*—of making it over for the

and disbursements of money in detail. The Check departments kept the rolls of the standing cavalry and infantry, the Pages, the Palace Door-keepers (*Ḳapîcîs*), and the personnel of the imperial stables—they were called 'Check' because persons of these categories entitled to pay could draw it only after obtaining countersignature of their certificates from these offices. The department of Contributions in Kind registered both the collection of these contributions from the provinces in war time and their distribution: in part these were stored in magazines at the capital and at fortresses on the frontiers, in part they were supplied direct to the commanders of forces on campaign. The Day-Book department, as its name implied, received daily accounts of receipts and expenses from all the other departments of the Finance Office, and once or twice a year produced a 'balance-sheet' (*ḫulâṣaî icmâl*)[1] for the perusal of the Sultan and the Grand *Vezîr*.

Of these four types of department only those called Accountancy need further description at this stage. For, on the one hand, there was never more than one department for contributions in kind, and, on the other, it seems probable that even in the days of the Conqueror there were, as later, only two 'check' departments, one for the infantry, the other for the cavalry and the various categories of palace employees. There were, it is true, also two 'Day-book' departments, but the second, called Little (while the chief one was called Great),[2] was probably a later creation, and by D'Ohsson's time had come to discharge duties quite inappropriate to its name.[3]

There were, eventually, five Accountancy departments, called *Baş* (Chief), *Anadolu* (Anatolia), *Ḥarameyn* (Holy Cities),[4] *Cizye* (Poll-tax), and *Küçük Evḳâf* (Small Endowments). These quite clearly fall into three groups: the first two together, the *Cizye* by itself, and the *Ḥarameyn* and *Küçük Evḳâf* together. The *Ḥarameyn Muḥâsebesi* cannot have been so called before the reign of Selîm I, when the Ḥijâz was added to the Empire. It seems likely that there was at first a single accountancy office for endowments —*Evḳâf Muḥâsebesi*—its concern being to keep registers of such imperial foundations and of the salaries provided from them for the 'learned men' that managed them, and to issue to the latter their certificates of nomination. But eventually there came to be

endowment of a religious or charitable institution. Similarly the official—of the *Defter-ḫâne*—that administered vacant fiefs (temporarily 'immobilized') was called *Mevḳûfâtçi*.

[1] *Ḫulâṣaî icmâl* (Arabic in Persian construction) means actually 'Quintessence of the Summary' (cf. *Icmâl* above, p. 127).

[2] *Küçük* and *Büyük* respectively.

[3] It then kept the rolls of the *Ḳapîcî Başîs* (see above, p. 83) and the *Levends* or marines (see above, p. 99). So D'Ohsson. Hammer, op. cit., 153, adds the rolls of sea captains, *Çâşnî-gîrs* and *Gedikli Za'îms* (See Appendix B (c) 7 (iv).

[4] i.e. Mecca and Medina. See above, p. 77, n. 1.

three departments concerned with these matters: the two we have mentioned and a third called *Ḥarameyn Muḳâṭa'asî*. *Muḳâṭa'a* means the lease of a tax-farm.[1] In later times, as we shall explain, the collection of tithes and dues accruing to the Treasury was not confided to salaried government employees but 'farmed out' to contractors. No less than nine departments of the Finance Office as constituted in D'Ohsson's days went, therefore, by the name of *Muḳâṭa'a* or Lease. One of these was created to deal with the lease of contracts for the farming of tithes and dues on property belonging to the imperial endowments of Mecca and Medina: the *Ḥarameyn Muḳâṭa'asî* in question. Whatever its scope originally, however, this came eventually to be confined to such leases as referred only to property of the kind in Asia, whereas similar property in Europe, as well as all property belonging to other imperial endowments, was then dealt with by the department that we have supposed to have been originally called *Evḳâf Muḥâsebesi* and which, owing to this connexion with the endowments of the Holy Cities, was later called *Ḥarameyn Muḥâsebesi*. Moreover, the issue of certificates of appointment to learned posts came to be similarly divided between the two departments: the *Ḥarameyn Muḥâsebesi* issued those that referred to Europe, the *Ḥarameyn Muḳâṭa'asî* those that referred to Asia. As for the Small Endowment department, its business was merely to keep registers of the salaries of persons attached to the service of such charitable establishments as hospitals, soup-kitchens, and asylums for the insane.

The secretaries of the *Cizye Muḥâsebesi* kept the rolls of the poll-tax imposed on *Ẕimmîs*, or non-Moslems,[2] and prepared the demand forms that were sent out yearly to the provinces shortly before the date of collection. Theirs was one of the few departments never burdened with supplementary and often anomalous duties. On the other hand, the *Baş Muḥâsebe*, which is said to have been the 'fundamental basis'[3] of the Finance Office, and its offshoot the *Anadolu Muḥâsebesi*, dealt between them with almost every variety of business other than those we have already mentioned and such tax-farm contracts as came under the 'Lease' departments.

Thus the *Baş Muḥâsebe* kept registers, first, of moneys received and disbursed by all the commissioners (*Emîns*), namely, those

[1] Arabic *ḳâṭa'a*, 'he made an engagement with a person on condition of an annual payment'—a post-classical use, probably related to *aḳṭa'a*, 'he granted (land) as a *ḳaṭîa* (or fief)'. For these leases resembled fiefs in that the holders of each were empowered to collect taxes and dues. Moreover, the Treasury received a fixed sum from the grant of such leases, instead of one proportionate to the yield of the dues, &c., imposed in the area concerned.

[2] For *Ẕimmîs* and the *Cizye* see below, ch. xiv.

[3] *Üssi esâsî*, see Aḥmed Râsim, ii. 378, note.

attached to the Household: the *Şehir Emîni*, the *Ḍarb-ḫâne Emîni*, the *Arpa Emîni*, and the *Maṭbaḫ Emîni*;[1] those attached to the *Ṭopçu* corps: the *Ṭop-ḫâne Nâẓiri* and the *Bârûd-ḫâne Emînis*;[2] and the Commissioner of the Admiralty (*Tersâne Emîni*).[3] It likewise kept registers, secondly, of money contributions received from the provinces; thirdly, of the pay of frontier garrisons; and fourthly, of munitions of war. It was further a depot of contracts for state supplies, and presumably in connexion with them received accounts payable by the Treasury, and prepared certificates, called *Mîrî Teẓkeresis*[4] authorizing their payment. These are said by D'Ohsson to have been the 'original' duties of the department. In later times, however, it was allotted still others, though special clerks grouped in 'sub-departments' were then appointed to deal with them. The first of these sub-departments was called *Mâlikâne Ḳalfasi̊*.[5] It registered such tax-farm leases as were granted, against an initial payment, to contractors for life. The second was called *Ẓimmet*[6] (obligation) because it kept accounts of state debts; and the third was called *Muḫallefât*,[7] because it registered revenues that accrued to the Sultan, and were paid not into the public but into the 'Inside' treasury, from successions and property confiscated from *Ḳapi̊ Ḳullari̊*.

The *Anadolu Muḥâsebesi* was perhaps the department at one time managed by the second *Defterdâr*. In the eighteenth century, however, it was by no means especially concerned with Anatolian affairs. It then merely kept the accounts of various tax-farms and imperial domains (*Ḫavâṣṣi̊ Hümâyun*), and the pay-rolls of veterans and troops garrisoned in the Archipelago.

As for the remaining departments, they consisted first, as we have indicated, of eight others for the registration of leases, of two called *Büyük Ḳal'a* and *Küçük Ḳal'a* (Great and Small Fortress), and of two called *Sipâh Ḳalemi* and *Si̊liḥdâr Ḳalemi* (*Sipâhî* and *Si̊liḥdâr* Bureaux). Three of the 'Lease' departments, called by place-names, Bursa, Avlonya, and Keffe, dealt merely with tax-

[1] i.e. the Commissioners of the City, the Mint, Forage Supplies, and the Kitchen (above, pp. 84–85).

[2] Above, p. 68.

[3] Above, p. 103. Hammer, op. cit., 147, groups the *Emîns* differently, stating that those of the City, the Admiralty, the Kitchen, and the Forage Supplies, were known as *Ümenâi Erba'a*, 'the Four Commissioners' *par excellence*.

[4] For *Teẓkere* see above, p. 49. The adjective *mîrî* here used substantivally, from Arabic *Emîr*, and hence meaning 'princely' or 'royal', was applied to the Treasury especially, which was commonly called simply 'the *Mîrî*'.

[5] i.e. 'Assistant of the Life Leases'. For *Mâlikâne* see below, p. 255, for *Ḳalfa* App. B (A). As explained below, each main department had several *Ḳalfas*; and when these sub-departments were added to them, each was managed by another.

[6] Cf. ch. xiv, below, for the *Ẓimmet* or *Ẓimma* contracted by *Ẓimmîs*.

[7] From Arabic *ḫallafa*, 'he left (something) behind him'.

farm leases in the provinces concerned. But the business of the others was more complicated. There was in the first place a *Baş Muḳâṭaʿa*, or Chief Lease, department, which was concerned with five different categories of leases. Thus certain particularly large tax-farms were called *Neẓâret* (Inspectorate), and leases for these, all apparently referring to districts situated on the right bank of the Danube, formed the chief category. The others were leases of farms for the collection of dues payable on rice crops (in Rumelia), salt mining, fishing (in the Black and Aegean Seas), and, lastly, timber-felling.[1] Probably the next most important of these departments was the *Maʿden Muḳâṭaʿasi̊* which existed primarily to register the leases of gold- and silver-mines.[2] But in time it had come to discharge other duties, totally unconnected with mining. Thus it also kept account, on the one hand, of tribute received both from the Hospodars and from the Gypsies (as a special category of *Z̲immîs*), and, on the other, of receipts from the yield of dues on the cultivation and transport of tobacco, and of the octroi imposed on commodities entering the principal cities of Rumelia, including the capital. A third department, the *Istanbul Muḳâṭaʿasi̊*, had duties scarcely less varied. Though it did in fact deal with the leases of tax-farms in the area surrounding the capital, it dealt also with certain others in western Thrace, and registered receipts from the market dues of Istanbul and Adrianople, and from dues on silk and objects made of gold and silver. The remaining two 'Lease' departments were called *H̱âṣṣlar Muḳâṭaʿasi̊* and *Sâliyâne Muḳâṭaʿasi̊* respectively, the first because the leases in question were those granted for the collection of tithes and dues in fiefs of the highest category, the second because it arranged for the payment of yearly salaries (*sâliyâne* meaning 'yearly')[3] to captains of the fleet, and of yearly pensions to the *H̱ans* of the Crimea and some of their officers. Why this department should have been called *Muḳâṭaʿa* is less evident. Perhaps it was that special revenues were set aside to meet the expenditure on these salaries, and that contractors (*mültezims*) leased the right of collection.

As for the 'Fortress' and 'Cavalry' bureaux, the *Büyük Ḳalʿa* kept rolls of garrisons and local levies stationed in fortresses on the frontiers in general and those along the Danube in particular, while the *Küçük Ḳalʿa* did the same for the local troops engaged to reinforce garrisons in Albania and the Morea. The bureaux of the *Sipâhs* and *Si̊li̊ḥdârs* existed merely to issue pay certificates to the men of these two *Bölüks*, which had to be countersigned at

[1] So D'Ohsson. Hammer, op. cit., 159, adds the leases of the customs in all ports on the Black Sea.

[2] *Maʿden* (Arabic), meaning 'a mine'.

[3] In Persian—from *Sâl*, 'year'.

the Cavalry Check department before payment might be obtained. The Four *Bölüks* had no corresponding bureaux in the Finance Office. Their certificates were prepared under the direction of their commanders, but had likewise to be countersigned at the Cavalry Check department.

These were all the departments of the Finance Office except its chancery, which was reckoned as one of them. Before we describe the latter, however, there is still a point to note—in connexion with the department of Contributions in Kind. This from some comparatively early date had been given the registration of revenues accruing from two taxes, levied on town dwellers, called *'Avâriḍ*[1] and *Bedeli Nüzûl.*[2] And later it was also, like the *Baş Muḥâsebe*, provided with three sub-departments for the registration of receipts from other taxes. One of these was a 10 per cent. commission[3] on the advance payments for 'life leases' (*mâlikâne*), one a due accruing from the Courier or Post system,[4] and the third a due on sheep.[5]

What we have called the Chancery of the Finance Office, the *Mâliye Ḳâlemi*, had as its chief function the drawing up of edicts regarding finance. These were signed by the *Defterdâr* and were adorned with the *ṭuğra*. But the department was also charged with the issue of diplomas to the learned men and pensioners that had received certificates from the three departments concerned with the registration of endowment funds. In late times the Chancery, again, had a sub-department attached to it. This was known as *Piskopos* (Bishop) *Ḳalfasi*,[6] and dealt with all matters concerning the finances of Christian churches and monasteries.

There were thus, in D'Ohsson's time, twenty-five main and seven subsidiary *ḳalems*, or departments. Each of the former was managed by a secretary (*Ḫoca*),[7] assisted by a *Kîsedâr*,[8] several *Ḳalfas*, and a number of clerks of two ranks. In the *Ḳânûn-nâme* of the Conqueror the principal *Ḫocas*, namely, those that managed Day-book, Check, and Lease departments, are shown as being

[1] Arabic, plural of *'âriḍa*, 'accident, unforeseen event'. This tax was originally levied to meet unforeseen expenses.

[2] That is, 'payment in lieu of lodging contributions'.

[3] Called *Ḳalemiye*, from *ḳalem* (see above, p. 127, note 9).

[4] Called *Menzil* (Arabic), 'travelling-stage'.

[5] Called *'Âdeti Ağnam*. For *'âdet*, 'custom', see above, p. 23. Here it means customary due on sheep—*ağnâm* (Arabic)—see below, p. 240.

[6] Cf. p. 133, n. 5, above.

[7] From Persian *ḫwâca*, meaning 'a man of distinction', but particularly a teacher. Under the Selcuḳids it had already come to be applied to officials of the *Dîvân*, so that the *Vezîr* was also referred to as *Ḫwâca-yi Buzurg*, 'the Great *Ḫwâca*'. In Ottoman usage *Ḫoca* was applied both to *'Ulemâ* that acted as preceptors, and to officials occupied in secretarial work, *Ḫocas* in this sense being contrasted with *Ağas*.

[8] For *kîsedâr* see above, p. 122, n. 5.

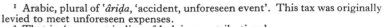

ranked in this order directly after the *Re'îsü'l-Küttâb* and the Secretary of the Janissaries, and above both the *Tezkerecis* and the secretaries of the *Re'îs*.[1] This list, however, omits the Accountancy *Ḥocas*.[2] But there is little doubt that the Chief Accountant (*Baş Muḥâsebeci*) was the most important of all the secretaries of the Finance Office. At any rate, in later times he ranked highest, being followed by the *Büyük Rüznâmeci*.[3] All these posts were then held by the year; and that of Chief Accountant was usually filled by such eminent persons as ex-*Kâḥyas*, ex-*Defterdârs*, and ex-*Re'îses*; its holder, moreover, was frequently promoted to the *Baş Defterdârlîḳ*.[4] In D'Ohsson's time the Finance Office employed over seven hundred secretaries and clerks, of whom four hundred and fifty belonged to the three principal departments—those of the Chief Accountant, the Great Day-book Keeper, and the Anatolia Accountant—in almost equal proportions.

All these departments were, of course, under the control of the *Baş Defterdâr*. But apart from them he had a special correspondence office, called *Oda*.[5] [6] This was managed by a functionary bearing the same title as the Secretary of the Grand *Vezîr*: *Mektûpçu*.[7] As well as discharging its general business, which included the drawing up of reports to the government, the clerks of the *Oda*, in later times, also prepared the life leases of tax-farms that we have already referred to. The *Baş Defterdâr* was further responsible for the State Treasury,[8] and consequently had a number of officials, other than those employed in the departments of the Finance Office, to assist him in matters affecting it. Thus the receipt and disbursement of actual specie were conducted by a Head Weigher (*Veznedâr Başî*) and fourteen assistants, their operations being recorded by an Inspector (*Sergi Nâẓiri*)[9] and his

[1] *Kâtibs* and *Şâgirds* (pupils or novices): see pay-list of reign of Murâd III given by Seyyid Muṣṭafâ, i. 138. He shows 16 *Kâtibânî Ḥazînei 'Âmire* and 133 *Şâgirdânî Ḥazînei 'Âmire*. This small number is accounted for by the fact that the clerks of the older *Ḳalems* were provided for from fiefs and so did not draw salaries. It is only those drawing salaries that are shown in this list.

[2] *O.T.E.M.*, No. 14, Appendix, 18.

[3] The *Ḳânûn-nâme* does, however, refer to the *Muḥâsebecis* in another passage, saying that the clerks of the *Re'îs* are eligible for promotion to the Treasury as *Muḳâṭa'acis* and *Muḥâsebecis*.—Ibid., p. 19.

[4] D'Ohsson, vii. 194; Aḥmed Râsim, ii. 315. The *Anadolu Muḥâsebeci* ranked third. Hammer, op. cit., 145 sq., however, places the *Büyük Rüznâme* first and the *Baş Muḥâsebe* second.

[5] Aḥmed Râsim, ii. 316, 318.

[6] For other uses of *oda*, meaning 'room', see above, pp. 62, 78.

[7] See above p. 120.

[8] *Ḥazînei 'Âmire*.

[9] *Sergi* (Turkish) means primarily a platform or booth on or in which wares are displayed for sale; and whether because coins were similarly set out in piles at the Treasury, it has as secondary meanings a public pay-office, and a note or cheque payable at such an office. It has also come to mean 'fair' or 'exhibition'. Hammer, op. cit., 146, states that the *Veznedâr Başî* and the assistant

clerk. The recovery of ordinary debts to the state, again, was confided to a Head Pursuivant (*Baş Bâḳî Ḳulu*),[1] who had at his command sixty men, and acted at the instance of the judge, called *Mîrî Kâtibi*,[2] who presided over the court attached to the Finance Office. Sums due from farmers of the poll-tax were likewise recovered by a special officer of the same type, the *Cizye Baş Bâḳî Ḳulu*. Finally two officials called *Kâğidi Enderûn Emîni* and *Kâğidi Bîrûn Emîni*[3] seem also to have come under the authority of the *Defterdâr*. The first was controller of stationery, issuing paper, pens, &c., to government offices as required. The second collected the dues imposed on newly appointed military fief-holders.[4]

VI. THE GOVERNMENT OF THE PROVINCES

As the area under the rule of the Ottoman sovereigns was gradually increased by conquest, they naturally found themselves obliged to divide it up into administrative districts. And to control each of these districts they appointed officers, who, as their representatives, enjoyed certain privileges indicative of this vice-royalty and exercised locally powers similar to those delegated, as regards the Empire as a whole, to the Grand *Vezîr*.

The Sultans of the 'Great' Selcuḳid dynasty had marked their sovereignty by the use, among other insignia, of standards and drums. Moreover, they would signalize the delegation of their powers to subordinate provincial rulers who acknowledged their suzerainty by granting them permission to use standards and drums also.[5] This usage was inherited in turn by the Sultans of Ḳonya and those of the House of 'Os̱mân. For the Sultanate of Ḳonya formed originally no more than a province of the 'Great' Selcuḳid empire; and its rulers came to enjoy the right of using standards and drums as representatives of their 'Great' suzerains.

of the *Sergi Nâẓiri* (called *Sergi Ḳalfasi*) were functionaries of the *Büyük Rüznâme*, and that the latter received payments small enough to be counted, whereas the former received larger ones, ascertained by weighing.

[1] So D'Ohsson, vii. 263, 371—'*Basch-Baki-Coulis*', and Hammer, op. cit., 164—'*Baschbaki Kuli*'. We have come across no other reference to this officer or his men, called '*Baki-Coulis*'. The meaning of the title is not clear. *Bâḳî* in Arabic means 'remaining', and hence the 'residue' of a debt.

[2] Literally, Secretary of the *Mîrî*.

[3] 'Commissioner of the Paper of the Inside' and 'Commissioner of the Paper of the Outside' respectively.

[4] For D'Ohsson's account of the Finance Office see vii. 261–73. Cf. Lybyer, 167–72. Hammer's account (op. cit., 137–69) does not differ materially from D'Ohsson's; and such differences as it exhibits may be due to modifications effected between the dates at which their works were written. Thus Hammer shows a 26th bureau, which dealt with 'shares' (*eshâm*) in tax-farms, introduced later than the period of our survey.

[5] See, for instance, 'The Last Buwayhids', *J.R.A.S.* 1931, p. 245. The standard was then called, in Arabic, '*alem*, the kettle-drum *kûs*.

Likewise the district ruled by ʿOsmân I is said by some even of the earliest Ottoman historians to have been a province of the Sultanate of Ḳonya, and ʿOsmân to have been granted a similar right as its ruler.[1] In any case, it is certain that under ʿOsmân's successors the officers that they appointed to control the districts into which their empire came to be divided were once more accorded the same privilege as a mark of their authority.[2]

Thus, up to the time of our survey, each of these officers still had in his employment a band of musicians who played, on pipes, horns, drums, kettle-drums, and cymbals, twice daily at his headquarters, at the hours of afternoon and evening prayer. The use of these bands, whose size was proportioned to the rank of the officer in whose honour they performed, represented the drum of the ancient privilege.[3] But it was rather by the use of standards that the Ottoman provincial governors were distinguished from the rest of the Sultan's servants. For these standards were described either by the Turkish word *sancaḳ* or by the Arabic *liwâ*; and the officers appointed to provincial governorships in the earliest days of Ottoman rule were known as *Sancaḳ Beyis*, or *Mîr Livâs*,[4] 'lords of the standard'.

These standards had, of course, a military as well as a royal significance—though, since Turkish, if not earlier Moslem dynasts, were essentially the leaders of their people in war, the royal to some extent presupposed the military. As we shall see, it was to the standards of the *Beys* that the provincial, and particularly the feudal, troops were summoned at the outset of a campaign, and round them that they fought. But owing to the fact that the *Beys* in peace time discharged what we should regard as civil functions in their capacity as governors, their standards acquired also a 'civil' significance—the 'civil' and the military thus making up the fully vice-regal. So, since they were known as 'lords of the standard' the original meaning of this title was extended: the words *sancaḳ* or *livâ* came to be applied also to the districts under their control. Up to the time of the conquest of Constantinople the *sancaḳ* (or *livâ*) was the principal administrative division of the Sultans' dominions. These divisions were, however, arranged in two

[1] *Encyclopaedia of Islam*, art. 'Sandjaḳ'; Tischendorf, 36.

[2] Zinkeisen, iii. 127.

[3] Aḥmed Râsim, ii. 117, note. The instruments were called: *zornâ*, *boru*, *ṭabel*, *naḳâra*, and *zel*. Cf. D'Ohsson, vii. 284, the band being described in this passage as consisting of *Chalumeaux*, *tambours*, *caissettes et cymbales*. Three *ṭuğ Paşas* employed nine players of each instrument—their bands hence being termed *doḳuz Ḳaṭ* (ninefold), two-*ṭuğ Paşas* six, and one-*ṭuğ Paşas* three. See also 'Ṭabl-Khāna' in Supplement to *Encyclopaedia of Islam*.

[4] For *Emîri Livâ*, a Persian construction of the Arabic *Emîru'l-Liwâ*. The *Sancaḳ Beyis* were also referred to, particularly in *ḳânûns*, simply as *Emîrs* (*Ümerâ*).

groups, European and Asiatic: the *sancaḳs* of Rumelia and the
sancaḳs of Anatolia; and the 'lords' of each group were subordinated to a 'lord of lords'—in Turkish *Beylerbeyi*, or in Turkicized Arabic *Mîrmîrân*.[1]

The first of these 'overlordships' or 'governorships-general' to
be created was that of Rumelia, in the reign of Murâd I (1360–89).
It was intended apparently to be held by a royal prince, for the
early Ottoman Sultans like other Turkish dynasts before them
were wont to confide the government of provinces to their sons
and brothers and were already, it appears, in the habit of entitling
their heirs *Beylerbeyi*.[2] Murâd's heir, however, afterwards Bâyezîd
the Thunderbolt, was still at this time a child. The governor-
generalship of Rumelia accordingly was conferred on his preceptor,[3] the general Lala Şâhîn together with this title,[4] which
thenceforth was applied no more to princes but only to such
governors-general. Royal princes continued to be given provincial
governments up to the sixteenth century, when the custom was
abandoned owing to the frequency with which they were apt to
rebel. In describing the system of local administration, however,
we shall ignore their participation in it as being, so to speak,
anomalous, except to remark here that the head-quarters staff of
each such prince seems to have resembled that of an ordinary
Beylerbeyi, except for the addition to it of a preceptor, who acted
as the prince's general adviser (or Grand *Vezîr*), and of a *Nîşâncî*.
No doubt also the princes maintained a more magnificent state
than ordinary governors, suitable to their august birth.

But here we must revert to the standard as an insignium of
royal authority. For though it was the word *sancaḳ* (or *livâ*) that
was used in describing the provincial governors as 'lords of the
standard'; though the object denoted by this word seems to have
been an ordinary flag; and though ordinary flags seem also to
have been used by them; the standard of the *Beys* or *Emîrs* was,
in fact, one much more peculiar, namely, the *ṭuğ* or horse-tail,
suspended from a pole and surmounted by a golden ball. This
was an ancient Turkish emblem, perhaps of totemic origin—*ṭuğs*
were originally made from the tails of yaks, not of horses. *Sancaḳ*
Beyis had a right to one *ṭuğ*, *Beylerbeyis* to two. Further, *Vezîrs*,
both of the *Ḳubbe* and provincial, had a right to three *ṭuğs*, and

---

[1] For *Emîri Emîrân*, a Persian modification of the Arabic *Emîru'l-Umerâ*.

[2] The title, in its Arabic form, was first used at the beginning of the tenth
century at the 'Abbâsid court for the generalissimos who soon came to dominate
the Caliphs. It was preserved under the Selcuḳids and so descended to the
Ottomans.

[3] *Lala*. Presumably Lala Şâhîn was so called on account of holding this
post. The *Lalas* of royal princes corresponded to the *Ata-begs* of the Selcuḳids.

[4] Belin, 'Essai sur l'Histoire Économique', *J.A.*, Serie VI, tom. 4, 274; Abdu'r-
Raḥmân Şeref, *Ta'rîḫi Devleti 'Oṣmaniye*, i. 102–3.

the Grand *Vezîr* to five. The Sultan himself would parade on campaign with as many as nine.[1]

The *ṭuğ* was thus a particular mark of royalty and vice-royalty. This being so, it is significant that the *Vezîrs* and *Beylerbeyis* were also, and they only, entitled *paşa*. For this word is usually said to be a contraction of the Persian *pâdişâh* 'sovereign'.[2] If this derivation is correct, therefore, we may note that the original full form was used of the Ottoman Sultans, and the contracted form of their chief provincial delegates.

The grading of provincial Governors in three ranks continued up to the period of our survey. Nevertheless, the rank of *Vezîr* was not of the same nature as those of *Beylerbeyi* and *Sancak Beyi*, since it did not in itself indicate that its holder governed any particular division of the Empire. The vezîrate, as it applied to provincial governors, was a merely honorific rank,[3] whereas *Beylerbeyiliks* and *Sancaḳ Beyiliks* were, essentially, posts. Indeed *Beylerbeyis* and, later, even *Sancaḳ Beyis* might also be *Vezîrs*, so that the vezîrate cut, as it were, across their hierarchy. Those that were granted vezirial rank became thereby automatically '*Paşas* of Three *Ṭuğs*', regardless of the posts they held.

The rapid expansion of the Empire in the latter part of the fifteenth and throughout the sixteenth century confronted its rulers with fresh problems. The newly added territories, unless, like the Rumanian Principalities, they were given a special status, were again divided up into *sancaḳs*. But these might no longer be conveniently grouped, so numerous were they now, in two *beylerbeyiliks*, according to their situation in either Europe or Asia. Indeed, the conquest of Egypt and some lands to the south

[1] *Encyclopaedia of Islam*, art. 'Ṭugh'.

[2] See Giese, *Das Problem der Entstehung des Osmanischen Reiches*. An alternative derivation is from the Turkish *baş ağa*, employed in the sense 'elder brother'. The title seems first, in the thirteenth century, to have been applied to the *dervişes* of the militant type (see below, ch. xiii), and next to the semi-religious, semi-military leaders of Turkish tribes in Asia Minor. Its application to officials and commanders under the early Sultans is further evidence of the religious character of the Ottoman movement. See *Encyclopaedia of Islam*, art. 'Turks'. Abdu'r-Raḥmân Şeref, op. cit. i. 102, explains its application first to the *Pervaneci* Çandârlî Ḳara Ḫalîl Paşa, and subsequently to the *Beylerbeyis* Lala Şâhîn and Timurtaş, by what he states was the Turkish custom of calling eldest sons *paşa*, this having led to its automatic application to the royal predecessors of these officers, 'Alâ'u'd-Dîn and Süleymân, respectively the reputed elder brother and the eldest son of Orḫan (1326–60). Cf. *Encyclopaedia of Islam*, art. 'Pasha', where it is stated that the title was first given to these *Beylerbeyis* and was a special attribute of that rank. The *Ḳânûn-nâmei Âli 'Osmân* (Part II—in *O.T.E.M.*, No. 15, Appendix, 12), however, seems to contrast both *Sancaḳ Beyis* and *Beylerbeyis* with *Paşas*—*Şol kimesneleri ki paşalar ve beylerbeyi ma'rifetile sancaḳ beyi ağriḳ ḥafẓi için ḳomuş ola* . . ., 'those persons whom the *Sancaḳ Beyi*, with the approval of the *Paşas* and *Beylerbeyis*, may have posted to guard the heavy baggage. . . '.

[3] Cf. above, p. 108.

of it, as well as of the Barbary Regencies, brought a large part of Africa under the Sultan's rule. Instead, other new *beylerbeyiliks* were formed, each consisting of a number of *sancaḳs*; and to these larger territorial divisions a new term was eventually applied—*eyâlet*, meaning 'rule' or 'government'.[1]

The governors of *Eyâlets* in later times seem to have been invariably *Vezîrs*.[2] And this being so, there would have been no *Paşas* of two *ṭuğs*—but merely *Vezîrs* entitled to three, and *Sancaḳ Beyis* entitled to one—had it not been for a further development. Though, as we have noted, a *beylerbeyilik* was essentially a post, it, like the vezîrate, came also to denote a rank which was conferred on deserving *Sancaḳ Beyis*.[3] So as early as the reign of the Conqueror we find that, though there were then no more than two of the governorships-general that were later to be termed *eyâlets*, yet there were enough persons holding the rank of *Beylerbeyi* to allow the inclusion in a *ḳânûn* of directions regarding their precedence, without reference to the provinces they governed.[4] That is to say, it is evident from this document that the officers referred to are not the actual governors-general of Rumelia or Anatolia, but others on whom the rank of *Beylerbeyi* has been conferred as an honour. Moreover, later at least the *Beylerbeyilik* of Rumelia in particular, as the senior governorship-general, was likewise conferred as an honourable rank on officers that had no connexion at the time with that province.[5] So there would be a *Vezîr* governing the *eyâlet* of Rumelia, and another officer, perhaps more than one, holding the rank of Rumelian *Beylerbeyi*.

In the hierarchy of officers and officials as defined in the *Ḳânûn-nâme* of the Conqueror, the *Beylerbeyis* ranked immediately after the *Vezîrs*. They were likewise entitled when in the capital to a seat in the *Dîvân*, and were apparently regarded as being on a par with the *Nîşâncî* and the *Defterdâr*. *Sancaḳ Beyis*, on the other hand, were obliged when attending the *Dîvân* to stand outside in the arcade. And their precedence depended on the

[1] D'Ohsson, vii. 277, states that it was only under Murâd III (1574–9) that the Empire was divided up into *eyâlets*. But contemporary historians make no reference to this reorganization—see *Encyclopaedia of Islam*, art. 'Sandjaḳ'. *Eyâlet* is from the Arabic *iyâla*, verbal noun of *âla*, 'he exercised power'.

[2] D'Ohsson, loc. cit.

[3] The result being, apparently, that in the end there were no governors of one *ṭuğ*—see D'Ohsson, loc. cit. The *Encyclopaedia of Islam*, art. 'Pasha', states that in later times a distinction was drawn between *Beylerbeyis* and *Mîrmîrâns*; and that it was the rank of *Mîrmîrân* that was then conferred on *Sancaḳ Beyis*.

[4] *O.T.E.M.*, No. 13 sq., *Ḳânûn-nâmei ʿÂli ʿOsmân*.

[5] See for instance the *Ḳanûn-nâme* of ʿAbdu'r-Raḥmân Tevḳîʿî (*Ḳânûn* of Feast-day Greetings), *M.T.M.*, i, 520, where the *Beylerbeyilik* of Rumelia is referred to as a mere rank, alternative to the vezîrate, that might be held by a *Defterdâr*: *Eğer defterdârîn vizâreti yaḫud Rumeli beylerbeyiliği pâyesi varşa. . . .* 'If the *Defterdâr* has the rank of *Vezîr* or *Beylerbeyi* of Rumelia. . . .'

extent of the revenues they had been granted. If these were below a certain figure, the *Sancaḳ Beyis* in question ranked after a certain category of 'learned men'.[1] Otherwise they ranked next to the *Beylerbeyis*; and all of them, as 'viceroys', were superior to all officers of the palace, commanders of troops, and officials of the administration whatever, except, of course, when these had been raised to the vezîrate.[2]

Though most of the *eyâlets* formed during the sixteenth century consisted of newly conquered territory, and, once constituted, remained unaltered as to their boundaries, some were also created by repartitioning.[3] The latter process, moreover, was repeated from time to time in the following centuries;[4] also *sancaḳs* were occasionally subtracted from one *eyâlet* and added to another,[5] so that the number of *eyâlets* in existence was not always proportionate to the size of the Empire. Thus, though the Empire was at its largest between 1590 and 1612,[6] the number of *eyâlets*, which then stood at thirty-five or thirty-six,[7] was smaller than

[1] *Taḫt Ḳâḍîs* (see below, ch. x, ii).

[2] *O.T.E.M.*, Nos. 13 and 14, pp. 13, 14, 20.

[3] Thus, during the sixteenth century both Bosnia and the *sancaḳ* of Gallipoli, originally included in Rumelia, were detached from it to form separate *eyâlets* (the latter, afterwards extensively added to, being governed by the *Ḳaptan Paşa*), whereas Buda and Temeşvar were separate though subordinate *Beylerbeyiliks* from the first.—Zinkeisen, iii. 131, 132.

[4] So, further *sancaḳs* were detached from Rumelia in the seventeenth century to form part, or the whole, of the new *eyâlets* of Silistria (or Oçakov) and the Morea.

[5] For instance, the *sancaḳs* of Iç Ili, Sis, Alâya, and Ṭarsûs, shown as belonging to the *eyâlet* of Cyprus by 'Ayni 'Alî, were later detached from it to form the *eyâlet* of Adana (formerly a *sancaḳ* of Aleppo), Cyprus itself and certain small neighbouring islands, including Paphos (Bâf) and Kerina, being later again attached to the *eyâlet* of the Archipelago (*Cezâ'iri Baḥri Sefîd*)—see D'Ohsson, vii. 301 sq. In Evliyâ Çelebi's list Aleppo, Adana, and Cyprus are shown as three separate *eyâlets*, but two *sancaḳs*—those of Sis and Ṭarsûs—appear under both Cyprus and Adana, the latter then possessing two additional *sancaḳs*, Ḳaraṭaş and Selefke.

[6] Owing to the inclusion in it between these dates of certain provinces conquered from the Persians in the war that preceded the earlier, and lost to them in the war that preceded the later, namely, Dâğestân, Şîrvân, Ḳaradâğ (the earlier Arrân), Erivân, part of Aẕerbâycân, and Lûristân. The dates given are those of the treaties by which the provinces were ceded and retroceded; but parts of the territory in question were occupied considerably before the first date. Dâğestân and Şîrvân were occupied in 1578, and Tabrîz in 1585. They were also for the most part lost before the second date. See *Encyclopaedia of Islam*, s.vv. We may also remark that though Georgia does not figure among the provinces won and lost at the dates mentioned, and is shown by Evliyâ Çelebi as an *eyâlet*, the Ottomans afterwards retained only a fairly precarious hold over those parts of the country that border the Black Sea, losing Tiflis itself. They regained control of Tiflis, however, in 1723, and their suzerainty over all Georgia was recognized by the Russo-Ottoman Treaty of 1724; but it was again made ineffective by the incursion of Nâdir Şâh, who retook Tiflis in 1734.—*Encyclopaedia of Islam*, art. 'Tiflis'.

[7] See Zinkeisen, iii. 133. This author's total of forty includes the three African regencies and Mecca, none of which were 'normally' governed. It also includes Ṣaydâ (Sidon), which, however, seems not to have been detached from

during the third quarter of the seventeenth century, when it stood at thirty-nine.[1] It is true that certain losses of territory sustained at the end of the earlier period were partially offset during the later[2]—for no Sultan actually ruled over the whole area included in the Empire at one time and another; and also that the increase in the number of *Eyâlets* between the two is accounted for partially by the fact that not all the territory lost was centrally governed,[3] whereas all the territory gained was. But repartitioning accounts for the rest of this increase; and it was accompanied, as was also the creation of new *Eyâlets* in the sixteenth century, by an increase proportionately even larger, in the number of *Sancaḳs*, effected likewise by the division of *Eyâlets* into ever smaller administrative districts.[4]

The loss of Hungary and Podolia at the end of the seventeenth century reduced the number of *eyâlets* again. By the time of our survey this seems to have stood at thirty-two.[5] Moreover, already during the seventeenth century in several of these *eyâlets* Ottoman rule had become no more than nominal.[6] And during the eighteenth, as we shall see, the area in which it was effective had shrunk still farther. The terms *Sancaḳ Beyi* and *Beylerbeyi*, also, were by this time little used in ordinary parlance for the provincial governors and governors-general, perhaps because of the equivocal significance that *Beylerbeyi* had meanwhile acquired. Governors-

Damascus till later (see below, p. 222). According to this list also Ṣan'â and Zebîd are shown together with the Yemen as forming three separate *eyâlets*. Perhaps, therefore, the total should be further reduced by two.

[1] Namely: 1. Bosna (Bosnia); 2. Temeşvar; 3. Budin (Buda-Pesth); 4. Varad (Varasdin); 5. Eğri (Erlau); 6. Ḳaniza; 7. Ujvar (Neuhausel;) 8. Yanova; 9. Ḳamnice; 10. Silistre or Ozu; 11. Keffe (in the Crimea); 12. Gurcistân (Georgia); 13. Rumeli; 14. Mora (the Morea); 15. Cezâ'ir (Archipelago and certain coast lands); 16. Anadolu (Anatolia); 17. Sivas; 18. Erḍerum; 19. Trabzon (Trebizonde); 20. Çildir; 21. Ḳaraman; 22. Diyâr Bekr; 23. Van; 24. Mer'aş (or Zu'l-Ḳadriye); 25. Mawṣil; 26. Şehrezur; 27. Adana; 28. Ḥaleb (Aleppo); 29. Ḳandiye (Crete); 30. Ḳibris (Cyprus); 31. Şâm (Damascus); 32. Ṭarabulus (Tripoli); 33. Raḳḳa; 34. Bağdâd; 35. Başra; 36. Mişr (Egypt); 37. Ḥabeş (Abyssinia—part of the present Eritrea); 38. Yemen; 39. Laḥsâ.—See lists of Seyyid Muṣṭafâ, Evliyâ Çelebi, *M.T.M.* i. 529–30; Tischendorf, 61 sq. D'Ohsson, vii. 277, states that the Empire at the time of its greatest extent had included forty-four *eyâlets*; but how he arrives at this figure is not clear. Possibly he, too, does so by including such provinces as the regencies, the principalities, and the Crimea that were not proper *eyâlets* at all.

[2] The loss of the six provinces mentioned above to Persia being offset by the conquest of Crete, of Podolia, and of certain parts of Hungary hitherto outside the area of Ottoman rule under Meḥmed IV.

[3] Of the six provinces lost under Aḥmed I only Dâğestân and Şîrvân seem to have been *eyâlets* proper—see Zinkeisen's list.

[4] *Şubaşiliḳs* (see below, p. 155) being erected into *sancaḳs*.—Zinkeisen, iii. 131–3.

[5] Made up of those shown above minus Nos. 3 to 9 (ceded by the Treaty of Carlovitz, 1699), minus Cyprus (cf. p. 142, n. 5 above); and plus Şaydâ (Sidon), detached from Damascus and consisting of the *Sancaḳs* of Şaydâ itself and Şafed (now in Palestine)—see D'Ohsson's list, loc. cit.

[6] For instance, in Ḥabeş, Yemen, and Laḥsâ.

general were now usually referred to by the Arabic word *Wâlî*, pronounced in Turkish *Vali*, and meaning 'ruler', governors of *sancaķs* by the word *Muteşarrif*, also Arabic, meaning 'one that enjoys a tenure'.[1] Now, moreover, in many *sancaķs* the administration was carried on by deputies of lesser rank than that of *Paşa*. But with these deputies we shall deal when considering the decay of the Ruling Institution as a whole.

The provincial governors in early times, notwithstanding their 'civil' functions, were essentially feudal officers. Not only was it to their standards that the *Sipâhîs* were summoned on the outbreak of war, and under their command that they fought, but the governors, like them, both subsisted on fiefs and were obliged to furnish *Cebelis*, tents, &c., in proportion to the revenues that their fiefs produced.[2] The fiefs in question were all of the *ḫâṣṣ* grade. It was laid down, though not always provided for in fact, that the revenues forthcoming from the *ḫâṣṣ* of a *Sancaķ Beyi* must amount to not less than two hundred thousand *aķçes*,[3] and those of a *Beylerbeyi* to not less than a million.[4] The longer their period of service the higher the revenues they were entitled to. Their *ḫâṣṣes* were gradually added to by the inclusion in them of hitherto separate *timars*. These additions, as in the case of ordinary *Sipâhîs*, were known as *teraķķîs*; so that the *ḫâṣṣ* granted to a *Sancaķ Beyi* on his first appointment corresponded to the *Sipâhî's ķiliç*.[5] Thus, if his predecessor had enjoyed revenues amounting to more than were the new *bey's* due, the Porte deprived the latter of the difference by detaching enough land from his *ḫâṣṣ* to effect the necessary reduction and converting it, until he should qualify for its gradual return, into ordinary *timars*. The persons[6] to whom

[1] *Encyclopaedia of Islam*, art. 'Sandjaķ'. Cf. below, p. 238, for peasants as '*Muteşarrifs*' of their holdings—which were called *taşarrufs*, 'tenures'. The word *Muteşarrif* was applied to *Sancaķ Beyis* only in the seventeenth century.

[2] According to the *Ķânûn-nâme Âlî 'Osmân* (*O.T.E.M.*, No. 15, Appendix, 12) a *Sancaķ Beyi* had to furnish one *Cebeli* for every 5,000 *aķçes* of revenue, a coat of mail (*gecim*) for every 50,000, and, in addition, two camel-drivers, three tents (one for himself, one so-called 'street' (*şokaķlî*), presumably for office purposes, and one for his treasury), a pantry (*kilâr*), a kitchen, and a saddlery. In the article 'Timar' of the *Encyclopaedia of Islam* it is stated that *Sancaķ Beyis* had to furnish a *Cebeli* for every thousand *aķçes*, but the figure 5,000 of the *Ķânûn-nâme* is confirmed by Evliyâ Çelebi, i. 101, 'Aynî 'Alî (in Tischendorf, 87), and Seyyid Muṣṭafâ, i. 120. It applied also to *Beylerbeyis*.

[3] Evliyâ Çelebi, i. 97; Tischendorf, i. 87; *Encyclopaedia of Islam*, art. 'Timar'. The list of *Sancaķ Beyis'* revenues supplied by 'Aynî 'Alî (and Seyyid Muṣṭafâ, i. 125 sq.) shows five *eyâlets* in which some amounted to less than the statutory figure—namely, Bosnia, Ķaraman, Erḍerum, Raķķa, and Diyâr Bekr.

[4] So the *Ķânûn-nâmei Âlî 'Osmân* (*O.T.E.M.*, No. 14, p. 28). Of the million *aķçes*, however, the *Beylerbeyis* had the use only of 800,000.

[5] See above, p. 51.

[6] They were usually, it appears, Janissaries or 'standing' cavalrymen that had earned the right to such small holdings.—'Aynî 'Alî in Tischendorf, 87.

such land was granted were compensated, when it was restored to the *Sancaḳ Beyi*, with other holdings.[1] Similarly, if by fortune or good management a *Beylerbeyi* was found to be deriving from his *ḫâṣṣ* larger revenues than he was entitled to, the Porte exchanged his lands for others not so unduly prosperous, to the benefit of the Imperial Domains.[2]

Originally the provincial governors seem to have been drawn from the feudal class itself, as their subordinate officers in the feudal hierarchy continued to be drawn even in later times. It seems possible even that each was appointed to command in the province in which he held a heritable fief, and that in some cases the office was itself hereditary.[3] After the institution of the *devşirme* system, however, which was itself due to the growing breach between the opinions and aims of the Court on the one hand and the Moslems of the provinces on the other, the Sultans, in order to maintain a closer hold on provincial affairs, and being jealous of family prestige in all high offices,[4] took to appointing *Ḳapî Ḳulus* to represent them in the *sancaks*. Nevertheless, until the last quarter of the sixteenth century the persons appointed continued normally to hold their posts for long periods:[5] until they were promoted to higher, were obliged to retire from old age, or died. Only in the reign of Murâd III (1574–95) was this practice abandoned. For reasons that will appear, the central government then became interested in contriving as frequent changes of office as it could. At first, thereafter, the viceroys would be dismissed every three years. But even this soon came to be regarded as too long a term; and the rule was then established that appointments should be made for one year only, though actually they were often prolonged by renewal.[6]

During the earliest period of Ottoman rule the *Sancaḳ Beyis* must have controlled the feudal system entirely. But when the first governorships-general were created, this control passed to the *Beylerbeyis*, who thenceforth until 1530 had the right both of granting all *zi'âmets* and *timars*, and, if the holders failed to per-

[1] *Encyclopaedia of Islam*, art. 'Timar'.

[2] *O.T.E.M.*, No. 14, Appendix, 28.

[3] See *Encyclopaedia of Islâm*, art. 'Turks'. The presumption that the early *Sancaḳ Beyi* was of the fief-holding class is supported by the fact that, as is explained below, his office and that of the *Alay Beyi*, who even in later times was always a feudatory, were originally one; and that, again even in later times, the sons of *Sancaḳ Beyis* and of *Beylerbeyis* were granted fiefs on their fathers' death (see Zinkeisen, iii. 160; Tischendorf, 48).

[4] Cf. p. 109, above, for the Sultan's jealousy of the Çandârli family of Grand *Vezîrs*.

[5] Ḳoçu Bey (Behrnauer, 277) states that twenty- or thirty-year terms were usual. Cf. Seyyid Muṣṭafâ, ii. 117.

[6] D'Ohsson, vii. 277; Belin, *La Propriété foncière*, 204; *Encyclopaedia of Islam*, art. 'Timar'.

form their duties satisfactorily, of depriving them.[1] The *Sancaḳ Beyis* seem to have been left, apart from their command of troops in war time and their 'civil' functions, with no more than a supervisory authority. If on the outbreak of war, for instance, a *Sipâhî*, being ill, desired to send a *Cebeli* to serve in his place, it was the *Sancaḳ Beyi* that decided whether he might do so. On the other hand, if any *Sipâhî* failed to furnish the correct number of *Cebelis*, his punishment rested with the *Beylerbeyi*.[2] The later *Sancaḳ Beyis*, being *Ḳapî Ḳulus*, again enjoyed (as indeed they were meant to) less influence and prestige locally than their feudal predecessors.[3] Moreover, possibly because the change was unwelcome to the feudatories over whom these *Ḳapî Ḳulus* were set, some of the duties performed by the earlier *Sancaḳ Beyis* were eventually confided to officers whom we have already mentioned as their subordinates, called *Alay* (or Muster) *Beyis*.[4] For the *Alay Beyis* were not *Ḳapî Ḳulus*, but *Za'îms*, or holders of *zi'âmets*, elected by their fellows[5] and so of the feudal class. Exactly when they were first appointed does not appear, though they were already in existence during the reign of the Conqueror.[6] But the appointment of an *Alay Beyi* to each *sancaḳ*[7] seems actually to have been decided on with the object of relieving its governor (now that he was by origin a *Ḳapî Ḳulu*) of the duties in question;[8] and as well as undertaking these, the *Alay Beyi* enjoyed some of the *Sancaḳ Beyi's* privileges: namely, the use, which we have characterized as in origin viceregal, of a standard and drum, though not that of a *ṭuğ*.[9] Each *Alay Beyi* had to assist him a standard-bearer (*Bayraḳ-dâr*) and a *Çavuş*, and like all the other military feudatories, was obliged to furnish a body of armed *Cebelis*. Though primarily, and probably more exclusively than the *Sancaḳ Beyi*, a military officer, he was also obliged to perform other duties in the *Sancaḳ* when ordered to do so by its *Paşa*, and in later times at least seems to have controlled the *Ṣubaşis* of the smaller districts composing it. The *Alay Beyis*, as their style implied, were charged in particular with mustering the feudal troops at the opening of a campaign and with ascertaining that applicants for military fiefs were eli-

[1] See above, p. 49.
[2] *Ḳânûn-nâmei Âli 'Oṣmân*, ii. (*O.T.E.M.*, No. 15, Appendix, 13).
[3] See *Encyclopaedia of Islâm*, art. 'Turks'.
[4] See above, p. 51.
[5] See above, p. 51. Cf. Belin, *Régime des Fiefs Militaires*, 231.
[6] There is one reference to them in the Conqueror's *Ḳânûn-nâme*, where they are ranked, together with the *Defter Kâḫyasis*, below a certain category of *Ḳâḍîs* (*O.T.E.M.*, No. 14, Appendix, 20).
[7] See Seyyid Muṣṭafâ, i. 121.
[8] Belin, op. cit. 231, note v: 'L'alaï-beïlik aurait, dans le principe, été attribué aux titulaires de sandjaq; plus tard, ces deux charges auraient été séparés. . . .'
[9] Ibid. 232, note.

gible.[1] As long as the *Sancaḳ Beyis* were themselves drawn from the feudal class no doubt they performed these duties themselves. But for *Ḳapi Ḳulus*, unused to local conditions when first appointed, the assistance of natives of the *sancaḳ* must have been necessary. It may be, indeed, that the *Alay Beyis* at first acted unofficially, for the references to them in the *Ḳânûn-nâmes* are strangely few. And they continued to represent the feudatories in each *sancaḳ*, whereas the *Sancaḳ Beyis* represented the central government. Only in the *sancaḳ* where the *Beylerbeyi* resided there was no *Sancaḳ Beyi* but only an *Alay Beyi*, the *Beylerbeyi* governing this province directly, as well as controlling the *eyâlet* as a whole.[2]

The *Alay Beyis* not only mustered the feudal troops for a campaign but also acted as their commanders, subordinate to the *Sancaḳ Beyis*. Unlike the latter, however, they seem never to have commanded independently; for a *Sancaḳ Beyi* would sometimes undertake minor operations with none but his own troops.[3] On the other hand, any governor might receive authority to command contingents furnished not only by his own province but by others, in which case the other governors concerned, provided their rank was not higher than his, were bound to obey him.[4] *Paşas* of three *ṭuğs*, somewhat similarly, carried their authority outside their own provinces in peace time. When travelling to or from the capital to their place of appointment they exercised full jurisdiction in all the *eyâlets* on their route, except those governed by officers of their own rank; whereas all lesser governors assumed authority only on reaching their place of appointment, and lost it immediately on dismissal.[5]

Most of the rules governing the administration of the provinces were naturally framed for the original *Beylerbeyiliks* of Rumelia and Anatolia. But they were applied also in most of those subsequently created, though not in all. For certain *eyâlets* (as they came to be called), of which Bağdâd and Egypt were the most notable, had little or no feudal organization;[6] a few, even, were not divided into *sancaḳs*;[7] consequently the *Paşas* that governed

[1] For the duties of the *Alay Beyi* see the *niẓâm-nâme* of 1777 (reign of ʿAbdü'l-Ḥamîd I), published in Cevdet, *Ta'rîḫ*, i. 317 sq. The instructions of which this is composed are based on earlier practice.

[2] D'Ohsson, vii. 278. Cf. Evliyâ Çelebi, i. 90 sq., where an *Alay Beyi*, but no *Sancaḳ Beyi*, is shown as resident at the head-quarters of most *eyâlets*.

[3] Tischendorf, 48.

[4] *M.T.M.* i. 500 (*Ḳânûn-nâme* of ʿAbdu'r-Raḥmân Tevḳîʿî).

[5] Ibid.

[6] Bağdâd, it is true, had fiefs in seven of its eighteen *sancaḳs*. But it was, nevertheless, *sâliyâneli* (see below, p. 148, n. 1).

[7] Such, apparently, were Georgia, Başra, Laḥsâ, the Yemen, and Ḥabeş. See Evliyâ Çelebi, i. 88, 95–6. The latter three, however, may have had *sancaḳs* in the preceding century.

them had to be provided for otherwise than by fiefs. In these *eyâlets*, and in certain non-feudal *sancaḳs* of *eyâlets* otherwise normal, the revenues that would else have accrued to the fief-holders of various grades were collected by agents for the local treasury. From these funds the governors were paid a fixed annual salary; and, after other local expenses had been defrayed, the surplus, if there was one, was sent to the capital. These provinces, *eyâlets* and *sancaḳs* alike, were for this reason called *sâliyâneli*,[1] that is, 'annual'. The sums they contributed to the central Treasury were called *irsâliye*.[2] In these *eyâlets*, again, the *Beylerbeyis* had the right of appointing the *Sancaḳ Beyis* (where such officers existed).[3] Elsewhere, as we have noted, the latter were, except during the earliest Ottoman period, appointed by the central government. They were promoted from very various posts, ranging from mere (though especially large) *zi'âmets* to *Ağaliḳs* of the Stirrup and high administrative appointments such as those of *Nîşânci* and *Defterdâr*.[4] And the amount of the revenues to furnish which they, as *Sancaḳ Beyis*, were granted *ḫâṣṣ* fiefs depended on the importance of their former posts. Thus mere *zi'âmet* holders promoted to a *sancaḳ* were entitled to no more than the minimum: two hundred thousand *aḳçes* (and, in fact, as we have noted, sometimes obtained even less). If, on the other hand, an *Ağa* of the Janissaries was so promoted, he was entitled from the first to as much as five hundred thousand.

In theory the governors' authority, though they represented the

[1] From the Persian *sâl*, 'year', and *sâleyâne*, 'annual'. In Turkish, therefore, *sâliyâneli* really means 'having an annual'—something.

[2] From Arabic *irsâl*, verbal noun of *arsala*, 'he sent'.

[3] Other *eyâlets* referred to as *sâliyâneli* were Başra, the Yemen, and Laḥsâ, as were also certain *sancaḳs* of the otherwise feudal *eyâlets* of Aleppo and the Archipelago. Other terms applied to these provinces were *maḳṭû'a merbûṭ*, 'obliged to pay tribute', and *Mîrîli*, 'of the *Mîrî*, or Treasury'. Crete, Cyprus, Varad, Kaffe, and the Morea are also said to have had no *timars*.—Evliyâ Çelebi, i. 88; Seyyid Muşṭafâ, i. 132; Hammer, op. cit., 244; Aḥmed Râsim, i. 347, note, 380, note; Tischendorf, 83–5; *Encyclopaedia of Islam*, arts. 'Sandjak', 'Timar'.

[4] The post-holders eligible for *sancaḳs* according to 'Aynî 'Alî (Tischendorf, 86–7) were the following: (1) *Za'îms* enjoying revenues amounting to 50,000 *aḳçes*, *Yaya Beyis* (see above, p. 54), *Timar Defterdâris* and *Defter Kâḫyasis* (see below, p. 150), *Seğmen Başis* (above, p. 60), and *Ağas* of the *'Ölûfecis* of the Right (above, p. 69). These all started at the lowest scale. (2) *Siliḥdâr Ağas* (above, p. 80), beginning with *Ḫâṣṣes* yielding 280,000 *aḳçes*. (3) *Ağas* of the 'standing' *Sipâhîs* (above, p. 69), beginning with *ḫâṣṣes* yielding 300,000 (above, p. 47). (4) Officers of the 'Outside' Service: *Mir Aḫors* (above, p. 83), *Çaḳirci Başis* (above, p. 86, n. 1), *Çâşnî-gîr Başis* (above, p. 86, n. 3), *Ḳapici Başis* (above p. 83), and *Mir 'Alems*, beginning with *ḫâṣṣes* yielding from 330,000, in the case of the first, to 450,000, in the case of the last. (5) *Nîşâncis* and *Defterdârs*, beginning with *hâṣṣes* yielding 450,000. (6) *Yeniçeri Ağasis*, beginning at 500,000. Evliyâ Çelebi's figures (i. 98) do not precisely agree with these; but the relevant paragraph, as translated, seems to need correction. Ḳoçu Bey (Behrnauer, 277) states that in earlier times *Sancaḳ Beyis* had been chosen from among the *Ḳapici Başis* and *Muşteferriḳas* (above, p. 87) of the court.

Sultan, was not all-embracing. On the one hand, the administration of the Sacred Law appertained not to them but to the *Kâḍîs* (judges) of their province. And on the other, all financial matters, including even those connected with the feudal system, were confided to special officials appointed to each province.[1] In practice, however, the respective jurisdictions of the 'lay' and the 'learned' officers were no more clearly defined in the provinces than they were in the capital: just as the Grand *Vezîr* had his law court in which he dealt with some cases himself and handed over others to the dignitaries of the *Şerî'a*, so did each governor in his *eyâlet* or *sancak*.[2] It seems probable, also, that even in early times his influence on the local finance officers was great enough to nullify such independence on their part as the regulations envisaged.[3]

Though few *eyâlets*, at any rate by the middle of the seventeenth century, were fully provided with them, the officials employed at its head-quarters might number eight besides the *Paşa* himself.[4] Of these, two were officers of the feudal troops, namely the *Alay Beyi* of the *Paşa's sancak* and the local *Subaşî* or *Çeribaşî*[5]—since each subdivision of a *sancak*, as we shall further explain,[6] had one of these officers; and one such subdivision included the *Paşa's* place of residence. Of the other six officers, three again, called collectively *Sipâhî Yazîcîlarî* (Secretaries of the *Sipâhîs*), were concerned with the registration of fiefs, namely

[1] Seyyid Muṣṭafâ, ii. 91.

[2] *M.T.M.* i. 528 (*Kânûn-nâme* of 'Abdu'r-Raḥmân Tevḳî'î).

[3] As early as the sixteenth century, at any rate, the provincial *Defterdârs*, instead of checking the *Paşas* in their misfeasances, would commonly abet them. See Zinkeisen, iii. 162. Indications on the one hand that *Defterdârs* were not over-scrupulous, and on the other that *Paşas* would bring pressure to bear on them, are contained in two documents of the reign of Süleymân the Magnificent, namely, a *ḳânûn* insisting that *Defterdârs* should be upright in their dealings, and a *fermân* to the *Beylerbeyi* of Rumelia prohibiting the diminution of fiefs held by the *Sipâhî Yazîcîlarî*.—Tischendorf, 46, 47.

[4] See Evliya Çelebi's lists (i. 90 sq.; text, i, 178 sq.). He states (p. 91) that each of the *sancaḳs* of Buda had its full complement of *Dîvân* officials, and specifies them as below. He shows only four other *eyâlets*, however, thus staffed, namely, Ḳaraman, Van, Şehrezûr, and Cyprus. For instance, of the two principal *eyâlets*, Rumelia and Anatolia, the first had no *Çavuşlar Kâḥyasî* (see below, p. 150) and the second no *Mâl Defterdârî* (unless perhaps the latter was represented in Anatolia by the official here listed as *Defter Muḥâsibi*, 'Accountant of the *Defter*'—Cf. *Muḥâsebe* (above, p. 130). In revenge these two provinces each had a number of supplementary officers: Rumelia a *Voynuḳ Ağasî* (see for the *Voynuḳs* above, p. 54) and seven *Yürük Beyis* (see above, p. 55), and Anatolia four *Müsellem Beyis* and eleven *Yaya Beyis* (see above, pp. 53–4).

Hammer, op. cit., mentions the presence in some *eyâlets*, namely Ḳaraman, Erḍerum, Diyâr Bekr, and Bağdâd, of a *Defterdâr des kaiserlichen Privatschatz*, and in Ṭarâbulus of a *Defterdar des Schatzes*. This may be a confusion with the *Mâl* or *Ḫazîne Defterdârî*—see below. On the other hand Evliyâ (text) also shows among the *dîvân* officials of the *eyâlet* of Temeşvar a *Mâlî Pâdişâhî Defterdârî*, a '*Defterdâr* of the Imperial Property', distinct from the *Ḫazîne Defterdârî*.

[5] See above, p. 51.

[6] Below, p. 154.

the *Defter Emîni*[1] of the *eyâlet* and his two assistants, the *Defter Kâhyasi*[2] for *zi'âmets* and the *Timar Defterdâri* for *timars*.[3] The fourth, who was in fact the highest of all in rank, was the *Mâl Defterdâri*[4]—that is to say, the Treasurer that dealt with money matters, the receipt and expenditure of cash, as opposed to the before-mentioned officials, who regulated what may be termed the feudal finances, since fiefs were created to furnish 'livelihoods' (*dirlik*)[5] in lieu of salaries. It will be seen that the *Mâl Defterdâri* and the *Defter Emîni* of an *eyâlet* corresponded to their homonyms of the central government,[6] which indeed had, as it were, given birth to these provincial governments by a process of division. This analogy holds good for the two remaining officers. These were an *Emîn* and a *Kâhya* of the local *Çavuşes*, who were primarily the governor's agents in the execution of the sentences pronounced by him and the *Şer'i* dignitaries in his and their law courts, just as the *Çavuşes* of the capital were the similar agents of the Grand *Vezîr*.[7] In the *Kânûn-nâme* of the Conqueror provincial *Defter Emînis* are not mentioned.[8] It is there laid down, however, that the *Timar Defterdâris* shall be recruited from among the salaried (*'ölûfeli*) *Muteferrikas*,[9] and shall rise to the post of *Defter Kâhyasi* and thence to that of *Mâl Defterdâri*.[10] *Timar Defterdâris* and *Zi'âmet Kâhyasis* lived, like the *Alay Beyis*, on the revenues of *zi'âmets*,[11] *Çavuşes* and other secretaries on those of *timars*.[12] The fiefs of these officials and *Çavuşes* were known as *kiliç yeri*.[13] They were under the control of the *Defterdârs*, the *Paşas* being forbidden by *kânûn* to interfere with them. Included presumably

[1] Or *Defter Müfettişi* (in the *Eyâlet* of Rumelia).

[2] Or *Zi'âmet Kâhyasi*—see Seyyid Muṣṭafâ, i. 121.

[3] *Encyclopaedia of Islam*, art. 'Timar'. The provincial *Defter Emînis* are not mentioned in the *Kânûn-nâme* of the Conqueror nor by 'Aynî 'Alî. Evliyâ Çelebi, however, shows one for most *Eyâlets* side by side with the *Defter Kâhyasi* and the *Timar Defterdâri*; and Feridun (see Belin, *Régime des Fiefs Militaires*, 230) states that the *Sipâhî Yazicilari* were the *Defter Emîni* and the *Timar Defterdâri* with their assistants, not mentioning the *Defter Kâhyasi*. Hammer, *Staatsverwaltung*, 245, mentions only the *Defter Kâhyasi* and a '*Zi'âmet Defterdâri*', stating that the former was the local representative of the *Mîrî*, whereas the latter was charged with the administration of feudal business. But in his *Staatsverfassung*, 350, he remarks that it was a duty of the *Defter Kâhyasis* when necessary to take the provincial *defters* to the capital for examination; and it seems probable that the *defters* in question were those in which feudal holdings were recorded.

[4] *Mâl* (Arabic), meaning 'property, money'. Evliyâ also calls these officials *Hazîne Defterdâris*, '*Defterdârs* of the Treasury'.

[5] Cf. above, p. 47.

[6] Above, pp. 127–8.

[7] Above, pp. 118–19.

[8] See above, n. 3. Possibly they were of later creation.

[9] See above, p. 88.

[10] *O.T.E.M.*, No. 14, Appendix, 19–20. *Timar Defterdâris* and *Defter Kâhyasis* might also, as we have noted (above, p. 148, n. 4), rise direct to being *Sancak Beyis*.

[11] Seyyid Muṣṭafâ, i. 121.

[12] *O.T.E.M.*, No. 14, Appendix, 28.

[13] i.e. 'substitute for a *kiliç*'.

among the provincial *dîvân* officials was the *Mevḳûfcu* (or *Mevḳûfâtî* or *Mevḳûfâtcî*).[1] It was his duty to recover taxes levied on the persons and the immovable property of the peasantry, and particularly to administer vacant fiefs for the benefit of the local treasury. It is stated that there was one *Mevḳûfcu* to each province, by which is presumably meant each *eyâlet*.[2] Possibly he was a subordinate of the *Mâl Defterdârî*. He does not, however, appear to have had a *dirlik* provided for him. Presumably, therefore, he either received a salary or lived on percentages of the revenues he recovered.

That many of the *eyâlets* had less than the full number of these '*dîvân*' officials (as they were called) was due generally to differences in their organization. Thus the *sâliyâneli eyâlets* (those in which the *Vâlî* was paid a yearly salary), since they contained no fiefs, required no officials to deal with them. It appears, again, that when *eyâlets*, such as that of Silistre, were carved out of others, the administration of their feudal and financial affairs was still conducted from the head-quarters of the 'parent' province: they therefore had no independent *dîvân* officials at all.[3] What seems stranger is that in several *eyâlets* there was no *Mâl Defterdârî*,[4] and that in others, while there were no officials for the administration of fiefs, yet there were *Alay Beyis* and *Çeri Başîs*.[5] Possibly in these places the duties of the missing functionaries were likewise performed by those of neighbouring provinces.

Just as the *Defterdâr* and the *Defter Emîni* of the central government each had his counterpart in the government of each *eyâlet*, so were the Grand *Vezîr's* staff and household models for the staff and household of every *Paşa*. In early times, it is true, the provincial governors kept up only a modest state, devoting the greater part of their revenues to 'public works' such as the building of mosques, colleges, and hospices, and to their military equipment. It was only during the sixteenth century, and particularly after it became common for *Vezîrs* to be given *eyâlets* and even *sancaḳs*, that the maintenance of large and magnificent households became fashionable among them; and the description that follows probably

[1] For the significance of *mevḳûf* see above, pp. 51, 130. *Mevḳûfat* is a plural; *cu, ci* the usual Turkish ending indicating an agent; *î* a similar Arabic ending. The last two forms are shown, for instance, by Belin, the first in the *Ḳânûn-nâmei Âlî 'Osmân*, ii. (*O.T.E.M.*, No. 15, Appendix). Possibly the *Mevḳûfcus* were connected with the bureau of the Treasury called *Mevḳûfât* (above, loc. cit.).

[2] Belin, *Régime des Fiefs Militaires*, 235.

[3] Adana and Raḳḳa were other such *eyâlets*.

[4] In, for instance, those of Sivas, the Archipelago, and Ṭrabzon.

[5] As in the *eyâlets* of Ḳarş, Çildir, and Mawşil. For this and the foregoing notes see the lists of 'Aynî 'Âlî and Evliyâ Çelebi. 'Aynî 'Âlî's shows the presence or absence only of *Mâl* (or, as he also terms them, *Ḫazîne*) *Defterdâris*, *Defter Kâḫyasis*, and *Timar Defterdâris*.

refers rather to the *Paşas* of these later times than to their more plain-living predecessors. But then at least a *Vezîr* of medium rank—for though no distinctions were officially recognized between one *vezîr* and another except in the case of *Ḳubbe Vezîrs*, the posts they held, the favour and fortune they enjoyed, and the services they performed, ranged them in a natural scale of consequence—a *Vezîr* of medium rank would then have his *Kâḫya*, corresponding to the Grand *Vezîr's Kâḫya Beyi*,[1] his *Dîvân Efendisi*, also called, like the Grand *Vezîr's* secretary, *Mektûpçu*,[2] but corresponding rather to the *Re'îs Efendi*, and his *Iç Ağas*, headed, like the *Iç Ağas* of both the Sultan and Grand *Vezîr*, by a *Silîḥdâr*,[3] who would carry the *Paşa's* sheathed sword before him on occasions of public ceremony.[4] Among these *Iç Ağas*, again, there would be a *Selâm Ağasî* (corresponding to the *Teşrîfâtçî* or Master of Ceremonies),[5] a Master of the Horse,[6] a *Kâḫya* of the Ushers,[7] a Treasurer,[8] a Butler;[9] like those of the Imperial Household his *Iç Ağas* would be slaves, trained by a system of apprenticeship to their predecessors in office.[10] As we have mentioned, every governor had his military band, of a size varying with the number of his *ṭuğs*.[11] But his rank was marked similarly by other privileges. Thus a *Paşa* of three *ṭuğs* had nine horses led before him, and was accompanied by six footmen called *Şâṭir*,[12] a *Paşa* of two *ṭuğs* six horses and four *Şâṭirs*, a *Sancaḳ Beyi* three horses and two *Şâṭirs*.[13] Otherwise he might employ as many attendants of various kinds as he could afford, such as grooms, tent-pitchers, linkmen, and watchmen, all corresponding to minor employees of the imperial Outside Service. A small number of archers called *ḳavvâs*[14]

[1] Above, p. 120. [2] Above, p. 120. [3] Above, p. 80 and App. C.
[4] D'Ohsson, vii. 285; Aḥmed Râsim, i. 455, note. [5] Above, p. 120.
[6] *Mîr Aḫor*, cf. above, p. 83. [7] *Ḳapîcîlar Kâḫyasî*, cf. above, p. 83.
[8] *Ḫazînedâr Ağa*. [9] *Kilârcî Başî*.
[10] Aḥmed Râsim, i. 455, note sq. The account given here of the training by the *Paşa's Ağas* of candidates for admission to their ranks, and the ceremony held when they were admitted, recalls the practices of the *dervişes*, the *Aḫis*, and the guilds (see below, pp. 283–4), as if there were, indeed, a guild or brotherhood of such *Iç Ağas*. Thus admission was signalized by the placing of a cap (*ḳavuḳ*) on the candidate's head, after the recitation of prayers. If an *Ağa* committed a serious crime, he would be solemnly deprived of this cap, and forced to turn to some other way of life, since thenceforward he could not hope to find employment in any 'household'.
[11] See above, p. 138.
[12] This word is apparently Turkish, though Arabic has one of the same form, meaning 'insolent, clever, tricky'. Hammer, loc. cit., puts the number of led horses, musical instruments, &c., that it was the privilege of three-*ṭuğ Paşas* to use, at seven.
[13] D'Ohsson, vii. 285, stating, however, that *Sancaḳ Beyis* were entitled to only one *Şâṭir*. But see *M.T.M.* i. 529, where the regulations (*Ḳânûn-nâme* of 'Abdu'r-Raḥmân Tevḳî'î) show two.
[14] Arabic, *ḳawwâs* from *ḳaws*, 'a bow'. The word means properly a 'bowmaker' rather than an archer. It is familiar in the spellings *ḳavass, cavass*.

acted, in early times, as the *Paşa's* aides-de-camp; later these *ḳavvâses* were employed in greater numbers as simple messengers. Finally, the *Paşa* had at his command, again like the Grand *Vezîr*, companies of *Tatar* couriers, of musketeers (*tüfengci*), and of mounted scouts (*deli*) each with its officer.[1]

Certain *Beylerbeyis* enjoyed special privileges. Those of Bağdâd, Cairo, and Buda, for instance, because these cities had all three been the capitals of monarchies, were permitted to use boats similar to those used by the Sultan,[2] to employ *Ṣolaḳ* and *Peyk* guards,[3] and to appoint certain officials without reference to the Porte.[4] The *Beylerbeyi* of Rumelia, again, because his was the senior *eyâlet*, might sit on a stool at the imperial *Dîvân*, took precedence of even the two *Ḳâḍî-'Askers* and was officially addressed, unlike the rest, as *Paşa*, with the phrase 'May his dignities endure!'[5] following his name.[6]

The *sancaḳ* was the smallest administrative district that was at the same time and in origin feudal. For, as we have mentioned, there were several *eyâlets* in which fiefs were non-existent, and even in an ordinary *eyâlet* the land was far from being entirely allotted to fiefs. If the *sancaḳ* was to be divided for administrative purposes accordingly, it was of necessity on a basis other than feudal. The basis, in fact, was judicial: the *sancaḳ* was divided into a number of districts in each of which there resided a Moslem judge, a *Ḳâḍî*, to administer the *Şerî'a*; hence each of these districts was termed a *ḳaḍâ*,[7] a judgeship or jurisdiction. Some of these *ḳaḍâs* were mainly or, in the case of large towns, entirely urban. Others were rural, being centred on villages. Sometimes, again, they were subdivided: the *Ḳâḍî* would be represented by a deputy in certain quarters of a city, or in rural districts called *nâḥiye*.[8] *Ḳâḍîs* were, of course, 'learned men' and as such not members of what we have called the Ruling Institution, from which their own was distinct. But though *ḳaḍâs* and their subdivisions were thus dependent on the 'Learned' rather than the

[1] See Appendix C. Aḥmed Râsim, i. 456–7, notes. Hammer, *Staatsverwaltung*, 246–7, in listing the members of a *Paşa's* staff—his *ḳapî ḫalḳî*, 'people of the gate'—mentions also an *Alay Beyi*, who, he says, led public processions and acted as his *Çavuş Başî*. But whether this was the feudal officer of the same title he does not state.

[2] Called a *ḳoçulu ḳayîḳ*. *Ḳoçu* means a 'closed carriage'. Presumably what is meant here is a barge, or gondola, with a covered saloon.

[3] See above, p. 87.

[4] Seyyid Muṣṭafâ, i. 127.

[5] *Dâmet ma'âlîhi* (Arabic).

[6] *M.T.M.* i. 527 (*Ḳânûn-nâme* of 'Abdu'r-Raḥmân Tevḳî'î).

[7] *Ḳaḍâ*, pronounced in Turkish *kaza*, is the verbal noun from *ḳaḍâ*, 'he decided (and hence) he judged, he acted as a judge', *ḳâḍî* being the present participle. It therefore means both 'a judgement' and 'the office of a judge'; and hence the area in which a judge exercises his office.

[8] Arabic 'vicinity, district'.

Ruling Institution, the latter was represented in them by the officers, called *Ṣubaşî*, one in each. We have already referred to these officers in connexion with the feudal system: they stood next below the *Alay Beyis* in its hierarchy. But *Ṣubaşîs* of this type naturally existed only in districts in which there were fiefs: they were called *Ehli Timar Ṣubaşîlarî*, '*Ṣubaşîs* of the Timariots', whereas those of other districts were called *Mîrî Ṣubaşîlarî*, '*Ṣubaşîs* of the Treasury'. These names probably indicate also that whereas the 'feudal' *Ṣubaşîs* subsisted, as they did, on the revenues of fiefs and were under the usual feudal obligations of furnishing *Cebelis*, &c., in proportion to their revenues,[1] the *Mîrî Ṣubaşîs* drew salaries from the Treasury; but both were also entitled to dues derived from fines imposed on offenders.[2] For not only the *Mîrî* but also the 'feudal' *Ṣubaşîs* were police officers, carrying out the sentences of the *Ḳâḍîs* in whose districts they worked, and being generally responsible for the maintenance of law and order. Apparently in places where Janissary detachments were stationed, they furnished police patrols, acting on the local *Ṣubaşî's* instructions, as in the capital, where the *Ṣubaşî* was one of several officers on whom such duties fell.[3] But whether in such places the *Ṣubaşî*, if he was of the *Mîrî* type, was likewise a Janissary himself does not appear.

In origin the office was in any case military. In earlier Turkish states indeed it had been of much greater importance. Under the Ğaznevids, for instance, the word (which means 'Head of an army')[4] had been applied to a general.[5] But already under the Selcuḳids of Ḳonya it had acquired a semi-'civil' significance: the Selcuḳid *Ṣubaşîs* were apparently military governors of cities.[6] Such military governors, however, were of necessity, by Moslem tradition, obliged to work with the judges of the *Şerî'a*. Whether or not, therefore, the Selcuḳids also appointed 'rural', and feudal, *Ṣubaşîs*, the division of the Ottoman dominions into *ḳaḍâs* led

[1] By the *Ḳânûn-nâmei Âli 'Oṣmân*, ii (*O.T.E.M.*, No. 15, Appendix, 12) *Ṣubaşîs* are required to furnish a *Cebeli* for every 4,000 *aḳçes* of revenue, a coat of mail (*gecim*) for every 30,000, and two tents if they derive more than this sum (? something appears to be omitted in the text here). According to Aḥmed Vefîḳ (in Belin, *Régime des Fiefs Militaires*, 234), *Ṣubaşîs* held *zi'âmets* including the head-quarters of their *ḳaḍâ*, which seems to indicate that the *zi'âmets* concerned were not heritable but resembled *hâṣṣes* in being the perquisites of offices (as did the *zi'âmets* that provided *dirliks* for the provincial *dîvân* officials). This supposition is borne out by the fact that special provision was made for the grant of *timars* to the sons of deceased *Ṣubaşîs*, in a manner similar to that in which the sons of *Beylerbeyis* and *Sancaḳ Beyis* were provided for.—Zinkeisen, iii. 157.

[2] *O.T.E.M.*, No. 14, Appendix, 28 (*Ḳânûn-nâme* of the Conqueror).

[3] See App. A (B).

[4] *Encyclopaedia of Islam*, art. 'Subāshī'.

[5] See, e.g., the *Ta'rîḫ* of Bayhaḳî.

[6] *Encyclopaedia of Islam*, loc. cit. Cf. Köprülüzade, *Salcuḳlular Zamânında Anadoluda Türk Medeniyeti*, 206, 219.

naturally to the appointment of a *Ṣubaşî* to act on the orders of every judge, whatever the character, urban or rural, of the area under his jurisdiction.[1] It was equally natural that these *Ṣubaşîs* should be placed in a position of superiority to the local *Sipâhîs*, and should be supported, like them, with fiefs. What seems less so is that these officers should have been obliged, as they apparently were, to go on campaign. For in their absence, unless they then appointed substitutes, the local *Ḳâḍî* must have been left with no one to execute his rulings.[2]

The conditions prevailing in such rural areas, however, are to be discussed in a later chapter. And in yet other chapters we are to describe the conditions under which the traders and artisans of the towns carried on their business;[3] the restrictions and penalties imposed on such peasants and townsmen as professed religions other than Islâm;[4] and the position of the *Ḳâḍîs* themselves in the hierarchy of 'learned men'.[5] We need do no more, therefore, in this place than mention the facts, first, that in cities and towns the *Ḳâḍî* had an adjutant other than the *Ṣubaşî*, called *Muḥtesib* or *Iḥtisâb Ağasî*, meaning 'Censor',[6] through whom he dealt with all matters concerning trade and industry; and, secondly, that the non-Moslem communities were represented in their dealings with the local authorities by functionaries chosen from among their members and called *Ḳoca Başîs*, or Chief Elders.

The governors imposed their authority in general by means of the feudal forces under their command. But in many important cities, some but not all of which were the capitals of *eyâlets*,[7] they had

[1] Actually, the urban *Ṣubaşîs* were in many cases first installed as the commanders of the garrisons placed in newly conquered cities, so that their position was similar to that of the Selcuḳid *Ṣubaşîs*.—*Encyclopaedia of Islam*, art. 'Turks'.

[2] During Selîm I's campaign in Syria, some of the Rumelian *Ṣubaşîs* seem to have remained at home, since, according to a story quoted by Tischendorf, 43, they were ordered by the Sultan to collect outstanding revenues on behalf of the *Sipâhîs* that had gone on campaign. The substitutes of others are also mentioned, however.

[3] Below, ch. vi. [4] Below, ch. xiv. [5] Below, ch. x, ii.

[6] For the word *muḥtesib* see below, pp. 279, 288.

[7] The towns that were at the same time the head-quarters of *eyâlets* (in the list supplied by Seyyid Muṣṭafâ, i. 91) were Bağdâd, Cairo, Damascus, Aleppo, Erḍerum, Ḳonya (of Ḳaraman), Kütâhya (of Anatolia), Cyprus (the capital being Nicosia—Lefköşe), Adrianople (Edirne—of Rumelia), Bosna (Serâyî) (Serajevo—of Bosnia), Temeşvar, and Buda. The others, all capitals of *sancaḳs*, were Brusa (of Ḫüdâvendigâr) in the *eyâlet* of Anatolia, Smyrna (Izmir—of Ṣağala) in the *eyâlet* of the Archipelago, and Salonika (Selânik) in the *eyâlet* of Rumelia. Also the capitals of the three Barbary Regencies. It is curious that in the three lists showing the distribution of Janissary *ortas* supplied by Aḥmed Cevâd, 164 sq., and referring respectively to an unspecified date during the reign of Meḥmed IV (1648–87), to 1723 and to 1750, no less than ten of the places shown above (including Cairo and the capitals of the Regencies) do not appear at all. The only places that figure in all four lists are Bağdâd, Damascus, and Serajevo, while Salonika appears in the two eighteenth-century lists as well as in that of Seyyid Muṣṭafâ. Most of the Janissary *ortas* seem

at their disposal as well several *ortas* of Janissaries and, in later times at least, detachments of 'standing' cavalry.[1] These forces had their own commanders,[2] responsible to the generals of their respective corps and so to some extent independent of the local governors, on whom they might, and were perhaps intended to, act as a check. They were nevertheless at the governors' immediate orders, as were also the wardens of fortresses[3] in frontier *eyâlets*, which were likewise garrisoned with detachments of the 'standing' *ocaḳs*. In peace time, therefore, the maintenance of law and order was well provided for, though even so it is not clear how, if in towns where Janissary *ortas* were stationed they furnished police patrols as in Istanbul, this service was supplied in towns where they were not stationed. Possibly their place was taken by watchmen, such as those maintained by the commercial and industrial guilds, or others in the service of the *Ṣubaşis* and *Muḥtesibs*.[4] This would have left such towns comparatively undisturbed by the departure of the troops to war. Not altogether, however: for the governor himself would go; and the neighbourhood would be temporarily denuded of the *Sipâhîs* and their officers. At harvest time, if the campaign was not yet finished, a few *Sipâhîs* would return to collect the tithes that were due to them and their fellows,[5] which seems to show that the mere presence of such members of feudal families as were left behind was insufficient to assure the proper ordering of these collections. During his absence however, a *Sipâhî* must have appointed some one to manage, if not his fief in general, at least the part of it in particular that he farmed directly. And it is to be presumed that just as the chief functionaries of the central administration, when they accompanied the Sultan or the Grand *Vezîr* on campaign, were replaced at the capital by deputies, so were the governors and their *dîvân* officers in the provinces.

Wars were of frequent occurrence, so that these upheavals were far from being extraordinary. It is remarkable, therefore, that

at all periods to have been stationed in places near the frontiers. Thus in the seventeenth-century list some nine places in Hungary, including Buda, are shown; while of the forty-two names common to the two eighteenth-century lists many are of places in the Caucasus and in the neighbourhood of the Crimea, most of the rest being of places along the Danube and near the Russian frontier or in Greece and the islands. Aḥmed Cevâd's first list is taken from Hezâr Fenn *apud* Hammer, op. cit., 221.

[1] See D'Ohsson, vii. 283. In earlier times, however, it appears that all the standing cavalry regiments were in peace time permanently stationed in or near the capital. See Tischendorf, 41.

[2] The commander of the local Janissaries was termed *Serdâr* (see above, p. 95), the commander of the local 'standing' *Sipâhîs*, *Kâḫya Yeri* (see App. A (c), and A (A) for the Janissary officer with the same title).

[3] The wardens were called *dizdâr* (*dez*, in Persian, meaning 'fort').

[4] See below, p. 288. [5] See above, p. 52.

the history of the Ottoman Empire up to the eighteenth century should have been marked with so few civil disturbances as it was, especially since, with the possible exception of Anatolia, all its provinces were inhabited by populations of which the majorities differed from their Ottoman rulers in either religion or race. The non-Moslem subjects of the Sultans in particular are usually represented as having been held down by a hideous tyranny. As a matter of fact, however, not only were such risings as did disturb the peace of the Empire during these centuries the work exclusively of Moslems, but they were hardly ever provoked by misgovernment. In early times the dominant motive in the launching of various revolts was, it is true, religious: their leaders still held the opinions that had animated the first Ottoman conquerors, but which the Sultans and the government had since discarded in favour of others less heterodox.[1] The last insurrections due to these differences broke out at the close of the sixteenth century.[2] Otherwise the chief causes of disturbance were the ambitions in earlier times of royal princes or pretenders such as Cem in the reign of Bâyezîd II, and Muṣṭafâ in that of Süleymân I, and, in later, of certain provincial governors themselves; as well, at all times, as the marauding propensities of Türkmen and other nomads. The latest semi-religious revolt was aided indeed by the severity of an army commander, as a consequence of which many of his soldiers deserted and joined the rebels;[3] and the persecution of the Durûz of Syria by one of his fellows seems to have contributed to another;[4] but these were not instances of provincial misgovernment in the ordinary sense. As for the subject peoples of Europe, and those few of Asia to whom Moslem control was new, they seem at first to have found Ottoman rule less irksome than that of their former sovereigns,[5] and for a long time received from abroad no encouragement to rise against it. The strength of the Empire declined, indeed, not because the peoples, Moslem or infidel, subject to the Ruling Institution and the learned profession rebelled against them, but because these bodies, as we shall show, were corrupted from within.

It was probably a weakness in the Ottoman polity that the line between rulers and ruled (which was far from coinciding with any more natural divisions of race or religion) was very sharply drawn.

[1] See above, p. 41.

[2] The risings of Ḳara Yazîcî at Urfa (Edessa) in 1599 and of Ḳalender Oğlu in Saruḫan (1606)—see *Encyclopaedia of Islam*, arts. 'Turks' and 'Ḳara Yâzîdjî'.

[3] Çiğala Sinân Paşa on the Hungarian campaign of 1596.—*Encyclopaedia of Islam*, art. 'Muḥammad III'.

[4] The persecution of the Durûz by Ibrahîm Paşa in 1585 being followed by the formidable rebellion of Faḫru'l-Dîn which was carried on for many years. —Ibid., arts. 'Murâd III' and 'Fakhr al-Dîn'.

[5] See Gibbons, *The Foundation of the Ottoman Empire.*

In the *Ḳânûn-nâmes* we find regulations defining minutely who are to be deemed *'askerîs*, that is (for our purpose), 'rulers' on the one hand, and *re'âyâ* 'peasants' or *şehirlis* 'townsmen' on the other;[1] and the latter, whose sole business, from the point of view of the state, was to pay taxes, were strictly forbidden to arrogate to themselves the privileges of the former, to ride a horse or wear a sword.[2] This rule seems to have been framed in the first place with the object of preserving the purity of the feudal class as one of fighters. It was feared, not that the *Sipâhîs* would mate outside their own class; for though many of them were of Turkish descent, so were some of the peasants over whom they lorded it; this was not in those days a matter of pride or concern; and in any case the *Sipâhis* were never restricted in the choice of wives or concubines. It was feared, on the one hand, that if the peasants rode horses and went armed, they would be less easy to master, and, on the other, that they would insinuate themselves into the *Sipâhî* class and dilute its martial vigour. By the time of Süleymân the Magnificent many fiefs were, in fact, in the hands of *Sipâhîs* of peasant descent; and the Sultan decreed that they were not on that account to be deprived, since all were alike his subjects.[3] But, though this view was new, and perhaps symptomatic, it scarcely compromised the principle at issue, since the *Sipâhîs* in question had won their holdings by serving in war, as volunteers, with distinction. By this time, also, the *Ḳapî Ḳulus* (who were *ipso facto 'askerîs*) had come to eclipse the feudatories in importance if not in numbers; so that the opposition of rulers and ruled was maintained hardly less sharply than before. Its result was double: to make all depend on the integrity of the rulers, and to render most of the ruled unfit to change their status. When, therefore, first the rulers' integrity was corrupted, for reasons to be described, and later the hitherto ruled were admitted to positions of authority, the effect was bound to be disastrous.

Though the segregation of rulers and ruled into closed castes was artificial, however, it had the virtue of leaving the ruled to pursue their avocations more peacefully than they would have been able to if it had not existed. This indeed was the justification of the ruling caste in its heyday: that, keeping all the instruments of force in its own hands, it both used them well in the maintenance of order, and reinforced in the ruled, by thus depriving them of the temptation to further their own ends by violent

[1] See the *Ḳânûnî Âlî 'Oşmân II* (*O.T.E.M.*, No. 17, Appendix, 39 sq.). Thus retired *Sipâhîs*, the emancipated slaves of the Sultan, the occupants of 'learned' posts at court, the children of *'askerîs* (as long as they do not formally become *re'âyâ*), and all women married to *'askerîs*, are to be accounted *'askerîs* themselves.

[2] See Ḳoçu Bey (Behrnauer), 276.

[3] Tischendorf, 44–5. This ruling was embodied in a *ḳânûn* of 1530.

methods, the traditions of peaceable behaviour already induced in them by their religious views and the corporative structure of their society. It was owing to the prevalence of these traditions that most of the rulers might, as we have mentioned, withdraw from a district without jeopardizing its internal security; and largely owing to their prevalence that even after the Ruling and Learned Institutions were corrupted, the Empire cohered for as long as it did, despite almost incessant wars and the intrigues of enemy states.[1] On the other hand, the main stream of Ottoman life naturally ran in the subject populations, in comparison with which the ruling caste, though much in evidence, was small in numbers; so that by its segregation it was to some extent isolated from this life. By the sixteenth century the Moslems and the Christians of the Ottoman Empire were alike separated by sectarian differences from their nearest co-religionists beyond its frontiers, with the result that a distinct culture, embracing both, was able to arise within them.[2] Nevertheless, the various races of which the subject populations were composed were not to be welded into a nation; and this largely for the reason that the ruling class, though to a great extent recruited from the Christian element,[3] on the one hand represented the political domination of Islâm, and on the other was isolated by its constitution from all the ruled of whatever faith.

At the same time, the ruling class was only one of many into which the Sultan's subjects were divided. For the ruled in turn were all organized into bodies such as trade guilds (to which, it may be remarked, Moslems and Christians would often belong indifferently);[4] and it was to these bodies rather than the state, or even the Sultan, that they were inclined to accord their most vivid allegiance. The guilds were, of course, essentially urban. Though in some places at any rate there were guilds of farmers, in general their place was taken in the country-side by village councils or, in the case of nomads, by their tribes. But all, guilds, village councils, and tribes, were to a great extent autonomous, though naturally they were supervised by the local governors; and their autonomy, which was reinforced by the fact that both towns and villages in most places tended to be economically self-contained, split up the subject populations into many semi-independent units, whose stability was little affected by the political vicissitudes of the Empire as a whole. Any wider allegiance that the individual members of these units might entertain was religious rather than political; and if for the more orthodox Moslems it might be centred

[1] Cf. Zinkeisen, iii. 135. [2] Cf. *Encyclopaedia of Islam*, art. 'Turks'.
[3] For the rules governing the *devşirme* see above, p. 43.
[4] See below, p. 289.

in the Sultan as *Imâm*,[1] in all cases it was weaker than their sentiment for the unit of which they formed part.

For these reasons the corruption of the Ruling and Learned Institutions was slow to affect the ruled. It is true that the virtual helplessness in which the latter were kept under the regime as at first constituted prevented them from rising against misgovernment. But if it had not been for the partial autonomy of the bodies in which they were organized, the depredations of the ruling class would have reduced them to ruin rapidly. In the end this corruption did in fact go far to destroy their prosperity and plunged many provinces, particularly in Europe, into a state of perennial disorder. But the process of decay was to some extent disguised by its gradualness, so that it was accepted by the Ottomans of every class with remarkable equanimity.

The superficiality of Ottoman rule, if it may be so described, was always more marked in the Asiatic provinces conquered after the fifteenth century than in the rest of the Empire, owing principally to the fact that these provinces had been for centuries under Moslem rule. For since the institutions already in existence in these provinces were naturally maintained with only such modifications as the assertion of Ottoman sovereignty necessitated, the Moslems that formed the majority in their populations looked to the government to preserve their traditions even less than did those of Anatolia and Europe. The institutions of the Empire itself, again, in so far as they were of Moslem origin, were derived immediately from Persia rather than from the countries conquered by Selîm I. But further contact with Persia was then interrupted owing to the establishment in that country of the heterodox Ṣafevid dynasty. Hence, if inspiration from the older centres of Islâm was still to affect the Ottoman 'homelands', it had to be drawn largely from the Arabic-speaking world; which, for this reason—and for the very reason that its inhabitants did speak the sacred language, while most of them at the same time professed the dominant religion—was regarded by the Ottoman ruling class, at least in the beginning, with a certain deference, which they did not accord to the rest of the Sultan's dominions. This being so, we are to devote a separate chapter to the government of the Arabic-speaking provinces. On the other hand, it was by the system we have described that most parts of the rest of the Empire were administered; and enough has been said concerning them—in view of the fact that, as has already been mentioned, other chapters again are to deal with particular aspects of provincial life—to present a general

[1] Even for the Orthodox Christians the Sultan is said to have acquired the attributes of a *Basileus.*—*Encyclopaedia of Islam,* art. 'Turks'.

picture of their administration. Here, accordingly, it remains only to deal, very briefly, with those parts of the Empire that were at once inhabited by populations other than Arabic-speaking and governed otherwise than by the system in question.

All these regions were on what were at one period or another frontiers of the Empire. Indeed, it was generally either on this account alone, or on account also of their physical conformation, that they were endowed with a special status. Some of them formed vassal states, more or less independent of the Porte according to the terms upon which their rulers or inhabitants had made their submission, and to the manner in which they had afterwards conducted themselves. But others were actually included in ordinary *eyâlets*.

Thus in several *eyâlets* lying to the east of Asia Minor and along what eventually became the Persian frontier there were regions governed by Kurdish chieftains. All but the more southerly parts of this territory had once formed part of the Kingdom of Armenia. But since the destruction of that Kingdom by the Selcuḳids in the eleventh century, the lands that it had included had been repeatedly overrun by Turkish armies and tribes. Even before the Ottoman conquest, therefore, there was a considerable Turkish element in the population of what had been Armenia. Moreover, its control by Moslem rulers of various lines and races, and the anarchical conditions created by the mutual struggles in which they engaged and by the Turkish migrations, had encouraged a movement into it from the south and east on the part of Kurdish tribes, so that by the end of the fifteenth century many of its districts were ruled by petty dynasts of that people. By this time, accordingly, it was hard to say where Armenia began and where Kurdistân came to an end.

The Ottoman conquest was effected by stages. It began (if we ignore the temporary acquisitions of Bâyezîd I in this area)[1] under Meḥmed the Conqueror, was continued by Selîm I, and was completed (except for a subsequent and also ephemeral extension under Murâd III) under Süleymân the Magnificent. The system by which much of this country came eventually to be governed, however, owed its origin to the conditions prevailing in the time of Selîm. For that part of it which he acquired fell to him on his defeat of the Ṣafevid Şâh Isma'îl, by whom it had been overrun shortly before. And Selîm found that the Kurds were antagonistic to Isma'îl both on religious grounds—since they were Sunnî, whereas the Ṣafevid movement was heterodox—and because Isma'îl had subjected them to government by Persian officers. Instead, therefore, of imposing on them governors appointed by

Armenian lands – occupied by many Kurds

[1] Lost owing to Bâyezîd's defeat at the hands of Timur.

the Porte as in most *sancaks*, Selîm set up in many parts of the area concerned a system of indirect rule, through the Kurds' own leaders; and this system was maintained even in regions that ceased to lie on the Persian frontier owing to further Ottoman conquests and was applied in other parts of Kurdistân incorporated in the Empire at later dates. By the middle of the sixteenth century there were at least thirty of these hereditary Kurdish governments established in various districts of Armenia and Kurdistân.[1] Nevertheless, the country had by then been divided also into *eyâlets*,[2] to which *Paşas* were appointed in the usual manner; and it became the policy of the Porte to increase the area of its direct rule at the expense of these semi-autonomous dynasts. This policy was no doubt aided by the conquest under Murâd III of further Ṣafevid territory.[3] The more easily accessible regions, particularly such as lay far from the border, seem then to have been converted into more or less ordinary *sancaks*. On the other hand, the Kurdish rulers of districts to which it was harder of application became actually freer of Ottoman control than they had been at first.[4] By the middle of the seventeenth century, when the Ottoman-Persian frontier had been drawn on a line that with one or two vicissitudes was to prove durable, the apportionment of Ottoman Kurdistân and Armenia into districts directly and more or less indirectly governed was also stabilized. Thus of the six *eyâlets* chiefly concerned, namely, Erḍerûm, Ḳarṣ, Çildir, Diyâr Bekr, Van, and Şehrezûr, whereas the first two were altogether 'normal', being divided into *sancaks* all of the usual type, each of the four others comprised some districts normally and others irregularly governed. Diyâr Bekr, for instance, besides eleven ordinary *sancaks*, had eight others ruled by Kurdish *Beys*, whose office was hereditary. These *sancaks* contained fiefs whose holders were commanded by the usual feudal officers and were obliged to serve in the usual way, only under their *Beys*. The latter might be dismissed by the *Paşa* for failure to perform their duties satisfactorily; but in such cases the *Paşa* was bound to replace the *Bey* dismissed by a member of the same family. These Kurdish *Sancak Beyis* had there-

[1] *Encyclopaedia of Islam*, arts. 'Diyārbekir' and 'Kurds', based largely on data supplied by the *Şeref-nâme* of Şeref Ḥan Bidlîsî. Cf. Seyyid Muṣṭafâ, i. 125. The settlement with the Kurdish chieftains was arrived at on the advice and by the agency of Mevlânâ Idrîs Ḥakîm of Bidlîs, a Kurd himself, at first in the service of the 'White Sheep' dynasty and afterwards in that of Bâyezîd II and Selîm I.—*Encyclopaedia of Islam*, art. 'Bidlīsī'.

[2] Or rather *Beylerbeyiliks*, if the date at which the term *eyâlet* was first used was later, as stated by D'Ohsson; see above, p. 141.

[3] See above, p. 142, n. 6. These conquests left the *eyâlet* of Van, for instance, far within the Ottoman frontiers.

[4] As in the case of the Süleymânî chiefs established at Ḳulp and Mayyâfariḳîn (whose name was changed to a corruption of theirs, Silvân) in the *eyâlet* of Diyâr Bekr.—*Encyclopaedia of Islam*, art. 'Maiyafāriḳīn'.

fore but little independence—unless they could defy the *Paşa*. But there were also in the *eyâlet* five so-called *ḥükûmets*, 'governments', whose rulers, Kurds also, were virtually autonomous, except for the obligation laid on them to furnish troops in war time. In these districts there were no fiefs; and all the proceeds of taxation went to the ruler, who had the privilege of being addressed as *Cenâb*.[1] There were four similar *ḥükûmets* in the *eyâlet* of Van, and another in that of Şehrezûr; while in the three provinces together there were some four hundred tribal chieftains holding hereditary *zi'âmets*, who were likewise obliged to supply troops to the *Bey* of their *sancaḳ*.[2] The position in Çildir is less clear. An account of the seventeenth century shows this *eyâlet* to have included only four hereditary *sancaḳs*,[3] whereas another, of the late eighteenth century, gives the number of its Kurdish *beyliks* as no less than nineteen.[4] Moreover, though Georgia is shown as an independent *eyâlet* in the seventeenth century,[5] and in the eighteenth the Janissary garrisons were stationed at Kutais and Bağdâdcıḳ,[6] it seems in fact to have been controlled from Çildir. It was to the *Paşa* of Çildir, for instance, that the *Beys* of Mingrelia made the annual gifts that marked their recognition of the Sultan's suzerainty.[7] After Şâh 'Abbâs recovered the provinces conquered from the Ṣafevids under Murâd III, indeed, the only parts of Georgia in its larger sense that continued to form part of the Ottoman Empire were those bounding the Black Sea;[8] and little attempt seems to have been made, until in the eighteenth century the Porte awoke to the danger of Russian expansion in those regions, to assert the Sultan's authority over them. We shall have occasion to describe later the efforts that were then made to repair this neglect.

But to return to the Kurds. As well as to the causes that we have already mentioned—their hostility to the Ṣafevids and the

[1] *Cenâb* (Arabic) means literally 'threshold', but is used as an honorific: so *Cenâbuka*, 'your Honour', 'your Excellency'.

[2] Evliyâ, i. 94; Seyyid Muṣṭafâ, i. 130; Hammer, op. cit., 259–60, 263–4, 266; *Encyclopaedia of Islam*, art. 'Kurds'; Isma'îl Ḥusrev, 165–6. Seyyid Muṣṭafâ describes the offices of these Kurdish chieftains as *yurtluḳs* and *ocaḳlıḳs*; see above, p. 48.

[3] Evliyâ, i. 95.

[4] D'Ohsson, vii. 298.

[5] By Evliyâ, loc. cit.

[6] Both in 1723 and 1750. See Aḥmed Cevâd's lists, pp. 167 sq. and 170 sq. Neither are shown in his earlier list from the Hezâr Fenn (pp. 164–5).

[7] Evliyâ, loc. cit. It may be noted also that whereas Evliyâ shows Şuşad as a district of Georgia, the earlier 'Aynî 'Alî (in Seyyid Muṣṭafâ, i. 130) attaches it to the *eyâlet* of Çildir.

[8] The omission from his lists by 'Aynî 'Alî of the districts of Georgia other than Şuşad shown by Evliyâ is due to the fact that he wrote before Murâd IV had recovered some of the territory lost to Şâh 'Abbâs, with the result that the Persian-Ottoman frontier was established, in 1639, on a line that gave the two states more or less what they had included before Murâd III's conquests.

difficulty of controlling them in the mountainous country they inhabited (a difficulty experienced, of course, equally in the case of the Georgians)—these regulations owed their origin partly to the fact that the Kurds were also for the most part wholly or half nomadic. This being so, it is not surprising to find that very similar regulations were applied in other districts, no less mountainous and inhabited by Türkmen and other nomads. In the *eyâlet* of Sivas, for example, six such districts were confided to the rule of a Türkmen *Ağa*,[1] and in the *eyâlet* of Adana, created only at the end of the sixteenth century, there were seven more whose tribal rulers were known as *Boy Beyis*.[2] This country—part of the ancient Cilicia—and that bordering it on the north-east as far as the Euphrates, had been left on their first incorporation in the Empire in the hands of local Moslem potentates of Turkish race, the former being ruled by the dynasty of the Ramaḍân Oğullarî during most of the sixteenth century, and the latter by that of the Ẕu'l-Ḳadr Oğullarî from near the middle of the fifteenth century up to the reign of Süleymân, when it was converted into an *eyâlet* called either Ẕu'l-Ḳadriye after them, or Merʿaş after its capital. These dynasties were both of a foundation later than the Ottoman,[3] which when it came in contact with them was already too powerful to fear them as rivals as it had feared and fought those Turkish dynasties that were established and formidable in the days when it was still comparatively weak. The incorporation of these two states in the Empire with their rulers as vassals was allowable on the same principles as allowed the small Kurdish dynasts to exercise a more limited authority over the territory inhabited by their tribesmen, and, as we shall see, was also applied in the Ḫanate of the Crimea. Up to near the end of the sixteenth century the Porte was less jealous than in later times of its authority in the provinces: as we have observed, the viceroys would then often remain in their posts for many years, and sons of the reigning monarch would usually be given provincial governorships. The maintenance in power of local dynasts such as the Ẕu'l-Ḳadr and Ramaḍân Oğullarî accorded with this atti-

[1] D'Ohsson, vii. 298. How long this régime had been in force does not appear.

[2] Evliyâ, i. 94. *Boy* (Turkish) has among other meanings that of 'clan'. The expression *Boy Beyis* was used of tribal leaders under the Selcuḳids of Rûm (see Köprülüzade, *Selcuḳliler Zamânında*, &c., 206).

[3] Little is known about the Ramaḍân Oğullarî before the second half of the fifteenth century. The Ẕu'l-Ḳadr dynasty was established about a hundred years earlier. The territory of the former comprised the districts of Adana, Sis, Ayas, Ṭarsûs, and the lands of the Varsaḳ Türkmen; the territory of the latter the later *sancaḳs* of Merʿaş, Malaṭya, 'Aynṭâb, Ḳarş, and Sumaysaṭ (Samosata). After their dispossession members of both houses were given employment as provincial governors. See *Encyclopaedia of Islam*, arts. 'Dhu'l-Ḳadr' and 'Ramaḍān Oghullarî'.

tude. But, for reasons to be explained, it later fell into disfavour: royal princes were then kept at the capital, and *Paşas* were posted about with ever-increasing frequency. It was natural, therefore, that the existence of the local dynasts also should have been deprecated. Those we have mentioned were, in fact, dispossessed; and it is probable that if the Porte had been in a position to do so, it would have imposed a unified and centralized rule also on every part of Armenia and Kurdistân and on other, similar, regions in which hereditary chieftainships had hitherto been allowed to subsist. What prevented it from doing so probably was the intractable temper of the tribesmen concerned and the mountainous formation of the country they inhabited. Before long, moreover, the corruption of the Ruling Institution resulted in a weakening of the central government, just as it sought to tighten its control over the provinces, so that it was faced with rebellions and the loss of all effective influence even in regions that had earlier been governed normally. The decay of the Ruling Institution cannot be said to have been due to this movement towards greater centralization; but its result was to cause the tranquillity of the provinces to depend much more intimately than heretofore on the good conduct of affairs at Istanbul, and to load the Porte with a burden that proved too heavy for it to bear.

A virtual autonomy somewhat resembling that of parts of the Armenian and Kurdish *eyâlets* was enjoyed also by many of the tribesmen of Albania and the inhabitants of Montenegro. Albania, however, was included in the *eyâlet* of Rumelia, of which the capital was Adrianople; and none of its *sancaḳs* were held officially on a hereditary term like the Kurdish *beyliks*; still less did it comprise any recognized *ḥükûmets*. Nevertheless, the social organization of all but the town-dwelling Albanians was tribal; and the tribesmen, particularly the Ghegs of the north, were of so warlike a temper that the Ottoman government was never able to subject them to a regular administration. Each tribe of the Ghegs, or 'mountain', as it was called, was divided into a number of clans under the authority of a *Bayraḳdâr*, who, since he held his office by inheritance, resembled, both in the nature of his office and its name, the Kurdish *Sancaḳ Beyi*.[1] Each clan had also a number of elders whose office was likewise hereditary. Assemblies of tribesmen were held under their presidency to settle matters of law. For the Albanians recognized only their customary law, though this was partially embodied in an unwritten *ḳânûn* of ancient native composition.[2] The clans were subdivided, each

[1] *Bayraḳ* and *sancaḳ* both signifying 'flag'.

[2] Called the *Ḳânûn* of Leke Dukagini, supposed to have lived in the thirteenth or the fourteenth century.

subdivision being controlled by another hereditary officer in whose hands lay the execution of justice, and who maintained direct touch with the representative of the tribe, called *Bölük Başi*, resident at Işkodra (Scutari), at least in late times. Revenues were obtained by the government from the tribes only when, which was seldom, it was strong enough to compel their payment. The difficulty of collecting them and of controlling the northern 'mountains' was such that in the middle of the sixteenth century all attempt to cope with it was abandoned. In return for exemption from taxation and governmental interference the tribesmen were engaged to supply the Ottoman armies with contingents of fighting men. These would sometimes assemble under the standards of the commanding *Paşas*. Otherwise they would join the raiding volunteers called *Akinci*.[1] Montenegro (Ḳaradağ) was included in the *sancaḳ* of Işḳodra. Ruled by its prince-bishops (whom we shall have occasion to mention later again), it was, if anything, even more lightly attached to the Porte than Albania proper. Among the Tosks of the south tribal life was more loosely organized, a number of great landlords exercising authority of a feudal character. In this part of the country as well, however, mountain tribes such as the Suliots were quite independent of governmental control, just as in what was equally in the beginning reckoned as a part of Rumelia, the Morea, the inhabitants of Maina were able to exact from the Porte a recognition of their autonomy in return for a payment of tribute.[2]

All the regions we have dealt with up to this point were at least included eventually, if not at first, in regular *eyâlets*, however irregularly governed they might in fact be. Those we are now to describe, on the other hand, were of an altogether different status. The Ḫanate of the Crimea, for instance, was a semi-independent state. Its connexion with the Porte resembled indeed that of the states governed by the Ẕu'l-Ḳadr and Ramaḍân dynasties. Unlike them, however, it was permitted by the Sultans to endure, partly no doubt because of its situation, since it continued, as they did not, to march with the dominions of foreign and hostile potentates. Though the north and centre of the peninsula had fallen into the hands of the Tatars as early as the thirteenth century, the Ḫanate was founded only about fifty years before the conquest of the Crimea by Meḥmed II, at the expense of the Genoese.[3] A part

[1] Seyyid Muṣṭafâ, i. 63.

[2] *Encyclopaedia of Islam*, arts. 'Arnautes' and 'Morea'; *Encyclopaedia Britannica* (11th ed.), art. 'Albania'.

[3] It had been founded by one Ḫâccî Girey, whose grandfather had been a prince of the Golden Horde, with the aid of the Grand Duke of Lithuania. The Genoese were expelled in 1434. The Ottoman conquest took place in 1475. *Encyclopaedia of Islam*, arts. 'Hādjdjī-Girāi', 'Kafa'.

of the country was on the Ottoman conquest formed into an ordinary *eyâlet* comprising three *sancaḳs*, with its capital at the principal port, Keffe (Theodosia). The remainder was left under the rule of the Girey Ḫans, whose residence was Bağçe Serâyi.[1] This arrangement was perhaps intended to afford the Porte a certain control over the Tatar state, while leaving it in the position of a buffer against attacks from the north: but the relations between the *Ḫan* and the *Paşa* of Keffe were left indeterminate; nor was it until near the end of the sixteenth century that the *Ḫans* formally acknowledged the suzerainty of the Sultan by causing his name to be mentioned in the *ḫuṭba*,[2] though from shortly after the conquest they had regularly been confirmed in power by the receipt of standards, *ṭuğs*, and written patents from Istanbul. The *Ḫan's* sovereignty extended beyond the limits of the peninsula as far as Bessarabia to the west and as far as Circassia, which indeed was regarded as a dependency of the Ḫanate, to the east. Moreover, on several occasions members of the Girey family were set up as *Ḫans* of Ḳazan on the Volga, while those of the Crimea continued to receive tribute from the Tsars of Moscow until the seventeenth century, from time to time enforcing their claim to it with raids. In the wars of the Porte with Austria and Poland the Tatar contingents played a notable part, gradually replacing the *Aḳinci* volunteers that in earlier campaigns had preceded the advance of the Ottoman armies proper, laying waste the country-side. On the other hand, the Nogay Tatars of Bessarabia were inclined to treat the Rumanians of Moldavia as inhabitants of the Domain of War, despite the fact that their country formed part of the Empire. Murâd III was able to insist on one occasion that the property and animals they had looted should be restored; but when in later times the authority of the Porte was weakened, the Principality suffered severely from the depredations of the Tatars. From early in the reign of Süleymân the *Ḫans* were provided with a considerable force of *seğmens*, artillerymen, armourers, and other types of soldiery from the capital, and received yearly a sum of money, called *seğmen aḳçesi*, to meet the expense of their pay. What was perhaps this subsidy to the *Ḫans*, though it may have been a separate payment of 1,000 *aḳçes* a day, was furnished by the revenues of Keffe.[3] In the course of its history the Ḫanate was often the object of contention on the part of rival members of the Girey family, who succeeded, not by right of primogeniture, but, like the later Sultans themselves, in order of seniority; and a deci-

[1] i.e. 'The Garden Palace'. The palace was originally built in a suburb of the town, then called Ḳirḳ Yer (Forty Places); but later this suburb became its centre; and the former name fell out of use. Ibid., art. 'Baghče Sarāi'.

[2] For *ḫuṭba* see above, p. 31.

[3] Seyyid Muṣṭafâ, i. 130.

sion in such cases was usually secured by the interposition of the Porte. Otherwise, however, the Ḫanate was governed independently on a tribal military basis. Two members of the ruling house besides the *Ḫan* himself held courts in other places than the capital, being provided with special revenues for the purpose. These were the *Ḫan's* first and second heirs, called respectively *Ḳalgay* and *Nûru'd-Dîn.*[1] The tribal chieftains, known as *Mîrzâs*, were commanded by two officers called *Şîrîn Beyi* and *Ma'sûr Beyi*, each of whom was appointed from a particular family.[2] The country's religious and legal needs were attended to by the usual 'learned men' organized independently of those appointed to places in the rest of the Empire and headed, it is notable, by a *Ḳâḍî-'asker*. Finally, an important official was the *Ḫan Ağasî*, whose office corresponded to that of a *muḥtesib*.[3]

The remaining four dependencies of the Empire that we must mention resembled the Crimean Ḫanate in this respect that they, too, were self-governing. Unlike its, however, their governments were Christian. As we have explained, the *Şerî'a* permitted the incorporation in the Domain of Islâm of states governed by 'scriptural' rulers on condition of their paying tribute to the *Imâm*. All four of these states, accordingly, were tributary to the Ottoman Sultans. Nevertheless, they differed one from another in the degree of control exercised over them in practice by the Porte.

The principalities of Wallachia and Moldavia[4] may be considered together, since not only were they inhabited by peoples of the same race, but were similarly governed and came eventually to stand in a similar relationship to the Porte. Historically, nevertheless, Wallachia was permanently reduced to a tributary status almost a century before Moldavia; and whereas the fate of Wallachia was settled by the final obliteration of Serbian independence in the fifteenth century, it was not until Süleymân had conquered the greater part of Hungary that the Ottoman hold on Moldavia became really firm. The terms upon which the original agreements to pay tribute and acknowledge the Sultan's suzerainty were concluded seem to have been more or less alike. The native princes, called *Hospodar* or *Voyvoda*, were to enjoy complete autonomy; the *Boyars*,[5] or land-owning nobles, of each principality were to elect them as heretofore from among the members of a

[1] This arrangement dated only from the last quarter of the sixteenth century.

[2] Evliyâ Çelebi, i. 93.

[3] Aḥmed Râsim, i. 289 sq., notes; Cevdet, i. 258 sq.; *Encyclopaedia of Islam*, arts. 'Girāy', 'Ḳrîm'.

[4] Called in Turkish Iflaḳ and Boğdan respectively.

[5] It may be noted that the words *Hospodar*, *Voyvoda* or *Voyevode*, and *Boyar* are all Slav. As we shall see, *voyvoda* was also used in Turkish for a certain type of government servant.

royal house; no mosques or Ottoman fortresses were to be built within their dominions; and no Moslems were to settle or purchase land in them. Even before Moldavia was finally reduced to paying tribute, however, Meḥmed II was provoked into invading Wallachia and interfering with the succession; and after Süleymân's invasion of Hungary Moslems began to settle and build mosques in both principalities. Both Hospodars were subsequently obliged to furnish contingents to fight with the Ottoman armies; and as time went on the Sultans demanded ever higher payments by way of tribute. Their hold on the principalities was strengthened by the construction of fortresses both on the Danube and, though this was contrary to the original agreement, on Moldavian soil, in Bessarabia,[1] the southern part of which was actually ceded to Süleymân after his invasion of the principality in 1538, by the then Hospodar, who went so far as to accept Islâm and received a Janissary guard in his capital. Before the end of the sixteenth century the Hospodar of Wallachia was also provided with a similar guard; indeed it was with a massacre of these Janissaries and other Moslems then resident in Tirgovişta[2] that in 1594 the Hospodar Michael the Brave began a revolt that ended in his uniting not only the two Danubian principalities but that of Transylvania in an ephemeral kingdom virtually independent of the Sultan, whose armies he defeated on more than one occasion after seizing several towns south of the Danube in Rumelia. Michael, however, was assassinated in 1601; and the principalities were restored to their former status.[3] In the course of the seventeenth century the Bassaraba family from which most of the Hospodars had hitherto been elected died out. Candidates for election had by now long taken to bribing the Sultan's ministers for their favour, which was decisive; and as a result the Porte had become interested in bringing about changes of tenure as often as it could. Already many of the Hospodars appointed were of other races than the Rumanian.[4] It was not, therefore, an abrupt reversal of practice when early in the eighteenth century the policy was adopted of choosing them exclusively from among the Greek aristocracy of the Phanar. The immediate cause of its adoption was the discovery that both

[1] Called in Turkish Bucaḳ.

[2] The Wallachian capital up to 1698, when the Hospodar transferred his headquarters to Bucarest, Tirgovişta being inconveniently near the frontier of Transylvania, now to be ceded to Austria.

[3] Michael began his adventure in concert with Aaron of Moldavia and Sigismund of Transylvania, Aaron also contriving a massacre of Janissaries and other Moslems at Yassy. On this Meḥmed III decided to convert Moldavia into an *eyâlet*, but owing to the defeat of his armies by the insurgents was prevented from doing so. Subsequently he was even obliged to recognize Michael's conquests.

[4] Hospodars of the following races had been appointed to Moldavia: a Saxon 1580), a Croat (1618), a Pole (1626), a Greek (1630).

Hospodars were in secret communion with Tsar Peter the Great, with whom the Sultan was then at war. It was evident that, in these times, when the Empire was in such evident decline, the Porte would be well advised to appoint Hospodars over whom it had some hold. The families of the Phanariots constituted, as it were, ready-made hostages. Moreover, the Phanariots by reason of their close connexion with the Patriarchate of Constantinople, which with the encouragement of the Ottoman government had extended its influence over various Orthodox communities of the Empire that had earlier been autocephalous, and had incurred the hatred of these communities by appointing Greeks to minister to their spiritual needs, had in the regions concerned come in some sort to be identified with the central administration, in which indeed some posts were habitually held by them. From 1716, accordingly, up to the time of our survey, the two principalities were invariably governed by members of these Phanariot families, in whom, for so long, the confidence of the Porte was on the whole justified, at least as regards their loyalty. Wallachia was the richer and more sought after of the two principalities; so that when as sometimes happened its Hospodar was replaced by the Hospodar of Moldavia, the change was regarded as a promotion for the latter. Since by now the post of *Dîvân* Dragoman was invariably held also by a Phanariot,[1] it was usual in the eighteenth century for the Hospodarships to be filled by persons who had previously enjoyed the opportunities it offered for familiarizing themselves with the conduct of affairs. These offices were all obtained as a rule by a combination of intrigue and bribery, which rendered their tenure highly precarious.[2] Each Hospodar kept himself informed of events at the capital and caused his interests to be watched by a representative called *Ḳapî Kâḫyasî*,[3] who made it his chief care to forestall the machinations of his master's rivals. These had as their aim the attraction of some minister's favourable attention, as his own were directed to holding it; and this could best be effected by the offer of money. Hence the Hospodars were put to enormous expense first in securing and then in retaining their offices; also they considered it due to the dignity of their rank to keep up an extravagant state.[4] The principal and often the only source on which they might draw to defray this expenditure was the wealth of the principalities themselves. And as, on the one hand, they

[1] See above, p. 123.

[2] It is said that the average tenure of a Hospodarship was two years and a half.

[3] i.e. 'Intendant of the Gate', their representatives at the Porte. All provincial governors and tax-farmers (*mültezims*) and the Greek-Orthodox and Armenian *millets* (see below, ch. xiv) kept similar *Ḳapî Kâḫyalarî* at the Porte to watch their interests.

[4] They were invested with honours comparable to those accorded to a *vezîr*.

could not look forward to any such long tenures of office as might have deterred them from risking its exhaustion, and, on the other, they enjoyed virtually unlimited power within the spheres of their jurisdiction, they were encouraged to extract as much as they could from their temporary subjects, whom their rapacity subjected to the severest suffering. For ever since the Hospodars had owed their appointment to the favour of the Porte, the Boyars had been unable to control them. They were now subservient in the extreme, and to escape their exactions themselves, joined with them in squeezing the peasants. The old constitution of Moldavia had provided for a division of powers between the Hospodar, the Church, and the Boyars, the most eminent of the latter forming a council; the three sat together in a high court of justice, the Metropolitan declaring the law, the Boyars deciding on the guilt or innocence of those on trial, and the Hospodar pronouncing sentence. But when the Hospodars became irresponsible this provision was naturally of little effect. The chief officers of state were a minister called by the Byzantine title of Logothete, a treasurer, and a commander-in-chief called Hetman; those of the court a chamberlain, a sword-bearer, and a cup-bearer. Under the Phanariot regime certain posts were still reserved for the Boyars; but the most influential were given to the Greek followers of the Hospodars. These followers often acquired Boyar status by marriage, with the result that the Rumanian upper class was progressively Grecized and so divorced in sentiment from the peasantry.[1]

The third of the four Christian dependencies of the Empire was the Kingdom of Transylvania.[2] On the first invasion of Hungary by Süleymân the Magnificent in 1526 all the parts of it then conquered were placed under the rule of Yanoș of Transylvania as the Sultan's vassal, with head-quarters at Buda. But when, on the Austrians' attempting to recover their losses, Süleymân was obliged to undertake another campaign in 1541, he made Buda the centre of an *eyâlet*, leaving only Transylvania to Yanoș's son and successor. From that date up to the end of the seventeenth century, accordingly, Transylvania remained a tributary vassal kingdom. For though, as we have mentioned, Michael the Brave of Wallachia incorporated it in his dominions for a few years at the end of the sixteenth century, it reverted to its former status on his death; and the only other event of major importance that befell it during its period of adherence to the Ottoman Empire was an invasion by the armies of Meḥmed IV under the command

[1] *Encyclopaedia of Islam*, arts. 'Iflāḳ' and 'Boghdān'; *Encyclopaedia Britannica*, art. 'Rumania'; Seton-Watson, *History of Rumania*, 34, 50 sq., 85, 126 sq.; Aḥmed Râsim, i. 290, note; iii. 1341 sq., notes.

[2] Called in Turkish Erdel.

of Köprülü Meḥmed Paşa in 1657—this was provoked by the disobedience of the then King, and resulted in an augmentation of the yearly tribute.[1] As regards the status of Transylvania under Ottoman dominion, it may be remarked that its kings were regarded as of higher rank than the Hospodars of the principalities, being invested with crowns instead of with the caps, called *ḳoḳa*, reserved for the latter; and that the fortresses on Transylvanian soil were manned with native instead of with Ottoman troops.[2] Transylvania was, of course, no longer Ottoman at the time of our survey, having been ceded to Austria by the Treaty of Carlovitz in 1699.

The republic of Dubrovniḳ, or Ragusa,[3] on the other hand—the fourth of the Christian dependencies—remained tributary to the Sultans until an end was put to its existence by Napoleon in 1804. As regards relations with the Porte, its history also is of greater interest and significance than that of Transylvania, or even, perhaps, that of the principalities. Dubrovniḳ was established as a free state, after having depended successively on Venice and Hungary, in the fourteenth century; and soon after, recognizing the advantages that a unification of the Balkan peninsula under Ottoman rule would offer to the commerce on which the republic chiefly subsisted, its rulers treated with the Sultans to such good purpose as in 1399 to obtain from Bâyezîd I the right for Ragusan subjects to trade unhindered in any part of the Empire. Subsequently Ragusan factories were established in many towns of the peninsula, and the Ragusans came to enjoy a quasi-monopoly of its trade. When, moreover, on the conquest of Serbia, Ottoman armies advanced to within striking distance of their territory, they hastened to offer the Sultans a yearly tribute; for by so doing they brought themselves into the Moslem legal category of 'tolerated infidel subjects', and acquired a title to protection by Ottoman forces. This arrangement proved so convenient to the Ragusans that, though in early times they were reproached by the Pope for their reprehensible friendliness for the infidel, they persisted in their attitude; and later, when in the wars that brought disaster on the Porte at the end of the seventeenth and the beginning of the eighteenth centuries the Venetians twice occupied the hinterland of Dubrovniḳ, the Ragusans contrived that by the treaties re-establishing peace this territory should be restored to Ottoman control. They were inclined, it is true, to withhold the payment of tribute, when the Porte seemed incapable of enforcing

[1] Evliyâ Çelebi, when stating (i. 92) that Transylvania had been conquered only in the reign of Meḥmed IV, is referring merely to this invasion.—Seton-Watson, op. cit. 119; *Encyclopaedia Britannica*, art. 'Austria-Hungary'.

[2] Aḥmed Râsim, i. 290, 291, notes.

[3] Under the Ottoman régime the name Dubrovniḳ was that officially used.

it; and the Ottoman ministers, on their side, insisted from time to time on increases in its amount. But only on two occasions were the Ragusans subjected to extraordinary contributions. From the Peace of Carlovitz onwards the tribute was brought to Istanbul every three years by envoys of the republic. These envoys, as also those that until its cession brought the tribute from Transylvania, were, at least by the late seventeenth century, received, like the representatives of foreign states, at assemblies of the *Dîvân* held either for audiences of the Sultan or for the payment of the troops. But the former were accorded no such honour as the latter dignitaries, the *ḳânûn* running: 'Infidel ambassadors over whom trouble must be taken are all except the ambassadors of Dubrovniḳ and Transylvania.'[1] The envoy from Dubrovniḳ was even excluded from the meal offered after the proceedings to the other ambassadors, who were invited to sit and eat with the Grand *Vezîr*. Nevertheless, relations between Dubrovniḳ and the Porte were peculiarly satisfactory. No doubt the geographical situation of the republic and its small size were partly responsible: for, in the first place, since it was surrounded by Ottoman territory, it was not called on to act as a buffer state, and, in the second, it was obliged to depend on some greater power and so was not tempted to strive for complete independence. Indeed, its example seems to show that the woes of, for instance, the principalities were to some extent due to the efforts made by their rulers to escape from Ottoman domination. For the Ragusans, who never made such efforts, who indeed clung to their position as Ottoman vassals, had no cause to complain of the treatment they received at the hands of the Porte; and there is no reason to suppose that, had the Hospodars remained equally loyal, the Sultans would have been less scrupulous in their regard. The prosperity of Dubrovniḳ did, it is true, decline during its long period of vassalage to the Porte. But it declined only as did that of its greater rivals in trade, Venice and Genoa, from causes that had nothing to do with Ottoman rule, and was further damaged by a disastrous earthquake in 1667.[2]

VII. THE DECAY OF THE RULING INSTITUTION

Some of the changes that overtook the Ruling Institution between the sixteenth and the eighteenth centuries have already been described; and some of the causes of its decay as a whole will already be apparent. It remains, however, to examine these causes somewhat further, and to complete our sketch of the condition to

[1] *M.T.M.* i. 514 (*Ḳânûn-nâme* of 'Abdu'r-Raḥmân Tevḳî'î).

[2] Forbes, Toynbee, Mitrany, and Hogarth, *The Balkans*, 103, 107; *Encyclopaedia of Islam*, art. 'Ragusa'.

which the Institution, and particularly the armed forces, had been reduced at the time of our survey.

A number of factors, which we can do no more than touch on, seem to have combined in the sixteenth century to make untenable the position of the Sultanate at the dizzy level attained by Süleymân the Magnificent. At first sight it would seem that the Empire, as a Mediterranean power, must have owed its decline, as the Italian maritime republics owed theirs, chiefly to the discovery of America and the Cape passages, by which trade between Europe and the Orient was gradually diverted from the overland routes. In the first place, however, the main land routes passed, not through the 'original' provinces of the Empire, but through Syria and Egypt, which were incorporated scarcely more than half a century before the decay set in. Gravely, therefore, though the latter countries suffered by the diversion, the decline of their prosperity, in so far as it was due to this cause, cannot have rendered the 'original' provinces less prosperous than they had been before the conquests of Selim, except in so far as their economy depended on their commerce with Syria and Egypt; and in fact such 'foreign' trade seems to have been comparatively unimportant to this economy as a whole. In the second place, Venice and Genoa owed their decline not only to the diversion of the Eastern trade from the overland routes, but to the competition of the Levant Companies chartered by the western powers, which from the end of the sixteenth century exchanged the manufactures of their countries both for the products of the Empire and for those of the East that were still carried overland—a development that, in comparison at least with its effect on the Italian republics, was beneficial to the Empire. It is true that, as time went on, the import of West-European manufactures led both to the ruin of native industries and the export of gold for the purchase of these imports. But this process became disastrous to the Empire only in the age of the industrial revolution—at least two centuries later than the beginnings of decay.

The discoveries of Columbus and Da Gama, therefore, can scarcely be regarded as the principal cause of this decay, if indeed they were even a very considerable cause. In any case, from the Ottoman point of view they constituted a factor of compulsion: as it were an act of God, beyond the Ottomans' control. And in this they contrasted with what does appear to have been its fundamental cause: the successive entertainment by the Sultans themselves of incompatible aspirations.

The first of these aspirations was the leadership of the popular-religious movement of conquest by which their empire was first expanded to considerable size. But their very success in this enterprise, the greatness of the position they attained thereby, induced in them a second ambition: to surround themselves with the traditional pomp of monarchy. Now their adoption of this aim cut them off from their former supporters in two ways. Not only did the Ottoman enterprise become predominantly dynastic; but the sultans followed the example of earlier Turkish dynasts in adhering to a strict orthodoxy. And this was not merely out of harmony with, but actually opposed to, certain religious beliefs, to the influence of which they owed in great part the foundation of their empire, and which were still entertained by a vast number of their Moslem subjects. As a result they were obliged again and again to suppress popular-religious risings. So the effect of this policy was to preserve and emphasize the military character of the Sultans' power, changed though this was in respect of its support. And being possessed of an efficient military instrument, the Sultans could not forbear to use it, till they had expanded their possessions far beyond what might have been the stable limits of Rumelia and Anatolia.

Their motive in doing so was not, to be sure, a mere love of aggrandisement: Selîm conquered not only Armenia and Kurdistân but also Syria and Egypt to prevent their conquest by the Ṣafevids; and Süleymân invaded Hungary to protect his European possessions from the Emperor. But Persia and Austria, by these extensions of Ottoman territory, were brought to march with it; and by the sixteenth century the Şî'î and Catholic worlds were no longer so much cut off one from the other that a combination between them was impracticable.[1] It is true that, had the Sultans refrained from expanding their empire in this way, these two opponents might still have hemmed them in on the smaller frontiers that would then have been theirs; and that their position relatively to Persia at least would in that case have been very much weaker than in fact it came to be. But the Austrian and Persian borders would not then have been separated by so vast a stretch of territory, cut by a sea and bestrewn with mountains, across which the Ottoman forces could not be moved with any rapidity. And, having less to defend, the Sultans might then perhaps have adopted with a greater degree of safety a way of life, consonant again with their aspiration to traditional monarchy, but unhappily incompatible with the command of armies: the retirement from the active conduct of affairs into a majestic seclusion. That they did adopt it, in the perilous position created by this expansion, seems to have been a prime cause in the decline of their power.[2]

[1] In 1599, for instance, Şâh 'Abbâs sent a mission to Europe, accredited to the courts of the Empire, the Vatican, and Venice amongst others; and in 1613–14 the king of Spain sent ambassadors, accompanied by several priests, to Iṣfahân —see Guy le Strange, *Don Juan of Persia* (London 1926).

[2] Koçu Bey, in his *Risâle* or tract setting forth the causes and course of the

Its consequences were in the event much mitigated by historical accidents: that in the early part of the seventeenth century the Thirty Years' War engaged most of the energies of central Europe, and that the power of the Safevids declined even faster than that of the Sultans themselves. Nevertheless, these consequences went far enough to show how disastrous the choice of such a seclusion might be. Indeed it was only this respite from external pressures, combined with attempts at recovery by certain Sultans and Grand *Vezîrs* (which constituted temporary reversals of this fateful policy) that saved the Empire from a swift disintegration.

Owing to the corporative structure of Ottoman society, the majority of the Sultans' subjects were, as we have remarked,[1] slow to be affected by the vicissitudes through which the Ruling Institution might pass. Nor did the conduct of individual Sultans produce much immediate effect on the tenor of their lives. On the other hand, the Ruling Institution itself depended absolutely on the Sultan, who was the head and centre of the 'corporation' it constituted. Naturally, therefore, the retirement of the Sultans from the direction of this corporation was calculated to result in its disorganization—unless their place might adequately be filled by their general deputies, the Grand *Vezîrs*. The attempt virtually to replace the Sultans by these ministers was in fact made: the Sultans' function in the state thereafter (except when, like the youthful 'Osmân II and his terrible brother, Murâd IV, they emerged to resume the leadership thus abandoned)[2] was limited to the approval or veto of their deputies' actions, and to ceremonial appearances in public. But, as we have explained, for the very reason that the ministers' authority was no more than delegated, and that they might at any moment be deprived of it, the Grand *Vezîrs* were as a rule too weak to direct the Ruling Institution satisfactorily. Moreover, the Sultans' retirement produced other

decline of the Ottoman power during the last quarter of the sixteenth and the first quarter of the seventeenth centuries, places the failure of the Sultans after Süleymân to attend to state affairs in person first on the list of such causes; see Behrnauer, op. cit. 275, 320. It is sometimes said (see, e.g. *Encyc. of Islam*, art. 'Turks' and cf. Cevdet, i. 106) that what caused the decline of the Empire was the difficulty its rulers experienced in converting it from a military into a 'civil' organization. But the Ottoman administration was in fact always as much 'civil' as 'military'. The real difficulty seems to us rather to have been that here described.

[1] Above, p. 160.

[2] 'Osmân II, known as Genç (Young) 'Osmān, partly to distinguish him from the founder of the dynasty, partly because he came to the throne at an unprecedentedly early age, reigned from 1618 to 1622, when he was deposed and murdered in a Janissary revolt. Murâd IV, who succeeded him after their imbecile brother Muṣṭafâ I had been restored for a few months and then deposed for a second time, was actually even younger, being only thirteen; but he later restored much of the lost fortunes of the Empire, retaking Bağdâd, for instance. He reigned from 1623 to 1640.

unhappy effects. As long as they took an active part in affairs, the influence exerted on them by the inmates of the *Ḥarem* and the personnel of the Inside Service was checked by their experience of the world outside the palace walls. Afterwards it was not: with the results that, in the first place, they yielded to the counsel of persons unfit to proffer it, and, in the second, they promoted to high offices of state persons unfit to fill them.[1] It thus came about that the incumbents of the Grand Vezîrate, who alone were in a position to supply the Sultans' deficiencies, not only lived in constant apprehension of dismissal, but were often inadequate to their employment. On the other hand, several Grand *Vezîrs* of the decadence showed themselves fully capable of replacing their Sultans at the head of affairs.[2] And the success of their efforts at conservation or reform, as of that which attended the vigorous rule of Murâd IV, is proof of the extent to which the Ruling Institution depended on its head—Sultan or Grand *Vezîr*—for its prosperity.

This dependence of the Ruling Institution on the character of the Sultan would probably have resulted in its eventual corruption in any case. It was, after all, a matter of chance that down to Süleymân the Sultans had all been adequate to their position; nor is there much reason to suppose that Selîm II would have been so successful a ruler as his forefathers, even if Süleymân had not already established the precedent of retiring from the direction of affairs. Again, it is probable that the decadence would have set in not much later than it did, apart from this dependence, owing to two other developments resulting from the conquests of the sixteenth century.

Both were due to the fact that the wars were immediately profitable. The acquisition of valuable spoils by the ruling class, headed by the Sultan, encouraged it to sustain a magnificence that, apart from being in itself a source of demoralization, could be supported only if this process were to continue indefinitely.[3] But it did not so continue: even during the reign of Süleymân warfare was not uninterrupted; and the campaigns of the end of the century were fought to maintain the frontiers already reached, and so yielded no booty from enemy territory; on the contrary, as the

Sultans

[1] Koçu Bey (see Behrnauer, op. cit. 276, 320, and cf. Cevdet, i. 95) considers the interference of court favourites in public affairs one of the major causes of decline. He traces it back to the reign of Süleymân and the promotion first of Ibrâhîm and later of Rüstem from the Inside Service to the Grand Vezirate. It was a tradition of Perso-Moslem statecraft that the monarch should be intimate only with powerless courtiers; see Niẓâmu'l-Mulk, *Siyâset-Nâme* (ed. Schefer), 82.

[2] Cf. above, p. 110.

[3] This is another of the points stressed by Koçu Bey, see Behrnauer, op. cit. 278, 321.

disorganization of the Ruling Institution developed, they began to result in defeats more often than in victories. The consequence was that, first, the ruling class took to supplementing its thus depleted resources by the acceptance of bribes in return for the favours that the privileged position of its members enabled them to confer;[1] and, secondly, the government, since it had come to depend largely on war booty for funds wherewith to pay the standing troops, was now, in searching for an alternative source, confronted with an all but insoluble problem, which it was nevertheless obliged to solve under ever recurrent threats of mutiny and riot.

The process of corruption began at the top. Based on the Sultan's right to a definite share in the spoils of war, a custom was established whereby military commanders, returning from a campaign, presented the monarch with the choicest booty they had secured; and this usage led in turn to the regular presentation of gifts by *Paşas*, even when no war had furnished the wherewithal.[2] From this stage it was an easy, a hardly perceptible step to another: the presentation of gifts in the expectation of a *quid pro quo*. And when once the Sultan or the Grand *Vezîr* had yielded to the temptation of accepting presents on this basis, the infection quickly spread to their inferiors of every rank. The acceptance of such 'considerations' was actually erected into a system, even in the reign of Süleymân. Thenceforward every candidate for office was required to pay a sum down for its grant—these payments being considered analogous, perhaps, to the advances payable by peasants on assuming a lease of agricultural land.[3] Such a system, however, was not merely open to abuses; it invited them. And though, during the reign of Süleymân, the competence of candidates for office, rather than their capacity to buy it, seems to have remained the criterion generally observed in their selection, later it was duly abused, with disastrous consequences. The object of such bribery as was not sanctioned was as a rule admission into, or advancement in, the government service. Its acceptance, therefore, implied that the organization of the Ruling Institution would be injured in two ways: the character of its personnel would be altered, and its rule of promotion by merit would be compromised.[4]

bribes

[1] Cf. Isma'il Ḫusrev, *Türkiye köy Iḳtiṣâdiyâti*, 171, referring to this development in connexion with speculation in land.

[2] Seyyid Muṣṭafâ, i. 115–16. Instances cited by this author are the presentation made to Süleymân by Barbarossa (cf. above, p. 92) and that of a million *lire* made by Ibrâhîm Paşa, Vâlî of Egypt.

[3] For *tapu* see below, p. 239.

[4] Seyyid Muṣṭafâ, i. 117–18. An anecdote is here quoted from the *Künhu'l-Aḫbâr* of the historian 'Alî about Şemsî Paşa of the Isfendiyâr Oğlu dynasty, who congratulated himself on causing Murâd III to accept a large bribe, since he judged that if the Sultans indulged in corruption their power, which had overcome that of his own ancestors, would decline.

As for the problem of the troops, this would perhaps have been less acute than it became, had not the Janissaries at least—if not the rest of the standing army—already long shown themselves all too apt for rebellion. The standing army, as we have remarked, had actually been created by the Sultans to free them from a dependence on popular support. And though the slave status of its members rendered it at first more tractable than the free-born Moslems of which the earliest Ottoman forces had been composed, by the end of the fifteenth century the Janissaries had grown conscious of their power as the Sultan's chief support, and had used it to bring about the deposition of Bâyezîd II and the accession of Selîm I. Selîm, again, on his Persian campaign, had been obliged to retreat after the victory of Çaldîran owing to their insistence. He had then, however, instituted new regulations for the corps, which, combined with his well-earned reputation for ferocity, kept them docile for the rest of his reign and for most of the reign of Süleymân. Nevertheless, early in the latter they had mutinied again; and on Süleymân's death had used the same means to force from his successor, Selîm II, a larger sum, by way of the now traditional accession bonus, than he could afford. Owing to the efficient rule of the Grand *Vezîr* Soḳollu they made no further trouble for the time being.[1] But in the following reign, in which these embarrassments reached a crisis, they began to terrorize the government in earnest, and in doing so to attract imitators among the rest of the paid corps.

Whether by a coincidence, or the decree of Fate, the Ottoman Empire began to decline almost exactly at the millenary of the Hegira—a date long awaited with apprehension by many of its Moslem inhabitants. For certain prophecies foretold that it would mark the ruin of Islâm at the hands of the Christians. The overthrow of the Emîrate of Granada, which was followed by migrations of Moors to Istanbul, and the defeat of the Ottoman arms at Malta and Lepanto, were interpreted as signs of impending doom. Alarums of Christian uprisings were so rife in many towns that the gates were shut at the hour of Friday Prayers, lest the faithful should be caught at a disadvantage.[2]

The fatal year (1591–2) came and went, it is true, without the occurrence of any catastrophe. Yet the reign of Murâd III, in which it fell, witnessed the infliction of irreparable damage to the Ruling Institution. The chief factors in this process were a threat to the system of the *devşirme*, and a growth of irregularities in that

[1] Seyyid Muṣṭafâ, i. 143.

[2] See Hasluck, *Christianity and Islam under the Sultans*, 721 sq., 751, 753. D'Ohsson, i. 245, states that public prayers of penance were first ordered by Murâd III, in September 1592, when he was alarmed by a conjunction of wars, civil disturbances, and plague. They were offered in the *Ok Meydânı*.

of fief-holding. The first was occasioned by the truculence of the Janissaries. The second was an effect of corruption.

It is true that the purity of *devşirme* recruitment had already been sullied by various devices. Christian parents had sometimes bought off their sons from conscription; Moslem, Jewish, and Gypsy youths had been substituted for Christian. But hitherto the government had punished severely most of such abuses when they were discovered. Nor had these abuses destroyed the discipline and fighting value of the corps.[1]

It appears, however, that Murâd III, observing how far the Janissaries—for it was against the Janissaries that the blow was directed—were the potential masters of the state, actually desired to corrupt their organization.[2] Hence in 1582, with the applause of his courtiers, but against the determined resistance of the Janissary *Ağa*, he allowed the admission of a large number of untrained recruits direct into the *ortas* of the corps.[3] Moreover, during the campaign with Persia that occurred in his reign, he permitted the enrolment of so many more, that by the end of it the personnel of the Janissaries had been more than doubled.[4]

This measure had a twofold effect. It compromised the *devşirme* system—since it was evident that, if such practices were repeated, this would become otiose—and it embarrassed the treasury as never before, since the funds at its disposal had scarcely sufficed for even the original establishment. Moreover, the second effect resulted eventually in an intensification of the first. The process was roughly as follows. In order to pay the enlarged army, the government resorted to a debasement of the coinage; and this occasioned revolts, first on the part of the Janissaries, and a few years later on that of the cavalry regiments, of the capital.[5] The soldiery thus came to feel its power more vividly than ever. Thenceforward it was ready to meet any opposition to its wishes with force. A second revolt of the cavalry in 1603 was, it is true, suppressed by means of the Janissaries;[6] but this was to render the Janissaries themselves the more intractable for the future. Os̱mân II made a serious effort to have done with the menace in 1622. But the Janissaries were too strong for him; and the struggle ended in his deposition and murder.[7] It was reserved for his brother

[1] *Encyclopaedia of Islam*, art. 'Dewshirme'. The only born Moslems that were legally permitted to enter the *ocaḳ* were the sons of retired Janissaries. Cevdet, i. 90.

[2] Cf. Juchereau, i. 40.

[3] Koçu Bey (Behrnauer, op. cit. 299–300); Cevdet, i. 95; Seyyid Muṣṭafâ, i. 140–1.

[4] Seyyid Muṣṭafâ, loc. cit.; Koçu Bey (Behrnauer, op. cit., 298).

[5] *Encyclopaedia of Islam*, art. 'Murad III'.

[6] Ibid., art. 'Muḥammad III'.

[7] See Eton, 152–8.

Murâd IV to succeed in curbing them, but only at the cost of still further destroying the basis of the Ruling Institution as it had formerly been constituted. For Murâd resorted to a suspension of the *devşirme* levy in order to reduce the establishment of the infantry.[1] Thereafter it was less and less frequently applied; and by the middle of the seventeenth century had become all but a dead letter.[2]

The disappearance of the *devşirme* system is hardly, perhaps, from a general point of view, a matter for regret. But it was fatal to the Ottoman power, because it involved the decline of the whole admirably arranged order of military and administrative training. Its effects might have been mitigated if at the same time the soldiery that it had been instituted chiefly to supply had been abolished and replaced by others properly exercised and disciplined. But though both Murâd IV and the Grand *Vezîr* Köprülü Fâḍil Aḥmed Paşa[3] formed bodies of fresh troops,[4] they were never sufficiently strong to abolish the Janissaries. And so the Janissaries continued in being, turbulent, expensive, untrained, consequently all but useless in war, and a fatal example of corruption and degeneracy to any rivals raised to supply their deficiencies.

For the abolition of the *devşirme* levies resulted in a recruitment of the Janissary *ocaḳ* entirely from among free-born Moslems—since only Moslems were eligible for service in the armies of the faith, and the conversion of *Ẕimmîs* had depended wholly on their conscription.[5] But these Moslem recruits were far less amenable to discipline than their predecessors of the *devşirme*. They soon

[1] *Encyclopaedia of Islam*, art. 'Murad IV'.

[2] Ibid., art. 'Dewshirme'.

[3] See above, p. 110, note 3.

[4] New formations were created by Murâd IV from among the *Cebecis* (above, pp. 66–8), the *Bostancis* (above, p. 84), and particularly the *Seğmens*; and Köprülü Aḥmed Paşa raised fresh troops under the names *beşli* and *gönüllü*—*Encyclopaedia of Islam*, arts. 'Murad IV' and 'Muḥammad IV'; Jorga, *Geschichte des Osmanischen Reichs*, iv. 161.

What precisely is intended by *Seğmens* here is doubtful. Jorga, op. cit. 158, states that the *Seğmens* were separated from the rest of the Janissaries (the number of whose *ortas* was thereby reduced to 176). But if so, they were later reunited. In other contexts the term *Seğmen* seems to be used vaguely for 'regular infantry'. Its use is compared by Hammer, *Staatsverwaltung*, 192, to that of '*chasseur*' in French.

Cevdet, i. 92, quoting Montecucculi, describes the *Beşlis* as mounted guards (*muḥâfaẓalilar*), adding that the hussars of Hungary were of this type. *Beşli* means 'of five', 'fiver'—possibly because these troops were paid at the rate of 5 *aḳçes* a day.

Gönüllü, meaning 'volunteer', was not a new name for troops. Jorga, op. cit. iv. 161, states that the function of the *Gönüllüs* was to raid ahead of the armies with the *Aḳincis* (see above, p. 56).

[5] Jorga, op. cit. iv. 158. Tott, *Memoirs*, ii. 70–1, emphasizes the fact that this whole development had come about because the Turks (i.e. Moslems) had been jealous of the privileges enjoyed by the Janissaries—'The Privileges granted them determined the Turks to have their Children enrolled'.

forced the abandonment of two cardinal principles of the Janissary organization, namely the prohibitions against marriage before retirement on pension and against engagement in any craft or trade. Janissary recruits of the new type were drawn chiefly from the artisan classes of the towns in which *ortas* were stationed, among whom, as among Moslems in general, early marriages were the rule. Consequently it became more and more unusual for them to live in barracks, more and more difficult to subject them to discipline and training, and more and more common for them to supplement their pay, and occupy the leisure thus created, with industrial or commercial activities.[1] Moreover, officials of influence, seeing that the standards of the corps were in any case neglected, used it to procure the enrolment of their servants and followers, and so to charge the state with their keep. Finally, in order to make room for such persons, able-bodied men were placed on the retired list.[2]

Very large sums set apart by the treasury for the payment of the Janissaries were thus expended without any return. The government made repeated attempts, accordingly, to reduce the number of men on the rolls. At the same time, however, during the latter half of the seventeenth century and the first forty years of the eighteenth, the Empire was seldom at peace. Hence a conflicting consideration was the provision of adequate reinforcements. It was probably in order to facilitate this provision that the government permitted a further development, which was again to have unhappy consequences. This was the affiliation to the *ortas*, in time of peace, of large numbers of unpaid men, who, when they were required, were formally enrolled by itinerant officers.[3] The arrangement was attractive both to the Janissaries and to the men so affiliated. For the latter were, so to speak, sworn in, after which they wore the emblem of their *orta* tattoo'd on their arms and legs.

[1] Thornton, 236; Juchereau, i. 44–5; Seyyid Muṣṭafâ, ii. 95, iii. 85.

The extent to which trading later became general among the Janissaries is shown by the following citation from de Tott, iv. 148: 'The Practice usual with the Turks, of keeping permanent Garrisons, added to the want of Discipline among the Troops, give them, in some sort, the Property of the Place at which they are stationed. . . . It is on this Principle that the Galiondgis [i.e. *Kalyoncus*—see above, p. 101] monopolize the sale of lambs, at Constantinople, and force the People to buy them. The Turkish soldiers, in every city, enjoy Privileges of the same nature. . . .' Cf. below, p. 295.

The difficulty of imposing discipline on the Janissaries was added to by the continual debasement of the coinage, since this virtually abolished the gradation of pay for good service.—Juchereau, i. 49–50.

[2] Seyyid Muṣṭafâ, ii. 93; Cevdet, i. 96. Ḳoçu Bey (Behrnauer, op. cit. 301), writing in 1630, already complains that with the neglect of the regulations there are 10,000 Janissary *Ḳorucus* and *oturaḳs* (See Appendix A) perfectly capable of service.—Cf. Jorga, op. cit. iv. 158.

[3] The operation of their enrolment on the outbreak of war was known as *taṣḥîḥ bi-dergâh*, 'verification at court'.—Seyyid Muṣṭafâ, ii. 95.

They then enjoyed a privileged position: they were immune, for instance, like Janissaries proper, from punishment by the civil authorities[1]—and could use the influence of the *ocak* for their own ends. On their side the Janissaries proper acquired an enormous reserve force, which enabled them more easily than ever to impose their will on the rest of the community.[2]

The regular infantry of the Sultans being reduced to such a parlous condition—and, as we shall see, the other arms were in no better case—it is remarkable that the Empire, up to 1739, when the wars in Europe came to an end, should have suffered no worse disasters than it did. The explanation appears to be that though in every other respect the series of campaigns in which it till then engaged were ruinous, they had the merit of supplying the army, to a considerable extent, with an effective, if unsystematic, training.[3] The one circumstance wanting, then, to reduce it to a condition near to absolute impotence was the occurrence of a comparatively long period of tranquillity, in which these active traditions should perish. This was duly supplied in the thirty-years' peace that ensued on the Treaty of Belgrade.

Disorganization could scarcely go farther than it had gone by now in the military system of the Janissaries. But until the conclusion of this peace the government at least attempted to get what return it could for the large sums it was obliged to spend yearly on the corps. Almost immediately after, however, it condoned another innovation, which ensured for the future that the bulk of these sums should, from a military standpoint, be completely wasted. This was the sale, to any one ready to purchase them, of the certificates with which every fully enrolled Janissary was provided, showing his title to draw pay.[4] It may be that this abuse had made such headway as to be incorrigible before the government was aware of it.[5] For the officers of the *ocak*, the *Ağa* himself, connived at it, because it was to their own advantage. By omitting to inform the registrars of vacancies in the strength they were able to issue fresh certificates, and either sell them, or draw the pay themselves. In any case these manœuvres resulted in the gradual,

[1] See above, p. 63, and cf. Juchereau, i. 11.

[2] Seyyid Muṣṭafâ, ii. 94–5, iii. 86; Juchereau, i. 43. Popular *ortas* would have as many as ten thousand adherents, unpopular as few as two hundred.

[3] Seyyid Muṣṭafâ, iii. 85. Cf. Jorga, op. cit. iv. 160, for the good quality of the army assembled by Köprülü Fâḍil Aḥmed Paşa (above, p. 181, n. 4), owing to the long service it had seen in Hungary, Crete, and Poland.

[4] Such a certificate was called an *esâme*, a word corrupted from the Arabic *esâmî* (plural of *ism*, 'a name'), originally meaning (in Turkish) 'a muster-roll'.

[5] The government made several attempts to suppress the practice and was not by any means wholly unsuccessful—temporarily. Thus the third Köprülü—Fâḍil Muṣṭafâ Paşa (above, p. 110, n. 3)—struck 20,000 false entries from the army pay-rolls—see Belin, 'Histoire Économique', *J.A.*, Série VI, tom. 4, 347; and again, in 1703, 2,400 others were detected and abolished.—Ibid. 370.

but by no means slow, transference of all these certificates to private persons. The famous Janissary corps came to consist almost wholly of officers. These and a small body of watchmen for police duties were the sole forlorn inhabitants of the great barracks in Istanbul. But they still had a supply of uniforms. And on solemn occasions, particularly at the quarterly parades in the palace courtyard for the distribution of pay, these would be brought out and placed on the backs of what men could be mustered.[1]

It might be expected that in these circumstances the Sultan would have abolished the *ocaḳ* and recognized the army on a new basis. But though few genuine paid Janissaries remained, the host of unpaid adherents attached to each *orta* had by no means diminished—on the contrary. And though these adherents were of little, if any, military value, they were admirably organized to oppose the least attempt to curtail, let alone abolish, their privileges.[2] Almost to a man they were artisans and as such members of trade corporations. The government had no independent force to pit against them; and with their barracks as rallying-points, and their officers to arm and direct them, they were masters of the situation.[3]

The disorganization of the 'regular' cavalry was by this time even greater, if possible, than that of the Janissaries. In the first place, it had begun earlier. Süleymân the Magnificent had been wont to select three hundred men from the cavalry corps to act as guards, and by way of reward had permitted them to undertake such civil duties as tax-farming and the collection of the *Cizye*. The advantages to be gained from such employments were so great that the cavalrymen sought, as time went on and the government grew both weaker and more corrupt, to secure more and more of

[1] Seyyid Muṣṭafâ, iii. 86, 89; Cevdet, i. 96; Juchereau, i. 44–5.

[2] Their rallying cry was '*Yoldaş yoḳmu?*', 'Have we no fellows?'—Cevdet, i. 97. In peace time they were now forbidden to carry fire-arms because of their propensity for rioting.—Juchereau, i. 45.

For the significance of *yoldaş* see above, p. 59, n. 1.

[3] Cevdet, i. 96–7. Juchereau, writing after the deposition of the reformer, Selim III (later than the period of our survey), and so having seen the power of the Janissaries exerted with disastrous effect, lays stress in more than one passage on the fact that the Janissary *ocaḳ* had come to include virtually the whole male Moslem population—of the towns, that is to say—and was practically all-powerful. Thus he writes of it (i. 43) that, '*identifiée avec la nation, elle fut entièrement sous l'influence des opinions populaires*', and (i. 52) describes it as '*semblable à une populace devenue souveraine*'. Cf. again, i. 56: '*Depuis que le corps est confondu avec la nation musulmane.*' Thornton, writing a few years earlier, likewise refers (preface, clxii–clxiii) to 'the populace of Constantinople, which does not consist of enervated artisans, but of men professedly soldiers, who are used to arms, and are scarcely inferior to the regular troops, especially since the general neglect of discipline'. The ever-hostile Eton, 59, on the other hand, regarding the affiliated 'civilians' as soldiers, finds that those of them that are not 'notoriously stigmatized for cowardice, theft, and the vilest of crimes' are 'enervated by a city life, and the practice of the lowest trades'.

them.[1] But these duties obliged them to live for the most part in the districts in which they were to be performed.[2] Many of them appeared in Istanbul only when pay-day came round;[3] and later, on account of the disturbances they were apt to create on these occasions, they were forbidden even to do this,[4] the distribution of their pay being confided to their officers.[5] In the second place, as in the case of the Janissaries and at the same time, their discipline had been compromised both by the gradual abandonment of the *devşirme* system and by the admission of untrained recruits; and their pay-certificates had likewise come to be sold to the public.[6] The process was hastened by the fact that their pay was in the hands of their officers, who were thus given every opportunity for playing tricks with it. Also in their case the government made no efforts to check the evil.

The action of the government, when in 1603 it suppressed a revolt of the cavalry by pitting the Janissaries against them, was imitated on several subsequent occasions, particularly under Murâd IV and Köprülü Meḥmed Paşa.[7] The former reduced their strength to its original level, and so far reorganized the 'Six Corps' as to place half the *'Ölûfecis* and *Ğurebâ* under the *Sipâhî* commander and half under the commander of the *Silihdârs*.[8] The action taken against them by Köprülü Meḥmed Paşa rendered them all but powerless. For unlike the Janissaries they had behind them no horde of 'adherents' to show fight at any threat to their estate. Indeed at the time of our survey the actual personnel of the cavalry corps resident in Istanbul—as distinct from that registered in the rolls[9]—was so small that the cavalry commanders

[1] Seyyid Muṣṭafâ, i. 145. Occasionally, as in 1654, efforts were made to forbid such employments—see Belin, op. cit. 329.

[2] Thus Ḳoçu Bey (Behrnauer, op. cit. 299) complains that instead of living near the capital, as they were supposed to live (cf. above, p. 70), the standing *Sipâhîs* would migrate as far afield as Hungary, Bosnia, the Morea, Georgia, or 'Persia', where they would set at nought the authority of the local *beys*, *Ḳâḍîs*, and tax-collectors.

[3] Seyyid Muṣṭafâ, ii. 92.

[4] See Juchereau, i. 87, who states that they were forced to disperse about Asia Minor.

[5] Cevdet, i. 99.

[6] Ibid.; Seyyid Muṣṭafâ, iii. 90. A partial reform of the cavalry certificate-traffic was effected by Çorlulu Aḥmed Paşa (cf. above, p. 76).—Belin, op. cit. 371–2.

[7] Seyyid Muṣṭafâ, ii. 93; Juchereau, i. 87; Belin, op. cit. 320.

[8] The *'Ölûfecis* and *Ğurebâ* of the Right being placed under the *Sipâhîler Ağasi*, those of the Left under the *Silihdârlar Ağasi*.—D'Ohsson, vii. 172, 366.

[9] The cavalry establishment fluctuated violently during the seventeenth century. According to Cevdet, i. 100, it had risen by the time of Aḥmed I (1603–17) from 7,000 to 21,000. Seyyid Muṣṭafâ, ii. 93, states that it was reduced by Murâd IV (1623–40) from about 30,000 to 5,000 or 6,000, and that at the accession of Süleymân II (1687) it stood at 15,000. Hammer, *Staatsverwaltung*, 270–40, citing Hezâr Fenn respecting a slightly earlier date, places it at 15,178; while D'Ohsson, vii. 367, remarks that, having risen during the reign of Meḥmed IV (1648–87) from about 26,000 to over 55,000, it was reduced under Aḥmed III (succeeded 1703) to 26,000.

were hard put to it to find men enough to parade for the receipt of pay.[1] Consequently the government had nothing to fear from them, and could easily have abolished them had it chosen to do so. It did not so choose for quite another reason—and one, it may here be added, that applied with equal force to any mooted abolition of the Janissaries—namely that the pay-certificates of both bodies were now held partly by government officials themselves[2] and partly by the general public; and it was thought with justice that neither were likely to submit without a protest, of incalculable effect, to being deprived of the income to which the purchase of these certificates entitled them.[3]

The history of the Ottoman artillery and its allied corps of Transportmen and Armourers was even gloomier. These bodies fell into total decay, however, only in the eighteenth century. For up to the Peace of Carlowitz (1699) the Sultans' artillery appears still to have been actually superior in some respects to that of their opponents, and their arsenals still to have been capable of providing arms for large forces.[4] Subsequently, however, and particularly during the long peace, all three corps were completely corrupted by abuses similar to those that had destroyed the efficiency of the Janissaries and the cavalry: their pay certificates were publicly bought and sold, and their establishment was consequently reduced to a skeleton. In their case, moreover, there seems to have been little affiliation of artisans, who might to some extent have maintained a tradition of training; and raw recruits hastily enrolled in an emergency were even more useless in this branch of the service than in those less technical.[5]

[1] So Seyyid Muṣṭafâ, iii. 90, stating that on some occasions, unless the sergeants in charge could offer convincing excuses for absentees, the same men had to appear twice. Cf. Jorga, op. cit. iv. 158. Perhaps D'Ohsson, vii. 368, who puts the number of *Sipâhîs* stationed in the capital at as much as 1,500, was deceived to some extent by these subterfuges.

[2] Cevdet, i. 96, states that most *esâmes* fell into the hands of dignitaries of the Inside and Outside Services, of the '*Ulemâ*, and of palace servants. In this case they were known as *Ḳapîli esâmeler*, 'Court certificates'.

[3] The abolition of these certificates was much discussed in connexion with the numerous plans for army reform projected under Selîm III, but was always rejected, on this score, as impracticable.

[4] Jorga, op. cit. iv. 160–1.

[5] See Cevdet, i. 98, who states that on the outbreak of war the officers, 'as at a shoot where the game is beaten' (*sürgün avi gibi*), would assemble a mob of vagabonds and hire the requisite transport waggons from shopkeepers and others, with the result that no more than half the ammunition supplied would reach its destination, the rest being abandoned *en route*, and that at the first sound of firing the said vagabonds would cut the harness of their transport animals and ride off on them, abandoning guns, waggons, and ammunition to the enemy. Cf. Juchereau, i. 62–3, 83, and Thornton, 270. Tott, iii. 9, likewise notes that on the outbreak of war in 1768 (?) (the terminal date of our survey period) the army left the capital with a 'prodigious train of Artillery, but which consisted of pieces ill mounted and full as ill served'. He also remarks, ibid. 132–3, that the Turks were far from wanting 'troops appointed for this service

As for the Sappers (*Lağimcîs*) and Bombardiers (*Ḫumbaracîs*), it is among them that we find the earliest instances of the training of Ottoman troops by foreigners. Thus the Sappers were already so trained during the Crete campaign (1644–69), by English and Dutch instructors, under whose direction they acquitted themselves with credit.[1] The 'westernization' of the Bombardiers was an affair of greater moment. It was undertaken in 1735 by the Comte de Bonneval, a French officer previously in the service of Louis XIV and later of the Emperor, of high rank and notable experience, who, on falling out with the Prince Eugène, sought employment with the Sultan in the hope of avenging the slights he had suffered at Vienna by reorganizing the Ottoman army as a whole. Thus, on soliciting engagement, De Bonneval described himself as possessing, apart from a general knowledge of military arts, a notable skill not only in the casting of cannon and grenades and the organization of batteries, but also in the dredging of harbours and the mining of metals. And it seems quite probable that he would have achieved this object had he not been hampered by frequent changes in the Grand *Vezîrate* (since by winning the confidence of one minister, he became automatically suspect to the next), and the opposition of officers that stood to suffer from his activities; so that, in the event, these were restricted to a reorganization of the Bombardiers. Before Maḥmûd I would accept his services, Bonneval was obliged to turn Moslem. Thereafter he was known as Aḥmed Paşa, since he was then raised to the rank of *Beylerbeyi*. His reform of the Bombardiers consisted in the recruitment and training of three hundred Bosnians extra to the former establishment. He himself was made *Ḫumbaracî Başî*, a post that he retained, with one short interval during which he was banished in disgrace to Ḳastamonu, until his death in 1747,[2] after

[the artillery]; more than forty thousand men, enrolled, and paid under the name of Topchi . . ., composed a Body, already too numerous; but, in reality, more expensive than useful', and goes on to describe their lack of discipline and the sale of their pay certificates. The brighter picture painted by Seyyid Muṣṭafâ (iii. 91), who says that in comparison with the Janissaries the artillery and allied corps were maintained in good order, and in particular that their pay certificates were not sold, evidently reflects conditions in the later seventeenth and earlier eighteenth century.

It may be noted that the Armourers (*Cebecis*), like most of the other corps, suffered by habitually receiving their pay in arrears. Thus in 1703, not having been paid for from 5 to 10 'quarters', they declined to embark, when ordered to do so, for Georgia, and headed a revolt that led to the deposition of Sultan Muṣṭafâ II—Belin, 'Histoire Économique', *J.A.*, Série VI, tom. 4, 363. The *Bostancis* (see above, p. 84) shortly afterwards revolted for the same reason.

[1] Jorga, op. cit. iv. 163.

[2] Juchereau, i. 71; *O.T.E.M.*, 1913, Nos. 18, 19, and 20; Meḥmed 'Ârif Bey, *Ḫumbaracî Başi Aḥmed Paşa*; Prince de Ligne, *Mémoire sur le Comte de Bonneval*; Vandal, *Le Pacha Bonneval*. Bonneval was buried next the *tekye* of the Mevlevî *dervişes* at Ğalaṭa, which was long, on this account, a place of

which the Bombardiers relapsed into an inefficiency no less complete than that of the rest of the armed forces.[1]

Having now described the effect of one of the factors in the process of decay that set in during the reign of Murâd III—the threat to the system of the *devşirme*, its eventual abolition, and the disastrous consequences of this measure to the whole paid standing army of the *Ḳapî Ḳullarî*—we may now turn to the other: a growth of irregularities in the holding of fiefs.

As in the case of the 'standing' army, such irregularities first occurred during the reign of Süleymân the Magnificent. A certain *Beylerbeyi*[2] then accepted bribes for the disposal of those falling vacant. But he granted them only to persons suitable to hold them; and such comparative scrupulousness was also observed in some cases of what were considered to be irregular grants of the reign of Murâd III.[3] Other grants of the time, however, were of a much more damaging nature, and opened the door to a corruption of the whole system: namely, the conversion of military fiefs either into 'civil' holdings[4] (it will be remembered that a large class of fiefs provided a livelihood for civil functionaries in any case) or into private property.[5] These conversions were effected, for their own benefit, chiefly at the instance of powerful courtiers, to whose influence Murâd was notably subject. But their example was quickly followed with increasing frequency by ministers and other functionaries, including the provincial governors, whose power was capable of abuse. Many of the fiefs thus converted were turned over, at least nominally, to the retainers of these functionaries, so that the true extent of their possessions might be concealed. Others, in order that their holders might not be deprived of them by confiscation, were illegally formed into *waḳfs* or pious foundations.[6]

This was one channel into which revenues intended for the

pilgrimage for slightly scandalized European tourists.—Cf. Hammer, *Staatsverwaltung*, 407.

[1] Juchereau, i. 472.

[2] Hüsrev Paşa, whom the historians point to as an early and unhappy example of promotion to a provincial governorship direct from the palace service.—Seyyid Muṣṭafâ, i. 123; Cevdet, i. 94.

[3] Namely those granted to his followers for good service in the Persian campaign by Özdemir 'Oşmân Paşa.—Ibid., cf. Ḳoçu Bey (Behrnauer, 294).

[4] i.e. from '*Kiliç*' holdings (see above, p. 49) into *arpaliks* and *başmaḳliḳs*—Ḳoçu Bey, loc. cit.; *Arpa* means 'barley' (cf. *Arpa Emîni* above, p. 85), *başmaḳ* 'a slipper' (both Turkish). These holdings were so called because the revenues they yielded were supposed to pay for the barley consumed in the stables of officers and officials, and for the slippers of the *Ḥarem* ladies.

[5] *Temlîk* or *mulk* (see below, p. 236).

[6] Seyyid Muṣṭafâ, ii. 96, iii. 76, 94–5; Ḳoçu Bey (Behrnauer, op. cit. 295); Juchereau, i. 125–6. Ismâil Ḫüsrev, 161, states that the *Sipâhîs* themselves used in later times to convert their holdings, which were state land, into private property. For the ingenious arrangement whereby the owners contrived to maintain control over property converted into *waḳfs* see below, ch. xii.

support of the feudal army were diverted. The other was the public treasure. We have remarked that the treasury was faced from the end of the sixteenth century with a declining revenue and mounting expenses, the latter being largely due to the growth in size of the 'standing' army. One way of solving the problem thus posed was a debasement of the currency. And though the expedient resulted in riots of the soldiery, and its advantage was nullified by the consequent necessity of raising their rates of pay, it was repeatedly resorted to.[1] In such circumstances the diversion to their own uses of some of the huge revenues collected and applied locally for the upkeep of the feudal troops was a perpetual temptation to the administrators of the Ottoman finances. The soldiery that they were obliged to pay in cash were in a strong position to enforce their will on the government, whereas the feudal troops were not. And so the government was inclined to allow feudal fief-holding to die, as it were, a natural death. Fiefs being within certain limits hereditary, they were permitted to remain in being until competent heirs died out. But when they did so, when the fiefs fell vacant, they were frequently assimilated to imperial domains, and, like these, entrusted by the treasury to tax-farmers.[2]

This evolution was made easier by the abrogation, under Süleymân, of the original practice whereby vacant fiefs lay in the gift of the *Beylerbeyis*.[3] The central government had assumed this duty because the *Beylerbeyis* had been prone to grant fiefs in return for bribes. But on the growth of corruption in the central government itself persons entitled to grants found themselves cheated again; and now their plight was worse than before, since they had then been able to appeal from the *Beylerbeyis* to Istanbul.[4]

On the other hand, the evolution was retarded to some extent by the very prevalence of corruption, since fief-granting was an obvious field for its exercise, and by the simple appropriation of fief 'title-deeds' at the death of the holder on the part of unauthorized persons.[5] Moreover, the mere persistence of *Sipâhî* families kept a great number of fiefs in being. In the eighteenth century, they still accounted for a considerable part of the agricultural land of the Empire. Their military value, on the other hand, was by then all but negligible.

[1] See below, ch. vii.
[2] Seyyid Muṣṭafâ, ii. 94.
[3] See above, p. 49.
[4] D'Ohsson, vii. 376, states that the practice whereby vacant fiefs were re-granted by the central government was revived under Muṣṭafâ II (1695–1703). But if it had fallen into disuse, this must have occurred a comparatively short time before, since Ḳoçu Bey, writing for Murâd IV (1622–40), refers to its disadvantages as here explained. Seyyid Muṣṭafâ, iii. 95, writes as if, nevertheless, the provincial governors had many opportunities of taking bribes for grants.
[5] D'Ohsson, loc. cit.

This was due to a number of factors. The first was the granting of fiefs to unsuitable persons, 'townspeople and farmers[1] of low extraction', even when they were such as to undertake military service at all. For of course neither the courtiers and officials that secured fiefs, nor their servants, ever even proposed to do so. The second was a deterioration in the quality of the officers promoted to be *Alay Beyis*. For when the *Beylerbeyis* began taking bribes for the appointment of *Alay Beyis*, it was only natural that the latter in turn should take bribes from the *Sipâhîs*; and a common aim of this corruption was the avoidance of war service. This practice resulted in the appearance at the seat of war of only the poorer fief-holders, who could not afford to indulge in it—and who were responsible at most for one armed attendant.[2] A third factor was again the effect of corruption. The official at the capital charged with the granting of fiefs did not hesitate to dupe applicants by allotting the same holding twice, or several times, over. Disputes concerning the tenure of fiefs were accordingly of frequent occurrence.[3] And this led to the failure of *Sipâhîs* to appear on campaign, since they feared with justice that if once they left their fiefs unguarded, some rival claimant, armed with a title equally good, might collect its yield of crops and dues for himself.[4]

The number of mounted troops yielded by the Ottoman feudal system at any period is hard to determine. In the time of Süleymân it appears to have been above two hundred thousand, if the armed attendants of the *Sipâhîs* are taken into consideration. But by the eighteenth century no more than five-and-twenty thousand, and perhaps fewer, could be mustered.[5] Moreover, being quite untrained and unused to one another's company, they were of little value in war.[6] Partly for this reason, and partly because no other troops were any longer available for the purpose, they were now often detailed for such unromantic duties as trench-digging and the hauling of cannon, which had earlier been discharged by the *Yürüks* and *Müsellems*.[7]

Some of these, as we have seen, were at one time employed with the fleet;[8] and during the seventeenth century all in one way or

[1] i.e. *re'âyâ*. It was the consequent confusion of *re'âyâ* and *'askerîs* (see above, p. 158) that was especially repugnant to the spirit of the original system.

[2] Seyyid Muṣṭafâ, ii. 96, iii. 95; Cevdet, i. 103; Isma'il Ḫüsrev, 168.

[3] Isma'il Ḫüsrev, 169, quoting Sakazov, *Bulgarische Wirtschaftsgeschichte*, for the simultaneous grant of a village to 18 or 20 persons.—Cf. D'Ohsson, loc. cit.

[4] Cevdet, 103; D'Ohsson, vii. 375–6.

[5] See, for estimates of their numbers at various times, Lybyer, 104; Seyyid Muṣṭafâ, iii. 94; Ḳoçu Bey (Behrnauer, op. cit. 296); followed by Cevdet, i. 103; Juchereau, i. 90; Jorga, op. cit. iv. 159; Isma'il Ḫüsrev, citing Sakazov.

[6] Cevdet, loc. cit. Cf. Seyyid Muṣṭafâ, iii. 95.

[7] See above, p. 55, and cf. Ahmed Refiḳ, *Anadoluda Türk Aşiretleri*, vi, viii; and Hammer, *Staatsverwaltung*, 235.

[8] Ibid. viii; cf. D'Ohsson, vii. 308–9. The name *Müsellem* was, nevertheless,

another seem to have lost their original status as organized *'askerîs*. The *Müsellems* and the *Yaya* militia of Anatolia, whose men, like them, held land tax-free in return for service, were merged either in the ordinary peasantry or in the *Sipâhî* class; while of the *Yürüks* those who settled were for a time given a fresh organization much like that of the original *Müsellems* (and subsequently underwent a similar evolution into *re'âyâ*),[1] whereas those who maintained their nomad habits took almost universally to brigandage, which the government was singularly unsuccessful in suppressing.[2] Another corps (if it may be so called) to disappear during the seventeenth century was that of the *Aḳincis*, the irregular unpaid cavalry which in earlier times had raided ahead of the Ottoman armies proper into enemy territory for the reward of booty. The place of the *Aḳincis* was taken thenceforward by Tatar horse from Bessarabia and the Crimea.[3]

still used for certain troops at a much later date. Thus Juchereau, i. 90, lists *Müsellems* with *Seğmens* as pioneers, stating that both were charged with the upkeep of roads and military works. Perhaps it was because of the nature of their duties, which resembled those of the original *Müsellems*, that these troops were so named.

[1] These *Yürüks* came to be called *Evlâdi Fâtiḥân*, 'The Sons of the Conquerors', and a *vezîr* was placed in command over them and called Evlâdi Fâtiḥân Ḍâbiṭi ('officer of', &c.). They were organized in *ocaḳs* of six, of whom one man, as *Eşkinci*, served at a time and was provided for by the others, as *Yamaḳs* (cf. above, p. 53). They were excused payment of all dues; but when no war was on hand the contributions that they would otherwise have paid to their *Eşkincis* went to defray the cost of frontier fortresses. They were commanded, as heretofore, by their own *Çeri-başis*.—Aḥmed Refiḳ, op. cit. viii–ix.

[2] Thus an attempt was made to settle some Anatolian *Yürüks* in the *sancaḳ* of Iç Ili; but they could not be prevented from raiding the settled population of that region; and at length in 1712 it was resolved to banish them by force to Cyprus. Most of them, however, escaped *en route* and dispersed in various provinces of western Anatolia, where, after being much harried, they were pardoned in 1714 on condition of taking up some honest occupations. In fact most of them eventually settled either as ordinary peasants or as sheep breeders or woodcutters. In later times, on this account, *Yürük* came to denote not necessarily a nomad, but rather a tribesman of strange beliefs, since even after their adoption of comparatively civilized ways these *Yürüks*, who had always resisted a thorough Islamization, remained very much more unorthodox in their religion than the normal *re'âyâ*.—Cf. Hasluck, *Christianity and Islam under the Sultans*, passim. A very similar fate was reserved for the many *Türkmen* tribes (*cemâ'ats*) of Southern and Western Anatolia, who appear to have differed from the *Yürüks* proper, chiefly in that their camping-grounds were outside the Empire when the original *Yürük* regulations were drawn up and in possessing a more definite tribal organization. When faced, in the seventeenth century, with the need of restraining their depredations, the government chose Raḳḳa on the Euphrates as a suitable centre at which to concentrate them; but though they, too, had shown some disposition to settle, it took a long time and the use of much force to reduce them to any kind of order. Many fled north again and joined other *Türkmen* tribes in Anatolia; and the government was reduced to taking guarantees in cash (*neẓir aḳçesi*) for their good behaviour. Most of these *Türkmen* tribes continued to lead their purely pastoral life, quarrelling over camping-grounds among themselves, and preying upon the neighbouring peasantry when the authorities were too weak to prevent them.—Aḥmed Refiḳ, op. cit. ix–x.

[3] Ḳoçu Bey (Behrnauer, 297); Juchereau, i. 99; D'Ohsson, loc. cit.

By the middle of the eighteenth century, then, the original military forces of the Empire, 'standing', feudal, and irregular alike, were not merely decayed, but were almost—if we except the remains of the feudal *Sipâhîs*—non-existent. If the Sultans should ever propose to fight again, therefore, it was evident that they would be obliged to rely on troops raised from other sources. There were in fact, apart from the Crimean Tatars, four main types available: first, the garrisons of the frontier fortresses; secondly, the troops of the provincial *Paşas*; thirdly, the private armies of the local grandees known as *Dere-beyis* (Lords of the Valleys); and, lastly, what levies the Janissary and other officers, touring the country-side on the outbreak of war, could attract to their standards.

The garrisons of the frontier fortresses were called *Serḥadd Kullarî*,[1] 'Slaves of the Frontier', to distinguish them from the *Kapî Kullarî*, 'Slaves of the Porte'. As we have mentioned, these fortresses were originally garrisoned by Janissaries, paid by the central government;[2] and even in later times it appears that Janissary officers, and even in some cases a few men, were still sent out from the capital to form the nucleus of such garrisons;[3] where they were supported nominally by the affiliated artisans of the town, who went by the name of *Yamaḳ*, 'assistant',[4] and actually by these 'Frontier Slaves', who were raised locally and paid from the local revenues which had always been allotted, under the names *Yurtluḳ* and *Ocaḳlîḳ*, to the needs of such fortresses.[5] According to Juchereau de Saint Denys,[6] they consisted of three types of infantry, called *ʿAzebs*, *Seğmens*, and *Müsellems* (all names we have already encountered in other connexions), and three types of cavalry: *Gönüllüs*[7] (heavy), *Beşlis*[8] (light), and *Delis*[9] (scouts). These *Müsellems* and *Seğmens* served, like the earlier *Müsellems*, as pioneers, being charged with the upkeep of roads and fortifications. The *ʿAzebs*, whom de Juchereau describes as 'élite', were presumably infantry proper. By the end of the eighteenth century the only satisfactory 'Frontier Slaves' were those drawn from Bosnia, Albania, and Macedonia, which were then capable of furnishing 10,000 cavalry and 40,000 infantry for the defences of the Danube. The Asiatic 'Frontier Slaves' were regarded as the worst soldiers in the Empire.[10]

[1] *Serḥadd* 'frontier', from Persian *ser* 'head' and Arabic *ḥadd* 'limit'.
[2] Above, p. 156.
[3] Seyyid Muṣṭafâ, iii. 93.
[4] Hammer, *Staatsverwaltung*, 216–17. [5] See above, p. 48. [6] i. 90.
[7] Meaning 'volunteers'; see above, p. 181.
[8] See above, p. 181, n. 4.
[9] *Deli* is contracted from *delîl* (Arabic), a guide.
[10] Juchereau, loc. cit. Cf. Jorga, op. cit. iv. 159, for the superiority of the Bosnian and Albanian troops in the wars of the late seventeenth century.

The *Paşas*' troops had consisted originally of the feudal *Sipâhîs* living in the district they governed, of the local Janissaries, artillerymen, &c., of detachments of the 'standing' cavalry, and of their personal retainers.[1] But as the Imperial armies became more and more disorganized, the *Paşas* were authorized by the central government to raise both cavalry and infantry locally for special purposes. These troops were paid partly out of the proceeds of government tax-farms, which, as we have mentioned, had increased at the expense of fiefs, and partly in an irregular fashion by forced contributions from local men of wealth and even from mosque funds.[2] In the eighteenth century cavalrymen raised by *Paşas* in this way went, like the cavalry of the frontier fortresses, by the names *Deli* and *Gönüllü*, and their infantrymen by that of *Tüfengci* (musketeer).[3] Such forces were raised either for war or for the suppression of rebellions on the part of other *Paşas*. But the effect of these manœuvres was to encourage provincial anarchy. For having a force at his disposal, a *Paşa* would be unwilling to disband it, and would often end by rebelling himself.[4]

The *Dere-beyis* indeed were no more than *Paşas* that had contrived to defy the government and their rivals long enough to

[1] See above, pp. 155–6.

[2] Juchereau, i. 92.

[3] For the *Tüfengcis* and *Delis* of the Imperial and Grand-Vezirial Households see Appendix B (B) 3 (iii) (6) and Appendix C.

Ordinarily each *Paşa* is said to have employed from 100 to 150 *Delis*, commanded by a *Deli Başi*, and the same number of *Tüfengcis*, commanded by a *Tüfengci Başi*; but the governors of certain eastern *eyâlets* might employ from three to five times this number of each, in which case the whole body of cavalry or infantry, as the case might be, would have a superior officer called *seri çeşme*. The *Gönüllüs* were apparently inferior in standing to the *Delis*, since their commander in each station, called *Gönüllü Ağasi*, was adjutant to the local *Deli Başi* (Seyyid Muṣṭafâ, iii. 83).

The employment by the provincial *Paşas* of these types of soldiery dates from about the beginning of the eighteenth century. During the seventeenth they had employed others: *Levends*, *Seğmens* (cf. above, p. 59, n. 4), and *Ṣaricas* (*Ṣari* means yellow; and this name perhaps refers to the colour of their standards)—Seyyid Muṣṭafâ, loc. cit.; Aḥmed Râsim, i. 501, note. Cf. Jorga, op. cit. iv. 161. *Levend*, as we have seen (above, p. 99), originally meant sailor or marine. But when other types of *'Askerîs* superseded these *Levends* in the Ottoman navy, they somehow preserved their identity as a distinct body and took instead to military service on land when they could obtain it, and, more often, to brigandage, when they could not. Owing to their insubordinate behaviour a decree was issued in 1695 abolishing the *Levends*, but giving them a chance to re-enrol as *Gönüllüs* or *Tüfengcis*. This order was largely ignored, however; and the *Levends* continued to add to the disorder prevailing in the provinces, particularly those of Asia, until past the terminal date of our survey—(Hammer, *Staatsverwaltung*, 234–5; Cevdet, ii. 40). D'Ohsson, vii. 379, indeed, states that the *Paşas* in his time still employed only *Levends* and feudal troops. But he seems to use the word loosely, to denote merely 'irregulars'. Finally, it may be remarked that as time went on the *Delis* and *Tüfengcis* became no less ill-disciplined than the *Levends* whom they had replaced (Seyyid Muṣṭafâ, loc. cit.). Cf. below, p. 218.

[4] Juchereau, i. 92.

found a dynasty. They do not appear, accordingly, before the eighteenth century, when the weakness of the government had gone far enough to permit their rise. At the time of our survey there were at least four major families of *Dere-beyis*, all in Asia[1]—even if we exclude the all but autonomous governors of ʿIrāḳ and Syria, who do not usually go by this (Turkish) name, and of whom we are to treat separately when considering the Arab provinces. Later, *Dere-beyis* were to appear also in Rumelia and to eclipse in political importance their Asiatic counterparts. It is a measure of the Sultans' enfeeblement that in the two wars of the later eighteenth century they had chiefly to rely on the troops supplied by such rebel dynasts. These troops seem to have been of the same types as those employed by the *Paşas* under the control of the Porte, and were supported by the revenues now collected within the area under the sway of each *Dere-beyi* for his own benefit.

Ad hoc enlistment of volunteers for campaigns had already been resorted to in the latter part of the seventeenth century on several occasions, in order to raise reinforcements for the regular army.[2] But it was not until after the long peace of our survey period that it became a chief method of recruitment for the Ottoman forces.[3] The recruiting officers were called *sürücüs*, 'drovers'. The volunteers, whom they enlisted for the duration of hostilities, were offered both daily pay and a bonus on enrolment,[4] and their enthusiasm was excited by 'learned men', who reminded them that any war engaged in by the Sultan was *ipso facto* holy. Being, however, wholly untrained and ill provided, they were difficult to control. Both on their way to the front and, in the case of the many who,

[1] These were (i) the Ḳaraman Oğullarï of Aydïn, Manise, and Bergama; (ii) the Çapar Oğullarï of Bozuḳ; (iii) the family of Canïḳlï ʿAli Paşa of Ṭrabzon; and (iv) the Elyas Oğullarï of Ḳuş Adasï.—See *Encyclopaedia of Islam*, art. 'Derebey'.

[2] As in 1689–90 when the third Köprülü, Fâḍil Muṣṭafâ Paşa (see above, p. 181, n. 4) recruited volunteers in both Rumelia and Anatolia—see Belin, 'Histoire Économique' (*J.A.*, Série VI, tom. iv. 346)—and again in 1695 on the capture of Chios by the Venetians.—Ibid. 350.

[3] The recruitment of volunteers by a general call to arms (*nefîri ʿâmm*) was resorted to on the declaration of war against Russia in 1769 by Muṣṭafâ III because of his well-justified reluctance to rely on the Janissaries, who, in addition to being no better trained, would be certain to demand constant increases of pay.—See de Tott, iii. 4–5.

[4] As in the last instance cited above, when each recruit was offered 7 *aḳçes* a day plus a bonus (*baḫşiş*) of 10 ḳuruş. During the war of 1769, when ninety-seven regiments of these *Mîrî ʿAskerîs*, 'Treasury Troops', were raised, each infantryman received 2½, each cavalryman 5 *ḳuruş* a month, a bonus of 25 *ḳuruş* on enlistment, rations, fodder, and, in some cases, a share in a tent. A condition of enrolment then was the possession of a gun, sword, lance, or pistols—to supplement, if not replace, the weapons provided by the government. Each regiment was commanded by a *Bin-başï*, 'Head of a Thousand', whose emolument was 1,000 *ḳuruş* a month and 10 per cent. of the troops' pay. D'Ohsson, vii. 381–2.

repenting their momentary ardour, deserted either before or after reaching it, on their way home they committed all manner of enormities in the villages, particularly where these were inhabited by Christians, through which they passed.[1] Nor were they less ready to mutiny and desert in the field; and though impetuous in attack, were easily routed when taken by surprise.[2] It was these untrained volunteers, and the equally untrained adherents of the Janissaries, who were now enrolled in very similar circumstances, and with them constituted the bulk of the Sultans' forces, that earned the Ottoman armies the evil reputation they enjoyed during the late eighteenth and early nineteenth centuries,[3] when their passage, it was said, came to be more dreaded by their fellow subjects in the provinces than that even of the enemy. It must be allowed, however, that the depredations in which they indulged were to some extent forced on them by the negligence of the authorities in arranging for their supply. Their treatment of the Christian peasantry also, where this was in fact worse than their treatment of their co-religionists, is partly to be explained, if not excused, on the one hand by the crusading spirit in which the Russians waged the wars in which these volunteers were engaged, and, on the other, by the corresponding spirit of Moslem fanaticism that was inculcated into them by the religious authorities of the Empire.[4]

Compared with the volunteers, the 'Frontier Slaves', the troops of the *Dere-beyis* and even those of the *Paşas*, though far less numerous, were well disciplined and equipped. None of them, however, were capable of withstanding successfully the trained armies against which they were pitted, far below the contemporary standard of West-European efficiency though even the latter might be. Soon after the outbreak of the war which ended our survey period, accordingly, it was perceived at Istanbul that what was needed if the Empire was to survive was some radical reorganization of the Sultans' armed forces. Unhappily, though in reality it scarcely existed, in theory the old 'standing' army still remained in being, to obstruct the efforts of those by whom this need was realized.

So much for the army. With the evolution of the Ottoman navy

[1] Eton, 25.

[2] Ibid. 67–8.

[3] See Thornton, 254, 260, who contrasts the indiscipline of the Turkish forces in his day with their former good order, remarked on by Busbecq and Rycaut.

[4] De Tott, iii. 8, notes that the volunteers were not all recruited at once, but that the strength of the army was continually being augmented by the arrival of fresh 'Fanatick Musselmen'. The Asiatic recruits, however, were not so 'Fanatick' as to neglect their own interests, and when passing through the Capital on their way to the front declined to budge before making terms with the government.—Ibid. 12.

we have already dealt; and our account of the Household is based chiefly on descriptions of it as it existed in the eighteenth century To complete our picture of the decay of the Ruling Institution, therefore, it remains only to note some late changes in the organization and conduct of the central and provincial governments.

Both were, of course, profoundly affected by the abolition of the *devşirme*. *Iç Oğlans* were still recruited to fill posts first in the Household and later in the army and the administration; but these recruits were now drawn, in theory from the Moslem population at large (though they were at the same time still regarded as the Sultan's 'slaves'), and in practice from among the relatives, friends, and *protégés* of those in a position to secure them places. The chief and most unhappy result of this innovation was a great and ever increasing multiplication of candidates, to satisfy whom, at least partially, a system of short alternate tenures of office was instituted: that is to say, whenever such a course was practicable, appointments would be given for one year only, after which the temporary holder of each such post would retire and await his next turn for employment. In the eighteenth century all the principal offices, not only in the central and provincial administrations but also in the army and the Household, were held on yearly tenures of the kind;[1] and, as we shall see, a similar system obtained in the learned profession. Add to this that these same posts were now conferred in return for bribes and that the main object of successful candidates was to recoup themselves for this initial outlay and to provide for the lean years they might expect to follow; and the welter of intrigue for the achievement of office, on the one hand, and the incompetence and venality of the office-holders, on the other, may well be imagined. Fortunately this system appears to have applied chiefly to the higher offices only, the subordinate secretaries and clerks remaining unaffected by this yearly general post and being promoted in a rational manner for good service and seniority.[2]

As we have pointed out, between the sixteenth and the eighteenth centuries the relative importance of many of the principal offices in the central administration had been completely altered. In the sixteenth century state business had been conducted by the Grand *Vezîr* sitting in the Imperial *Dîvân* with *Vezîrs* of the Dome, the *Ḳâḍî-ʿaskers*, the *Ḳaptan Paşa*, the *Nîşâncî*, and the *Defterdârs*. In

[1] See D'Ohsson, vii. 191 sq.
There were then eighty-five of these 'alternating posts (*menâşibi devrîye*) at Istanbul, divided into six categories, and including not only the three 'ministers', the six 'secretaries of state', the three *Defterdârs*, the *Nîşâncî*, the *Defter Emîne*, and the heads of the Finance Office departments, but also the Commissioners of the Household and the Generals of the infantry and cavalry corps.
[2] Hammer, *Staatsverwaltung*, 163.

the eighteenth the *Vezîrs* of the Dome had been abolished; the office of *Nîşâncî* had become a sinecure; the *Kâhya Beyi* and the *Re'îs Efendi*, formerly no more than leading officers of the Grand *Vezîr's* Household, had become ministers of an importance at least equal to that of the *Defterdâr*; while correspondent with these changes, Imperial *Dîvâns*, though still held, were held more and more infrequently and merely for show; and state business was in fact conducted in the course of daily meetings at the Sublime Porte.

This development corresponded to a growth, at least during the earlier part of the period during which it took place, in the power of the Grand *Vezîr*. But it marked also a growth in what we may call caprice in government. Under the old régime, governmental initiative was exercised within an uncommonly rigid framework of *Ḳânûns* with a semi-religious basis. As the Sultans retired from active rule, however, and the Grand *Vezîrs* assumed a greater independence, it became more and more common for the latter to issue special edicts, under the name of Imperial or Noble Rescripts (*Ḫaṭṭi Hümâyûn* or *Ḫaṭṭi Şerîf*).[1] These, it is true, embodied the Sultan's right of action by *'urf*,[2] which had always been recognized. Nor was there any conscious, or at least acknowledged, lessening of respect for *Ḳânûns*: indeed, reforms were almost invariably represented as a restoration of the conditions envisaged in the *Ḳânûns* of the glorious past. But each of these Rescripts was naturally regarded as a peculiarly solemn, and, as the latest, so the most reverend, formulation of the Sultan's will: with the result that ordinary *firmâns*, or commands, which were meant to, and as a rule did, require no more than the observance in particular cases of general rules already laid down by *Ḳânûn*, came to engage comparatively little respect. Rescripts, no less than *Ḳânûns*, were supposed to conform to the *Şerî'a*, but they became in fact an instrument of tyranny (in its strict sense); and so, during the period of change, we may observe that the Ottoman government became decidedly less 'constitutional' than it had been.[3]

The abolition of the *devşirme*, apart from its effects on the organization of the army, affected the government of the provinces, as it affected the central administration, chiefly by multiplying the candidates for high office and by elevating to this position many persons who had undergone none of the strict training of earlier days but had made their way up the ladder of state employment by cajolery and corruption. From these there followed two further

[1] *Ḫaṭṭ*, Arabic, 'a line' and hence 'a signature, an autograph'.

[2] See above, p. 23.

[3] Hammer, *Staatsverfassung*, 73–4. *Ḫuṭûṭu Hümâyûn* were introduced under Murâd III (1574–95).

results. In the first place provincial governors lived in a constant state of apprehension at the intrigues of their rivals, and where they had sufficient forces at their command to risk the adventure were tempted to maintain themselves in office by defying the Porte to dislodge them at the end of their term in favour of the next aspirants on the list:[1] it was on such defiance, as we have remarked, that the *Dere-beyis* founded their power. In the second place the title of *vezîr* came, with the multiplication of office-holders, to be conferred more and more lavishly; and since there were not enough *eyâlets* to go round, some had to be content with mere *livâs*. In some cases one or two *livâs* would be amputated from an *eyâlet* to compose a worthier holding. In others *livâs* and even simple *ḳaḍâs* would be placed under the control of *paşas* governing territories not even adjacent, whose yield was insufficient for their needs.[2] Hence it became common for *paşas* to appoint agents for the administration of these detached districts, under the names *mütesellim*[3] for *sancaḳs* and *voyvoda*[4] for *ḳaḍâs*, and to share with them the revenues derivable from the tax-farms which the *paşas* now frequently held themselves on a life-tenure.[5] The sole interest of these agents was to make as much money as they could while the opportunity was still theirs.

Another development of the seventeenth and eighteenth centuries was the rise to power of a class of provincial notables—*A'yâns*.[6] Originally, it appears—though at what date we are uncertain (the scheme of the Ruling Institution in its prime not, so far as we know, providing for their activities)—these notables were elected by the people of each region,[7] presumably to represent them *vis-à-vis* the governmental authorities, perhaps on the analogy of the *ḳoca-başîs*, who headed the local Christian communities.[8] Once chosen, the *A'yâns* were appointed by *firmân* and were addressed in form: 'Notables of the *Vilâyet* and Elders of Affairs.'[9] In any case the *A'yâns* of later days appear generally to have been landowners and to have owed much of their influence to this fact. In the eighteenth century it was the *A'yâns*, we are told, who controlled the civil and financial administration of the towns, so that the *Ḳâḍî* confined himself to matters of *Şer'î* justice. Juchereau,[10] indeed, maintains that the *A'yâns* had control also of military forces; but it appears from what he goes on to relate that he saw

[1] Juchereau, i. 178, 180–1.
[2] Cf. above, p. 144.
[3] *Mütesellim*, Arabic, 'one that accepts delivery of something'.
[4] See above, p. 54.
[5] i.e. *mâlikâne* (cf. below, p. 255). These were sold by auction at the Capital. For their purchase by *paşas* see Juchereau, i. 178.
[6] *A'yân*, plural of Arabic *'ayn*, in the sense 'principal personage'. In Turkish this plural is used in the same sense as a singular.
[7] Isma'il Ḥüsrev, op. cit., 170.
[8] See above, p. 155.
[9] *A'yânî vilâyet ve iş erleri.*
[10] i. 180.

no very clear difference between the *A'yâns* and the *Dere-beyis*, of whom there were in his day many more than at the time of our survey.[1]

This completes our sketch of the decay. The Ruling Institution had thus, by the eighteenth century, undergone as complete a transformation as was compatible with the maintenance of most of its original forms. Instead of being manned almost exclusively by slave converts, it was now manned entirely by free Moslems. Instead of inspiring its members to earn merit by the exercise of talent and virtue, it taught them that they must look to corruption for advancement, and might safely neglect the duties that should have been concomitant with their privileges. Finally, instead of providing the Sultans with an efficient instrument for the preservation and extension of their power, it was now scarcely strong enough to maintain their authority at home, and had become an engine of feeble tyranny over those of their subjects that were unable to combine against it.

[1] For further details concerning the *A'yâns* see below, pp. 256–7.

CHAPTER IV

GOVERNMENT AND ADMINISTRATION IN THE ARAB PROVINCES

I. THE OTTOMAN REGULATION

THE aims of Sultans Selîm and Süleymân in the organization of their Arab provinces were to maintain them in the condition in which they were taken over and to preserve the supremacy of the Ottoman Sultanate. The modest ambitions which had contented the Conqueror and the Lawgiver remained the highest ideals of their weaker successors. The keynote of Ottoman administration was conservatism, and all the institutions of government were directed to the maintenance of the *status quo*. Since the *ḳânûns* of Selîm and Süleymân were regarded as the embodiment of the highest political wisdom, amelioration could have no meaning except the removal of subsequent abuses. The exercise of public spirit and initiative on the part of governors or lesser officials was thus not so much discounted as maimed and circumscribed, and a vast network of vested interests created by the conquests placed an all but insurmountable obstacle in the way of the would-be reformer.

If, however, we base our view, not upon the eighteenth-century doctrines of the Social Contract and the Rights of Man, or their later successors, but upon the considerations which may reasonably appear to have guided the Ottoman Sultans, we shall find that their system was eminently practical, and neither harsh nor unjust. They accepted the traditional and recognized division of mankind into a variety of social orders: 'men of the sword', 'men of the pen', merchants, artisans, cultivators, *ḏimmîs*, slaves. To each order were assigned its functions, and regulations were drawn up to ensure the proper carrying out of those functions, and that none should interfere with or infringe the functions or rights of others. It was taken as axiomatic that each order and each province should, as far as possible, pay for the upkeep of its own administration and contribute an equitable proportion to the Imperial Treasury. So far from overburdening their subjects, the Sultans had the wisdom to realize that light taxation and simple forms of direct administration were in the interests both of the Treasury and of the population. Before the Ottoman conquest the lands of Western Asia were divided into a number of independent states, and cultivators were rack-rented and merchants fleeced to pay for the upkeep of large and expensive armies and extravagant courts. As provinces of a vast empire with far-flung frontiers, and at peace with one another, their military establishments were reduced to small garrisons, sufficient to maintain internal order and supply a few regiments for the Imperial army when required. Finally, by its strict adherence to the doctrines and principles of the Şerî'a, its patronage of both the orthodox learning and the Ṣûfî teachings, and its organization of the judicial service, the Ottoman state sought to foster the religious life of all its subjects and to maintain a high standard of justice, as the moral sanctions of its rule.

While these measures reflect the more positive and favourable aspects of the Ottoman regulation, another group reflects the maxims of the traditional Perso-Turkish political philosophy, reinforced by the experience of the Empire itself. Its ruling idea was distrust—fear of treachery or of unregulated ambition on the part of the officers of the Empire—and its methods were directed to centralization and the balance of forces. We have already described the division of the provinces into *eyâlets*, theoretically equal in status and each to a large extent self-governing under its *Paşa* or *Wâlî*. Though the latter united in himself the supreme military and civil authority, and was responsible for public order and security, for the collection of taxes[1] and the remittance of the stipulated annual tribute or contribution to Istanbul, and for the public administration generally, his tenure of office was precarious, and by the eighteenth century was renewable only from year to year. Even within his province, his capacity for effective control was weakened by a variety of contrivances, apparently designed to prevent him from exercising any form of direct administration. The accounts of the *Paşalik* were kept by the *defterdâr* or 'book-keeper', who held his office independently by *firmân* from Istanbul;[2] and the other branches of administration were in the hands of the *Paşa's kethudâ* or 'steward' (called vulgarly *kâhyâ* or *kihyâ*), also appointed on annual tenure. While the *Paşa*, in accordance with the traditional Islamic system, possessed wide judicial powers, the *ḳâḍî* and the other religious dignitaries enjoyed, and exercised, the right of sending protests and memorials direct to Istanbul, seldom without effect.[3]

But these were minor checks compared with the relations between the *Paşa* and the armed forces of each *eyâlet*, and between the constituent sections of the armed forces themselves. At each

[1] At Aleppo a separate officer, the *muḥaṣṣil*, was appointed from Istanbul direct for this purpose (cf. Volney, ii. 41). Very occasionally the *taḥṣîl* and *paşalîk* were united, perhaps not before 1180/1766; cf. Ğazzî, iii. 305.

[2] e.g. Seyyid 'Alî b. Ḥasan, who was *defterdâr* of Damascus for eighteen years (1717–35: Murâdî, iii. 211), and Muḥammad b. Farrûḫ, who held the same office for thirty years from 1746 without interruption (ibid. iv. 38).

[3] See below, chap. ix.

head-quarters a body of Janissaries and other troops was established as a permanent resident garrison, their functions being inherited by their descendants. These troops were usually distributed in two or more *ocaḳs*, mainly of foot, more rarely of horse, musketeers, &c., each commanded by its own *ağa*, *kâḫyâ*, *defterdâr*, and other officers, who seem to have been confirmed in office, but not nominated, by the *Paşa*. His authority over them was restricted in various ways: by *ḳânûns* which attached specific duties and rights to particular *ocaḳs* or officers,[1] by limitations upon their use for local operations,[2] and above all by the provision that the garrison of certain citadels (including those of Aleppo and Damascus) should be formed of imperial troops under the command of special officers nominated by the Porte.[3] In Egypt, which, unlike the Asiatic provinces, formed a single *eyâlet*, a further restriction was imposed by the institution of a *dîwân* or council, composed of the *Paşa's* officers, the principal military officers, and chief religious dignitaries, which met four times a week or oftener and came to a decision on all matters of administration; but though the final executive authority rested with the *Paşa*, he was not permitted to attend the *dîwân* in person, and it was presided over by his *kâḫyâ*.[4]

The Janissaries and other *ocaḳs*, in turn, did not constitute the entire military forces of each province. As we have seen, it was one of the characteristic features of the Ottoman system that the greater part of the cultivable land was assigned in the form of life-holdings to the feudal *sipâhîs*, and this system was extended also to the incorporated Arab provinces, excluding those in Arabia proper. Three of the *eyâlets*, however, contained neither *zi'âmets* nor *timars* of the ordinary type, namely Egypt, Bağdâd, and Başra. In Bağdâd a number of *sipâhîs* were settled as farmers of crown lands in several departments or *sancaḳs*; in the small province of Başra the whole district was held by the *Paşa* as an *iltizâm* or farm. The organization of Egypt is dealt with in detail later in this volume.[5]

[1] In Egypt, for example, the *ocaḳ* of the *Çawuşîya* had the duty of collecting the taxes and that of the Janissaries (*Inkişarîya*) of policing the towns. The *ağa* of the latter, besides his prerogative of leading the expeditionary forces dispatched from Egypt to join the Imperial army when required, thus became *ex officio* chief of police. Cf. above, p. 66.

[2] Cf. Ḥaidar, i. 45.

[3] Cf. Volney, ii. 49. Similarly the *ḳapudan* of Suez, as commander of the Red Sea fleet, but not the *ḳapudans* of Alexandria and Damietta (Combe, 65). Süleymân's *Ḳânûn-Nâma*, however, prohibited the *Paşa* and the Beys from giving the command of the maritime ports, or the administration of revenues, to persons in their private service (*ap.* Digeon, ii. 253).

[4] For details regarding the 'Great *Dîwân*' and 'Little *Dîwân*' see Marcel, *Histoire de l'Égypte*, 194, and Combe, 58–9. Unlike other governors, the *Paşa* of Egypt could not leave Cairo, and was indeed confined to the Citadel by the *Ḳânûn-Nâma* (Digeon, ii. 253).

[5] Below, pp. 259 sqq.

Apart from the advantages of the *timar*-system in providing for the upkeep of a large militia force, it ensured the existence in each province of a strong element almost exclusively of Turkish extraction, whose interests were bound up with those of the Empire, and who in an emergency could serve as a counterpoise to the local Janissaries. Each provincial group of *sipâhîs* had its own administrative organization, with a separate *defterdâr* and a recognized *bey* or *emîr*.[1] Although the majority of the feudal *sipâhîs* were not permanently under arms, reference is made to a body of them which carried out certain duties at Damascus.[2]

Still a third military force was constituted in most provinces by the private retainers of the *Paşa*, the Beys, and the *Defterdâr*. Each *Paşa* and Bey, on appointment to his post, took over automatically the official *ḫâṣṣ* allotted to the office, with the usual obligation of providing so many men for military service. The average *ḫâṣṣ* of a Beylerbeyi was sufficient to maintain between 150 and 200 horsemen, that of each *Sancaḳ-beyi* from 30 to 80 horsemen, and that of the *Defterdâr* from 20 to 25 horsemen.[3] The *Paşa* of Egypt had neither *ḫâṣṣ* nor private retainers.

A special difficulty confronted the Ottoman Sultans in the existence of nomad and semi-nomad tribes occupying lands within or on the frontiers of the provinces, and more especially of the Arab provinces. In Northern Syria the Türkmens, in Mesopotamia (Diyâr Bekr) and ʿIrâḳ the Kurds, and in Egypt, Syria, and ʿIrâḳ generally the Beduin Arabs, all constituted refractory elements, openly hostile to the authority of Turkish *Paşas* and Beys. In the northern provinces a half-hearted attempt was made to attach them to the Empire by the creation of special hereditary *ṣancaḳs* and semi-independent *ḥukûmets*, the latter paying no revenue to the central government and exempt from military service.[4] In Egypt the Sultans apparently trusted to the continuance of the old Mamlûk control.[5] On the occupation of ʿIrâḳ, however, the problem seems hardly to have been faced, and it was left to the *Paşas* to adopt what measures of control—or, if need be, of resistance and retaliation—they could. It may even have occurred to the Sultans that the presence of the nomads placed yet another obstacle in the path of ambitious or rebellious *Paşas*. But the absence of a definite policy towards the Kurds and nomad Arabs, or rather the policy of *laissez-faire* alternating with savage

[1] See above, pp. 146, 150, and cf. Murâdî, i. 275.

[2] Murâdî, iv. 16. The *sipâhîs* at Bağdâd, on the other hand (Longrigg, 87), were apparently regular troops.

[3] See p. 144, above. For the private armies of the *Paşas* see above, p. 193.

[4] See pp. 162–3, above.

[5] See the regulations for the conduct of the 'Arab *şeyḫs*' in the *Ḳânûn-Nâma*, *ap*. Digeon, ii. 204–8.

repression,[1] was to prove one of the cardinal weaknesses of Ottoman rule in Arab Asia.

A system so balanced and counterweighted depended for its maintenance upon the quality of the Imperial supervision and upon the character of the *Paşas* and *Defterdârs*. It was too much to expect that it would work without constant friction and overhaul, and the history of the Ottoman provinces in Asia during the sixteenth and seventeenth centuries is very largely taken up with the encroachment of one or other of the parties upon the prerogatives of the remainder or of the central government, and of occasional—but at best only temporarily successful—efforts to restore the balance. Scenes of violence, of factions between the local troops, and of risings against local governors, fill the monotonous chronicles of the period, which in their preoccupation with these more striking, but generally superficial, events seldom furnish evidence of the slow accumulations of change. As to the method there can be little doubt. The acquisition of a privilege here, the usurpation of a right there, were of far greater importance than the more spectacular outbreaks; sanctified by tradition, each supplied one more weapon or one more outwork in the constant struggle for supremacy. It is true that at the centre the rot had set in by the end of the sixteenth century, but much sound wood remained. Weak and vicious governors there were in plenty, but the annals of the provinces bear, on the whole, favourable testimony to at least the half of the *Paşas*,[2] and show that, minor incidents excepted, the public and financial administration was reasonably honest and the cultivators were less oppressed than under either the previous or the succeeding régime. The central government had not yet become unmindful of its obligations to its subjects; complaints of ill usage resulted in the prompt suspension of the offending governors,[3] and measures destructive of the economic stability of the provinces were severely punished.[4] The physical conditions of the Empire precluded the exercise of a more direct and rigorous control over its functionaries, nor could even the *Paşas*, in their extensive provinces (least of all the captive *Paşa* of Cairo), keep a watch over all the activities of their subordinates.

We must also be careful not to import a Western European, and that a nineteenth-century, standard into our judgement, and it may be as well to emphasize here a point which has a close bearing on the development of administrative institutions in Arab Asia for the

[1] Cf., e.g., Ğazzî, iii. 288–90.

[2] e.g. Combe, 21–39 (Egypt); Longrigg, 31–50 and 81–95 (ʿIrâḳ); Ğazzî, iii. 251–92 (Aleppo).

[3] e.g. Ğazzî, iii. 281; cf. also Longrigg, 49.

[4] *Paşas* guilty of adulterating coinage executed: Ğazzî, iii. 287 (a *paşa* of Aleppo in 1660); Combe, 32 (a *paşa* of Egypt in 1635).

greater part of our period. The conception of authority implied in the minds of the subjects themselves an assertion of power accompanied by a certain measure of harshness and violence. '‘Abd el-Ra'ûf Paşa (says the Christian chronicler Michael of Damascus)[1] was mild, just, and peaceloving, and because of his exceeding justice the people of Damascus were emboldened against him.' The Egyptian chronicler el-Cabartî is even more emphatic:[2]

'If the peasants were administered by a compassionate *multazim*, they despised him and his agents, delayed payment of his taxes, called him by feminine names, and hoped for the ending of his *iltizâm* and the appointment of some tyrant without fear of God or mercy for them, so as to gain by that means their private ends by the alighting of his violence upon some of their number. Likewise also their *şeyhs*, if the *multazim* were not an oppressor, were [not] able in their turn to oppress their peasants, for they gained no profit except when the *multazim* demanded excesses and fines.'

The prevalence of such a conception of authority may, at first sight, be put to the account of long centuries of misrule and oppression, supplemented by the tradition of quietism which was inculcated by the religious authorities and, by an acquired habit of stoicism, passing into fatalism. But this explanation by no means covers all the facts. It seems rather to be a development of the basic idea that authority confers privilege,[3] and three elements in particular may be discerned as contributing to its general acceptance. One was the purely selfish element of material ambition, common to men in all grades of society, which Cabartî illustrates in his reference to the village *şeyḫs*. There was none so low as might not hope, by some turn of fortune's wheel, to be set in a position of authority, however subordinate, and so to share in its perquisites. A second element was derived from the unstable and transitory nature of most forms of authority. Those whose turn had come[4] enjoyed an opportunity which would probably be brief and therefore to be made the most of. The victims of their extortions would be the first to exclaim at their folly if they neglected to do so, and the demands of equity were met when the deposed tyrant was called to account and deprived of his wealth and sometimes of his life by his successors or superiors. Yet public

[1] *Ta'rîḫ ḥawâdiṯ el-Şâm wa Lubnân*, ed. Ma‘louf (Bayrut, 1912), p. 49.

[2] iv. 208, 10–15/ix. 90 (the translation is not good). The same observation is made by Estève, in *Description de l'Égypte, État Moderne*, i, Part I (Paris, 1809), p. 321. For *multazims* and *şeyḫs* see pp. 262–3, below.

[3] Even in the nomad Arab tribe, the chief enjoyed exclusive privileges, including the right to a quarter of the booty taken on a raid or in battle.

[4] It is significant that the Arabic word *dawla*, of which this is the primary meaning, acquired the sense of 'authority, rule, dynasty', and was the term commonly used in the Arabic-speaking provinces to designate the Ottoman Empire. Cf. above p. 19, n.2.

opinion recognized certain limits to tyranny and exploitation. One may even speak of 'permissible extortions' or 'recognized abuses' as we shall see later, in the sense that they had become traditional usages. Moreover, public opinion required the abuse of authority to be offset by other qualities, such as liberality, accessibility, bravery, and a certain magnanimity. When these qualities were lacking, or when tyranny violated the unwritten laws which governed the exercise of authority, the limits of quietism were reached, and vengeance was demanded and exacted.[1]

The passage quoted above from Cabartî, it may have been remarked, bases the toleration of abuses of authority upon yet a third reason, the violence of factional spirit. It is in fact difficult to overestimate the part which was played in all aspects of the administrative and social life of the Arab provinces by family, group, or tribal rivalries. It was these that stirred the deepest passions of the soul; personal ambitions, let alone moral and religious ideals, counted for nothing beside them. The senseless and ceaseless tearing of faction against faction, with all its attendant violence to persons and property, was restrained neither by scruples of religion and humanity nor by consideration of economic and political consequences. Over and over again in our survey we shall have occasion to recur to this ingrained characteristic of the social organization in the Arabic provinces. Yet, although it is probably the most powerful single factor in the social life of our period, it is by its very nature the most difficult to seize and the most rebellious to analysis and precision of statement. Our documentary sources furnish singularly little assistance in explaining the factions which divided the local troops and resulted in the furious *émeutes* of Janissaries against Seyyids at Aleppo, of Janissaries against *Ḳapiḳul* at Damascus, of *ocaḳ* against *ocaḳ* (and later of *Mamlûk* party against *Mamlûk* party) in Egypt, in spite of their ample details. For the *Ḳeys* and *Yemen* feud which distracted the country regions of Syria we have a few casual references and the notices of travellers. The rest has to be put together mainly by analogy and conjecture.

Given such a view of authority and its prerogatives, the rule of the average Turkish *paşa* and *bey* of the older school, for all his unprogressiveness, lack of ideals, and acquiescence in abuses, was more acceptable to the mass of subjects and more agreeable to their humour than is generally supposed. He possessed to the full, and put to good use, the personal qualities which gained their respect; he was careful to acquire positive merit by constructing or repairing

[1] e.g. the numerous cases when a master was assassinated by his slaves or retainers, villages rebelled against a tax-collector and defied the government, and *paşas* were ignominiously driven out of their cities.

such public works as canals, dykes, quays, *ḫâns*, and religious edifices, and by the creation of endowments; and by his neutral attitude to the violent local feuds and personal antagonisms of his district he rendered a service to public security and private property, while none knew better how to play off the rival parties for his own ends.

The radical weakness of the Ottoman administration, on the other hand, is to be found in precisely the same characteristics. Lacking any real consideration for the welfare of the subjects, losing little by little any moral ideals which might have inspired them in the earlier stages, the officers of the administration were, by their very virtues, led insensibly to adopt a cynical view of their functions and responsibilities. Their world was divided into *ḥukkâm*, 'governors', and *re'âyâ*, 'subjects', the latter of whom existed, by divine providence, to supply the needs of the former. The practical outcome of this cynical view was the universal substitution of monetary standards for the old standards of efficiency. The 'good' *paşa* was one who remitted promptly and in full the sums and deliveries in kind required by the Imperial Treasury. From this it was but a step to the corruption described in a previous chapter.[1] By the beginning of the eighteenth century it had become the established practice to give promotion by favouritism and bribery, and to put up to auction offices (not only administrative, but also judicial and theological), lands, and concessions of all kinds. Cynicism had taken such root that it had ceased to be immoral and become second nature. To maintain discipline over the Turkish soldiery, when its natural foundations in respect for superior ability were absent, became an all but impossible task. The impotence of the *paşas* to prevent abuses, and the probability that they would be condoned at a price, encouraged lawlessness and rebellion, which became gradually more violent and widespread. Yet such was the natural talent of the Turkish governing classes, and so ingrained the conviction of their superiority, not only amongst themselves, but also in the minds of their subjects, that (apart from the turbulence of the Janissaries) it was not until the middle of the century that the system began seriously to be challenged and to show alarming symptoms of breakdown. Before we go on to deal with this, however, it is desirable to investigate in rather fuller detail the traditional relations between the government and the social organization, in view of the capital importance which these relations are destined to assume in our study.

[1] See above, p. 196.

II. GOVERNMENT AND THE SOCIAL STRUCTURE

The Western observer, accustomed to an organized social hierarchy, and inclined to pursue the ideal of stability through a system of mutual rights and duties between the different classes and social groups, braced by legal safeguards and checks, and sanctioned by some participation in the control of the legislating and administrative bodies, can find nothing comparable to such a system in the Ottoman Empire. He is therefore apt to conclude that the Ottoman régime was essentially a system of exploitation, injurious to the social and economic welfare of the subjects, that it not only lacked any guarantees for life and property against the violence, cupidity, or caprice of the soldiery, but in effect made agriculture, industry, and commerce their helpless victims. Legal redress, it was assumed, could not be looked for from courts whose officers were a byword for venality and corruption, and whose decrees, moreover, were illusory, since they depended for enforcement upon the goodwill of the very administration and soldiery against whom they were directed. Such is the impression conveyed by all, or almost all, the travellers and writers of the eighteenth century.[1] More especially do they marvel that any people could endure the rule of such a caste as the Mamlûks, in which the ordinary evils of the Ottoman administration were intensified by the servile origin and violent character of the governors and by the instability of their power.[2]

A perusal of the contemporary oriental documents and of the careful descriptions and analyses which were compiled by the French officials during their period of administration of Egypt[3] makes it clear that the Turco-Mamlûk administration was in itself by no means the capricious and irresponsible tyranny which has so frequently been held up to obloquy. It is true that, theoretically, no system of government could be worse or could more quickly lead to economic disruption and anarchy than that of foreign slave-born military despots, linked by no ties of nature to the country and

[1] But it must be remembered that their statements relate almost entirely to the last half of the eighteenth century, when the old structure was being rapidly undermined by the factors already mentioned.

[2] Of the numerous amiable descriptions of the Egyptian Beys, that of George Baldwin may serve as a sample: 'The Mamaluks, a set of swineherds, vagabonds, any thing; kidnapped in the mountains of Mingrelia, Circassia, Georgia, and brought young into Egypt; sold, circumcised, and trained to the career of glory; their road to honour, apostacy; their title to power, assassination and a contempt of death; no stability, no order, no character among them, but a constant thirst and jealousy of command' (*Political Recollections relative to Egypt* (London, 1801), Preface, 50–1).—Cf. Volney, i. 157–8; and Lockroy, *Ahmed le Boucher*, pp. 4–6, whose account is false in all material particulars.

[3] Although they too shared the general opinion of the Turco-Mamlûk administration.

people they exploited, and with no ambitions but power and wealth. Yet, in fact, by the middle of the eighteenth century, Egypt had lived for more than five hundred years under the Mamlûk system, and was still far from relapsing into anarchy.[1] The level of her economic prosperity had undoubtedly declined during this half-millennium (in large measure owing to causes external to Egypt itself),[2] large areas of land had gone out of cultivation, and it is probable that the population had been appreciably reduced.[3] Had it not been for the Ottoman conquest, a breakdown might perhaps have taken place much earlier; but we have seen reason to believe that, by reducing the crushing burden of taxation and by maintaining a fairly regular system of administration, the establishment of Ottoman supremacy guaranteed (at least down to the beginning of the eighteenth century) to the population of the Arabic provinces a period of relative tranquillity after the disasters of the later Mamlûk, Timûrid, and Türkmen régimes.

Yet the paradox remains of a government, generally apathetic, unprogressive, and careless of the welfare of its subjects, and often arbitrary and violent in its dealings with them, and a society upon whose institutions and activities such a government had little or no effect. The explanation is to be found in the very lack of a complex, all-embracing political organization. As we have already suggested,[4] we may visualize Moslem society as composed of two coexisting groups, the relations between which were for the most part formal and superficial. One group formed the governing class of soldiers and officials, the other the governed class of merchants, artisans, and cultivators.[5] Each was organized internally on independent lines, and neither group interfered with the organization of the other in normal circumstances. From time immemorial the governing class had lived on a percentage of the produce of the land, supplemented by various duties on goods, and the social structure of the other class had accommodated itself to this situation. In spite of political and dynastic revolutions, stability was ensured by the fact that under all changes of sovereignty the exist-

[1] The Mamlûk system of 'fiefs' or 'assignations' was introduced into Egypt by Saladin (regn. 1171–93) and with subsequent modifications (in 1315 and again, after the Ottoman conquest, in 1517 and 1526) remained substantially the same until the period of Meḥmed 'Alî.—Cf. C. H. Becker, 'Steuerpacht und Lehnswesen' in *Islamstudien*, i. 234 sqq. and the monographs of Poliak.

[2] The most serious blow being the opening up of the Cape route to India in 1497, with the consequent diminution of the Indian transit trade in the Red Sea.

[3] It is scarcely possible to gain more than a very rough idea of the population of Egypt in the Middle Ages, but in the fourteenth century it is not likely to have exceeded four millions. In 1800 it was estimated, after careful calculation, at a little over 2,400,000 (Chabrol, 8), but reasons will be given later for regarding this figure as an underestimate.

[4] See pp. 158–160, above.

[5] The place held by the 'men of religion' is discussed below (ch. viii).

ing bureaucracy remained in being, and maintained the traditional practices with a minimum of alteration. The new masters stepped into the places vacated by their predecessors; the titles to assignments of land were redistributed, but the relations between landlord and peasant, official and artisan, remained on the whole unchanged. The extreme conservatism of the bureaucracy is nowhere more clearly seen than in Egypt, where the respective functions of the Moslem accountants, the Jewish gold-dealers and book-keepers, and the Coptic tax-assessors and collectors in the eighteenth century were practically what they had been in the tenth. From the outside it looked as though the *Paşa* or Bey could do as he pleased; in practice he was restrained from excessive abuse of his power partly by his own reverence for tradition and acceptance of traditional usage as binding,[2] partly by the steady pressure of the bureaucracy, who had learned by experience that a certain standard of agricultural and industrial productivity was in their own best interests. Changes of dynasty, even, were not without their compensations. During a long period of uninterrupted dynastic rule, abuses naturally crept in and multiplied, sometimes to an extent which threatened social stability. The advent of a new dynasty swept these away and revitalized the old system; usually the energy and foresight of its founder resulted in a number of minor reforms in addition. Such had been the case in the Ottoman conquest, and the real defect of Ottoman rule was that it had lasted too long.

A further consequence of this state of affairs was that the Ottoman conquest did not result in the Ottomanization of the Arabic lands. A Turkish military aristocracy was no new phenomenon in either Egypt or Arab Asia, but even the bureaucracy never became thoroughly Turcicized. On the contrary, we find that the Turkish (or rather Bosniak) garrisons, intermarrying generation after generation with the Arab inhabitants, became absorbed into the local population, apparently even to the extent of forgetting their Turkish tongue. The old administrative cadres retained both their traditional functions and their Arabic idiom. The careful reader of Cabartî's chronicle cannot fail to be struck by the persistence of the technical administrative terms of the medieval Mamlûk Sultanate, and it is very questionable whether a knowledge of Turkish ex-

[1] Hence the indifference shown by the population of Egypt to political changes and the quarrels of the Beys, remarked on by all travellers; e.g. Sonnini: 'The tradesman neither quitted nor shut up his shop; and the mechanic worked coolly at his door, without giving himself the smallest concern respecting the combatants' (English trans., p. 428). But the factional feuds of the Janissaries at Damascus and elsewhere were a different matter.

[2] It may be thought that this could hardly apply to the Mamlûks, but on the contrary they were, as many passages in Cabartî show, equally strongly attached to tradition.

tended far outside the ranks of the senior officials. The increasing predominance of the Mamlûk troops[1] still further, if anything, counteracted any tendency towards Ottomanization, since they deliberately cultivated the tradition of pre-Ottoman times.[2] In Syria, however, Ottoman influence was much stronger, but here too, except in Aleppo and the northern districts,[3] it scarcely penetrated below the ranks of the governing class. Even the aristocratic families among the *'ulemâ* of Damascus, though in frequent relations with the Turkish *'ulemâ* and intermarrying with Turkish families, resented the introduction of Turkish usages,[4] and only those who had studied in Constantinople were familiar with the Turkish language.[5]

The interposition of the bureaucracy thus shielded the mass of the population—cultivators, artisans, merchants—from the effective intervention of the military power in their organization and activities. Over a long period of centuries they had created an independent organism, so solidly based and yet so resilient that its stability was never in danger. On this social and economic basis the structure of Islamic society was built up; the foreign slaves, foreign rulers and administrators, and foreign merchants formed only the superstructure, which could be supported without risk of collapse, so long as the foundations remained intact.

To describe the structure of this society in any detail would as yet be premature. It is evident upon closer examination that we have to deal, not with a closely knitted organism, even within the restricted limits of a single province, but rather with a vast number of small social groups, which may almost be described as self-governing. A recent investigator has defined such a society as 'consisting mainly of territorial and genealogical communities, rooted in thousands of more or less isolated centres, mostly villages, which are autonomous units, almost self-sufficient in their religious, social, political, and economic life'.[6] It will be part of our task to

[1] It is remarkable that as late as the eighteenth century they were still called, even in Syria, by the medieval name *Ğuzz*.—Ḥaidar, i. 93; Cab., *passim*; Lane, *Mod. Egypt*, chap. iv, first sentence.

[2] The most striking illustration of this is the inscription of 'Alî Bey in the Mausoleum of the Imâm el-Şâfi'î in Cairo, where he is called by the ancient wazirial and Caliphial titles '*'azîz miṣr . . . al-mutawakkil 'ala'llâh . . . al-ḥâkim bi'amri'llâh*' (G. Wiet in *Bull. de l'Inst. d'Eg.*, xv. 182–3).

[3] The famous Turkish historian Na'îmâ (d. 1716) was a native of Aleppo, and Murâdî mentions several Turkish poets at Aleppo and its environs. Since the Middle Ages there has always been a considerable Turkish element in the population of Northern Syria.

[4] e.g. Murâdî, ii. 98.

[5] Cf. Murâdî, ii. 187 foot.

[6] A. D. A. de Kat Angelino, *Colonial Policy* (tr. G. J. Renier, The Hague, 1931), i. 67–8. The passage quoted continues as follows (slightly abridged): 'Great religions like Islam have superimposed a common veneer of general religious culture, without, however, causing them to lose the peculiar shade of mystical-magical feeling of their own particular life. Tradition, status, and the

analyse more fully in the following chapters the triple relationships involved in this system—those between the individual and the group, between the groups themselves, and between the different groups and the administration, but certain common features may be indicated here.

In the first place the groups carried none of the social and religious exclusiveness of the Indian castes, and are not to be regarded as in any way analogous to the latter. There is indeed a tendency towards the marking-off of the military forces as a superior caste, but even this is offset very considerably by their normal social relationships; and amongst the social groups themselves any similar tendencies seem to be foreign to the mentality of Western Asia. This is again reflected in the religious equalitarianism adopted by Islâm, which has in turn strengthened the resistance to caste ideas, if it has not wholly prevented the classification of social grades. The absence of rigid caste barriers gave sufficient flexibility to the system to allow exceptional talent or personality to make its way up; and there are enough examples in our very restricted material of persons who, born into one group, attained to some position in another, to justify us in asserting that there was at all times a certain movement within and between the individual groups.

Nevertheless, for the enormous majority of persons, their station in life, their occupation, and their economic position were regulated by the accident of birth. A son normally followed his father, a daughter was generally married within the village or craft group. Consequently where these groups were of long standing (and there were few which were not), the tie of common occupation was almost always strengthened by that of blood, and the craft or village community—if not too large—was constituted by members of a single family more or less widely branched. Such a constitution enabled the effect of the rigid Islamic law of inheritance, namely to decompose property into minute fractions, to be mitigated by constant recombination, and rendered the community more compact and homogeneous. On the other hand, the already powerful control of tradition over the conduct of the individual member of the group was intensified by the family ties which linked him to the other members, and by the disciplinary sanctions which the family was in a position to exercise. In these circumstances initiative was not so much stifled as non-existent, since every consideration combined to persuade each member that in the maintenance of the established order lay his own best interests, and

interests of the group determine the place and function of the individual, and as a rule heredity transfers them. Aptitude and inclination are not consulted, so that talent is rarely given the chance of unfolding itself.'

nothing ever came to his observation or knowledge which might induce a belief that a better order could exist.

The relations in which the separate groups stood to one another were less uniform. Groups with different economic functions—such as cultivator and artisan, artisan and merchant—were obviously linked by the natural or traditional economy of their provinces, which was almost always of a simple and direct kind. The normal interchange of services was conducted in the cities usually on a money basis, in the country districts very often for produce in kind. Except for these, and for the common participation of local groups in local religious ceremonies or the more specialized association of two or three groups in a religious fraternity, there seems to have been extraordinarily little direct contact between the various groups. Each inhabited its own quarter in the city, or its own village or section of a village in the country, and, in certain districts at least, the existence of factional feuds set up a positive barrier to social intercourse.

Administratively, each group had a chief member, an elected or appointed *şeyẖ* or leader, through whom all its relations with the governing authorities were conducted. The holder of an assignment of land acted through the village *şeyẖ* or *şeyẖs*, who were held responsible for the maintenance of order and the collection of the taxes. Each industrial and merchant corporation had likewise its *şeyẖ*, with the same administrative and taxing functions, who dealt with the relevant officer of government either directly or through a superior *şeyẖ* possessing jurisdiction over a number of corporations. In every case, again, these relations were fixed by tradition, and for the most part strictly adhered to. The very looseness of this organization was one of the chief safeguards of the social structure. Any violence on the part of a military officer, a government official, or a band of Arab marauders could normally affect only individual groups; when it expended itself, the groups rapidly recovered. In extreme cases, if the original group were entirely dissolved, a fresh group was formed, and—provided the violence was not renewed—set to work to rebuild the shattered economic tissue. When this happened too frequently (as was the case in the later medieval period) it caused a shrinkage in the numerical strength and economic capacity of the social structure as a whole, but did not destroy it. In general, therefore, the conduct of government touched only the surface of its life; here and there temporary dislocations might be caused, and a grasping and short-sighted policy might and did produce local contractions by allowing land to fall out of cultivation or forcing the stoppage or transfer of a branch of industry. But so long as the groups themselves, with their traditional organs of administration, remained intact, and so long as the intervention and extortions of the military governors were limited to the profits and spared the capital and the means of livelihood themselves, the social organism showed a marvellous power of recuperation.

The predominating role of traditional usage in all these relations, internal and external, has been sufficiently emphasized above. Its precise character necessarily varied from group to group and from place to place, even within the same district. There can be little doubt that in many groups this tradition went back far behind the Islamic era; in Upper Egypt, especially, its roots lay in the ancient Pharaonic civilization. Among the industrial groups, on the other hand, the traditional usages as a whole derived from the Middle Ages, though specific practices might be of earlier origin. But it was not merely the fact of its antiquity that made traditional usage all but absolute; indeed it was generally quite sufficient for a usage to be once established, even at a most recent date, for it to enjoy the same prescriptive character. Its potency lay in its association with the religious ideas of governors and governed alike; not primarily in the sense that the religious authorities of Islâm gave a religious or quasi-religious sanction to each and every usage,[1] but rather that reverence for tradition was the doctrine most characteristic of and most strongly stressed in Islamic teaching. The close association of the religious and social structures will be examined later, but enough has been said to show that, for all its apparent fragility, even a Turkish or Mamlûk governor might hesitate to lay a sacrilegious hand on tradition.

It is not surprising that so intimate an association, governed by unwritten sanctions, should have escaped the notice of European travellers, whose contacts with Moslem society were of the most superficial.[2] But it is of importance for us to appreciate it thoroughly, as it is typical of the institutions of Islamic society and government generally. 'Point de lois fixes. . . .' No written laws, whether with penal or other sanctions; in their place a network of traditional relations, maintained only by the common will, yet which had survived eight centuries of dynastic vicissitudes and conquering armies, and still regulated the conduct of both society and government. Similarly in other fields, where at first sight

[1] It might be questioned whether they ever expressly sanctioned a great many of the traditional usages in village and town, but there can be no doubt that the local men of religion, whether of the *'ulemâ*, or of the Ṣûfîs, or of both, did in fact throw their weight upon the side of tradition, and officially condoned the traditional usages even when (like those at the cutting of the Ḫalîc at Cairo) they were pre-Islamic and animistic in origin.

[2] Cf., e.g., Volney's generalization: 'Il n'y a point de lois fixes; et ce cas, qui est commun à toute l'Asie, est la cause radicale de tous les désordres de ses gouvernemens' (i. 455). The statement is, in point of fact, not inaccurate, but it sees only the negative and not the positive side of the relationship.

there appears to be nothing but unregulated confusion, and even, to the Western eye, a total disregard of law and justice, we shall find custom and tradition setting recognized limits to conflicting jurisdictions and dictating what may not be done and what may be done, even though technically against the written law. In the last resort, it is a difference in the conception of law, and in the function of administrative law in particular, that is at the bottom of the misunderstanding.[1]

Such a system, on the other hand, possessed serious and inescapable drawbacks, quite apart from the personal suffering and economic loss resulting from its repeated violation by members of the governing and military classes. It perpetuated the gulf which separated the people from the government,[2] producing at best an apathetic acquiescence in it on their part, as a necessary evil, but not infrequently offering a foothold to elements of social opposition. Their direct relations with it were limited to the field of taxation, often extorted with violence[3] and supplemented by oppressive *avanias*. On the side of the government we have already seen its results in a similar apathy towards the interests of the subjects and an absence of all incentive to improvement or reform. But since the situation could not long remain stationary, the balance was continually shifting against the people by constant small encroachments. One institution, it is true, remained to form a positive link between them, and in a measure endeavoured to redress the balance—the religious institution. How far it succeeded in carrying out these functions will be considered in due course.[4]

The second criticism to be brought against the system is its hostility to change and consequent stifling of initiative. If we may judge by the analogous situation in intellectual life, originality was not wholly non-existent but it was suppressed in the supposed interests of the group, or if it could not be suppressed was ignored, and its achievements suffered to disappear.[5] We shall never know, in any probability, whether some Arab Jacquard devised an improved loom or some Turkish Watt discovered the power of steam, but we can confidently assert that, if any such invention had

[1] See ch. x, i.

[2] It did not, however, create this gulf, which was a legacy to Islamic civilization from its imperial predecessors in Western Asia, deepened by the establishment of Turkish military hegemony from the eleventh century.

[3] So traditional had this practice become that observers agree in asserting that the Egyptian peasant refused to pay his taxes until they were exacted by violence, and was regarded with contempt by his fellows if he did so.—(See also p. 205).

[4] See chs. viii and ix, below.

[5] A typical example is offered by the physician Ibn el-Nafîs (d. A.D. 1288), who discovered the principle of pulmonary circulation; but it was entirely ignored by the physicians of the following generations, and his name and work were both forgotten.—(See *Supplement* to *Encyc. of Islam*, s.v.)

occurred, it would have been entirely without result. The whole social organism, in fact, was one characteristic of, and only possible in, a stationary or retrograde civilization, and herein lay its essential weakness. It is not an exaggeration to say that after so many centuries of immobility the processes of agriculture, industry, exchange, and learning had become little more than automatic, and had resulted in a species of atrophy that rendered those engaged in them all but incapable of changing their methods or outlook in the slightest degree.[1]

It was this incapacity, rather than unwillingness, to learn[2] that above all characterized Asiatic Moslem society in the seventeenth and eighteenth centuries. Its sterilized brain could not effectually conceive any idea that lay outside the narrow range of its experience and tradition, nor could it meet any situation which deviated from the path traced by routine. So long as the Ottoman provinces lived in a closed intellectual, economic, and social order, the system continued to serve its purpose, though with steadily diminishing returns. But during the course of the eighteenth century various factors combined to disturb the existing equilibrium, more especially in the economic and military spheres, and created new problems which the old organization was totally unable to deal with. The result was to render the social order the helpless victim of violent solutions by which its protective covering of tradition was torn away and its institutions were exposed to destruction.[3] The nature and effects of this process will be examined in detail in the following chapters, after its causes have been indicated in a summary account of the main political, military, and economic developments during the eighteenth century.

III. THE ARAB PROVINCES IN THE EIGHTEENTH CENTURY

At the root of the disorders which afflicted both subjects and administration in nearly every part of the Empire was the conflict between the central authority, represented by the *Paşa*, and the ambitions and feuds of the local troops, supplemented in all the Arab provinces by the lawlessness of the Beduin tribes, and in

[1] See below, pp. 264 and 296, n. 2.

[2] But it encouraged an unwillingness to learn, out of an exaggerated estimate of its own perfection. A striking example is given by the historian Cabartî, who asserts (as an explanation of the mechanical advances made in Europe) that in 1159/1746 a number of Franks came to study mathematics under his father and on their return to Europe taught what they had learned, and 'translated it from theory into practice, inventing by means of it marvellous devices such as windmills, machines for drawing heavy weights, for raising water from wells, &c.' (i. 397, foot/iii. 191).

[3] Compare Cabartî's grievance against 'Alî Bey that 'he rent established customs and violated usages, destroyed ancient houses, and abolished the old sound ways' (i. 258/ii. 235), although, in comparison with subsequent events, he looks back to his time with regret (i. 383 foot/iii. 162–3).

Northern ʿIrâḳ by the intransigeance of the Kurds. The equilibrium which the *ḳânûns* of Süleymân had aimed to establish, always difficult to preserve, had almost everywhere been lost by the failure of the *Paşas* to counteract the encroachments of the Janissaries,[1] who, for their part, disliked both the disciplinary and financial control to which they were subjected, and endeavoured to increase their influence and share in the local administration. In the early years of the eighteenth century the conflict became more intense, and often led to armed struggles between the parties. The Porte, growing alarmed at the increasing violence and disorder, hesitated between maintaining its traditional policy of frequent changes, and leaving in his command a *paşa* who had shown his competence to curb the spirit of rebellion. More often than not, in consequence, its hand was forced. In ʿIrâḳ the energy of Ḥasan Paşa (appointed to Bağdâd in 1704) in subduing and punishing the Arab tribes made him irreplaceable, the more so that he regularly dispatched the tribute due from his provinces.[2] The devolution of his commands to his son Aḥmed in the crisis of a Persian war (1724) laid the foundations of a dynasty. Ḥasan and Aḥmed had organized a private Mamlûk force on the model of the Ottoman *Serây*, and one of the Mamlûks in particular, Aḥmed's *kâhyâ* and son-in-law Süleymân Ağa, had made a name for himself in the Arab wars and received promotion to the rank of *Paşa*. On Aḥmed's death in 1747, the Porte attempted to reassert its control, but the Bağdâd Janissaries resisted the claims of the Porte's nominees, and in 1749 Süleymân, already *Paşa* of Başra, re-entered the city as the first of a line of Mamlûk *paşas*, whose all but independent rule lasted till 1831.[3] Moşul, gravitating in the orbit of its greater neighbour, continued formally to receive *paşas* annually from Istanbul, but remained for a century the almost exclusive appanage of the Calîlî family.[4]

While ʿIrâḳ was thus favoured with a government which, if not more enlightened than the Ottoman, was, at least until the end of the century, more stable and resolute and in its remoteness little

[1] The term 'Janissaries' is frequently used by both European and Arabic writers in the eighteenth century to denote the local regiments or *ocaḳs* collectively, although the *Yeni-çeri* or *Inkişarîya* proper formed only one *ocaḳ* amongst others.

[2] He and most of his successors held also the governorships of Başra and Mârdîn.—See for this period of ʿIrâḳî history generally Longrigg, pp. 123 sqq.

[3] Although nominally liable for the payment of the regular contributions from their provinces, the Mamlûks were for the greater part non-tributary vassals (see also Longrigg, 199). The transmission of authority in such a Mamlûk system was 'hereditary', not in the sense of descending from father to son, but from master to freedman (who was frequently a son-in-law at the same time).

[4] Cf. Olivier, ii. 361–3, and his outspoken admiration for Muḥammad Paşa Calîlî (1789–1807).

troubled by external events, Syria suffered the full effects of the nerveless and venal rule of Istanbul.[1] On the other hand, Syria had probably benefited materially more than any other Asiatic province from incorporation in the Ottoman Empire, as a result of the commercial connexions thus formed,[2] and enjoyed a fairly flourishing social and economic life. In spite of the military riots, the rapacities of *Paşas*, tax-collectors, and Arabs, the plagues and famines, that fill the annals of Aleppo and Damascus, there is little to suggest that down to about 1750 the interior organization of the country suffered any serious blow. In both cities the standing military forces were divided into two camps. At Aleppo the Janissary troops were at feud with the local militia, who prided themselves on descent from the Prophet and were consequently known as Seyyids or Aşrâf. At Damascus the opposing factions were the Imperial Janissaries or *Ḳapîḳul*[3] and the local or *Yerlîya* Janissaries. For the purpose of preserving some sort of order the *Paşas* were obliged to maintain a private army, the cavalry of which (called *Delîs* or *Levends*)[4] they recruited mainly from the Türkmens or Kurds of the north, and the infantry from Algerian and Tunisian immigrants, known as Barbaresques or *Mağâriba*.[5] This expedient was not wholly successful, since under weak governors it merely added a third faction to the existing two and produced a fresh crop of *émeutes*.[6] In spite of constant repression, the violence of the Şerîfs and Janissaries, especially at Aleppo, increased almost year by year, disorganizing the administration and, together with the inroads of the Arabs (to be touched on at the end of this chapter), depopulating the country-side. Volney in 1785 asserts (probably with some exaggeration) that of over 3,200 villages in the province of Aleppo listed in the registers of taxation, scarcely four hundred then existed, and that the greater part of the depopulation had taken place in the preceding twenty years.[7]

[1] Or, as it is always called in contemporary Syrian writings, Islâmbûl, 'The City of Islam', or in Turkish 'Islâm abounds'. The term first occurs regularly on the coins of Aḥmed III (1703–30).—Lane-Poole, *Coins*, p. xv.

[2] See pp. 304–5, below.

[3] Murâdî (ii. 61) defines the *Ḳapîḳul* as the troops and government servants employed in the government offices at Damascus. They were generally allied with the garrison in the citadel, but it is not clear whether these were technically included in the *Ḳapîḳul* or not.

[4] See above, p. 193.

[5] Cf. Volney, ii. 46; Ḥaidar, i. 40, 45; Murâdî, i. 107; Lockroy 38. Ḥaidar, i. 104, mentions an instance when a Druse chief hired Mağribine troops from the governor of Damascus.

[6] Cf. Ğazzî, 306–7. On several occasions the *paşas* of Aleppo were refused entrance and forced to besiege the city: ibid. Executions of large numbers of Janissaries at Aleppo: ibid., 299. Massacre of the Şerîfs (Aşrâf): Olivier, ii. 309–12.

[7] Volney, ii. 46–7; cf. Russell, 15–16, Olivier, ii. 312. On the ravages of the Arabs, cf. Ğazzî, 295–8, and Olivier, ii. 301; on the revolt of the Aşrâf in 1770, Charles-Roux, *Échelles*, 213–15.

While Damascus shared most of the misfortunes of Aleppo, it was spared their worst effects by the emergence of a remarkable family whose members and clients all but monopolized the *Paşalıḳs* of southern Syria for some sixty years. Like the dynasty of Ḥasan Paşa in ʿIrâḳ, it owed its establishment to the services rendered by its founder at a critical moment. During the governorship of ʿO̱tmân Paşa, known as Abû Ṭawḳ (*c.* 1721–4), the disorders between the *Ḳapıḳul* and the *Yerlîya* Janissaries reached an unprecedented height. But the Porte could not afford to regard such a state of affairs in Damascus with the same apathetic eye that it turned on similar disorders elsewhere. The Sultan's prestige as temporal head of Sunnî Islâm was bound up with the Pilgrimage to Mecca, and Damascus was the rendezvous and starting-point of the great pilgrim caravan from all the northern provinces. The *Paşa* of Damascus held, *ex officio*, the coveted title of *Amîr el-Ḥacc*, 'Commander of the Pilgrimage', and was charged with the duty of making arrangements for the convoy and provisioning of the caravan,[1] and of personally conducting it with a force of troops sufficient to protect it from the covetousness of the Beduins of Arabia.

A serious and long-continued outbreak of disorder at Damascus therefore menaced the security of the Pilgrimage, and in 1724 ʿO̱tmân Paşa was replaced by a certain Ismâʿîl, known as al-ʿAẓm,[2] the son of a former trooper in the garrison, and at that time *Paşa* of Ṣaydâ. He suppressed the outbreak, executed the chief offenders, and with the aid of his body of Bosniak mamlûks and Mağâriba maintained order in the city until his supersession in 1730.[3] After a short interval, his brother Süleymân was appointed to the *Paşalıḳ* and asserted his authority by banishing a large body of Janissaries. These took refuge in the Lebanon and maintained themselves by plundering until they were allowed to return, only to be subsequently seized and put to death. His government coincided with the rise of Şeyẖ Ẓâhir al-ʿOmar in northern Palestine, and it was while besieging Ẓâhir in Tiberias that Süleymân met his death in 1742.[4] He was succeeded by his nephew Asʿad Paşa al-

[1] The greater part of the revenues of the *eyâlet* were earmarked for this purpose.—See below, ch. vii.

[2] The local Syrian pronunciation is ʿAḍm; similarly Ẓâhir (see below) was locally known as Ḍâhir.

[3] Murâdî, ii. 84; Kurd ʿAlî, ii. 289. The origin of the ʿAẓm family is not known with certainty, but they are believed to have been Türkmens, who established themselves at Maʿarra where Ismâʿîl was born about 1660. Pococke, ii. 124, states that the Bosniak troops of the *Paşa* were frequently changed to prevent their forming connexions in the city.

[4] Ḥaidar, i. 34; Volney, ii. 3. According to Murâdî, iii. 184, he was poisoned by one of his suite at the instigation of Ẓâhir (the text has ʿAkka by mistake for Tiberias). For Ẓâhir al-ʿOmar see below, pp. 222–3.

'Aẓm, formerly *Paşa* of Ṣaydâ, whose difficulties with the *Yerlîya* were intensified by hostilities against the Druses of the Lebanon.[1] The *Yerlîya* were protected by the *Defterdâr*, Seyyid Fetḥallâh, the head of a wealthy and long-established family in official service at Damascus. Finally As'ad Paşa was driven to seek authority from Istanbul to use extreme measures, and in 1746 Fetḥallâh was executed and a large number of the *Yerlîya* Janissaries massacred, to the joy and relief of the population.[2] A new *Defterdâr* was sent from Istanbul, and for the remaining ten years of his tenure of the *paşalık* the government was orderly and quietly conducted. Volney highly praises As'ad Paşa: 'he did an infinity of good and established such discipline among his troops as to protect the peasantry from their ravages.'[3] But the services which the 'Aẓm *paşas* had rendered to the province of Damascus and to the Porte could not overcome the suspicion with which the Dîwân looked upon the dynastic tendency. During As'ad's long tenure of Damascus, the *paşalıks* of Ṣaydâ and Tripoli had been given mainly to his relatives and dependents, on the pretext of containing the ambitions of Ẓâhir al-'Omar, and in 1755 the *paşalık* of Aleppo also was conferred upon him. At the same time, however, Ḥuseyn Ağa, known as Ibn Makkî, his deputy in Jerusalem, was raised to the rank of *Paşa* and made independent of Damascus, and in 1756 Ḥuseyn was installed in Damascus,[4] while As'ad fled into the desert.[5] This attempt to break the power of the 'Aẓm family proved disastrous. Ibn Makkî scarcely set foot in Damascus before the military feuds and disturbances broke out with renewed violence; to make matters worse, the Pilgrim Caravan, returning from Mecca in the late summer of 1757, was set upon by the Arabs, besieged at Tabûk, and plundered.[6] The *Paşa* fled to Gaza,[7] and Damascus was given

[1] Ḥaidar, i. 34.

[2] Murâdî, iii. 286–7; iv. 38. According to Murâdî As'ad paid a thousand purses to the Porte for the *firmân* authorizing the massacre and the seizure of Fetḥallâh's property.

[3] Volney, ii. 137. Cf. also Murâdî's very favourable notice of Darwîş, the Ağa of the *Yerlîya* after 1746, praising his strict control over his troops.—Murâdî, ii. 108. (It is true, however, that Darwîş was Murâdî's maternal uncle.)

[4] Ḥuseyn's grandfather was a rich merchant of Gaza, whose son Muḥammad took service under the *Paşa* of Damascus, rose to be *kâḫyâ* of As'ad Paşa, and obtained Gaza as a *mâlikâne*. Ḥuseyn's career began with the government of this place; subsequently he was appointed to Jerusalem and early in 1756 was made *Paşa* of Ṣaydâ (Murâdî, ii. 60–1). Volney, ii. 139–40, gives (on rather dubious authority) an account of the intrigues preceding his appointment to Damascus.

[5] He was afterwards accused of connivance with the Arabs and murdered at Ankara, and his fortune, estimated at some three million piastres, confiscated by the Porte: Murâdî, iv. 210; Ḥaidar, i. 55; Volney, ii. 242. The fortune of his predecessor, Süleymân, had also been confiscated on his death.—Murâdî, iii. 286.

[6] Murâdî, ii. 61–2, 111; Volney, ii. 140.

[7] He was afterwards restored to favour, and held the *paşalık* of Mar'aş, but retired eventually to Gaza, where he maintained a private army, and was killed

over to confusion and disorder, in which even the Druses took a hand by aiding the *Yerlîya* against the *Ḳapîḳul*. It was not until the end of 1758[1] or early in 1759 that the Porte transferred ʿAbdallâh Paşa Çatacî from Aleppo to Damascus; he brought a strong force with him, joined hands with the *Ḳapîḳul* and after severe fighting (in which he was not always successful) succeeded in restoring order.[2] On his death in 1761,[3] the ʿAẓm régime was restored; for ten years Damascus was governed by ʿOṯmân Paşa, surnamed el-Ṣâdiḳ ('the True'), a former Georgian Mamlûk of Asʿad Paşa. The growing power of Ẓâhir al-ʿOmar compelled the Porte to consent to the appointment of other members and dependents of the ʿAẓm family (including ʿOṯmân's own sons) to the *paşalîḳs* of Ṣaydâ, Tripoli, and even at times of Aleppo; the pilgrim road was refortified, and fair order re-established,[4] except for constant raiding and fighting in the valley of the Biḳâʿ between the *Paşa's* forces and the Druse Amîrs.[5] The invasion of Syria by the mamlûks of ʿAlî Bey of Egypt, led by Muḥammad Bey Abû Ḏahab, in concert with Ẓâhir al-ʿOmar, took both ʿOṯmân and the Ottoman government by surprise, and Damascus surrendered after the briefest of resistances in 1771. But Abû Ḏahab unexpectedly retired, and another ʿOṯman, known as al-Miṣrî, was appointed to Damascus, with the task of settling scores with Ẓahir al-ʿOmar.[6] His ignominious failure led to the appointment in 1773 of Muḥammad Paşa, descended from the ʿAẓm family on the maternal side, who for ten years maintained internal and external order in his *paşalîḳ* and died in 1783, leaving the reputation of having been 'the best of all governors of Damascus' during the century.[7]

The death of Muḥammad Paşa al-ʿAẓm marked the end of the relative immunity of Damascus. The familiar disorders revived; Ibrâhîm Delî Paşa (1786–90) was, after a long struggle with the citizens, driven out and only regained the city after an investment with troops brought from Ḥomṣ and Ḥamâh.[8] He was succeeded

in fighting a raiding force of B. Ṣaḫr Arabs in 1783, his property being as usual confiscated (Murâdî, ii. 62).

[1] A contemporary description of this year of rioting is quoted by Kurd ʿAlî, *Ḫiṭaṭ el-Şâm*, ii. 296–7 (dated by error 1161).

[2] Murâdî, i. 98, iii. 207; Ğazzî, iii. 301; Ḥaidar, i. 45. Volney, ii. 146–7, praises ʿAbdallâh Paşa very highly, but the romantic story which he relates (pp. 143–5) of his origin and earlier history seems to be false.

[3] According to Volney (ii. 147) he was poisoned by his nephew.

[4] Although their government in the provinces was by no means free from abuses; cf. Kurd ʿAlî, ii. 291.

[5] Murâdî, iii. 161; Ḥaidar, i. 35, 66–7, 90, 92; Volney, ii. 13.

[6] Ḥaidar, i. 92–104. Cf. Lockroy, 52–65, who does not, however, distinguish between the two *Paşas* of like name.

[7] Murâdî, iv. 97–102, a judgement confirmed by the Christian Michael of Damascus (ed. Maʿlouf, p. 2).

[8] Mich. Dam. 5–6; his deputy's good administration at Baʿalbek: Ḥaidar, i. 149. Since 1730 Ḥamâh and Ḥomṣ had been attached to Damascus as crown

by Aḥmad Cezzâr, *Paşa* of Ṣaydâ, with whose five years' tenure of the *paşaliḳ* a new and melancholy page in its history opened.

The first Ottoman reorganization of Syria allowed only for three *eyâlets*: Aleppo, Şâm (Damascus), and Tripoli. In 1660, after the final liquidation of the revolt of the Maʿnid Druse amîrs in the Lebanon,[1] a fourth *eyâlet* was formed of the coastal regions of the former *eyâlet* of Şâm, with its head-quarters at Ṣaydâ (Sidon). The function of the new *eyâlet* was to keep the Druse and Maronite population of the Lebanon range under surveillance, and, in conjunction with the province of Tripoli, to prevent any further outbreak. To be effectual, this involved also co-operation with Damascus, and in times of danger, as has been seen, one or both of the coastal *paşaliḳs* became in practice (though never in theory) subordinate to the *paşas* of Şâm. Nevertheless, during the second half of the eighteenth century, its renewed difficulties with the Druse and other chieftains in the highlands, its closer relations with Egypt, and its openness to intercourse with European merchants[2] combined to give the *paşaliḳ* of Ṣaydâ unexpected significance as a focus for the new tendencies which began to manifest themselves from this time in the Asiatic provinces, and which were first exploited by Şeyḫ Ẓahir al-ʿOmar.

The beginnings of Ẓahir's career are connected with the Ḳeys and Yemen feud which distracted the Lebanon and southern Syria. In 1698 the Şîʿî *mutawâlîs* or *metâwila*, who inhabited the mountainous country between the Sea of Galilee and Ṣaydâ, rose under the leadership of a Yemenî *şeyḫ*. The Druse amîr Başîr I, of the Ḳeys or Red party, in alliance with the *Paşas* of Ṣaydâ and Tripoli, put down the revolt and installed Ẓâhir, who came of a locally influential Sunnî and Ḳeysî family, as *şeyḫ* of Ṣafed.[3] In 1705 he was appointed governor of Ṣafed and ʿAkka,[4] and for over thirty years applied himself to strengthening his position, keeping out of local feuds as far as possible, paying his tribute regularly, and gaining over the Metâwila. By 1742 he was strong enough to occupy Tiberias and resist Süleymân Paşa of Damascus[5], and about 1750 he refortified ʿAkka against the eventual attacks of his

fiefs (*mâlikânes*) of the *Paşas* and had had the advantage of their protection. Both towns, however, and more especially Ḥamâh—which Pococke (ii. 144) had found about 1730 'in a very flourishing condition'—suffered from the depredations of the Arabs.—Cf. Murâdî, iii. 161, and iii. 12, 15; Volney, ii. 173.

[1] For the revolt of Faḫr ul-Dîn (II) b. Maʿn (1585–1635), see H. Lammens, *La Syrie* (Bayrut, 1921), ii. 66–90; F. Wüstenfeld, *Fachr ed-Din der Drusenfürst* (Göttingen, 1886).

[2] Although there were European consuls and establishments at Aleppo, it had proved impossible to maintain either at Damascus.—Cf. Volney, ii. 152.

[3] The family were known as the Banû Zeydân.—Cf. Murâdî, iii. 184; Ḥaidar, i. 6.

[4] Ḥaidar, i. 8. (Ḥaidar is not always reliable, however, in his dates or facts.)

[5] See above, p. 219.

former overlords, the Druse amîrs.[1] Here he set himself to attract the European merchants and under the tuition of his Syrian Christian factotum, Ibrâhîm el-Ṣabbâğ,[2] initiated the fatal practice of monopolizing the principal productions of his territory, in order to maintain his quite considerable army.[3] The suspicions and hostility of the Porte were aroused, and as a result of his conflict with ʿOṯmân Paşa el-Ṣâdiḳ Ẓâhir allied himself with ʿAlî Bey of Egypt and contributed to the success of the Mamlûk invasion in 1770–1. Nevertheless, on his occupation of Ṣaydâ in 1772 he was formally recognized as governor of the *paşalîḳ*.[4] In the following year he allied himself with the Druse Amîr Yûsuf, inflicted a total defeat on the army of Damascus, and with the aid of a Russian squadron drove the future Cezzâr Paşa out of Bayrût.[5] In 1774 he received a formal *firmân* of pardon.[6] In 1775 a second Mamlûk invasion destroyed his power, and the *coup de grâce* was delivered by the Ottoman *ḳapudan-paşa* Ḥasan, who besieged and captured ʿAkka in the same year.[7] Ẓâhir himself was assassinated by mutineers amongst his own *Mağâriba*; Ibrâhîm el-Ṣabbâğ was seized and his fortune confiscated.[8]

The material and administrative legacy of Ẓâhir al-ʿOmar was gathered by Aḥmad Cezzâr, who after an adventurous career was promoted to the *paşalîḳ* of Ṣaydâ on its recapture.[9] Without

[1] Ḥaidar, i. 43.—Cf. Lockroy, *Ahmed le Boucher*, pp. 33 sqq.

[2] He was a Melkite (Uniate Greek): Ḥaidar, i. 113; Lammens, ii. 105. See his portrait in Volney, ii. 36: 'Jamais il ne portait que des habits sales et déchirés. À voir ce petit homme maigre et borgne, on l'eût plutôt pris pour un mendiant que pour le ministre d'un état considérable.' Lockroy (p. 43) erroneously calls him a Jew.

[3] Volney, ii. 29; Charles-Roux, *Les Échelles de Syrie*, 68. Volney estimates his forces in 1770 at 1,500 horsemen from Ṣafed, 1,200 *metâwila* cavalry, and 1,000 Mağribine infantry (i. 110), but in 1772 at 5,000 to 6,000 horsemen and 1,000 *Mağâriba* (ii. 22). His picked *metâwila* warriors were called *fidâwîs*—a curious relic of the terminology of the Ismâʿîlî 'Assassins' of crusading times.—Murâdî, i. 57; Ḥaidar, i. 79.

[4] So Ḥaidar, i. 100, who adds that he undertook to pay an annual tribute of 450 purses, *plus* 1,000 purses of arrears.

[5] Ḥaidar, i. 98–9, 103–4; cf. Lockroy, 86–97.

[6] Quoted in full by Ḥaidar, i. 107–8.

[7] Ḥaidar, i. 112–13, dates this under 1189/1775; Murâdî, iii. 184, gives 1190/1776.—Cf. Lockroy, 120.

[8] It was estimated at '20 millions de France' [= 8,000,000 piastres].—Volney, ii. 36.

[9] Of Bosniak origin, he served first under ʿAlî Bey in Egypt, where he gained the *sobriquet* of el-Cezzâr, 'The Butcher', by his treatment of the Beduins of the Delta. Subsequently he joined the Druse Amîr Yûsuf, and was appointed to command Beyrût by him (so Ḥaidar, i. 97, and cf. Olivier, ii. 257), but on attempting to make himself independent there, he was driven out by Ẓâhir al-ʿOmar with Russian assistance. After a short stay with Ẓâhir at ʿAkka, he fled to Damascus, regained the favour of the Porte, and shortly before the capture of ʿAkka was promoted *Beylerbeyi*. See Ḥaidar, i. 97–9; Lammens, ii. 112 sqq. E. Lockroy, in *Ahmed le Boucher* (Paris, 1888), has written a highly coloured, but on the whole accurate, account of Cezzâr, mainly from French sources.

delay, he resumed and improved on the programme of Ẓâhir; he rebuilt the fortifications of ʿAkka more strongly than before, raised a private army of some four thousand Bosniaks, Arna'uṭs, Mağâriba, and Beduins,[1] established monopolies of all produce,[2] and opened up commercial relations with European merchants. He also began to build a fleet, and systematically farmed out the districts and customs of his *eyâlet* at ruinous rates.[3] Not content with the enormous profits thus acquired, he obtained the *paşalîḳ* of Damascus in 1790 (retaining at the same time both Ṣaydâ and Tripoli), and repeated his extortions there.

'In truth (says the Damascus chronicler), during Cezzâr's government of Damascus, which lasted for about five years, the people had not one month of rest—firstly from unjust demands for money, and secondly from repeated debasement of the currency, which resulted in enormous loss, then by forced sales of all sorts of goods which were plundered from different quarters and thrown on the market at low prices, over and above a multitude of afflictions of various kinds.'[4]

The Jewish bankers who kept the government's accounts were the special objects of his extortions, and when one escaped from his confinement the Jewish quarter was sacked and looted.[5] Added to all this was his callous cruelty and disregard of life, which did not spare even his own mamlûks.[6] Small wonder that on his deposition in 1795 'the streets of Damascus were decorated and the shops illuminated'.[7] Twice again, in 1799, and in his last year of life (1803–4), Cezzâr was appointed to Damascus, and by his exactions and cruelties drove most of those who had anything to lose to seek refuge in Aleppo or the Lebanon.[8]

The situation in Egypt had in the meantime developed along parallel, but somewhat different, lines.[9] It will be recalled that Sultan Selîm had established six corps or *ocaḳs* of Turkish (or rather Bosniak) troops in Egypt after the conquest, but that he and his successor Süleymân had at the same time perpetuated the Mamlûk system, by which the surviving Mamlûk amîrs (and later on the officers of the *ocaḳs*) purchased Circassian and other white

[1] Charles-Roux, *Les Échelles*, 136. Volney estimated his army in 1784 at about 900 Bosniak and Arna'uṭ horsemen and 1,000 Mağribine infantry (ii. 76). Ḥaidar (i. 118) states that he took into service about 600 *Levend* cavalry who had recently been disbanded from the Ottoman army, while Muḥammad Paşa al-ʿAẓm enrolled about 300 of them.—See also Ḥaidar, i. 162; Lockroy, 146 sqq.

[2] Charles-Roux, 134, 140.

[3] See below, ch. vii.

[4] Mich. Dam. 6–7.

[5] Ibid. 8.

[6] See the portrait and descriptions given (from hearsay) by Olivier (ii. 264–76), who asserts that the entire population of Syria regarded Cezzâr Paşa as a sorcerer; and cf. Miḫâ'îl Muşâḳa, pp. 47 sqq.

[7] Mich. Dam. 9.

[8] Ibid. 13–14.

[9] For the external history of Egypt under the Ottoman *Paşas* see J. J. Marcel, *Égypte Moderne* (Paris, 1848), and the more recent, and in many respects more satisfactory, account by E. Combe, *L'Égypte Ottomane* (Cairo, 1933).

slaves, who constituted a standing force of horsemen, and served as a counterbalancing element to the *Paşa* and the Janissaries. The distinction between the regular *ocaklîs* and the Mamlûks became still more marked, when in course of time large numbers of the former, by intermarriage with the Egyptian population and infiltration into the craft guilds,[1] were merged into the citizen population and (though still retaining their regimental privileges) lost their military character. Though the military forces were therefore in no case composed of native Egyptians, yet they were totally distinct from the Turkish regiments of Anatolia and Rumelia, and the lapse of two centuries had made them still more conscious of their individuality.[2] The social organization in Egypt had accommodated itself with little difficulty to this situation, and the distance of Constantinople and comparatively light yoke of Turkish suzerainty predisposed the population to accept the Ottoman connexion without cavil or regret and to a certain unenthusiastic loyalty to the Sultan, as the embodiment of secular authority.[3]

While the former Turkish immigrants, now naturalized, formed a relatively stable element, there might be ground for regarding the Mamlûks as much less reliable and less amenable to the influence of tradition and religious sanction.[4] Though the Mamlûk system went back more than three centuries before the Ottoman conquest, its nature was such that the Mamlûks could not strike roots in the country. Each generation was freshly imported from abroad, and had to be converted afresh to Islâm.[5] The strength of the system lay in the strict training which the young Mamlûks had to undergo before they entered on their military career. On this we have apparently no direct information, but two illuminating passages in Cabartî throw enough light to enable us to reconstruct its main features. 'The traditional usage was that Mamlûks should

[1] For the relations between the *ocaks* and the artisan corporations see below, p. 295.

[2] They were collectively known as *Mişrlîya*, 'Egyptians', and Cabartî in many passages shows that they were sharply distinguished from 'Ottomans, Turks, and strangers from Syria and Aleppo' (iii. 260/vii. 212).

[3] But this does not prevent Cabartî from expressing a little mild sarcasm at the orders of the Porte.—ii. 156 foot/v. 18.

[4] Why did the Mamlûks never succeed in perpetuating their race beyond the second, or at the most the third, generation, while the Turkish *ocaklîs* had six or seven generations behind them by the middle of the eighteenth century? The reason can only be sought for in certain special (and now obscure) circumstances of their mode of life, amongst possible factors being the circumstance that they did not marry Egyptian wives, the prevalence of unnatural vice amongst them (cf. Volney, i. 158; Olivier, ii. 145–6), and the kind of life led by the Circassian women.

[5] This did not necessarily detract from their religious enthusiasm (the zeal of converts being well known), but certainly cut them off from any fundamental assimilation of Islamic tradition.

never ride alone through the city without their patrons, but this custom had now [i.e. in 1787] fallen into disuse and was no more than a memory. They now left their patrons' houses, married, had houses and attendants of their own, rode on horseback through the streets, gave dinners, came, went and smoked on the street, not realizing that they were flouting convention, although they were nothing more than slaves'.[1] From this passage we may gather the strict discipline which was enforced on them down to the eighteenth century (since Cabartî implies that the change had taken place in the lifetime of persons then elderly); from the other we gain a glimpse of their literary and religious education. When Ismâʿîl Bey imported troops from the Balkans, the Egyptians found them irreligious and unprincipled, and it struck them particularly that 'he employed them from the very first in military exercises, without having trained them in polite accomplishments or in any knowledge of religion'.[2] It is therefore unjustifiable to regard the Mamlûks as an illiterate and undisciplined body,[3] and this conclusion is fortified by numerous facts and judgements recorded in the same historian's critical and sober pages,[4] although there was undoubtedly a falling off from earlier standards in the middle of the eighteenth century.[5]

[1] Cab. ii. 145/iv. 284.

[2] Id. ii. 180/v. 72; cf. also ii. 214/v. 136; iv. 25–6, 27/viii. 55–6, 58.

[3] See, for example, Volney's account of their regular exercises.—i. 151.

[4] e.g. i. 179/ii. 87–8: ʿO̱tmân Bey D̲u'l-Fiḳâr, Şeyẖ el-Beled from 1729 to 1743, was just and upright; he took no bribes and would not allow his subordinates to accept them, and never extorted money; ii. 5–8/iii. 239–44: ʿAbdar-Raḥmân Kâẖyâ (d. 1776) was one of the most remarkable builders in the history of Cairo, being reckoned to have built or restored eighteen large mosques and a vast number of small mosques, schools, &c.; even the notorious Murâd Bey rebuilt the mosque of ʿAmr at Old Cairo—Marcel (*Égypte Moderne*, 248), it is true, represents this as a treasure hunt, but his version can hardly stand against Cabartî's formal statement (iii. 170/vi. 318) that he rebuilt the mosque with great magnificence and that it was destroyed in the following year by the French. Other examples of public utility works by Mamlûks: iii. 173, 176, 219/vi. 322, 327; vii. 103–4. Of their patronage of letters less can be said, the Turks being evidently more interested in learning than either the Mamlûks or the Egyptians. But even here there were exceptions, and Muḥammad Bey Abû D̲ahab's action in buying the original copy of Şeyẖ Murtaḍâ's famous commentary on the dictionary called *al-Ḳâmûs* from the author for 100,000 *dirhams* of silver (Cab. ii. 199/v. 108), recalls the vanished magnificence of Bağdâd. Of the last of the Mamlûks, Murâd's colleague Ibrâhîm Bey, Cabartî records that he was 'characterized by courage and gallantry, steadfast under adversity, patient and forbearing, easily led to the right, averse to jesting, disliking to shed blood' (iv. 263/ix. 210). Compare, finally, the tone of his account of the massacre of the Mamlûks in 1811, with his frequent references to 'long-established families' and almost complete identification of the Mamlûks and old Turkish families with the people of Egypt (iv. 127–32/viii. 286–98).

[5] Several factors no doubt contributed to this decline, but a peculiarly remarkable one was the appearance of non-military 'patrons' about this time. Thus we hear of two Egyptians of humble birth: Şâliḥ, a peasant, and Aḥmad al-Gelfî, a porter, both of whom became wealthy capitalists and money-lenders, who bought Mamlûks and placed them in the ranks of the *ocaks* and thus

By custom a certain number of the provincial governorships and other offices were held by Mamlûks, on the usual yearly tenures, and their continued influence in the administration of the country was thus assured. As the control of the *Paşas* and the power of the regular *ocaḳlîs* declined, that of the Mamlûks grew. The principal Bey held the office of Governor of Cairo, with the title of *Şeyḫ el-Beled*, and already by the beginning of the eighteenth century his authority rivalled that of the *Paşa*. The Mamlûks enrolled in rival *ocaḳs* formed two opposing factions, between whom armed disputes were of constant occurrence;[1] and the leader of the winning faction automatically became Şeyḫ el-Beled for the time being. Whether he ruled well or ill, maintained himself for a long term of years, or was killed or driven into exile by the opposing faction, the *Paşas*, with rare exceptions, looked on impotently. Orders from the Porte for the execution of sundry Beys led only to the summary deposition of the too-enterprising governor who attempted to enforce them.[2] Yet the administration remained on the whole orderly and reasonable in its treatment of the subjects. Except for certain increases in taxation, and the growing power of the Beduins, there was little alteration in the traditional structure of government and society down to the end of the seven years' rule of Ibrâhîm Bey and Riḍwân Bey (1747–54). The increasing concentration of authority in the hands of the Şeyḫ el-Beled, however, inevitably led to more ambitious plans, which began to be realized when 'Alî Bey, the successor and avenger of Ibrâhîm, seized the office for the second time in 1767.

The Mamlûk Beys were not the only inhabitants of Egypt who had gained by the decline of Ottoman control. From time immemorial the semi-sedentary Beduin Arabs formed a disturbing element in the agricultural economy of both the Delta and Upper Egypt,[3] and by their numbers, mobility, and warlike character[4] they were frequently able to defy the efforts of the governors to control their depredations. Even in the days of the former Mamlûk Empire the revolts, actual and threatened, of the Beduins had constituted one of the standing preoccupations of the

founded influential Mamlûk groups. Cabartî explicitly charges the former with ruining many powerful families by his usury (Cab. i. 203/ii. 141; Marcel, op. cit. 225).

[1] Their miniature battles were, however, fought outside the city walls, and so scarcely affected the ordinary life of the citizens. For all the apparent anarchy of these proceedings, there was a recognized 'code of honour' (called by them *adiguą kabza*) which was punctiliously observed.

[2] It was one of the curiosities of the government of Egypt that the Beys had acquired the prescriptive right of deposing the *Paşas* without consulting the Porte. But even after deposition, the *Paşas* were usually treated with ceremony, and there are few instances of display of violence towards them.

[3] See pp. 266–7, below.

[4] The phrase must be understood, of course, *à l'Arabe*.

Sultans,[1] and in more recent centuries their numbers had been reinforced by the immigration of new fractions from the West. In several regions Beduin *Şeyḫs* took advantage of the weakening of the central power and the feuds of the Mamlûks to extend their authority over entire provinces. By the middle of the century the Beys found their pretensions challenged on two fronts. In Upper Egypt, Ḥumâm, *şeyḫ* of the Hawwâra tribe, held the entire country south of Asyûṭ,[2] and in the Delta the provinces of Buḥayra, Şarḳîya, and even Ḳalyûbîya immediately to the north of Cairo, were overrun by tribes who were independent in all but name.

The sudden re-emergence of the Mamlûk state is probably not unconnected with this revival of the Beduin menace. At all events, the first activities of ʿAlî Bey were directed to the crushing of the Beduin tribes. In 1769 an expedition commanded by Muḥammad Bey Abû Ḏahab destroyed the power of Ḥumâm, and broke up the Hawwâra confederation; simultaneously the future Aḥmad Paşa Cezzâr, then one of ʿAlî Bey's Mamlûks, distinguished himself by his suppression of the Beduins of Buḥayra.[3] These operations alone demanded a considerable increase in military effectives, and a still greater increase was required in order to carry through the expeditions which followed into the Ḥijâz and Yemen in 1770 and into Syria in 1771. It will be recalled that the Ottoman regiments in Egypt were established there primarily for purposes of defence, and though contingents were liable to be called up for service in the imperial army they did not constitute in themselves a strong offensive force.[4] Since, moreover, in conformity with the Ottoman system, their maintenance was provided for by assignments of land, such revenues as the central provincial treasury disposed of were insufficient to support the upkeep of a regular army.[5] In order, therefore, to carry out his ambitious projects of expansion and independence, ʿAlî Bey was faced with a double problem. He had on the one hand to create an army capable of taking the offensive, and on the other hand to find the financial resources for its maintenance.

To solve these problems was utterly beyond the capacity of the relatively efficient but routine-bound bureaucracy of Egypt, more

[1] See A. N. Poliak, in *Revue des Études Islamiques*, 1934, 257–65.

[2] The sources are unanimous as to his equitable rule; by his policing and control of the Arabs, maintenance of the irrigation canals, and mild government, he brought about a sudden burst of prosperity in his provinces and created for himself an immense reputation.—See Girard, 510–12, 560; Lancret, 246; Estève, 323.

[3] See p. 223, n. 9, above.

[4] All the less so that a large proportion of the *ocaḳlis* were no longer on the effective military strength; cf. the Ḳapudan-Paşa Ḥasan's disgust at their uselessness.—Cab. ii. 135/iv. 260.

[5] For the similar position in Turkey see Thornton, *Present State*, ii. 1–2, 64–5.

especially in view of the economic difficulties to be described shortly. 'Alî Bey was accordingly driven to crude and violent solutions, which set the example for his successors also, and launched the country on the headlong rush towards economic ruin and social disintegration which marks the last decades of the eighteenth century. It never, apparently, entered the head of any Turk or Mamlûk to utilize the Egyptians as soldiers. Consequently 'Alî Bey, besides making large purchases of Mamlûks, began to enrol bodies of foreign mercenaries in his service, and supplemented these with Nubians and Arabs from Arabia.[1] He also organized a corps of artillery (probably manned by Greeks), which contributed not a little to his success in Syria.[2] Abû Ḏahab enlisted Turkish and Greek soldiers and sailors,[3] and placed his artillery under an English officer, though without much success.[4] These developments were accelerated by the Turkish reoccupation of Egypt under the Ḳapudan-Paşa Ḥasan in 1786 and 1787. His fortified line south of Cairo, his flotillas on the Nile, and his devices for raising money supplied the rivals Ismâ'îl Bey and Murâd Bey with new ideas, which they practised assiduously after his recall. Ismâ'îl brought in recruits from the Balkans and Albania (Bosniaks and Arna'uṭs), whose irreligious and overbearing conduct rendered them thoroughly odious to the population;[5] Murâd brought in Greeks and Cretans[6] and with their aid

[1] Cabartî, under 1183/1769, speaks of '*delîs*, Druses, Mutawâlîs and Syrians' (i. 335; the translation (iii. 55) has 'Russes, Albanais, Metwalis, et des chrétiens Syriens'!). The army sent to Arabia in 1770 consisted of 'Turks, Mağribîs [i.e. Mağribine infantry], Syrians, Mutawâlîs, Druses, Ḥaḍramîs, Yemenîs, Sudanese, Abyssinians and *delîs*' (id. i. 350/iii. 91), and that sent to Syria in 1771 of 'Mağribîs, Turks, Indians, Yemenîs and Mutawâlîs' (i. 364/iii. 115). (It may be noted that an earlier Bey, Ḳaṭâmiş, had already formed a corps of negro Mamlûks: i. 174/ii. 77.)

Volney (i. 109) estimates the army sent to Syria at about 40,000 men in all (Murâdî, i. 54, gives the same figure), of whom about 20,000 were fighting men (including 5,000 Mamlûk cavalry and about 1,500 Mağribine infantry). The *delîs* in Egypt were mostly Syrian mountaineers.—Cab. iv. 226/ix. 132. For 'Alî Bey's military and economic measures see also Ḥaidar, i. 76.

[2] Cf. Murâdî, i. 54–6; Ḥaidar, i. 85; the garrison of Damascus surrendered almost at once. But, contrary to the general belief, artillery was by no means unknown in Egypt and Syria even before this time. The citadels of Aleppo and other towns were armed with cannon (cf. Ğazzî, iii. 267 (in 1600) and 299); according to Volney, however, they were mostly useless and badly handled (i. 147; ii. 48; for Alexandria, i. 7). Volney quotes an eyewitness for Süleymân Paşa's use of cannon at Tiberias in 1742 (ii. 2), and artillery is frequently mentioned in sieges and field engagements after 1771 (Ḥaidar, i. 92, 93, 98, &c.). In 1783 Volney refers to a factory of coarse gunpowder in Egypt (i. 174), and found Suez guarded by six bronze cannon manned by two Greek artillerymen 'qui tirent en détournant la tête' (i. 185).

[3] Cab. ii. 107/iv. 186. Ḥaidar (i. 110) estimates his army in 1775 at over 60,000 men.

[4] Volney, i. 126, 128; cf. Murâdî, i. 57.

[5] Cab. ii. 180/v. 72; joy in Cairo when they were ordered to leave the country after Ismâ'îl's death.—Id. ii. 195/v. 100.

[6] Cab. iii. 41/vi. 87.

built foundries and powder factories and created a new fleet.[1] The latter was captured by a former subordinate of the Ḳapudan-Paşa, Nicolas of Chesmé,[2] who, though by no means a docile officer,[3] made his force sufficiently formidable to be avoided even by the French during the later operations in Upper Egypt.[4] It would appear too that the number of Mamlûks was gradually increased.[5]

In order to find the means to keep up these mercenary forces and armaments the Beys had recourse mainly to extortions and the imposition of new taxes. 'Alî Bey began the disruption of the old land system by seizing the estates of his opponents,[6] and of the economic structure by extraordinary levies on the villagers, extortions from the merchants and non-Moslems,[7] and the setting up of monopolies in favour of privileged merchants.[8] It is with justice that the Egyptian historian, *laudator temporis acti semper*, complains that 'Alî Bey 'rent established customs and violated usages, destroyed ancient houses and abolished the old sound ways',[9] although, in comparison with later events, he looks back to his time with regret.[10] His successors pushed extortion to still greater lengths,[11] but in Egypt the conservatism of the Mamlûks themselves and of the bureaucracy preserved the old forms down to the end of the century, in contrast to the radical changes introduced by Cezzâr Paşa in southern Syria. It was, moreover, probably as much for economic reasons as through mere ambition that 'Alî Bey attempted to extend his authority over the Arabian

[1] Cab. iii. 168/vi. 315; Browne, *Travels*, p. 81; Olivier, ii. 69; Auriant, 'Ahmed Aga le Zantiote' in *Aventuriers et Originaux*; Politis, *L'Hellénisme et l'Égypte Moderne*, i. 89–95. The Italian merchant Rossetti imported arms from Italy for Murâd, who is said also to have employed Italian mechanics and gunners in his new arsenal at Gîza, and some Italian officers and pharmacists in his army (Balboni, i. 206, 215). Prior to this the Egyptian fleet consisted of some twenty-eight small vessels built and stationed at Suez and armed with 'four rusty swivel-guns' each (Volney, i. 222).

[2] A. Boppe, *Le Colonel Nicolas Papas Oglou et le Bataillon des Chasseurs d'Orient*, Paris, 1900.

[3] Cab. iii. 168/vi. 316.

[4] Denon, *Travels* (Eng. tr.), iii. 102 (although Nicolas had himself by then joined the French forces (Politis, loc. cit.)).

[5] In 1783 Volney estimated the total Mamlûk forces, including youths, at 8,500. They were armed with English carbines of wide bore and two pistols, in the use of which they were regularly exercised, battle-axe, and sabre (i. 143, 149–51). The upkeep of each Mamlûk he put at from one to two thousand piastres per annum (i. 156). In 1798 the number of Mamlûks and *ocaḳlis in Cairo* was estimated at 10,400 (Jomard, 'Description de la Ville . . . du Kaire', *Description, &c.*, ii. 2, 694).

[6] Cf. Ḥaidar, i. 76. 'Alî Bey was himself enrolled in the Janissary *ocaḳ*.

[7] Cab. i. 309, 351/iii. 15–16, 93; for the expenses of the Syrian campaign a special contribution of 103 dollars (about 220 piastres) was levied on each village, 100,000 dollars extorted from the Copts and 40,000 from the Jews. According to Volney (i. 122) the cos of the expedition to Mecca was eleven million piastres.

[8] Volney, i. 122.

[9] i. 258/ii. 235.

[10] i. 383/iii. 162–3.

[11] See ch. vii, below.

coast of the Red Sea and southern Syria,[1] and though the later Beys did not venture to repeat his open challenge to the Sultan's authority, it is significant that Murâd was already playing with the idea of an expedition to the gold country of the south when he was surprised by the arrival of the French.[2]

From this brief survey two main points disengage themselves. The first is that the old system did not break down by its own weight or inertia. Apart from the weakening control of the Porte, there is practically no indication prior to 1760 or so that a crisis was so near at hand. The *causa causans* of the catastrophe both in Egypt and Syria was the gradual substitution for the old *ocak*-organization of a new type of army composed of mercenaries. It was the expense of these new military establishments—and not the greed or luxury of the Mamlûks and *paşas* themselves—that was at the bottom of the repeated extortions and *avanias* that fill the pages of the chronicles of the period, and which, combined with the economic factors to be discussed in a later chapter, undermined the stability of the social order. The second point is that many of the tendencies and factors that play so large a part in Meḥmed ʿAlî's administration of Egypt—the economic exploitation, the military reorganization, the introduction of European technical experts, the attempt to shake off Ottoman suzerainty and to extend Egyptian control over the neighbouring provinces—are already visible in Egypt and Syria during the last decades of the eighteenth century.

Before bringing this section to a close, it remains to consider briefly the relations of Egypt and the Syrian *eyâlets* to the Porte during this period. However loosely Ottoman control was exercised, and however much it might appear in retrospect that the Arab provinces were in effect breaking away from Constantinople, the contemporary sources give us no ground for thinking that either the Ottoman authorities or their subjects were exercised about the possibility of a dissolution of the tie. It had never been the practice of the Ottoman Sultans to place too strict an interpretation upon the obedience of their governors, and provided that due ceremonial was observed, and especially that the provincial revenue was punctually dispatched, they could afford to wait until a favourable opportunity of intervention presented itself. Volney, with his usual acuteness, summarized the situation in a few phrases:

'La politique des Turks n'est point de tenir leurs vassaux dans une stricte obéissance; ils ont dès long-tems calculé que s'ils faisaient la guerre à tous les rebelles, ce serait un travail sans relâche, une grande

[1] See pp. 311–12, below.

[2] Auriant: 'Ahmed Aga le Zantiote' in *Aventuriers et Originaux.*

consommation d'hommes et d'argent, sans compter les risques d'échouer souvent, et par là de les enhardir. Ils ont donc pris le parti de la patience; ils temporisent; ils suscitent des voisins, des parens, des enfans; et plus tôt ou plus tard, les rebelles qui suivent tous la même marche, subissent le même sort, et finissent par enrichir le sultan de leurs dépouilles.'[1]

Their experience during the eighteenth century had done little or nothing to destroy the belief of the Ottoman authorities in their capacity to assert their authority in the last resort. Apart from the special case of the Mamlûks of 'Irâḳ, the calculations enunciated by Volney practically never failed to prove exact. The only governors who openly rebelled were 'Alî Bey and Ẓâhir al-'Omar; both ventured on this step only because the hands of the Porte were tied by war in Europe; and in both cases its authority was vindicated without excessive delay and at little cost to itself. The insolence of the Egyptian Mamlûks was chastened by the Ḳapudan-Paşa's occupation of Cairo in 1785 and 1786,[2] and though Murâd and Ibrâhîm sent a very much reduced *Ḫazne* to Istanbul, they were careful always to account for the missing sums,[3] and to meet special demands when these were made.[4] Moreover, the Porte held a strong guarantee for the submission of the Mamlûks in its power to stop the export of white slaves to Egypt. The 'Aẓm *paşas* were on the whole model vassals in the discharge of their duties, and the Porte readily consoled itself for their incorrigible dynastic tendency by sequestrating their fortunes. The same expectation caused it to shut its eyes to the enormous disproportion between the total revenues of Cezzâr and the annual tribute which he dispatched to Istanbul, and its ears to the bitter and justified complaints of his subjects. And if this may be regarded as a confession of moral bankruptcy, it might be retorted that the Porte was preferable to its own *Paşas* or to the Mamlûks. It is indeed among the most striking indications of the decline of political morality and genius for government in the Ottoman ruling class that not a single governor in the century established his rule on any other basis than that of force, that none inspired his subjects with devotion, that none was mourned for his own sake. Consequently, the ultimate moral authority of the 'Dawla' was never challenged; to *Paşas* and people alike it stood for final retribution and the redress of abuses. Finally, the religious institution also, at least in its upper ranges, threw its influence on the side of the Ottoman supremacy. Although the classical doctrine of the Caliphate was

[1] Volney, ii. 5.

[2] It is noteworthy that Ḥasan Paşa arrived at Alexandria with but a single vessel and a few hundred marines.

[3] See ch. vii, below.

[4] Cab. ii. 351/v. 198–9.

still in abeyance,[1] the psychological basis of Pan-Islamism was already present in the universal reverence for the Sultan as the representative and defender of the Sunnî faith against the infidels of Europe and the heretics of Persia.

Nevertheless, there were two features in the political life of the century which, though they do not bulk very large in our sources, may have shaken the confidence of the Porte and caused some misgivings for the future. The first of these was the negotiations which were opened up between 'Alî Bey and the Russian command, followed by the alliance between Ẓâhir al-'Omar and the Russian fleet.[2] It is true that they came to nothing and that the Ottoman authorities, in their blind belief in their own strength, were not yet conscious of the extent to which the European powers had surpassed them in resources and in military science. But they carried the moral that the Ottoman Empire was no longer a self-enclosed entity, isolated from the outside world, and that sooner or later the problem of imperial unity would be complicated by the intrusion of elements from beyond its borders.

The second portent was the increasing pressure and organization of the Beduin Arabs, ever refractory to Ottoman suzerainty and contemptuous of its pretensions. Simultaneously with the local recovery of the Beduins in Egypt,[3] but entirely unconnected with it, a period of effervescence had set in amongst the tribes of the Syrian desert. During the sixteenth and seventeenth centuries, the northern ranges of the desert had been in a sense policed by the great confederacy of the Mawâlî. Their chief, who had the hereditary title of Abû Rîṣa, ruled over the whole area from a 'capital' at Âna on the Euphrates, and enjoyed a regular income from tolls on caravans and Ottoman annuities. At this time their relations with the Turkish authorities were relatively good, and they played a notable part, chiefly on the Turkish side, in the history of 'Irâḳ.[4] But the decline of the desert route and the brutalities of the *paşas* were already driving them to brigandage, when the entire tribal system of the Syrian desert was disorganized by the slow but relentless northward migration of the 'Anaza. About the beginning of the eighteenth century these, one of the largest tribal groups in Northern Arabia, had been set in motion by some obscure train of causes. By the middle of the century they had cut off the Mawâlî from the Euphrates and forced them westwards towards the regions of Aleppo and Hamâh,[5] with the inevitable consequences

[1] See above, ch. ii.

[2] See an article by Auriant, 'Catherine II et l'Orient, 1770–1774' in *L'Acropole*, v. 188–220 (Paris, 1930); Lockroy, 73 sqq.

[3] Above, pp. 227–8.

[4] Longrigg, 39, 67–71; Oppenheim, *Die Beduinen*, i (Leipzig, 1939), 305 sqq., 312 sqq.

[5] Oppenheim, op. cit. 68 sq.

of pillage and destruction in the invaded districts. The Ottoman government found it politic to recognize the situation and turn it to profit. It conferred upon their chiefs the title of Beg, with the duty of guarding the desert frontier between Aleppo and Damascus. In return, they were permitted to levy duties upon the caravans, which they interpreted to include also the levying of contributions upon Ḥamâh and other towns.[1] In the southern districts, the leading tribe was that of the Ṣaẖr, who ranged over Palestine and Transjordan. During the wars of Ẓâhir al-ʿOmar, the Ṣaẖr became his allies and were furnished by him with arms.[2] Meanwhile, in the Arabian desert itself, but outside the range of direct Ottoman contact and Ottoman prevision, the Wahhâbîs were building up their first empire under the house of Saʿûd. Until the end of the century they were almost less than a name in Syria and Egypt,[3] and to the Ottoman authorities they were little more than a frontier problem to be dealt with by the *Paşa* of Bağdâd.[4] Not even the most far-sighted could have foretold that the Wahhâbî movement would, in the course of the next twenty years, affect—by its fall even more than by its rise—the structure and cohesion of the Empire.

[1] A. de Boucheman, in *Revue des Études Islamiques*, 1934, 23–4; Volney, ii. 173, where the *şeyẖ* Muḥammad al-Ḫorfân is said to have had at his disposal 'up to 30,000 horsemen'. For their exemption from taxation in Mesopotamia on condition of supplying escorts to caravans cf. Rousseau, 94.

[2] Volney, ii. 8.

[3] Cabartî does not mention them until 1802, and then as a new movement which emerged from Nejd 'about three years ago'; they are not mentioned at all by Murâdî, except for an indirect reference (iv. 31–2).

[4] Longrigg, 212–16.

CHAPTER V

THE PEASANTRY. LAND TENURE AND AGRICULTURE

In describing the peasantry of the Ottoman Empire—and with it various other inhabitants of the country-side that cannot strictly be included in that term—we have divided our account into two sections, dealing with the non-Arabic-speaking and the mainly Arabic-speaking peoples respectively. For not only did the physical conditions in which peasant life was lived and agriculture was carried on in the two areas concerned differ very greatly from one another and so render them largely unlike, but it was only comparatively late in the history of the Empire that they were united within it, so that principles originally determined by conditions in the 'home' provinces—that is, Anatolia and Rumelia—could not be applied with rigour to the accessions of the sixteenth century, the more so in that these were predominantly Moslem in population and had been included for centuries within the Domain of Islam.

Moreover the available information regarding the two areas is not, so to speak, parallel. We have at our disposal more detailed accounts, for instance, of the state of the peasantry in Egypt and some of the other Arab provinces in the eighteenth century than we have of those in the 'home' provinces. On the other hand, the *Ḳânûns* regulating landholding that were promulgated in the sixteenth century reflect the conditions then prevailing in the 'home' provinces; and it is chiefly by inference from the available accounts of the breakdown of the system that they embodied, taken together with others of peasant life as it is lived to-day in parts of the same area, that we can arrive at some notion of the state of the country-side in the mid-eighteenth century. Finally, since some of the provisions originally drawn up for the 'home' provinces—particularly those regarding land-tenure—were subsequently applied to some extent in the Arab provinces, we devote our first section to the former, and our second section to the latter.

I. RUMELIA AND ANATOLIA

The conditions in which agriculture was carried on in these provinces were largely determined by their geography and climate. For large areas in both were exceedingly mountainous. Hence communications, except along their coasts, were little developed. And hence again, owing to the difficulty of transporting them farther than the nearest town, in most regions crops were grown only for local consumption; indeed the bulk was grown for consumption by the growers themselves. Since, therefore, the country people produced very little for sale, their resources for buying clothes, utensils, and foodstuffs were correspondingly meagre. They were obliged to make almost everything they required at home. And so it came about that the breeding of animals for hides, wool, &c., as well as for labour, played a larger part in the agricultural economy of the country than did the growing of crops.[1]

This appears to have applied to the whole area. But naturally the relative importance of stock-breeding and agriculture proper varied from region to region. In the most mountainous parts stock-breeding engaged the inhabitants' attention almost exclusively, being accompanied only by 'subsistence' cultivation; whereas in such parts as were most fertile and best situated as regards communications—that is either near some port or along one of the more important caravan routes—cultivation attained almost to an equality with stock-breeding. The rest varied between one extreme and the other.

Now, surveying the two provinces as a whole, the Ottoman authorities regarded them as being divided up into different categories of land. Three of these do not concern our present description: namely, first, land so arid or marshy that it could not be used for agricultural purposes, or the more inaccessible parts of the mountain ranges; secondly, mineral-bearing tracts; and, thirdly, urban areas. There remained forest land, pasture land, arable land, vineyards and orchards, land on which hay was cut, and, finally, the emplacements of villages including vegetable plots. These six varieties are our present concern.

We have remarked earlier in this survey that in the sixteenth century all agricultural land in the two provinces was declared to appertain to the state, unless it had been devoted to a religious endowment.[2] All such land, therefore, was, in Ottoman terminology, either *mîrî* or *wakf*. But what was meant by agricultural land was only the second two of our six categories: pasture and arable land. Of the remaining four, forest lands were also *mîrî*/*wakf*; but the remainder were, essentially, not. Thus the sites of houses in villages were private property—*mulk*, and each house had attached to it a half-*dönüm* of land that was likewise *mulk*. Again every village had a tract from which hay was cut; and this was the common property of the villagers. The status of the remaining category, that of vineyards and orchards, was more

[1] Owing to the circumstances in which these pages were sent to press, the notes to pp. 236–48 of this chapter have been added at the end of the volume (Appendix D).

doubtful. They, as we say, were essentially *mulk*. That is to say that the trees were private property. But unless they were included in the small area that constituted the village emplacement—it was known as *Tetimmei-Suknâ* (the Complement of Habitation)[1]—the ground in which they were planted was *mîrî/wakf*.[2] In many cases, of course, this distinction mattered little. If the only produce of a vineyard were its grapes, and they were *mulk*, the vineyard itself was virtually *mulk*, and often, apparently, came to be so regarded. But if a peasant chose to cultivate the ground, it *ipso facto* became *mîrî* (unless it was *wakf*) whatever its status had been before. Buildings erected on *mîrî* ground were likewise *mulk* in most cases. As will appear, these distinctions were fraught with confusion.

To turn now to the peasants themselves. The term used to denote a peasant was *ra'îya* (plural *re'âyâ*), an Arabic word meaning originally 'cattle at pasture'. Strictly speaking, when applied to human beings, it embraced all the ruler's subjects: he was the shepherd and they were the flock. In Ottoman parlance, however, it denoted only settled free farmers and their families, whether Moslem or *Dimmî*. The *re'âyâ* were thus contrasted on the one hand with all the Men of the Pen and the Men of the Sword (including the nomad *Yürüks* who originally performed special services for the state and were hence regarded as 'soldiery'), and on the other with the artisans and merchants of the towns.

The status of the *re'âyâ* was bound up with that of the lands they inhabited, which we have just described. And since this was partly '*mulk*' and partly '*mîrî/wakf*', they were proprietors of that which came under the first heading, but only tenants of that, far the larger, which came under the second. But apart from this classification by status, the land was divided in another way. As we have also mentioned, the great bulk of *mîrî* land was apportioned into fiefs, appertaining either to the Sultan, to members of his family and household, to civil functionaries, to the upkeep of frontier fortresses, or to the feudal *Sipâhîs* and their superior officers (most of whom were at the same time provincial governors).[3] Likewise *wakf* lands were divided into properties, the revenues of which were devoted to the object, a mosque, say, or a *madrasa*, for which they had been designed. Now all these fief-holders, it will be remembered, were tax-collectors in person or by proxy: they received the taxes in lieu of pay; and so were the intendants or *Mütevellîs* of each *wakf* property. The revenues of remaining lands, those not constituted into fiefs together with the Sultan's domains, were collected by tax-farmers for the Treasury and the Privy Purse respectively. The chief, if not the only, function of the *re'âyâ*, therefore, from the point of view of the government, was to supply these various collectors with their dues. Hence every peasant was inscribed as the *ra'îya* of either a fief-holder, of a *wakf*, or of the *mîrî*. The term employed for the 'lease' upon which he held such of his land as was not private property was '*taṣarruf*' or 'use'.[1] It was not, however, only in respect of the land so held that the fief-holders and *Mütevellîs* had the right of tax and due collection. For private property also was subject to some taxation; and they had the right to collect its proceeds from their *re'âyâ* as well as that on *taṣarruf*-holdings. This was due to the fact that in constituting both fiefs and *wakfs* the government willed away its rights of collection on any private property included within their boundaries.

Although fief-holders were really no more than 'tenants-in-chief', they were commonly called 'landowners' (*Ṣâḥibi-Arḍ*).[2] And though the *Mütevellîs*, who collected taxes and dues on behalf of the *wakfs*, and the tax-farmers (*Mültezims*), who, from the mid-sixteenth century onwards, did likewise on behalf of the Treasury, were not of course in quite the same position, yet they had rights over the peasantry very similar to those enjoyed by the landowners proper. We need not, therefore, in describing the relations of the peasants to their immediate superiors (for, as will appear, these various categories of 'tax-collectors' had other than purely fiscal rights over them), deal separately, in general, with the landowners on the one hand, and these two classes of officials on the other; but may content ourselves with noting such peculiarities in the authority of *Mütevellîs* or *Mültezims* as distinguished them from the holders of fiefs. We may, indeed, begin by noting one or two such distinctions. First, the holding of military fiefs—*Timars* and *Zi'âmets*—by *Sipâhîs* was hereditary up to a point: they passed normally to *Sipâhîs'* sons if the latter were eligible for military service, though this did not apply, of course, to any fiefs—even military *Ḫâṣṣ* fiefs—that were the perquisite of an office. Secondly, every fief contained what may be described as a 'proprietary nucleus' called *Ḫâṣṣa Çiftlik* (private farm) which the holder worked in person or through an agent for his own benefit. Finally, fiefs of all kinds were distinguished from the properties administered by *Mütevellîs* or the areas 'farmed' by *Mültezims*, in being called 'livings' (*Dirlik*), a term which emphasizes the fact that the revenues of each were intended to provide the holder with a livelihood, whereas the bulk of those collected by *Mütevellîs* went to the foundation of which they constituted the endowment, and those collected by the *Mültezims* had to be set against the sums they had already paid to the Treasury by way of speculation.[3]

Just as the enjoyment of *dirliks* by *Sipâhîs* was up to a point hereditary, so was the *taṣarruf* of fields and pastures by peasants.

Indeed the principal reason for the declaration that no agricultural holdings were private property appears to have been the desire of the authorities to permit the inheritance of peasant holdings while avoiding the inconveniences of the Sacred Law in this respect. For according to a series of highly complicated provisions embodied in the Sacred Law, at least two-thirds of all private property was divided up in fixed proportions among the heirs of its owner on his death, so that it tended to become split up into minute and unmanageable fragments. The Law made no provision for the inheritance of *taṣarrufs*, however. So the Sultans could regulate it as they chose.[1]

As regards peasant *taṣarrufs* they instituted the following regulations. Provided the peasant continued to discharge his duties properly (we shall come to these in a minute), his holding passed on his death to his sons without the payment of any special due. But if he left no son the position was different. In order that another member of his family might inherit it, the latter must pay another 'advance' (*ṭapu*),[2] estimated by 'disinterested' Moslems in some cases, equal to one year's dues in others, priority of claim depending upon the relationship of the heir to the deceased holder in this order: his daughter, his brother, his sister, his father, his mother. If he or she paid the new *ṭapu*, the relative in question might not be excluded. No more distant relatives, on the other hand—except grandsons in special circumstances—had any claim, and could not prevent the re-letting of the *taṣarruf* outside the family. Inheritance of *taṣarrufs* from women, on whom by these rules they often devolved, was restricted to sons; and they were obliged in this case to pay the *ṭapu*. *Taṣarrufs* were sometimes held, again, by two or more peasants, whether related or not, in partnership. In such cases the share of each passed to his heirs (as here defined); but in default of such heirs, the remaining partner or partners had the right to take over the vacant part of the holding on payment of *ṭapu*.[3] Finally, the landowner might dispose of a *taṣarruf* to an 'outsider'—the resident of another village—only after offering it to the peasants of the village to which the land in question was attached.[4]

By these regulations the authorities desired at once to prevent the splitting up of *taṣarruf* holdings and to ensure the continuity of peasant families in their enjoyment. Other regulations emphasize the latter point. The foundation of the system was the family homestead. Holdings were actually worked by families. If a man had several sons they took over the *taṣarruf* jointly on his death; and if later any of them wished to dispose of his share to an outsider, the other brothers could prevent it. If a man left no sons and the *taṣarruf* was assumed by his daughter, it was, of course, her husband that took control. In the cases of both sisters and grandsons they had actually to be resident in the homestead in order to make good their claims.[1]

Peasant families were thus secure against arbitrary ejection from their holdings by the landowner. But only so long as they discharged their duties. These duties consistedin the proper cultivation of the arable land of which they enjoyed the *taṣarruf* and in the payment of numerous taxes and dues.[2] Moreover, they were bound to inform the landowner of, and obtain his consent to, any transactions they might wish to effect in connexion with their holdings, such as the sale of their *taṣarrufs*. This was a cardinal principle. Any transactions carried out without the landowner's consent were invalid.[3]

The dues and taxes payable may be classified in two categories, those levied on the holding or its produce, and those levied on the peasants personally. The former category may again be divided into taxation on stock-breeding and taxation on cultivation. The principal dues levied in connexion with stock-breeding were the sheep custom (*'âdeti ağnâm*), the sheep-pen due (*ağîl resmi*) and various pasturage dues. In fiefs the sheep custom was levied in kind at the lambing season (originally at the rate of one *akçe* for every two sheep); while the pen due was payable when the sheep were folded for breeding. The latter, however, was not current in all fiefs, and was considerably lighter than the sheep custom, only 5 *akçes* being exacted for every 300 sheep.[4] As for pasturages, the landowner was authorized to levy dues on any peasants that made use of the areas in his fief or property set aside for summer and winter grazing. Apparently they had to pay according to the number of animals so pastured, but how, whether in cash or in kind, or on what scale does not appear.[5]

The principal impost on cultivation was the tithe (*'uşr*), which, as we have explained, was properly termed *ḫarâcî mukâsama* (or Yield Levy). The tithe, which was, of course, a contribution in kind, was appropriated by the collectors at the time of harvest before reaping. But the peasants were obliged to bring their whole crop for threshing to the landowner, and to transport that part of the grain taken as tithe either to the nearest weekly market or to the village granary. The proportion of any crop taken by way of tithe varied from province to province from one-tenth to as much as one-half. As the Empire had been built up, registers had been made of the dues and taxes to be levied in each province, no doubt based on conditions already obtaining. Periodically these registers were revised, but only to bring them up to date. No attempt was made to alter the bases of provincial taxation in the interest of uniformity.[6]

The landowner was also entitled to collect tithe on wheat, barley, and rye straw (this being known as *salâriye*);[1] likewise on fruit and vegetables grown by peasants on *mîrî* soil (i.e. anywhere but in the small plot allowed to each household as private property) and even on such produce grown on these private plots as might be offered by the peasants for sale, provided only that the vineyards, orchards, or vegetable gardens were not already registered for the payment of a fixed due.[2] Bee-hives, again, if they were kept on *mîrî* land, were subject either to a fixed yearly due, or to a tithe on the honey produced; and so, if the local register contained provisions to this effect, were the grape products known as *pekmez* and *kufter*.[3]

So much for tithes. We now come to fixed dues (*rasm*, plural *rusûm*). As we have just mentioned, vineyards, fruit-orchards, and vegetable gardens (on *mîrî* or *wakf* land) were normally registered for such fixed annual payments; and there were many others, such as a due on mills (levied according to the number of months each was in use) and on 'roofs' (for though the peasants' houses and sheds were private property, they were nevertheless subject to this tax, payable to the landowner).[4] The landowner's consent to peasants' transactions in connexion with their *taṣarrufs*, again, could only be secured on payment of a fee (called *maʿrifet akçesi*—acknowledgement money).[5] And this brings us to personal taxation.

Here we at once come up against religious distinctions. As we have already pointed out, *Dimmîs* began by being subjected to the *cizya*, or tribute. This, however, had nothing to do with the 'landowners', being collected on behalf of the government. But religious distinctions as regards taxation did not by any means stop here. To start with the 'farm money' (*çift akçesi*). This, it may be remembered, was one of the popular names for what was properly called *harâcî muwaẓẓaf*, which was a fixed due exacted yearly from all peasants enjoying *taṣarrufs*, according to the amount and quality of the land included in their holdings.[6] All peasants, however, did not possess holdings; many worked on those belonging to their relatives. And *taṣarruf*-less peasants were also subjected to fixed taxes, though lighter, which in the case of Moslems were of two kinds, according to whether they were married or single. The tax imposed on such married Moslems was called *benâk*, that on bachelors, *mucerred*. In the sixteenth century the sums exacted from each man under these heads were respectively 12 and 6 *akçes* a year. Now the dues called *çift akçesi*, *benâk*, and *mucerred* were all applied only to Moslems. But *Dimmîs* were subjected in fact to similar imposts, though on a higher scale. And all three dues went in their case by the same name: *ispence*. The *ispence* was of course imposed in the case of *Dimmî taşarruf*-holders according to the extent and quality of their land. In that of 'landless' male *Dimmîs*, however, it was uniformly (at the same period) 25 *akçes* a year, whether they were married or not. On the other hand *Dimmîs* in one case came off more lightly than True-Believers. This was the marriage due (*'urûs resmi*). Whenever a peasant married he was bound to pay the 'landowner' a due; and here Moslems had to pay twice as much as infidels.[1]

We have now sketched the obligations of the peasant to the landowner in the latter's capacity of tax-collector. Next, accordingly, we may deal with the questions: what constituted the proper working of a *taşarruf*, and what happened if a peasant failed in this duty.

Proper working as regards crop cultivation consisted chiefly in sowing not less than a definite amount of seed, and in not failing to sow any part of the holding for more than two consecutive years. The latter provision was designed to admit the custom of leaving fields fallow two years out of three. If this period was exceeded, the peasant forfeited his *taşarruf*-rights, unless he paid a 'neglect due' (*çift bozan*, or *boz hakkî*), which, however, he might do for any length of time. When a peasant forfeited his rights in this way, the landowner was at liberty to 're-let' the holding on *ṭapu* to another. But at the same time he (the original peasant) had first claim on the new 'lease', provided he paid both the 'neglect due' and the *ṭapu*. Failing this, peasants of the same village had a prior claim to the lease, before, that is to say, 'outsiders'. For in the hierarchy of agricultural life, the village stood, as a unit, next above the family.[2]

The rights and duties of the peasants were thus well balanced. But now we come to the forfeiture of the former by failure to discharge the latter. Peasant families might wish to abandon their holdings, and migrate to other fiefs or properties where they would be welcome because they must pay *ṭapu* before acquiring a new *taşarruf*, or take up other ways of life. Such movements, however, were not at all to the government's taste. Its object was to keep its feudal cavalry and the other beneficiaries of the fief-system properly supplied with revenues. Hence *Ḳânûns* were promulgated that virtually bound the peasantry to the soil, except in so far as landowners sanctioned migration. The latter might force migrant peasants to return to their original holdings up to ten years from the date of their departure. Peasants were thus obliged to work and provide revenues for the landowners, unless they chose to starve: in fact they were virtually serfs, even in theory. And though they might submit any disputes arising between them and the landowners (who strictly speaking had no judicial authority over them) to the decision of the local *Ḳâḍî*, the landowners must in fact have confined their freedom of action within very narrow limits. The only inducement to the landowners to permit any changes, indeed, lay in the dues they received for their recognition of transactions and for the re-grant of *taṣarrufs*. So, somewhat paradoxically, these must to some extent have told in favour of peasant freedom. Landowners, again, could not of course force peasants to take up vacant *taṣarrufs*. But otherwise the stability of the agricultural system was as far assured as laws could make it.[1]

Indeed, a notable feature of the *Ḳânûns* that regulated it is the emphasis laid in them on the necessity of observing established custom—what has been done in the past must be done now and for ever. Perhaps the most far-reaching prescription of the kind is that which forbade, in general, the conversion of pasture into arable land, and vice versa.[2] Only one exception was permitted in each case. If arable land, though left fallow longer than the canonical two years, was so well watered that it might qualify as meadow-pasture, its holder was entitled to maintain it as such, paying the appropriate dues. On the other hand, where the arable land of a village was situated in a valley, peasants were encouraged to extend the area under cultivation by 'opening up' unused tracts 'on the mountain-side'.

Possibly these rules were framed with the object of counteracting a tendency that the peasantry of the less developed parts of Anatolia displays to-day, and presumably displayed in earlier ages, to devote little or no attention to maintaining the fertility of their fields, and when this is exhausted to open up fresh ground instead. But here we come to the question how far the past may be judged from the present. Unhappily, apart from *Ḳânûn-nâmes*, we have few documents relating to agricultural conditions in the Ottoman Empire up to the nineteenth century. The author of a recent survey, however, is of the opinion that, owing to the uneven development of communications in Anatolia, the regions that are still badly served provide us with a picture of peasant life as it was lived before the construction of railways and the consequent growth of an agriculture based on the sale of produce instead of on its consumption by the producer.[3] No doubt this is true up to a point. We must, however, make allowances also for the decay of the feudal system that we have described. On the other hand, the place of the railways was taken up to the end of the eighteenth century and beyond it to a certain extent by the caravan routes, which later fell into disuse owing, quite apart from the rivalry of railways and before their construction, to the ruin of Ottoman industries by Western competition.[4] In those areas where it was already possible to transport agricultural products to a market, agriculture would appear already to have developed beyond the 'subsistence' level. But they were comparatively few.

Taking present conditions to represent those of the past with these reservations, then, we may suppose the *reʿâyâ* to have been animated hardly at all by any idea of gain, and to have worked their land with a minimum of effort and very little knowledge. Thus they do not appear to have made any use of manure for preserving the fertility of their fields, depending for this entirely upon various systems of fallow. The peasants in such regions when their fields ceased to be fully productive would, if they were allowed to, simply clear and plough up fresh tracts, even of forest land where no other was available. Or, according to another scheme, they would cultivate a field for one year and leave it fallow for two—possibly this was the regular system under the 'feudal' régime, as it would account for the provision for a two-year fallow. In areas where the possibilities of selling produce were greater, a somewhat more advanced system was followed, called *nadas*. Here fields would be cultivated in alternate years; but those left fallow would be twice ploughed up, to preserve moisture and keep down weeds. Finally in still more advanced districts crops would be grown in more or less regular though unscientific rotation.[1]

The initiative of individual peasant families appears to have been exceedingly restricted. For their holdings were contiguous; hence it was essential that they should all plough and sow simultaneously, and should all grow the same crops, or at least crops that should be harvested at the same time, in order to obviate the necessity of passing over crops standing in one holding in order to reach another.[2] How far under the old régime the 'landowner' directed their activities is not clear. Since a large part of his revenues were collected in kind he had an intimate interest in them. In some places to-day, however, there exist village elders (*Köy Büyükleri*) who settle what each producer is to grow; and as it would seem that in the old days villagers were inclined to deal in a body with their *Sipâhî*, at any rate in such matters as disputes over the payment of tithes, their leaders may also have had authority under him.

In 'subsistence' areas crops were, of course, grown in accordance with the customary diet and habits of the peasantry. Nowadays this diet consists mainly of farinaceous products: maize or barley bread, rye soup, a crushed-wheat *pilâv* called *bulğur*, together with a form of liquid *yoğurt* called *ayran*. Meat is eaten only on feast-days. Sweet-stuffs were perhaps supplied either by honey, or, as in one area to-day, by sugar extracted from beetroot. Most of the peasant's clothing was of wool, hair, or leather. But even now in many places cotton is grown by farmers for spinning and weaving at home; and this does not seem to be an innovation.

All farm implements, again, ploughs, harrows, threshing sledges, &c., were likewise home-made, mostly of wood. Indeed the wooden plough is still universally employed in all regions where modern agricultural machinery has not been introduced. These ploughs were drawn as a rule by oxen, since horses were used only for riding and as pack-animals. Owing to the badness or absence of roads, carts were little used, loads being transported by camels, donkeys, and mules. Finally, the buildings owned by each peasant family consisted of a dwelling-house, a stable, and a granary, built partly of mud and partly of wood.

The ordinary peasant of the 'subsistence' areas was, as we have seen, even more dependent upon the animals he raised than upon the crops he grew. He was a shepherd or goatherd as well as, or even more than, a cultivator. In the winter months the flocks would pasture near the villages in low-lying tracts, which was convenient, since this was the time of greatest labour on the land. In the summer, however, they had to be taken farther afield, when those who tended them were obliged to live in tents—another home-made article. The peasants depended as well as for some of their food—milk and milk products, for instance—for almost all their clothing on their flocks, which furnished them with skins, leather, and wool or hair, which the women spun, wove, and dyed at home (nearly every house containing a loom), into material for garments or these tents, or into carpets and mats. Indeed, so self-sufficient was their economy that they could almost have done without money, had it not been that their dues, as distinct from their tithes, were payable in coin. To obtain the necessary cash they would offer some part of what they produced in the nearest weekly market. As the townspeople depended for their part on the peasantry for the supply both of their food and the raw materials for local industries, the peasants could be assured of obtaining the necessary funds. In the more accessible regions, moreover, the peasantry were inclined to buy town products instead of depending entirely on those they could make at home. These transactions, however, were largely carried out by barter, if modern practice supplies a true indication, sometimes on a credit basis. The peasant wishing to buy something in the market would pledge himself to deliver so much farm produce at the time of harvest.[1]

It appears from some *Ḳânûn-nâme* provisions that peasants occasionally experienced difficulty in finding the money to pay their dues with. In this case it was decreed that they should pay tithe instead—though such a transaction was possible only when the due was paid as an alternative to tithe. On the other hand, in some cases they would contract to make a fixed payment, assessed annually, in lieu of tithe. But this practice was probably confined to areas of 'market' economy; indeed, it was most usual in connexion with vineyards, which played little part in the economy of the subsistence areas. In this connexion we may remark that whereas *mîrî* lands, on which *taṣarruf*-holders had to pay dues according to its quality and extent, were surveyed for assessment, *mulk* lands as a rule were not. It was only when peasants contracted to make fixed payments instead of *ʿuṣr* that their *mulk* holdings had to be surveyed so that the payment in question might be determined. As we have remarked above, where vineyards, olive groves, or fruit orchards were planted on *mîrî* land, the produce of the trees was, nevertheless, *mulk*. And it would appear from the frequent references to *mulk* vineyards, &c., in the *Ḳânûns*—which can scarcely all refer to genuine *mulk* properties, since, as we have seen, these were confined to the 'complement of habitation'—that the status of such 'mixed' holdings was apt to cause confusion. Yet the fact that genuine *mulk* properties had not to be surveyed shows that normally they were subject only to the payment of tithe, whereas these 'mixed' holdings, like all *mîrî* lands, were subject also to that of dues. On the other hand the tithe on vines, &c., was never, presumably, more than one-tenth, as ordained by the Sacred Law; in other words it was the genuine *ʿuṣr*, not a variable proportion like the *ḫarâcî muḳâsama* that also went by this name.[1]

The determination of the authorities not to suffer the inconveniences of the Law in respect of inheritance is shown in other ways than their erection of all agricultural land into state property. Thus, though they declared peasants to own the various kinds of private property that we have described, yet they insisted that this should not be split up by inheritance. In one ruling it is stated in so many words that though buildings and trees, being *mulk*, should pass to a peasant's heirs according to the Law, yet this principle must be disregarded, 'in order not to diminish the land of the heir resident in the homestead',[2] that is of the heir that inherits the *taṣarruf*. Moreover, if a peasant's only heirs were of a relationship more distant than would entitle them to inherit his *taṣarruf*, the landowner might exclude them from the inheritance of such *mulk* property as they were entitled to under the provisions of the *Şerîʿa*, unless they were resident on the homestead. As regards the produce of vines, &c., each legal heir was entitled to his share; but the tithe was to be collected from them all, as a body. The authorities were thus prepared to flout the *Şerîʿa* where its provisions endangered the maintenance of homesteads intact. But the circumstance that *taṣarrufs* were worked by whole families together must have rendered the occasions of such illegal action much rarer than they would have been otherwise.[1]

The ownership of some private property by the peasants might have given them some slight independence of the landowner, had the dues and tithes on it been collected on behalf of the Treasury. As it was, the landowner collected these as well as the contributions from *taṣarruf*-holdings. Moreover, if peasants failed to discharge their obligations in respect of their *taṣarruf* holdings, the landowner was entitled to 'interfere' with their private property—though the precise meaning of this sinister phrase is not made clear.[2] And so, as a rule, there can be no doubt that the peasantry were virtually at the mercy of the landowners, despite various regulations intended to circumscribe their authority.[3] It seems likely that the least happy of the peasants were those of the lands whose contributions were farmed by contractors for the Treasury; for most of these contracts were short-term, so that the tax-farmers had little interest in tempering their harshness with an eye to the future. The most rigid of the 'landowners', on the other hand, seem to have been the *waḳf* authorities. *Mütevellîs*, for instance, were obliged to see that no lands were 'let' against a *ṭapu* payment less than what had been established by precedent, and in cases where their agents effected such transactions, to overrule them. *Sipâhîs*, on the other hand, were forbidden to exact further payments from peasants, once the deeds regarding a *ṭapu* lease had been drawn up and registered by the *Ḳâḍî*.[4]

Of all the categories of landowners the *Sipâhîs* were the most closely connected with the peasants. In the first place they were in one aspect no more than superior peasants themselves—indeed various rulings show that it was by no means unheard of for *Sipâhîs* to become peasants proper—by registration—and for peasants to become *Sipâhîs*—by the grant of a fief.[5] In the second place the inheritance of fiefs by *Sipâhî* families, restricted though it was to competent sons, and in special circumstances to grandsons, and that of *taṣarrufs* by peasant families, gave rise to strong sentimental ties between the two classes, ties which though they had their origin in the almost total subordination of the *reʿâyâ* to the *Sipâhîs*, yet fostered a valuable solidarity. And in the third place *Sipâhîs* sometimes held land in partnership with peasants, supplying them with cattle and seed, in which case they took half the proceeds.[6]

As regards the restrictions placed upon *Sipâhîs*' freedom of action, we may mention the obligation under which they were placed not to undertake the exploitation of vacant *taṣarruf* lands themselves.[7] Their own farming activities were confined to their 'private farms'; it was no doubt on these, for instance, that in the days of the *devşirme* they set to work the '*Acemioğlans* sent to them for preliminary training. *Sipâhîs* were, of course, bound also by all the regulations that we have mentioned: they might not eject peasants from their holdings without cause, exclude legal heirs, or exact more than they were entitled to by way of tithe or due. And even in minor particulars they were restrained by *Ḳânûns*: thus they might not graze their animals on peasants' fallow, or 'let' any part of the village pasture on *ṭapu*.[1]

The rule in military fiefs was that every peasant should be registered as the *ra'îya* of one *Sipâhî*. But there were exceptions to it. For some fiefs were held in partnership by two or more *Sipâhîs*; in which case they would exercise joint authority over their peasants, the decision of one, however, being binding on his partner or partners. And, on the other hand, some peasants were registered as the *re'âyâ* of two independent *Sipâhîs*, who divided the dues payable between them.[2] Finally, some peasants were unattached to any *Sipâhî*, but only, it appears, landless men; and in their case the *benâk* due, to which they were subject, was collected by the *Mevḳufcu*, the agent of the *mîrî*.[3]

The authorities thus sought to endow the *Sipâhîs* and other fief-holders with powers sufficient to ensure their enjoyment of the revenues provided by the labours of the *re'âyâ*, but no greater. The system they adopted was in fact well balanced as regards the rights and duties it conferred and imposed on both the fief-holders and the peasants. But its balance was one that might be maintained only so long as the central government kept the fief-holders in effective control. And actually, as we have seen, from the end of the sixteenth century not only was this control more and more relaxed, till by the eighteenth it was in many regions non-existent, but the whole feudal system was corrupted by the shifts to which the government resorted in its permanent financial embarrassment. Before considering the effects of these developments on the lives of the peasants, however, we must consider the position in the country-side of certain "'*Askerîs*', whom we have already mentioned as forming part of the armed forces of the Empire.*

The '*Askerîs* in question were the *Müsellems*, the *Yayas*, the *Voynuḳs*, the *Doğancîs*, and the *Yürüks*. As has been indicated in our former reference to them, their status resembled that of the *Sipâhîs* in many respects, and particularly by the very fact that they were reckoned as troops, since the main division of the inhabitants of the country-side was between '*Askerîs* and *re'âyâ*. The regulations governing the rights and duties, as farmers, of the *Müsellems* and *Yayas* seem to have been much alike. As long as they worked only the farms allotted to them, both were exempt from the pay-

* See above, pp. 53–4.

ment of all dues and tithes, except that the *Yayas* resident in certain *Sancaks*[1] had to furnish their *Sancak Beyis*, while those elsewhere had to furnish their *Yaya Başis* with forty *akçes* a year per *ocak* by way of 'wheat and barley money',[2] and the former were also subject to the payment of marriage dues and certain other contributions in kind.[3] It would appear that both *Müsellems* and *Yayas* sometimes farmed *ra'îya taşarrufs* adjacent to their own holdings, in which case the *Kânûn* enjoined care in distinguishing between the two for purposes of taxation, for in taking up such extra holdings they assumed the liabilities as regards them, of *re'âyâ*.[4] Sometimes, again, *Müsellems* would permit other persons to farm their land and pay them tithes and dues, thereby assuming the position of *Sipâhîs* in this respect. Indeed, the government seems to have encouraged this approximation by depriving *Müsellems* of the right of ejecting such cultivators, unless for some misdemeanour, after they had fulfilled their obligations for ten consecutive years.[5] The *Yayas*, on the other hand, were strictly forbidden to let their lands on *ṭapu*, or, *a fortiori*, to sell them; and presumably this latter prohibition applied to the *Müsellems* likewise.[6] *Yayas* that abandoned their holdings might be forced by their *Sancak Beyis*, like fugitive *re'âyâ* by their *Sipâhîs*, to return to their holdings. *Yaya* holdings that fell vacant were handed over to another member of the *ocak* to which the owner had belonged.[7]

The *Voynuks* were allotted certain tracts in Bulgaria suitable for their duty of breeding and tending horses.[8] These lands, on which they too paid no taxes,[9] might be held only by persons of this class, so that any transference of its ownership, whether by sale or inheritance, was illegal. *Voynuks* might allow the temporary working of their land by 'outsiders';[10] but no length of use by the latter could

[1] The *O.T.E.M.* (as below), pp. 46–7, refers to 'the *Bey* of the *Yaya Sancak*' (*Yaya sancaği beyi*) and later to 'the *Yayas* in the *Sancak* referred to' (*mezkûr sancakta olan yayalar*). Presumably, therefore, there were *sancaks* in which most if not all the cultivators were *Yayas*. On the other hand, not all *Yayas* resided in them, for we read of '*Yayas* dependent on *Yaya Başis*' (*Yaya Başilarina muta'allik olan yayalar*), who are contrasted with those dependent on the *Sancak Beyi*.

[2] *Buğday ve arpa akçesi.*

[3] See *O.T.E.M.*, *Kânûn-nâme*, p. 47: *Yayalar döttügü vaşak ve kaplan derisine yaya sancaği beyi muteşarriftir*, 'The *Bey* of the *Yaya Sancak* enjoys the lynx and leopard skins contributed by the *Yayas*'.

[4] See *M.T.M.* i. 311.

[5] *M.T.M.* i. 311. The 'outsider' in this case being a *Yürük*.

[6] Indeed, it is stated by Aḥmed Refik, *Anadoluda Türk Aşiretleri*, vii, that they were also forbidden both to let and sell.

[7] *O.T.E.M.*, 1912, No. 17, 46 sq.

[8] See above, p. 54. The *Kânûn* requires that only prairie, not marsh, land be granted to *Voynuks*.

[9] Their land—like *mulk* land (see above, p. 246)—not even being surveyed.

[10] The latter paying them *'uşr*. If they objected on the ground that no taxes were payable on *Voynuk* land they were to be ejected—so the *Kânûn*. *Voynuks*

establish their claim to it. Men of the *Voynuḳ* reserve—they were known as *Voynuḳ* Supernumeraries[1]—were, if Christian, subject to the payment of *cizya*;[2] and *Voynuḳs*' relatives, if they worked *Voynuḳ* land, were subject not only to the *cizya*, but also to the *ispence*, which, as they were not registered as the *re'âyâ* of any *Sipâhî*, they paid to the *Sancaḳ Beyi*. *Sipâhîs* were strictly forbidden to interfere with *Voynuḳs* and their reserve men and relatives, unless, as sometimes happened, these took up the *taṣarrufs* of already cultivated fief-lands. In this case they were liable in respect of such land for all the ordinary dues.[3] If they opened up new fief-land, they did so on terms similar to those in force for *re'âyâ*.[4] As for the *Doğancîs*, their position seems to have been similar. Their privileges might also be transmitted to their heirs provided that the latter carried out the duties that went with them. Ordinary *re'âyâ* appear on occasions to have sought admittance to the *Doğancî* corps (if it may be so called), presumably to escape their obligations. For the *Ḳânûn* lays it down that by so doing they were not to be regarded as losing their *ra'îya* status.[5]

The *Yürüks*, being of no settled habitation, were not subject to any *Sancaḳ Beyi*, but were dealt with by the *Subaşîs* of whatever district they passed through or chose for summer or winter encampment. Thus it was the *Subaşîs*' duty to see that on their journeys they remained at no stage longer than three days, and committed no depredations on fief or *waḳf* lands. In case of crime or insubordination also it fell to the *Subaşîs* to punish them, after obtaining—such was the law at least—a written ruling (*ḥucca*) from the local *Ḳâḍî*.[6]

The *Yürük* tribesmen lived normally by stock-raising. Hence they were taxed with the payment of pasture (*otlaḳ*) and sheep dues (*'âdeti ağnâm* and *ağil resmi*), the actual payments being made to the *Sancaḳ Beyi* of the district they had chosen for their summer encampment in fleeces in September. Moreover, provision was made for the service of five men from each *ocaḳ* of thirty in war-time by the payment of 50 *aḳçes* from the remaining twenty-five, whilst a smaller contribution—600 *aḳçes*— in cash was exacted from the whole thirty in years of peace. Those going on service were further excused for the time being from payment of

thus receiving *'uşr* were temporarily in the position of *Sipâhîs*, like the *Müsellems* just mentioned.

1 *Voynuḳ Zevâ'idi*.

2 The *Ḳânûn* has *ḫarâc*—but it is evident that the word is here used in its popular sense, since it is mentioned together with *ispence*.

3 Aḥmed Refiḳ, *Türk Idâresinde Bulğaristân*, 4, states that they paid only half-*'uşr*. But the *Ḳânûn* (*M.T.M.* i. 308) merely says *'uşr*.

4 *M.T.M.* i. 101, 108, 308–90; Aḥmed Refiḳ, *Türk Idâresinde Bulğaristân*, 3, 6.

5 *M.T.M.* i. 312.

6 Ibid. 306, 307, 308; Aḥmed Refiḳ, op. cit. vi.

the sheep due. The *Yürüks* were exempt, on the other hand, from all the agricultural contributions exacted from the peasantry, including the marriage due, which was not imposed even in the case of a *Yürük* woman's marrying a *ra'îya.*[1]

There was evidently a tendency at least as early as the sixteenth century for these nomads to settle. We find, accordingly, in the *Ḳânûns* various regulations governing such settlement. If *Yürüks* merely took up ordinary peasant land, they automatically became *re'âyâ* of the *Sipâhî* (or other 'landowner') concerned, and were obliged, after ten years' residence, to have themselves inscribed as such. If, however, they opened up uncultivated land in a fief, they paid only half the sums imposed on peasants that did likewise. On the other hand, once they had given up their *'Askerî* status, *Yürüks* were no longer liable to the payment of the pasture (*otlaḳ*) due, which was not applicable to *re'âyâ.*[2] It would appear from these provisions, therefore, that the authorities desired to encourage the settlement of nomads, but were not ready to sacrifice any revenue in so doing.

The Chevalier D'Ohsson refers to these various categories of *'Askerîs* as having existed under the earlier Ottoman Sultans, and gives the numbers of some of them. Thus he places the *Müsellems* at three thousand and the *Yayas* at twenty thousand. The *Yürüks* he describes somewhat misleadingly as Rumelian infantry, but gives no figure for their strength. The *Voynuḳs* numbered, according to him, six thousand.[3] On the other hand, from Turkish sources we learn that the *Yürüks* and *Müsellems* of Rumelia together numbered forty thousand,[4] and the *Yayas* and *Müsellems* of Anatolia twenty-six thousand,[5] their *Yamaḳs* in both cases being counted in. As regards their status in general, it will be seen that they were rewarded for their duties on much the same principles as those on which the *Sipâhîs* were rewarded for theirs. The *Müsellems*, *Yayas*, *Voynuḳs*, and *Doğancîs* have to incur less expenditure than the *Sipâhîs* when serving the Sultan on campaign. Therefore they are rewarded like the *Sipâhîs* with the enjoyment of an agricultural holding on which they do not have to pay taxes, but, unlike them, do not receive contributions from other taxpayers—except when they actually go on campaign. On the other hand, they have to toil to obtain a living, whereas the *Yürüks* merely have to guard their flocks. Hence the *Yürüks*, to make up for their comparative leisure,[6] are not tax-free: they have to pay the dues enumerated above. Such was the system. It now remains for us

[1] Aḥmed Refiḳ, op. cit., vii–viii.
[2] *M.T.M.* i. 306–7.
[3] D'Ohsson, vii. 308–9, 378–9.
[4] Aḥmed Refiḳ, *Anadoluda Türk Aşiretler* vi, quoting Ḳoçi Bey.
[5] Ibid. viii, quoting *Ḳânûnnâmei 'Âlî 'Oṣmân.*
[6] Cf. Isma'îl Hüsrev, 58.

to see how the countrymen, *re'âyâ* and *'Askerîs* alike, fared in the days of decay.

Since most of the *'Askerîs* disappeared early from the scene, let us take them first. When in the sixteenth century the necessity for employing marines on a considerable scale was first felt, the *Müsellems* were called on for this service, which they discharged under the conditions laid down for their former duty.[1] But later, being found unsuitable, they were permitted to pay a due in lieu of service, and so were approximated to the status of ordinary *re'âyâ*, among whom, as time went on, they were insensibly merged, their holdings becoming common *mîrî* land, of which the revenues nevertheless continued to fall to the Admiralty. The *Yayas* seem merely to have been abolished—whether they were allowed to remain on their holdings as *re'âyâ* does not appear. But their lands were first formed into ordinary fiefs, which were subsequently grouped into fourteen lots; and these, under the name of *Beylik*, went to supply pensions for retired Janissary officers.[2] The *Doğancîs* seem to have declined with the popularity of hawking, which was not a sport pursued by any of the later Sultans.[3] The *Voynuks*, on the other hand, were still at least in existence in the eighteenth century.[4] During the thirty years' peace, however, they ceased for some reason to breed horses for the army, as they were meant to do. When war broke out again in 1767, accordingly, the supply had to be made up by requisitions.[5]

As for the *Yürüks*, they too ceased to perform their auxiliary duties with the army towards the end of the sixteenth century. In course of time a considerable number of them appear gradually, by settling, to have been absorbed into the ordinary peasant population. As we have mentioned, the government seems from early times to have favoured such settlement, since the nomads were naturally harder to manage and only too ready to cause disturbances. And in later centuries it pursued the same policy, attempting at the same time, though not always with success, to restrict the still migratory tribes to certain areas.[6] Apart from their turbulence, the *Yürüks* continued to be distasteful to the Sultans on account of their heterodoxy. For they preserved the beliefs of their conquering progenitors in greater purity than their settled kinsmen—so much so that *Yürük* became all but a synonym for

[1] Seyyid Muṣṭafâ, iii. 92. [2] D'Ohsson, vii. 308–9. [3] D'Ohsson.

[4] See Aḥmed Refiḳ, *Türk Idâresinde Bulğaristân*, and D'Ohsson, vii. 378–9. It is usually difficult to be sure whether D'Ohsson is speaking of something which actually exists (in his day, that is to say), has existed, or should exist. But this passage reads as if the six hundred *Voynuḳs*, under their *Voynuḳ Ser-'Asker*, who came to Constantinople to put the horses of the great to grass, actually did so in his time.

[5] Seyyid Muṣṭafâ, iii. 111.

[6] See Aḥmed Refiḳ, *Anadoluda Türk Aşiretleri*.

heterodox, or *Ḳizil-baş*.[1] Though they led no more risings after that of the Celâlîs at the end of the sixteenth century, they remained sufficiently warlike to cause the authorities no little anxiety from time to time. Moreover, those of them that still went by the name of *Türkmens* actually furnished troops in time of war. D'Ohsson puts the number of the latter at ten thousand.[2]

By the eighteenth century, therefore, the agricultural holdings actually worked in earlier days by *ʿAskerîs* (as distinct, that is to say, from *Timars*, which were merely 'owned' by *Sipâhîs*) had nearly all been converted, by one process or another, into ordinary peasant land. All that remained of the *ʿAskerîs* of the country-side (again excepting the *Sipâhîs*) were some *Voynuḳs*, who were neglecting their duties—and, presumably for this reason, disappeared also, soon after, from the scene—and a large number of turbulent *Yürüks*, scarcely under control of any kind, either still nomad or in various stages of settlement.

The chief factor in the disruption of the order we have depicted, as far as the peasantry proper was concerned, was the extension of the tax-farming system to almost every variety of land-holdings. In the earlier centuries of the Empire's existence no taxes had been farmed. Even on the Imperial *Ḫâṣṣes* and state-lands taxes and dues had been collected by salaried officials called *Emîns*. But during the reign of Süleymân the Magnificent the Imperial *Ḫâṣṣes* had been 'let' to tax-farmers; and the system had gradually been extended to state-lands, fiefs, and even *waḳf* lands. In these circumstances it made little difference to the peasantry who owned the lands they inhabited: in all cases they had to deal with the tax-farmers, the *Mültezims*, whose interest it was to wring as much as possible from them, in order to render profitable the bargains they had struck.

Simultaneously, nevertheless, the original system of land-holding had been very considerably transformed; and this too had affected the peasantry adversely. To begin with, a certain amount of fief land had been converted, either legally—by imperial grant—or illegally—by mere seizure—into private property; and some of this had in turn been converted by its new proprietors into *waḳfs*.[3] Moreover, the Sultans had continued to create *waḳfs* from state property,[4] whereas no *waḳf* property had been converted to other uses.[5] Hence *waḳf* lands came to account for a higher proportion of the total than formerly.

[1] See Hasluck, *Christianity and Islam under the Sultans*.

[2] D'Ohsson, vii. 379.

[3] Ismaʿîl Hüsrev, *Türkiye Köy Iktisadiyati*, 169, 173; see Cevdet, i. 102.

[4] Cevdet, ibid.

[5] Seyyid Muṣṭafâ, iii. 176, notes that early in the eighteenth century the administration of the *waḳfs* appertaining to the Imperial mosques of Fatih,

But these conversions, in so far as they were made on state lands, diminished the revenues accruing to one or other of the treasuries, which, as we have noted, grew in any case more and more embarrassed from the end of the sixteenth century, owing both to the cessation of conquests and so of windfalls in the shape of booty, and to the increase of expenditure alike on the administration and the army. Hence the *mîrî* resorted to the abolition of fiefs. When a *Sipâhî* died and left no suitable heir, so that his fief fell vacant (*mahlûl*), instead of regranting it, as the *Ḳânûn* required, the Treasury retained it and put it out to farm. In this way the strength of the *Sipâhî* cavalry diminished till in the eighteenth century it stood at no more than a quarter of what it had once been.[1] But this was a matter of indifference to the Treasury, which now had at its disposal the revenues that had formerly been collected direct by the vanished feudatories. Nor was it only *Sipâhî* fiefs that were so abolished. The majority also of those that had originally been devoted to the support of officials both of the central and of the provincial governments[2] were likewise converted into state lands. So, again by the eighteenth century, no *Ḫâṣṣes* of this type remained but those appertaining to the Grand Vizir, the *Ḳaptan Paşa*, and the *Nişancî*.[3] This process had been made feasible only by another contravention of the *Ḳânûn*. According to the *Ḳânûn* the grant of *Sipâhî* fiefs at least had lain with the provincial *Beylerbeyis*.[4] From the end of the sixteenth century, however, the latter had taken to rewarding their followers with vacant fiefs, and even to accepting bribes for them, granting them to the highest bidder, whether he were a person capable of discharging *Sipâhî* duties or not.[5] Hence a decree had been issued removing the right of grant from the provincial governors and conferring it on the authorities of the Porte. But this measure, intended as a reform, resulted only in further abuses. First, it enabled the Porte officials to carry out the conversion of fiefs into *mîrî* lands that we have referred to. Secondly, it deprived persons to whom fiefs were due—namely the *Cebelis*, the senior of whom in any fief,

Sultan Selim, and Süleymaniye was handed over to the Grand Vizir in order to increase his revenues. It was, however, only the surplus that he was entitled to use, after the necessary expenditure had been met.

[1] Seyyid Muṣṭafâ, iii. 94. A shortage of *Sipâhîs* had been experienced as early as the campaign of 1593.—Ibid. i. 123; Cevdet, i. 103.

[2] That is to say *Ḫâṣṣes* and *Ziʿâmets* for the more important, *Ḫizmet* (*Ḫidma*) *Timars* for the less.

[3] Seyyid Muṣṭafâ, iii. 76.

[4] Ibid. i. 121.

[5] Ibid. i. 123, ii. 96. The taking of bribes for fiefs began as early as the reign of Süleymân himself. More ominous was the conversion of seventeen highly productive *Timars* into Imperial *Ḫâṣṣes* by the Vizir Sokollu in the reign of Murâd III, during which, in disregard of the *Ḳânûn*, the Sultan also pensioned off certain deserving officers with *Timars*.—Cf. Cevdet, i. 101.

was entitled, on its falling vacant, to promotion as a *Sipâhî*—of the redress, in case of a wrongful grant, that had formerly been afforded them by appeals from *Beylerbeyis* to the Porte.[1] The consequence, accordingly, of these various transactions, was that not only were fiefs greatly reduced in numbers, but that a high proportion of those that remained in being fell into the hands of persons incapable alike of military service and of the proper conduct of an agricultural holding.

However, as we say, the actual ownership, or holding, of *ra'îya* lands came to be more and more a matter of indifference to the peasantry, owing to the extension of the tax-farming system. This was universal on the now swollen state lands; general on lands held as fiefs by persons other than genuine *Sipâhîs* and on those converted, legally or otherwise, into private property; common on *wakf* lands; and by no means unusual on ordinary *timars*.[2] By the time of our survey, therefore, the old feudal system had all but disappeared, except on the fiefs of those *Sipâhîs* that still kept the collection of the revenues in their own hands.

In all other places the *re'âyâ* had now to deal with the tax-farmers, called, on the imperial *Ḥâṣṣes*, *Muḥassils*,[3] and elsewhere *Mültezims*, whose sole concern it was to wring as much from them as possible. No doubt the conduct of the *Mültezims* depended to some extent on the source of their contracts. That is to say, if they had contracted with a fief-holder or a proprietor, they were obliged to be circumspect, owing to the interest of such persons in their property and its prosperity. For though, theoretically, the *Mültezims* were entitled to exact from the peasantry only the legal dues, yet they assumed with their contracts some of, if not all, the authority formerly enjoyed by fief-holders,[4] and used it wherever they could to render their bargains as profitable as might be. And since, simultaneously with their rise to power, the administration of justice, as it appertained both to the '*Ulemâ* and to the provincial military governors, had fallen into the hands of persons, in the shape of *Nâ'ibs* on the one hand, and of *Mütesellims* and *Voyvodas* on the other, who were often unfit to carry it on, the *re'âyâ* could no longer be even so sure as formerly that in appealing to the law against illegal exactions they would obtain redress.

Matters in respect of the *Mültezims* had nevertheless been worse towards the end of the seventeenth century than they were in the eighteenth. For after the Peace of Carlovitz the Treasury had introduced the system of life farms called *mâlikâne* for the tax

[1] Cevdet, i. 101; Isma'îl Hüsrev, op. cit. 168.
[2] Seyyid Muṣṭafâ, ii. 96.
[3] Cf. Isma'îl Hüsrev, op. cit., 170.
[4] Cf. Isma'îl Hüsrev, op. cit., 170. They came to be regarded, as the *Sipâhîs* had been regarded, as the actual landowners (*Ṣâḥibi-Arḍ*).

contracts in its grant. And this measure seems in fact to have improved the condition of the peasantry, as it was intended to. For tax-farmers who had a life interest in their contracts naturally kept an eye on the future. Instead of wringing the last grain and *akçe* from the peasants under their control, as their predecessors had done when their contracts ran for a term of one or two years, they were circumspect in their exactions, seeing that their own subsequent prosperity depended on that of the peasants.[1] It is true that most of these 'life-farms' were held by officers and officials of the palace and the Porte, who delegated their administration. But their interest in the yield of the farms seems to have caused them to curb the rapacity of their representatives, at all events to some extent. Yet the system of *mâlikâne* tax-farming was no satisfactory substitute for that of *Sipâhî* land-ownership, which, though it kept the peasantry in a state not far removed from serfdom, yet endowed them with masters whose attitude in general was paternal, who shared their point of view, and whose position was sanctified in their eyes by long establishment.

The spread of tax-farming accounted more than any other cause for the disruption of the order that had formerly ruled in the provinces. But what rendered the pursuit of agriculture difficult, and in many cases finally impossible, was the provincial anarchy that resulted from the weakening of control by the central government, and the consequent emergence of petty dynasts. We have already had occasion to describe the rise of the *Dere-beyis*. Here, accordingly, it is enough to note that in the areas over which they exercised a somewhat uncertain sway, they were inclined, depending as they did on at least a measure of popular support, to consider the interests of the peasantry on the whole rather more sympathetically than the local governors that represented the Sultan. None of them, it appears, made any attempt to introduce administrative innovations. They contented themselves with collecting the regional revenues for their own benefit. The decay of order in the provinces led, however, to the rise of another class of local magnates called *Aʿyâns*, who as time went on added their contribution to the woes of the peasants.[2]

The *Aʿyâns* were persons of consequence in their districts: rural notables. They were not government employees; and the manner in which they first attained to notability is not clear. Possibly it was by means of the legal and illegal conversion of fief and other lands into private property, since in the original scheme of landholding there would appear to have been no place for such persons. The *Aʿyâns* first appear on the scene as representatives of the local population in their dealings with the government. But in the

[1] Cevdet, iv. 286. [2] See above, pp. 198–9.

original scheme, again, no such representation was necessary. As we have noted, however, the *Beylerbeyis* and *Sancaḳ-beyis*—now usually called *Vâlîs* and *Mutaṣarrifs* respectively—had been obliged, owing to their being given control simultaneously, for revenue purposes, over two or more separate districts, to employ substitutes for the government of those in which they did not reside. And it was perhaps because of this development, because these substitutes—*Mutesellims*, in the case of *Sancaḳs*, *Voyvodas*, in the case of *Ḳaḍâs*—were invested with no more than a part of the authority of the officers that appointed them, that the *A'yâns*, newly established as private property owners, asserted themselves as representatives of the people *vis-à-vis* the government, and equally as representatives of the government *vis-à-vis* the people. It is true that, to begin with, the *A'yâns* were elected by the people, though by what process does not appear. At the same time they seem to have enjoyed their status apart from this election—possibly because the descendants of elected *A'yâns* came to be regarded, whether elected or not, as *A'yâns* themselves. And in the second half of the eighteenth century certain governors attempted to control their appointment and exact payment in return for it.[1] In the meantime the *A'yâns* of many districts had contrived, partly owing to their already recognized position, partly owing to the relaxation of governmental control, to secure to themselves the management of local affairs, particularly in the matter of taxation, and now joined with complaisant officers of the law in fleecing the peasants, who were thus left defenceless.[2] Moreover, in the general decay of law and order, other agents, such as the *Mubâya'acîs*, or grain purchasers, who had authority in certain regions to buy supplies at a price fixed by the authorities for the victualling of the capital, or, in the case of *Ḍimmî* peasants, the *Cizyedârs*, or collectors of the poll-tax, were more or less free to exert what pressure they could on the unhappy *ra'âyâ*;[3] with the result that desertion of holdings became more and more common.

As early as the middle of the seventeenth century two celebrated writers[4] remark on the number of deserted villages they had come across on their travels in the provinces. And though the process of depopulation may have been momentarily arrested, or at least retarded, by the institution of the *mâlikâne* life-farm system, it was vastly accelerated during the eighteenth century, particularly

---

[1] Cevdet, iv. 286.
[2] Ismaʿîl Ḥüsrev, op. cit. 170; Cevdet, iv. 285–6, vi. 65. The *A'yans* are referred to by Seyyid Muṣṭafâ, iv. 98, as magnates of cities and towns. But Cevdet, loc. cit., records their co-operation with venal *Ḳâḍîs* and *Nâ'ibs* in collecting excessive *saferiye* (war dues) from peasants, thereby causing many to abandon their holdings. [3] See Cevdet, iv. 287, 290–1.
[4] Ḥacci Ḥalîfe (Hajji Khalifa) and Ḳoçu Bey.

in its second half.[1] The depopulation both of Rumelia and of Anatolia is attested not only by European observers of the time,[2] but by decrees passed to prevent the influx of peasants into Istanbul. No doubt, when they abandoned their holdings, peasant families would sometimes migrate to others more favourably situated. Many of them, however, if they did not swell the brigand bands of which more and more came into being in both provinces at this time, left country life altogether and sought their fortunes in towns and cities.[3] No statistics of population exist, of course, for this period. It seems clear, however, from these indications that the classes that lived on the contributions furnished by way of dues and taxes were engaged during the seventeenth and eighteenth centuries on a long-drawn-out strangling of the unfortunate geese that laid their golden eggs.

II. THE ARAB PROVINCES

The description given in the preceding section may be applied in its main outlines also to the Asiatic provinces. In all of these the unit of agricultural economy was again the village, with its assigned cultivable lands and pastures. The lands were held likewise by the three types of proprietors with which we have already become familiar, namely the cultivators themselves (here generally referred to, not as *re'âyâ*, but as *fellâḥîn*), the tenants-in-chief, represented either by *Timariots* or *Multazims*, and the beneficiaries of *wakf* endowments. Excluding for the present the last of these, which entered into the average village economy in very unequal degrees, we may concentrate upon the relations of the two former and their tenants.

The position of the *fellâḥs vis-à-vis* the tenants-in-chief was similar to that of the *re'âyâ* in the home provinces. The majority in each village were effective owners in the sense that they were at liberty to bequeath them and to alienate them to other *fellâḥs*. But each parcel of land belonging to a *fellâḥ* was burdened with a tax payable to the tenant-in-chief, who held the land as a grant from the state.[4] On the other hand the tenant-in-chief might not deprive a *fellâḥ* of his land, except for non-payment of taxation.

[1] Isma'îl Ḫüsrev, op. cit. 171–2. Ḥacci Ḫalîfe remarks on the contrast between the country which he saw flourishing on the Persian side of the frontier, and that on the Ottoman side.

[2] e.g. Eton 259, sq. References to vanished villages, known to have existed in the first half of the eighteenth century along the roads from Istanbul to Ankara and from Istanbul to Belgrade.

[3] Eton 248, 259.

[4] It was assumed by the legists that all ancient rights of property in the soil had by now been extinguished through failure of heirs or for other causes, and that the land, having been resumed by the public treasury, could be disposed of by the sovereign in whatever way he considered best; see Ibn Nuceym, *el-Baḥr el-Râ'iḳ*, v. 118, and Ibn 'Âbidîn, *Minḥet el-Ḫâliḳ*, v. 114.

As in the home provinces again, side by side with the fief-holders or *timariots*, the *multazims* (or *ḍâbiṭs*, as they were called in ʿIrâḳ) of public lands and *mâlikânes* had acquired, in virtue of their right to collect the taxes on agricultural land, a position that approximated so closely to that of the former as to be almost indistinguishable from it. The tax-farm or *iltizâm* was originally held on yearly tenure only, but this system appears to have been gradually modified in most districts by usage. In 1104/1692 it was decreed that *mâlikânes* were to be regarded as the property of the holder during his lifetime; that he was at liberty to alienate them by sale, subject to state confirmation; and that on his death the estates should be put up to auction, preference being given to his sons.[1] Thus by the eighteenth century it may be assumed that, as in the home provinces, most *iltizâms* of state lands (as distinct from the farming of private estates) were held on life tenures.

When, however, we pass from generalities to details we are faced by a bewildering complication. Village rights and usages differed so greatly, not only from province to province but even within the same district, that the details might require to be greatly modified for any one region. In certain parts of Syria and Palestine, for example, as also in Upper Egypt, village lands were held in common and the taxes were paid largely in kind;[2] in Lower ʿIrâḳ the villagers cultivated only very small plots of land, and agriculture was carried on mainly by the semi-nomadic herdsmen.[3] But the importance of tradition and traditional usage was common to all, and may be very well illustrated by the peculiar usages in force in the greater part of Lower and Middle Egypt.[4] It is, at the same time, essential for our purpose to summarize these in some detail, in view of the changes introduced by Meḥmed ʿAlî.

After the Ottoman conquest of Egypt the entire cultivable land (other than *waḳf* lands) was divided into parcels and distributed amongst the members of the *ocaḳs* and other persons as *multazims*.[5]

[1] Ğazzî, iii. 292, who adds that this change was a great boon to the cultivators (though it obviously failed to remedy the wider abuses of tax-farming). At the same time, each village was rated at a fixed annual amount, to be collected by the owners in three instalments.—Cf. also Murâdî, iv. 130; Poliak, *Feudalism in Egypt, etc.*, 62. For *mâlikânes* see above, pp. 255–6.

[2] See for Palestine and Syria details in *Revue des Études Islamiques*, ix (1935), 240; for Upper Egypt, Lancret, 245–7.

[3] Rousseau, 62–3.

[4] Full details are to be found in three fundamental articles in the *Description*: M. A. Lancret, 'Mémoire sur le système d'imposition territoriale, etc.' (i. 1, pp. 233–60); le comte Estève, 'Mémoire sur les finances de l'Égypte, etc.' (i. 1, pp. 299–398, esp. 310–14); and P. S. Girard, 'Mémoire sur l'agriculture, l'industrie, et le commerce de l'Égypte' (ii. 1, pp. 491–714, esp. 491–589). See also the exhaustive monograph of S. de Sacy, 'Recherches sur la nature et les révolutions du Droit de Propriété territoriale en Égypte', republished in *Mémoires*, &c., vols. i–ii (Paris, 1818–23).

[5] The original instructions issued by Süleymân provided that the *Defterdâr* should estimate the revenue of each village, regulate its *iltizâm* accordingly, and

In the course of the seventeenth century[1] these tax-farmers acquired the right of hereditary succession, and by the eighteenth century the *multazim* appears as effective owner of his assignment in the sense that he had the power to augment or diminish certain impositions, to give or to sell it to other *multazims*, or bequeath it to his son or daughter, or burden it with an irrevocable endowment, subject to confirmation by the state[2] of the title or grant in all three cases. His position was, in consequence, similar to that of the *timariot*, but at the same time resembled that of the ordinary *multazim* in Europe or Asia in that his primary duty was to collect and transmit the revenue due from his village or villages to the provincial and central treasuries. The rights and duties of the Egyptian *fellâḥ* were, for the rest, much the same as those of the other *re'âyâ*.

Thus it appears that though the Egyptian *fellâḥ* could not freely dispose of his land, he was able to alienate it temporarily,[3] and was also at liberty to choose his own crops for cultivation, without interference from the *multazim*,[4] even if in practice the rotation of crops was doubtless fixed by local usage. On the other hand, there can be no doubt that he was tied to the soil, and that in spite of the fact that any system of villeinage is repugnant to the *Şerî'a* so far as Moslem cultivators are concerned. The *Ḳânûn-nâma* of Süleymân is categorical on the point: 'When a field remains fallow through the fault of the cultivator, they [the *kâşifs*,[5] inspectors, &c.] will make all the searches necessary to discover him, and having brought him back to his village and punished him, they will compel him to sow his field.'[6] The historian Cabartî also says: 'When the *fellâḥ* fled from his village to another, the *multazim* would search for him and send agents from the *kâşif* of the district to fetch him.'[7] Since the historical evidence shows that the 'fugitive' problem was one of the standing difficulties of Egyptian governments from the very first century of Moslem rule,[8] it appears that the system of villeinage in Egypt was based upon

assign it 'to rich and upright private persons', who might hold more than one village at a time (Digeon, *Canoun-Namé*, 210–11; de Sacy, i. 105).

[1] This appears from a passage cited by de Sacy, i. 139–40.

[2] i.e. by the Paşa and finance department at Cairo, on payment of the usual 'advance', here called *ḥulwân*.

[3] This is asserted by Estève (p. 304) and Chabrol (p. 246), while both deny the statement made by Lancret (p. 235) that he was at liberty to sell his land.

[4] Lancret, 236; and cf. Cab. iv. 254/ix. 190.

[5] The *kâşif* was a district governor of lower rank than a bey.

[6] Digeon, 243–4; cf. also 246: 'Peasants who have left their villages after the date of the [Ottoman] conquest shall be compelled to return to them, whatever pretext they may allege.'

[7] iv. 109/viii. 244; cf. also iv. 207/ix. 88, and below, ch. vii.

[8] H. I. Bell, 'The Administration of Egypt under the Umayyad Khalifs', in *Byzantinische Zeitschrift*, xxviii. 3–4, p. 284.

ancient usage, and was taken over by the Ottomans in this instance from the existing practice.[1] Whether its extension to parts of Syria and Palestine dates from the Mamlûk or the Ottoman period it is difficult to discover. But it is to the credit of the religious authorities that some at least of them protested energetically against this 'tyrannical' abuse.[2] And in spite of the prohibition of desertion of villages, it always recurred during periods of agricultural misrule, as we shall have occasion to observe more than once in the course of our study.

In all but a few villages a proportion of the cultivable land, averaging one-tenth of the lands held by the *fellâḥs*, was set aside as seignorial land (*arḍ al-waṣîya*), and farmed out or cultivated by the *multazim* or *multazims*. The obvious danger that *waṣîya* land would in time swallow up the *fellâḥs*' lands was avoided by an ingenious 'usage'. The *fellâḥs*' lands and *waṣîya* land in each village were divided into twenty-four 'carats' (*ḳîrâṭ*), either belonging entirely to one *multazim* or divided between several. Each *multazim* owned the same number of carats (and fractions of carats) of *waṣîya* land as of *fellâḥs*' land, and could not sell any portion of the latter without at the same time selling an equal portion of his *waṣîya* land.[3] The balance of interests was thus maintained, for while *waṣîya* lands were most profitable to the *multazim*, they were most onerous to the cultivators, who were bound in many parts to cultivate them by *corvée*.[4] This in itself would scarcely have preserved the system, however, had it not been for its

[1] Information is supplied from a trustworthy Egyptian source that on old deeds of grants of land it is specified that so many *feddâns* and so many Copts are assigned to the grantee. This would suggest that originally it was only the Coptic cultivators who were tied to the land, and that the system was extended to the Moslem cultivators by a strictly illegal and oppressive 'usage'.

[2] Ibn Nuceym, v. 118: 'The land of Egypt is not now tribute-land, but rentage-land; there is therefore no claim against the cultivator if he leaves it uncultivated, unless he is the tenant of it, and there is no compulsion upon him by reason of the land. If, consequently, any cultivator abandons his cultivation and comes to dwell in Cairo, there is no claim against him, and the action of the oppressors in subjecting him to compulsion is illegal, especially if he wishes to engage in study of the Ḳur'ân and learning like the students at the mosque of el-Azhar.' (Ibn Nuceym, who died in 1563, was the most celebrated Ḥanefî jurist in Egypt in the Ottoman period.) But there is no evidence that *fellâḥs* on lands held by *şeyḫs* were freer than *fellâḥs* on other lands.

[3] On the other hand, he might constitute part or all of his *waṣîya* lands as an endowment (*waḳf*), but rarely devoted any of his *fellâḥs*' land to the same purpose (Lancret, 239).

[4] This was by no means universal, however, the usage varying as between districts (consequently the dark picture drawn by Cabartî, iv. 207/ix. 88, must not be generalized). In some parts the *multazim* farmed out his lands to the village *şeyḫ*, or had them cultivated by his *fellâḥs* on payment in money and kind. The *fellâhs* were also required to clean private canals, but were paid for their work at fixed rates (Lancret, 243), and Süleymân's *Ḳânûn* authorizes the *kâşifs* to make a levy on the villages for the maintenance and repair of the dykes (Digeon, 200–1).

usefulness in circumventing the conflict of interests between seller and buyer.

It is not easy to describe in a few lines the elaborate system by which the total sum of taxation for which each village was assessed was repartitioned between the inhabitants.[1] This was the work of a committee consisting of a Coptic *ṣarrâf* (financial intendant) representing the *multazim*, the *şeyẖ el-beled* (village headsman), chosen by the *multazim* from among the richer families of his tributary *fellâḥs*, but in practice usually hereditary,[2] and the *ṣâhid* or village lawyer, whose function it was to guard the interests of the *fellâḥs*. In the repartition of the old-established taxes[3] the *waṣîya* land was included as well as the *fellâḥs*' lands;[4] the 'additional' taxes were borne by the latter only. The taxes were payable by the cultivators individually in money, and by instalments. In theory, only irrigated land was liable to tax; in the event of a low or excessive Nile, the uncultivated area was measured, and a corresponding proportion deducted from the total village dues (the *mîrî*, however, remaining unchanged).[5] In practice, while the *multazims* had to be content with a temporary decrease of revenue in a bad year, the deficiency was frequently added to the amount exacted in the next good year.[6] It is one of the most striking indications of the strength of 'custom' that, in spite of the universal cultivation of the date-palm, no tribute was exacted on its produce.[7]

Each village was thus a self-contained unit, the routine of whose life was governed by a body of traditional usages, and little affected by external events. Its relations with the government were limited

[1] Detailed account with specimen statements of taxation in Estève, 312 sqq.

[2] Each *multazim* appointed a *şeyẖ el-beled* for his own tributaries, and if a single *multazim* owned a large holding he might appoint several to different sections. Consequently there were usually several *şeyẖs* in each village.—Lancret, 241.

[3] As will be seen below (ch. vii), the total of the imposts levied at the end of the eighteenth century on the villages in Egypt included:

A. Taxes established by the Ottoman regulation of 1526, collectively termed *mâl el-ḥurr*; this included the *mîrî* or land-tax payable to the Sultan, together with certain fixed sums payable to the local authorities.

B. Additional taxes exacted since the beginning of the eighteenth century, known generally as *barrânî* or 'extraordinary' taxes.

[4] From the table published by Estève (pp. 314–17) it appears that *waṣîya* lands were often undervalued, and the *fellâḥs*' land overvalued for taxation purposes, while for taxation purposes the *feddân* was reckoned at 5,353 square metres, instead of its proper figure of 5,929 square metres (Girard, 505–6). Girard also mentions cases of abusive reductions of the *feddân* to less than twenty-four carats in the Delta.

[5] Lancret, 242. Cabartî mentions only a single instance of remission of *mîrî* on account of drought, in 1106/1694–5 (i. 25/i. 60); a petition for its remission in 1206/1791–2, on the same grounds, was rejected (ii. 226/v. 157). Elaborate regulations for the measurement of irrigated lands are given in Süleymân's *Ḳânûn-nâma* (Digeon, 234–41).

[6] Estève, 331; Lancret, 250.

[7] Girard, 551, is categorical on this point, though according to Lancret, 243, date plantations paid duty to the *multazims*.

almost exclusively to payment of the taxes demanded and, apart from occasional interferences by the *multazims* or other military officers, it was in practice all but self-governing. The keystone of the village community was the *şeyẖ el-beled*. Each *şeyẖ* policed the *fellâḥs* who cultivated the lands under his charge, and the principal *şeyẖ* acted as magistrate and arbitrator, with authority not only over the cultivators but over all the inhabitants.[1] Though often harsh and tyrannical, it was he who kept the village together, and his position was respected not only by the villagers but also by the *multazims*. Stability was further ensured by the tendency of the offices of *şeyẖ*, *şâhid*, and the other village functionaries[2] to remain within given families, and by the uniformity of the population. Within the villages, lands might constantly change hands, proprietors sink to day-labourers, and labourers become proprietors, but there could be little alienation to outsiders.[3] Its simple needs were supplied by one or two shopkeepers, potters, and other artisans,[4] and each village also supported out of its own resources an *imâm* for the service of the local mosque (and Koran school, if any), a barber, and a carpenter, besides maintaining patrols of *Ḫafîrs* (guardians) to guard the crops and granaries, give warning of the approach of Beduin marauders, patrol the dykes, and generally prevent disorders.[5]

Although, as will appear later, the taxes established by the Ottoman legislators in Egypt were not excessive in themselves, the Egyptian cultivators, like their fellows in the other provinces of the Empire, were oppressed by burdensome and arbitrary demands dictated by the cupidity and venality of their administrators. More especially was this the case during the eighteenth century and its latter decades, when the fabric of government and economic life seemed to be on the point of collapse. Yet, while

[1] Lancret, 241, 244. He enjoyed also certain pecuniary advantages, including the exemption from tax of a portion of his holdings as compensation for the entertaining of officials, &c., which was one of his principal duties (cf. Cab. iv. 61/viii. 132). But he was prevented from becoming too rich and powerful by occasional *avanias* on his personal property, and in some villages his authority was held in check by a rival party headed by some rich cultivator (Lancret, 244).

[2] Such as the *ḫawlî*, who superintended the measurement of the village lands and the cultivation of the *multazim's* lands (Lancret, 242).

[3] A *fellâḥ*, if unable to cultivate all his holding, could engage a part against a sum of money sufficient to enable him to cultivate the rest, his lands being restored on payment of this sum (Lancret, 236). If he were unable to pay the debt, his personal property (including cattle and agricultural implements) might be seized and sold: 'mais, comme le législateur recommande au créancier la plus grande modération envers son débiteur, celui-ci obtient presque toujours un délai pour satisfaire à ses engagements, ou bien il s'arrange à l'aimable' (Chabrol, 263).

[4] Lancret, 244. There seems to be no information as to whether the village shopkeepers at this period were Moslems, Jews, or Copts, and what their relation was to the village community as a whole.

[5] Estève, 311–12.

these external factors cannot be minimized, it would be unjust to lay the blame for the backwardness of agriculture upon the exactions of the Turks and Mamlûks, without qualification. For centuries before Ottoman Turk and Mamlûk entered Egypt, the peasant had pitted his craft against the exploiters and had failed;[1] and failing, the genius of the race, inferior to no other in capacity and depth of feeling, had turned in upon itself in bitterness and sought revenge, as it were, in limiting production to the minimum of its requirements, in a tenacious opposition to all changes, and an almost deliberate harshening of all its conditions of life. The fertility of the soil served only to raise up oppressors on every side, and since, in the *fellâḥ's* experience, it seemed that only by oppression could anything be gained, he also, by a natural reaction, became an oppressor of his own kind. The primitive character of his agricultural implements and methods[2] was doubtless due to poverty, yet we hear of rich cultivators and of the wealth amassed by village *şeyẖs*. The real causes were lack of incentive to invention, since the implements served well enough,[3] and a refusal, amounting almost to inability, to depart from traditional usages. The experiments made by Mehmed ʿAlî show that, even had new tools and new methods been brought within reach of the *fellâḥîn*, they would have been unheeded, and possibly even regarded with suspicion as a means for getting more out of them. And finally, physical undernourishment and malnutrition, one of the main underlying factors which had brought the Moslem civilization to a standstill, limited the capacity of the cultivator, hardy as he was, to a certain standard of exertion.[4] The standard of living of the Egyptian *fellâḥ* may be

[1] It is historically false to regard the *fellâḥîn* of the Delta and a large part of Middle Egypt as lineally descended from the ancient Egyptians and inured to tyranny. The population of these districts was completely recreated by a continuous process of Arab settlement from the middle of the seventh century, and from that time almost down to the Ottoman conquest there was no lack of agrarian revolts; cf. Poliak in *R.E.I.*, 1934, 251–73.

[2] e.g. Girard, 501–2; Volney, ii. 266–7.

[3] The use of deep ploughs, for instance, would naturally be injurious to cultivation in the Nile irrigation basins and on the Syrian hill-sides. The cheapness of labour also militated against the introduction of more elaborate machinery, and still more the fact that local materials, means of construction, &c., were strictly limited, especially in Egypt, with few minerals and metal workers. The relatively primitive *sâḳiya*, raising some seven hundred kilograms of water per minute, was not at all ill adapted to a system of irrigation which lacked proper arrangements for drainage. It is now well established that the cause of the decay of agriculture in the Tigris–Euphrates basin was not either misgovernment nor Mongol destruction (real enough though both these causes were) but principally the overcharging of the soil with mineral deposits due to an uneconomic system of irrigation, without due regard to drainage and manuring.

[4] See the curious calculation in Girard (p. 501): a single labourer working a counterweighted bucket (*şadûf*) raised 143 kilograms per metre per minute; when the *şadûf* was employed experimentally in France the average amount raised by a single labourer was 220 kilograms per metre per minute. One man,

gauged from the following statements and calculations of Girard.[1] A daily labourer in Upper Egypt received 5–8 paras (roughly one-fifth to one-quarter of a franc) per day, in the Fayyûm and the Delta from 8 to 19 paras (one-quarter to two-thirds of a franc). The daily food of a single labourer in Upper Egypt was estimated at 3 paras. His single body garment was a *cibba*, which cost from 300 to 350 paras (about 11 or 12 francs) and lasted him a year or more, together with a woollen shawl costing about 180 paras and a head shawl costing 100 paras. Thus his annual upkeep—for himself alone—averaged about 540 paras for clothes and 1,095 paras for food, to which Girard adds about 360 paras for occasional expenses (coffee, meat, &c.): a total of close on 2,000 paras or a little over 70 francs a year. In the Delta food and upkeep cost rather more, but in any case meat was rarely eaten by the villagers except on festival occasions.

Amongst the various agencies which contributed to depress the cultivator, opinions differ as to the responsibility of the Coptic *ṣarrâfs* or financial intendants. The Comte d'Estève, while admitting that the *ṣarrâf* made a handsome profit on his transactions,[2] declares that their administration was preferred to that of the local *ṣeyḫs* because they were not only zealous and loyal, but impartial, whereas the *ṣeyḫs* were inclined to espouse local quarrels.[3] Girard, on the other hand, declares bluntly that the discouragement of agriculture and depopulation of the country were due in the main to 'the fraudulent manœuvres of this class of financiers'.[4] It is surprising that no source makes other than casual reference to debt as a burden upon the Egyptian cultivator,[5] since the experience of similar communities and the fact, vouched for by Volney,[6] that

with a plough hauled by two oxen, ploughed a *feddân* (about an acre) in two days or two days and a half (id. 508).

[1] Girard, 507–8. It must, however, be borne in mind that these figures relate to a period in which the depreciation of the para had probably raised the cost of living to some extent.

[2] Estève, 319–20: dues payable by each cultivator on receipt of demand note and on each instalment paid and final receipt; commission made by charging the cultivators a higher rate of exchange for the dollar (or *pataque* = Abû Ṭâḳa), in which all taxes were assessed, than the rate at which they paid the proceeds to the *multazims* (cf. Cab. iv. 109/viii. 244); by speculation, advances against high interest, &c.

[3] Estève, 313.

[4] Girard, 589: 'Nous avons dit qu'il y avoit au moins un de ces écrivains dans chaque village; ils étoient au nombre de trois ou quatre dans quelques endroits, et tous avoient une famille à entretenir et des domestiques à leurs gages. Je ne crois pas donc m'écarter de la vérité en portant à trente mille le nombre des individus qui vivent en Égypte de la perception des droits du fisc, et en avançant que le découragement absolu de l'agriculture et le dépeuplement des campagnes sont moins le résultat du despotisme des beys que des manœuvres frauduleuses de cette espèce de financiers.' Cabartî also (in an indignant mood: iv. 207/ix. 88) accuses *ṣeyḫs*, *ṣâhids*, and *ṣarrâfs* equally of oppressing the peasantry.

[5] Estève (above, n. 2); Chabrol (above, p. 263, n. 3).

[6] Volney, ii. 265: 'Quand les paysans ont besoin d'avances pour acheter des semences, des bestiaux, etc., ils ne trouvent d'argent qu'en vendant en tout ou

'usury carried to the most crying excess' was to be regarded as 'the greatest scourge of the country-side in Syria', would lead us to expect a parallel condition in Egypt. One can only suppose that while the Coptic *ṣarrâf* was able to make a certain amount of profit on loans, any extensive burdening of the land with debt was rendered unprofitable by the very small margin of income which could be attached, and by the very narrow circle within which village lands could be disposed of. For the last thing which the moneylender desired was to take over the property or the cultivation of it himself, nor was it in the *multazim's* interest that the village economy should be disturbed by too frequent changes in the distribution of property.

A more obvious and, in its cumulative effect, even more exhausting scourge in all the Arab provinces was the ravaging of the cultivated lands by the Beduins, and their high-handed oppression of the cultivator. Among the most fertile districts of Syria several, including the coastal plain of Palestine and Ḥawrân, were exposed to raids from the neighbouring deserts. The latter enjoyed some protection from the proximity of Damascus, as it was the chief source of grain supplies not only for the city but also for the annual pilgrim caravan. Since the Beduin tribes of the southern districts had an economic interest in the Pilgrimage (for which they supplied the camels and escorts in return for a subsidy), the *Paşas* were in a position to bring peaceful pressure to bear upon them, supplemented by military force if necessary, although neither means was sufficient to prevent occasional raids. Palestine, however, was too distant and too poor to receive similar protection, and is described as being in consequence 'one of the most devastated regions of Syria'.[1] With the decline of the central power, the Beduin raids became bolder and more frequent, and there were probably many towns and villages in Syria besides Ḥamâh and Aleppo which were forced to pay protection money to the tribes in their vicinity as an insurance for their crops and livestock.[2] Volney draws a vivid picture of the peasants in the threatened regions 'forced to sow with musket in hand', and hastily reaping the yellowing crop to hide it in underground matamores.[3] The villages of

en partie leur récolte future au prix le plus vil. . . . L'intérêt le plus modique est de douze pour cent; le plus ordinaire est de vingt, et souvent il monte à trente.' This statement refers primarily, however, to the Lebanon and Northern Palestine (i.e. Maronite, Druse, and Metâwila country, all of which lay outside the Moslem system proper); but Olivier (ii. 306) records that the Jews at Aleppo lent money at usurious rates to the cultivators of the neighbourhood and were repaid in produce. In Egypt, the chief debts contracted by the peasants were on advances of seed and grain from their *multazims*; cf. Poliak, *Feudalism*, 68–9.

[1] Volney, ii. 199; see also Murâdî, ii. 62. But Maundrell in 1697 found the plain East of 'Akka 'fertile beyond imagination'.

[2] Volney, ii. 173; Olivier, ii. 301.

[3] Volney, ii. 267.

Egypt, more especially those of the Delta, suffered in the same way from the Beduin tribes of the flanking deserts, and all observers agree as to the extensive and constant depredations committed by the Arabs in all parts.[1] But it is probable that the sedentary *fellâḥîn* of Egypt suffered even more from the violence of the semi-sedentary Beduins. Girard describes the tyranny of the settled Arabs in the districts immediately to the south of Cairo: they seize by force the best lands, direct and interfere with the water-courses during the inundation, break down the dykes, resist the payment of taxation, which has then to be made good by their unfortunate *fellâḥ* neighbours, and even seize the harvest of other villages if their own is insufficient.[2]

On the other hand, it must not be overlooked that the Beduins played an indispensable part in the economic life of the Arab provinces. By their camel-breeding they supplied the sole means of transport for caravans of travellers and merchandise;[3] they policed trade-routes as well as robbing on them; and they supplied several of the materials of commerce and industry (reeds, alkali, wool, and camel hair) as well as of food (mutton, butter, and cheese) to the towns.[4] Even their agriculture contributed a by no means negligible proportion to the total produce. More especially in Lower ʿIrâḳ, the tribesmen were the chief cultivators—the Ḫazâ'il of the marsh region, for example, furnished almost all the rice consumed in the province of Bağdâd[5]—and several of the tribes, both Arab and Türkmen, were engaged mainly in sheep-rearing.[6] As regards Egypt in particular, it is not improbable that during the greater part of the Ottoman period the Beduins—apart from the purely nomadic tribes on the fringes—were becoming an increasingly sedentary and productive section of the population, and that it was largely the Mamlûk persecutions which were responsible for the conditions described by the French writers at the close of the century.[7]

Apart altogether from Beys, Mamlûks, tax-farmers, *ṣarrâfs* and

[1] Lancret, 250–1; Girard, 512–13; cf. also *Description, &c.*, i. 1, pp. 293–8 (where the number of the Beduins on the borders of Egypt is estimated at 40,000), and Cabartî, passim.

[2] Girard, 512–13. But see above (p. 228) on the good administration of Şeyḫ Humâm of the Hawwâra tribe.

[3] In Egypt camels sold in the market at from thirty to sixty dollars: Girard, 555. The Beduins also reared most of the horses in Egypt (where they fetched forty to sixty dollars) and in the Arab provinces.

[4] Cf. Russell, 18 and 53.

[5] Rousseau, 59; also the Lâm on the Tigris.—Id. 80.

[6] Cf. Volney, i. 360. According to Girard (556) the Arabs in Egypt also supplied the markets with cattle, either of their own raising or plundered from other villages.

[7] Cf. Volney, i. 67–8. See also the regulations applicable to the Arab *şeyḫs* in the *Ḳânûn-nâma* (Digeon, 204–8).—de Sacy, i. 96–103.

Beduins, however, the villagers themselves contributed in no small measure to their own misfortunes, and by their rivalries played into the hands of their despoilers. The most characteristic feature, not only of village but even of urban life to a certain degree, in southern Syria and Lower Egypt was the division of the population into two factions, in alliance with corresponding factions amongst the Beduins.[1] In Syria these bore the historic names of *Ḳeys* and *Yemen*,[2] or, amongst the Druses of the Lebanon, 'Red' and 'White' respectively. Neighbouring towns belonging to opposite factions engaged in frequent hostilities with one another and with the surrounding villages,[3] and the military expeditions of *Paşas* and governors were at times frustrated because local levies would not fight against rebels of their own faction.[4] The consequence was, in Volney's phrase, 'a ceaseless civil war'.[5] It became a point of honour to destroy the rival village's crops, injure its fruit-trees, guide, support, and in case of retaliation protect the Beduin raiding parties of their own faction. A similar state of affairs is attested by Girard in the Egyptian Delta, where the rival Arab factions were known as *Sa'd* and *Ḥarâm*.[6] The *şeyḫs* of rival villages 'used on the slightest pretext to arm their peasants against

[1] Various theories have been put forward to explain the existence of these factions. They appear throughout the Near East and North Africa, among both Berbers and Arabs, apparently as a legacy from nomadic life, carried over into semi-nomadic life and thence into the sedentary population. For the *leffs* and *ṣoffs* of the Berbers in Kabylia and Morocco see E. Masqueray, *La formation des cités chez les sédentaires de l'Algérie* (Paris, 1886), and R. Montagne, *Les Berbères et le Makhzen* (Paris, 1930); for the Hinâwî and Ğifârî factions in Arabia, B. Thomas, *Arabia Felix* (London, 1932), p. 111; and see a recent study relating to Northern Syria, A. de Boucheman, 'Note sur la rivalité de deux tribus moutonnières de Syrie', in *Revue des Études Islamiques*, 1934, 11–58.

[2] For the Ḳeys and Yemen feud which broke out between the Arabs in the seventh century and led to the downfall of the Umayyad Caliphate of Damascus, see J. Wellhausen, *Das arabische Reich und sein Sturz* (Berlin, 1902).

[3] e.g. Bethlehem (Yemenî) and Hebron (Ḳeysî); cf. Volney, ii. 194–5, 197.

[4] e.g. the attack of 'Otmân Paşa el-Ṣâdiḳ on Nâblus in 1764; Volney, ii. 177.

[5] Volney, ii. 197: 'Cette discorde qui règne dans tout ce pays, depuis les premiers tems des Arabes, y cause une guerre civile perpétuelle. A chaque instant les paysans font des incursions sur les terres les uns des autres, et ravagent mutuellement leur blés, leurs doura, leurs sésames, leurs oliviers, et s'enlèvent leurs brebis, leurs chèvres et leurs chameaux. Les Turks, qui partout répriment peu ces désordres, y remédient d'autant moins ici, que leur autorité y est très-précaire; les Bedouins, dont les camps occupent le plat pays, forment contre eux un parti d'opposition, dont les paysans s'étayent pour leur résister, et pour se tourmenter les uns les autres, selon les aveugles caprices de leur ignorance ou de leurs intérêts. De là une anarchie pire que le despotisme qui règne ailleurs.' Cf. also ii, 203, on the destruction of olive-trees at Ramleh by peasants of rival factions.

[6] Cabartî does not mention these factions in the Delta, but indicates in one passage (i. 31/i. 50) that the guilds of artisans in Cairo were already divided into *Sa'd* and *Ḥarâm* factions at the time of the Ottoman conquest, and in another (i. 209/ii. 157) appears to suggest that during the later Mamlûk rivalries even the *'Ulemâ* took sides for and against *Sa'd* and *Ḥarâm*. The names gradually passed out of memory and are only rarely found in later writers, e.g. Rifâ'a Bey Râfi', *Anwâr Tawfîḳ el-Calîl*, i. 482 (Bulaḳ, 1285).

one another', besides supporting the Arabs of their own faction in their plundering raids on the villages of the other.[1] Rival irrigation interests in the flood season further embittered and gave opportunity for the display of inter-village factions, resulting often in bloody disputes, there being no police to intervene.[2]

While it is quite impossible to paint a roseate picture of village life in any of the Ottoman provinces, and European travellers and oriental writers unite in representing the villagers as a miserable and downtrodden class,[3] it is equally clear that their situation was by no means so intolerable and so devoid of guarantees for life and property as has generally been asserted.[4] Nothing can be held to mitigate the evil effects of the system of tax-farming, where it was in force,[5] but where lands were held by a *timariot* or *multazim* with a reasonable prospect of hereditary transmission, the relationship between cultivator and tenant-in-chief was frequently softened by a perception of their common interests. The possession of land entailed social duties, sanctified by custom and by the ethical teachings of their religion, and there is sufficient evidence that the harshness of the peasants' lot was to some extent alleviated by consideration on the part of the landholders, within the measure of their powers and their preconceptions. Their fortunes, unlike those of the *Paşas* and Mamlûk Beys, were bound up with the yielding capacity of a given piece of land, inherited from father to son, and which they had no wish to see diminished in any way.[6] The *multazim* was, indeed, as much a victim of the process of

[1] Girard, 514; cf. also 556: horses were too expensive to be employed in cultivation, but were a highly esteemed possession because in the village feuds success usually went to the village which had the greatest number of horsemen. See also Volney, i. 172. According to Chabrol (pp. 24–5) the feuds were put down by 'Alî Bey and became much less violent after his time.

[2] Girard, 498.

[3] e.g. Cabartî, iv. 207/ix. 88–9, speaking of the tyranny of the *multazims*, village *şeyḫs*, &c., says: 'Many other unreasonable ways and acts also, to which they have been brought up and become accustomed, they take no objection to and see no disgrace in; for God has set in authority over these *fellâḥs* men who treat them without mercy or leniency, because of their evil doings, their lack of piety, and their treachery and injury to one another.'

[4] Chabrol's outburst: 'Dans cette malheureuse contrée, le paysan n'est pas propriétaire, ne peut jamais le devenir; il n'est pas fermier; il est serf-né de la faction qui opprime sa patrie: c'est l'Ilote des anciens Spartiates; c'est l'esclave infortuné des colons de l'Amérique' is not description, but rhetoric.

[5] See, for example, Rousseau's indictment of the system in 'Irâḳ, as equally ruinous to cultivator, tax-farmer, and agriculture (pp. 65–6).

[6] There is an interesting passage on this subject in Cabartî (iv. 109/viii. 243–4 [translation very inaccurate]): 'The *multazim*, on learning of the assessment of the tax, promptly went to the *dîwân* of the clerks, and having ascertained the sum levied on his parcel (*ḥiṣṣa*), gave guarantees for it and had a delay of a fixed period granted him, leaving a written undertaking with them in return. He would then endeavour to recover the sum from his *fellâḥs*, and if they paid no heed to his claims for payment and turned the demands back to him, he paid it out of his own pocket, if he was possessed of sufficient means, or borrowed it,

spoliation during the last decades of Mamlûk rule as were his *fellâḥs*, and if he was unable to meet the demands made upon him—at the expense, of course, of his peasants—he was himself evicted from his holding.[1]

It would seem, then, that the main charges to be brought against the agricultural administration of the Turks are more negative than positive. That the government meant well on the whole is shown by the injunctions which are uniformly found in works on public administration. But good intentions were paralysed by weakness and inertia, by failure to prevent peculation and oppression by its official agents and to maintain order and security (especially against the Beduin Arabs), and by neglect of the utilities and public works necessary to agricultural welfare. Yet, thanks to the steadying influence of long-established usages, the system maintained itself without excessive hardship to the peasantry so long as the central government kept the fief-holders, and still more the *paşas* and local authorities, in effective control. By the middle of the eighteenth century its power to do this was completely non-existent in Egypt and ʿIrâḳ, and gravely weakened in Syria. The ensuing disorders were due mainly to the action of those *Paşas* and Beys who sought to take advantage of the weakness of the Porte and to build up a military power on a scale too great for the economic resources of their provinces. Like the feudal system in the directly administered provinces, the whole structure of agriculture in the quasi-independent *paşaliḳs* was being thrown into ever greater confusion by the shifts to which these despots resorted in order to obtain increased revenues. It was only in the last years of the eighteenth century that a régime of extortion became all but universal,[2] and the frequency with which the peasantry were deserting their lands bears eloquent

even at interest. Then subsequently he would recover it in full from the *fellâḥs* little by little, from a desire to preserve the welfare of the peasants of his holding, to give them security, and keep them settled on their lands, in order that they should produce the required sum for the *mîrî* and something [over and above] upon which they and their families might live. If this was not done, the duty of recovering the sum was transferred to the *kâşif* of the district, who appointed agents in the district to make urgent demands, together with [demands for] the additional sums levied for the agents' *ḥaḳḳ el-ṭarîḳ* and expenses. If payment were delayed, the missions and demands were repeated again and again in the same way, so that the distress [of the *fellâḥs*] was multiplied many times, and often the amount of the original sum due was expended in the process many times over . . . until the *fellâḥ* was reduced to bankruptcy, sold his crops and his cattle, and fled from his village to another.'—Cf. also id. i. 305/ii. 308.

[1] e.g. Cab. ii. 74, 152–3; iv. 109/iv. 107; v. 8; viii. 244–5.

[2] There were, however, limits to neglect of public works, since *multazims* and beys suffered in the last resort as much as the cultivators. Even Murâd and Ibrâhîm, alarmed by the increasing decline of agriculture in the eastern Delta and consequent fall in revenue, took measures to restore some of the canals to service (Olivier, ii. 63).

testimony to the extent to which the old economy was breaking down.[1]

The principal crops raised both in Egypt and in Syria were as follows: for internal consumption: millet (*dura*), lentils, beans, maize, onions, and other root crops; for consumption and export: wheat and rice; for fodder (chiefly in Egypt): barley, clover, fenugreek, vetch; economic cultures: colza, lettuce, and sesame for their oils, flax, cotton, safflower, indigo, sugar-cane, tobacco, roses.[2] No figures are, of course, available of the absolute or relative acreage devoted to each, but it should be remembered that the greater part of the irrigated land in Egypt bore two crops annually, and a small proportion (from 15 to 25 per cent.) three crops.[3] Most of the economic cultures were peculiar to certain localities or districts. Indigo was grown, for example, in Upper Egypt and in the Beysân district of Palestine, and was introduced into Lower ʿIrâḳ only about the end of the century.[4] Rose-cultivation for the perfume industry was confined to the Fayyûm.[5] Cotton, on the other hand, was grown almost everywhere, in Upper Egypt in the form of tree cotton (*gossypium arborescens*), elsewhere as an annual (*gossypium herbaceum*),[6] while flax, though grown in most parts of Egypt, was little grown outside.

The selection and rotation of crops was probably regulated by rigid custom, but this did not exclude the possibility of adaptation to changes in the market. The culture of flax, for example, was stimulated or depressed by the opening or closing of the export market, since it was most profitable when a proportion of the output was exported.[7] The most remarkable example of change of culture in the Ottoman period was the introduction of tobacco into Syria during the seventeenth century. Although its cul-

[1] Cf. Cab. iv. 109/viii. 244: 'The lands of Syria and Rumelia were filled with peasants from the villages of Egypt' (confirmed, as regards the famine year 1784–5, by Volney, i. 164); also ii. 83/iv. 129; Lancret, 247 (desertion of villages in the Fayyûm), 250.

[2] Girard, 515–50; Volney, i. 315–17; Russell, 16–17. In Mesopotamia and ʿIrâḳ the same staples (wheat, rice, barley, millet, maize) were cultivated (Rousseau, 8, 56, 61, &c.) together with cotton, tobacco, sesame, and madder (ibid.; Olivier, ii. 444). Outside Egypt natural pasturage replaced most of the fodder crops.

[3] Girard, 499 sq., 558–65.

[4] Olivier, ii. 444. The indigo plants in Upper Egypt lasted from two to five years.

[5] Girard, 549–50. The bushes were renewed every five years, and produced about eight *ḳanṭârs* of rose-leaves per *feddân*.

[6] The former were renewed every eight or ten years, and their average produce when in full yield (in the third year) was 300 pounds per *feddân*, whereas the annual cotton harvest yielded up to 240 pounds per *feddân* (cf. on the cotton culture at Lâḏiḳîya, Olivier, ii. 283). Very little raw cotton was exported from Egypt, but a considerable amount from Syria; cf. however Blumenau, 134, where he speaks of Egyptian cotton as 'a profitable article of trade'.

[7] Girard, 563.

tivation was hindered by religious and administrative opposition to begin with,[1] it rapidly established itself as a main culture in the region of Lâḏiḳîya (Latakia), and as a subsidiary culture (with a much inferior product) in most other parts of Arab Asia and Egypt. Generally speaking, however, the poverty of the cultivators restricted their choice to those crops which required the smallest outlay for seed and labour of cultivation,[2] and yielded the largest relative profits. The very careful computations made by Girard of costs of cultivation and profits of each crop grown in Egypt[3] are exceedingly enlightening in this, as in many other respects. His figures establish the following as the crops which yielded the highest percentage of profit on outlay: clover 612 per cent.;[4] colza 500 per cent.; beans 353 per cent.; lentils 350 per cent.; tobacco 318 per cent.; fenugreek 304 per cent.; wheat 285 per cent.; onions 247 per cent.; lettuce 208 per cent.; barley 203 per cent.; lupins and vetches 193 per cent. On the other hand, none of these crops, with the exception of tobacco and onions,[5] yielded an absolute profit of more than fifteen dollars per *feddân*, and barley, lentils, and lupins yielded only from five to six. Nothing can show more eloquently how pitifully small were the individual earnings of the cultivator, even under the most favourable Egyptian conditions, and how narrow the margin of livelihood upon which tax-farmer, *ṣarrâf*, and Mamlûk were speculating.

It is, however, important to observe that the three most profitable economic cultures, which required also a certain organization of capital, namely sugar, indigo, and rice, were already at this time well represented in several districts, and even fairly flourishing in Egypt.[6] Small quantities of sugar-cane were, indeed, grown every-

[1] A Sultanian decree published in 1040/1630 formally prohibited the practice of smoking tobacco, and Murâd IV in 1638 executed at Aleppo twenty persons suspected of smoking *in private*: Ġazzî, iii. 280–1; cf. p. 291, below. For the tobacco culture at Lâḏiḳîya see Olivier, ii. 281–3; Russell, 17.

[2] The labour of harvesting and threshing was usually paid for in kind, and therefore less onerous to the cultivator.

[3] Girard, 566–84 and 701–11.

[4] This yielded two or three cuttings and was largely consumed as green fodder (G. 532–3), hence its high profits. The percentages given above for clover, beans, lentils, wheat, and barley apply to naturally irrigated winter crops (*bayâḍî*) only; the labour required for artificial irrigation under other conditions more than doubled the expense of cultivation.

[5] And onions and tobacco were precisely those of the cultures in the above list which were least extensively grown because their relatively high cost of cultivation put them out of reach of the ordinary cultivator.

[6] According to Girard's figures, the expenditure, produce, and profit respectively of these cultures over an area of ten *feddâns* were as follows:

Sugar:	839 dollars;	2,010 dollars;	profit 1,171 dollars.
Indigo (yearly averages):	961 " ;	1,504 " ;	" 543 "
Rice (with clover)	1,054 " ;	1,417 " ;	" 363 "
Rice (with wheat):	1,034 " ;	1,393 " ;	" 319 "

where, but only for sale as a raw sweetmeat.[1] Its cultivation for economic exploitation was confined to a small area in Upper Egypt, where it was conducted as a joint enterprise between a group of Mamlûks and manufacturers.[2] Indigo, with even heavier initial expenses, was grown not only by rich proprietors, but also by 'associations of *fellâḥs*'.[3] Unfortunately no further information is given on this interesting and rather unexpected instance of agricultural co-operation. The rice plantations were on a much larger scale than either of the foregoing, and occupied a considerable area in the regions of Rosetta and Damietta, and in Lower ʿIrâḳ, with smaller plantations in Syria (Hûleh). In the Nile Delta the operations of irrigation, cultivation, threshing and bleaching required a large outlay on oxen, machines, and labourers, the last named being engaged on annual wage-rates, not as day labourers. The culture of rice thus approached much more closely than other branches to European farming methods, and the similarity was increased by the fact that the expenses involved by the upkeep of machinery, men, and animals were met by loans, on which interest was paid at 10 per cent.[4] In ʿIrâḳ on the other hand, the cultivation was carried on by the riverain tribes in the marshy regions of the two rivers and of the Kârûn; little outlay was required, and there appears to be no reference to the existence of husking machines.

The cultivation of fruit-trees and of fruit generally was of secondary importance in Egypt, except for the universal date-palm, and such fruits as melons. Only in the Fayyûm were there extensive plantations.[5] In Syria, on the other hand, fruit was one of the principal cultivations: olives in the coastal areas and around Nâblus,[6] lemons and oranges around Jaffa and Tripoli,[7] vines (and

[1] Girard, 547; Olivier, ii. 172, adds for the manufacture of syrup. The cultivation of sugar-canes begun by some peasants in a marsh near Yabnâ (Southern Palestine) about 1780, and brought to an end in the second year by extortionate taxation (Volney, ii. 206), was probably only for the same purpose.

[2] Girard, 586; see below, p. 298, note 4.

[3] Girard, 545. In the summary reports of the proceedings of the Institut d'Égypte there is a reference to a Frenchman named Porte, who had engaged in the cultivation and manufacture of indigo before the French expedition (*Memoirs relative to Egypt*, London, 1800, p. 15). The Egyptian indigo was of excellent quality, but suffered from the very rough methods employed in its manufacture (cf. Girard and Olivier, ii. 170–1).

[4] Girard, 521–5, 577 sqq. The average wage of the labourers in 1798 was five to six pataques per annum in addition to their food. Descriptions of the husking and blanching machinery, ibid.; M. Jollois, 'Notice sur la Ville de Rosette', *Description*, ii. 2, p. 342; Atlas of *Arts et Métiers*, planche ix; and in most of the works of travel.

[5] Girard, 552–3; Savary, i. 424–5. Of these, the vines were the most important, the grapes being exported to Cairo.

[6] Olivier (who was, however, personally acquainted only with Northern Syria) represents the olive cultures of Syria as languishing, ii. 284–5.

[7] Cf. Russell, 29. The fruit gardens of Jaffa were completely destroyed by the

also white mulberry for silk-rearing) in the Druse country, pistachios at Aleppo, and fruit of all kinds at Damascus,[1] especially apricots, which were made into a kind of dried apricot paste, much appreciated by travellers and of which large quantities were used on the Pilgrimage and exported.[2] The date-palms of Lower 'Irâḳ have always been justly famed, and furnished almost the only natural product of the country which was exported in any quantity. The province of Bağdâd, however, possessed also large plantations of citrus fruits.[3]

Apart from the rearing of camels, horses, and sheep by the Beduins,[4] stockraising played a much smaller part than in Europe as a supplement to agriculture. Very little meat was consumed by the population, and that mostly in the towns.[5] In the second place, the poverty of the *fellâḥs* limited to a minimum the number of animals employed for cultivation.[6] Agricultural operations were carried out mainly by oxen (and in Lower Egypt and 'Irâḳ by buffaloes[7]); for the transport of crops the cultivators hired camels from the Beduins, at the rate (in Egypt) of twenty-five to thirty paras per day.[8] For the conveyance of persons and small loads each peasant owned one or two asses, the price of each averaging ten to twelve dollars.[9] But this comparative absence of stock resulted in a serious deficiency of manure, especially in those parts where dung was valued as a fuel, and still further diminished the fertility of the soil. Egypt alone escaped these consequences owing to the natural fertilizing qualities of the Nile mud and by the use of nitrates derived from ruins and rubbish heaps.[10] Goats were raised in Upper Egypt for their milk and for making waterskins.

Egyptian Mamlûks, particularly on their second invasion in 1775, when they cut down all the orchards, Volney, ii. 201; but by 1799 the 'bois d'orangers' at Jaffa was again large enough to cover the movements of the French troops, *Agenda de Malus* (Paris, 1892), p. 131.

[1] Volney, i. 316–17. Volney also speaks with particular admiration of the orchards in the Orontes valley, in which the trees were planted in quincunxes (ii. 54), but the olive-trees in this district were liable to damage by exceptional frosts (Olivier, ii. 295).

[2] It was (and is) called *Ḳamar el-dîn* or *cild el-faras* ('horse-hide'); see Burton, i. 191.

[3] Olivier, ii. 443. [4] See above, p. 267.

[5] The chief source of the meat supply of Cairo was the herds of half-wild buffalo which lived in the vast marsh to the east and south-east of Lake Burlus (Girard, 554). Elsewhere the principal supply came from the flocks of the nomads.

[6] Girard, 556.

[7] The prices of these rose from sixty dollars in the extreme south of Egypt to about double that amount in the Delta, and the average cost of forage (clover, dried clover, chopped straw and beans) for each animal was about ten paras per day: Girard, 553–4.

[8] Girard, 555. Wheeled vehicles were unknown in Egypt and 'Irâḳ, and rarely seen in Syria (cf. Russell, 56). [9] Girard, *loc. cit.*

[10] For the manuring of ordinary (summer) crops in Egypt cf. Savary (Eng. tr. [2]), i. 74; Olivier, ii. 164.

Large numbers of sheep were raised also in the Fayyûm, there being an average of 800 sheep per village of two thousand *feddâns*. In this province the sheep were shorn twice annually for the village weaving industries, a good fleece weighing four or five pounds. Elsewhere in Egypt the sheep, which were mostly brown, were shorn only once, the fleece, weighing two to four pounds, being sold in the open market at forty to fifty paras the pound.[1] In all provinces pigeons played an important part in the village economy, both as food and for their manure, the latter selling at ninety to a hundred paras the *ardebb*[2] and being used chiefly for date-palms, melons, and vines.[3] Bees were kept for their honey and wax,[4] and hens in Egypt chiefly for the incubation industry.[5]

[1] Girard, 555–6.

[2] The *ardebb* varied slightly in different provinces, the standard *ardebb* of Cairo measuring 184 litres or about half a bushel (Girard, 506).

[3] Girard, 552.

[4] According to Olivier (ii. 178–9) bees were owned in Egypt exclusively by Copts, who began in the Ṣa'îd in the autumn and gradually moved down to the Delta, but owing to the heavy taxes latterly imposed by the Mamlûks, the industry was very greatly reduced.

[5] Girard, 556–7; cf. below, p. 298. Elsewhere they were kept mainly for food. The *ḳâḍî* of Aleppo, by an 'ancient usage' was supplied with fowls by the villagers of Cebel Sim'ân every three months, until this tax was abolished on the *ḳâḍî's* initiative in 1699: Ğazzî, iii. 293.

CHAPTER VI

THE CITY: INDUSTRY AND COMMERCE

I. THE STRUCTURE OF THE CITY

THE contrast which exists between the rural community and the city in every society was rarely more striking than in the medieval Islamic world. Here it was not merely a contrast between isolation and congregation, between the dispersed economy of the village and the concentrated economy of the town, between oppressed poverty and relative freedom and wealth, between producer and consumer. It was a contrast of civilizations. The medieval Moslem culture was above all an urban culture. While Islâm but lightly touched the secular life of the country-side, it rebuilt and refashioned the cities from their foundations, and stamped them with an individual impress which has persisted even to the present day. Between the Egyptian or Syrian city and its country districts there was little or no tie but the economic one[1]—indeed, the possibility of any stronger tie was all but ruled out by the contempt with which the townsman regarded the peasant—while the cities of widely distant countries shared a common culture, a common order of life, a common disposition of mind, and a sense of unity fostered by these joint possessions and traditions, even when physical intercourse between them was relatively limited. There is a marked change of spiritual atmosphere in the cities; though they share in the general decline of the eighteenth century, there is something of independence in the bearing of the townsmen, a conviction of their dignity as citizens of Islâm, and a readiness to assert their rights, even though it might degenerate into mere rioting and mob demonstrations. This change of tone and of bearing struck even the European travellers in the eighteenth century, although they cannot explain whence it comes.[2]

[1] This all but complete dissociation is strongly reflected in Islamic literature, which is a literature of townsmen from beginning to end. Even for the eighteenth and nineteenth centuries it is only from the works of European writers that it is possible to gain an insight into the life of the agricultural communities.

[2] Cf. Rousseau: 'En général les habitans de Bagdad, bien loin d'être de vils esclaves, sont fiers, entreprenans, actifs, et enclins à la mutinerie. Toutefois, dans la commerce ordinaire de la vie, on les trouve civils, spirituels, généreux, et obligeans envers les étrangers' (Bagdad, p. 9). Volney regards it as simply due to maladministration: 'Les artisans et les marchands, rassemblés dans les villes, échappent plus aisément, par leur foule, à la rapacité de ceux qui commandent. C'est-là une des causes principales de la population des villes dans la Syrie, et même dans toute la Turkie: tandis qu'en d'autres pays les villes sont en quelque sorte le regorgement des campagnes, là elles ne sont que l'effet de leur désertion. Les paysans chassés de leurs villages, viennent y chercher un refuge; et ils y trouvent la tranquillité, et même l'aisance' (ii. 268). But he does not explain how

In spite of the existence of a sense of unity, however, the Islamic city was not in any respect an organic unity. The social organization, as it had been built up under political and economic pressure, and reworked and vitalized by religious influences, was one of dislocated, self-contained and almost self-governing groups, subject only to the overriding authority of the temporal and spiritual powers, represented by governors, police officers, and *ḳâḍîs*. Its characteristic feature was the corporation (*ṭâ'ifa*), whose social importance can hardly be overestimated. If religion was the cement of the Islamic structure, the corporations were the bricks of which it was built. Not only the artisans and merchants, but all who were engaged in any occupation were members of a recognized corporation, with regular statutes, chiefs, and tax assessments.[1] There were, for example, corporations of students and teachers, of domestic servants, of water-carriers—even, as we shall see, of beggars,[2] thieves, and prostitutes.

The corporation served many purposes. It offered the means by which the humblest citizen could give expression to his social instincts, and be assured in return of his place in the social order. This was his field of citizenship, and if he was rarely called upon to play any part in outward political life, he was, on the other hand, little interfered with by his political governors, who respected in general the independence and the traditional usages of the corporations. The social function of the corporations was enhanced (not in all, but in most, especially of the craft-corporations) by their religious affiliation, usually to one of the great religious orders.[3] The moral effect of this religious personality, as it were, was incalculable; it encouraged the qualities of honesty and sobriety which all observers agree in attributing to the Moslem artisan, and to it is probably due the remarkable tenacity of the corporations

this economic miracle was operated. He is fully justified, however, in his next remarks on the care taken by the *paşas* and the administration to see that supplies were abundant in the cities and prices kept low.

[1] The methods of taxing the corporations varied greatly, and will be dealt with in the appropriate contexts. Few were assessed directly for *mîrî* (e.g. the *şeyḫ* of the brokers at Rosetta, Estève, 361); more usually they paid a fixed annual contribution to the administrative officers from whom they depended. Thus in Egypt the pedlars and sellers of ironware formed, together with the strolling players (*muḥabbezîn*), snake-charmers (*ḥuwâh*), monkey-keepers (*ḳirdâtîya*), singing-girls (*mağânî*), jugglers (*melâ'ib*), wrestlers (*pahâlewîn*), dancers (*raḳḳâṣîn*), and troupes (*cink*), the *Ḫurda* corporation, which paid a tax of the same name to the intendant of the *'azeb-ocaḳ* (Estève, 360; Cabartî, iii. 229/vii. 132).

[2] In 1718 the corporation of beggars in Cairo gave Ibrâhîm Bey a horse and saddlery to the value of 22,000 paras (Cab. i. 105/i. 243).

[3] See the following section. Cabartî regularly includes them under the general term *'aşîra* = lodge of *dervîşes*. But the exact mechanism of this affiliation has not yet been established; possibly the *şeyḫ* occupied a definite place in the hierarchy of the order.

over so many centuries. It supplied the moral and religious foundation for the discipline which was exercised by the craft-organization over its members; and in spite of, or perhaps even because of, the differences in wealth and sometimes in condition between the members, it made for social solidarity and emphasized social duty.

From the members' point of view, the corporations maintained the standard of craftmanship, prevented underhand competition, and served the purposes of an insurance or friendly society. It is not to be denied, on the other hand, that they tended to stereotype the processes of industry and to imprison the workman in a narrow rut. But in a stationary civilization this must be accounted a minor drawback, and it was offset by the protection which they gave to the civil population as a whole[1] against the petty tyrannies and oppressions of the rulers and the military.

From the rulers' point of view, they maintained order and discipline amongst the artisans and other elements of the city populations, and provided a convenient means of administration and of bringing pressure to bear on them, through the *şeyẖs*. The latter (or their *kâẖyâs*) represented the corporations in all their relations with the government, and not only distributed the tax-quotas of their members but were personally responsible for their payment.[2] The *şeyẖ* of each corporation was also administrator and arbitrator in its internal affairs, deciding disputes between the members, maintaining order, and punishing misdemeanours.[3] Complaints against any member of a corporation were addressed to the *şeyẖ*, who rarely failed to obtain satisfaction from the offender, even in the criminal corporations.[4] But he had far from autocratic powers, and if his exactions went beyond reasonable limits, or if for any reason the members of the corporation were dissatisfied with his administration, he was removed from office and another *şeyẖ*, chosen by them, installed in his place.[5] Within the limits imposed by religion, tradition, and 'usage', therefore, the corporations were relatively free and autonomous, a fact which explains the (at first sight surprising) stability and adaptability to political circumstances shown by industry in all Islamic countries, though it was inevitably affected by general economic conditions and by local measures.

The physical organization of the city reflected this social consti-

[1] Not, however, to the individual workman, who was never secure against arbitrary police action or victimization, and could rarely count on obtaining redress.

[2] If any or all of the members were non-Moslems, the *şeyẖ* also collected the poll-tax (*ẖarâc*, properly *cizya*) due from each.

[3] Chabrol, 322; cf. Cab. iii. 119/vii. 64.

[4] Cf. Lane (*Mod. Egypt.*, chap. iv) on the corporation of thieves, and Bowring, 117.

[5] Chabrol, 323. In general the office of *şeyẖ* was hereditary in a given family.

tution.[1] Beneath the external unity of emplacement, represented by the city wall, and of function, represented by the main *sûḳs* or bazaars, the urban area was subdivided into a large number of separate quarters, called *ḥâra*, each self-contained, with its own communal buildings (mosque, bath, market) and its own gates, by which it asserted and maintained its separate existence.[2] Each *ḥâra* formed an administrative unity under its own *şeyḫ*, and was inhabited by families between whom there existed some natural tie, either of origin, occupation, or religion, thus constituting a homogeneous group.[3] Since the number of *ḥâras* was less than the number of separate corporations, it would appear that the *ḥâra*-system was superimposed on the corporative system, but did not conflict with it, the *şeyḫ* of the *ḥâra* having rather police (and, if necessary, military) functions. At Cairo there was a 'chief *şeyḫ* of the *ḥâras*', who had a recognized position as leader and spokesman of the city population.[4] At Damascus his place appears to have been taken by the *ra'îs*, who was one of the principal religious dignitaries and exercised control over all the corporations.[5] The general responsibility for policing was shared by the market superintendent (*muḥtasib* or *emîn iḥtisâb*, formerly a religious office, but now apparently held by a civil or military officer) and by an *ağa* or *kâḫyâ* of the local Janissaries, known as the *Şubaşi* or *Wâlî*.[6]

In spite of the division of the city population into close communities, occupational and domiciliary, and the frequent existence

[1] See, for a recent comprehensive description of Cairo in the Ottoman period, M. Clerget, *Le Caire*, i. 178–87.

[2] Cairo had fifty-three *ḥâras* in the eighteenth century: Jomard, *Description . . . du Kaire*, p. 661, where a brief description is given. For the *ḥâras* of Damascus, see J. Sauvaget, in *Revue des Études Islamiques*, 1934, 450 sqq., with plan. De Kat Angelino, *Colonial Policy*, i. 78, in reference to this structure uses the phrase 'agglomeration of villages, quarters, and streets', which probably represents the process in the reverse order, so far as the cities of Western Asia are concerned.

[3] 'Ces espèces d'enclos sont habités, soit par des ouvriers d'une même profession, soit par des étrangers d'un même pays on d'une même religion, mais toujours par des hommes exerçant aux mêmes conditions, ayant les mêmes droits aux privilèges, et ainsi réunis dans un même intérêt': Jomard, loc. cit.; cf. Sauvaget, p. 453.

[4] *Şeyḫ meşâyiḫ el-ḥârât*; Cab. iii. 53, 240; iv. 174/vi. 106; vii. 162; ix. 16; Bowring, 121. From Cabartî's expressions it is evident that each of the main *sûḳs* also had its *şeyḫ* (presumably the *şeyḫ* of the relevant corporation). The non-Islamic communities were organized in *ḫuṭṭs*, under a *kebîr* or *ra'îs*; but the term *ḫuṭṭ* appears to have been synonymous with *ḥâra* (Lane, *Mod. Eg.*, chap. xxv). There is no reference to a chief *şeyḫ* of the corporations at Cairo prior to the period of Meḥmed-'Alî.

[5] Murâdî, i. 62; ii. 71 (the Ḥanefî muftî). In the early part of the nineteenth century the office of *şeyḫ el-meşâyiḫ* or *ra'îs* was hereditary in the family of the *Naḳîb el-Aşrâf* (Qoudsi, p. 10). *Ra'îs* at Jerusalem: Murâdî, iii. 132; at Nâblus, id. i. 11.

[6] Cab. i. 102; ii. 107/1. 237; iv. 186, &c.; *Ḳânûn-nâma* (Digeon), 249, 260; Deny, 39–40. See above, pp. 154–5.

of rival factions amongst them,[1] it would be a mistake to assume that there was no organization for common action. It is true that municipal institutions, in the strict sense, were lacking, and that any association of the general population in the government of the city would have been regarded with suspicion, if nothing more, by the authorities. At the religious festivals, and on such public occasions as the accession of a Sultan,[2] however, the corporations marched in procession; and the citizens were liable to be called out *en masse* for the defence of the city in an emergency.[3] Since they were armed,[4] the rulers always went in fear of a popular rising, and the function of the police was as much (or more) to keep them under control as to preserve public order.[5] Nevertheless, arbitrary or tyrannical conduct on the part of the governors or their subordinates was liable to provoke, and did in fact provoke, retaliatory action until justice was done on the offender.[6] The history of Syria, in particular, affords numerous examples of such concerted action by the citizens, and though rarer in Egypt, it was destined to play a decisive part at critical moments in the future course of Egyptian history. Besides this drastic method, another and more frequent form of objection was simple passive resistance. It was one thing for *Paşas* and governors to issue an order, but if they wished it to be obeyed vigorous action and some exemplary punishments were generally required.[7] Much of the apparent passivity and immobility of the population is in fact to be put down to the natural instinct of self-preservation under arbitrary rule.

As regards the population of the cities, all estimates have to be accepted with caution, and are often contradictory. In 1798 Cairo was reckoned to contain 263,000 inhabitants,[8] but it was still suffering from the effects of the famines and plagues of the previous fifteen years. Aleppo is credited by Olivier with 150,000,[9]

[1] e.g. at Nâblus: Joliffe, i. 48. For Cairo see above, p. 268, n. 6.

[2] e.g. Mich. Dam. 21, and the Maḥmal festival at Cairo.

[3] Ismâ'îl Bey called up a levy of all the inhabitants of Cairo—'*ḳâḍî*, *şeyḫs*, merchants, artisans, magribines, and "folk of the *ḥâras* and bands" '—to defend the city against Murâd and Ibrâhîm, but retained only the magribines and *ocaklîs* (Cab. ii. 13/iii. 258); another levy on the approach of the French (iii. 6–7/vi. 13–14).

[4] Cab. iii. 240; iv. 223/vii. 162; ix. 126. It must be remembered that a large proportion of the artisan population belonged to the *ocaḳs*. The lower classes, however, had no weapons other than clubs.

[5] Hence the violence shown by the police, remarked on by all travellers and residents; cf. Jomard, 725.

[6] e.g. at Alexandria (Cab. ii. 93/iv. 150); at Cairo, ii. 189/v. 85–6; at Aleppo (Ğazzî, iii. 293); and frequent risings in Syria against governors, e.g. Murâdî, ii. 32; Ḥaidar, i. 204, 205; Volney, ii. 16, 68; Olivier, ii. 335 (Urfa). It was more usual, however, to appeal to the religious leaders to intervene on their behalf with the authorities.

[7] Cf. Cab. i. 102–4; ii. 178/i. 238–40; v. 67, and ch. x, i, below.

[8] Jomard, 694 (cf. Chabrol, 8–10), *plus* 24,000 at Bûlâḳ (Jomard, 748).

[9] Olivier, ii. 301; Volney, ii. 50, estimates 100,000, but his figures are generally

Damascus and Bağdâd with about 100,000 each,[1] and the coastal towns of Syria with 5,000 to 15,000.[2] Urfa, with 30,000 to 40,000, and Moṣul, with some 65,000 inhabitants,[3] were the only large towns in the interior; the remainder were little more than large villages.[4]

II. INDUSTRY

Of all the social institutions of the Islamic East, that of industry remained, until well into the nineteenth century, the most faithful to its traditional organization and usages. Impoverished and debased though their livelihood and products might be, by comparison with the great industrial revival in the East during the tenth to the thirteenth centuries, the artisans of the eighteenth century preserved, with none but minor changes, the craft-guilds[5] and industrial processes of their medieval predecessors. The smaller village industries, where one or two craftsmen supplied local needs for pottery, wooden utensils, baked or unbaked bricks and coarse fabrics,[6] may be left out of account here, as forming rather an appendage to the structure of village life, the organization to which they belonged being that of the village, not of the craft. Similarly the weaving industries carried on in the tribes, mainly by women, important though their products might be in commerce,[7] belong to the tribal organization.

The citizen craft corporations (*aṣnâf*) varied in the details of their organization from place to place, but all followed the same general system. Each consisted of masters, journeymen or master-apprentices, and ordinary apprentices, called in Turkish *usta*, *ḳalfa*, and *çirak* respectively, organized in a rigid hierarchy under

lower than those of others. Ğazzî, i. 331, on the other hand, gives the impossible figure of 400,000, and asserts (iii. 301–2) that 87,000 perished in the famine of 1759. Russell in 1753 computed the population at about 235,000.

1 Volney, ii. 151: 80,000 at Damascus; Rousseau, 9; Olivier, ii. 388.

2 Alexandria, 20,000: Olivier, ii. 7; Rosetta, formerly 25,000: Olivier, ii. 51. Baṣra, on the contrary, is credited by Rousseau (p. 32) with 45,000 to 50,000, and Tripoli, in 1715, with 80,000 (Charles-Roux, *Les Échelles*, 8).

3 Olivier, ii. 328, 357.

4 Volney, ii. 172, 173, gives 'not more than 2,000' for Ḥomṣ and 4,000 for Ḥamâh—both figures probably very greatly underestimated—and 12,000 to 14,000 for Jerusalem (ii. 179).

5 The Arabic name was *ṣinf* or *ḥirfa*, in contemporary sources generally *ṭâ'ifa* or *kâr*. The term 'guild' is not quite satisfactory as a translation of these terms, since the powers of the medieval guilds in Europe in controlling the industry were much wider than those of the Islamic corporations. The study of these craft corporations has not progressed beyond the initial stages; see the article 'Ṣinf' in *Enyc. of Islam* (Massignon); Girard, 598 sqq.; Bowring, 117; Clot Bey, ii. 300–2.

6 See Girard, 'Mémoire sur l'Agriculture etc.', 591, 593, 594–5; and cf. Denon's *Travels* (Eng. tr. i. 210), where the village artisans are described as 'the most abject class'.

7 Especially the carpets woven by the Türkmen women in Northern Syria.—Volney, i. 360. Cf. above, p. 245.

a *şeyḫ* or head member. Every apprentice was obliged from the first to attach himself to some master, who would teach him the mystery of the craft and the traditions of the corporation, and who would vouch for him when he attained proficiency and was eligible for promotion. Only masters were permitted to open shops; and the number of shops sanctioned for each guild was strictly limited.

The privilege of owning a shop, or the authority to pursue any industrial or commercial calling, was called in Turkish *gedik*.[1] The actual premises were never the property of the shopkeeper, but were held by him on lease with an annual payment of rent. The *gedik* itself, however, was a form of property, capable of being pledged or sold (to a suitable purchaser), and passed on a master's death to his heirs. A son could step into his father's place, if he were properly qualified—that is, had attained the rank of master-apprentice in the same guild. Otherwise the *gedik* was sold by the heirs to another competent member. Fresh *gediks* could be acquired only by the payment of an advance to the Treasury, the applicant having to prove that he was in possession of the implements required for carrying on his craft. *Gediks* were of two kinds, one allowing the holder to pursue his calling wherever he wished, the other attaching him to a definite place.[2] The transferable kind seems always to have been rare, however, and to have become rarer still as time went on, no doubt because of the government's desire to maintain a firm control of the number of artisans operating in any quarter.[3]

The initiative allowed to members of guilds was, indeed, extremely small. For their transactions were limited in other ways. In the first place, no commodity of any kind might be sold above the price periodically fixed by the government. In the second, no craftsman or merchant might make or sell anything else than that sanctioned for his guild.[4] And in the third, no changes of fashion were allowed—thus stringent orders were issued soon after the beginning of our period to the cobblers and shoe-sellers of Istanbul against the manufacture by the former, and the sale by the latter,

[1] Literally 'breach', hence privilege—said to be the Turkish equivalent of the Arabic *farc*. The use of the word in this sense appears to have originated only about the year 1140 (1727–8), when it replaced the term '*ustalıḳ*' (Mastership). '*Gedik*' had until then been used to denote the custom by which trade implements were handed over without payment to purchasers or inheritors of *ustalıḳ* rights. *Belediye*, i. 652–3, 658–9. Cf. Belin, *La Propriété Foncière*, 264. The latter author was told by the historian Cevdet Paşa (about 1860) that *gediks*, in the new sense, had then been in existence for from 150 to 200 years.

[2] Called '*Havaî*' and '*Mustaḳarr*' respectively.

[3] *Belediye*, i. 659; Belin, op. cit. 266, 269. *Havaî gediks* still existed, nevertheless, into the nineteenth century.

[4] *Belediye*, i. 646. Documents of 1039 (1629–30) and 1074 (1663–4) cited.

of boots, shoes, and slippers with pointed toes,[1] 'against the ancient mode'.[2]

In the matter of price-fixing—*nerh*[3] or, in the Arab provinces, *tes'îr*—the government's aim was to defend the consumer. For the price fixed was one *above* which no wares might be sold. Vendors were at liberty to sell *below* it, if they chose; but this appears to have been uncommon. There seems to have been little or no competition between members of a guild, who had their shops all together in one street or quarter.[4] The imposition of a *nerh* was directed rather against the abuse of its monopoly rights by the guild as a whole than against price raising by individuals.

Guilds had existed in Islâm long before the foundation of the Ottoman Empire.[5] But in the latter they had developed principally from the Society of Chivalry or Virtue,[6] as represented by the *Aḫis* of Anatolia, whom we have referred to in connexion with the army. For the Ottoman guilds, like the dervishes, had at first a *ṭarîḳat*, a "way" which was none other than that of this society;[7] and though most of them had become much 'secularized' by the eighteenth century, considerable vestiges of their former organization lingered on. Thus every guild still had as it were a patron 'saint' (*pîr*), often two. These were personages of religious lore, the major being generally a Hebrew patriarch, and the minor a Companion of the Prophet. Those of the first category were believed as a rule to be the inventors of the craft or trade carried on by the guild in question. Until late in the nineteenth century every Moslem shopkeeper continued to display in his booth a verse in which the name of his *pîr* was mentioned.[8]

Again, the promotion of apprentices was signalized by the performance of a binding ceremony of initiation,[9] which took place in the presence of all the officers and masters of the guild, similar to that whereby in the mystical orders a novice became a full-fledged dervish.[10] The original ceremonies were extremely complicated,[11]

[1] '*Sivri burunlu.*'

[2] Ibid. 650. *Irade* to the *Istanbul Kazisi* dated 1222 (1807).

[3] A word of Persian origin, properly *nerḫ*. The institution of the *nerh* does not derive from the *Şeri*, and is said to have been condemned by the Prophet. Nevertheless it dates from the early days of the Caliphate; cf. Poliak, in *R.E.I.* 1936, 261. *Belediye*, i. 394. For *Kanunî Nerh* see *M.T.M.* i. 505.

[4] See above, p. 279.

[5] See *Encyclopaedia of Islâm*, iv. art. 'Ṣinf' by L. Massignon. They are thought to date from the III/IX century. Also von Kremer, *Kulturgeschichte*, ii. 186, and B. Lewis in *Economic History Review*, Nov. 1937, pp. 20–37.

[6] '*Fütüvvet*' (Arabic, *Futuwwa*). See above, p. 59.

[7] *Belediye*, i. 518, 537. Hence the masters were also called '*ehli ṭarîḳ*' (Arabic *ahl al-ṭarîḳ*). Cf. Thorning, Beiträge, 115–16.

[8] *Belediye*, i. 518, 522–4; Thorning, 83, 84.

[9] Called in Turkish '*şed bağlamak*'. *Belediye*, 8, 524.

[10] Thorning, 71, 123 sq.

[11] They involved considerable study on the part of the candidate, who was put

but with the relative 'secularization' of the guilds they were simplified.[1] The term '*peştemallîk*', used for the purchase money of a shop, is a relic of this initiation ceremony, the *peştemal*, or towel, being the object with which the candidate was bound.[2] And, if this was not the case with all, certain guilds, namely the Tanners, Cobblers, and Saddlers—the largest and most powerful—who also preserved the name '*aḫi*' for their elders, continued to use the *peştemal* in the promotion of apprentices until quite recent times.[3]

In the eighteenth century the affairs of each guild were managed by two officers, the *Kâḫyâ*[4] or steward, and the *Yiğit Başî*[5] or Chief Fellow, together with a council of elders (*iḫtiyârîye*),[6] formed by some or all of the masters. In earlier times the guild hierarchy had been headed by a number of other officers, including a *Şeyḫ* as the principal and a *Duacî*, or reciter of prayers.[7] But even where, as in the case of the Barbers' guild, these officers were still appointed as late as the last quarter of the eighteenth century, the *Kâḫyâ* and the *Yiğit Başî* now took precedence over them.[8] All the officers were originally elected by the guild elders from among their own numbers; and this procedure was still followed in the case of the *Yiğit Başî*, and often in that of the *Kâḫyâ*. But the latter post was in later times frequently given to retired officials, by way of providing them with a livelihood—a change due also partly to the fact that the *Kâḫyâ* was the representative of the guild in its dealings with the government, as well as the general manager of the guild's internal business.[9] Owing to this semi-official position, the *Kâḫyâ* was in some sense, even when he had risen from it, felt to be outside the body of the guild; so the members, in turn, dealt with the *Kâḫyâ* through the *Yiğit Başî*.[10] The word *yiğit* is another vestige of the Society of Virtue,

through an examination. Also expressions, ordinarily unintelligible, were used and interpreted by the officer called *nakîb* (see below, n. 7). Thorning, 107, 110.

[1] The absence of the necessary officers is enough to prove this.

[2] *Belediye*, i. 518. In earlier times aprons, girdles and other objects were also used, see Thorning, 140 sq. and p. 293, below.

[3] *Belediye*, i. 537.

[4] A Turkish corruption of the Persian *kat khudâ*, 'master of the house'. Though thus pronounced, the word was spelt *kethüda* in Turkish documents.

[5] See below, p. 285.

[6] The use of the word *iḫtiyâr* to mean 'old' in Turkish appears to have come from its application to these elders. As a chosen body they were called *Iḫtiyârîye*, from the Arabic *Iḫtiyâr*, 'choice'. *Belediye*, i. 578; Thorning, 13 sq.

[7] *Belediye*, i. 560. Other officers were the *nakîb*, who managed guild affairs on the *Şeyḫ*'s behalf, and whose duties later devolved on the *Kâḫyâ*; and the *çavuş*, whose duties as usher and doorkeeper were later assumed by the *Yiğit Başî*. *Belediye*, i. 561, 563, 565. For a discussion of the original officers see Thorning 99 sq. D'Ohsson, *Tableau Général*, iv. 228, is aware only of the *Kâḫyâ* and *Yiğit Başî* as guild officers.

[8] *Belediye*, i. 563.

[9] Ibid. 564–9—eighteenth-century documents cited, 574.

[10] Ibid. 574.

whose members had been called *fatâ*, a word meaning, in Arabic, an honourable and generous man. *Yiğit* is its Turkish equivalent; the guild members were *yiğits*; and the *yiğit-başi* was their head.

The relative secularization of the guilds in the eighteenth century is shown by the use of the word *lonca*, commonly derived from the Italian *loggia*,[1] for the masters' place of meeting. In earlier times this had been described by various words used for centuries before the foundation of the Ottoman Empire to denote the habitat of *Sûfîs*.[2] The change appears to have been made towards the end of the seventeenth century.[3] But why this foreign word was adopted is not clear. Nor has the whole question of the 'secularization' of the guilds been adequately explained. The author of the *Mecellei Umuru Belediye* suggests two reasons for it, namely that the old ceremonies required a higher standard of education for their proper performance than was to be met with among artisans in later times, and that the membership side by side of Moslems and unbelievers in one guild necessitated the abandonment of specifically Moslem ceremonies by these bodies.[4] But the disorganization in the seventeenth century of the *medrese* system of education, intended as it was for the training of divines, can scarcely have affected the artisan class; and there is no indication that as time went on non-Moslems came to form a larger element in the guilds than they had at first. It is true that relations between Moslems and Ḏimmis in the guilds show a definite worsening from the seventeenth century onwards, as we shall see. But the remedy applied by the government was to segregate the parties within their guilds; and this measure could only have facilitated the performance of religious ceremonies by the Moslem section. Perhaps a partial explanation may be sought, on the other hand, in the custom that grew up at the same period, according to which artisans would affiliate themselves to the corps of the Janissaries. Actually the majority of the metropolitan artisans were so affiliated in the eighteenth century;[5] whilst at the same time these artisans constituted the greater part of the Janissary corps.[6] For this attachment must have carried with it to some degree an adherence to Bektaşism. It may be, then, that the guilds no longer felt the need for an elaborate religious organization of their own.

[1] Cf. B. Kerestedjian, *Dictionnaire Étymologique de la Langue Turque*, 26, 317. But more probably it is the Spanish *lonja*, 'exchange', introduced by the Jewish refugees.

[2] Viz. *zaviye* (Arabic, *zâwiya*) and *ḫankâh* (Persian). Later also *Meydân*, *Maydân* Ali, *Meydân Odasi*. See Thorning, 121, 220.

[3] Since Evliya Çelebi (d. 1679), who deals at great length with guild affairs, makes no mention of it.

[4] *Belediye*, i. 575. [5] Ibid. 619.

[6] Seyyid Muṣṭafâ, *Netâicülvuḳûât*, iii. 85–6; Cevdet Paşa, *Tarîḫ*, i. 96.

The religious practices of the guilds had in any case a heterodox tinge—their initiatory ceremonies for instance gave a pre-eminent position to the first three *Imâms* of the Şî'a;[1] and the saint, Aḫi Evren, to whom the Tanners and the Saddlers—the strongest of all the guilds—were attached, was a focus of religious ideas of the same order as those connected with *Ḥaci Bektaş*.[2]

Again, apart from Bektaşism, the connexion between the *dervîşes* and the guilds, in so far as these were Moslem, remained close. In the first place the orders recruited their members chiefly from the artisan class.[3] And in the second, many members of the Guilds were adherents of 'Melâmism', that school of secret virtue, of which there was a centre at Istanbul.[4] It may therefore be that, though the guilds to some extent lost their character as centres of religious life, this implied no more than a reorientation of their members' devotion.

The members of the Society of Virtue had lived almost communistically, pooling their profits for their common advantage. And this principle survived among the later corporations in the maintenance of a common assistance fund,[5] to which all members made a weekly or monthly contribution. This fund, which was controlled by the *Kâḫyâ*, the *Yiğit Başî* and the masters, was used partly for religious purposes—for example yearly readings at the mosque of Eyup in Ramazân, accompanied by a distribution of *pilâv* to the public—and partly for the aid of guild members in case of illness or other distress. Again, if any member died indigent, his funeral expenses would be defrayed from this source. Finally, those members who were in temporary need of funds, particularly if they wished to extend their business, might borrow from the common fund at a rate of 1 per cent.

The fund was further enlarged by special contributions. Thus masters who desired to advance apprentices or master-apprentices to a higher rank would contribute certain fixed sums towards the expenses involved in the ceremonies by which this advancement was accompanied.[6] Every few years, again, sometimes ten, sometimes twenty, the guild would hold festivities, lasting for more than a week, at some delectable spot such as the Kâğidḫane.[7] These entertainments were not only a pleasure but also a source

[1] Thorning, 60–1, 81, 85–6, 149; *Belediye*, i. 523; cf. Abdulbaki, *Melâmilik ve Melâmiler*, 167–8.

[2] *Belediye*, i. 548. Cf. Hasluck, *Christianity and Islam under the Sultans*, 505, for observations on Aḫi Evren. For Ḥaci Bektaş see p. 64, above.

[3] Thorning, 74.

[4] *Belediye*, i. 552 sq., see ch. xiii below.

[5] *Ta'âvun Sandiği*. Cf. Cab. iii. 6; iv. 198/vi. 14 (erroneous); ix. 67.

[6] 50 *kuruş* in the case of an ordinary, 300 *kuruş* in that of a master-apprentice (date not specified).

[7] The 'Sweet Waters of Europe'.

of profit to the members, as they fulfilled the functions of a modern exhibition or advertising campaign. This applies as well to the participation of the guilds in the official rejoicings ordered by the sultans from time to time, generally on the occasion of the birth, or circumcision, of royal children. The guilds would then parade with their emblems,[1] and, as when they held their festivities, would, if their craft were such as to make them acceptable, present the Sultan and the chief ministers with examples of their work. The expenses both of the festivities and of the parades were defrayed by special levies on the members. The guilds also owned common property in the way of 'plate' and cooking utensils. These were either bought, or received by way of a return gift from some Sultan, and were used on their days of festival.[2]

The regulation of guild affairs by the government was in the hands of the *ḳâḍî*. Thus all orders from the Sultan or the Sublime Porte regarding the guilds of the capital were addressed to the Istanbul *Ḳazisi*. Originally the latter's authority extended only to Istanbul proper, the 'Three Towns'[3] of Eyup, Ğalaṭa, and Uskudar having each its own *ḳâḍî*. But in guild matters it was found to be more practical for the Istanbul *Ḳazisi* to deal with the artisans and merchants of the whole area, chiefly because by far the greater number were to be found in Istanbul itself. The matter was never definitely regularized, however; and except in cases regarding which special orders were issued, the other three *ḳâḍîs* conserved their respective jurisdictions.[4] The Istanbul *Ḳazisi* had also several deputies stationed in various quarters of the city, as well as other 'roving' deputies to survey on his behalf the conduct of the guilds in matters of prices, weights, and measures. The responsibility for this surveillance rested in principle with the *ḳâḍî*; but in fact it was checked by no less than three other officials. Thus both the Grand *Vezîr* and the Ağa of the Janissaries would, like the *ḳâḍî* himself, make periodical rounds of the markets, accompanied by men with scales, to see that no shopkeeper was giving short weight; and a still closer and more regular watch was kept by the officer known as *Muḥtesib*, or Inspector, and his men.[5]

[1] Cf. D'Ohsson, *Tableau*, iv. 410, '*Tous sont richement vêtus, et chaque corps avance séparément à la tête d'une espèce de char de triomphe décoré des symboles, des instrumens, et des productions même de chaque art et de chaque métier.*'

[2] *Belediye*, i. 579–83. Cf. account published in *Revue du Monde Musulman*, ix. 171 sq. (1909).

[3] *bilâdi selâsa.*

[4] *Belediye*, i. 302–3; cf. D'Ohsson, *Tableau Général*, iv. 228.

[5] This multiplication was due to the fact that the Grand *Vezîr* was responsible for all governmental affairs, whether they were delegated to subordinates or not, and that the *Ağa* of the Janissaries was responsible for the general policing of Istanbul proper, with the exception of certain quarters round the palace. *Belediye*, i. 885. Though the word *Muḥtesib* (Arabic, *muḥtasib*), an inheritance

Throughout the Empire to all cities and towns that boasted a *ḳâḍî*, there was also appointed one of these inspectors.[1] The *Muḥtesib* was concerned, unlike the *ḳâḍî*, exclusively with the affairs of the guilds and with the collection of various dues on commodities and transactions.[2] A special due was levied on all shopkeepers to furnish a salary for him and his men; and, since one of the Inspector's duties was to collect this revenue, it had come, like other revenue-collecting posts, to be farmed out by the year.[3] In Istanbul the Inspector had under his command a force of thirty-one men, known as *Kol Oğlans*.[4]

The Inspector had authority to punish offending shopkeepers summarily, his office differing in principle from that of the *ḳâḍî* thereby, since the *ḳâḍî* was supposed to decree penalties only after hearing witnesses in his court.[5] It appears, however, that when the *ḳâḍî* made his rounds he dispensed with formalities no less than did the other officials—for the procedure of the Grand *Vezîr* and the *Yeniçeri Ağasî* was similar to that of the Inspector.

The punishment of offending guild members was greatly complicated by the enrolment of the greater number in the corps of the Janissaries. For an ancient *ḳânûn* laid it down that a Janissary might be punished only by his own officers; and this still held good, though the Janissary guildsmen were soldiers only in name. If one of them was brought to the *ḳâḍî*'s court charged with some offence, therefore, the *ḳâḍî* was obliged to hand him over to the Janissary officers. This enrolment also undermined the authority of the *Kâḥyâs* and elders to some extent. For by their original regulations they were empowered, without appeal to any higher authority, to suspend offending members from the pursuit of their craft.[6] The lightest offences, when dealt with by the other officers, were punished by beating. The culprit was forthwith bastinadoed in front of his shop. For more grievous misdemeanours, and especially when they were committed not for the first

from the early days of Islam, was also used in Ottoman official language, a more usual designation of this functionary was *Iḥtisâb Ağasi*. Cf. M.T.M. ii. 504–6, *Kanunî Divanî Çarşembe* (for *Vezîrs* rounds).

[1] *Belediye*, i. 327.

[2] This was an Ottoman peculiarity. Under the caliphate the *Muḥtasib* was a general censor of morals, charged with the promotion of good and the prevention of evil. See e.g. al-Mâwardî, *Al-Aḥkâm al-Sulṭâniya*.

[3] *Belediye*, i. 327–9.

[4] Fifteen of these men were called '*Gedikli*', because they held their posts by virtue of a *gedik*, which like the *gediks* of shopkeepers was hereditary. In the event of a *gedikli's* dying without a son, the place was filled by the senior of the other sixteen men, who were called '*Mülâzim*'. The number of *Kol Oğlans* was increased during the eighteenth century to fifty-six.

[5] *Belediye*, i. 309.

[6] A man so suspended was said to be '*yolsuz*'—without a way. For more serious offences, such as theft, the culprit might even be expelled from the craft—Qoudsi, 32.

time, the penalty was imprisonment, with or without hard labour, for two or three months, or indefinitely. Janissary and ordinary guild members were supposed to be on the same footing in this respect, though they were confined in different prisons.[1] In cases where guildsmen were discovered selling badly or wrongly made goods, these were seized and destroyed as well.[2]

Most of the trades and handicrafts of the Empire were carried on by Moslems and Dimmis alike. Certain guilds, however, were reserved to Moslems only, for instance those of the druggists and house-painters; whilst about nine-tenths of the trade in foodstuffs was also kept in their hands.[3] In other trades Moslems and Dimmis at first belonged to the guilds without distinction. Although Mehmed the Conqueror had formed the various categories of Dimmis into 'nations', self-governing in religious affairs, the Christian guilds already existing in Constantinople were merged in those of the victors. There seems to have been a strong resemblance, as in so many Byzantine and Moslem institutions, between the guild-systems of the two communities. But one of these resemblances lay in the religious character of both;[4] and it has yet to be discovered how the resulting obstacles to union were overcome. The mystical, comparatively latitudinarian nature of the '*Ahi*' cult may have made matters easier. In any case, united they were. From about the middle of the seventeenth century relations between the two sections grew less amicable, however. Though as usual, this development was not uniform throughout the whole range of guilds, the two classes then took to meeting in separate lodges; and later the Dimmis acquired the right of electing their own *Yiğit Başis*. Until much later the *Kâhyâs* continued in all cases to be Moslem; but eventually this office as well was granted in some instances to non-Moslems.[5] And during the eighteenth century the Dimmis of some guilds appealed to the *Dîvân* for permission to hold their periodical festivities apart. They complained that their Moslem colleagues—who no doubt used their name of Janissary in this as in other matters to terrorize their victims—had sought to make them bear the whole cost.[6]

A more fundamental division of the guilds than this of religion was that between merchants and craftsmen.[7] Thus it was not until the word *gedik* had lost its connexion with the implements

[1] *Belediye*, i. 637–40. Janissaries were imprisoned in the Rumeli Hisar for slight, and at Kilidülbahir in the Dardanelles for grave, offences. Ordinary artisans were imprisoned at the Ağa Kapisi jail.

[2] See *Belediye*, i. 639, for an order dated 1131 (1718–19) of the *Istanbul Kazisi* for some copper vessels, on sale though unfit for use, to be thrown into the sea. Sometimes they were exposed outside the offender's shop—Qoudsi, 32.

[3] Ibid. 645. [4] Thorning, 79. [5] *Belediye*, i. 570, 574, 577.

[6] Ibid. 584 sq. Eighteenth-century documents cited.

[7] A great many of the craftsmen, however, sold their own products; and

of a craft[1] that it might properly be used of merchant guilds. In their case, moreover, apprenticeship necessarily played a less important part especially since the opportunities for skilful dealing were so much circumscribed by government control. But there were also guilds of persons outside both these categories. For on the one hand certain 'intellectual workers', such as secretaries, physicians, panegyrists and even students, had each their corporation with its patron, its officers, ceremonies, &c., so, on the other, did the farmers—at any rate those of the district round Istanbul.[2] Indeed, even the pursuit of disreputable and criminal callings was organized in the same way; so there were guilds of beggars, prostitutes, pickpockets, thieves, and other evil-doers. The criminal guilds had of course no *Kâhyâs* recognized by the authorities, though they paid taxes to the police, and some of them proudly acknowledged patron 'saints'.[3]

Hostility to governmental control was to be expected in the criminals; but in fact it was to some extent traditional in the guilds as a whole. For not only was it a revolutionary movement that had first brought guilds into being in Islâm;[4] but the '*Ahi*' organization, from which the Ottoman guilds were immediately descended, had had its heyday in the anarchy that followed the Mongol invasion of Asia Minor in the thirteenth century. One of its very aims at that time, indeed, was to organize opposition to all government agents;[5] and in the neighbourhood of Ankara and Sivas some groups of *Ahis* had even set up their own administration.[6] No doubt it was partly for this reason that the Ottoman authorities sought to maintain so tight a hold on all the activity of the guilds. Yet, even so, some of them maintained relics of their former independence in certain privileges. Thus both the Tanners and the Saddlers of the Capital had been able to exact an order

'retail' shopkeepers who carried on no craft themselves were not designated by the word for merchant, *tâcir*, which was reserved for certain large-scale dealers, particularly in morocco leather and oil. *Belediye*, i. 668.

[1] See above, p. 282.

[2] *Belediye*, i. 500.

[3] Ibid. 501. Cf. *Revue du Monde Musulman*, ix. 148. Criminal guilds were an inheritance from the pre-Ottoman world of Islâm—see Thorning, 211, and von Kremer, *Kulturgeschichte*, ii. 187. Several of the great fairs dedicated to *dervîş* saints in Egypt, notably those of Sîdi'l-Bedawî at Ṭanta, were (even down to the middle of the nineteenth century) utilized as occasions of public display by the guilds of jugglers, prostitutes, &c. (cf. e.g. Denon, *Travels*, iii. 93–4; Couvidou, *L'Égypte Contemporaine* (*c.* 1870), 236–7; Cab. i. 230–1; iii. 39–40/ii. 178; vi. 84–5). The prostitutes paid an annual rent to the keepers of the shrine of Ṭanta, which rent was abolished (but only temporarily) by 'Alî Bey (Cab. i. 306/iii. 7–8). When a *Paşa* of Egypt in 1730 abolished the drinking-shops and prostitutes' booths in Cairo, he found it necessary to recompense the intendant of the police and his subordinates for their loss (id. i. 144/ii. 1).

[4] That of the Carmathians. Cf. *Encyclopaedia of Islam*, art. 'Ṣinf' referred to above.

[5] See Ibn Baṭṭûṭa, ii. 261. [6] *Belediye*, i. 550.

from Mehmed the Conqueror forbidding the police to enter their markets, which was regularly confirmed by his successors. Other quarters in Istanbul enjoyed a like privilege, namely the Egyptian Market, the *Bezistân*,[1] and the street of the linen-weavers. The Tanners also, both of the capital and of Edirne, preserved another remarkable custom of the Society of Virtue. If any murderer or thief fell into their clutches, instead of delivering him up to the authorities, they would take him in hand themselves and train him till he could take his place among them as an honest artisan.

The power of individual guilds in preserving such rights depended of course on their size: those of the Tanners and Saddlers happened to have an especially large membership, whereas others were comparatively small. Certain guilds engaged in cognate crafts and trades, however, gained in importance by being organized in groups. Thus in Istanbul the cobblers, Moslem and Ḏimmi, engaged in the making of various kinds of boots, shoes, and slippers, together with the vendors of these products, were so linked together, the *Kâẖyâ* of the shoemakers in the Great Market being the head of all the subsidiary guilds as well as of his own, with the right of entry to their lodges, where he would inspect wares for sale. Such groups of guilds would often acknowledge a patriarch as their common patron, each having as its subsidiary patron a companion of the Prophet. How dependent the smaller guilds were upon Government support may be seen from the case of the tobacco-sellers. Tobacco smoking had been introduced into the Empire early in the seventeenth century, and was for a long time prohibited by the government. The then world of Islam, however, was one in which no innovations were provided for; the Gate of Interpretation was firmly shut; and no certain estimate of the standing of tobacco was obtainable. The doctors disagreed; but the public welcomed the new pleasure with growing enthusiasm; the Divan was obliged to lift its ban; and the trade developed. The tobacco sellers, however, though they might be privately organized, could obtain no redress against surreptitious sale by other tradesmen. It was not until 1725 that they procured the appointment of a *Kâẖyâ* and were formally recognized as a guild.

The strict control of guild affairs exercised by the government was not, however, wholly directed to curbing their tendency to insubordination. It had another object in view, namely the protection of the workers themselves. Thus it would sanction the creation of fresh *gediks* for the opening of shops and workshops only when the demand for the commodities to be sold or produced

[1] Or *Bezâzistân*, or *Bedisten*, literally 'Cloth-hall', the repository of precious merchandise, such as jewels and rich stuffs. Each was in charge of two *Kâẖyâs* appointed by the government.—D'Ohsson, iv, 209.

in them justified such a measure; and would seek to prevent unemployment in one place by prohibiting the importation of competing wares from another. It also guarded their interests by regulating the rents paid for *gedik* establishments, which were all either *wakf* or private property. Moreover, though the government dealt with the guilds in all ordinary cases through their *Kâhyâs*, and on its own behalf appointed the *Muhtesib* and his men to scrutinize their transactions, the guild elders were at perfect liberty to appeal to the *kâdî* in his court, and frequently did so, for the redress of wrongs committed by both these officers.

In the days of the Society of Virtue apprentices entering a guild were given two 'fathers in the path' and two 'brothers in the path', to supervise their training and conduct. The relationship between a master and his apprentice bore also a close resemblance to that of a *dervîş* adept to his novice. A very strong sentiment of solidarity was thereby induced among the members of a guild, which, rather than the state or religion, became their focus of loyalty; and this sentiment survived the process of secularization. The adherence of large numbers of artisans to the Janissaries must have divided their allegiance in some measure; but their solidarity was fostered by the proximity of their shops. Moreover the severe restrictions imposed by the government on their operations made competition between them all but impossible, and gave their desire for gain a minimum of outlet. Their attitude is strikingly illustrated by the custom that prevailed until the guilds fell into decay. Shopkeepers who had already made their first sale of the day would hand on a prospective purchaser till he came to one of their fellows that had not yet done so. In general, moreover, the level of honesty among the guildsmen was notably high, the Moslems here contrasting favourably with unbelievers in the opinion of European observers.

In the Arabic provinces, so far as our scanty information goes, the industrial organization seems to have been on the whole freer than it was in Istanbul.[1] Its pre-Ottoman basis had been relatively little affected by the peculiarly Turkish usages derived from the *ahîs*, here, as elsewhere, the Turkish governors having been content to leave old custom undisturbed. Hence the crafts were still administered each by its *şeyh* or *kebîr* (whose office was nominally elective, but in practice often hereditary within a given family),

[1] The corporations are referred to in almost all works relating to Egypt, &c., but usually without much detail, e.g. Lane, chap. iv; Clot-Bey, i. 336; Bowring, 117; Chabrol, 321–3 (and cf. 268); Jomard, 698–9. The only detailed source is Elia Qoudsi, 'Notice sur les Corporations de Damas', publié par Carlo Landberg (in Arabic), in *Actes du VIème Congrès des Orientalistes*, 2me Partie (Leiden, 1885). On the craft corporations at Cairo see now also M. Clerget, *Le Caire*, ii. 130–7.

assisted by a *ṣâwîṣ*.[1] To a great extent the whole organization was hereditary, so much so, indeed, that certain specialized crafts were limited to a few families, or even to a single family.[2] The functions of the *ṣeyẖ* are defined as: to hold and preside at meetings of members of the craft, to keep the corporation together and to punish those guilty of acts to its prejudice, to find work for the artisans and assign masters to them, and to discuss with the authorities all matters connected with the corporation. The chief of these matters was the annual tax, imposed upon the members of the corporation collectively, which the *ṣeyẖ* repartitioned amongst the members proportionately to their resources.[3]

Down to the eighteenth century, the religious affiliations of the crafts remained intact. They were manifested outwardly at the public religious festivals, when each corporation paraded under its banner,[4] but were naturally more intimate in private gatherings and ceremonies. In spite of their possibly heretical origins, the craft lodges in the Arab lands seem by now to have been (like el-Azhar) thoroughly orthodox, in the *Ṣûfî* interpretation of the term at least. Here, as in Turkey, the principal ceremony was that of 'binding' (*ṣedd*) an apprentice on admission to the corporation.[5] Although the details varied, the following is stated by Qoudsi to have been typical of the ceremonies at Damascus. At a meeting of the craft, the candidate for admission was invested by the *naḳîb* (here the representative of the Chief Şeyẖ of the Corporations) with a shawl or girdle, in which three or more knots were tied, symbolic of the oaths of brotherhood to be taken and given. The knots were untied by the *ṣeyẖ* of the craft, the *ṣâwîṣ*, and the candidate's master, with appropriate formulae. One of the masters was then designated as his 'craft-father', and the new member took the oath of loyalty to the craft and made symbolic presents to the officers. The ceremony ended with religious recitations and prayers, and a simple festival given by him to all the members.[6] Several candidates might be admitted at the same

[1] The *ṣeyẖ* was elected by agreement, never by majority vote. If the masters failed to agree, the *ṣeyẖ el-meṣâyiẖ* appointed one of the candidates. The election was followed by a ceremony of confirmation, at which the *ṣeyẖ* took an oath (Qoudsi 13–14). The *ṣâwîṣ* also was elected by the craft, and acted as the *ṣeyẖ*'s agent and messenger, but had no judicial authority (id. 15). The 'crier' (*munâdî*) of the Cairo corporations (Cab. iv. 99/viii. 221) was probably the same officer.

[2] e.g. the art of wall-painting in gilt was preserved at Damascus in one family (hence called el-D̲ahabî), and was lost about the beginning of the nineteenth century (el-Maʿlûf, p. 24) (see p. 294, n. 2).

[3] The corporation of linen-weavers in the Fayyûm, for example, was taxed at 20,000 paras annually (Girard 598); cf. also Jomard, 698.

[4] See the descriptions in Lane's *Modern Egyptians*, chap. xxv.

[5] Although Girard says (p. 603) that there was no apprenticeship in the strict sense, the control exercised over learners was very strict; cf. Qoudsi, 16.

[6] Cf. Lane's description of the ceremony of admission into certain of the

time, and any member of the craft was at liberty to oppose the admission of a candidate by displaying a specimen of faulty work done by him. A second ceremony of 'binding' was held when an artisan was promoted to master, but it was less elaborate, the candidate simply promising to observe the usages of the craft.[1]

Here, too, the non-Moslem members and corporations[2] were placed in a somewhat anomalous position as a result of these religious associations.[3] They were not, however, excluded from participating in the craft ceremonies and organization, and non-Moslem members of a mixed corporation were assigned Moslem 'craft-fathers'. On the other hand, their religious usages were respected, the Lord's Prayer, for example, being substituted for the Moslem oaths on the admission of a Christian candidate.[4]

Arab lands

The number[5] and organization of the craft corporations gave them a considerable influence in political life; and since the *şeyḫs* of corporations had the right of entry to the *Paşa* in the time of Meḥmed ʿAlî,[6] it may safely be assumed that they possessed the same right in the eighteenth century, and exercised it upon occasion.

Their influence upon the administration and conduct of the governors (as well as the mutinous character commonly attributed to their members) was enhanced in the Ottoman period by the merging of the Janissary and other local *ocaḳs* into the craft corporations. Parallel to the development which we have already

crafts in Cairo (chap. xxvii ad fin.), and the diploma of admission into the corporation of bow-makers quoted by Cabartî (ii. 214–16/v. 136–9), which brings out very clearly the moral character of the rite. Qoudsi estimates the expense to the candidate at from forty to a hundred francs all told.

[1] Qoudsi, 28.

[2] Such as the Christian corporations of masons and sculptors at Damascus and the Jewish slaughterers at Aleppo. The masons' and builders' corporation at Aleppo was apparently composed of Moslems and Christians. The shoemakers were divided into several craft sections; certain kinds of shoes were made by Moslems only, other kinds by Christians only, and some by both and by Jews as well, but they apparently formed a single corporation. Amongst other mixed corporations were those of scribes and calligraphers, jewellers, coppersmiths, and carpenters (see Ǧazzî, i. 101 sqq.; el-Maʿlûf, 'Industries of Damascus' in *Journal of the Damascus Chamber of Commerce* (in Arabic), 1922). One very curious mixed corporation, whose existence is characteristic of the tolerant social conditions in the Moslem cities, was that of the 'bouffons, farceurs and parasites' at Damascus, with one Moslem and one Christian şeyḫ, and a burlesque ceremony of admission (Qoudsi, 30).

[3] It is not unlikely that one of the objects underlying the formation of these religious affiliations in the first place (during the Middle Ages) was the peaceful conversion of the artisan class to the Islamic faith.

[4] Qoudsi, 29.

[5] An exact enumeration is not yet possible; Cabartî usually mentions 70 or 72 corporations at Cairo, but in one passage (relating to 1814) seems to imply the existence of as many as 106 (iv, 198–200/ix. 67–72). Bowring (in 1838) gives the number at Cairo as 164 (p. 117), but this figure is perhaps accounted for by monopolizations. In any case many of these were mercantile or other non-artisan corporations.

[6] Bowring, 117.

traced in Istanbul itself,[1] the *ocaḳs* of Cairo, Damascus, Aleppo, Bağdâd, and the lesser cities had gradually filtered into the local crafts and in many cases controlled or even monopolized the corporations. At the beginning of the eighteenth century, it could be asserted that the corporations of Cairo were composed mainly of soldiers and soldiers' sons,[2] and although in practice these artisans (who were called by the Turkish name of *yoldaş*, Arabicized as *îlḍâş*[3]) were exempt from military service, their names were still inscribed on the registers of the *ocaḳs*, they still enjoyed a share in the distributions made to the troops, and they retained a claim to the protection of their regiments.[4] At Bağdâd the population is said to have been 'almost entirely composed of Janissaries, engaged in commerce and industry'.[5] The same feature is also attested in Syria[6] and was particularly marked at Tripoli.[7]

Compared with their medieval antetypes, the industrial products of Egypt and Western Asia at the end of the eighteenth century were on the whole primitive and coarse. For this regression there were several causes. The general economic exhaustion of the Near East, caused by the wars and natural disasters of the fourteenth and fifteenth centuries, had been reinforced by the transference of the bulk of the Indian trade to the African sea-route in the sixteenth. The hereditary structure of industry made easy the transplanting of whole crafts, particularly the finer and more specialized crafts, the secrets of which were jealously guarded by a few families.[8] Apart from such administrative interference, it not infrequently happened that a craft limited to a single family died out, and occasionally a larger but still specialized craft was destroyed by a natural catastrophe.[9] An insidious factor was the

[1] See p. 182, above.

[2] Cabartî, i. 37/i. 88; cf. Volney, i. 143: 'Aujourd'hui les janissaries, les azabs, et les cinq autres corps ne sont qu'un ramas d'artisans, de goujats et de vagabonds qui gardent les portes de qui les paye' (an obvious exaggeration since 'les cinq autres corps' would include the Mamlûks themselves). Similarly the Janissaries at Alexandria: Volney, i. 7.

[3] Cab. ii. 131, 135; iii. 92, &c.; see above, p. 59, n. 1.

[4] Cf. the attempt of the *ḳapudan paşa* Ḥasan to regulate this situation: Cab. ii. 135/iv. 260 (very loose). It was apparently the regular practice of Ottoman troops, on entering a city, that each soldier associated himself with a local member of his own craft, and assured him 'protection' in return for a half-share in his profits, much to the indignation of the local artisans and tradesmen (Cab. ii. 116; iii. 89/iv. 209; vi. 169).

[5] Rousseau, *Bagdad*, p. 9.

[6] 'Ces prétendus soldats ne sont plus que des artisans et des paysans aussi ignorans que les autres, mais beaucoup moins dociles. Lorsqu'un pacha commet des abus d'autorité, ils sont toujours les premiers à lever l'étendard de la sédition' (Volney, ii. 43). But it is difficult to believe that the janissaries engaged in agriculture as well as industry.

[7] Volney, ii. 68.

[8] Tîmûr, for example, carried off large numbers of craftsmen from Damascus to his capital, Samarḳand; and the transfer of the capital from Cairo to Istanbul involved some transplanting of industry, even if there is no truth in the story that after the capture of Cairo Selîm removed a great many artisans to Istanbul.

[9] Such as the great earthquake of 1759 in Syria, which is supposed to have

growing competition of European goods—especially textile fabrics—with native products, owing to the preference which the wealthy and powerful families showed for the former.[1] But there can be little question that the main reasons were political and administrative—the lack of positive encouragement of industry, except by rare governors, the languishing economic conditions of the Near East as a whole under Ottoman rule, and the conservatism of the corporations and artisans,[2] supplemented by the exactions and peculations of Turkish and Mamlûk governors and officials. On the other hand, the absorption of all the Arab lands in the same imperial structure, together with the lands on the northern coasts of the Mediterranean Sea, opened up new paths of economic intercourse, which stimulated industry; and it would not be surprising to find (if only reliable data were available) that what they had lost in the quality was offset by some considerable increase in the quantity of their manufactures. Nor were all the movements of industry in the one direction only; in Syria at least, new crafts or sections of crafts were introduced during the Ottoman period either from other centres or to meet new needs.[3]

In general the industries of the Ottoman lands stood upon a sound economic basis, each area utilizing mainly the raw materials produced in it, and where necessary importing from the neighbouring regions what it required in exchange for its finished products. The provincial towns were engaged mainly in the working up of local products for consumption within their own districts, but in the principal cities and a few other centres the main industries were organized on a large scale for export. In most cases, it is clear that we have to do with corporations of small master-craftsmen, carrying on their trade as a house industry, although many may have had relatively large installations or establishments served by a number of journeymen and apprentices.[4] The mention of weaving 'factories' at Damietta and Rosetta[5] also suggests a concentration of looms under one roof and organized on capitalist lines.[6]

destroyed the ateliers of the makers of *ḳâṣânî* tiles at Damascus (al-Ma'lûf, op. cit. 16–17), and which ruined the town of Ba'albek (Volney, ii. 183).

[1] Cf. Girard, 590.

[2] All observers comment on the routine character of industry, the worke possessing a mechanical but unintelligent skill developed to 'a kind of instinct' (Denon's *Travels*, i. 277), and completely ignorant of the principles of their art (Thornton, *Turkey*,[2] i. 101); cf. Volney, i. 174, ii. 285; Bowring, 57.

[3] e.g. importation of new tailoring crafts at Damascus by Ottoman pashas: al-Ma'lûf, p. 33 (perhaps—to judge by its Turkish name of *alâca* ('striped')—the important industry of manufacturing striped cotton and silk garments was one of these); an example of a new industry was that of making mouthpieces for water-pipes, at Aleppo.

[4] Cf. Murâdî, i. 167 (Seyyid Maḥmûd al-Falâḳasnî).

[5] Girard, 601–2.

[6] The daily wage of a weaver was from eight paras upwards: Girard, 595, 597, 605.

The leading industry in most centres was, as it has always been, the manufacture of cotton, wool, and silk textiles. The spinning was usually done by women as a household occupation. Cotton stuffs were woven in all important centres in ʿIrâḳ, Syria, and Egypt. It was the principal industry at Ṣaydâ and Gaza,[1] and there were extensive cotton manufactures at Maḥallet el-Kebîr, Benî Suêf, and in Upper Egypt. When local supplies of cotton ran short, it was imported by Cairene merchants from Syria.[2] Linen-weaving was from time immemorial a staple industry in Egypt, especially in the Delta, where every town of any size had several hundred looms. Their products, as well as the coarse linen packing-cloth of the Fayyûm, had a steady market in Syria and Turkey.[3] Wool-weaving was carried on in the Fayyûm and the Delta, the former specializing in white shawls (the weekly export of these to Cairo sometimes reached as many as two thousand shawls), the latter in woollen garments;[4] also in Northern Syria and ʿIrâḳ.[5] Silk-weaving was carried on not only in Syria, but the raw silk was exported also to Egypt and worked up into a variety of articles in Cairo and the towns of the Delta, part of the produce being re-exported to Syria.[6] The silk-weaving industry supported also a number of auxiliary trades: dyeing (the rose dye of Cairo being especially noted), embroidery, and tassel-making,[7] and the manufacture of gold and silver thread (at Cairo and Aleppo). The cotton and wool industries similarly gave employment to large corporations of carders. In addition to textiles, the weaving industries included mat-making, generally carried on as a local industry, but specialized in a few places where mats of a superior quality were manufactured.[8]

[1] Volney, ii. 99, 208; he estimates about five hundred looms in Gaza.

[2] Girard, 594–7, 601; about two thousand cotton weavers in M. el-Kebîr, and five to six hundred at Benî Suêf. It is important to note that the cotton industry in Egypt was in a flourishing condition long before the period of Meḥmed ʿAlî. Thornton (*Turkey*², i. 67) cites 'the silk, linen, and cotton stuffs of Cairo' among the most highly skilled manufactures in the Ottoman dominions. Cf. also Volney on the quality of the cotton fabrics of Damascus (ii. 155).

[3] Girard, 597–600. The prepared flax was bought by the women in the markets, and the spun thread sold by them at four paras the skein.

[4] Girard, 598–600: the Fayyûm industry was taxed at two paras per loom per week.

[5] The data for Aleppo are taken mainly from Ğazzî, i. 101 sqq.; those relating to ʿIrâḳ from Rousseau's *Description du Pachalik de Bagdad*.

[6] Girard, 601–2; Olivier, ii. 9; Blumenau, 306. According to Jewish sources, most of the silk weavers at Cairo were Jews.

[7] These were carried out at Aleppo mostly by women, according to Ğazzî (loc. cit.), but at Cairo there was a corporation of silk cord and tassel-makers (ʿ*aḳḳâdîn*: Cab. i. 350/iii. 89).

[8] e.g. in the Fayyûm and at Menûf in the Delta, the latter occupying six or seven hundred workmen. The reeds were supplied by the Gawâbît Arabs from the Wâdî Naṭrûn, and the mats were exported to Cairo, Syria, and Turkey—Girard, 604–5.

The manufacture of oil and oil products occupied several industries. In Egypt, oil was manufactured in most towns for local consumption from the seed of lettuce, carthamus, colza, flax, or sesame, lettuce oil being also exported to Arabia from Upper Egypt. This manufacture was remarkable for requiring the most expensive machines used in Egypt, the price of an oil-press rising to four hundred dollars.[1] In Syria the universal culture of the olive supplied the raw materials for an extensive soap-making industry, especially in Palestine and Aleppo,[2] where there was also a smaller candle-making industry. Among the lesser industries may be mentioned the distillation of rose-water in the Fayyûm;[3] the manufacture of loaf sugar and molasses in Upper Egypt;[4] the manufacture of sal-ammoniac, chiefly from refuse dumps, in Cairo and the Delta;[5] the production of salt by evaporation, and of saltpeter;[6] and iron-smelting in the Lebanon.[7] An important Egyptian industry, the incubation of chickens, was largely a monopoly of the provincial governors, who farmed out the incubators to intendants, that of Luxor, for example, at a rate of thirty dollars a month.[8]

The minor and more specialized arts and crafts were confined to the principal cities. The wood and metal-working crafts were as strongly represented at Cairo, where practically all the raw materials had to be imported, as in the Syrian towns; but there was little demand for luxurious or artistic furniture, and these

[1] Girard, 605–7. In general, the employment of machines was hindered not only by the cost of installation and working, but also because the labour of men and animals was less expensive, owing to the cheapness of living and low wages.

[2] The soda was supplied by Beduin Arabs, who obtained it by burning the alkaline desert plants (Volney, ii. 196; Russell, 18). Alkali was even exported from Alexandria to Syria for this purpose (Savary, i. 44), but Alexandria itself maintained a number of soap factories with oil imported from Crete (Olivier, ii. 9).

[3] Girard, 609.

[4] At Farşût and Aḫmîm; an interesting case, since it was a joint enterprise between a group of Mamlûks and manufacturers, the former supplying land, buildings, and materials, the latter the workmen, who received a daily wage of six paras: Girard, 586, 610–11. The average sale price of loaf sugar was ten dollars per *ḳanṭâr* of 150 *roṭls*; according to Jomard (716) the finest refined sugar 'qui approche de celui de Hambourg' sold at 60 paras the roṭl. On the increased demand for Egyptian sugar in the nineties see Olivier, ii. 172.

[5] Girard, 611–13. The factory at Manşûra occupied thirty workmen, who were paid 2½ dollars per month in addition to their food. Sal-ammoniac was one of the principal exports of Egypt, which at one time supplied the whole of Europe; but Blumenau (p. 308) remarks that owing to its impurity it required a second sublimation at Marseilles.

[6] Girard, 616–17.

[7] al-Ma'lûf, 13–14. A subsidiary of this was the manufacture of fire-arms. Volney describes the primitive methods used in founding the iron, and compares them with the *fonte catalane* of the Pyrenees (ii. 287).

[8] Girard, 613–15. Eggs were bought at eight to ten paras per hundred plus one-quarter of the chickens hatched; the workmen also were paid in chickens.

industries were everywhere in decay.[1] Syrian Christians and Armenians almost monopolized the profession of jeweller in all countries, the Jews having a special function in Egypt as brokers of the precious metals.[2] Glass-making was a traditional industry in Hebron, and was introduced from there into Damascus in the early Ottoman period.[3] Each industry was concentrated in a special quarter of the town, or in a separate *sûḳ* (bazaar), in accordance with the traditional corporative organization.[4]

While fishing was everywhere engaged in, organized fisheries existed only on Lakes Burlus and Menzâla in the Delta. The fishing rights on the former were farmed out for 3,300 dollars annually to a bey, who employed about four hundred fishermen. Additional men were engaged in the middle of spring for the catching and preparation of botargo.[5] The fishing on Lake Menzâla appears to have been carried on mainly by an association of fishermen, centred in the township of Maṭarîya, who paid a boat tax to the *Paşa.* Such fish as were not sold fresh were sent to Damietta for curing and exported thence to Cairo and various parts of the Levant, chiefly for the use of the oriental Christians.[6] Lastly, the large number of boats employed for all transport services on the Nile and its canals provided a valuable—indeed indispensable—occupation and source of income for the mass of those villagers who were engaged in agriculture during the winter only, and whose profits on their crops were swallowed up by the heavy taxation.[7] A proportion of the population of the coastal towns also served as seamen in the coasting vessels.[8]

III. COMMERCE

Compared with the structure of agriculture and industry that of commerce was complex and multiform.[9] The internal com-

[1] The art of the coppersmiths alone was allowed by M. Girard to have been *assez avancé*—Girard, 617–19. At Aleppo the coppersmiths were Christians for the most part; at Damascus they were (and are) Jews.

[2] Samuel-Bernard, *Monnoies*, p. 399; cf. *Ḳânûn-nâma*, ap. Digeon, 276, and Cabartî, iv. 205/ix. 82.

[3] Volney, ii. 196; al-Ma'lûf, 34.

[4] Russell, 6. A large number of industries have been omitted, as calling for no special remark: e.g. the making of garments, head-gear, and shoes; building and carpentry; rope-making.

[5] Prepared from the roe and milt of a grey mullet (*mugil cephalus*) which spawns in these waters.

[6] Girard, 615–16; Savary (Eng. tr.², i. 318, 334). The corporation of sellers of salted fish (*fasîḫ*) and botargo (*baṭâriḫ*) was one of the lowest in rank of the corporations of Cairo (Cab. ii. 152 [not in trans.]). Nevertheless, there were several wealthy members, and it is related that one of them was robbed of four thousand dollars during the riots of 1815 (Cab. iv. 227/ix. 134).

[7] Girard, 621. [8] Olivier, ii. 8.

[9] The fullest account of Egyptian commerce is contained in the already frequently quoted monograph by Girard, *Description*, ii. 1, pp. 621–87. No such survey exists for Syria or 'Irâḳ. For the European commerce see especially

merce of each region was conducted mainly through weekly markets in all towns and agricultural centres,[1] where the surplus produce of the district was exchanged for goods from the capital. At the latter similar weekly markets were held for the disposal of provincial imports,[2] while the main *sûḳs* were alimented by the regular output of the regional industries. The wholesale trade and the larger operations of exportation and importation were carried out in the spacious *ḫâns* (called in Egypt *wekâlas*, and by the Franks *okels*) with which the chief cities were abundantly provided.[3]

Internal and inter-regional commerce, though flourishing up to a point, was handicapped by several factors. The general poverty of the population and its declining standard of living made any prospect of expansion exceedingly remote, and tended also to stereotype the range and quantity of commercial exchanges. The backwardness of means of communication and transport,[4] and the constant insecurity of travellers from highwaymen and robbers[5] resulted not only in heavy personal losses but in a general slowing down of the tempo of commerce. Merchants preferred to wait until a large caravan was ready to travel in company, for the sake of the security offered by numbers.[6] The neglect of the governors to prevent the silting up of canals and harbours, and the formation of dangerous shoals at the mouths of the Nile,[7] was probably more harmful to commerce than the taxes on *wekâlas*[8] and the

P. Masson, *Histoire du Commerce français dans le Levant au XVIIe siècle* (Paris, 1896); *Histoire . . . au XVIIIe siècle* (Paris, 1911).

[1] Supplemented by annual or semi-annual fairs, the most famous being the two fairs of Sîdî Aḥmad el-Bedawî at Ṭanta at the spring equinox and summer solstice. Interchange of produce between Beduins and settled population at local markets—Girard, 622–3; Pococke, ii. 144.

[2] Girard, 626. It is not quite clear, however, to what extent merchants acted as middlemen between producer and artisan, or the larger producers marketed their produce directly.

[3] Jomard (*Description du Kaire*, 727) asserts that, reckoning in all the smaller private establishments, the number of *wekâlas* at Cairo probably reached 1,200 to 1,300. Lane (chap. xiv) estimates about two hundred in Cairo. For the *ḫâns* at Ṣaydâ, see Olivier, ii. 226.

[4] In Egypt and ‘Irâḳ there were no roads to speak of; all communications were by water, often involving trans-shipment. On the other hand, this allowed the carriage of goods in bulk, whereas in Syria camel-transport was the only available means, wagons being unknown (cf. Volney, ii. 271).

[5] For the piracy practised by ‘certain villages’ on Nile craft see Girard, 628; Savary (Eng. tr.[2], i. 74); brigandage on the Tigris and Euphrates, Rousseau, 52. On the insecurity of the roads in Palestine: Volney, ii. 199; Murâdî, iv. 228; between Aleppo and the coast: Volney, ii. 56; Olivier, ii. 296–7; 301–2; in ‘Irâḳ: Rousseau, 90, 94. Cf. also Masson[2], ii. 284–6. On the main roads posts of guards (*ḫaffârs*) were established; but their activities were often confined to exacting sums of money from travellers; cf. Olivier, ii. 294.

[6] Hence the prominence given in the Arabic sources to the action of governors who restored order and made the roads safe; e.g. ‘Alî Bey: Ḥaidar, i. 76, 77; Muḥammad Paşa al-‘Aẓm—Murâdî, iv. 101.

[7] Savary, i. 35, 53–5, 310; the harbours of Lâḏiḳîya and Beyrût—Volney, ii. 69, 78; Olivier, ii. 276. [8] Estève, 361.

levying of market dues. Export and import duties, however, in the hands of unscrupulous agents and in times of political disturbance, were a crushing burden.[1] How far the activities of Moslem merchants were hindered by the lack of organized banking facilities is difficult to estimate. Although the Islamic law, as is well known, forbids usury in any shape or form, and is consequently opposed to the charging and taking of interest on loans, the prohibition was by no means universally observed. There were several methods by which the law could be evaded,[2] and those whose consciences would not allow them to do so could always have recourse to the Jews or Copts. Girard mentions, in connexion with the rice plantations, that to take interest over 10 per cent. was regarded as usurious, and elsewhere that the regularity of commercial relations between Egypt and the Barbary States allowed merchants to trade either for cash or on credit for one year, the interest in the latter case varying between 7 and 12 per cent.[3] The same principle presumably applied also to commercial relations with Syria and Turkey. There is enough evidence in the Arabic sources to confirm that the placing out of money at interest was by no means uncommon amongst Moslems.[4] But even this provision of credit did not offset for the Moslem merchant the advantages which his European competitor reaped from his more flexible banking system, although it was due rather to the special privileges which (as will be seen later) were enjoyed by the latter and their protégés that they began to supplant the Moslem merchants to an increasing extent in the eighteenth century.

On the other hand, the respect for the rites and usages of Islâm, which the Ottoman government was always careful to show, actively favoured the most remarkable and extensive of the commercial operations in Moslem society. When even the lesser annual fairs held under the patronage of a noted saint were free of duty,[5] few Ottoman governors would venture to place obstacles in the way of the pilgrim to the Holy Cities. The connexion between the Pilgrimage to Mecca and petty commerce has always been very close in Islam. Practically all pilgrims chaffered their way to and from the Ḥijâz. Starting out with the merchandise of their native countries, they sold most of these on the journey and with the proceeds they purchased at Mecca the spices, pearls, and coffee of Arabia and the muslins, shawls, and pepper imported

[1] See below, pp. 311–12 and ch. vii.
[2] Descriptions in Chabrol, 261 sqq.
[3] Girard, 577, 647.
[4] e.g. Cabartî, i. 191/ii. 121; and the fortune of two thousand purses (fifty million paras) left by Muḥammad Çorbaci 'the usurer' (d. 1138/1725: id. i. 137/i. 315–16).
[5] Girard, 627.

from India, and disposed of these on their way home.[1] Both Egypt and Syria profited greatly from this trade. The goods of pilgrims were allowed to enter Egypt not only free of duty, but without inspection by the customs authorities,[2] whether they came by land caravan, or, as the majority of pilgrims even from the Barbary States now did, by sea.[3] The importance of the Barbary trade to Egypt is shown by the action of the Sultan of Morocco, who in 1746, in consequence of the molestation of the pilgrims by the Egyptian *amîr al-ḥacc*, wrote a letter to the *ʿulemâ* of Egypt reproaching them for permitting these acts of impiety, and refused to allow the Moroccan caravan to join the Pilgrimage of that year; in the meantime, the offending *amîr* was put to death.[4] Syria, and especially Damascus, profited still more, the Syrian caravan being the premier caravan in size and importance. The furnishing of the multitudes of pilgrims with the quantities of provisions required for a three months' journey to and from Mecca, and of thousands of them with means of transport and camping materials, was, indeed, the foundation of the economic prosperity of Damascus during the Ottoman period.[5] ʿIrâḳ also shared in this traffic,[6] though to a much smaller extent; but it found compensation in the arrival of large numbers of Persian pilgrims, alive and dead, to visit the Şîʿî shrines of Najaf, Kerbelâ, and Kâẓimeyn, and a lesser but persistent, stream of Sunnî pilgrims, especially from India, to the tombs of Abû Ḥanîfa and ʿAbd el-Ḳâdir el-Gîlânî at Bağdâd.

The organization of the mercantile communities in the eighteenth century is somewhat obscure, and the very sparse information available suggests that in both Egypt and Syria it was by no means so rigid as that of the artisans. Whether this applied also in earlier centuries, or whether the mercantile system, the most sensitive part of the Islamic social structure, was already feeling the approaching storm, is, with our present knowledge, difficult to say. Several corporations of retail merchants are mentioned in the sources,[7] and as the merchants of each commodity were

[1] Cf. Volney, ii. 154. Süleymân's *ḳânûn-nâma*, however, protests energetically against this 'abuse', and orders that the customary duties should be exacted from all merchandise and slaves for sale imported by pilgrims of every rank—Digeon, 227.

[2] Girard, 642; Estève, 348.

[3] Generally via Leghorn (Girard, 643). It is noteworthy that in medieval times duty was generally levied upon the goods of pilgrims passing through Egypt, even under a ruler of such scrupulous orthodoxy as Saladin: see Ibn Jubair 239–40 (paraphrased in Carra de Vaux, *Les Penseurs de l'Islam*, ii. 89–91).

[4] Cabartî, i. 174/ii. 77–9.

[5] Cf. Sauvaget in *Revue des Etudes Islamiques*, 1934, pp. 469–70.

[6] Cf. Rousseau, 119 (re-exports from Arabia).

[7] e.g. tobacco-sellers and soap-sellers (Cab. iii. 107–8/vi. 207), cloth-sellers (ii. 224/v. 153), coffee and spice merchants and grain merchants (ii. 151–2/v. 5–7).

usually grouped together in the markets, the organization by *sûḳs*, each with its *şeyḫ*,[1] was probably identical with the corporative organization. We have no knowledge, however, of admission ceremonies into these corporations, corresponding to those in the artisan guilds, and they may have been merely administrative groupings. The head of the mercantile community, usually the wealthiest of the merchants, was known in Cairo as the *Şâh-bandar*;[2] his duties were 'to exercise authority over all the merchants, artisans, and retail dealers in their disputes and internal regulations'.[3] A similar office existed in Damascus, and it is recorded that during a riot in 1793 the governor ordered him to put a stop to it, whereupon he 'separated the combatants'.[4]

The merchants, though by no means exempt from *avanias* and extortions, formed a wealthy and respected section of Moslem society.[5] Together with the secretaries and a section of the *'ulemâ* they constituted a real middle-class, and were often able to bring pressure to bear on the administration. The principal merchants were reckoned amongst the *a'yân* or 'notables' of their city, and several merchant families, even in the eighteenth century, acquired immense fortunes and intermarried with the Beys and aristocratic military and *şeyḫly* houses.[6] The founder of the Şarâ'ibî family in Cairo, Muḥammad el-Dâda (d. 1724), left 1,480 purses in gold and a vast amount of movable and immovable property, including a fleet of three vessels in the Red Sea.[7] The Safarcalânî family at Damascus built and endowed several mosques.[8] Such merchant houses naturally maintained branches or agencies in other cities,[9]

[1] Cab. iv. 250/ix. 182. There are also references to corporations of traders in specific sûḳs—iv. 199/ix. 69: *tuccâr el-Ğûrîya, tuccâr Ḫân el-Ḫalîlî, tuccâr el-Ḥamzâwî* (the last named probably being Greeks).

[2] The term does not occur in Cabartî prior to the appointment of Seyyid Muḥammad el-Maḥrûḳî in 1813—iv. 176/ix. 90; but it is found in the *Thousand and One Nights* (the text of which dates from the eighteenth century), see Lane's translation, ii. 361, and the duties of the office are confirmed by Jomard's statement (p. 724) that his father, Seyyid Aḥmad el-Maḥrûḳî 'préside un tribunal de commerce'.

[3] Cabartî, *loc. cit.* The extension of his authority over the artisans may have been an innovation by Meḥmed 'Alî.

[4] Mích. Dam. 7; he is here called *el-Mutaḳaddim beyna 'l-tuccâr* ('premier merchant').

[5] Various reasons may be assigned for this: the absence of a real feudal system, the connexions formed between the merchants and the *şeyḫs* and *'ulemâ*, the influence they acquired by their wealth, the association of commerce with the Pilgrimage, and (probably not the least important) the fact that, since Muḥammad himself had been a merchant, commerce was always regarded in Islâm as an honourable occupation.

[6] e.g. Cabartî, ii. 221/v. 148. For the *a'yân* see above, p. 198.

[7] Cab. i. 87/i. 203; cf. also i. 176, 204/ii. 80–1, 144–5. Other wealthy Cairene families (of Magribine origin): i. 375; ii. 218–19/iii. 141; v. 142.

[8] Murâdî, i. 15–16. 'Umar el-S. (d. 1700) left 65,000 piastres in cash in addition to goods, buildings, and landed estates (ib. iii. 187).

[9] e.g. Cûḫî family of Aleppo—Murâdî, iv. 131.

and in view of the dangers of the road were sometimes under the necessity of engaging armed retainers.[1] It was not uncommon for *şeyẖly* families to engage in trade and to make considerable profits,[2] although in some cases, particularly among the strict Ḥanbalî school, they preferred 'honest' trade to the holding of posts paid out of revenues acquired by means of doubtful legality, in the eyes of the Canon Law.[3]

From Syria Egypt imported large quantities of silk yarn[4] and other raw materials as required for its textile factories (cotton, gall-nuts, dye), indigo, sesame seed, a considerable range of Syrian textiles, soap, olive oil, dried apricots and figs, and tobacco. These goods were mainly transported by sea from the Syrian ports to Damietta either on Greek or Turkish vessels or European coasting-vessels. Small caravans were occasionally convoyed by the Arabs of Sinai from Palestine.[5] They carried in return mainly food-stuffs: rice, beans, lentils, and wheat, if required; some manufactured linen and silk fabrics, indigo, sal-ammoniac, sugar, hides, and mother-of-pearl shells,[6] and a small proportion of Sudanese products. The average profits made either way were from 10 to 30 per cent.[7] From the European provinces of Turkey and Smyrna the chief imports were textiles, dried fruits, furs, tar, wood, and arms, in return for rice, wheat, dates, sugar, saffron, skins, woven fabrics, cotton and linen yarn, senna, coffee, and Indian and Sudanese products, including slaves.[8]

For the local trade between Syria and Turkey and 'Irâḳ no detailed figures are available. The principal local exports were, as before, textiles, silk, gall-nuts, tobacco, indigo, and dried fruits. Aleppo was the centre of an extensive trade in pistachio nuts,[9] and one of the principal markets of white slaves from the Caucasian regions.[10] 'Irâḳ exported few of its local products, except the dates of Baṣra, the lading of its caravans coming almost entirely from India, Persia, and Arabia (pearls, coffee, and spices).[11]

[1] See Rousseau's account of 'Ebn Rezk' at Başra (p. 45).

[2] Murâdî, i. 175, 250.

[3] Murâdî, i. 68.

[4] About three thousand bales of 135 lb. weight, mainly from Tripoli and Beyrût. On the poor quality of the silk of Tripoli see Volney, ii. 67.

[5] Girard, 644–7; Volney, i. 177. There was also a regular contraband traffic via Lake Menzâla—Girard, 649.

[6] 100,000 to 200,000, together with 200,000 *dôm*-palm nuts and 25 tons of a grain called *bezrebât*, all used for making chaplets, &c., for Christian pilgrims. According to Volney (ii. 181–2) this was the principal industry of both Moslems and Christians at Jerusalem. Large quantities were also exported from Jerusalem to Turkey and the Mediterranean countries, and the convent of Terra Santa alone was reputed to gain 50,000 piastres a year from this trade.

[7] Girard, 647–9.

[8] Chabrol, loc. cit.; Volney, i. 177.

[9] Volney, ii. 49–50, 155; Olivier, ii. 308. It is evident that Damascus and Southern Syria traded chiefly with Egypt, Aleppo with Turkey and 'Irâḳ.

[10] Ǧazzî, i. 148.

[11] Rousseau, 10, 44.

Internal commerce, however, formed only a relatively small proportion of commercial relations in the Ottoman Empire. Severely though Egypt and the other Arab lands had suffered from the transference of the main Indian trade to the Cape route, their geographical position still conferred upon them immense natural advantages as centres of the entrepôt trade between Europe, Asia, and Africa. The main points of convergence of the trade-routes were Cairo and Aleppo, with a secondary centre at Bağdâd. Cairo possessed a monopoly of the caravan trade with the Eastern Sudan and (except for such commodities as were exported by the pilgrim caravans through Damascus and 'Irâḳ) of that with the Arabian provinces on the Red Sea. Aleppo[1] was the gateway of the trade route to Bağdâd, which served as the main channel for commercial relations with Persia and the Persian Gulf. But these relations in themselves would have had little importance had it not been for the outer termini of the chain: Europe, Persia, and India. The produce of Egypt and Syria entered into all these transactions in very unequal proportions—a fact which the sequel will show to have had serious, and in the end disastrous, consequences for the structure of internal commerce as well. Even in internal commerce, by the end of the eighteenth century, a very large, possibly the greater, proportion of local produce in Egypt was exchanged for European goods, such as cheap ironmongery and glass, and to a lesser extent for Indian stuffs.[2] The preponderating, and indeed indispensable, place which they held in the entrepôt trade will be appreciated best from a brief survey of the principal exchanges.

The annual caravans from Dârfûr and Sennâr, which brought ivory, tamarind, hides, tiger-skins, gum, cassia, ostrich feathers, gold dust, and natron, as well as negro slaves,[3] took back with them little of Egyptian manufacture except cotton goods and other textiles. The great bulk of their purchases were of Indian or European origin: silks, muslins, shawls, glass-ware, mirrors, razors, files and other metal goods,[4] guns and gunpowder, and a

[1] It is significant that all the vast *ḫâns* still to be found in Aleppo date from the Ottoman period. See generally J. Sauvaget, *Alep* (Paris, 1941), 186 ff., and for relations between Aleppo and the interior Charles-Roux, *Les Échelles de Syrie* (Paris, 1928), Annexe VII. Detailed accounts of the routes are given in Christina Phelps Grant, *The Syrian Desert* (London, 1937).

[2] Girard, 626, 628. See also the lists of Egyptian imports and exports in Chabrol, 286–97 and 300–3.

[3] For a detailed statement of the average imports and exports of these caravans see Girard, 629–40. The Dârfûr caravan brought annually about five or six thousand slaves (over four-fifths of them female), those from Sennâr a few hundreds in the year.

[4] The Dârfûr caravan, for example, took 25 tons of Venetian glass, 4,000 packages of razors and 1,000 of files, the Sennâr caravan 5 tons of glass-ware and 18,000 mirrors.

variety of materials for ornaments and cosmetics. In return for the oil, honey, butter, tarbushes, morocco slippers, and woollen shawls and cloaks imported from the Barbary States, Egypt exported a much larger volume of goods, the major portion consisting of linen and cotton stuffs.[1] The remainder, except for some sal-ammoniac and occasionally dried rose leaves, was made up of coffee and spices from India and Arabia. The Moroccan land caravan took about equal quantities of Syrian and Egyptian textiles.[2]

The maritime commerce between the Red Sea ports of Suez and Ḳuṣayr and the Arabian ports of Yanbuʿ and Jedda was still fairly extensive. The import trade at Ḳuṣayr consisted almost exclusively of coffee from the Yemen via Jedda, some ten or twenty vessels arriving each month;[3] that of Suez, in addition to coffee, gum, incense, and other South Arabian products was supplemented by the muslins and other Indian fabrics brought to Arabia by the pilgrims from the East, and by a small trade with Jedda by Arab and Malay vessels.[4] Goods landed at Ḳuṣayr were transported on hired camels to Ḳenâ and thence by river to Cairo, those landed at Suez were conveyed to Cairo by four Arab tribes for a hire of ninety paras per camel.[5] In return, Egypt exported to Arabia forty to fifty thousand *ardebbs* of wheat, beans, and lentils, as well as oil, sugar, safflower, and linen fabrics through Ḳuṣayr, and from Suez considerable quantities of European goods: Venetian glass-ware and coral, cochineal, saffron, iron, lead, copper, paper, gilt and silvered thread, to a total value well exceeding a quarter of a million dollars.[6]

At the other extreme, Baṣra and Baǧdâd imported an extensive

[1] Ten to twelve shiploads annually to Tunis, three or four to Algiers, and two or three to Tripoli, each carrying from 150 to 400 bales of woven fabrics, a small quantity being of Syrian manufacture. The bale of ordinary linen and cotton stuffs contained three to four hundred pieces, valued at from 60 to 200 paras the piece (Girard, 642).

[2] Girard, 641–4. Volney (i. 76) estimates the Barbary caravan at 3,000–4,000 camels.

[3] These vessels were open sailing-ships ('dhows'), built mostly in India, and of 70 to 80 tons burthen, the largest being of 90 tons. There was also at the end of the century a shipyard at Jedda, the materials being supplied by the English from India. The cost of a dhow was 4,000–5,000 piastres (Girard, 655). The harbour at Ḳuṣayr was a shallow open roadstead, and vessels were unloaded by porters in the sea.

[4] Girard, 650–7. A large proportion of Indian goods, however, came overland with the pilgrim caravan, since they were allowed in duty-free, whereas at Ḳuṣayr they paid an import duty of 10 per cent. In 1798 the value of Indian imports by caravan still amounted to between 250,000 and 300,000 dollars, and twenty-five years earlier was much greater.

[5] A sum of twenty-three piastres per camel was paid as protection-money to the ʿAbabda Arabs, through whose ranges the route to Ḳuṣayr ran, and an additional import duty of 3½ piastres per hundredweight was levied at Ḳenâ.

[6] Girard, 658–61.

variety of products from India, Persia, and Arabia, mostly for transport to Aleppo and Damascus, which were paid for almost entirely by European goods and coin, except for the local produce of dates and tobacco.[1]

The European trade itself reveals a similar tendency. The principal imports into Egypt were heavy fabrics and satins, paper, glass-ware, metals and ironmongery, arms, spices, and wood;[2] into Syria, woollens, dyes, sugar, West Indian coffee, paper, metals and ironmongery, and luxury articles.[3] In return, Egypt exported a small proportion of its native products (principally safflower, sal-ammoniac, senna, natron, hides, and some linen and cotton fabrics),[4] the remainder consisting of re-exports from Arabia (coffee, incense, gum, and drugs) and from the Sudan (ivory, gum, tamarind, ostrich plumes). From Aleppo, the exports included re-exports from Persia and Arabia as well as gall-nuts and copper, but Southern Syria offered nothing but its own raw materials, chiefly cotton and silk.[5]

It is obvious from this survey that the external commerce of the Arab countries was of little benefit to them, and in so far as the imports consisted of manufactured articles and luxury goods for the rich, while the exports consisted of raw and unworked materials, it was directly injurious to their industry and to their economic wellbeing.[6] In addition to this, it placed a strain upon their

[1] Rousseau, 44–5, 119–20. The principal imports were: From India and the Archipelago—indigo, shawls, silks and cottons, spices, and sugar; from Persia—silk, wools, lambskins, pipe stems, shawls, saffron, tobacco, sulphur, nitre, fabrics, dried fruits, carpets, metals, and various drugs; from Arabia—coffee, pearls, incense, myrrh, drugs. The European goods exported in exchange were woollens, satins, galloons, jewellery, coral, gold and silver cloth, ironmongery, &c.

[2] Details in Girard, 662–78. These were brought to Egypt almost exclusively on vessels from Venice, Trieste, Leghorn, and Marseilles, the products of other than French and Italian origin utilizing the most convenient of these services (e.g. metals and ironmongery from the Empire through Venice, English arms and general merchandise through Leghorn, English and Swedish metals and Dutch spices via Marseilles). In the nineties some forty voyages were made annually from these ports to Alexandria (6–7 from Venice, 12–15 from Leghorn, and about 20 from Marseilles, ships of 200–400 tons burthen).

[3] Mainly by French vessels (see Charles-Roux, *Les Échelles*, and Report of Chamber of Commerce at Marseilles, appended to Volney, ii. 340–60), but English and other goods reached Alexandretta from Leghorn. There were also a large number of French vessels engaged in cabotage in the Levant (ibid.; Girard, 675), and a few English vessels (Charles-Roux, 82).

[4] Leghorn, however, took large quantities of flax and cotton thread. The export of wheat by European merchants was subjected to such stringent regulations as to be practically prohibited (cf. Digeon, 221).

[5] Report of Chamber of Commerce of Marseilles (loc. cit.); cf. Volney, ii. 279; Charles-Roux, 7–8.

[6] 'Si l'on considère qu'une grande partie des marchandises de l'Inde et du café, passe à l'étranger; que la dette en est acquittée avec des marchandises d'Europe et de Turkie; que la consommation du pays consiste presque toute en objets de luxe qui ont reçu leur dernier travail; enfin, que les produits donnés en retour sont, en grande partie, des matières brutes, l'on jugera que

monetary equilibrium, which was probably one of the chief factors in the steady depreciation of the silver currency during the century.[1] On the one hand the local currency was struck in insufficient quantities to meet the needs of this commerce, and every year a large amount of currency was exported to the Levant from France and Italy.[2] On the other hand the Indian and Arabian trade caused a ruinous drain of gold and silver from Egypt, Syria, and 'Irâḳ alike, since few of their own products were taken in exchange, and what of the balance was not met by European wares was taken out in coin.[3] And to make matters worse, both Arabs and Indians were unwilling to accept any silver other than the Imperial (or Hungarian) thaler, known as *Abû Ṭâḳa* or 'pataque'.[4]

The economic disadvantages to Egypt and Syria of the European and Eastern trade might have been offset to some extent, materially if Egyptian and Moslem Syrian[5] merchants had taken a large share in it, intellectually if intercourse with European merchants had broadened the outlook of even small sections of Moslem society, and dispelled some of the ignorance of the world that was so strikingly characteristic of it at this time. But neither condition was fulfilled, and it would not be altogether unreasonable to see in this double deficiency the prime cause of the violent dislocation of Moslem society in the following century.

The European trade was entirely in the hands of Christians (European and Levantine) and Jews. The French Levant Company dealt exclusively with French business houses and Levantine protégés in the *échelles* of Egypt and Syria. The Venetian cargoes were addressed (at the end of the century) to four Venetian and four Jewish firms at Alexandria and Cairo. The Tuscan trade was maintained not only by the few Italian (other than Austrian) merchants in Egypt and Syria, but even more by Jewish merchants at Leghorn, who acted as agents for European exporters of all

tout ce commerce s'exécute sans qu'il y en résulte beaucoup d'avantages pour la richesse de l'Égypte et le bien-être de la nation': Volney, i. 178; cf. for Syria ii. 281. The same sentiment is expressed by the French ambassador at Constantinople, Choiseul-Goffier, in a letter to Montmorin (January 25th, 1788): 'Si les Turcs sont les plus incommodes alliés . . . ils doivent aussi être considérés comme une des riches colonies de la France' (quoted in Masson, ii. 279).

[1] See below, Chap. vii.

[2] It seems impossible to obtain any accurate computation of the amount involved. Even the figures of official French reports differ widely: cf. Masson, ii. 506–8. The figure given in the Report of the Chamber of Commerce at Marseilles (*apud* Volney, ii. 347–9), namely, one million francs per annum to Syria and Egypt alone, is probably the best average. But the Hungarian and Spanish currency was imported mainly from the Italian ports, so that the grand total may be three or four times that amount. Cf. also Girard, 662 sqq.: Chabrol, 285.

[3] Cf. Chabrol, 287; Denon's *Travels*, ii. 227; Rousseau, 45; Olivier, ii. 452.

[4] Masson, ii. 507.

[5] The significance of the religious qualification will appear below.

nationalities and were in correspondence with Christian merchants at Damascus and Aleppo.[1] The greater part of the commerce with the Barbary States also was carried on via Leghorn or by French vessels on cabotage. The Sudanese and Arabian trade (apart from the Pilgrimage caravan) was in the hands of Arab merchants from these countries.[2] The commerce between Aleppo and Bağdâd was conducted mainly by Armenians,[3] that between Iran and ʿIrâḳ by Persian merchants domiciled at Bağdâd;[4] that of the Persian Gulf was monopolized by Arabs and English.[5] Nor was even the internal and inter-regional commerce a preserve of the Moslem merchants. Although the greater part of the freight carried in the European coasting-vessels belonged to Turkish merchants,[6] a proportion—difficult to estimate at the beginning of the century, but steadily growing as it advanced—of the local trade of Egypt, Syria, and Turkey was in the hands of Christian Syrians, Greeks, Jews, and Armenians.[7] So long as all were fellow subjects of the Ottoman Empire with their Moslem competitors, little harm was done, but before the century was out, these confessional differences began to assume grave significance.

The main cause of these developments is to be sought, not in any deep-laid scheme of foreign merchants or governments, but in the exclusiveness of Moslem society. The oriental non-Moslems had, as will be seen, recognized social functions and a corresponding status, but the Franks were relegated to the margins. In spite of their privileges they were subject to numerous legal restrictions,[8] which were, however, probably less prohibitive of intercourse with the Moslems than was the reserve which the latter maintained, for all their outward courtesy. It was not the same in all cities; Aleppo, for example, was distinguished for the tolerance

[1] See generally Masson, Girard, Wood, and Charles-Roux, 48–9, 184.

[2] Girard, 651–2.

[3] Olivier, ii. 306; Charles-Roux, 202.

[4] Rousseau, 10: 'pour la plupart des gens instruits, probes, sincères et doués de toutes les qualités essentielles aux négocians étrangers'.

[5] Rousseau, 37.

[6] 'La caravane ou cabotage côtier, est une branche d'industrie précieuse en ce que, devenant les voituriers des Turks et de leurs marchandises, nous retirons sans aucun risque le salaire et l'entretien de nos bâtimens et de nos matelots. . . . On estime à cent cinquante voiles les caravaneurs qui partent soit de Marseille, soit d'Agde, des Martigues, de la Ciotat ou d'Antibes; ils sont expédiés pour deux ans; en supposant qu'il en rentre cent par an avec chacun 20,000 francs de profit, c'est un total de 2,000,000': Report of Marseilles Chamber of Commerce, Volney, ii. 258; cf. Olivier, ii. 6. In 1798 Girard (p. 675) estimated about 100 French vessels on cabotage in the Levant.

[7] On the other hand, it is totally false to represent them as practically monopolizing the internal commerce, as Volney does (ii. 277): cf. Olivier, ii. 307.

[8] Volney, i. 196, calls it 'une détention habituelle', and though this phrase refers to the situation of the merchants after 1777 matters were little better at an earlier period; cf. Masson and Charles-Roux, 33.

of its inhabitants,[1] Damascus for their intolerance,[2] while Cairo occupied an intermediate position. This situation had the two serious results already indicated. Since the Frank merchants had need of local agents, interpreters, and *fournisseurs*, they had no alternative but to make use of those sections of the population which were ready to associate with them. In Egypt these were mainly Jews, until the middle of the century;[3] in Syria, mainly Christians of the coastal regions, especially the Melkites (Uniate Greeks), together with Armenians in Aleppo. In spite of the efforts of the European merchants, especially in the French *échelles*, to restrict these 'protégés' to their role of agents, many of them, having once gained a footing in the European trade, developed it on their own account.[4] In this they were aided by their assimilation to the nationality of their protectors, by virtue of the usages in force under the Capitulations, whereby the Ambassadors at Constantinople were empowered to grant *berâts* or patents of protection issued by the Porte to a number of selected persons in their service.

In the latter half of the century, the commercial activities of the Syrian Christians and the Armenians in particular were intensified and extended, both in external and internal trade. Two factors contributed to this development. One was the abuse of the ambassadors' privilege to grant *berâts*. 'Twenty years or so ago', writes Volney in 1785, 'they were given to understand that it was more lucrative to sell them. The present price is from five to six thousand livres.'[5] And since each ambassador had fifty *berâts* placed at his disposal, and the gift was renewed on each fresh appointment, it is not surprising that the number of such protégés, assimilated to French, Austrian, Swedish, British, and other European nationalities, and sharing the same consular jurisdiction, mounted rapidly. The extent of the abuse may be gathered from the report that in 1793 the *Paşa* of Aleppo complained to the Porte that the number of consular 'dragomans' in Aleppo amounted to about fifteen hundred, all exempted from taxation and engaged in commerce. A special commissioner was sent from Istanbul to make investigation, with the result that all but six were deprived

[1] Cf. Volney, ii. 51: 'Les habitants musulmans ou chrétiens passent avec raison pour les plus civilisés de toute la Turkie'; Masson, ii. 286; Olivier, ii. 313. But the latter singles out the population of Bağdâd as more polished, educated, active, and tolerant than that of any other city: ii. 388.

[3] Cf. Volney, ii. 151.

[3] The Copts being engaged in land revenue operations, and little given to trade.

[4] See Masson, ii. 167–8, on the contradictory policy of the French authorities towards the 'étrangers protégés'—'Juifs, Arméniens ou autres, tous commerçants habiles, peu scrupuleux et envahisseurs'.

[5] Volney, ii. 278; cf. Wood, *Levant Company*, 135.

of their *berâts* (real or fictitious), and, in spite of their offers of bribes, were sent to Istanbul for punishment.[1]

By assimilation to a European nationality, former Ottoman subjects gained a twofold advantage. In the first place they gained the protection of the consuls of the European states, and of the means of redress which the consuls were frequently able to employ, against the interminable extortions and *avanias* which the caprice and greed of customs officers and of governors inflicted upon all branches of trade,[2] and which were often transformed by repetition into regular duties. Not that they escaped entirely, any more than their European protectors, from these exactions, but at least they fared better than Ottoman subjects, whose only protection and resource were the law-courts; and though the law-courts might deal more or less satisfactorily with ordinary civil and commercial suits, they were powerless against the arbitrary tyrannies of the later Mamlûk Beys, *Paşas* of the type of Aḥmad Cezzâr, and their agents.[3] In the second place, they became entitled to the privileges granted to European merchants under the Capitulations, and more especially to the lower range of duties upon their imports and exports.[4] By this means they were enabled to undercut their competitors of Ottoman nationality and to acquire towards the end of the century a quasi-monopoly of the wholesale trade within the Empire.[5]

The second factor which contributed to the concentration of the Egyptian and Syrian trade in particular in the hands of Syrian Christians was their sudden (and as yet unexplained) ousting of the Jews from the posts in the financial administration which they had hitherto held in Egypt and Southern Syria, about the 'sixties of the century.[6] Their capture of the Egyptian customs[7] gave them control of one of the key positions in commerce, and with the well-known tendency in each of the non-Moslem minority groups to favour their fellow sectaries, the number of Syrian

[1] Ǧazzî, iii. 311.

[2] On the *avanias*, 'les vers rongeurs du commerce du Levant', see Charles-Roux, *Les Échelles*, 53–4, 183–4, and on the 'customary gifts' to officials, ibid. 51–2.

[3] Girard, 649; cf. also 662: '[Leur commerce] supportoit par celà seul toutes les redevances qu'il plaisoit à l'autorité de lui faire subir, et ces redevances imposées par le caprice n'avoient des bornes que celles de l'avidité des exacteurs'.

[4] See Chap. vii.

[5] Cf. Volney's remark that almost all the commerce of Syria was in the hands of Franks, Greeks, and Armenians, and formerly also of Jews. But he can find no better explanation of this situation than that the government 'finds it more lucrative to sell to foreigners the rights and the industry of the Moslems' (ii. 277).

[6] See below, Chap. vii.

[7] 'Alî Bey gave the farm of the customs in Egypt to a Syrian, Ḥannâ Faḫr, and it will be recalled that at the same time the all-powerful minister of Ẓâhir al-'Omar in Southern Syria was a Syrian Melkite (see above, p. 223).

Christian traders in Egypt began to increase rapidly from that moment.[1] Another, and perhaps unexpected, result of their success was that they (or some of them) utilized their offices and influence to create difficulties for the European merchants, and it is even asserted that it was the Christian traders who instigated several of the *avanias* to which the French colony was subjected.[2]

On the other hand, the European merchants were beginning, by the last decades of the century, to seek a greater share in the profitable eastern and intermediate stages of the entrepôt trade. Since 1780 the East India Company had acquired a preponderating position in the Persian Gulf, and was represented by a protégé at Bağdâd.[3] Even before this, it had penetrated into the Red Sea as far as Jedda, where some three or four vessels a year discharged Indian stuffs and shipbuilding material, and in all probability utilized the money received for these to purchase coffee at Mokha.[4] They were prohibited by the Ottoman government from sailing to the north of Jedda, but during the short reign of ʿAlî Bey an attempt was made to reopen the Suez route to English commerce, upon the advice of an enterprising Italian merchant, Carlo Rossetti, consul of Venice and Austria at Cairo.[5] After a promising beginning (for in spite of the protests of the Porte, Muḥammad Bey Abû D̲ahab continued ʿAlî Bey's policy in this respect), it was brought to a stop by a combination of interests, backed up by the disastrous fate of a caravan between Suez and Cairo in 1779.[6] Rossetti himself was, in the meantime, studying the interior commerce with a watchful eye, thanks to the influence which he enjoyed with the Mamlûk Beys; and already before the close of the Mamlûk period he had begun to intervene in it for his own profit, by acquiring the monopoly of the import of senna.[7]

But while the European trade, thanks to the fact that a large

[1] Cf. Volney, i. 190–1; Carali, i. 1, 85. By the end of the century the Egyptian trade with Leghorn was conducted by fifteen to twenty Syrians and two or three Jews—Girard, 672.

[2] Estève, 350; Masson, ii. 304.

[3] Longrigg, 188, 253–4.

[4] Girard, 652–3, 655.

[5] For Rossetti's part as counsellor of ʿAlî Bey, promoter of his relations with Russia and of his projects for commerce with India, see Volney, i. 100, note (information derived from Rossetti himself).

[6] See on these events Girard, 657–8; G. Baldwin, *Political Recollections*; Charles-Roux, *Autour d'une Route*, esp. pp. 26 sqq.; H. H. Dodwell, *The Founder of Modern Egypt*, 4–5; A. C. Wood, *Levant Company*, 167–72. Although the plan was nominally pursued under English auspices, the British ambassador at Constantinople (who was hostile to the scheme) declared that the real promoters were 'a group of adventurers, composed of Greeks, Armenians, subjects of most of the European nations, and some English subjects' (Charles-Roux, p. 101). Baldwin was, in fact, the only English merchant in Cairo at that time (ibid. p. 110).

[7] For Rossetti's role in encouraging Murâd Bey to attempt an expedition to Dârfûr in order to exploit the gold mines see Auriant, *Aventuriers et Originaux*, pp. 14–21.

proportion of its imports was destined for the personal consumption of the governing classes, either directly or by exchange for Sudanese, Indian, and Persian products,[1] escaped the worst effects of the anarchy of the latter decades, it, too, suffered from the exactions and innovations which were on the point of destroying the traditional economic structure of the Moslem society.[2]

[1] Girard, 590: 'Le luxe des familles riches et puissantes est entretenu par le commerce étranger'; cf. Volney, i. 156–7, and Cabartî, ii. 224, 227/v. 153, 159.
[2] See the following chapter.

APPENDIX A

THE ARMY

(A) THE JANISSARIES

THE *ortas* of the three divisions of which the Janissary corps was eventually composed were all organized alike. The mere existence of these divisions in later times, therefore, seems to show that they were of independent origin. The *Seğmens*, indeed, are known to have been originally an independent force.[1] And it seems possible that the later *Bölük* represented the force first used as a body-guard for the Sultan at his head-quarters, and the *Cemâʿat* that employed for garrison duty in the provinces. For, in the first place, the *Cemâʿat* was almost twice as large as the *Bölük*.[2] Secondly, D'Ohsson[3] not only states that in his time more than half the *Bölük ortas* (thirty-one out of sixty-one) were stationed in Istanbul, as against only eleven of the then hundred *Cemâʿat ortas*, nine of which were commanded by officers having special functions in the *ocaḳ*,[4] but he gives us to understand[5] that whereas some *ortas* were permanently stationed at the capital, others were permanently stationed in the provinces, remarking further[6] that one *orta* of the *Cemâʿat* had never moved from Vidin since its conquest in the fourteenth century, and that the provincial *ortas* '*restent en permanence dans les places fortes qui leur ont été assignées*'[7]. Thirdly, the name *Bölük* seems significant. It was that given also to the cavalry divisions stationed at head-quarters. Unhappily the tables supplied by Aḥmed Cevâd,[8] showing the number of men stationed at various places in the provinces at some date during the reign of Meḥmed IV, and again in 1723 and in 1750, make no mention of the *ortas* concerned. Also the Janissary organization was already corrupted even at the earliest of these dates. They show, nevertheless, an increase in some garrisons and a decrease in others over this period. Moreover, Janissary *ortas* were sent to garrison such places as Crete, conquered only after the Empire had begun to decline. It looks, therefore, as if the *ortas* were left in permanent stations as a rule, but were moved if necessary. Fourthly, the *Bölük* was controlled by the *Ḳul Kâḫyasi*, a title probably abbreviated from *Ḳapi Ḳulu Kâḫyasi* (Intendant of the *Ḳapi Ḳulus*); and the Janissaries of the body-guard were *Ḳapi Ḳulus par excellence*. Moreover, the *Ḳul Kâḫyasi* commanded not only the whole division but also its first *orta*, which the Sultan himself honoured with his mem-

[1] See p. 59.

[2] Comprising one hundred and one *ortas* (before the abolition of the sixty-fifth under Murâd IV), against sixty-one of the *Bölük*.

[3] vii. 312–13.

[4] The *ortas* in question were the 60th, the 61st, the 62nd, the 63rd, i.e. the four *Ṣolaḳ* companies (see below, p. 321), the 64th, that of the *Zagarcis*, the 71st, that of the *Ṣamsuncus*, the 73rd, that of the *Ṭurnacis* (for these see below, p. 315), the 94th, the *orta* of the *Ocaḳ Imâmi* and, finally, the 101st, that of the *Beytü'l-Mâlci* (for these see below, p. 316).

[5] Loc. cit. [6] vii. 316. [7] vii. 321. [8] Aḥmed Cevâd, 164–71.

bership,[1] and though inferior in rank to the *Ağa*, enjoyed greater prestige in the *ocaḳ*, the consent of whose members had to be obtained before he might be dismissed. Finally, according to Aḥmed Cevâd,[2] the men of *Cemâʿat* were called *Yaya Beyleri*; and this may indicate that it was they that replaced the early *Yayas*, who, owing to their feudal status, were essentially provincial.

As for the *Seğmens*, it may be remarked that not only does the Persian word of which this is a corruption, *Sägbân*, mean dog-keeper, but three companies, afterwards reckoned as of the *Cemâʿat*, of, respectively, greyhound-, mastiff-, and crane-keepers,[3] are said to have been created simultaneously by Bâyezîd I.[4] It would seem, therefore, as if the Janissary corps in its final form comprised part, at least,[5] of what had originally formed the Sultan's hunt service.

The *Seğmens* were amalgamated with the Janissaries proper by Meḥmed II, in the hope that they would induce in the *ocaḳ* as a whole a spirit of greater docility than it had hitherto exhibited. And until Selîm I began appointing officers of the Household to the *Ağaliḳ* with a similar aim, the *Seğmen Başis* regularly succeeded to that post.[6] The *Seğmen* division, however, comprised far fewer *ortas* than the *Bölük*, and of these only one was (in later times, at least) stationed at the capital.[7] Moreover, the *Ḳul Kâhyasi*, the *Bölük* commander, enjoyed a much greater esteem than the *Seğmen Başi* in the corps itself—a prestige, indeed, even greater than that of the *Ağa* himself. Further, he controlled all appointments in the *ortas* except those of their commanders; he was responsible for the economy of the *ocaḳ* in general; it was by him and the *Ağa* that most questions affecting the Janissaries were settled; and by him that operations in the field were directed. It is even said[8] that he might not be dismissed without the consent of the *ocaḳ*. It is not surprising to find, therefore, that eventually he rose to second place in the Janissary hierarchy. When towards the end of the sixteenth century Murâd III was obliged to return to the older practice, and appoint *Ağas* from within the corps, the *Ḳul Kâhyasi* shared with the *Seğmen Başi* the privilege of eligibility for this promotion, and later supplanted the *Seğmen Başi* as the *Ağa*'s chief adjutant.[9]

The three other officers that formed the *Dîvân* of the *ocaḳ* were the commanders of the 'hunting' *ortas* mentioned above. They were called *Zagarci Başi*, *Ṣamsuncu Başi*, and *Ṭurnaci Başi* respectively. But

[1] D'Ohsson, vii. 315.
[2] Aḥmed Cevâd, 28.
[3] *Zagarcis*, *Ṣamsuncus*, and *Ṭurnacis*.
[4] *Encyclopaedia of Islam*, art. 'Segbān'.
[5] Only part, evidently, since four companies of Falconers were still attached to the Household (see below, p. 347).
[6] Aḥmed Cevâd, 51; D'Ohsson, vii. 314.
[7] D'Ohsson, vii. 313.
[8] By Hammer, cited by Aḥmed Cevâd.
[9] Aḥmed Cevâd, 40, 51; D'Ohsson, vii. 314–15, 334. D'Ohsson places the *Seğmen Başi* still first, and the *Ḳul-Kâhyasi* second after the *Ağa* in his list of Janissary officers (314–15), but states that the *Ḳul-Kâhyasi* was the *Ağa*'s first lieutenant (334), *Ḳâ'im-maḳâm* (Arabic), 'standing in the station (of)'. Ṣari Meḥmed Paşa, author of the late seventeenth-century *Neṣâ'iḥü'l-Vüzerâ*, in dealing with the Janissaries, mentions the *Ağa* and the *Ḳul Kâhyasi* as joint managers of the corps, ignoring the *Seğmen Başi* altogether. See Wright, *Ottoman Statecraft*, text, 64 sq., trans. 110 sq.

besides these *Ocak Ağasis*, there were several other officers, inferior to them, that had also to do with the affairs of the corps as a whole. These were the *Beytü'l-Mâlci*[1], or Treasurer, the *Kâhyâ Yeri*, or Deputy *Kâhyâ*,[2] and the *Yeniçeri Kâtibi*, or Secretary. The first two of these three each commanded an *orta*[3] stationed in the capital, the Treasurer being aided in his work by a *Kassâm*, or Apportioner of Inheritances, a 'learned man'.[4] The *Kâhyâ Yeri* represented the *ocak* *vis-à-vis* the *Ağa* himself, whom, when absent, he replaced at councils of state; orders addressed to the Janissaries by the government were headed by his name; and it was he who conveyed the *Ağa*'s commands to the wardens of fortresses and subordinate generals on campaign.[5] The Secretary, on the other hand, was not a Janissary at all, but a 'civil servant'. He kept the rolls with the assistance of a large staff of clerks. The appointment was, in later times at least, annual.[6]

Next after these officers we may place others, whose authority, while extending beyond individual *ortas*, affected only those stationed in the Istanbul area. The first of these was the *Baş Çavuş*, who besides commanding the fifth *orta* of the *Bölük*, was provost of the *ocak*, and as such had at his orders three hundred sergeants called *Kul Çavuş*.[7] The *Baş Çavuş* presented petitions from Janissaries at the *Ağa*'s Council, and marshalled the *ortas* three times a year at the palace to receive their pay.[8] Equal in rank with him was the *Muhḍir Ağa*, or Summoner.[9] Besides acting as captain of the *Ağa*'s guard, which was furnished by the *orta*, the twenty-eighth of the *Bölük*, under his command, and as controller of the prison situated at the *Ağa*'s head-quarters, the *Muhḍir Ağa* represented the *ocak* in dealings with the government.[10] A third officer of this class, though of less importance, was the commander of the fifty-fourth *orta* of the *Bölük*, called *Ta'lîm-ḫâneci*, or Director of the House of Instruction.[11] It was he that supervised the military training of the local Janissaries.[12] Finally, the latter had as their *Imâm*, or

[1] From Arabic *Bayt al-Mâl*, 'the House of Wealth', a traditional name for the Public Treasury.

[2] *Yer* (Turkish), 'place', here 'substitute'.

[3] The *Beytü'l-Mâlci* commanded the hundred and first *orta* of the *Cemâ'at* (D'Ohsson, vii. 318), the *Kâḫya Yeri* the thirty-second *orta* of the *Bölük*. (So D'Ohsson, vii. 319, the thirty-third according to the pay-table of 1634 supplied by Aḥmed Cevâd, 144.)

[4] Appointed by the *Ḳâḍî-'asker* of Rumelia.

[5] Aḥmed Cevâd, 42–3; D'Ohsson, vii. 319.

[6] D'Ohsson, vii. 322–3. Up to the reign of the Conqueror the Secretary *had* been appointed from among the *orta* commanders. Aḥmed Cevâd, 43, states that he had three (principal?) clerks (*yazicis*), one for each division. The Secretary was also called *Yeniçeri Efendisi* (*O.T.E.M.* No. 14, Appendix, p. 26, note 1, and Aḥmed Cevâd, 35).

[7] For the significance of the word *Çavuş* see below, p. 349. These were called *Kul Cavuş* to distinguish them from the *Çavuşes* of the Household (above, p. 87).

[8] D'Ohsson, vii. 318; Aḥmed Cevâd, 29, 42.

[9] *Muhḍir* (Arabic) participle from *aḥḍara* 'he caused to be present'. Pronounced *Muhzir* in Turkish.

[10] D'Ohsson, vii. 318; Aḥmed Cevâd, 32, 41.

[11] *Ta'lîm* (Arabic), verbal noun from *'allama* 'he taught'.

[12] His *orta* was the 54th of the *Bölük* (D'Ohsson, vii. 319), not the 55th of

Prayer-leader, another *orta* commander, though the discharge of such a duty by any one not a 'Learned Man' was something of an anomaly.[1]

Of greater consequence than these but with a more restricted jurisdiction was the *Istanbul Ağasî*, the *Ağa* of İstanbul. For it was he that supervised the thirty-four *ortas*,[2] supplementary to the establishment of the *ocak* proper, in which the *'Acemî Oğlans* were given their education and preliminary training. He himself while commanding their thirty-fourth *orta* in person, had as his assistants two officers, one to deal with recruits conscripted by *Devşirme* in the European provinces, and hence called *Rumeli Ağasî*, the other, the *Anadolu Ağasî*, to deal with those so conscripted in Asia. Each had authority over seventeen of these *ortas*, grouped in two so-called *Meydâns*.[3] The recruits on reception were instructed in the principles of Islâm, and given the rudiments of a more general education, by special *Hocas* or professors. They were not forced to apostatize, but might not hope for high advancement unless they did so. After undergoing their training they

the *Cemâ'at*, as stated by Aḥmed Cevâd, 32. The latter was not stationed at Istanbul (cf. D'Ohsson, vii. 312, note 3).

[1] His *orta* was the 94th of the *Cemâ'at*, not the 84th as stated by Aḥmed Cevâd, 32. The 84th was not stationed at the capital (cf. again D'Ohsson, vii. 312, note 3). The *Imâm*, while holding this office, wore the type of turban distinctive of the Learned Profession, but abandoned it, together with his religious functions, on being promoted in the *ocak* hierarchy. D'Ohsson, vii. 317–18.

[2] So D'Ohsson, vii. 312, 313. In reckoning the total number of *ortas* as two hundred and twenty-nine, he is allowing for the abolition of the 65th of the *Cemâ'at* (see above, p. 60, n. 2). According to Aḥmed Cevâd, 257, there were at one time fifty-nine *'Acemî Oğlan ortas*, thirty *Bölük*, and twenty-nine *Cemâ'at*. He draws this conclusion from pay-lists that he had seen; but if the table supplied by him on p. 259, concerning the distribution of pay in 1623, represents one of the said pay-lists, it does not bear him out, showing thirty-one items under *Bölük* (this number corresponding with that of the *Bölük ortas* proper, according to D'Ohsson, vii. 313) and thirty-eight under *Cemâ'at*. His account altogether seems somewhat confused. We have therefore followed D'Ohsson's.

[3] *Meydân* (Arabic), an open space, arena, or parade ground. This word was used also by the *Aḫis* for their meeting-place. Perhaps, therefore, we may see in this usage another link between their organization and that of the Janissaries. It may be significant in this connexion that the *ortas* of the *'Acemî Oğlans* were the most ancient of all (D'Ohsson, vii. 313).

Aḥmed Cevâd, 156, quoting a table showing the accession money given to the Janissaries by Murâd III (1574), shows as well as the *Rumeli Ağasî* and the *Anadolu Ağasî*, and as superior to them but inferior to the *Istanbul Ağasî*, a *Gelibolu Ağasî*, or *Ağa* of Gallipoli. Certain *Acemî Oğlans* were certainly sent to Gallipoli for training (cf. Seyyid Muṣṭafâ); so presumably this was their commander. On p. 257 he also mentions a *Meydân Kâḫyasî* as an officer of each *'Acemî Oğlan orta*, equivalent to its *Oda Başî*. But it seems more probable that this was either another name for the *Rumeli* and *Anadolu Ağasîs*, or else that each of these *Ağas* had an assistant so-called, especially since the *Ḳapîcî*, whom he states to have been another *orta* officer, had clearly to do with the whole division of the *'Acemî Oğlans*: Aḥmed Cevâd himself comparing him to the *Muḥḍir Ağa*.

Again, Aḥmed Cevâd states (187) that the *'Acemî Oğlans* that were recruited from among the prisoners of war were supervised by an officer called *Ḳul Oğlu Baş Çavuş*. But this name—literally Head *Çavuş* of the Slaves' Sons—seems more applicable to an officer supervising the sons of pensioners (who were called thus: *Ḳul Oğlu*) admitted as a favour into the *ocak*.

were promoted to service in any of the three corps of the *ocaḳ* indifferently. Such promotions took place every seven years.[1]

The remaining officers of the *ocaḳ*, other than simple company commanders, were stationed at fortified points on the frontiers, whence they were called *Ser-ḥadd Ağasis*.[2] Each of these garrisons included a number of Janissary *ortas*, which, as we have indicated with reference to provincial garrisons in general, tended to remain in permanent residence. In war, of course, these garrison *ortas* might be called to fight elsewhere than in their stations; and strategic necessity might demand the increase of one garrison at the expense of another. Again, quarrels between *ortas* sometimes led to the removal of one or both from the scene of their disagreement. But otherwise few alterations in their disposition were made.[3] There were in all thirty-two *Ser-ḥadd Ağasis* equal in rank, with the exception of the Commandant of Vidin on the Danube. He enjoyed a pre-eminence and the title of *Ṭurnaci Başi*, like the member of the Janissary *Dîvân* mentioned above.[4] He was superior also to the latter, owing to the fact that all officers had to attain the rank of *Dîvân Ṭurnaci Başi* in order to be eligible for appointment to the command of garrisons.[5]

Despite the fact that the Janissary corps consisted of three originally distinct divisions, all the *ortas* into which it was further divided, except a few employed for special duties, were commanded by similar sets of officers. This hierarchy in each *orta* was of an unusual kind. It consisted of seven or eight officers only, none of whom were equal in rank, thus contrasting with most military organizations, in which the officer in command has under him two or more officers, of inferior but equal rank, each of whom again has authority over several officers of still lower rank, and so on. The Janissary officers, on the contrary, seem each to have had a special function in relation to the *orta* as a whole. No doubt this peculiarity was due to the circumstances in which the Janissary *ocaḳ* was first formed: of small companies then numbering no more than fifty men apiece. This would account for the fact that their officers were not ranged in a 'pyramidal' hierarchy: the commander, indeed, would scarcely have required as many as half the subordinate officers with which he was supplied to control so few men, even if they had been so ranged. But, as we have remarked, it seems almost certain that, apart from certain cavalry divisions,[6] the Janissaries were the first troops to be paid and rationed by the budding Ottoman government. This being so, it would be natural for especial attention

[1] D'Ohsson, vii. 316–17, 327–8. Aḥmed Cevâd, 247 (citing Na'îmâ regarding seven-year period), 256–7.

[2] *Ser-ḥadd*, a hybrid term: Persian *sär* 'head' plus Arabic *ḥadd* 'limit'. Hence 'frontier'.

[3] See above, p. 314.

[4] See above, p. 315. The *Ṭurnaci Başi* was the lowest in rank of the three commanders of 'Hunting' *ortas*.

[5] It was under the supervision of *Ṭurnaci Başis* and officers of equal rank that the *Devşirme* conscription was carried out, according to Aḥmed Cevâd, 250, 251. Which *Ṭurnaci Başi* is intended is not clear, nor what officers were of equal rank. Possibly the *Ser-ḥadd Ağasis* are intended.

[6] See above, p. 58.

to be paid to the problem of feeding them; since the feudal troops received not only no pay, but also no rations from the state. And the titles by which several ranks in the officer hierarchy were designated seems to indicate that the chief function of their holders was, at first, to cope with this problem. For the *orta* commanders were called *Çorbacis* (literally, soup-men, purveyors of soup);[1] and two of the inferior officers in each *orta* were called respectively *Aşçi* (cook)[2] and *Baş Ḳara Ḳulluḳçu* (head scullion).[3] Further, the under-officers, or sergeants (*Çavuş*)[4] of the *orta* were called *Ḳara Ḳulluḳçus* (scullions); and its most treasured possession, revered even more than its standard, was the huge copper cauldron (*ḳazğan*), in which its ration of *pilâv*[5] was cooked. It is not clear whether in later times these 'cooks' and 'head scullions' were still what these designations imply, or acted also, or exclusively, as subordinate commanders.[6] The only *orta* officer whose title indicates a purely military duty was the *Bayraḳdâr*,[7] or standard-bearer. For the remaining officers were also concerned, if their titles of rank are to be taken as describing their functions, with the *orta*'s material or spiritual well-being. They were called, respectively, *Oda Başi*,[8] which we may translate as Chief of the Barrack-room, *Vekil Ḫarc*,[9] or quartermaster, *Saḳḳâ* (Water-carrier)[10] and *Imâm* (Prayer-leader).[11] Each *orta* had also a clerk, who kept its rolls.[12] Two *ortas*, those commanded by the *Ḳul Kâḫyasi* and the *Baş Çavuş*, had each an extra officer, called *Zenbilci*.[13]

It is not clear in what order these various offices were ranged,[14] but

[1] See above, p. 61. [2] Cf. below, p. 321.

[3] So translated by D'Ohsson, vii. 320, '*premier marmiton*'. Redhouse has merely 'subaltern officer of the old Janissaries, who commanded a patrol-party or the guard of a guard-house', but this is clearly not the primitive meaning of the word. If it is derived from *Ḳul* (slave) it would mean literally 'man of the black servitude, or service', and so be quite applicable to a scullion. *Ḳulluḳçu*, which we shall meet later (see e.g. below, p. 334), would then mean simply servant (literally, service-man).

[4] Cf. above, p. 316.

[5] Boiled rice, prepared with butter.

[6] The 'scullions' certainly had military duties—see above, note 3,

[7] *Bayraḳ* (Turkish) 'flag', plus *dâr* (Persian) 'having'. Cf. above, p. 83. *Mir 'Alem* (for Arabic *Amîr al-'Alam*), 'Commander of the Standard'. The *Bayraḳdârs* were also, hence, called *'Alemdârs*. We shall meet with a famous *'Alemdâr Paşa* (vol. ii). The ending *dâr* appears also in such words as *Ḫazinedâr*, *Defterdâr*, likewise compounded with Arabic nouns.

[8] See for *Oda*, p. 62, above.

[9] For *Wakîl al-ḫarc* (Arabic) 'agent of expenditure', 'steward'. *Ḫarc* may mean either 'revenue' or 'expenditure' in Arabic, only the latter as used in Turkish.

[10] One who distributes liquid for drinking.

[11] Cf. above, p. 62.

[12] According to Aḥmed Cevâd, 43. D'Ohsson, vii. 323, states that there were in all sixty such *Oda Yazicis*, headed by a *Baş Yazici*.

[13] *Zenbîl*, a basket.

[14] Moreover, the authorities do not exactly agree on their names. Thus D'Ohsson shows *Ustâ* as another name for the *Aşçi*, whereas Aḥmed Cevâd shows no *Ustâ*, and Seyyid Muṣṭafâ no *Aşçi*; Aḥmed Cevâd, on the other hand, identifies the *Baş Ḳara Ḳulluḳçu* with the *Baş Eski* ('head senior'), though D'Ohsson shows the office of the latter as separate, Seyyid Muṣṭafâ ignoring it. The most likely order seems to be the following: (1) *Çorbaci*,

certain that promotion was from one to the other by seniority of service. Only the *Çorbacî* was appointed from outside the *orta*. *Çorbacîs* were appointed indifferently to any of the three divisions of the *ocak*, and in the provinces were frequently changed. Those that had begun by commanding *ortas* of the *Cemâʿat* in the capital, had the privilege, however, of remaining attached to that division.[1] The *ortas* of the *ʿAcemî Oğlans* were also commanded by *Çorbacîs*.[2] But whether their subordinate officers were of ranks similar to those of the Janissaries proper does not appear.[3]

The men of each *orta*, except those of the *ʿAcemî Oğlans*, were from the reign of Süleymân the Magnificent divided into three grades. The highest was that of the pensioners (*Oturaḳ*),[4] whom wounds or old age had rendered unfit for war; the middle that of the veterans (*ʿAmel-mânde*);[5] the lowest that of the 'campaigners' (*Eşkinci*).[6] They were under the immediate control of the sergeants mentioned above. Promotions to the rank of *Çavuş* or *Ḳara Ḳulluḳçu* were by a combination of seniority and good service. And presumably the officer proper of the lowest rank in each *orta* was chosen from among the *Çavuşes*. The *ʿAmel-mânde* men of the *ortas* stationed in Istanbul were known as *Ḳorucus*, and though living in the Janissary barracks[7] were employed under an officer of the Household as inspectors of the aqueducts that brought its water-supply to the capital.[8] Other men of each *orta* acted

(2) *Oda Başî*, (3) *Vekil Ḫarc* (called *Mütawallî* by Seyyid Muṣṭafâ), (4) *Bayraḳdâr*, (5) *Aşçî Ustâ* (placed above *Oda Başî* by Seyyid Muṣṭafâ, below *Baş Ḳara Ḳulluḳçu* by Aḥmed Cevâd), (6) *Baş Ḳara Ḳulluḳçu* or *Baş Eski*, (7) *Saḳḳâ*. Only Seyyid Muṣṭafâ shows an *Imâm*, ranking him after the *Bayraḳdâr*. D'Ohsson, vii. 320; Seyyid Muṣṭafâ, i. 142; Aḥmed Cevâd, 46. The *Koca Seğmen Başî* in his epistle (*Risâle*) addressed to the future Muṣṭafâ IV in 1804 refers to *orta* officers, though casually, as follows: '*Oda Başî Ağa*, *Saḳḳâ Baba*, *Aşçî Ustâ* (cf. above), and *Baş Ḳara Ḳulluḳçu* . . . '. (Cevdet, vii. 293.)

[1] D'Ohsson, vii. 321–2.

[2] Aḥmed Cevâd, 257.

[3] As explained above, p. 317, n. 3, the other officers mentioned by Aḥmed Cevâd seem rather to have belonged to the *ʿAcemî* 'sub-*ocaḳ*' as a whole than to have been *orta* officers.

[4] Or *Muteḳâʿid*, equivalent terms derived respectively from *oturmaḳ* (Turkish) and *ḳaʿada* (Arabic) 'to sit'. There were *Oturaḳ* officers as well as men.

[5] A hybrid term, from *ʿamal* (Arabic) 'work' and *mânde* (Persian) 'remaining' (in reserve). The *ʿamel-mândes* seem to have differed from the *Oturaḳs* in having earned the right by their valour to perform special duties, whereas the *Oturaḳs* had earned the right to retire from service altogether. If married *Oturaḳs* left orphan children they were supported at the expense of the government. Such children were called *Fodule Ḫorân* 'bread-eaters' (from *faḍla* (Arabic) 'surplus' and *ḫordan* (Persian) 'to eat'). The word *Fodule* was originally applied to surplus rounds of bread distributed to the poor from pious foundations, and then to a particular kind of bread, fine and white (cf. Aṭa, 279, for the *Fodules* prepared in the Privy Kitchen of the Palace, see below, p. 336). The *Fodule-Ḫorân* of the Janissaries had a special secretary to deal with their affairs, Aḥmed Cevâd, 34, 142, 185.

[6] From (Turkish) *eşmek* 'to amble' on a horse, especially to war. The term *Eşkinci* was also, and more properly, applied to feudal *Sipâhîs* (see above, p. 50, n. 4). But it had already acquired a more general sense of 'one that goes on campaign' on horseback or not.

[7] D'Ohsson, vii. 321.

[8] Seyyid Muṣṭafâ, i. 142.

as 'helps' *Yamaḳ* to the *Aşçi*,[1] some of them apparently specializing in various branches of cookery.[2]

In war, when operations requiring especial intrepidity were on hand, volunteers were enrolled from among the Janissaries. These were called 'Head-riskers' (*Serden-geçti*)[3] or 'Bare Swords' (*Dal Ḳiliç*). They were promised an increase of pay; and those that survived were thenceforth permitted to wear a special cap, the significance of which was known to all beholders.[4] A number of the *ortas*, also, apart from those that we have already mentioned individually as being commanded by general officers of the *ocaḳ*, had special names. Six of these were stationed at the capital, namely, first, four of the *Cemâʿat*, the sixtieth to the sixty-third, which under the name *Ṣolaḳ* furnished part of the Sultan's body-guard, each *orta* being commanded by a *Ṣolaḳ Başi*, with two lieutenants. We have referred to these guards above, when considering the Household.[5] Secondly, the men of the nineteenth *orta* of the *Bölük* were known as *Bekçis*, or Sentinels, because they furnished guard-posts for the army when encamped in war time.[6] Thirdly, the men of the thirty-third *orta* of the *Seğmen* division were called *Avcus* (huntsmen). They were commanded by an *Avcu Başi* or *Ser Şikârî*, and spent the summer at Istranca, near the Black Sea coast.[7] Of the provincial *ortas*, two of the *Seğmen* division, again, were named after its secretary (the eighteenth) and its *Kâẖyâ* (the twentieth),[8] officers about whom we have no other information: possibly they ceased to be more than ordinary *Çorbacis* after the amalgamation of the *Seğmens* with the rest of the Janissaries. The remaining *ortas* with special names were all of the *Cemâʿat*, namely, the first four, whose men were called *Devecis* (Camel drivers), the fourteenth, that of the *Ḫâṣṣekis*,[9] the seventeenth, that of

1 Aḥmed Cevâd, 46. Young Janissaries acting as scullions were called *Cevelik*—ibid. 191.

2 Aḥmed Cevâd, 48, at least, quotes Cevdet as stating that there were men subordinate to the *Aşçi Başi* (*sic*) called *Çörekçis* (*çörek* means a bun) and *Güzlemeci* (*güzleme* being a special kind of cake). He includes among these men, however, one called *Oturaḳci* (i.e. a member of the pensioner class, or possibly the controller of the pensioners), another called *Ḳoltuḳçu* (or Hawker), and a third called *Tellâl* (from Arabic *dallâl*, a town crier) and classes them all as *Ḳalfas*. Perhaps, therefore, they are not to be identified with the *Yamaḳs* of the *Aşçi*. They may all have been sub-officers of the pensioners, on the assumption that the latter, being no longer under training for war, were allowed to earn their livings in petty trades; or these offices may have been unofficially created in later times when the *ocaḳ* developed into a mere centre for the tradesmen who affiliated themselves to its various *ortas* (see above, p. 182). We have not succeeded in identifying the citation from Cevdet.

3 (Turkish) literally, 'He renounced (his) head'.

4 So Seyyid Muṣṭafâ, i. 142. ʿAṭâ, i. 23, refers to the *Serden-geçti* and *Dal Ḳiliç* men as volunteers enrolled by the Janissary commanders after the decay of discipline in the *ocaḳ* (cf. Cevdet, i. 97). Aṭa states further that this was a practice of the eleventh century of the Hegira, being abandoned after 1100, i.e. A.D. 1689.

5 See above, p. 87.

6 D'Ohsson, vii. 343.

7 Ibid. 313, 319–20, 343.

8 *Kâtibi Seğmenân Ortasi, Kâẖyai Seğmenân Ortasi*—*Encyclopaedia of Islam*, art. 'Segbān'.

9 See below, pp. 350–1. So called, according to D'Ohsson, vii. 343, because

the *Çergecis* (Ceremonial tent-pitchers),[1] the twenty-eighth, that of the *Okçuṣ* (Archers),[2] and the thirty-fifth, called confusingly enough the *Seğmen Avcîsîs'* company.[3] The *Çorbacîs* of the four *Deveci ortas* are said to have been accounted superior to all their colleagues of this rank.[4]

As for the guilds, called *Ordu Eṣnâf*, that were attached to the Janissary corps, a document of the end of the seventeenth century[5] in which it is remarked that for guilds from Istanbul, Adrianople, and Brusa to accompany the army was an old custom, shows a list of twenty-two. They represented the following trades: wool-carders, sword-makers, bow-makers, saddlers, linen-drapers, cobblers, barbers, blacksmiths, candlemakers, cooked sheep's head sellers, makers of iron strips for shoe heels, druggists, goat's-hair cloth makers, slipper-makers, *Kaftan*-makers, silk-merchants, trouser-makers, coppersmiths, tinsmiths, and bakers.[6] Unfortunately the information at our disposal regarding them dates from a time when the discipline of the *ocak* had already been somewhat corrupted.[7] But by the eighteenth century these *ocak* guilds seem to have been placed on a permanent footing. They then numbered thirty-four, each having its workshop (*Kâr-ḫâne*) and consisting of some thirty artisans directed by an *Ustâ*.[8] By that time, however, their position had become somewhat anomalous, since most of the men that then claimed to be Janissaries were in reality artisans themselves.

the *Ḥâṣṣekis* of the palace, who were then reckoned as *Bostancîs* (see above, p. 84), were recruited from this *orta*. Aḥmed Cevâd, 29, states that three other *ortas* of the *Cemâ'at* were also called *Ḥâṣṣeki*, namely, the forty-ninth, the sixty-fifth, and the sixty-seventh, and mentions (41) two general officers of the *ocak*, called *Büyük* and *Küçük Ḥâṣṣeki*, whom he places (35) above the *Baṣ Çavuṣ* (see above, p. 316) in rank. The officers, he says, each commanded an *orta*, were charged with the command of frontier expeditions, and were sent out from the capital to deal with problems that arose among the Janissaries of the provinces. Neither D'Ohsson nor Seyyid Muṣṭafâ makes any mention of them; and we have therefore omitted them from our account. It is to be noted, moreover, that the sixty-fifth *orta* of the *Cemâ'at* there stated by Aḥmed Cevâd to be one of those termed *Ḥâṣṣeki* was that abolished by Murâd IV (cf. above, p. 60, n. 2).

[1] Aḥmed Cevâd, 31. Their *Çerge* or ceremonial tent was set up opposite that of the Sultan, on campaign, so that he had to pass through it.
[2] So D'Ohsson, vii. 343. *Okçu* usually means a maker or seller of arrows (*Ok*).
[3] *Seğmen Avcisi*: Dog-keeper—huntsman (cf. above, p. 315). Confusingly because this *orta* was not of the *Seğmen* division, but of the *Cemâ'at*—like the *orta* of the *Zağarcis* (see above, p. 315).
[4] Aḥmed Cevâd, 29. In the pay-list of 1634 referred to above (p. 316, n. 3) he shows also a number of other *ortas* of the *Cemâ'at* as being called *Devecis* or rather *Şütürbân* (Persian for camel-driver). The table, according to his reading, moreover, gives special names to still other *ortas*, but the evident difficulty he experienced in deciphering the script in which the tables were set out, added to the general inaccuracy of his book, makes us hesitate, especially in this case, to adopt his conclusions.
[5] An *Irâde* to the *Kâḍî* of Istanbul dated 1697, published by 'Oṣmân Nûrî, i. 631-2.
[6] Two guilds omitted. For guilds in general see Chapter VI.
[7] Cf. 'Oṣmân Nûrî, i. 627.
[8] D'Ohsson, vii. For the word *Ustâ* see above, p. 281.

(B) THE JANISSARIES AND OTHER TROOPS AS POLICE

As we have explained when discussing the administration of the provinces, all those parts of the Empire that were governed by officials appointed from Istanbul were divided into so-called *Eyâlets*.[1] A considerable area surrounding Istanbul on both sides of the Bosporus, however, was excluded from the two neighbouring *Eyâlets* and depended immediately on the capital. This area was itself divided into four judgeships—those of Istanbul and the so-called 'Three Towns', Eyyub, Ğalaṭa, and Üsküdar.[2] But at the same time it was policed by soldiery under the command of no less than five officers, the limits of whose respective jurisdictions did not coincide with those of these judgeships. With two of these officers, the Head Gardener[3] and the Admiral,[4] we have dealt elsewhere. The greater part of the area, indeed, was policed by a force at the orders of the Head Gardener. Those parts of it under the jurisdiction of the three remaining officers, the *Ağa* of the Janissaries, the *Ṭopçu Başî*, and the *Cebeci Başî* were confined to Istanbul itself and part of the judgeship of Ğalaṭa. The methods used by all five, however, were similar. In describing those used by the *Ağa* of the Janissaries, therefore, we may to some extent show also how the other officers exercised their authority.

The offences that it was the aim of the authorities, and the duty of these troops in their capacity of police, to prevent were those defined by the *Şerîʿa*, *Ḳânûns*, and *ʿÂdât*;[5] as were likewise the punishments applied to persons that committed them. In general, moreover, it was by order of the learned men who administered the Sacred Law, the *Ḳâḍîs* and their substitutes, that, when they had established the guilt of a person apprehended, these punishments were applied. As we have had occasion to explain when dealing with provincial government, however, high 'lay' officers and officials were also endowed with authority to punish offenders, even without the concurrence of such learned men, though not, in theory at least, in such a way as to run counter to the provisions of the *Şerîʿa*. *Ḳapî Ḳullarî*, in particular, were subject entirely to the authority of their superior officers, who, and not the 'learned men' in question, judged and punished offenders among them.[6] Moreover, persons of the tolerated religions were to a great extent controlled by the dignitaries of their own denominations. Not only, therefore, was there more than one 'code' of law current: first, the *Şerîʿa*, secondly, the *Ḳânûns* and respected *ʿÂdât* by which it was amplified, and thirdly, the codes of rival religions as applied to their adherents; but there were at least three types of officials: the learned men of the *Şerîʿa*, the 'lay' officers referred to, and the dignitaries of the tolerated religions, concerned with the execution of these codes. This being so, the troops that performed police duties were obliged to act in concert with these various authorities. So, in the parts of Istanbul with which we are here concerned, though all persons so engaged were either

[1] See above, p. 141.
[2] Cf. below, ch. x.
[3] *Bostancî Başî* (see above, p. 84).
[4] *Ḳaptan Paşa* (see above, p. 104).
[5] See above, p. 23.
[6] For this privilege as it regarded the Janissaries see D'Ohsson, vii. 353.

actual Janissaries, or accounted as Janissaries owing to their being so engaged, some of them acted principally at the orders of the *Ḳâḍî* and his substitutes. The dual authority of the 'learned' and 'lay' officers was exemplified particularly in the round of inspection made every Wednesday by the Grand *Vezîr* accompanied by the *Ḳâḍî*, the *Ağa*, and a large train.[1] But the *Ağa* was obliged also to make independent rounds at least twice a week,[2] while lesser officers controlled their subordinates chiefly by the same method.

Six of the general officers of the *ocaḳ* apart from the *Ağa* were concerned with police, as distinct from their military duties. These were the *Seğmen Başî*, the *Istanbul Ağasî*, the *Muḥḍir Ağa*, the *Ta'lîm-ḫâneci*, and two that we have not yet mentioned called *Çardaḳ Çorbacî*[3] and *'Assâs Başî*.[4] The *Seğmen Başî* was responsible to the *Ağa* in peace time for the good conduct of all the subordinate officers engaged in police work, and, acting as the *Ağa*'s substitute when the latter went on campaign, he was then left in charge of the area normally under the *Ağa*'s jurisdiction.[5] The *Istanbul Ağasî* was responsible for such *ortas* of the *'Acemî Oğlans* as performed police duties: as we have mentioned, they took the place of ordinary *ortas* ordered to the front; whether any districts were patrolled by them otherwise does not appear.[6] The *Ta'lîm-ḫâneci* and the *Çardaḳ Çorbacî* were each in control of a special district, the former of that surrounding the *Oḳ Meydanî*,[7] where his school of instruction was situated, the latter of one called *Çardaḳ* (whence his name) on the Golden Horn, where his *orta*, the fifty-sixth of the *Bötuk*, was permanently stationed.[8] It was, moreover, by the *Çardaḳ orta* that the guard for the *Ağa*'s headquarters or Door (*Ağa Ḳapîsî*), a palace near the Süleymâniye mosque, were furnished, as were also the men that rowed his barge.[9]

[1] See *M.T.M.* i. 503 sq., for the *Ḳânûn* of the Wednesday *Dîvân*.

[2] Aḥmed Cevâd, 37; 'Oṣmân Nûrî, i. 888; cf. *M.T.M.* i. 524—*Ḳânûn* of the *Yeniçeri Ağasî*.

[3] Or *Çarṭaḳ*—from the Persian *Çähâr Ṭâḳ*, 'four arches or vaults'. See note in 'Oṣmân Nûrî, i. 799.

[4] Arabic, 'one that goes rounds of inspection at night, night-watchman'. Commonly written *'asses* in 'old' Turkish.

[5] 'Oṣmân Nûrî, i. 888–9.

[6] The *Istanbul Ağasî* appears in the long list of officers responsible for the preservation of law and order in the capital supplied by 'Oṣmân Nûrî, i. 884, and also in that supplied by 'Aṭâ, i. 290, of persons connected with the *Şehir Emini* (see above, p. 84).

[7] 'Oṣmân Nûrî, i. 885. The *Ta'lîm-ḫâneci* is said by this author to have been assisted in this duty by the *Ḳorucus* of the *ocaḳ* (see above, p. 320). He adds that they executed civilian criminals by lashing them to a tree with a bow-string and shooting them with arrows. Soldier criminals they executed by hanging, this being a privilege granted by Meḥmed the Conqueror. *Oḳ Meydanî*, 'Arrow parade-ground'.

[8] D'Ohsson, vii. 319. 'Oṣmân Nûrî, i. 799, note, states that there were two *iskeles*, or wharves, called *Çardaḳ*, one that of *Yemiş*, the other that of the *Un Ḳapanî* (the fruit wharf and the wharf of the flour-weighing office respectively). That referred to in the title of the *Çorbacî* seems to have been the first. The word *Çardaḳ* was used indeed as a synonym for *Ḳapan*, the latter, derived from the Persian *Käpân* meaning 'scales', coming also to denote the vaulted building (see note 3 above) in which the public weighing of commodities was carried on.

[9] Aḥmed Cevâd, 32, citing Hammer. The *Ağa Ḳapîsî* was used after the

The *Muhḍir Ağa* was the representative of the Janissaries on the staff of the Grand *Vezîr*, part of the guard of whose residence was furnished by his *orta*. But he had at his orders also a company of halberdiers (*Ḥarbacis*),[1] drawn again from the *orta* of the *Çardaḳ Çorbaci*,[2] and two bodies of under-officers called *Ḳapi Kâhyasis* (Intendants of the Door) and *Mumcus* (Matchlock-men).[3] For he was one of three officers whose business it was to see that sentences pronounced by the principal magistrates (learned men) and the Grand *Vezîr* were carried out;[4] and it was the *Ḳapi Kâhyasis*, who numbered sixty, and these *Mumcus* by whom, at his command, such sentences were executed. Five of the *Ḳapi Kâhyasis* were armed with rods (*falaḳa*), and were hence known as *Falaḳacis*. One or more of them accompanied the Grand *Vezîr* and the *Ağa* on their rounds, to apply the bastinado to offenders summarily sentenced by those dignitaries. The *Muhḍir Ağa* was further the inspector of a prison attached to the Grand *Vezîr*'s residence, which, as we have seen, also included many of the government offices.[5]

The *'Assâs Başi* was the second of the officers under whose supervision sentences were carried out, the third being the *Subaşi* of Istanbul,[6] who though also, apparently, a Janissary,[7] was not one of the general officers of the *ocaḳ*.[8] The *'Assâs Başi* and the *Subaşi* worked largely together, and depended more exclusively on the *Şerî'a* authorities than did the *Muhḍir Ağa*,[9] though they worked partly at the orders of the *Ağa* and the *Seğmen Başi*.[10] They went on rounds of inspection, arresting

suppression of the Janissaries as the head-quarters of the *Şeyhü 'l-Islâm*, until the abolition of that office on the declaration of the republic.

[1] From the Arabic '*Ḥarba*', a short lance.

[2] Aḥmed Cevâd, loc. cit., puts the *Ḥarbacis* at 100 and states that they were furnished by the 56th *orta*. D'Ohsson, vii. 325, does not say from what *orta* they were drawn, and puts them at 60.

[3] From *Mum* 'candle'—here meaning 'wick' or 'match'.

[4] D'Ohsson, vii. 167.

[5] Ibid. 318, 325. The *Mumcus* numbered eighty-four in all and were headed by a *Mehter Başi* (Head door-keeper—*Mehter*, from the Persian *Mehtär*, meaning literally 'superior', hence a superior servant, a groom, a bandsman, a door-keeper—cf. below, p. 337). Not all of them were attached to the *orta* of the *Muhḍir Ağa*, some being attached to those of the *'Assâs Başi* and the *Kâhyâ Yeri* (see above, p. 316). Two officers of the *Muhḍir Ağa*'s *orta*, called *Tüfengci Başi* (Head Musketeer) and *Maṭaraci Başi* (Head Water-skin carrier) marched on either side of the Grand *Vezîr* when he went on his rounds (D'Ohsson, vii. 172; cf. 'Oṣmân Nûrî, i. 83). For the attendance of *Falaḳacis* on the Grand *Vezîr* see D'Ohsson, vii. 325. For their attendance on the *Ağa* see 'Osmân Nûrî, i. 888; Aḥmed Cevâd, 37.

[6] D'Ohsson, vii. 167. We have already referred to other officers called *Subaşi* as controlling the feudal *Sipâhîs*, and as performing police duties in rural districts. The two types had, in fact, sprung from one: in earlier times the title had been applied to Turkish army commanders (the word *su* being thought to mean not 'water'—*Şu* is the ordinary word for water—but army). It was so used under the Ğaznevids (see e.g. the eleventh-century Persian *Ta'rîhi Bayhaḳî*). But already under the Selcuḳid régime in Asia Minor *Subaşis* were charged with the maintenance of order in cities. In the earliest Ottoman period the title was still one of some grandeur, degenerating subsequently, and particularly after the conquest of Constantinople, as is the manner of titles (see 'Oṣmân Nûrî, i. 903–4). *Encyclopaedia of Islam*, art. 'Subāshī'.

[7] See 'Oṣmân Nûrî, i. 900, 902.

[8] See D'Ohsson's list, vii. 313–20.

[9] 'Oṣmân Nûrî, i. 884, 902.

[10] Ibid. 900.

persons suspected of or caught in the commission of offences, and when such cases had been dealt with by the *Şerî'a* authorities, inflicted the punishments decreed by them. The principal prison, called Baba Ca'fer, situated near the Fruit Wharf (*Yemiş Iskelesi*),[1] was under their joint control, being managed by the *Subaşî* but guarded by the *'Assâs Başî*.[2] The *'Assâs Başî* had further the particular duties of keeping the streets clear of impeding crowds on occasions of ceremony,[3] and of executing criminals in public.[4]

What with the surveillance exercised ordinarily by the *ortas* posted in *Ḳulluḳs*, the *'Assâs Başî*, the *Subaşî* and their men, and extraordinarily by the Grand *Vezîr*, the *Ağa* of the Janissaries, the *Seğmen Başî*, &c., the immoral and criminal propensities of the population were already subject to a multiple scrutiny. Even this, however, was not held to guarantee their suppression; they were watched for by still other members of the Janissary *ocaḳ*, namely spies in disguise called *Ṣalma Tebdîl Çoḳadarîs*,[5] and *Böcek Başîs*.[6] The first, who submitted daily reports to the *Ağa*, were especially concerned with the prevention of such gambling as might lead to public disturbances, and of the neglect of their religious duties by artisans.[7] They also saw to it that the men of the *ocaḳ* behaved themselves in public, and that children made no noise in mosques during *Ramaḍân*. The *Böcek Başîs* had as their especial charge the prevention of robbery and the punishment of thieves. It is notable that they employed women in their detective work, and are said to have been highly successful in obtaining the restitution of stolen property.[8]

(C) THE CAVALRY

Each of the six cavalry divisions was, as we have remarked, commanded by an *Ağa* appointed from the Imperial Household. It had further, as its general officers, a *Kâḫyâ*, a *Kâḫyâ Yeri*—who represented it on the staff of the Grand *Vezîr*,[9] just as the *Muḥḍir Ağa*

[1] Baba (Father) Ca'fer was the patron 'saint' of prisoners (cf. above, p. 283, for *Dervîş* saints and the patrons of guilds). A hermitage (*Zâviye*) adjoined it, whose *Mütawallî* supervised the distribution of food given in charity to the prisoners (see 'Oṣmân Nûrî, i. 911, for document dated 1766–7 regarding the maladministration of the prison). The city gate at the *Yemiş* wharf was also called *Zindân Ḳapîsî* (Prison Gate) owing to the proximity of this establishment. *Encyclopaedia of Islam*, art. 'Constantinople'.

[2] D'Ohsson, vii. 319, states somewhat misleadingly that the prison in the control of the *'Assâs Başî* was in the centre of the city.

[3] 'Oṣmân Nûrî, i. 902, 954.

[4] D'Ohsson, loc. cit.

[5] More or less literally, 'valets disguised for going on rounds of inspection'—*Çoḳadar* 'a valet, a lackey', from Turkish *çoḳa*' (broadcloth) plus Persian *dâr* (keeping); *Tebdîl*, Arabic verbal noun from *baddala* 'he changed, replaced', hence, in Turkish, 'a change of costume or appearance, a disguise'; *Ṣalma*, Turkish, 'a round of inspection'. The word *Tebdîl*, often corrupted to *Teptil*, is used simply for 'spy'. These men were also called *Ṣalma Baş Çoḳadarîs* and *Ṣalma Tebdîl 'Askerîs*. They numbered between twenty and forty.

[6] *Böcek*, Turkish, 'an insect', because they 'wormed their way' into criminal secrets, hence *Böcek Başî* 'a detective'.

[7] They would beat such men as disregarded the *Âẓân*, or Call to Prayer, and force them to go to mosque.

[8] 'Oṣmân Nûrî, i. 901.

[9] D'Ohsson, vii. 172. In D'Ohsson's time the four *Bölüks* had been amal-

represented the Janissaries[1]—a *Baş Çavuş*, a *Baş Bölük Başi*, one or more secretaries,[2] and, presumably, since each had its particular standards, a number of *'Alemdârs*.[3] Though each of the six divisions was called a *Bölük*, this word was also used for sections of each division, and in the divisions of the *Sipâhîs* and *Silîḥdârs*, if not of the others, these sections consisted each of twenty men, commanded by a *Bölük Başi*.[4] The presence of a *Çavuş Başi* among the general officers perhaps indicates that each squadron had also one or more *Çavuşes*. It may be remarked that an Ottoman historian of the seventeenth century[5] criticizes the organization of the standing cavalry as providing it with too few officers for the proper preservation of discipline.

No doubt the fact that the men of the four higher divisions each had several armed retainers made them peculiarly hard to control. The number of such slaves maintained by each man was apparently proportionate to the scale on which he was remunerated.[6] Thus the *Sipâhî-Oğlans*, who were the highest paid, had to maintain five or six, the *Silîḥdârs* four or five, the *Ölûfecis* only two or three. The *Ğurebâ*, who were the least well paid, were under no obligation to maintain any at all.[7]

In spite of the *Sipâhîs*' numerical and social superiority to the Janissaries, their commanders, who were drawn from the highest category of the Sultan's pages, were yet placed below the *Ağa* of the Janissaries in order of precedence. Indeed, a number of officials and officers of the Household came between him and them in this

gamated with the *Sipâhîs* and *Siliḥdârs*, so only the *Kâḫyâs* of the latter two divisions were thus employed. 'Os̱mân Nûrî, i. 883, mentions the *Kâḫyâ Yeris* of the *Sipâhîs* as among the officers attached to the Grand *Vezîr*.

1 See above, p. 325.

2 Ramberti (Lybyer, loc. cit.) mentions *Kâḫyâs* and *Yazicis* or secretaries; Seyyid Muṣṭafâ, i. 144, adds *Çavuşes*; and D'Ohsson, vii. 364, *Kâḫyâ Yeris* and *Baş Bölük Başis*.

3 Cf. p. 319, n. 7 above. The *Sipâhîs*, *Silîḥdârs*, *'Ölûfecis* and *Ğurebâ* had, respectively, red, yellow, red-and-green, and white-and-green standards. Zinkeisen, iii. 176; cf. D'Ohsson, vii. 368, and Seyyid Muṣṭafâ, i. 144.

4 Lybyer (Ramberti), 251; D'Ohsson, vii. 364, 365.

5 *Ḥâccî Ḫalîfe*, the *'Kâtib Çelebi'* (Seyyid Muṣṭafâ, loc. cit.).

6 So Lybyer, 98, citing foreign sixteenth-century accounts. Neither Seyyid Muṣṭafâ nor D'Ohsson refers to these armed slaves.

7 Ibid. 100. Whether the *Sipâhîs* themselves, or the Treasury, paid their attendant men-at-arms does not indeed appear to be quite certain, though, if the *Sipâhîs* paid them, as we presume, this would perhaps account for the silence of our Turkish authorities regarding these slaves. Lybyer, however, cites one Venetian author (Garzoni, 1573) as stating that 40,000 cavalrymen were paid by the Treasury. Seyyid Muṣṭafâ, i. 144, states that when in the reign of Murâd III the establishment of the *Bölüks* was raised to 20,000, their yearly pay amounted to over 130,000,000 *aḳçes*. This is equivalent to about 20 *aḳçes* a man a day, and so evidently provides only for the *Sipâhîs* themselves, not for their followers. For though it is true that Seyyid Muṣṭafâ, i. 145, states that the daily pay of the *Sipâhîs* and *Siliḥdârs* was 13 *aḳçes*, that of the *'Ölûfecis* 11, and that of the *Ğurebâ* 9, he adds that this scale was applicable only to newly joined men, the rest receiving supplements for war service; and Zinkeisen, iii. 176, states that, under Selim I, the *Sipâhîs* and *Siliḥdârs* received from 20 to 40 *aḳçes* a day and the *'Ölûfecis* and *Ğurebâ* 15 to 20, while Ramberti's scale (Lybyer, 250–1) is *Sipâhîs*, 40, *Silîḥdârs*, 25, *'Ölûfecis*, 8 to 16, and *Ğurebâ*, 7 to 14.

order.[1] For the Janissaries enjoyed peculiar esteem as a corps: when, for instance, three times a year the pay of all the standing troops was distributed at the palace, it was to their officers alone that this distribution was made in detail. The *Ağas* of the cavalry *Bölüks* each merely received a lump sum, which they distributed later at the palace of the Grand *Vezîr*.[2] One privilege, however, they shared with the infantry *ocaḳs*. Offending *Sipâhîs* might be punished only by their own officers,[3] though the latter performed no such police duties as the *Ağa* of the Janissaries and the *Ṭopçu* and *Cebeci Başîş*.

Since not only the six *Ağas* but also most of the men of the first four *Bölüks* were recruited from the Household, it was natural that their relations with the Sultans should have been close. As we have seen, the Sultan had a special mounted body-guard, independent of them, which accompanied him on campaign and was regarded as peculiarly 'noble'.[4] Nevertheless, Süleymân the Magnificent chose to form yet another corps from favoured men of the *Bölüks*, whom under the name *Mülâzim*[5] he employed as personal aides-de-camp. These numbered three hundred; and by way of reward they were permitted, at the close of the campaign during which they had performed this service, to undertake remunerative 'civil' duties, such as the administration of the estates of princesses, or that of tax-farms, or the collection of the poll-tax from non-Moslems. Such 'standing' cavalrymen as showed promise were in any case often promoted to minor provincial governorships, which entailed the conduct of civil as well as military affairs. Possibly, therefore, the purpose for which Süleymân so rewarded these *Mülâzims* was to prepare them for such promotion. From regarding this employment as a privilege, however, the *Sipâhîs* came in time to regard it as a right; and their insistence on it greatly contributed to the confusion into which both their own organization and that of the government was later thrown.[6]

[1] The order of precedence as shown in the *Ḳânûn-nâmei Âli 'Oṣmân* is as follows:

Yeniçeri Ağasi (after the *Sancaḳ Beyis*, see above, p. 138).
Mir 'Alem, Ḳapici Başi, Mir Aḫors, Çaḳirci Başi, Çaşnigir Başi—all these being officers of the 'Outside Service' of the Household (see above, p. 83).
Bölük Ağasis.
Çavuş Başi.
Ḳapicilar Kâḫyasi (see above, p. 83).
Cebeci Başi.
Ṭopçu Başi (*O.T.E.M.*, No. 13, pp. 10–12).

In another passage (p. 22) the *Defter Emini* and *Şehir Emini* are said to have had precedence of the *Bölük Ağasis*; and in the later *Ḳânûn-nâme* of 'Abdu'r-Raḥmân Tevḳi'î, the *Ağas* of the Four *Bölüks* are placed after the *Çavuş Başi* and the *Ḳapicilar Kâḫyasi*—only, however, in a section dealing with *Dîvân* dress (*M.T.M.* i. 526).

[2] See Aḥmed Cevâd, 116 sq. Cf. D'Ohsson, vii. 222 sq.

[3] See *M.T.M.* i. 510 (*Ḳânûn-nâme* of 'Abdu'r-Raḥmân Tevḳi'î).

[4] The *Muteferriḳa* guard—see above, pp. 87–88.

[5] 'Attaché' or 'adjutant' (Arabic). The word was also used in the learned profession (see Chapter VIII). In the army as reorganized during the nineteenth century it was applied to the lowest two ranks of officers, and so corresponds to 'lieutenant'.

[6] Seyyid Muṣṭafâ, i. 145; Aḥmed Râsim, i. 381. These civil employments were called *Ḫidmet* 'Service'.

APPENDIX B

THE IMPERIAL HOUSEHOLD

(A) THE BLACK EUNUCHS

THE black eunuch last arrived in the *Ḥarem* service was known as the *En Aşaği*, or Lowest, *Ağa*. After being presented to the *Ḳizlar Ağasi* he was taken by the latter's *Oda Lalasi*,[1] the Supervisor of the *Ağa's* apartments, to the principal officer of the eunuch guards, called *Baş Ḳapi Ğulâmi*[2] in whose presence his name was entered on the rolls. He was then made to kiss the hand of a sub-officer of *Ḥâşilli* or *Ortanca*[3] rank, who was appointed as his *Lala*, or Supervisor. His duties were to serve the eunuchs of the next lowest category to his own, who were called *ʿAcemî* (that is 'foreign') *Ağas*,[4] and their sub-officers, the *Nevbet Ḳalfasis*[5] (Substitutes of the Watch), whose duty it was to command in turn the eunuchs on duty at the *Ḥarem* doors, placing himself at these officers' command. The Lowest *Ağa* was himself put on guard duty at the hours of Ablution (*Âbdest*) and prayers.[6] The rest of his time was spent in learning the principles and *Ḳânûns* of the *ocaḳ*.

As soon as another eunuch was received into the service, the former 'Lowest *Ağa*' became automatically a 'Foreign *Ağa*', yielding his former title to the new-comer. How many Foreign *Ağas* were employed at a time is not mentioned; but they were eventually promoted in order of seniority, when vacancies occurred, to be *Nevbet Ḳalfasis*. Such promotions were notified to the *Ḳizlar Ağasi* and *Baş Ḳapi Ğulâmi* by the officer responsible for the discipline and cleanliness of the corps, called *Müsândereci Başi*.[7]

There were five *Nevbet Ḳalfasis*, four of whom, numbered by seniority, took duty in turn, the fifth and most important controlling the others in their dormitory and doing guard duty only occasionally, when the Sultan and the *Ḳadins* went for an outing to one of the garden pavilions.[8] The *Nevbet Ḳalfasis* had special charge of the *Ḥarem* door keys. There were four of these doors, two of iron and two of bronze, one behind the other in the single passage by which the *Ḥarem* might be entered.[9] The *Nevbet Ḳalfasi* on duty received the keys of these doors from the *Ḳizlar Ağasi* early in the morning and returned them to him at night.

[1] See below, p. 331. [2] See below, p. 330. [3] See below, p. 330.

[4] Just as the Janissary novices were called *ʿAcemî Oğlans*—presumably because the eunuch *ʿAcemî Ağas* were, like them, of non-Moslem birth.

[5] *Nevbet* (Arabic *Nawba*) meaning 'turn' in the sense of recurrent occasion or action. *Ḳalfa* is a Turkish corruption of the Arabic *Ḥalîfa*, successor, deputy (whence Caliph).

[6] Presumably because his seniors all wished, or were obliged, to attend services, preceded by ablutions, in their mosque.

[7] See below, p. 330.

[8] These excursions, which were attended with complicated ceremonies, went by the term *Ḥalveti Ḥümâyûn* (Imperial retirement).—Cf. D'Ohsson, vii. 82.

[9] See D'Ohsson, vii. 70.

Next above the *Nevbet Ḳalfasîs* ranked four sub-officers called *Ortanca*,[1] and next above them again twelve others called *Ḥâṣilli*[2] who controlled the *Nevbet Ḳalfasîs*. Promotion went again by seniority, except that both *Ortancas* and *Ḥâṣilli* might refuse to receive the senior *Nevbet Ḳalfasî* or the senior *Ortanca* into their grade if they chose. On reception into both grades the eunuch promoted was received by the *Ḳîzlar Ağasî*, whose robe he kissed, after which he went to the eunuchs' mosque, where he distributed largesse.

The senior *Ḥâṣilli*, again, was eligible, on the occurrence of a vacancy, to become second officer of the guard, called *Yayla(ḳ) Baş Ḳapî Ğulâmî*, and the latter to become first officer, *Yeni Serây Baş Ḳapî Ğulâmî*. These titles mean respectively Summer Head Slave of the Door and Head Slave of the Door of the New Palace.[3] The former was so called because he remained in command when the Sultan went in the summer to Beşiktaş or another of the palaces other than the *Ṭop Ḳapî Serâyî*. The offices of the two *Baş Ḳapî Ğulâmîs* were the highest in the *ocaḳ* to which eunuchs could rise by mere seniority. The rest were all conferred by favour, even some that ranked below these two. Thus every separate 'apartment' (*Dâ'ire*) of the *Ḥarem*—those, for instance, of the *Vâlide* and the *Ḳadîns*—was provided with a *Baş* (Head) *Ağa*,[4] chosen usually from among the *Ortancas* or *Ḥâṣillis*, and also with several minor eunuchs chosen from among the *'Acemîs* and *Nevbet Ḳalfasîs*, called *Ḥarem Ağasîs* by way of distinction from those of the watch, under him. All these eunuchs continued to advance in seniority despite their special work. The remaining posts, on the other hand, stood outside the hierarchy that we have described altogether. Nor were they arranged, so it appears, in an independent hierarchy. They were of three types: those of the *Müsânderecis*, headed by the *Müsândereci Başî*, those of the *Muṣâḥibs*, headed by a *Muṣâḥib Başî*, and those of the Treasurer, *Ḫazînedâr Ağa*,[5] and his deputy, the *Ḫazîne Vekîli*.[6] The duty of the *Müsânderecis* was,[7] as we have mentioned, to see that the eunuchs kept themselves clean, observed the regulations, and fulfilled their religious duties. All eunuchs up to the

[1] Meaning 'Middle', i.e. between the *Nevbet Ḳalfasîs* and the *Ḥâṣillis*.

[2] Meaning perhaps 'fully trained'. *Ḥâṣil* (Arabic) means 'produce', 'result', and hence 'profit', also 'what is left after a process of purification'.

[3] *Ğulâm* (Arabic), though meaning secondarily 'slave', is equivalent to the Turkish *Oğlan*, 'boy'. D'Ohsson, indeed, uses *Oğlan* instead of *Ğulâm* for these titles.

[4] The *Baş Ağa* of the *Vâlide* acted as assistant to the Chief of the eunuch guard, the *Baş Ḳapî Ğulâmî*.

[5] Cf. above, p. 74, the *Ḥarem* lady called *Ḫazînedâr Ustâ*.

[6] *Wekîl* (Arabic) means simply deputy—and so *Ḫazîne Vekîli* (Deputy of the Treasury).

[7] The significance of this word is obscure. Redhouse states that *Müsendere* is a corruption of the Arabic *Maṣdara*, and means 'The fixed slab at the end of a Turkish sofa'. This is not enlightening in connexion with our word. Moreover, *Maṣdara* itself is not a classical word, nor is it shown by Dozy, *Supplément aux Dictionnaires Arabes*. *Muṣâdara*, however, means 'exacting with importunity', and hence (in 'Abbâsid usage at least—see e.g. the *Kitâb al-Wuzerâ* of Hilâl al-Ṣâbi') 'imposing a fine'. And since the transition from the idea of fining to that of imposing punishments in general seems a not impossible one, it may be that *Müsânderici* is *Muṣâdere-ci* in disguise.

rank of *Ḥâṣilli* were punished by beating. Those above it were merely admonished, or, if their fault was serious, were banished to Egypt. It was the duty of the *Muṣâḥib Baṣî*[1] to remain in perpetual attendance on the Sultan while in the *Ḥarem*, to convey his orders to the *Ḳîzlar Ağasî*. The ordinary *Muṣâḥibs* numbered eight or ten. They took duty two at a time, accompanying the Sultan and their chief, and carried orders to the Lady Intendant. The Treasurer and his deputy were, as we have mentioned, responsible for the economy of the *ocaḳ*. The Treasurer ranked as the *Ağa's* lieutenant, immediately above the *Muṣâḥib Başî*.[2]

Apparently the other palaces, and certainly the Old *Serây*, had similar eunuch guards, headed by a *Baş Ḳapî Ğulâmî*. Whether eunuchs passed from one service to another does not appear. Not only they, however, but also such eunuchs as were employed in the households of princes and princesses seem to have come under the authority of the *Ḳîzlar Ağasî*. Each princess had not only a *Baş Ağa* like the *Vâlide* and the *Ḳadîns*, but a *Baş Ḳapî Ğulâmî* and a *Mâbeynci*,[3] the head of ten or twelve *Ḥarem* eunuchs. Finally, each prince, in his 'cage' had a black eunuch as one of his tutors or supervisors (*Lala*).

The *Ağa's* own 'household' included a number of *Nevbet Ḳalfasîs*, one of whom remained on duty at night in case the *Ağa* were required in an emergency, a number of slave-girls,[4] and a whole court of attendants and guards of various types, not all of whom were eunuchs themselves.[5] They were all under the direction of his Room-Supervisor,[6] who though he had no high official position, in fact took charge of the palace in the *Ağa's* absence. When an *Ağa* was dismissed he too was exiled to Egypt, and replaced either by the *Baş Ḳapî Ğulâmî* of the old *Serây* or by the governor of Medina, a post which, as we have mentioned, was conferred in later times on negro eunuchs of the *Ḥarem* service.[7]

(B) THE INSIDE SERVICE

1. *The White Eunuchs*

Up to near the end of the sixteenth century the Inside Service as well as the *Ḥarem* was dominated by the White Eunuchs. Their chief,

[1] *Muṣâḥib* (Arabic) means 'Companion'—and here evidently 'Attendant in Waiting'.

[2] See D'Ohsson, vii. 55. D'Ohsson calls him *Baş-Muṣâḥib*.

[3] For *Mâbeyn*, cf. above, p. 72. The *Mâbeynci*'s duty was to carry a lantern or torch before the *Damad*, the princess's husband, when he visited his *Ḥarem* at night, and to carry messages from him to the princess when he was in his *Selâmliḳ* or reception-room.

[4] This is mentioned by D'Ohsson, vii. 54, as a peculiar privilege for a eunuch.

[5] 'Aṭâ mentions the following:
a *Kürkçü Başî* (Head Fur-pelisse Keeper);
a *Ḳuşçu Başî* (Head Cook; cf. below, p. 351);
a *Ḳahveci Başî* (Head Coffee-maker);
a *Baş Çoḳadâr* (Head Valet);
a *Ḥeğbeci*, a *Zülüflü Balṭaci*, and a *Ḳizbekci*.
For the latter three types of guards see below, pp. 353, 359, 361. These at least were evidently not eunuchs.

[6] *Oda Lalasi*.

[7] The above account is taken from 'Aṭâ, i. 257 sqq.

the *Bâbü's-Se'âdet Ağasi* or *Ḳapi Ağasi*[1] had five principal white-eunuch lieutenants, one for each of the three superior chambers called:

(1) For the *Ḫâṣṣ Oda*, *Ḫâṣṣ Oda Baṣi*,[2]
(2) For the *Ḫazîne*, *Ḫazînedâr Baṣi*,[3]
(3) For the *Kilâr*, *Ḳilârci Baṣi*;[4]

one for the two chambers (called *Büyük* (Great) and *Küçük* (Little) *Oda*),[5] in which prospective pages continued their education already begun either at Ġalaṭa Serâyi or elsewhere before being admitted into the Service proper, namely:

(4) The *Serây Ağasi* (*Ağa* of the Palace), who was also responsible for the safety of the establishment, commanding for this purpose a guard of forty subordinate eunuchs; and

(5) The *Serây Kâḫyasi* (Intendant of the Palace),[6] whose duties are not specified.

Below these ranked in turn

(6) Five *Köṣe Baṣis* (literally 'Heads of the Corner'), whose duty it was to see that their subordinates behaved themselves and discharged their duties properly;[7]

(7) An unspecified number of *Baş Eskis* ('Head Seniors'), the highest in rank of whom was called *Oda Kâḫyasi* (Intendant of the Chamber); and (8) Two *Üzengi Ağasis* (*Ağas* of the Stirrup—not to be confused with the officers of the Outside Service bearing the same title[8]), one called 'Right' and the other 'Left'—presumably because they marched on either side of the Sultan when he rode.[9]

The subordinate White Eunuchs that presided over the *Iç Ağas'* messes were called *Ṣofra Eskisis* ('Seniors of the Table').[10]

The first loss of influence by the White Eunuchs to the Black occurred during the reign of Murâd III, when in 1582 the office of *Dârü's-Se'âdet Ağasi*, hitherto appertaining to the *Ḫazînedâr Baṣi* or the *Serây Ağasi*, was given to a negro.[11] It was restored some ten years later to a *Serây Ağasi*; but passed finally to the Blacks on the accession of Meḥmed III in 1595, when the control of the *Ḥarem* and the Inspectorship of some of the Imperial *Awḳâf* were removed from the *Ḳapi Ağasi* for good. No doubt this change resulted also in a weakening of the White Eunuchs' control of the Pages; but it was not until a century later that the management of the Inside Service was taken out of their

[1] i.e. *Ağa* of the Gate of Felicity, or *Ağa* of the Gate.—Cf. above, p. 76.

[2] Apparently in early times the *Ḫâṣṣ Oda Baṣi* was often a page and not a eunuch—see Lybyer, 127, and notes to the *Ḳânûn-nâme* of the Conqueror (*O.T.E.M.*, No. 13, Appendix, 14). Nevertheless, it is to be noted that in this document the *Ḫâṣṣ Oda Baṣi* is placed between the eunuchs *Ḳapi Ağasi* and *Ḫazînedâr Baṣi* as if he were one himself.

[3] For *Ḫazînedâr* (Treasurer) see above, p. 74.

[4] *Kilârci*, one that looks after a *Kilâr* or larder—a butler.

[5] 'Aṭâ refers only to the *Küçük Oda*; but both D'Ohsson (vii. 47) and the editor of the *Ḳânûn-nâme* of Meḥmed II (*O.T.E.M.*, No. 13, Appendix, 15, note) refer to a *Büyük* as well.

[6] So 'Aṭâ, i. 164. D'Ohsson, vii. 56 sq., does not mention the *Serây Kâḫyasi*.

[7] This is not stated of the eunuch *Köṣe Baṣis*, but is said to have been the duty of *Ḫâṣṣ Odalis* similarly entitled.—Cf. below, p. 342.

[8] See above, p. 82.

[9] 'Aṭâ, loc. cit.

[10] 'Aṭâ, i. 160.

[11] Cf. above, p. 76.

hands and confided to the Pages themselves.[1] Thereafter the duties of the *Ḥâṣṣ Oda Baṣî* were restricted to investing dignitaries such as the Grand *Vezîr* and the *Şeyḫü'l-Islâm*, and certain officials of the Palace itself, with pelisses of honour: he is said to have become Master of Ceremonies for the Inside Service (*Enderûn Teşrîfâtçî*); and those of the *Ḥazînedâr Baṣî* and the *Kilâr Baṣî* to inspecting the catering for their respective 'Dormitories'. The *Serây Ağasî* continued to act as commandant of the Palace in the absence of the Sultan and the officers that accompanied him;[2] and Ğalaṭa Serâyî was still committed to the care of a White Eunuch. But the White Eunuchs had by now entirely lost their former dominant position. D'Ohsson states that in his time only about eighty were employed, as against about two hundred Blacks.[3]

2. *The Lower Chambers*

Most of our information regarding the organization of the Inside Service refers to the eighteenth century, when it was no longer under the White Eunuchs' control. The removal of this control no doubt involved a certain amount of reform. Nevertheless, most of the posts in the three higher chambers seem to have been created during the reigns of Meḥmed II, Bâyezîd II, and Selîm I;[4] and though the *Seferli* Chamber was actually created only later, under Aḥmed I, to replace the 'Little Chamber' (*Küçük Oda*),[5] which was rather a general school for the training of the Pages than a regular department of the Service, it was already old-established by the time of this reorganization.

The three lower Chambers, *Ḥazîne*, *Kilâr*, and *Seferli*,[6] were in their final form organized very similarly. Thus certain men in each *Ḳoğuş* or Dormitory were called *Biçaḳlî*, because they wore gold- or silver-plated daggers (*Biçaḳ*) in their belts; while others, inferior to them, were known as *Ṣoyunaḳs*,[7] because they were allowed to wear night-clothes when off duty. There appear to have been eleven *Biçaḳlîs* to every nine *Ṣoyunaḳs*, the total numbers not being given.[8] Each *Ḳoğuş* is said again to have had twelve *Ḳalfas* (*Ḫalîfes*), who received a yearly gratuity beyond the ordinary salary of the Pages. These *Ḳalfas* aided the visiting *Ḫocas* (professors)[9] to teach the novices. Finally, apart from its *Kâḫyâ*, each department had a considerable number of officers and under-officers, divided into two sections according to the nature of their promotion.

[1] Owing to the enterprise of Çorlulu 'Alî Paşa—see above, p. 76.
[2] This according to D'Ohsson, vii. 57.
[3] Ibid.; cf. 'Aṭâ, i. 164–5.
[4] See 'Aṭâ, i, 30, 72, 73, 94, 98.
[5] 'Aṭâ, as noted above, ignores the *Büyük Oda*. D'Ohsson, vii. 48, states that both these chambers were suppressed by Meḥmed IV, whereas 'Aṭâ, i. 154, puts the conversion of the *Küçük* into the *Seferli Ḳoğuş* down to Aḥmed I, in 1606 or 1607.
[6] So called by 'Aṭâ *passim*. D'Ohsson, vii. 44, has *Séfer* ('*Séfer-odassi*') translated '*Chambrée de Campagne*'). *Sefer* (Arabic) means 'journey' and hence 'campaign'; *Seferli* (with Turkish ending) 'appertaining to a campaign'
[7] From *ṣoyunmaḳ* (Turkish) 'to undress'.
[8] So, according to 'Aṭâ, i. 138.
[9] 'Aṭâ, i. 75. Presumably these were senior *Lalas*.—Cf. above, p. 331.

The *Kâhyâs* themselves were former members of the *Hâss Oda*, and inferior only to the principal page, the *Silihdâr Ağa*, whose lieutenants they were. Each was appointed to the chamber in which he had begun his service. The *Kâhyâs* of the *Kilâr* and the *Seferli*, therefore, might have little hope of further promotion in the *Serây* service. The *Kâhyâ* of the *Hazîne*, on the other hand, habitually succeeded to the post of *Silihdâr*.[1]

As for the lesser officers of each chamber, those promoted by mere seniority were called *Biçaklî Eskis* and were appointed from among the ordinary *Biçaklîs* mentioned above. There were twelve in each chamber,[2] the top two in the *Hazîne* and the *Seferli*, the top five or six in the *Kilâr*, having special titles;[3] while the untitled *Biçaklî Eskis* in each chamber acted as under-officers.[4] The remaining officers were appointed for skill and merit by favour—the numbers of such posts differing in each department. At the same time each department had ten officers with corresponding titles, the first of whom only was a *Biçaklî Eski*, the rest being appointed by favour.

These first ten were:

(i) The *Göç Eskisi* ('Removal, or Travel, Senior')[5]—so called because he deputized for the *Kâhyâ* of his chamber when the Sultan left the Palace for some other residence;

(ii) The *Baş Kullukçu* (Head Servant);[6]

(iii) The *Nevbetçi Başî* (Chief of the Watch);[7]

(iv) and (v) The *Kullukçus* or servants of (ii) and (iii);

(vi) The *Pâris Kâhyasî* (Intendant of the Sick-room);[8]

(vii) The *Kâhyâ's Imâm* (Prayer-leader);

(viii) The *Kâhyâ's Kullukçu*;

(ix) The *Kâhyâ's Kilârcî* (Butler);

and (x) The *Kâhyâ's Hoftâncî* (Wardrobe-master).[9]

The officers particular to each Chamber were the following:

(i) *In the* Hazîne (*Treasury*)

(i) The *Giyim Başî* (Head Robe-master)[10]—the *Kâhyâ's* deputy;

(ii) The *Baş Yazicî* (Head Clerk), also called *Baş Efendi*;

(iii) Three minor clerks, called Second, Third, and Fourth *Yazicîs*;

(iv) Three assistant *Yazicîs*.

It was the duty of these seven clerks to maintain the registers of objects conserved in the treasury, marking those removed and acquired.

[1] D'Ohsson, vii. 44.

[2] 'Aṭâ, i. 96; D'Ohsson, vii. 45.

[3] See 'Aṭâ, i. 165–6. He states that there were six entitled *Biçaklî Eskis* in the *Kilâr*, but shows only five titled. It is not clear, therefore, in which respect he is wrong.

[4] According to D'Ohsson, loc. cit., all the *Biçaklî Eskis* were '*sous-officiers*'.

[5] *Göç* means 'the act of changing one's place, a move, a migration'—from the Persian *Koç*. The *Göç Eskisis* of each department were among its *Biçaklî Eskis*.

[6] For the meaning of *Kullukçu*, see above, p. 319.

[7] For *Nevbetçi*, cf. above, p. 329, n. 5.

[8] *Pâris* (not given by Redhouse) is perhaps a corruption of *Mâriḍ* (Arabic) 'sick'.

[9] *Hoftân*, properly *Kaftân*, 'a coat'.

[10] Or *Güğüm Başî*. Though the pronunciation *Güğüm* appears to have been usual (cf. D'Ohsson, vii. 41), 'Aṭâ, i. 165, prefers *Giyim*, since *Giyim* means 'clothing', whereas *Güğüm* means 'kettle'. The *Giyim Başî* was a *Biçaklî Eski*.

(v) The *Kütüb Ḥâfiẓi* (Librarian). He was responsible to the *Kâhyâ* for the maintenance in good order of the various libraries in the Palace.

(vi) The *Çanṭaci* (Purse-keeper).[1] This officer and the *Kâhyâ's Ḥoftânci*[2] had the joint inspection of the Cupboard of the Privy Purse (*Ḥarci Ḥâṣṣe Dolâbi*) and were charged with the maintenance of its registers. They, the clerks, and the *Baş Ḳullukçu* of the *Ḥazîne*[3] were responsible to the *Kâhyâ* for the Treasury itself as opposed to the personnel of the Chamber. The *Baş Ḳullukçu* had another duty: of registering and inspecting all the hangings, carpets, and other objects supplied to the various departments of the Inside Service from the Tailors' Workshop (belonging to the Outside Service).[4]

The Treasury was originally founded to house the valuables acquired by the Sultans after the conquest first of Constantinople and later of Syria and Egypt. But it also housed the Sultan's jewels and furs, a portrait of each monarch from Meḥmed II onwards,[5] and even stores of objects in everyday use by the *Ağas* of the Service and the inmates of the *Ḥarem*.[6] Its entire contents were checked whenever the *Kâhyâ* was changed, by a process that it took several months to apply. During his term of office the *Kâhyâ* was obliged to furnish the Sultan with monthly statements of accessions and removals, drawn up by the first two clerks. Careful precautions were taken against theft. Thus, whereas the *Kâhyâ* kept the signet of Selîm I with which the doors were sealed, the Head Clerk kept their keys, so that the Treasury might be opened only with the concurrence of both. And when it was opened, for the introduction of new, or the removal of old, objects, or for the periodical cleaning of its contents, these operations were carried out under the eyes of all the principal officers of the department.[7]

As well as the officers of the *Ḥazîne* listed above D'Ohsson mentions six others, not referred to by ʿAṭâ, namely:

(i) The *Anaḫtar Ağasi* (*Ağa* of the Key)[8]—the police officer of the Chamber;

(ii) The *Serğuççu* (Keeper of the Imperial Aigrettes);

(iii) The *Ḳapaniçaci* (Keeper of the Sultan's fur-lined gala robes);

(iv) The *Ṭabaḳ Eskisi* (Senior of the Dishes)—keeper of the porcelain dinner services;

and (v) Two *Tüfengcis* (Gun-keepers)—who carried the Sultan's sporting guns when he went shooting.[9]

[1] *Çanṭa* (Turkish) 'purse, pouch, bag'.

[2] i.e. No. 10 of the officers common to all three departments.—See above.

[3] No. 2 of such officers.

[4] See below, p. 361.

[5] D'Ohsson, vii. 39; cf. ʿAṭâ, i. 57.

[6] Thus objects required for the *Ḥarem* were applied for by the *Ḳizlar Ağasi*, writing materials were applied for by the *Sirr Kâtibi* (see below, p. 343), arms by the *Tüfengci Başi* (see below, p. 344), &c.—ʿAṭâ, i. 199–200. All these objects are now to be seen in the museums of the old *Serây*.

[7] ʿAṭâ, i. 172–3; D'Ohsson, vii. 39–41.

[8] ʿAṭâ, on the other hand, shows an *Anaḫtar Ğulâmi* as belonging to the *Kilâr*, whereas D'Ohsson does not. Possibly this officer was the head *Köşe Başi*—see above, p. 332.

[9] D'Ohsson, vii. 42–3.

(ii) *In the* Kilâr (*Larder*).

(i) The *Peşkir Başî*. *Peşkir* (Persian *Pîş-gîr*) means 'napkin', and so *Peşkir Başî* 'Chief (Attendant) of the Napkin'. It was his duty to supervise the food and drink prepared for the Sultan and to keep the vessels in which these were served. He was also charged with the education and discipline of the *Ağas* of this department. His deputy and substitute for summer excursions was the *Göç Eskisi* of the *Kilâr*,[1] who was also called *Mum Başî*, or 'Chief (Attendant) of the Candle'.

(ii) The *Tepsici Eskisi* (Senior of the Tray-carriers). It was the duty of this officer to hand his silver tray and spoons to the Sultan, and to serve the *Ağas* with the white-flour cakes called *Foḍule*. He was also in charge of the kitchen called *Ḫarcî Fîrîn* or Ordinary Oven, a department of the Outside Service.[2]

(iii) The *Mum Şagirdi* (literally 'Pupil of the Candle'), whose duty it was to tend the candles of the Chamber of the Prophet's Cloak (*Ḫîrḳaî Seʿâdet Odasî*).

(iv) The *Anaḫtar Ğulâmî* (literally 'Page of the Key'). His duty was to patrol the dormitory at night together with a number of watchmen.[3]

(v) The *Şerbetçi* (Sherbet-maker). He accompanied the Sultan whenever he left the Palace, whether in state or incognito, with such food, drink, eating and washing utensils as might be needed, loaded on two mules.

(vi) The *Yemişçi* (Fruit-server).

(vii) The *Ṭurşucu* (Pickle-server).

(viii) The *Ṣu Ḳullukçu* (literally 'Water Servant'). He acted at the orders of the *Mum Başî*, causing the *Bostancîs* of the *Saḳḳâ Ocağî* to bring sweet water on mules from Çamlica to the Palace.[4]

The remaining officers were, first, the servants (*Ḳullukçus*) of the *Peşkir Başî*, of the *Tepsici Eskisi* and the *Mum Şâgirdi*, secondly, the *Şerbetçi* of princes (sons of Sultans reigning and deceased), and lastly, the *Kilâ ci* of the *Silîḥdâr Ağa*, the chief page.[5]

Responsibility for the Sultan's meals was thus divided among a number of *Ağas* under the authority of the *Kilâr Kâḫyasî*. In early times, before the creation of the posts just listed, the *Kilâr* had been managed by the *Baş Ḳullukçu*[6] of the department under the supervision of the white-eunuch *Kilârcî Başî*.[7] Subsequently, however, the *Baş Ḳullukçu* was left with no more than one or two dishes for which he was responsible. Another important officer was the *Nevbetçi Başî*[8] of the *Kilâr*. For, in the first place, he had charge of the gold and silver plate and the porcelain services in which the Sultan's meals were dished up—registers of their component pieces being kept under the direction

[1] i.e. No. 1 of the officers common to all three departments—see above, p. 334.

[2] 'Aṭâ, i. 166. *Fîrîn* is the Turkish pronunciation of the Arabic *Furn*, 'an oven'.

[3] See above, p. 335, n. 8; 'Aṭâ, i. 73–4.

[4] All the *Ağas* of this department so far listed were *Biçaḳlî Eskis* (see n. 3 on p. 334 above). Hence there were only six others.—'Aṭâ, i. 166.

[5] 'Aṭâ, i. 167.

[6] No. 2 of the officers common to all three departments.

[7] See above, p. 332.

[8] No. 3 of the officers common to all three departments.

of the *Kâhya*, the *Peşkir Başî*, and the *Nevbetçi* himself; and, in the second, he kept a medical store in which drugs and instruments for cupping and bleeding were preserved for the use of the *Ağas*. The fall of the White Eunuchs resulted in the assumption by the various officers mentioned above, but particularly by the *Nevbetçi Başî*, of most of the duties formerly performed by the *Kilârcî Başî*.[1]

(iii) *In the* Seferli (*Campaign Chamber*).

(i) The *Câmeşûy Başî* (Chief of the Laundrymen).[2]
(ii) The *Mehter Başî* (Chief of the Bandsmen).
(iii) The *Ḥammâmcî Başî* (Chief of the Bath-keepers).
(iv) The *Ṣarîḳçî Yamağîs* (Assistants to the Turban-folder).

That the duties performed by members of the *Seferli* department were highly varied was due to the circumstance of its having been created to replace the *Küçük Oda*, which, as we have remarked, was a general training school for the *Ağas*. The four principal types of service discharged by its members are said to have been: 'Drum-beating (*Ṭablzenlik*), the folding of turbans, head-shaving, and the cleaning of the royal clothes.'[3] When it was first formed, its pages used to wash the Sultan's clothes on campaign. Hence its name (*Seferli*) and the title of its principal officer (Chief of the Laundrymen). In peace time, on the other hand, these pages used only to wash various types of towels and napkins; and since the muslin turban-cloths (*Ṣarîḳ*) used by the Sultan—which, as well as his towels, continued to be washed by the *Baş Ḳullukçu*[4] of the department[5]—were not unlike these napkins, fifteen of them took over the duty (hitherto performed by certain *Ağas* of the *Ḫazîne*) of re-folding them, after washing, into the prescribed modes. These fifteen pages were the Assistants of the Turban-folder, the latter, the *Ṣarîḳçî Başî* (Chief Turban-folder) being a member of the *Ḫâṣṣ Oda*,[6] chosen from among them.[7] Twenty other pages, with ten assistants, similarly took over the duty of shaving the heads of the Service personnel, hitherto performed by such *Ağas* of the *Ḫazîne* and *Kilâr* as happened to exhibit an aptitude for this art. They acted under the orders of the Chief of the Bath-keepers, who in turn was second-in-command to the *Berber Başî* (Chief of the Barbers),[8] another member of the *Ḫâṣṣ Oda*, who shaved the Sultan himself. The *Ağas* were shaved once a month at the great bath (*Ḥammâm*) built next the *Ḫazîne* by Selîm II. This was heated for the occasion under the direction of the *Ḥammâmcî Başî* by galley slaves supplied by the Admiralty.[9] As for the duty of drum-beating—which was extended to the playing of music in general—this was discharged by the *Mehter Başî* and his bandsmen.[10] Apparently these bandsmen were drawn from

[1] 'Aṭâ, i. 174–5.
[2] From the Persian *Câme*, 'garment' and *Şûyîdän*, 'to wash'. This officer is evidently reckoned by 'Aṭâ as a *Biçaḳlî Eski*.
[3] 'Aṭâ, i. 154.
[4] No. 2 of the officers common to all departments.
[5] So 'Aṭâ, i. loc. cit.; cf. D'Ohsson, vii. 44.
[6] See below, pp. 338, 343.
[7] 'Aṭâ, i. 194–5.
[8] See below, p. 345.
[9] 'Aṭâ, i. 198.
[10] Ibid. i. 154.

among the *Ağas* called *Çavuşes* of the department. We shall have occasion to describe the *Çavuşes* of the Court, when considering the Outside Service and the Central Administration.[1] From 'Aṭâ's account it would seem that even those of the Inside Service had originally been employed, like the others, as couriers. In later times, however, though they still acted as messengers within the palace,[2] most of them were trained either as musicians, or, if they were endowed with fine voices, as *Mü'ezzins* (Callers to Prayer) or ceremonial applauders. Others are said to have acted as supervisors and as trainers of pupils in these arts.[3] Though the bandsmen proper belonged to the *Seferli* chamber, *Çavuş* musicians were also numbered, according to D'Ohsson, among the *Ağas* of the *Ḥazîne* and the *Kilâr*.[4] The *Çavuşes* of the Inside Service were headed by a *Baş Çavuş*, who ranked as one of the assistants to the pages of the *Ḥâṣṣ Oda*.[5]

3. *The* Ḥâṣṣ Oda

Just as, in the lower chambers, the officers of each were divided into two categories by the manner in which they obtained their appointments—whether by seniority or by favour shown for merit—so were those of the *Ḥâṣṣ Oda*. Thus those offices whose performance required no special skill or training were to be attained in the normal course of promotion by seniority from the '*Biçaḳlî Eski*' offices of the lower chambers; and the holders of the highest of these offices in the *Ḥâṣṣ Oda* were likewise regarded as its *Biçaḳlî Eskis*.[6] The offices of the other category—which did require skill or training in some art (such as, say, coffee-making or secretaryship)—were filled by *Ağas* other than the *Biçaḳlî Eskis* of the lower chambers. Some of the latter promotions were invariable—as, for instance, that of the *Ṣarîḳçî Başî*, who was always chosen from among the *Ṣarîḳçî Yamağîs* of the *Seferli* chamber[7]—and some variable—the post in the *Ḥâṣṣ Oda* being conferred on any *Ağa* considered suitable. The offices for which skill was needed were those known in the eighteenth century as '*Mâ-beynci*'; their holders were the Sultan's personal attendants *par excellence*, discharging their duties in the *Mâ-beyn* or Intermediate Apartments[8]—between the *Ḥarem* on the one hand and the Third Court (the sphere of the Inside Service as a whole) on the other. It appears that before the reorganization consequent on the fall from influence of the White Eunuchs, all the principal pages of the *Ḥâṣṣ Oda*, if not the others as well, were regarded as *Mâ-beyncis*. But after that event the *Biçaḳlî Eski* pages ranked above the *Mâ-beyncis*,[9] so that the offices of the chamber were virtually divided into three grades: the highest was that of the *Biçaḳlî Eskis* or Superior *Ağas*; the second was that of the *Mâ-beyncis*;

[1] See below, pp. 349–50, and p. 118 above.
[2] Thus D'Ohsson, vii. 46, states that two from each chamber were always in attendance on the *Silîḥdâr Ağa*, to convey his orders to the subordinate pages.
[3] 'Aṭâ, i. 170. [4] D'Ohsson, vii. 46. [5] 'Aṭâ, i. 168.
[6] According to 'Aṭâ, i. 188, 192. D'Ohsson makes no reference to *Biçaḳli Eskis* in the *Ḥâṣṣ Oda*. [7] See above, p. 337.
[8] *Mâ-beyn* meaning, in Arabic, 'what is between'.
[9] See 'Aṭâ, i. 190, 201.

and the third that of the Inferior *Ağas*. who seem to have gone by no distinct appellation.[1]

The *Ḥâṣṣ Oda* was created by the Conqueror, in whose *Ḳânûn-nâme* its four chief office-holders are mentioned by title.[2] Its personnel is said to have been fixed at forty by Selîm I, when he constituted the pages that composed it guardians of the Prophet's Cloak.[3] According to D'Ohsson, it still stood at forty in his day, this auspicious number then including the Sultan himself—so that of the pages there were no more than thirty-nine.[4] ʿAṭâ, on the other hand, gives us to understand that the pages themselves numbered forty apart not only from the Sultan (of whose inclusion he makes no mention) but also from the *Silîḥdâr Ağa*, usually reckoned as the principal page.[5] Otherwise their accounts, though ʿAṭâ's is far fuller, differ on only a few points, the main discrepancy between them lying in the number of *Ağas* to be placed in each of the three grades.

There seems to be no doubt, nevertheless, that, whether included in the forty[6] or not, the *Silîḥdâr* came at length to be regarded as of an eminence that placed him above even the category of the superior *Ağas*, just as the *Kâḫyâs* of the lower chambers stood apart from their subordinate officers. Indeed, the *Silîḥdâr* and the *Kâḫyâs* may be said to have formed a category of their own, the *Kâḫyâ* of the *Ḫazîne*, as we have noted, being generally appointed to succeed to the post of *Silîḥdâr* when this fell vacant. We therefore place the *Silîḥdâr* in a section by himself.

(i) *The* Silîḥdâr Ağa (*Sword-keeper*).

The *Silîḥdâr's* original duties were to carry the Sultan's sword hanging from his left shoulder (except at ceremonies, when he carried it over his right shoulder); and to guard and keep in good trim all the Sultan's armour and weapons.[7] After his advancement to first place in the Service, however, he was charged with many others. He then remained in perpetual attendance from the time when the Sultan appeared for early morning prayer until his retirement late in the evening. All communications (*Telḫîṣ*) from ministers and others were presented by him; and all the Sultan's commands (*Irâde*) were conveyed by him to the officers or officials concerned. He further supervised the conduct of all ceremonies in which the Sultan took part; had joint charge, with the *Kâḫyâ* of the *Ḫazîne*, of the Privy Purse Cupboard already mentioned;[8] was responsible for the good behaviour of all the pages—relying on the *Kâḫyâs* of the three inferior chambers to maintain discipline on his behalf; received novices into the Service, and arranged pensions for *Ağas* on their retirement; and commanded the Outside-Service corps of the *Zülüflü Balṭacis*.[9] His importance was reflected in

[1] ʿAṭâ's references to the inferior *Ağas* are somewhat confusing. See below, pp. 345–6.

[2] See *O.T.E.M.*, No. 14, Appendix, 23.

[3] ʿAṭâ, i. 30, 94.

[4] D'Ohsson, vii. 34.

[5] See ʿAṭâ, i. 188, 192, where the page highest in rank mentioned is the *Çoḳadâr Ağa*.

[6] Or thirty-nine.

[7] D'Ohsson, vii. 34–5.

[8] Above, p. 335.

[9] See above, p. 86.

the large size of his entourage. This consisted of five *Lalas*,[1] a *Ḫoftâncı*,[2] a *Kilârcı*,[3] a *Tütüncü*,[4] nine *Çoḳadârs* (Valets), who also acted as Falconers,[5] three *Zülüflü Balṭacıs*, six *Ṣofalıs*, two *Yedekçis*, two *Heğbecis*, one *Ṣaḳḳâ*, and five *Aşçıs*.[6] When dismissed, the *Sılıḥdâr*, unless pensioned off, was usually given Egypt or some other important provincial governorship.[7]

(ii) *The Superior* Ağas, *or* Biçaḳlı Eskis *of the* Ḫâṣṣ Oda.

(1) and (2). The *Çoḳadâr Ağa* (Valet) and the *Rikâbdâr Ağa* (Stirrup-holder). After the reorganization the offices of these *Ağas* became all but sinecures. Çorlulu 'Alî Paşa when *Sılıḥdâr* had insisted on their holders' performing *Mâ-beynci* duty; but by the end of the seventeenth century the former practice by which pages were quickly promoted from the Inside Service to some State employment had fallen into desuetude, with the result that promotion within the Service was far slower than formerly, and *Ağas* could not easily attain to high posts such as these before they were sixty years old and more; at this age *Mâ-beynci* duty was too strenuous for them; and they were therefore excused all service but that of acting as the *Sılıḥdâr's* adjutants at public ceremonies. They used also, in company with the *Sılıḥdâr* and the White Eunuch *Ḫâṣṣ Oda Başı*, to attend the Sultan when he travelled by water.

Before the reorganization it was the duty of the *Rikâbdâr* to accompany the Sultan when he went for otherwise solitary rides in the palace grounds or elsewhere, and to hold his stirrup when he mounted and dismounted. In later times the *Çoḳadâr* used to walk on the Sultan's right in processions, carrying the Privy Waterproof (*Ḫâṣṣ Yağmurluḳ*), and to scatter handfuls of newly minted silver among the crowd when the Sultan rode to mosque.[8] Before the reorganization he may perhaps have been the direct superior of the *Mâ-beynci* called, confusingly enough, *Baş Çoḳadâr* (Head Valet), whose[9] duties really had to do with the Sultan's clothes. In early times the *Rikâbdâr* was the senior of the two in rank;[10] but in the eighteenth century the *Çoḳadâr* not only deputized for the *Sılıḥdâr* in the latter's absence, but habitually succeeded him in office. The *Rikâbdâr* was then likewise the *Çoḳadâr's* deputy and heir to his post. Of all the *Ağas* these two and the *Sılıḥdâr* alone had the privilege of wearing turbans, their inferiors wearing embroidered caps.[11]

[1] See below, p. 331. [2] Cf. above, p. 334.
[3] An officer of the *Kilâr* department—see above, p. 336.
[4] *Tütün* means 'tobacco'.
[5] *Çaḳir-ṣalan*—for Falconers see below, pp. 347–8.
[6] For the *Ocaḳs* of the *Ṣofa*, the *Yedekçis*, the *Saḳḳâs*, and the *Aşçıs* see below, pp. 354, 357, 361.
[7] 'Aṭâ, i. 209–12; D'Ohsson, vii. 34–5; *O.T.E.M.*, No. 14 Appendix, 23, notes.
[8] *O.T.E.M.*, No. 14, Appendix, 23–4, notes.
[9] See below, p. 342.
[10] See *O.T.E.M.*, No. 14, Appendix, 14.
[11] 'Aṭâ, i. 208–9; D'Ohsson, vii. 35; *O.T.E.M.*, No. 14, Appendix, 23–4, notes.

(3). The *Dülhend Ağasi* (*Ağa* of the Turban).[1] 'Aṭâ and D'Ohsson are at variance in their explanation of this page's title. D'Ohsson states that he and another *Ḫâṣṣ Odali* followed the Sultan in processions carrying imperial turbans which they inclined to spectators for their salutes.[2] 'Aṭâ states that the *Dülbend Ağasi* was the Sultan's deputy for the service and inspection of the Chamber of the Prophet's Cloak (*Ḫirḳai Seʿâdet Odasi*), and that when visitants kissed the blessed garment, he would wipe it with an embroidered turban-cloth. According to this account, not only was he responsible for the cleaning of this Chamber and for the lighting of its candles (with the assistance of the *Mum Şâgirdi* of the *Kilâr*),[3] but arranged the order in which the *Ḫâṣṣ Odalis* should perform in it the perpetual recitation of sacred texts that was one of their principal functions. They would remain on duty for this purpose for twenty-four hours, two at a time;[4] and the *Dülbend Ağasi* would report shortcomings in their performance to the *Silihdâr*.[5]

(4). The *Anaḫtar Ağasi* (*Ağa* of the Key).[6] After the reorganization it was by this officer that the eunuch *Ḫâṣṣ Oda Başi* was replaced as controller of the highest chamber.[7] His office corresponded to those of the *Kâḫyâs* of the lower chambers. His chief duty was to ensure the proper performance of their services by the *Ḫâṣṣ Odalis*, to apportion these services between them, to see that they went to mosque on being woken in the morning, to receive their applications for sick-leave, and to supervise the cleaning of their place of assembly, called *Yeşil Direk* (The Green Pillar).[8] D'Ohsson states that he also acted as housekeeper (*économe*) to the Chamber and as intendant of the Sultan's table.[9]

(5). The *Baş Peşkir Ağasi* (Head *Ağa* of the Napkin).[10] After the reorganization this officer seems no longer to have performed the duty implied in his title—of presenting the Sultan with a napkin on which to wipe his hands after washing them.[11] Instead he now acted as deputy for the *Anaḫtar Ağasi* when the Sultan left the palace for some other residence in the summer. For neither the *Anaḫtar Ağasi* nor the three *Kâḫyâs* of the lower chambers went on these visits. The *Baş Peşkir Ağasi* therefore controlled all the *Ḫaṣṣ Odalis* that accompanied the Sultan, and received the reports both of the *Göç Eskisis* that then deputized for the *Kâḫyâs* and of the white eunuchs—*Serây Kâḫyasi*[12]

[1] *Dülbend*, from the Persian *Dolbänd*, is probably the word from which our 'turban, turband' is derived—*Encyclopedia of Islam*, art. 'Turban'. It is the equivalent of the Turkish *Ṣariḳ*—see above, p. 337.

[2] D'Ohsson, vii. 35.

[3] See above, p. 336.

[4] Cf. D'Ohsson, vii. 38.

[5] 'Aṭâ, i. 207–8.

[6] *Anaḫtar* (written *Anaḫdar* by 'Aṭâ) is from the Greek.

[7] 'Aṭâ, i. 164.

[8] Ibid. 206.

[9] D'Ohsson, vii.

[10] Cf. with the *Peşkir Başi*—above, p. 336.

[11] Perhaps he was formerly merely the superior of the *Peşkir Başi*, just as the *Çoḳadâr Ağa* may have been the superior of the *Baş Çoḳadâr*—see above, p. 340.

[12] 'Aṭâ has *Serây Ağasi*; but as we have noted above, p. 333, the *Serây Ağasi*, according to D'Ohsson, vii. 57, in fact commanded at the Palace when the Sultan was away.

and *Kilârcî Başî*—that likewise deputized for the *Ḳapî Ağasî*. On these occasions the *Baş Peşkir Ağasî*, like the *Anaḫtar Ağasî* at other times, was of course responsible to the *Silîḥdâr Ağa*.[1]

(6). The *Biniş Peşkir Ağasî* (literally 'Riding *Ağa* of the Napkin'). This officer was the adjutant of the *Baş Peşkir Ağasî*. What was meant by '*Biniş*' was the Sultan's appearances outside the *Serây* on horseback. Possibly the *Biniş Peşkir Ağasî* was responsible for any *Ḫâṣṣ Odalîs* of rank inferior to his own that took part in these cavalcades.

(7). The *Ibrîḳdâr Ağasî* (*Ağa* of the Ewer). ʿAṭâ does not mention this page. But D'Ohsson states that his office was to pour water over the Sultan's hands when he wished to wash them.[2]

(8) and (9). Two *Köşe Başîs* (literally 'Heads of the Corner'), called by ʿAṭâ *Köşe Peşkir Ağaşîs* (literally 'Corner *Ağas* of the Napkin'). D'Ohsson calls them the police officers of the Chamber; and ʿAṭâ, who notices them together with the *Biniş Peşkir Ağasî*, specifies it as their duty to accompany the Sultan wherever he went, and, while resting under umbrellas set up in the corners of such places, to supervise the 'standing in a row' of the *Ḫâṣṣ Odalîs* in attendance and the decent behaviour of those awaiting their turn.[3]

(iii) *The* Mâ-beyncis.

(1). The *Baş Çoḳadâr* (Head Valet). The *Mâ-beyncis* as his personal attendants came into closer contact with the Sultan than the 'Superior' *Ağas*, and so in a way enjoyed an esteem almost as great as theirs. The *Baş Çoḳadâr* as their head was, at least in the eighteenth century, an officer of importance scarcely less than that of the *Silîḥdâr*, to whom he acted as assistant for the affairs of the *Mâ-beyn*. His duties were very various. To begin with, he had under him forty subordinate *Çoḳadârs* of two grades,[4] members of the three lower chambers, the

[1] ʿAṭâ, i. 206; D'Ohsson, vii. 36.

[2] D'Ohsson, vii. 36. This statement seems open to suspicion. Such a duty would imply that its performer was a *Mâ-beynci*. But the *Ibrîḳdâr Ağasi* is not included by D'Ohsson among the *Mâ-beyncis*.

[3] There is some confusion in ʿAṭâ's references to these officers. In one passage (i. 205) he states that the three subordinates of the *Baş Peşkir Ağasi* were called *Biniş* and *Köşe Peşkir Ağasis*; but goes on to describe their system of promotion, which, he says, was from the rank of *Biniş Peşkir Ağasî* to that of *Göç* (not mentioned before) and then to *Baş Peşkir Ağasi*—implying presumably that the four officers concerned were called, in order of diminishing importance,

(1) *Baş Peşkir Ağasi*,
(2) *Göç Peşkir Ağasi*,
(3) *Biniş Peşkir Ağasi*,
and (4) *Köşe Peşkir Ağasi*.

In another passage (i. 192) he refers to the *Baş Peşkir Ağasi*, three *Köşe Peşkir Ağasis* and four *Köşe Başis*, stating that these eight officers with their superiors, the *Çoḳadâr Ağa*, the *Rikâbdâr Ağa*, the *Dülbend Ağasi*, and the *Anaḫtar Ağasi*, were the twelve *Biçaḳli Eskis* of the *Ḫâṣṣ Oda*. Finally, in yet a third passage (i. 192–3) he states that of eight *Ḫâṣṣ Odali* office-holders three were called *Peşkir Ağasis* and five *Köşe Başis*, the *rest* being called *Biçaḳli Eskis*. This being so, we have followed D'Ohsson.

[4] The first twenty were accoutred with finery supplied from the *Ḫazîne*; the second twenty, who were regarded as their *Mülâzims* (i.e. candidates for succession to their posts) had to supply their own.

senior of whom was entitled *Ikinci*, or Second, *Çoḳadâr*, and the next in rank *Cizmeci* (Boot-holder), because when the Sultan went riding he carried his boots in a bag, while the Second *Çoḳadâr* likewise carried his slippers.[1] The *Baş Çoḳadâr* further commanded a number of *ocaḳs*, or corps, of the Outside Service,[2] and was Inspector of the treasury attached to the Imperial Stables.[3] He and his subordinates had the privilege of receiving the Grand *Vezîr*, the *Şeyḫü'l-Islâm* and the *Ḫâns* of the Crimea when they came to the *Serây* for investitures. When the Sultan rode in public, it was they who collected petitions presented to him *en route*. The Second *Çoḳadâr* controlled the subordinate *Çoḳadârs* as his second-in-command; the *Cizmeci* controlled the nine crews, each of twelve men, who rowed the Palace boats called *Ṣandal*.[4]

(2). The *Sirr Kâtibi* (literally 'Clerk of the Secret'—or 'Secretary' in its strict sense). Though ranking after the *Baş Çoḳadâr*, this page came to be respected more than any of the other *Mâ-beyncis*, owing to his knowledge of state secrets. D'Ohsson, indeed, lists him above the *Baş Çoḳadâr*. One of the *Yazîcîs* of the *Ḫazîne* was usually promoted to this post. It was the *Sirr Kâtibi's* duty to break the seals of *Telḫîṣes*[5] presented by the *Silîḥdâr Ağa* and hand them to the Sultan. When after reading one the Sultan would write a reply, the *Sirr Kâtibi* would seal and dispatch it by a messenger of the Outside Service. He had also to preserve papers not immediately dealt with, and submit them later, when necessary, for the Sultan's reconsideration. Further, he would cause his *Yamaḳ* or Assistant to make précis of the petitions collected by the *Çoḳadârs* on the Sultan's public appearances, and present them together with the originals. This latter duty appertained before the reform to the *Ḳapî Ağasî* and was assumed under the régime of Çorlulu 'Alî Paşa by the *Silîḥdâr*.[6] The *Sirr Kâtibi* used also to follow the Sultan in processions, carrying his writing materials in a gold-embroidered bag, and wore in his belt as a badge of office a golden pen-case.[7]

(3). The *Ṣarîḳçî Başî* (Chief of the Turban-folders). As we have stated, this officer was promoted from among the fifteen *Ṣarîḳçî Yamağîs* of the *Seferli* chamber, who worked at his orders. They kept turbans of every description for the Sultan to wear by way of disguise on gilt stools in a room called the *Ṣarîḳ Odasî*, overlooking the southern mouth of the Bosphorus.[8] A turban once worn would be undone and repaired, the cap (*Ḳavuḳ*) about which it was wound being handed over for attention to another *Ağa* called *Ḳavuḳçu Başî*. When new cloths had to be bought, the *Ṣarîḳçî Başî* informed the *Baş Ḳulluḳçu* and the

[1] D'Ohsson states that the slippers (or sandals) were carried by the *Baş Çoḳadâr*.

[2] See below, pp. 351–62. 'Aṭâ here states that he also commanded the *Peyks* and *Ṣolaḳs*—see above, p. 87.

[3] See below, p. 355.

[4] See below, p. 351. He evidently controlled them as deputy for the *Baş Çoḳadâr*, who was their official controller.—'Aṭâ, i. 201–4; D'Ohsson, vii. 36–7.

[5] See above, p. 122.

[6] 'Aṭâ, i. 200–1.

[7] D'Ohsson, vii. 36.

[8] In later times, that is to say. Earlier these turbans were kept in a pavilion called Revân Odasî ('Aṭâ).

Ḫoftânci of the *Ḫazîne*, in the registers of which these purchases were recorded.[1]

(4). The *Ḳahveci Başi* (Chief of the Coffee-makers). It was the duty of this *Ağa* to prepare and serve coffee, first, to the Sultan after morning prayer and after the midday and evening meals, and, secondly, to such dignitaries as the *Şeyḫü'l-Islâm*, the *Ḫân* of the Crimea, *Vezîrs* and *Ḳâḍî-'askers*, who assembled when the Sultan rode out from the Palace. According to 'Aṭâ, in early times he was not always given *Mâ-beynci* rank, and though later he invariably held it, he then ceased in fact to perform *Mâ-beynci* duties, serving coffee himself only when the Sultan appeared in public on occasions of ceremony. The *Ḳahveci Başi* had charge of all the vessels and utensils used for coffee-making. These were registered in the *Ḫazîne*, and if broken had to be replaced by him at his own expense.[2]

(5). The *Mü'ezzin Başi* (Chief of the Callers to Prayer). The duties of a *Mu'ezzin* we shall describe when considering the Learned Profession.[3] Suffice it to remark here that the *Mü'ezzin Başi* officiated in whatever Imperial Mosque the Sultan chose to visit on Fridays. He was the head of a corps of minor *Mü'ezzins*, chosen for their melodious voices from the *Çavuşes* of the lower chambers.[4] His second-in-command was called *Baş Mü'ezzin* or *Seri Maḥfil* (Head of the Box—that is, the private box behind the grille of which the Sultan followed the services in Imperial Mosques). The *Seri Maḥfil* trained the *Çavuşes* that were candidates for posts as *Mü'ezzins*, and recommended those that showed an aptitude to the *Mü'ezzin Başi* for appointment when a vacancy occurred. He also arranged the minor *Mü'ezzins*' time-table of duties. By becoming *Mü'ezzins* the *Ağas* chosen were admitted into the Learned Profession, and so, strictly speaking, ceased to be *Ḳapi Ḳulus*. Thus the *Mü'ezzin Başis* were often promoted to the Imperial Imâmate (a Learned post of the Outside Service) and might thence rise to even the august rank of *Ḳâḍî-'asker*.[5]

(6). The *Tüfengci Başi* (Chief of the Gun-keepers).[6] This *Ağa* was assisted by twenty other *Tüfengcis*, drawn from the three lower chambers,[7] among whom he himself had formerly served. The Sultan's sporting guns, which it was their province to look after, were kept in a cupboard by the entrance to the Chamber of the Prophet's Cloak. On the monarch's monthly shooting expeditions the *Tüfengci Başi* would cause these guns to be taken by three attendants called *Avadan Bostancis*[8] to the ground, where he and his assistants, who also carried the targets for range-shooting, would prime and adjust them. The game shot was delivered to him. The *Tüfengcis* further attended to all the fire-arms used in the Inside Service, causing ammunition of the

[1] 'Aṭâ, i. 194–5; D'Ohsson, vii. 37.
[2] 'Aṭâ, i. 196–7; D'Ohsson. vii. loc. cit.
[3] Below, Chapter IX.
[4] Cf. above, p. 338.
[5] 'Aṭâ, i. 169; D'Ohsson, vii. 36. D'Ohsson places the *Mü'ezzin Başi* first in the list of *Mâ-beyncis*, above the *Sirr Kâtibi* and the *Baş Çoḳadâr*.
[6] D'Ohsson calls him '*Porte-Arquebuse*'.
[7] See above, p. 335, for the two *Tüfengcis* stated by D'Ohsson to be officers of the *Ḫazîne*.
[8] Or *Işlikçis*—see below, p. 353.

requisite calibres to be cast for them. The powder used was supplied by the *Silihdâr Ağa.*[1]

(7). The *Berber Başi* (Chief of the Barbers). This *Ağa* was appointed to the *Ḫâṣṣ Oda* from among the barbers of the *Seferli* chamber with whom we have already dealt.[2] It was his duty to shave the Sultan in person. The hair shaved was carefully preserved in a box and sent yearly with the *Ṣurra* (the purse containing the Sultan's annual present to the *Şerîfs* of the Ḥijâz) to Medina, where it was honourably interred. ʿAṭâ states that the *Berber Başi* was not invariably of *Mâ-beynci* rank.[3]

(8). The *Ṭirnaḳçi* (Manicurist).[4] He used to pare the Sultan's nails on Thursdays.[5] This page is not mentioned by D'Ohsson.

(9). The *Baş Lala* (Head Tutor). This officer kept a special medicine chest—of drugs rarer than those conserved by the *Nevbetçi Başi* of the *Kilâr*. He had a *Ḳulluḳçu* and five other attendants drawn from various *ocaḳs* of the Outside Service, one of whom, a *Zülüflü Balṭaci*, used, with the *Ḳulluḳçu*, to make up prescriptions from these drugs under the direction of an apothecary acting at the orders of the *Ḥekîm Başi* (Chief of the Physicians—another 'Learned' post of the Outside Service).[6] When ready the medicines in question were sealed jointly by the Chief Physician and the *Baş Lala*. The *Baş Lala* used also to be present at all the Sultan's meals. Apparently his post, since it carried a salary only of the second scale, used sometimes to be held together with that of *Ḳahveci Başi*.[7] Possibly for this reason D'Ohsson ignores it. He refers indeed to *Baş Lalas* as tutors (*gouverneurs*) of princes, stating that they were *Ḫâṣṣ Odalis*;[8] but presumably the pages to whom such offices were given were, so to speak, seconded from the *Ḫâṣṣ Oda* and so were supplementary to the thirty-nine or forty of its establishment proper.

The remaining three *Mâ-beyncis*, if there were twelve, as is stated by D'Ohsson,[9] had no titles. Indeed, D'Ohsson, who, as we say, omits the *Ṭirnaḳçi* and the *Baş Lala* from his list, leaves the last five untitled. ʿAṭâ makes no references to *Mâ-beyncis* other than those already mentioned. This being so, we may pass on to the inferior *Ağas*.

(iv) *The Inferior* Ağas.

These, according to D'Ohsson, numbered seventeen. Unhappily he supplies us with no further information about them; and that which may be deduced from ʿAṭâ's account is not only scarcely more considerable but also highly confused. Thus in one passage[10] he states that the establishment of forty was made up of five *Ağas* (omitting the assistants of the *Baş Peşkir Ağasi*), eight *Mâ-beyncis* (omitting the *Ṭirnaḳçi*) and twenty-seven other '*Gediklis*'; in another[11] that the *Ḫâṣṣ Odalis* inferior to the twelve *Biçaḳli Eskis* consisted of eight ordinary *Biçaḳlis* and twenty '*Gediklis*', who in turn had fifteen *Mülâzims*; and in a third[12] that, according to some accounts, the forty were divided

1 ʿAṭâ, i. 195–6. 2 Above, p. 337. 3 ʿAṭâ, i. 198.
4 *Ṭirnaḳ* means 'finger-nail'. 5 ʿAṭâ, i. 198.
6 See below, Chapter XI. 7 ʿAṭâ, i. 193–4. 8 D'Ohsson, vii. 97.
9 D'Ohsson, vii. 38. 10 ʿAṭâ, i. 191. 11 Ibid. 192. 12 Ibid.

into an upper and a lower twenty. In both the last two passages he makes no reference to the *Mâ-beyncis*, and so leaves us in ignorance of the manner in which they fitted into the scheme of the *Biçaḳlis*. It appears that the *Biçaḳli* pages, namely those that were promoted by mere seniority, enjoyed automatic increases of pay according to the rank, rather than the post, that each attained; whereas each *Mâ-beynci* post seems to have carried a specific rate of pay.[1] Possibly, therefore, the *Biçaḳli* system applied only to the non-*Mâ-beynci Ağas*, who would thus be divided into the two sections we have called superior and inferior (i.e. to the *Mâ-beyncis*). Putting the two accounts together, accordingly, and supposing that there were, in fact, twelve superior *Ağas*, as is stated by ʿAṭâ, and twelve *Mâ-beyncis*, as is stated by D'Ohsson, we are left with either fifteen or sixteen inferior *Ağas*, of whom eight may have been ordinary *Biçaḳlis*.

As we have noted, ʿAṭâ also refers to fifteen *Mülâzims*, extra to the forty *Gedikli* posts. In fact, he refers to them at least twice;[2] and it is possible that among these *Mülâzims*, or even among the inferior *Ağas* themselves, there may have been included such assistants of the more important pages as the Second *Çoḳadâr* and his colleague the *Cizmeci*, the *Baş Çavuş*, the *Seri Maḥfil*, the *Yamaḳs* of the *Sirr Kâtibi* and the *Tüfengci Başi*, and the falconers of the *Siliḥdâr* and the other principal *Ağas*. ʿAṭâ certainly refers to these office-holders, and others, such as an *Imâm* of the *Ḫâṣṣ Oda*, as if they were no longer connected with any of the lower chambers.[3] Unfortunately he is no more explicit than this.

(C) THE OUTSIDE SERVICE

1. *The* Ağas *of the Stirrup*

In the *Ḳânûn-nâme* of the Conqueror[4] the following persons are listed as *Ağas* of the Stirrup:

1. *Yeniçeri Ağasi.*
2. *Mîr ʿAlem.*
3. *Ḳapici Başi.*
4–5. *Mîr-Aḫor* (later two).
6. *Çaḳirci Başi.*
7. *Çaşnî-gîr Başi.*
8–13. Six *Ağas* of the Cavalry *Bölüks*.
14. *Çavuş Başi.*
15. *Ḳapicilar Kâḫyasi.*
16. *Cebeci Başi.*
17. *Ṭopçu Başi.*

The non-military *Ağas* were then, therefore (1) the *Mîr-ʿAlem*, (2) the *Ḳapici Başi*, (3) the Great *Mîr-Aḫor*, (4) the Little *Mîr-Aḫor*, (5) the *Çaḳirci Başi*, (6) the *Çâşnî-gîr Başi*, (7) the *Çavuş Başi*, and (8) the

[1] See ʿAṭâ's contrasted lists of persons eligible for the two types of promotion —i. 165–8.
[2] Another reference being i. 190.
[3] See the headings of the lists—i. 168–9.
[4] *O.T.E.M.*, No. 13, Appendix, 11–12.

Ḳapicilar Kâhyasî; and the four of these seven who had lost the rank of *Ağa* by the eighteenth century were the *Ḳapici Başî*, the *Çaḳirci Başî*, the *Çâṣnî-gîr Başî*, and the *Çavuş Başî*.

The change was evidently made at some date after 1677, since all these functionaries still appear as *Ağas* of the Stirrup in a *Ḳânûn* of that year—possibly it was made during the reign of Aḥmed III (1703–30), when many alterations in ancient procedure were effected. According to this same *Ḳânûn* some of the *Ağas* had it as their privilege to assist the Sultan in mounting his horse. Then the Great Master of the Horse held the near, and the chief *Ḳapici Başî* (for, as we shall see, there were then a large number of *Ḳapici Başîs*) the off-stirrup, the Standard-bearer holding the reins, the *Çâṣnî-gîr Başî* supporting the 'Blessed Elbow', and the Little Master of the Horse (here called *Aḥor Ḳalfasî*) holding the animal's head.[1]

We propose here to amplify the account already given of the *Ağas* of the Stirrup and of the men that they commanded. Since those that had lost this rank by the eighteenth century have not yet been considered at any length, we therefore begin with them.

2. Former Ağas *of the Stirrup*

(i) *The* Ḳapici Başi.

There was thus originally only one *Ḳapici Başî* or Head Doorkeeper. But before long the post was doubled; and as time went on there were created at first four such posts, later ten, and finally, by the time of D'Ohsson, no less than a hundred and fifty. They thus formed a corps, for which a post of commander was created called *Baş Ḳapici Başî* or Chief Head Doorkeeper. At the same time they were made dependent on the *Mîr-ʿAlem*; and the original eminence of the employment was to some extent maintained in that only such eminent persons as the sons of *Beys*, *Paşas*, and other notables were admitted to the corps. The fact again that the original *Ḳapici Başî* was a doorkeeper was reflected in the nightly attendance of one[2] of their number at the *Orta Ḳapi*, the great door leading into the second court of the *Serây*. Otherwise the later *Ḳapici Başîs* were employed chiefly as chamberlains at palace receptions, and for particularly important and secret missions to the provinces. Twelve of them accompanied the Sultan when he went to mosque on Fridays.[3]

(ii) *The* Çaḳirci Başi.

Çaḳir means 'falcon'. The *Çaḳirci Başî* was therefore the Chief Falconer. In the time of the Conqueror he was in charge of all the palace falconers; but in the course of the sixteenth century when hawking was at its most popular at court, three other posts of more or less equal status were created, namely those of *Şahinci Başî*, *Doğanci Başî*, and *Atmacaci Başî*—*Şâhîn*, *Doğan*, and *Atmaca* meaning respectively peregrine, lanner, and sparrow-hawk; and the *Çaḳirci Başî* not

---

[1] *M.T.M.*, i. 526.
[2] D'Ohsson. ʿAṭâ, i. 61, states that two went on night duty by hours.
[3] D'Ohsson, vii. 14, 18–19; *O.T.E.M.*, No. 13, Appendix, 11, note.

only lost his pre-eminence, but fell to second place, ranking after the *Şahinci Başî*. During or after the reign of Selîm II (1566–74), again, the sport fell into disfavour with the Sultans; while their subjects found that to kill game was impious, as requiring a payment of alms in expiation of the cruelty involved, and to eat it imprudent, since the game might itself have been contaminated with some impure substance.[1] Though, therefore, the four Chief Hawkers were still maintained, and though each of the principal pages continued to count a falconer in his suite,[2] these offices had become by the eighteenth century pure sinecures, and then ranked as we have mentioned after those of the Commissioners, in the third category of the Outside Service. The *Doğancî Başî*, it may be remarked, was responsible for the Bulgarian *'askerîs*, also called *Doğancî*, that were charged with raising falcons for the *Serây*.[3]

(iii) *The* Çâşnî-gîr Başî.

Çâşnî-gîr in Persian means 'taster'. The *Çâşnî-ğir Başî* in the time of the Conqueror, as an *Ağa* of the Stirrup, was an officer of considerable importance. By the time of D'Ohsson, however, he ranked only as of the fifth category in the Outside Service, being subordinate to the Commissioner of the Kitchen and the eunuch and page of the Chamber of the Larder.[4] Nevertheless, he had under his control about fifty lesser tasters, whose duty it was to bring in, under his directions, the trays of food from which the Grand *Vezîr* and other ministers should eat on days of *Dîvân*. Moreover, he had charge of part of the imperial kitchen called *Ḥalvâ-Ḫâne*, or Sweet-House, together with two other officials called *Ḥalvâcî Başî* (Chief Sweet-maker) and *Ḫoş-Âb Başî* (Chief Syrup-maker). Once a year at a night known as *Ot Gecesi* (literally 'Fire Night') the personnel of this department distributed special sweet pastes flavoured with peppermint and other condiments to all the inmates of the *Serây*, and were rewarded by witnessing a performance by the jugglers and conjurers under the control of the Head Gardener. Their services might also at other times be hired by the Palace *Ağas*; and perhaps because they were thereby brought into contact with the eminent it was not uncommon for members of the *Ḥalvâ-ḫâne* to rise in the palace service with unaccustomed rapidity. A notable case of such swift promotions was that of the celebrated Grand *Vezîr* Köprülü Meḥmed, who began his career as one of these sweet-makers.

D'Ohsson does not mention the Chief Syrup-maker, but states that the Chief Sweet-maker, who was also an officer of the fifth Category, had about one hundred and fifty assistants.[5] According to the *Ḳânûn-nâme* of 'Abdu'r-Raḥmân Tevḳî'î, the tasters were also employed

1 D'Ohsson, iv. 25–6.

2 'Aṭâ, i. 168. These were *Şahincis*, not to be confused with the *Ḳuşçus* (see below, p. 350).

3 D'Ohsson, vii. 20; *O.T.E.M.*, No. 13, Appendix, 12, note; cf. above, p. 54.

4 Cf. above, p. 332 and below, p. 357.

5 *O.T.E.M.*, No. 13, Appendix, 12, note; 'Aṭâ, i. 297–8; D'Ohsson, vii. 22–3.

as messengers, to whom, as to the *Muteferriḳas*, missions of secondary importance were entrusted.[1]

(iv) *The* Çavuş Başî (*and the* Çavuşes).

Çavuş means 'herald, messenger, or pursuivant'.[2] The employment of *Çavuşes* by the Ottoman Sultans has been ascribed to their imitation of Byzantine usages; but this ascription has been proved false, since it has been shown that functionaries bearing this name were also employed by various pre-Ottoman Moslem governments.[3] The first Ottoman *Çavuşes* appear to have discharged the duties of ushers, messengers, and guards. As we shall explain, the early Sultans were in the habit of giving public audiences nearly every day, partly for the transaction of State business, partly for the reception of distinguished guests, and partly for the administration of justice. The *Çavuşes* and their captain the *Çavuş Başî* attended these assemblies to usher in guests, officers, officials, and litigants, and to carry the Sultan's orders to their recipients whether in the capital or in the provinces. Again, when the Sultan left the palace, the *Çavuşes* headed his cavalcade as part of the body-guard, and accompanied him when he went on campaign.[4]

By the second half of the fifteenth century, there were already two types of *Çavuş*: those that were paid by the Treasury, called '*Ölûfeli* (i.e. 'pay-drawers') and those that subsisted on fiefs, called *Gedikli* (i.e. 'reserve')—the latter name seeming to show that the original *Çavuşes* were all paid.[5] Whether there was any difference between the duties performed by one type and those performed by the other does not, however, appear. What is certain is that as time went on both were supplanted as couriers by other functionaries—*Ḳapîcî Başîs*, *Ḫâṣṣekîs*, and *Muteferriḳas*,[6] and that apart from their continued participation in the Sultan's public processions, they came to be attached to the service of the Grand *Vezîr* (who eventually discharged all the Sultan's other public duties) rather than that of the palace. Hence the loss of Stirrup rank by the *Çavuş Başî* and his classification by D'Ohsson[7] as a minister of state rather than a court official. That he continued to act jointly with the *Ḳapîcîlar Kâhyasî*[8] as master of ceremonies at *Dîvâns* did not mean that he was thereby properly a member of the Outside Service, since the *Dîvâns* were now presided over not by the

---

[1] *M.T.M.* i. 526.   [2] See Redhouse.

[3] Köprülüzade, 'Bizans'in Osmanli Muesseselerine Te'sîri' in *Türk Ḥukûk ve Iḳtiṣât Ta'rîhi Mecmû'asî* i. 211 sq.

[4] There are no references in the *Ḳânûn-nâme* of the Conqueror to the duties of *Çavuşes*; but 'Ata, i. 169-70, for instance, states that they were used as messengers in early times, and the *Ḳânûn-nâme* of 'Abdu'r-Raḥmân Tevḳî'î describes the attendance of *Çavuşes* at Friday *Dîvâns* and at processions for planting the *ṭuğs* on the outbreak of war, and their marshalling of petitions at Imperial *Dîvâns*—*M.T.M.* i. 501-2, 508, 531.   Cf. D'Ohsson, vii. 33

[5] This is clear from the *Ḳânûn* of the Conqueror and 'Abdu'r-Raḥmân, the former referring to the *Timars* (fiefs) of *Çavuşes* (*O.T.E.M.*, No. 4, Appendix, 28) and the latter to '*Ölûfeli* and *Gedikli* Çavuşes (*M.T.M.* i. 543). At the latter date the 'feudal' *Çavuşes* numbered two hundred.

[6] See 'Aṭâ, i. 61, 170.   [7] vii. 166.   [8] See D'Ohsson, vii. 17.

Sultan, but by the Grand *Vezîr*. For this reason we include the further description of his duties and those of the *Çavuşes* themselves in that of the central administration.

3. *The* Ağas *of the Stirrup in the eighteenth century*

(i) *The* Bostanci Başi.

After the promotion of the *Bostanci Başi*, he ranked next after the *Mîr-ʿAlem*. In the *Ḳânûn-nâme* of the Conqueror the *Bostanci Başi* is referred to not among the officers of state but immediately after and apparently in connexion with the pages of the Inside Service;[1] 'A (or the) *Bostanci Başi* has been placed in charge of the garden. When the barge is rowed, the *Bostanci(s)* row, he steers.'[2] Even as late as the second half of the seventeenth century the *Bostanci Başi* had no place in court ceremonial. Thus in the *Ḳânûn-nâmẹ* of ʿAbdu'r-Raḥmân Tevḳîʿî no reference is made to him at all; and the only mention of any of his subordinates is to the *Bostanci Oda Başisi*[3] as attending Wednesday and Friday *Dîvâns* for police purposes.[4] The rise of the *Bostanci Başi* to Stirrup rank was evidently due to his assumption of duties earlier performed by other functionaries. Thus his duty of presiding over punishments and executions had earlier been discharged by the *Baş Ḳapici Başi*,[5] who, it may be noted, is ranked still by ʿAṭâ, most of whose account of palace institutions refers to the eighteenth century, as an *Ağa* of the Stirrup in the *Bostanci Başi's* place.[6]

As for the corps of which he was head, the senior men of the *Bostancis* were known as *Ḫâṣṣekîs*, a term that, as we have mentioned, was also applied to certain ladies of the *Ḥarem*[7] with an implication of special distinction. These men were regarded as forming a separate *ocaḳ* within the *ocaḳ* as a whole. Both ʿAṭâ and D'Ohsson describe it,[8] though their accounts differ in most respects. D'Ohsson states that the *Ḫâṣṣekis* were three hundred '*sous-officiers*', sixty of whom formed part of the Sultan's body-guard; that they were commanded by a *Baş Ḫâṣṣekî*; and that they had three other officers: the *Kirecci Başi* (Chief Lime-farmer) who enjoyed the right of farming the excise on the production of lime; the *Baliḳ Emîni* or Fish Commissioner, who likewise farmed the fisheries in the neighbourhood of the capital; and the *Şarâb Emîni*, or Wine Commissioner, who regulated and levied dues for his own benefit and that of the *Bostanci Başi* on the production of wine. ʿAṭâ, on the other hand, limits the number of *Ḫâṣṣekîs* to just over a hundred men, of whom twelve, called *Tebdîl Ḫâṣṣekîs*, accompanied the Sultan wherever he went as plain-clothes detectives;[9] and mentions others called *Ḳuşçus*,[10] whose duty it was to apprehend and

[1] *O.T.E.M.*, No. 14, Appendix, 24.

[2] '*Bağçeye Bostanci Başi ḳonulmuştur. Ḳayiğa ḳonulduḳta Bostanci kürek çekip, ol dümen ṭuta.*'

[3] See below, p. 351.

[4] *M.T.M.* i. 504, 508.

[5] See Lybyer, 131, note 2, citing Spandugino.

[6] ʿAṭâ, i. 74.

[7] See above, p. 73.

[8] See ʿAṭâ, i. 293, and D'Ohsson, vii. 29–30.

[9] Cf. the Janissary *Şalma Tebdîl Çoḳadâris*, above, p. 326.

[10] *Ḳuş* means 'bird' (Turkish) and *Ḳuşçu* either 'dealer in birds' or 'falconer'. Presumably it is in the latter sense that the word is to be understood here,

punish any *Ḫâṣṣekîs* that misbehaved themselves. It is evident from ʿAṭâ's account, however, that he treats as *Ḫâṣṣekîs* all the senior officers and men of the *Bostanci* corps as a whole. Thus his list of the *Ḫâṣṣekî* officers corresponds in part with D'Ohsson's list of the *Bostanci* officers.[1] And since D'Ohsson agrees that the *Bostanci Başi*'s second-in-command was called *Ḫâṣṣekî Ağa*, it seems probable that ʿAṭâ is right in so treating them. Other officers mentioned by both authors are (1) the *Kâḫyâ* of the *ocaḳ*, (2) the *Bostancilar Oda Başisi*, who represented the corps in the suite of the Grand *Vezîr*,[2] (3) the *Ḳara Ḳulaḳ* of the Grand *Vezîr*, whose duty it was to carry messages between that minister and the Sultan;[3] and (4) the *Ağa Ḳara Ḳulaği*, who resided at the head-quarters of the *Ağa* of the Janissaries to give warning of fires in the city. D'Ohsson mentions two other *Bostanci* officers, the *Ḳuşçu Başi*, the inspector of the forests under the *Bostanci Başi*'s supervision, and the *Terekeci Başi*,[4] who collected the *Bostanci Başi*'s dues. Finally, both accounts agree that it was common for *Ḫâṣṣekîs* to be used as couriers for the conveyance of dispatches to the provinces.

The men of the *Bostanci ocaḳ* are said by D'Ohsson to have numbered about two thousand five hundred; to have been divided like the Janissaries into *ortas*; and even to have been reckoned as forming part of the Janissary corps.[5] From the information supplied by ʿAṭâ, however, the impression is given that the *ocaḳ* was, in fact, made up rather of a number of sub-*ocaḳs*, whose men perhaps all wore the distinctive red cap of the *Bostancis*, but each of which constituted a distinct body; and D'Ohsson's description in some measure confirms this impression, since he enumerates the very varied duties that the *Bostancis* were called in to perform. Though the *Ḫâṣṣekîs*, as we have remarked, were reckoned as forming one of such sub-*ocaḳs*, theirs was clearly of a nature different from and superior to the rest. Thus though the *Bostanci Başi* was in some manner responsible also for all the others, in many cases he shared this responsibility with one or more other high officers. For most of these sub-*ocaḳs* had not only a Commandant (*Emîr*), but also an Inspector (*Nâẓir*) and a controller (*Ḍâbiṭ*). The *Bostanci Başi* might hold any one of these three offices.

One of the more important of these sub-*ocaḳs* was that of the *Ḫünkâr Ṣandalcis*, or Imperial Boatmen. *Ṣandal* means a rowing-boat of European type as distinct from the native *Ḳayiḳ* (*caïque*). Nevertheless, the head-quarters of this *ocaḳ* was called *Ḳayiḳ-ḫâne* (caïque-house); and

though why these men should have been called falconers it is hard to say. It may be noted, however, that the *Bostanci* officer called *Ḳuşçu Başi* was inspector of forests (see below).

[1] The only officer mentioned by ʿAṭâ and not by D'Ohsson is the *Baş Tebdîl* or Head Detective.

[2] See above, p. 350, for mention of his attendance on the Grand *Vezîr* at Wednesday and Imperial *Dîvâns*.

[3] See below, p. 364, n. 4, for an explanation of this term, which means 'Black Ear'.

[4] D'Ohsson does not specify what dues; but *Tereke* means 'an estate left at death'.

[5] D'Ohsson, vii. 27–8. D'Ohsson classifies the *Bostancis* as 'Gardes du Palais'.

the *Ṣandalcis* also rowed types of boat called *Filûḳa*,[1] likewise of European design, and *Zevreḳ*,[2] a smaller vessel of Eastern origin. Their officers were called *Ḥamlecis* (meaning Stroke oarsmen), their Controller being the *Baş Ḥamleci*, while their Commander was the *Baş Çoḳadâr*[3] and the *Bostanci Başi* their Inspector. The *Ṣandalcis* rowed not only the Sultan's boats, but also those of the principal officers of the palace. When the Sultan travelled by water, his boat was steered, still in the eighteenth century as in the fifteenth, by the *Bostanci Başi* in person.[4]

Of the other sub-*ocaḳs* the following are listed by 'Aṭâ:

(*a*) Those whose men looked after the palace grounds and pavilions. Several of these *ocaḳs* were named after these pavilions, viz. Gül-ḫâne,[5] Isḥâḳîye, Sepeciler Köşkü, Yali Köşkü, and Ṣoğuḳ Çesme. The men of another, that of the *Bamyacis*,[6] as well as guarding the pavilion of Sinân Paşa tended its gardens, living on what they sold of their produce. The men of the Şevḳîye *ocaḳ* did the same for the pavilions called Incili and Iftârîye. The *Bağcis* and *Işlemecis* watered the trees of the palace gardens in general. All these *ocaḳs* were 'controlled' by the *Bostanci Başi* and 'commanded' by the *Baş Çoḳadâr*.

(*b*) *Ocaḳs* named after gates in the palace wall.

1. The *ocaḳ* of the *Cizme Ḳapisi* (The Gate of the Boot). Its men guarded a pavilion near this gate, where the pages and hospital guards took their recreation. They were 'commanded' by the Chief White Eunuch.[7]
2. The *ocaḳ* of the *Ṭop Ḳapi* (Cannon Gate).[8] Its men were charged with preventing unauthorized persons from entering the palace ground by landing from the sea.[9]
3. The *ocaḳ* of the *Baliḳ-ḫâne Ḳapisi* (Gate of the Fish-house). Its men guarded the prisoners landed at this gate, acted as watchmen, and went fishing when the wind was favourable.[10]
4. The *ocaḳ* of the *Otlaḳ Ḳapisi* (Gate of the Pasture). Its men furnished guards to the stables, and were 'commanded' by the Master of the Horse.[11]

[1] i.e. Felucca. *Filûḳa* is the more usual spelling. 'Aṭâ has *Felüke*.

[2] From the Arabic *Żawraḳ*.

[3] One of the principal 'Inside' pages of the *Ḫâṣṣ Oda*.

[4] 'Aṭâ, i. 300; D'Ohsson, vii. 37.

[5] It was this pavilion that gave its name to the famous Decree of 1839.

[6] Bamya=Okra (*Hibiscus Esculentus*). The men of one of the companies of cavalry (*cündîs*) formed by Meḥmed I were also called *Bamyacis*, those of the other being called *Laḥanacis* (*Laḥana* meaning 'cabbage'). They received these names for the reason that one company trained near Amasya in a place where okra was much cultivated, while the other trained at Merzifon, where there was an equally remarkable growth of cabbages ('Aṭâ, i. 177). Whether the *Bamyacis* of the pavilion of Sinân Paşa were connected with these others does not appear.

[7] 'Aṭâ, i. 304.

[8] When in the nineteenth century the Sultans ceased to live in the old palace, it was naturally no longer referred to as the *Serây par excellence*, but to distinguish it from the Sultan's actual residence—Dolma Bağçe or Yildiz Köşkü—came to be called, after this gate, 'Ṭop Ḳapi Serâyi'.

[9] 'Aṭâ, i. 304.

[10] Ibid. i. 305. Possibly there was some connexion between this *ocaḳ* and the *Baliḳ Emîni* (see above, p. 350).

[11] Ibid.

5. The *ocaḳ* of the *Fîl Ḳapîsî* (Gate of the Elephant). Its men were guards of this gate.[1] Their commander was the Intendant of the Doorkeepers.

(*c*) Those whose men guarded and policed the landing-stages round the Bosphorus and the Golden Horn, called after the places in question: Dolma Bağçe, Ḳara Yalî, Beşiktaş, Ḫayr ed-Dîn, Orta Köy, Ḳuru Çeşme, Bebek, Yeni Köy, Ḳalender, Büyük Dere, Ṣarî Yar, the two Ḳavaḳs, Beğkoz, Ṭoḳad, Sulṭanîye, Paşa Bağçesi, Incir Köyü, Çubuḳlu, Gök Ṣu, Ḳule Bağçesi, Çengel Köyü, Ḳuzğuncuḳ, Üsküdar, Ayazma, Ṣîlacîḳ, Ḥayder Paşa, Taziciler, Ḳaḍi Köyü, Fenar Bağçesi, Nerdebanlî, Eren Köyü, Bostancî Başî Köprüsü, Bulğurlu, the two Çamlîcas, Filuriye, Davud Paşa, Ṭopçular, Veydos, 'Alî Bey Köyü, Kâğid-ḫâne, Behâriye, Ḳara Ağaç, Ḫâṣṣ Köy.[2] This list is far, of course, from accounting for all the places under the inspection for police purposes of the *Bostancî Başî*, since the area of his jurisdiction ran up to the Black Sea on each side of the Straits and extended to the boundaries of the *Eyâlet* of Rumelia which ran at a considerable distance to the north and west of the Capital.[3] In this area every village had its squad of *Bostancîs*, headed, but only in the larger places, by an *Ustâ*.

(*d*) *Ocaḳs* of porters. There were two that we may place under this heading, namely (1) that of the *Heğbecis*. *Heğbe* is a Turkish corruption of the Arabic *Ḥaḳîba*, a saddle cushion or truss. Each of the principal inside officers, including the two Chief Eunuchs, had a *Heğbeci* in his service. They were commanded by the principal Page, the Sword-bearer, the *Bostancî Başî* being their controller (*Ḍâbiṭ*);[4] and (2) that of the *Yişlikçis* or *Işlikçis*. This consisted of only twelve men, also known as *Avadan Bostancîs* (*Avadan* apparently meaning 'artificer'). Six of them went on duty daily, three to carry whatever weapons—such as bows and arrows—the Sultan might require when he rode out, as ordered by the *Çoḳadâr Ağa*, the other three remaining at the orders of the *Tüfengci Başî* to carry arquebuses and ammunition.[5] It was the latter officer's duty to present the Sultan with his musket when he went shooting.[6]

(e) *Ocaḳs* of grooms. There were also two of these, namely the *Yedekçis* (meaning 'spare-horse-leaders') and the *ocaḳ* of the *Serrâc-ḫâne* (saddlery). These men groomed the horses of the principal pages of the Inside Service and of the eunuchs.[7]

(*f*) Supply *ocaḳs*. There were five of these, all 'controlled' by the *Bostancî Başî*, viz.:

1. The *ocaḳ* of the *Ṭavuḳ-ḫâne* (Chicken-house) whose men reared chickens for the Imperial Kitchens at a place below the Mosque of Sulṭân Aḥmed. They were inspected by a page of the inside service called *Ṭavuḳçu Başî* (Chief Chicken-raiser).[8]
2. The *ocaḳ* of the *Ṣayî* (Number).[9] The men of this *ocaḳ* pastured

[1] 'Aṭâ, i. 305.
[2] Ibid. i. 310; cf. 'Os̲mân Nûrî, i. 919.
[3] See 'Os̲mân Nûrî, i. 918, where Çaṭalca is mentioned as having a *Bostanci* post.
[4] 'Aṭâ, i. 305.
[5] 'Aṭâ, i. 300.
[6] D'Ohsson, vii. 37.
[7] 'Aṭâ, i. 308.
[8] Ibid. 308–9.
[9] Spelt wrongly *Saye* by 'Aṭâ.

sheep brought to the capital from Rumelia at a place called Rami Çiftliği above Eyyûb on the Golden Horn. They reckoned the number required for the palace (hence their name), and drove the rest to market in the city. Their Commander was the Commissioner of the Kitchen, and their Inspector the Chief Butcher.[1]

3. The *ocaḳ* of the *Ḫâṣṣ Bağçe* (Privy Garden). Its men grew fruit and vegetables for the Kitchens, selling the surplus for their own advantage. They were commanded by the Sword-bearer.[2] Since in the *Ḳânûn* of the Conqueror the *Bostanci Başi* is referred to as being placed over the *Bağçe*,[3] it may be that this *ocaḳ* was the nucleus of the whole *Bostanci* corps.

4. The *ocaḳ* of Gümüş Ṣuyu (Water of Silver), a spring above Eyyûb, from which its men drew water for making the Sultan's coffee. It was commanded by the Page called *Ḳahveci Başi* (Chief Coffee-maker).[4]

5. The *ocaḳ* of the *Ḳuş-ḫâne* (Bird-house)—not to be confused with a part of the Kitchens also bearing this name.[5] Its men reared birds, especially a kind called *Kuhu*, for feathering arrows. They were commanded by the Sword-bearer.[6] Whether the *Bostanci* officer called *Kuşçu Başi* and the under-officers called *Ḳuşçus*[7] had any connexion with this *ocaḳ* does not appear.

(*g*) The *ocaḳ* of the *Saḳḳâs* or water-carriers. Their head-quarters was opposite the great gate of Aya Ṣofya. On the outbreak of fires in the city they used to load their animals with water-skins and attempt to extinguish the flames with hoses. On feast days they had the duty of cleaning the palace. Two of them also used daily to clean the dining-rooms of the various 'dormitories' of the Inside Service before and after meals, in rotation, and to help themselves to any food left over. They acted at the orders of the Water Inspector,[8] but apparently[9] had a chief, the *Saḳḳâ Başi*, and a *Kâḫyâ* of their own. At Imperial *Dîvâns* the *Saḳḳâ Başi* used to serve the *Vezîrs* with musk-scented sherbets or sweets according to the season, while they were waiting for the proceedings to start, and had the duty of warning them of the Grand *Vezîr's* approach. He and his men used also to hand round the basins, covers, and napkins to the ministers who dined after the business of the *Dîvân* was concluded.[10]

(*h*) The *ocaḳ* of the *Mezbele-Keşân* or Refuse-heap Removers. Its men were charged with removing refuse from the Palace, two at a time, and throwing it into the sea. They were commanded by the *Çoḳadâr Ağa*.[11]

[1] 'Aṭâ, i. 309.
[2] Ibid. 304.
[3] Cf. above, p. 350.
[4] 'Aṭâ, i. 309.
[5] See below, p. 357.
[6] 'Aṭâ, i. 309.
[7] See above, pp. 350–1.
[8] 'Aṭâ, i. 309. For the Water Inspector (*Ṣu Nâẓiri*), see below, p. 357.
[9] It is not quite clear whether the *Saḳḳâs* that appeared at *Dîvâns* were the same as those with whom we are dealing. Presumably they were.
[10] See the *Ḳânûn-nâme* of 'Abdu'r-Raḥmân Tevḳî'î, *M.T.M.* i. 507, 509.
[11] 'Aṭâ, i. 303.

(ii) *The Masters of the Horse.*

The staff of the Imperial Stables (*Iṣṭablî ʿÂmire*) constituted an *ocaḳ* called *Ḫâṣṣ Aḫor*[1] *Ocaği* (*ocaḳ* of the Privy Stable), commanded by its own officers under the *Çoḳadâr Ağa*, and 'inspected' by the Great Master. The next most important officer below the Little Master appears to have been the Secretary (*Ḫâṣṣ Aḫor Kâtibi*), who had five assistants called *Ṭavla Ḳâtibi* (Stable or Picket Secretary), *Arpa Kâtibi* (Barley Secretary), *Ṣaman Kâtibi* (Straw Secretary), *Giyâh Kâtibi* (Hay Secretary) and *Serrâclar Kâtibi* (Secretary of the Saddlers). Since the Stables comprised a Treasury in which were deposited such decorative and precious objects as gold and silver encrusted saddles and other harness, their staff also included a Treasurer (*Ḫâṣṣ Aḫor Ḫazînedâri*). This treasury was inspected jointly by the *Baş Çoḳadâr*, the two Masters and the Secretary; while the registration of its contents was carried out by a special clerk called *Raḫt Kâtibi* (Furniture or Equipment Secretary), supplied by the Department of the public Treasury called *Baş Muḥâsebe*.[2] Other officers of the Stable *ocaḳ* mentioned were a Head Saddler (*Serrâc Başi*), a Head Shoesmith (*Naʿl-bend Başi*), the Senior of the Privy Stable (*Ḫâṣṣ Aḫor Eskisi*), and a number of Detective Seniors (*Tebdîl Eskisis*).[3] The functions of these Seniors are not described.[4]

(iii) *The Intendant of the Doorkeepers.*

The Doorkeepers (*Ḳapicis*) were under the joint control of their Intendant and the Chief White Eunuch. Their seniors, eighteen in number, formed a sub-*ocaḳ* called, strangely enough, the *ocaḳ* of the Father of the *Ağa* (*Ağa Babasi Ocaği*).[5] These were lodged in a tower of the *Orta Ḳapi*,[6] the main gate leading into the second court of the *Serây*, and acted as controllers of the palace porters. When a porter was required in any department, application had to be made to this *ocaḳ*, where the porters were registered and by the senior officer of which they were, when necessary, punished. These *Ağa Babasi* Doorkeepers wore a special head-dress. Their senior officer was privileged to act as the Sultan's messenger on days of parade.[7] Two of the senior *Ḳapicis* also had special titles, namely *Iskemleci Başi* (Chief Stoolcarrier) and *Düşelikçi Başi* (Chief Carpet-spreader).[8] The first used to present a silver mounting-block to the Sultan when he went riding, and returned petitions favourably received to suppliants.[9] The *Düşelikçi Başi* acted as *Çavuş* to the *Ḳapici Başis*.[10]

[1] *Iṣṭabl* is the Arabic, *Aḫor* the Persian for 'stable'.
[2] See above, p. 132.
[3] Cf. above, p. 350.
[4] ʿAṭâ, i. 290, 308.
[5] The significance of this name is obscure; perhaps *Babasi* = *Bâb Ağasi*.
[6] Meaning 'Middle Gate'.
[7] Such is apparently the meaning of this passage, which reads 'The senior of the Ağa Babasi Ocaği has the duties of giving and obtaining information in the order of preparation for the parades of the (Prophet's) Birthday, *Ḳader*, the two Feasts and the Distribution of Pay'.
[8] Redhouse does not give the word *Düşelik*; but *Düşek*, *Düşeklik*, and *Düşeli* mean anything spread, especially for sleeping upon.
[9] Aḥmed Râsim, ii. 133–4, note.
[10] ʿAṭâ, i. 290, 302.

4. *The Commissioners*

(i) *The* Şehir Emîni.

As we have mentioned, the *Şehir Emîni* not only controlled the erection of new and the repair of old buildings in the capital, but was also responsible for its water-supply.

As regards building, the supply of material and labour rested with the *Şehir Emîni* himself, whereas his chief assistant in this sphere, the *Mi'mâr Başî* or Chief Architect, provided the scientific and artistic knowledge required.[1] Building was controlled with the utmost rigour. No new constructions or repairs to old on any ground whatever, whether belonging to the state, to a pious foundation, or to a private person, were permitted without the Chief Architect's sanction; and when this had been obtained, the concurrence of a number of other authorities had further to be obtained.[2] The *Mi'mâr Başî* had on his staff two assistant architects[3] and a number of building foremen and inspectors.[4] Moreover, when any important edifice was erected special commissioners were appointed to supervise it.[5] The division of responsibilities between the *Şehir Emîni* and the *Mi'mâr Başî* was not always, particularly in later times, determined with precision.[6] Thus other officials, such as the Chief Lime-farmer (*Kirecci Başî*),[7] the Director of Repairs (*Ta'mirât Müdîri*), and the Director of Stores (*Enbâr Emîni*) appear as subordinate sometimes to the one, sometimes to the other.[8] All the greatest mosques of Istanbul were designed by architects that were *Ḳapî Ḳullarî* proper, that is to say, men recruited for the Sultan's service as slaves by ***Devşirme***, capture or purchase, the most celebrated being Sinân Ağa, the author of the Süleymânîye and Şâh-zâde mosques, who worked under Süleymân the Magnificent and his successor. After the abandonment of the ***Devşirme***, however, it became usual to employ *Z̤immîs* (that is to say, persons of the tolerated religions). Thus the mosques called Lâleli and Nûrî 'Os̱mânîye, built during the period of our survey, and exhibiting an Italianate character, were designed by a Christian named Simeon Ḳalfa.[9]

The water-supply of the capital was derived from springs outside the walls. Some of the reservoirs in which the water was conserved, the aqueducts and channels by which it was conveyed to the city, and the cisterns and fountains from which it was there drawn, dated from Byzantine times; others had been constructed by Sultans and private

[1] 'Os̱mân Nûrî, i. 1361. [2] Ibid.

[3] Called *Ser Mi'mâr* and *Mi'mâri S̱ânî*, ibid. 977; cf. 'Aṭâ, i. 290.

[4] *Kâẖyas* and *Çavuşes*. It was their duty to keep up a perpetual inspection of buildings of all kinds, public and private, in the capital—'Os̱mân Nûrî, i. 977–8. [5] Ibid. 977. [6] Ibid. 978; cf. 1362.

[7] As we have noted, the *Kirecci Baci* was a *Ḥâṣṣekî* officer subordinate to the *Bostancî Başî*; see above, p. 350.

[8] 'Os̱mân Nûrî, i. 978; cf. 'Aṭâ, loc. cit.

[9] 'Os̱mân Nûrî, i. 978. The author is surely wrong in stating that the great earlier architects were all 'Turks and Muslims'. Sinân was certainly a *Devşirme* recruit (see Aḥmed Refiḳ's biography, *Mi'mâr Sinân*), and so must have been a Christian by birth—and presumably the origin of the others was similar. It is true that they were Muslim converts, as were most, if not all, of the *Ḳapî Ḳullarî*.

persons. Hence these waterworks were all regarded as pious foundations (*Awḳâf*), and were managed as such by curators (*Mutawallîs*) and due-collectors (*Câbîs*).[1] Thus for each foundation the donor provided funds to support one or more supervisors,[2] who had under them a number of so-called watercourse men (*Ṣu Yolcus*) of two grades,[3] paid by the beneficiaries of the supply. But both the supervisors and their men (whose posts were hereditary) were also controlled by three classes of government officials, responsible to the *Ṣu Nâẓiri*, the *Şehir Emîni's* principal adjutant in this department. These were: first, the reservoir guardians (*Bend Muḥâfiẓis*);[4] secondly, the *Ḳorucus*,[5] who were responsible for the aqueducts and channels outside the walls; and thirdly, the *Çavuşes*,[6] who were responsible for their prolongations within. The chief concern of the officials was to maintain a constant and uncontaminated flow and to apportion the supply equitably between the proprietors of vineyards and produce-gardens outside the walls, and between the various quarters of the city, where the most liberal consumers were the proprietors of inns[7] and bath-houses.[8]

(ii) *The* Maṭbaḫ Emîni.

The *Maṭbaḫ Emîni*, as we have stated, was responsible for the palace kitchens. These were divided into four departments, viz. (1) the Bakeries;[9] (2) the Sweet-house (*Ḥalvâ-ḫâne*),[10] where drinks as well as confectionery were prepared; (3) the Lower Kitchen (*Aşaġî Maṭbaḫ*) or *ocaḳ* of the Cooks;[11] and (4) the so-called Aviary (*Ḳuş-ḫâne*),[12] from which the Sultan's own meals were served. The Bakeries were managed by a Head Baker,[13] the Sweet-house by the Head Taster, a Head Sweet-boiler, and a Head Syrup-maker,[14] and the Lower Kitchen by a Head Cook,[15] all of whom were included in the fifth category of Outside Service officers.[16] As such they were subordinate to the Page and the White Eunuch[17] who managed jointly the Chamber of the Larder, but

[1] See for *Awḳâf* and their management, Chapter XII below. *Mutawallî* (Arabic, 'curator') was pronounced *Mütevelli* in Turkish.

[2] Called *Bölük-başi* in the case of Imperial, and *Ustâ* in the case of private *Awḳâf*.

[3] *Ḳalfas* and *Çiraḳs* (apprentices).

[4] *Bend* (Persian) meaning anything that binds or holds together, here a dyke or reservoir.

[5] Guards, particularly of meadow- or forest-land (*Ḳoru*).

[6] *Çavuş*, a herald, messenger, or pursuivant (Redhouse). As we have seen, this word was used for various other types of functionary.

[7] *Ḫân*.

[8] *Ḥammâm*—'Oṣmân Nûrî, i. 1220–4.

[9] The Bakeries comprised two departments, namely the *Ḫâṣṣ Firin* or Privy Bakehouse, and the *Ḫarci Firin* or Ordinary Bakehouse—see 'Aṭâ, i. 297—but their personnel seems to have formed a single *ocaḳ*.

[10] See above, p. 348.

[11] *Aşçilar Ocaġi*—'Aṭâ, i. 299. The food eaten at night during *Ramaḍân* was prepared in this kitchen.

[12] Apparently because it was managed by two of the *Zülüflü Balṭacis* (see below, p. 359) called *Ḳuşçu*—literally bird-men, falconers.

[13] *Ekmekçi Başi*.

[14] *Çâşnî-gîr Başi*, *Ḥalvâci Başi*, and *Ḫoş-âb Başi*; cf. above, p. 348.

[15] *Aşçi Başi*.

[16] Cf. D'Ohsson, vii. 22–3—though he does not mention the *Ḫoş-Âb Başi*.

[17] i.e. the *Kilâr Kâḫyasi* and the *Kilârci Başi* (see above, pp. 332, 336).

were also directed by the Commissioner of the Kitchen and his assistant. The staff of the 'Aviary', which came also, presumably, under this mixed jurisdiction, was made up of talented cooks promoted from the Sweet-house and the Lower Kitchen.[1] The Commissioner further commanded the *ocaḳs*, controlled by the *Bostancî Başî*, from which the kitchens were supplied with mutton and fowls.[2]

5. *Officers of the Fourth Category of the Outside Service*

These, who, as we have remarked, were all four subordinate to the Chief Eunuch, were the following:

(*a*) The *Çadîr Mehteri Başî* or Chief Tent-pitcher.[3]

The *Çadîr Mehteri*'s original duty was to set up and strike the Sultan's tents when he went on campaign.[4] And even in late times when the Sultans no longer led their armies to battle, the *Çadîr Mehteris* used still to pitch the royal tents in the gardens of the palace or elsewhere in the neighbourhood of Istanbul when the Sultans went on excursions for pleasure. In the eighteenth century there were no less than eight hundred of them, divided into four companies. Some of them, however, discharged curiously incongruous duties. Thus forty of the seniors among them formed an *ocaḳ* of 'weighers' (*Veznedâr*) headed by a Chief Weigher (*Veznedâr Başî*), inspector of the Public Treasury situated in the first court of the Palace,[5] who acted at the orders of the Minister of Finance (*Defterdâr*).[6] On the other hand, the men of the lowest grade of these tent-pitchers acted as hangmen or executioners, four or five of them remaining always in readiness at the gate of the second court to carry out the orders of the Sultan or his ministers.[7]

(*b*) The *Ḫazînedâr Başî* or Chief Treasurer.[8]

The Treasury in the keeping of this official was situated next the *Dîvân*-chamber, and to distinguish it from those of the *Enderûn* and the *Ḥarem* was called *Dîş Ḫazîne*, 'Treasury of the Outside'.[9] In it were kept the archives of the Finance Department; the fur pelisses and other 'robes of honour',[10] which, in accordance with ancient Moslem custom, were presented to dignitaries both native and foreign on occasions of ceremony; and the cloth-of-gold bags in which orders were dispatched to provincial governors. This treasurer had twenty assistants.[11]

[1] 'Aṭâ, i. 297.

[2] i.e. the *ocaḳs* of the *Ṭavuḳ-ḫâne* and *Ṣayi* (see above, pp. 353–4).

[3] *Çadîr* means 'tent', *Mehter* 'groom'.

[4] *O.T.E.M.*, No. 13, Appendix, ii. note.

[5] Cf. below.

[6] See above, p. 129.

[7] D'Ohsson, vii. 21.

[8] Not to be confused with the eunuch of this title—see above, p. 330.

[9] See the *Ḳânûn-nâme* of 'Abdu'r-Raḥmân Tevḳî'î (*Ḳânûn* of the Imperial *Dîvân*—*M.T.M.* i. 507). When the Grand *Vezîr* has entered the *Dîvân*-chamber, the *Ḫazînedâr Başî* of the *Dîş Ḫazîne* presents him with the wax seals of the door, which, after kissing them, the Grand *Vezîr* breaks and hands back. Again, in the same *Ḳânûn* (p. 509), it is laid down that after the Grand *Vezîr* and other functionaries have dined, the *Çavuş Başî* shall seal this treasury—here referred to as the *Mâlîye-Defterḫânesi ve Ḫazîne* (The Archive-store of the Finance Department and the Treasury)—with the Imperial Ring.

[10] *Ḫil'a*—from the Arabic root meaning to take off a garment, because originally such robes were discarded by the sovereign, who by wearing them endowed them with some of his glory.

[11] D'Ohsson, vii. 21–2.

(*c*) The *Bâzergân Başî* or Chief Purveyor (of textiles to the Palace); and

(*d*) The *Pişkeşçi Başî*, or Chief Guardian of Gifts presented to the Sultan.[1]

6. *Officers of the Fifth Category*

We have already dealt with four of these, namely the *Çâşnî-gîr Başî*, the *Ekmekçi Başî*, the *Aşçî Başî*, and the *Ḥalvacî Başî*.[2] Of the remaining two yet another was connected with the food-supply of the Palace, viz. the *Kilâr Ağasî* (*Ağa* of the Larder), who was assisted by about a hundred *Kilârlîs*; and all five were dependent on the White Eunuch and the Page who were jointly responsible for the Chamber of the Larder.[3]

The sixth officer of this Category was the *'Alem Mehteri Başî*[4] or *Mîri Mehterânî ṭabl u 'alem*,[5] the Chief Bandsman. As we have noted,[6] the use of military bands, and particularly drums, had for long been a sign of royal authority in Islam. The Sultan's bandsmen numbered sixty-two in peace time; but their establishment was doubled when he went on campaign, when they used to play before his tent at prayer-time. The *'Alem Mehteri Başî* was subordinate to the Standard-bearer, and had as his assistant the *Sâzende Başî* (Chief Instrumentalist).[7]

7. *The 'Independent' Ocaḳs of the Outside Service*

(i) *The* Balṭacîs.

Some of the *Balṭacîs* of the New *Serây*, the *Zülüflü Balṭacîs*,[8] were employed in special duties. Twelve of them in particular, distinguished by their literacy and known as *Ḳalfas*,[9] attended the Sultan on journeys, accompanied by thirty of their subordinates, to guard his standard, and on feast days and other occasions of ceremony brought out his throne from the Inner Treasury to the Council Chamber.[10] They also carried the effects of the *Ḥarem* on the Sultan's summer excursions, and instructed the minor Black Eunuchs in reading and writing. One of them, again, acted as *Ḳuşçu*, or falconer, to the *Ḳîzlar Ağasî*; while two others, also called *Ḳuşçus*, supervised the 'Aviary' Kitchen, whence its name (*Ḳuşḫâne*).[11] Apart from the *Ḳalfas*, each of the *Ḫaşş Odalîs*, the White

[1] Ibid.; cf. 'Aṭâ, i. 290. Officers mentioned by 'Aṭâ but not by D'Ohsson are the *Ḳaşşâb Başî* (Chief Butcher), the *Bâzâr Başî* (Chief Marketer?), the *Taḫtrevancî Başî* (Chief Palanquin-carrier), and the *Ḳavuḳçu Başî* (Chief Cap-maker).

[2] Above, p. 357.

[3] i.e. the *Kilâr Kâḫyasî* and the *Kilârcî Başî*. D'Ohsson, vii. 22–3.

[4] 'Chief of the Standard Grooms.'

[5] 'Chief of the Grooms of the Drum and Standard.' [6] Above, p. 137.

[7] D'Ohsson, vii. 14, 23; cf. *O.T.E.M.*, No. 13, Appendix, 11, note. The 'Standard' were thus distinguished from the 'tent' grooms. See above, p. 358.

[8] See above, p. 86.

[9] They were taught by the *Ḫocas* of St. Sophia.

[10] Their third officer on this account was called *Dîvân-ḫânecî*.

[11] See above, p. 357. Redhouse gives as a secondary meaning for *Ḳuş-ḫâne*, a small saucepan. But it seems more probable that this should have been derived from the name of this once-famous kitchen than vice versa. 'Aṭâ writes of

Eunuch officers and the *Kâhyas* of the three lower chambers had a *Baltaci* in attendance on him.[1] The Sword-bearer (*Silihdâr Ağa*), who 'commanded' this division of the corps, was attended by a *Baş Baltaci* and three men, the *Hazîne Kâhyasi* (head page of the Treasury Chamber), who 'inspected' it, by two men. Subordinate officers of the division were its *Kâhya*, a second *Baş Baltaci*, the *Dîvân-hâneci* mentioned above, and the *Baltaci* of the *Kilarci Başi* (White Eunuch), who controlled the Lower Kitchen and the Bakeries.[2]

The other division of the original corps was in later times commanded by the *Kizlar Ağasi*. But since some of its senior members assisted that dignitary in his management of the pious foundations of the Holy Cities and other places,[3] it seems likely that these *Baltacis* were earlier controlled, like the foundations themselves, by the *Kapi Ağasi*. Indeed, another of the White Eunuch officers, the *Serây Ağasi*,[4] continued to exercise some authority over them, together with the black *Baş Kapi Ğulâmi* of the Old *Serây*,[5] where their quarters were situated, and the *Harem* of which it was their first duty to guard and serve. Many of the senior men, however, were employed as Chief Coffee-makers[6] to the *Vâlide*, the princesses, the *Kadins*, and the *Kizlar Ağasi*; while the latter and the other Black Eunuch officers each had another of them in his service as a robe-keeper.[7] It was likewise in the New *Serây* that those who assisted in the management of the pious foundations had their office. These secretaries, seven in all,[8] were chosen for their proficiency in study,[9] and often rose to hold high posts in the public administration.[10]

these men performing *Kuşçu* duty (*Kuşçuluğu hidmetinde bulunur*) without indicating its nature. D'Ohsson merely states that the '*Couschdjis*' took messages from the *Silihdâr* to the Sultan.

[1] Those that so served the White Eunuchs were termed *Kandillis* (lamp-carriers). The *Baltacis* served coffee to the *Hâşş Odalis* after meals, under the direction of the *Kahveci Başi*.

[2] All this according to 'Atâ, i. 290, sq., 297, 299. D'Ohsson's account differs from this, as explained below.

[3] See above, pp. 76–7.

[4] See above, p. 332.

[5] See above, p. 330.

[6] *Kahveci Başi*.

[7] *Hoftanci* from *hoftan*, robe, properly *kaftân*.

[8] The *Baş Yazici* (literally, Head Writer) and six *Kalfas*. D'Ohsson mentions two *Baltaci* officials connected with the foundations, namely the *Hâşşekî Başi*, the collector of the dues accruing to the *Ağa*, and the *Hâşşekî Baş Kâtibi*, his first secretary, who are perhaps to be numbered among these *Kalfas*.

[9] They were taught by the *Hocas* of the Bâyezîd mosque.

[10] D'Ohsson, vii. 30–2, and 'Atâ as above and i. 305–7, differ in their accounts of the two divisions of the *Baltacis*, D'Ohsson giving to those of the Old *Serây* some of the offices and duties stated by 'Atâ to belong to the *Zülüflüs*, as, for instance, the *Kâhyâship*, and carriage of the *Harem* effects. No doubt this confusion is due to the facts that some of the *Baltacis* of the Old *Serây* were employed at the New, and that some of the *Zülüflüs* were under the orders of the *Kizlar Ağasi*. D'Ohsson puts the numbers of the *Baltacis* at four hundred, and that of the *Zülüflüs* at one hundred and twenty. 'Atâ may be partly at fault; for instance, in enumerating the *Zülüflü* officers he calls their second-in-command simply *Baltacilar Kâhyasi*, not *Zülüflü Baltacilar Kâhyasi*, which may indicate that D'Ohsson is right in allotting this office to the other division. In this uncertainty we have followed 'Atâ's description, since, not having been translated, it is the less accessible.

(ii) *The* ocaḳs *of the* Ḳizbekçis, *the* Dolab, *the* Ṣofa *and the* Ḥaṭab Enbârî.

The *Ḳizbekçis*[1] supervised the water-supply, offered the Sultan drinking and washing water at ceremonies, spread his carpet when he went to mosque, and swept the saloon where he mounted his horse. The men of the *Dolab ocaği* apportioned the supply between the various departments of the Palace. They also guarded and cleaned a pavilion, near their quarters, belonging to the *Ḳapî Ağasî.*[2] The men of the *Sofa*[3] *ocaği* were for the most part employed in the service of the *Ḥâss Odalîs* and some of the inferior *Iç Ağas*, one to each, and had the special duty of bringing to the second court the sheep sacrificed by the Sultan at the *Ḳurban* Feast.[4] The Wood-store[5] men in general distributed fuel to the various departments of the Palace. But some of their seniors[6] performed the oddly anomalous service of directing the cleaning of the Palace hospital by prisoners of war that were brought up for this purpose from the Admiralty. When any of the *Ağas* fell ill, again, he was conveyed from the *Orta Ḳapî* to this hospital in a special carriage, which the men of the Wood-store had the duty of dragging.[7]

(iii) Ocaḳs *of Artisans.*

The Tailors' Workshop (*Terziler Kâr-ḫânesi*) occupied part of a church, the remainder having been converted into a mosque, just outside the Imperial Gate. It was organized by Selîm I, and consisted of forty tailors, headed by a Head Tailor (*Terzi Baṣî*) and a Head Carder (*Ḥallâc Baṣî*). The tailors supplied the Serây personnel with all that was needed in the way of clothes, quilts, &c.[8]

The *ocaḳ* of the mat-makers (*Ḥaṣîrcîs*) was situated in the wood-store. Its members' chief duty was to weave mats, changed once a year, for the Chamber of the Prophet's Cloak, and for mosques.[9]

---

[1] So called, according to a possibly apocryphal story, because their first commander prevented a mad *Ḥarem* girl (*Ḳîz*) from escaping—*bekçi* meaning guard, watchman. The *ocaḳ* was formed by Meḥmed the Conqueror towards the end of his reign, and consisted of forty men headed by a *Ḳizbekçi Baṣi*. The name was in later times corrupted to *Ḳuzbekçi*. D'Ohsson does not mention the *ocaḳ*, though it remained in existence until after his date.—'Aṭâ, i. 294 sq.

[2] 'Aṭâ, i. 301. *Dôlâb* (Persian—written in 'old' Turkish *Ṭolab*) means a water-wheel or other turning machine.

[3] Properly *Ṣuffa*, meaning an ante-chamber surrounded with 'sofas' (whence our word). This *ocaḳ* took its name from the neighbouring mosque called *Ṣofa Câmi'i*, within the palace grounds. Both mosque and *ocaḳ* dated from the reign of Süleymân the Magnificent.

[4] 'Aṭâ, i. 298–9. The *Ḳurbân Bayrami* (Sacrifice Feast) is held on the 10th of *Ẕu'l-Ḥicca*, the month of the Moslem year during which the ceremonies of the Meccan pilgrimage are performed. In Arabic it is called *'Îd al-Aḍhâ* or *al-'Îd al-Kabîr*. The sheep in question were reared by the *Ḳurbân Ocaği*. (See above, p. 86.) [5] *Ḥaṭab Enbârî.*

[6] Called *Vardiyan*, from the Italian *guardiano*. Functionaries, &c., connected with the Admiralty were apt to have appellations derived from Italian, as we have seen.

[7] 'Aṭâ, i. 301. [8] Ibid. 310.

[9] Ibid. 299–300. D'Ohsson, referring to these artisans, states that they numbered about three hundred—tailors, furriers, shoemakers—vii. 25.

(iv) *The* Muteferriḳas.

Like the *Çavuşes* the *Muteferriḳas* were divided at least from the time of the Conqueror into 'pay-drawing' (*'Ölûfeli*) and 'exceptional' (*Gedikli*), i.e. feudal.[1] Again like the *Çavuşes*, the feudal *Muteferriḳas* came to be attached to the service of the Grand *Vezîr* rather than to that of the Sultan. When the fiefs on which they subsisted were of the size called *Zi'âmet*, they were also commonly called *Gedikli Za'îms*.[2] They had an independent commander, the *Muteferriḳa Başi*, one of the Grand *Vezîr's* adjutants.[3] In the second half of the seventeenth century there were two hundred feudal *Muteferriḳas* and an unspecified number of those drawing pay.[4] In D'Ohsson's account the latter are not mentioned at all, and had presumably by that time been abolished. The number of the former still stood at two hundred.

[1] The term *'Ölûfeli Muteferriḳa* is used in the *Ḳânûn-nâme* of the Conqueror (pp. 18, 20, 25) in contrast with both *Za'îm Muteferriḳas* and *Timar Muteferriḳas* (Muteferriḳas of Timars). As in the case of *Çavuşes* the term *Gedikli* perhaps came into use only later. We find it in the *Ḳânûn-nâme* of 'Abdu'r-Raḥmân Tevḳî'î (*M.T.M.* i. 543). D'Ohsson, vii. 377, is evidently wrong, therefore, in stating that the *Gediklis* were created only in 1597.

[2] See D'Ohsson, vii. 168, 173, 377—the *Çavuşes* holding *Zi'âmets* were likewise called *Gedikli Za'îms*.

[3] D'Ohsson, vii. 173.

[4] According to the *Ḳânûn-nâme* of 'Abdu'r-Raḥmân Tevḳî'î. According to Zinkeisen, iii. 182, there were between 300 and 400 in 1640, and 631 in 1660. By 1698 the *Muteferriḳas* and *Çavuşes* together numbered 500.

APPENDIX C

THE HOUSEHOLD OF THE GRAND *VEZÎR*

THE household of the Grand *Vezîr*, like the households of most of the Sultan's richer subjects, was modelled on that of the Palace. Only the Grand *Vezîr* enjoyed such large revenues that his was better able than any one else's to emulate the Imperial household in size. It fell far short of it in this respect: his *Ḥarem*, for instance, was guarded by no more than four or five eunuchs. But it was similarly organized in an Inner and Outer Service. The former was headed by twenty-four pages, of whom the chief was a *Silîḥdâr Ağâ*[1] and the others bore titles similar to those of the Sultan's *Ḫâṣṣ Odalîs* and lesser attendants;[2] and it comprised, on the Imperial model, a number of deaf-mute messengers.[3] The Outside Service, again, like the Sultan's, had its Treasurer, Master of the Horse, Intendants of the Doorkeepers and Kitchens, and several 'Learned Men'.[4] Moreover, it resembled its model in comprising persons employed in public business, so that the line of demarcation between this part of the minister's household and the officials and soldiers that were attached to his service was somewhat indistinctly drawn. It depended, rather than on the nature of the duties discharged by these functionaries, on the source of the emoluments they received: whether this was the Grand *Vezîr's* purse or the public treasure. The eight footmen (*Ṣâtir*) by whom it was his privilege to be accompanied in public were clearly his private servants. But the forty doorkeepers[5] of the Porte, in that it housed most of the government departments, were less so, as were his forty *Ağas*, who were often employed in carrying dispatches to the provinces, his twelve *Çavuşes*, who directed the march on occasions of public procession,[6] and his two hundred valets (*Çokadârs*), the two senior of whom were employed as detectives with the duty of reporting to the prime minister's second-in-command.[7]

For in the eighteenth century (to which the foregoing applies likewise) the persons definitely regarded as public employees attached to the Grand *Vezîr's* department consisted largely of other guards and couriers. Among the latter, for instance, were the *Gedikli Muteferriḳas*,[8] and a corps of two hundred Crimean Tatars, on whom the services originally performed by the *Çavuşes* had devolved. The commanders

[1] Cf. above, p. 339.

[2] For instance, the Grand *Vezîr* had a *Çoḳadar Ağa*, a *Peşkir Ağa*, a *Ḳahveci Başi*, a *Ṣariḳci Başi*, a *Berber Başi*, and an *İbrîḳdâr Başi*, corresponding to the Sultan's *Ḫâss Odalis* with the same titles. He also had a *Miftâḥ Ağa* corresponding to the *Anaḫtar Ağa* of the Sultan (*Miftâḥ* in Arabic, *Anaḫtar* in Turkish, meaning 'Key').—D'Ohsson, vii. 179–80.

[3] Ibid. 180.

[4] Ibid. 178–9. D'Ohsson does not give the Turkish titles of these functionaries. His 'Almoner' and *Mu'eẓẓins* were presumably *'Ulemâ*.

[5] *Mehter*.

[6] For this reason they were called *Alay Çavuşus* (*Alay* meaning parade, cf. above *Alay Beyis*, p. 51).

[7] The *Kâhya Beyi*—see above, p. 120.

[8] See above, p. 362.

of these bodies, called respectively *Muteferriḳa Başi* and *Tatar Ağa*, and those of two small bodies of cavalry,[1] were members of the Grand *Vezîr's* staff, which was otherwise made up of three officials and fifteen officers of the *Çavuşes*.[2] The first two of these three officers, the *Telḥişçi*[3] and his substitute,[4] were charged with delivering to the Chief of the Black Eunuchs, the *Ḳîzlar Ağasî*, the communications addressed by the Grand *Vezîr* (as he alone might address them) to the Sultan. The third was the *Ḫoftancî Başî*,[5] or Head Keeper of the Pelisses presented by the minister to all persons appointed to fresh offices. Finally, attached to the staff as aides-de-camp were representatives of each of the 'standing' *ocaḳs*, infantry and cavalry (though the latter had by this time been reduced to two).[6] The aide-de-camp representing the Janissaries was the *Muḥḍir Ağa*, whose *orta*, the twenty-eighth of the *Bölük*, formed a guard for the Porte.[7] The aide-de-camp of the *Bostancîs* was the *Oda Başî* of that corps;[8] and it may be remarked that just as the *Bostancî Başî* steered the Sultan's barge,[9] so this *Oda Başî* steered that of the Grand *Vezîr*—further evidence that the *Vezîr* was privileged to imitate the Sultan on a lower level of grandeur.[10]

---

[1] *Gönüllüs* (volunteers) and *Delis* (scouts). Those in the Grand *Vezîr's* service numbered fifty each. Their commanders were entitled *Gönüllüler Ağasi* and *Deliler Ağasi* respectively.

[2] *Bölük Başis*. They were the commanders of the fifteen companies of *Çavuşes*; see above, p. 119.

[3] From Arabic *Laḫḫaṣa*, 'He presented a résumé', whence (the verbal noun) *Telḫiş*, 'a résumé or report', applied to the communications addressed to the Sultan by the Grand *Vezîr*. As we shall note in describing the Learned Institution, the *Şeyḫü'l-Islâm* also had a *Telḫîsçi*.

[4] Called *Vezîr Ḳara Ḳulağî*, on account of the cap of lynx-fur that he wore. *Ḳara Ḳulaḳ* means literally 'Black Ear', and was applied to the Asiatic lynx (hence the name caracal from the Turkish).

[5] Cf. above, p. 334.

[6] The *Sipâhîs* and *Silihdars* were represented by their *Kâhya Yeris* (above, p. 326); the *Cebecis*, *Ṭopçus*, *Ṭop 'Arabacis* by *Ḳapi Çavuşus* (Porte *Çavuşes*). Another *Ḳapi Çavuşu* is shown by D'Ohsson as representing the '*Emirs*', but who are intended is not clear. These *Emirs* can hardly be the descendants of the Prophet that went by that title, or the *Sancaḳ Beyis* (see above p. 139) who were likewise called *Emirs*.

[7] Above, p. 316.
[8] Above, p. 350.
[9] Above, p. 350.
[10] D'Ohsson, vii. 172–3, 177–9.

APPENDIX D

NOTES TO PAGES 236–48

p. 236, *n.* 1. Isma'il Ḫüsrev, *Türkiye Köy Iḳtiṣâdiyâtî*, 20 seq., 32, 45 seq.
n. 2. *M.T.M.*, i. 51, 56–7.

p. 237, *n.* 1. See e.g. *M.T.M.*, i. 105.
n. 2. Ibid. i. 84.
n. 3. Isma'il Ḫüsrev, op. cit. 158.

p. 238, *n.* 1. See *M.T.M.*, i. 51–2.
n. 2. Arabic *ṣâḥibu 'l-arḍ*, 'owner of the land'. Cf. Isma'il Ḫüsrev, op. cit. 159.
n. 3. Ibid. 158–9, 161.

p. 239, *n.* 1. *M.T.M.*, i. 57–8.
n. 2. Ibid. i. 54.
n. 3. Ibid. i. 76–7.
n. 4. Ibid. i. 78–9.

p. 240, *n.* 1. Ibid. i. 58, 59, 63, 71.
n. 2. Ibid. i. 55.
n. 3. See ibid. i. 52: *sipâhîden izinsiz olan mu'âmelât külliyen bâṭildir.*
n. 4. Ibid. i. 107–8, 542.
n. 5. Ibid. i. 97. These dues are referred to in the *Ḳânûn* as *yaylaḳ*, *ḳîşlaḳ*, and *otlaḳ resmi* or *ḥaḳḳî*, 'summer pasture, winter pasture, and pasture-dues'.
n. 6. Ibid. i. 51, 103, 104.

p. 241, *n.* 1. Ibid. i. 102.
n. 2. Ibid. i. 104.
n. 3. Ibid. i. 101, 106–7. Cf. Isma'il Ḫüsrev, op. cit. 163.
n. 4. *M.T.M.*, i. 83, 104, 108.
n. 5. Ibid. i. 84.
n. 6. Ibid. i. 51.

p. 242, *n.* 1. Ibid. i. 109–11.
n. 2. Ibid. i. 55, 111–2.

p. 243, *n.* 1. Ibid. i. 305–6. Cf. Isma'il Ḫüsrev, op. cit. 160–1.
n. 2. *M.T.M.*, i. 55–6.
n. 3. Isma'il Ḫüsrev, op. cit. 41.
n. 4. Ibid. 32, 114.

p. 244, *n.* 1. Ibid. 40 seq.
n. 2. Ibid. 29.

p. 245, *n.* 1. Ibid. 22 seq.

p. 246, *n.* 1. *M.T.M.*, i. 101.
n. 2. *Yurt yerinde olan vâriṣin yerine naḳṣ gelmemek için* (ibid. i. 74).

p. 247, *n.* 1. Ibid. i. 74.
n. 2. See ibid. i. 85: *ṣâḥibi arḍa ḥaḳḳ vâṣil olmadîğî ḥâlde daḫle ḥaḳḳ dîr.*
n. 3. Cf. Isma'il Ḫüsrev, 159–60.
n. 4. *M.T.M.*, i. 95.
n. 5. Ibid. i. 310, 311.
n. 6. Ibid. i. 103.
n. 7. Ibid. i. 59, 78–9.

p. 248, *n.* 1. Ibid. i. 85.
n. 2. Ibid. i. 93.
n. 3. Ibid. i. 310. Cf. Bélin, *Du régime des Fiefs militaires*, 235.

INDEX OF ARABIC AND TURKISH TERMS

INDEX OF PERSONAL NAMES

INDEX OF PLACE-NAMES

SET IN GREAT BRITAIN
AT THE UNIVERSITY PRESS OXFORD
AND REPRINTED LITHOGRAPHICALLY BY
JARROLD AND SONS LTD,
NORWICH